THE
ENCYCLOPEDIA OF
WORLD FAITHS

THE CONTRIBUTORS

Revd Duane Wade-Hampton Arnold
Executive Minister
First Congregational Church of Detroit
Michigan
USA

The Independent Churches of Eastern
Christianity
Antecedents to the Reformation
The Lutheran Churches

Dr Bryan W. Ball
Principal
Avondale College
Cooranbong
New South Wales
Australia

The Seventh-day Adventist Church

Dr Eileen Barker
Senior Lecturer in Sociology & Dean of
Undergraduate Studies
London School of Economics

The Unification Church
New Religious Movements in Modern
Western Society

Dr Peter D. Bishop
Senior Lecturer in the History of
Religions
Brighton Polytechnic

The Nature of Religion
Religion in the Modern World

Professor Mary Boyce
Professor emeritus of Iranian Studies
University of London

Zoroastrianism

Revd Dr Raymond Brown
Principal
Spurgeon's College
London

The Baptist Churches

Professor F. F. Bruce
Professor emeritus
University of Manchester

The Brethren

Dr John H. Chamberlayne
Part-time Lecturer
University of London & Open
University

Taoism

Dr W. Owen Cole
Head of Religious Studies
West Sussex Institute of Higher
Education

Sikhism

Michael Darton
Freelance publisher & writer

General editor

Revd A. Ian Dunlop
Retired Minister of the Church of
Scotland

The Calvinist Churches

John Ferguson
Formerly President
Selly Oak Colleges
Birmingham

The Buddha

Revd Professor Duncan Forrester
Head of Department of Christian Ethics
and Practical Theology
University of Edinburgh

The Church of Scotland

Revd A. Raymond George
Warden
John Wesley's Chapel
Bristol

The Methodist Church

Dr Ian Hazlett
Lecturer in Theology
University of Birmingham

Christianity to the Eleventh Century

Dr Walter J. Hollenweger
Professor of Theology
University of Birmingham

The Pentecostal Churches

Rabbi Dr Louis Jacobs
Rabbi of the New London Synagogue

Judaism

Major Clifford W. Kew
Editor
The Officer
Salvation Army Headquarters
London

The Salvation Army

Dr Ursula King
Senior Lecturer
Department of Theology and Religious
Studies
University of Leeds

Hinduism
Jainism

Dr Alan Kreider
Tutor & Director of Cross-Currents
Programme
London Mennonite Centre

The Mennonite Church

Revd Fred Linyard
Minister
Moravian Church
London

Chairman
Provincial Board of Moravian Church in
Britain

The Moravian Church

Rose-Marie Loft
Assistant Director of Public
Communications
Church of Jesus Christ of Latter-day
Saints
London Mission

The Church of Jesus Christ of Latter-
day Saints

Revd Arthur J. Long
Principal
Unitarian College
Manchester

Hon. Lecturer
Department of Theological Studies
University of Manchester

The Unitarians

Mahinda Palihawadana
Buddhist scholar from Sri Lanka
teaching at Colegate University
Hamilton
New York

Theravada Buddhism

Muriel Poulter
Formerly Lecturer
Woodbrooke College
Selly Oak
Birmingham

The Society of Friends

Dr Andrew Rawlinson
Lecturer in Buddhism in the
Department of Religious Studies
University of Lancaster

Mahayana Buddhism

Revd Dr Bernard M.G. Reardon
Formerly Head of Department of
Religious Studies
University of Newcastle Upon Tyne

The Church of England and the
Anglican Communion

David Sibrey
Jehovah's Witnesses Information Office

The Jehovah's Witnesses

D. Howard Smith
Formerly lecturer in Comparative
Religion
University of Birmingham

Confucianism
Shinto

Dr Peter Smith
Lecturer in Religious Studies
Mahidol University
Bangkok-Salaya
Thailand

Research Fellow in Sociology
University of Lancaster

Babism
Baha'i Faith

Revd Dr Colin Thompson
Chaplin and lecturer in European
Studies
University of Sussex

The United Reformed Church

Dr Jack Thompson
Assistant Director
Centre of New Religious Movements
Selly Oak Colleges
Birmingham

New Religious Movements among
Primal Peoples

Michael J. Walsh
Librarian
Heythrop College
University of London

The Roman Catholic Church

Professor Montgomery Watt
Formerly Professor of Arabic & Islamic
Studies
University of Edinburgh

Islam

Revd Canon Hugh Wybrew
Secretary of the Fellowship of St Alban
& St Fergus

The Eastern Orthodox Churches

THE ENCYCLOPEDIA OF WORLD FAITHS

AN ILLUSTRATED SURVEY OF THE WORLD'S LIVING RELIGIONS

GENERAL EDITORS

PETER BISHOP & MICHAEL DARTON

Macdonald Orbis

A Macdonald Orbis BOOK

© Macdonald & Co (Publishers) Ltd 1987

First published in Great Britain in 1987
by Macdonald & Co (Publishers) Ltd
London & Sydney

A member of BPCC plc

British Library Cataloguing in Publication Data
The Encyclopedia of world faiths: a survey
   of the world's living religions.
   1. Religions
   I. Bishop, Peter D.   II. Darton, Michael
   291   BL80.2
   ISBN 0 356 14062 8

Typeset by Bookworm Typesetting, Manchester

Printed and bound in Spain by Graficromo SA

Editor: Gillian Prince
Art Director: Dave Goodman
Designer: Frances Austen
Picture Researcher: Jane Williams

Macdonald & Co (Publishers) Ltd
Greater London House
Hampstead Road
London NW1 7QX

CONTENTS

INTRODUCTION

THE
NATURE OF RELIGION

Religion is a nearly-universal phenomenon, extending as far back in history as we can trace human activity, and manifested among people in every part of the world. Religious activity, religious rites and religious language are woven into the fabric of most great civilizations, and the study of religions is part of any comprehensive attempt to understand history and society. Religion is also an enduring vehicle for expressing some of the most private of human experiences, in our sense of wonder and mystery, in times of sorrow and bereavement, and in moments of great joy. The universality of religion, however, results in a great variety of beliefs and practices, and the identification of religion with social activity on the one hand and with deeply personal feelings on the other leads almost inevitably to paradox.

This confronts us with the question: what is religion? Are we able to say anything coherent about so varied a phenomenon? Many attempts have been made to define religion. Some attempts assume that there is a common element among the great variety of religious phenomena, and so seek to provide a description which can express the essential nature of religion. Other definitions are more simply the result of scholars in particular fields (social anthropology, for example) clearing the ground by saying what they mean when they use the word 'religion'.

So difficult is it to produce a clear and accurate definition of religion that actually fits the facts, that critics may be excused for thinking that there is no such thing; or rather, that while it may be possible to speak about particular religions, or certain kinds of religious phenomena, the attempt to speak about religion as though it were one particular kind of thing is doomed to failure. Is it the case that while religions exist, religion itself does not? I think not. There are common elements amidst the vast variety of the world's religions, and we shall look at some of these later.

Some attempts to define religion reveal more about the inclinations, backgrounds and perhaps also the cultural contexts of those framing the definitions than they do about religion itself. A

nineteenth-century apologist for Christianity, Schleiermacher, could define religion in terms of 'the feeling of absolute dependence upon God', and in many parts of the world a connection between religion and God may appear to be unexceptional. But a Theravada Buddhist, for example, might remind us that early Buddhism appears to have taken no account of the question of God, and certainly did not teach or require belief in God. By universal consent, Buddhism is a religion. Is that the result of a mistaken understanding, and should Buddhism be described as something else? Or should we revise our definitions in the light of the actual existence of Buddhism? However we respond to the questions, the difficulties of definition appear immediately. The historical and cultural context in which we live is likely to have considerable influence upon our understanding of what religion is.

Other attempts at definition reveal other presuppositions or approaches. For the philosopher A. N. Whitehead, religion was 'what the individual does with his solitariness'. Certainly, any careful and sympathetic study of religion will reveal much that is concerned with deeply personal feelings, expressed in prayer and meditation as well as in the individual's search for meaning and identity. But the inadequacy of the phrase as a definition of religion is obvious. It ignores completely social, ethical and other important facets of religion. The limitation is revealed starkly when one compares it with the definitions provided by some modern social anthropologists who refer to institutions and to 'culturally postulated' supernatural powers. Language, as well as content, may reveal a certain kind of sociological approach, and while it is legitimate for the social anthropologist to concentrate upon social manifestations of religion, for the rest of us other features may be equally, or more, important.

The reflection of particular schools of thought in particular definitions of religion is common. Sir Edward Tyler, a great figure in the nineteenth-century development of the study of religions, found the beginnings of religion in what he called 'animism'. He believed that primitive man, searching for answers to questions about what constitutes the difference between the living and the dead, or sleeping and waking, and asking himself what reality could be accorded to human and animal forms that appeared in his dreams, came to attribute 'shadows', or spirits, to humans and animals and then by extension to trees, plants and inanimate objects. As a result of his reflections upon what he saw as its origins, Tyler produced a 'minimum definition' of religion as 'belief in spiritual beings'. Another great nineteenth-century pioneer of the study of religions was Sir James Frazer, whose massive and erudite work, *The Golden Bough*, brought together a vast collection of information about religious rites, beliefs and practices. Frazer came to the conclusion (now generally discredited) that religion had arisen by an evolutionary process out of a preceding age of magic, and that attempts to control the powers changed gradually into attempts to placate them, so that the essence of early religion was in sacrificial acts designed to appease the god or gods. Hence his definition of religion as 'a propitiation or conciliation of powers superior to man'.

These definitions reflect particular schools of thought, often with distinctive theories about the origins, and therefore also about the essential nature, of religion. Some also reflect particular cultural contexts. For Europeans and Americans it has been natural until recent times to think of religion in terms of belief in God and of institutional forms which reflect a Judaeo-Christian heritage. In other parts of the world perceptions of religion are necessarily different. In India, the very word 'religion' is a relatively recent projection on to the immensely varied systems of belief and practice which we now commonly know by the name of Hinduism. The Hindu sacred language, Sanskrit, has no exact equivalent of 'religion', and Hindus themselves have traditionally known their faith by the term *Sanatana dharma*, which means something like 'the eternal law'. So this reflection on the difficulties of simple definitions leads naturally to a suggestion which might guide a reading of all that follows in later chapters: that is, that the same word in English may not mean the same thing in different contexts, especially when the contexts are the great religions of the world. 'Religion' is likely to have different connotations for adherents of different faiths. For the Jew it will mean something slightly different than for the Christian; for the Muslim something different than for the Hindu; for the Buddhist something different than for the Sikh. And for the modern secularist, something different again than for all the others. It was William Blake who wrote: 'If the doors of perception were cleansed everything would appear as it is, infinite.' Cleaning the doors of our perception to look at religions, those traditional vehicles of the infinite, is a difficult task. But it is one which we have to attempt, by imaginative, informed and sympathetic enquiry if we are to come near to understanding what the great world religions have to say.

Definitions are difficult, but there are ways of clarifying what it is that is comprehended under the term 'religion'. One example of such an attempt which has gained much acceptance is that made by Ninian Smart in *Secular Education and the Logic of Religion* (1968) and *The Religious Experience of Mankind* (1969). Smart suggested six 'dimensions' of religion which could be used to identify what may properly be regarded as religion, particularly by way of contrast with an ideology such as Marxism. The question of whether there are essential differences between ideologies and religions is one which has arisen in recent times with the rise of powerful political ideologies. Marxism and Fascism have both been described as 'quasi-religions', most notably by Paul Tillich, who believed that these two opposed ideologies of the twentieth century were essentially 'religious', with emotional as well as rational appeal. For Tillich, religion was whatever concerns people ultimately, and his notion of 'ultimate concern' encouraged him to consider seriously whether ideologies which exercise great influence over the hearts and minds of millions should not be regarded as religions. Clearly there are areas of overlap, and these in both directions.

THE SIX DIMENSIONS OF RELIGION

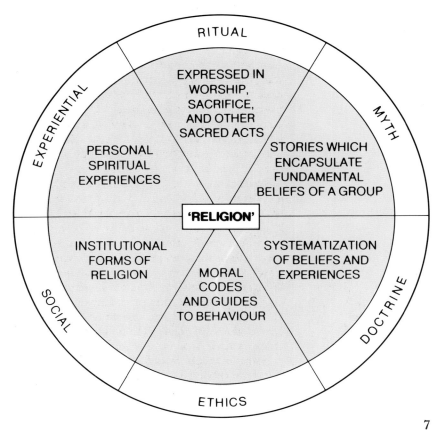

7

Ideologies incorporate some of the features of religions, and religions themselves impose their own ideologies. It was partly to provide a set of criteria to distinguish between religion and ideology, and partly to clarify the word 'religion', that Ninian Smart set out six different categories which seemed to him to be present in everything that could properly be called a religion. His six categories, or dimensions, were the ritual, mythological, doctrinal, ethical, sociological and experiential. A reflection upon these six dimensions may help us to clarify what religion is, and to rid ourselves of the limited view often contained in formal definitions.

To begin with the ritual dimension, it is clear that ritual plays an important part in all religions. It can be traced far back in history, and deduced not only from texts but also from artefacts and archaeological remains which reveal buildings and implements which seem to have been connected with the corporate enactment of sacred rites. The 'great bath' at Mohenjo Daro in the Indus Valley (see 'Hinduism', page 186) is one example of an archaeological find which is thought to reflect ancient ritual use. The large and presumably public building contained an oblong pool with small cubicles around it, and is most likely to have been used for some kind of ritual ablution. Ritual may have been an instinctive reaction to great events, and some rituals (rain-making, for example) mimed the event they wished to come to pass.

Sacrifice is another form of ritual discerned in ancient societies through the mists of time but persisting into the present. Sacrifice takes various forms. An honorific sacrifice is one in which God or the gods are presented with gifts, sometimes as a thank-offering and sometimes in expectation of a reward or blessing from the god in return. In propitiatory sacrifice an offering (or victim) is given in the belief that the powers will be appeased by the appropriate offering made in the correct way. Sacrifice has always played an important part in Indian religion. It was a vital part of the religion of Vedic times and it persists in various forms in modern Hinduism. In Christianity, the concept of sacrificial worship has been given a particular, and often highly allegorized, interpretation in the central service of the Mass, or Holy Communion.

In course of time rituals become strictly formalized, and one problem of ritual in changing societies is that the original intentions and feelings which the action sought to express and enhance may be diminished or even forgotten as thought-forms and modes of expression change. On the other hand, one of the values of ritual is that people are able to engage in actions which,

Located in present-day Pakistan Mohenjo Daro is an important site of the Indus Valley civilization (c 2000 BCE). The 'Great Bath', one of the buildings on the citadel, reflects the importance of ritual in the life of early man.

even though imperfectly understood, may provide a vehicle for deeply-felt longings and hopes which are less easy to express in more literal and concrete forms.

The second dimension identified as an essential element in religion in Ninian Smart's scheme is mythology. An examination of the texts and beliefs of the great religions shows that myths do indeed play a part in them all, even in those religious traditions which most strongly claim an origin in an objective act of revelation. The word 'myth' has come to be used popularly, especially in the West, for something that is not true or that is at best a kind of fairy story. It is important to recognize that this is not the way the word is used in religious discourse. A myth is a story which encapsulates something believed to be true by a large group of people bound together by common belief or commitment (a nation, or the followers of a particular religion). In using the form of a story a myth does not concede that it is 'only a story', but tries to find a way of conveying a truth too profound to be dealt with in matter-of-fact terms. The western world, perhaps because of the dramatic impact made there by science and scientific method, has become suspicious of what is not literally true, or what cannot be measured or analysed in an empirical way. So myths tend to be misunderstood, and too hastily discarded. In traditions which originate in the East, on the other hand, the place of myths appears to be more readily accepted. In the Hindu tradition stories such as those contained in the *Ramayana* and the *Mahabharata* can be acknowledged to be not literally true, and yet valued as expressions of truths in story form.

The best known, as well as the most controversial, example of myth in Judaism and Christianity is probably the material found in the first four chapters of the book of Genesis. Within that fascinating collection of material some quite fundamental beliefs are expressed: the belief that the universe has its origin in God; beliefs about the nature of human beings and their relation to God and to the natural world; about the essential fallenness of human nature; about the reflection of that human condition in jealousy and anti-social behaviour. Some Christians take the stories to be literally true, and so as expressions not only of religious truth but also of secular truth. Other Christians accept in a post-Darwinian age that the stories of creation, for example, cannot serve as a scientific account but nevertheless see them as expressing essential religious truths. Certainly myths can function to convey religious ideas in a non-literal form. But myths have also functioned to bind people together and to express the shared convictions of civilizations and societies in ways that enable different people to relate to and take from the stories whatever is appropriate to their own spiritual and intellectual development.

A third common feature of religion was said to be a doctrinal dimension. In doctrines, or theological statements, beliefs and religious experiences are systematized and put into a form in which their importance can be preserved and their meanings transmitted to the community of believers. Doctrines, therefore, tend to arise after the events which they enshrine, and to represent ordered reflections upon mysterious and largely inaccessible phenomena. Doctrinal statements of one kind or another are found among all the great religions, although the ways they are arrived at and the importance attached to them may differ considerably between different religious traditions. In the religions of Semitic origin, belief in revelation is of fundamental importance. So, for example, much critically important Christian theology is concerned with the nature of Jesus Christ and his relationship to God the Father. The belief that God spoke uniquely through Jesus was defined in increasingly careful and precise terms during the first four centuries of Christian history until the major creeds came to be accepted as authoritative. The task of doctrinal definition continued, however, and theological debate on Christological and other matters is clearly of great

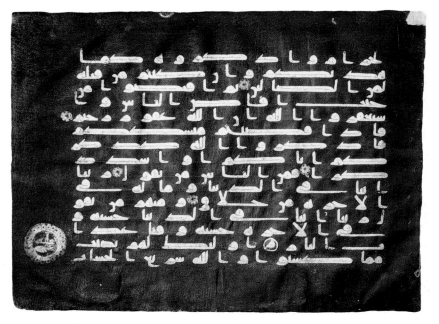

A 9th-century Qur'an in the early Kufic script which originated in Kufa on the Euphrates river. As the revealed word of God to Muhammad the Qur'an provides the basis for the religious and moral standards of Islamic life.

interest and concern among Christians in the twentieth century.

Among Muslims also the understanding of revelation has led to much theological activity, and the experiences of Muhammad have been interpreted doctrinally in ways that have made it possible for the community of Islam to embrace and share beliefs in, for example, the sovereignty of Allah, the finality of revelation through his prophet Muhammad and the nature of the Qur'an as the unmediated word of Allah.

Doctrinal statements are also to be found in abundance among the great religions of the East, although there the word 'theology' is not always appropriate since not all are agreed on the existence of *theos*, or God, around whom doctrines might be formulated. In Hindu traditions doctrines tend to reflect schools of thought, and since there is no Church or equivalent institution to pontificate on agreed or orthodox doctrine, variety in belief is both acceptable and common. The traditional western division between doctrine, or theology, and philosophy is also less clear in India, since the major 'schools' of Hinduism are schools of philosophy, although it seems reasonable to suggest that the differences between, say, *Advaita* and *Visishtadvaita* represent differences of doctrine as well as those of philosophical interpretation.

It should also be clear to any perceptive observer of religions that the formulation of doctrinal standards by official bodies cannot ensure similarity of beliefs among their members. Believers may affirm the same creeds and doctrinal statements with sincerity and yet differ widely in the ways in which they understand and interpret those same beliefs.

Religions also have in common a tendency to incorporate moral codes into their religious teaching, and so all religions have their ethical dimension. The moral codes of religion often have to do with social behaviour, and in that respect religion may function as a form of social control. But the ethical precepts of religions also relate to personal conduct and to matters that are regarded as important for self-control and so for spiritual development. Families of religions often reflect very similar moral codes. In Judaism the Torah includes among many other things the ten commandments which Christians traditionally have accepted as a set of basic precepts applicable to Christians as well as to Jews, and very similar commands appear in the Qur'an. In addition the three Semitic religions have developed their own distinctive ethical teaching, as well as interpreting in their own ways their common heritage. All are agreed that murder, adultery, stealing, giving false evidence and coveting the property of others are wrong. The Qur'an places a particularly strong emphasis upon the regulation of family relationships; and the New Testament provides the Christian with the positive injunction to 'love one's neighbour', which although very broad and imprecise is supported by many vivid illustrations. The notion of 'divine command' in relation to ethics is naturally strong in these three religions, although it should be noted that all three possess developed systems of ethical teaching which are not simply confined to statements of the original texts of the Hebrew Bible, the New Testament, and the Qur'an.

The Indian family of religions has also produced clear and concise ethical rules, although in some respects these differ from the Semitic or western models. Hinduism (from about 600 BCE), Jainism and Buddhism all teach the importance of *ahimsa* (non-violence), of truthfulness, of not stealing, and of not misusing sex, and to these four Jainism and Hinduism add a fifth precept which has to do with the restraint of selfishness. Buddhism, in which the restraint of selfishness is a fundamental part of its overall teaching, substitutes for the fifth precept an injunction to refrain from the use of alcohol (a teaching also found in the Qur'an). In religiously-based ethical systems, the narrow line between conduct which might be thought to impinge directly on other people's welfare (murdering, lying, etc.) and conduct which is thought conducive to spiritual growth, is illustrated by the practice of *ahimsa*. *Ahimsa* discourages violence against people, and this aspect of Hindu and Buddhist ethics has been evident in a number of modern examples, from the life of Mahatma Gandhi to Buddhist monks in nuclear disarmament demonstrations. *Ahimsa* also discourages violence against all kinds of living creatures and so has encouraged vegetarianism which in turn has become one of the signs of religious orthodoxy in some Indian traditions. Religiously-based ethics may serve to sharpen the self-image of a religious community; they may help to perpetuate a religious tradition by encouraging its adherents to conform to an acceptable pattern of behaviour; and on occasions they may challenge accepted conventions in the name of revealed truth. All religions have their ethical prescriptions, and most claim that they are based upon revelation or that they reflect the essential nature of reality. But practice and theory often diverge. The acceptance of moral codes by believers may be an indication of the ideals they admire, but of course it is not inevitable that all the believers will even attempt to put the precepts into practice. It is also a difficult and delicate question how far religious experience and teaching create ethical values or to what extent religion simply provides an additional sanction to moral rules originally based upon other grounds.

Religions also tend to be organized, often in institutional form, and so there is a sociological dimension to them all. In the West people naturally think of the Church when an institutional form of religion is mentioned, and clearly the whole nature and history of Christianity is linked inextricably to the Church in its varied forms. The social forms of religion often are the easiest to define and measure, and perhaps nowhere more clearly than in the case of Christianity. It could be argued that a 'Christian' is a member of the Christian Church, and 'Christianity' is what the Church is and does, although many Christians

寺法妙山本日
Nipponzan Myohoji

no doubt would object to that kind of simple definition, suggesting any number of ideal qualities which constitute the true Christian or genuine Christianity.

Institutional forms of religion are not always of a churchlike nature. Hinduism, which is diverse in belief and applies no credal tests to its adherents, does exhibit an important, indeed vital, connection between religious practice and the social institution of caste. Traditionally to be a Hindu has been to be a member of a particular caste, and caste relates to defined levels of religious purity as well as positions in a social system.

The social aspects of religion are often the most amenable to objective study. It is possible to be clearer about the nature of an institution, whether it is growing or declining, and the roles its members perform, than about the quality of belief or the nature of religious experience.

All the five dimensions discussed so far can be found in all the major religions and can help us to appreciate the multi-faceted nature of religion and to consider it in all its aspects. The great movements we call religions exhibit these five elements, together with one more. But all five, it might be argued, are found in phenomena which are not usually considered to be religions. An ideology, such as communism, may have its own equivalents of rituals, and its own kind of mythology. Certainly, in its political philosophy, it will have doctrine; ethical judgements will be regarded as of great importance; and social institutions, whether party, cadre, government, or state, will give practical expression to the ideology. Is religion, then, in any way distinctive?

As a social phenomenon and a means of reinforcing moral rules religion, although of great importance, need not be regarded as unique. But there is one other dimension to religion which provides it with its distinctive character, and that is religious experience. The feelings of awe and wonder, the sense of approaching a mystery, the apprehension of some power or quality greater than oneself, all believed to be intimations of a supernatural power or reality, are fundamental parts of religion and are what most clearly distinguishes religion from other areas of human life.

In an important book on religion, published in English in 1923, Rudolf Otto wrote about 'the idea of the holy' as the elemental fact of religion, and defined religion as 'a unique, original feeling response . . . which claims consideration in its own right'. There is great importance in this. However strong or magnificent religious institutions may have become, however powerful their influence on conduct or their interpretations of the world, there has been, so far back as one can see, a recognizable religious sense much like that defined by Otto which even when articulated only in the lives of exceptional people has preserved the notion

that at the heart of religion is something distinctive, powerful and of great importance in human experience. The phenomenon is seen most obviously in mysticism of various kinds, but not only there. Religions with an emphasis on social and corporate expressions also show an awareness of the importance of personal spiritual experiences. So the biblical saga of Jacob includes the story of his dreaming, at a time of great personal crisis, and waking with the comment 'Surely, the Lord is in this place, and I did not know it'. His response to a rare religious experience involved other dimensions of religion. In an act of ritual, presumably intended to help him act out some of the feelings of a mysterious experience, he is said to have built a pillar of stones, poured oil on it, and made a vow. Similar examples can be found in all religious traditions. Prayer and meditation, spiritual exercises and yoga, incorporate systematic methods which are calculated to enhance perceptions of a power or reality beyond normal sense experience. It may be argued that experience of this kind is not a category unique to religion. But among the characteristics of what many religions would regard as genuine religious experience is a tendency for the experience to lead to a commitment to a way of life, a particular ethical position, and often to the acceptance of some kind of personal renunciation. It is not simply the experience enjoyed for its own sake, but the connection between experience and commitment that characterizes religious experience in many of the traditions.

These six dimensions of religion, then, help us to know what to look for when we attempt to identify a 'religion', and in the case of the experiential dimension suggest a means of distinguishing between religion and a secular ideology.

As one might expect, not all scholars are entirely happy with Ninian Smart's categorization of religion into six dimensions. Eric Sharpe, for example, declares himself unhappy with the possibility that Smart's scheme might encourage a grading of the dimensions into an order of importance. This of course I have myself done in suggesting that the category which distinguishes religion from other human experiences and movements is what Smart called the experiential dimension, and such a judgement, while open to debate, seems to me to be necessary if we are to be clear about what, if anything, is distinctive in religion. Eric Sharpe's objection, if I understand him correctly, is not directed against this, but against emphasizing one mode of religion in a way that suggests that it is more worthy of study than others. This I should wish to avoid. Every aspect of religious life and all religious phenomena must be studied if we are to have a rounded picture of what religion is and of what is important and influential in any one form of religious tradition.

Eric Sharpe's more substantial objection to the six dimensions is that the mythological and ritual appear to be different kinds of categories, concerned more with content than with fundamental qualities, and that other examples of this kind of dimension could just as well be cited on the grounds that religions might be said to have a musical dimension, a legal dimension, and so on. In *Understanding Religion* Sharpe produces his own scheme, consisting of what he calls four 'functional modes': the existential mode which would include faith and that essential element of religious experience described above; the intellectual mode, which would include formal statements of belief; the institutional mode, which would include the organizations which contain and transmit faith and belief; and the ethical mode, concerned with conduct. As the phrase 'functional mode' suggests, this scheme is concerned more with analysing the way religions function than with the attempt to recognize what a religion is. It supplies a useful criticism of Smart by suggesting that not only is religion difficult to define but also that its many dimensions or aspects may baffle explanation.

Eric Sharpe also rightly points out that among religious believers different people will make different estimates of what is the most important 'mode' in their own religion. Some will emphasize religious experience, and many assert that those who do not speak of a similar kind of experience are not true believers. Others will emphasize right belief, and assume that whatever else a religion gives, it must provide a framework for true belief. For others, the emphasis and the test of the true believer may be found in right behaviour. And for yet others, attention may focus chiefly upon an organization, perhaps as the bearer of revelation or the transmitter of religious experience. This is a useful reminder. In studying religion we need to beware not only of generalizations made in the comparison of religions (as though the word 'God' means the same thing in widely different religious traditions) but also of generalizations about believers. It is tempting to assume that all Christians, all Muslims, all Jews, all Hindus, must believe the same things in the same way, and place the same kind of importance on teaching about religious practice and right behaviour as their co-religionists. In fact, closer examination often reveals great variety of emphasis and interpretation of what is judged to be of central importance, and what is deemed peripheral among people who make the same confessions of faith and follow the same pattern of teaching.

Generalizations about single religious traditions may obscure significant differences, and generalizations about religion may lead to gross over-simplification, although it is possible that some generalizations will help us in identifying

THE FOUR 'FUNCTIONAL MODES' OF RELIGION

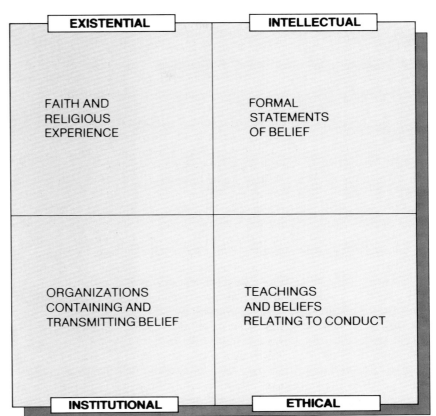

EXISTENTIAL	INTELLECTUAL
FAITH AND RELIGIOUS EXPERIENCE	FORMAL STATEMENTS OF BELIEF
ORGANIZATIONS CONTAINING AND TRANSMITTING BELIEF	TEACHINGS AND BELIEFS RELATING TO CONDUCT
INSTITUTIONAL	ETHICAL

certain dominant features among the great variety of religious phenomena.

Some much-respected scholars have generalized on a grand scale in attempting to categorize religions and to draw attention to particular features of major religious systems. R. C. Zaehner continued the use of a very broad classification of religions (which goes back at least to Heiler in 1918) when he described the Semitic religions of Judaism, Christianity and Islam as 'prophetic' and the Indian religions of Hinduism and Buddhism as 'mystical'. There is substance in the point he makes by doing this. The religions in the Semitic group all claim their origin in an act or acts of revelation, and so the notion of a prophetic message which proclaims the will of God is central to them all. The Indian group of religions contains many examples of religious practice which concentrates on meditation and on refining and heightening a divine sense or essence which is believed to be an integral part of human nature. But when we look in detail at any particular religious tradition within these categories we find ourselves confronted with many specific examples which contradict Zaehner's general classification. Christianity fits into his prophetic category, and clearly is based upon a belief in revealed truth. Yet Christianity also has mystical traditions which have been and still are of great importance. Many aspects of

Hinduism fit into the 'mystical' category, and yet Hindus also claim that the Vedas are revealed truth. There is something in what Zaehner says; but these very broad categories probably do more to mislead than to inform. Major religious systems are complex and multi-faceted, and only detailed study of actual practices and doctrines can do justice to them.

ORIGINS

The articles that follow deal in particulars, outlining the main features of religions rather than engaging in comparisons or seeking to establish broad principles that could apply to religion generally. In discussing dimensions and modes of religion, however, we have seen already that there are common features of religions that can be identified, providing frameworks for systematic study and understanding. Another way of seeking a common thread running through the varied phenomena of religions is to look back and ask whether and in what ways traces of religious activity can be discerned in pre-history.

It is in the nature of archaeological evidence that the earliest indications of religious belief occur not in written documents but in the remains of burials. As long as 100,000 years ago a creature we know as *Homo neanderthalensis* (after the Neander valley in Germany, where the first traces were found) used to bury his dead. In this act is something which generally distinguishes people from animals: animals leave their dead; humans appear always to have felt a need to dispose of their dead with care and dignity, suggesting not only a lingering affection for the person who has died but also probably a feeling (belief at this early stage may be too strong a word) that death may not be the end, and that provision for or protection against the dead is therefore appropriate. This early man, or pre-man, buried his dead with care, and placed within reach of the body implements, such as stone weapons, which might have been thought useful for some future existence or might simply have been a memorial of an aspect of the person's daily work. Later discoveries of the Palaeolithic, Mesolithic and Neolithic periods confirm that the practice of burying bodies with artefacts, most likely intended as tools for an after-life, continued down to the period of documented history. In the Palaeolithic period most burials were of bodies carefully arranged in particular ways, often in a crouching position and sometimes with the knees drawn up tightly against the chest. We can only speculate about the reasons. This type of burial might suggest an attempt to place the body as though in sleep, or in the position of an embryo in the womb, and either reason might well indicate a belief that the dead

Even the earliest human burials disposed of the dead with care and dignity. The body was placed in a crouching position, or simply as though asleep. Either position might indicate a belief that the dead would awake once more; that death might not be the end.

would wake from sleep, or be born into a new life. But the binding of a body before burial necessary to achieve such a posture might also suggest a fear of the dead, and an attempt to protect the living from any return of the dead person to their midst.

Many of these early burials also pointed the body along an east-west axis, and some have seen in this an attempt to link the progress of the soul with the course of the sun. Another interesting feature of burials from very early times was the smearing of the body with red ochre, a practice found not only in Europe but also in Africa, Australia and the Americas. Was this, perhaps, an attempt at contagious magic? The use of a substance which in colour resembled blood might have been thought of as a means of re-animating the dead person after burial.

The mystery of birth and death, and of what may lie on either side of them, appears to be not only a perennial human concern but also a fundamental element in religious feeling and thinking. One of the notable contributions of S. G. F. Brandon to the study of religions was in his insistence on the importance of people's consciousness of time in their religious thinking. He supported his view by reference to evidence from the earliest times in human history of the care taken over burials and of the placing of implements and provisions in the grave, with their implications of a concern to provide for and deal with the mystery of death in the belief that it is not the end. From the beginning of human history there has been an apparent unwillingness among the majority of people to accept the idea that death involves the annihilation of a person. The belief that the meaning of life is not extinguished by death, and that in some form and by some means life continues beyond the grave, has been a persistent feature of human experience and one of the most important elements in religious belief and practice in many of the world's religious traditions.

The tantalizingly limited evidence from prehistoric times also suggests that belief in a human cycle of birth, death and rebirth was linked to the rhythm of the natural world and of vegetation. Observation of the plant that died, was buried in the form of the seed, and then burst into new life in another season, supported or perhaps determined the view that this too was the fate of men and women. This association is particularly evident in the Mesolithic and Neolithic periods with the increasing location of people in settled communities and the development of agriculture. Human fertility was also linked to this rhythm of nature, as is evidenced by the discovery at Palaeolithic sites of figurines of women. The figures are very simple, with blank faces but heavily emphasized sexual features, suggesting that they were not portraits but symbols of women's reproductive power and therefore of the promise of new life beyond the mystery of death.

A dominating concern with death and the prospect of life beyond it is also the most obvious feature of the oldest religion of which we have substantial and decipherable documentary evidence, that is, Egyptian religion. One of the clearest indications of Egyptian belief about death and what lies beyond is found in the legend of Osiris, a very ancient story which appears to have been current even in the pre-dynastic period, that is before c. 2,500 BCE. The story is alluded to in the Pyramid texts, which were written c. 2,400–2,300 BCE, and incorporated into the mortuary rituals for Pharaohs and other privileged members of Egyptian society. Osiris, according to the

story, was a good and wise king who lived long ago in Egypt. He was hated by his brother, Set, who found the opportunity to murder Osiris and then threw his dismembered body into the Nile. Isis, the wife of Osiris, searched for her husband and, with the help of her sister and of the gods, she was able to find the body which was reconstituted and raised to life. Instead of returning to the land of the living, however, Osiris then became the god of the dead. This legend became the basis of the funerary ritual which was designed to reproduce ritually what were thought to have been the events of Osiris's death and resurrection. In the process of embalming the body texts were recited which recounted what had happened to

A fertility figure of a standing woman from Catal Huyuk in Turkey (c 6000 BCE). Such figurines were not intended as portraits but as symbols of woman's reproductive power and linked her with new growth from the seed each year, and to a cycle of birth, death and rebirth.

Osiris and suggested that the efficacy of his death and resurrection would be available for the dead person who was ritually associated with Osiris. The name of Osiris was actually added to the name of the dead person, and in the Pyramid texts the climax of the ritual seems to occur with the statement: 'As you do not die, Osiris, so this man does not die.'

At first, the ritual was designed to ensure immortality for the Pharoah, and it is this with which the Pyramid texts are chiefly concerned. But there is evidence of a gradual democratization. The Coffin Texts of the Middle Kingdom (c. 2160–1788 BCE) indicate that leading members of society were buried with the same formula as that used for the Pharaohs. The Book of the Dead, the original title of which was the more positive 'The Coming Forth to the Day' (a product of the New Kingdom, c. 1600–1090 BCE), suggests that the use of the ritual had spread more widely and that anyone with sufficient financial means might employ the ritual and hope to share in the after-life.

The Egyptian concept of life after death was still a fairly materialistic one. The person was regarded as a psycho-physical unity, and the body thought of as essential to life after death. The Coffin Texts show great concern that sufficient food and drink should be provided for those in the after-life. Papyrus rolls were placed in coffins to help guide the dead on their journey, and the funerary texts as a whole are much concerned with advice to help the dead with practical difficulties they may encounter, such as having to cross waters or pass watchmen.

In later Egyptian texts Osiris also appears to have assumed the character of a nature god, dying in the autumn and rising to life again in the spring. In this he was also identified with the Nile, the waters of which were believed to flow from Osiris. The analogy with nature was sometimes dramatized in the tomb by placing a table there, on which would be seeds set in earth and watered. The rapid germination that followed represented the resurrection of Osiris.

The records of ancient Egyptian religion combine with archaeological discoveries to suggest how great was the concern of ancient people and their religions with the mystery of death and the expectation of some life beyond. The instinct that resists the apparent finality of human mortality has remained an important part of religions. For the Christian, it is expressed in terms of death and resurrection which is believed to mirror and be the consequence of the resurrection of Christ. The Christian hope is expressed in terms of eternal life, a concept of a quality which begins in this world but is not confined to it. For the Muslim, it relates to the promise of a paradise in which rewards and compensations for faithfulness to Allah and suffering in this life can be given, an assurance of justice and of the irresistible power of Allah which even death cannot overcome. In the Semitic and western traditions the general expectation is of the continuation of personal identity in a way that expresses the psycho-physical unity of the human personality. This, rather than the notion of a disembodied soul, has been reinforced by belief in resurrection and in a paradise pictured in earthly terms. In India, while notions of heaven and hell can be found in the traditions, the dominant idea has been of a spiritual entity, or soul, which inhabits the human body and is constrained by material influences. The soul, it is believed, is reborn after death to dwell in another body and to continue a round of birth, death and rebirth that may be almost endless. Differences exist between Hindu and Buddhist traditions about the nature of the soul that is reborn and the degree of continuity between one life and the next; but the essential belief in rebirth, or transmigration is common, and appears to continue to be an important element in living faith in the Indian traditions.

The question of whether or not death is the end of all human experience remains an important question for all religions, and all present their own answers to the problems of time and mortality. In spite of the differences between them they all affirm some post-mortem reality and so continue to give expression to that hope which appears to have been an instinctive response of people to their environments since human history began.

Other evidence of possible religious ideas held by the earliest human inhabitants of the earth comes from cave art. Remains of Palaeolithic works of art have been found in many parts of Europe, and especially in Spain, France and southern Italy. The supposition that these were not intended simply for public display is based upon the fact that most of the drawings are in places to which access is difficult, in some cases hundreds of metres in from cave entrances, and at Lascaux, France, in a gallery to which access is by rope ladder through a shaft over six metres deep. A number of the paintings and clay figures discovered at the sites are of wild animals transfixed with arrows, and it has been suggested that these may represent a kind of hunting magic, depicting scenes in a way that sought to bring about on an actual hunt the results shown in paintings and figures. It has been suggested that rituals may have been performed by hunters in front of the paintings before embarking on a hunt. A painting that has attracted much interest is of the figure known as The Dancing Sorcerer or The Great Magician in the Trois Frères cave at Lascaux. The figure is human in shape, but has a furry skin, an animal's tail, the eyes of an owl, and a stag's antlers. Its posture suggests that it is engaged in a dance, and scholars have speculated that here in

FAITH AND LIFE

Religion is not only a subject of historical interest and concern: it is also a living reality. Despite increasing secularism in Europe and North America (matched even there by growth in less structured religious practices) religion worldwide continues to flourish. Religion also impinges upon other areas of life, stimulating social and political reform, encouraging anti-establishment judgements on such matters as war, economic development and racial equality. Campaigning about such issues may be an essential religious duty. Religion also provides a powerful impetus for the public expression of conservative political and social views, as in the modern Islamic revival in Iran

Varanasi (or Benares) is one of the great holy cities of India. This picture of a Hindu ascetic was taken outside the temple of Shiva on the campus of Benares Hindu University. Renouncing the normal pleasures of life to become a sadhu *or a* sannyasi *remains an important part of Hindu life.*

or neo-fundamentalism in North America. Religion remains a vital part of people's lives in more traditional ways — in acts of charity and learning; in pilgrimage and devotion; and in proclamation. This section illustrates religion in the modern world and the ways in which faith and life interact.

17

RIGHT *The modern world offers many attractive alternatives to the life of a monk, or* bhikkhu, *but Buddhism continues to influence society by the association between the general population, the Buddhist laity, and the* sangha (*the community of monks*). *Boys like those pictured here can join the* sangha *for life; but many enter for a few years and then return to lay life, imbued with a deeper knowledge of Buddhism and of monastic discipline and practice.*

LEFT A Parsi boy reads a sacred text from the Avesta. *The Parsi community of India is the main living exponent of the ancient Middle Eastern religion of Zoroastrianism (named after the prophet Zoroaster). Driven to western India by persecution in Persia (hence 'Parsi'), they have maintained their religious beliefs and practices. In modern times their religion's emphasis on education, purity and integrity has encouraged their emergence as a vigorous, well-educated and commercially successful people.*

BELOW The association of deep religious feeling and national sentiment is a feature of religion in the modern world which is illustrated in this picture of Jews praying at the Western (or 'Wailing') Wall in Jerusalem. The Wall is a remnant of the Jewish Temple destroyed by the Romans in 70 CE. It is a reminder of Jewish history in Israel and of survival in dispersion, and a place to pray for faith and nation.

ABOVE This Buddhist monk, or bhikkhu, a member of a Japanese order, is engaged in the dedication of the London Peace Pagoda. The Pagoda, in Battersea Park, London, is a witness to the concern for peace in a world threatened by nuclear war. The rejection of violence and the positive acceptance of ahimsa (non-violence) are important precepts in Buddhist teaching. Reflecting this tradition, Buddhists are often found to be active in peace movements.

RIGHT A Khalsa Sikh winding his turban. A fully-initiated, or Khalsa, Sikh customarily wears or carries on him five symbols of his commitment (see the 'five Ks', page 269). The uncut hair and beard were one of the signs enjoined on Sikhs who became full members by Guru Gobind Singh when he initiated the Khalsa on Baisakhi Day, 1699. The turban, worn to keep the hair tidy, has become a symbol of Sikh identity.

LEFT A member of a Pentecostal Church takes her message to the streets of New York. The slogan illustrates the problem of interpreting the Book of Revelation, which was written probably in the last decade of the first century CE and intended through its symbolic language to provide comfort for persecuted Christians of the time. Now, however, it is understood by some as a message intended to apply literally to modern-day events. In some circles 'the Rapture' conveys the idea of a cataclysmic end to world history in which the 'saved' will be miraculously removed from the earth before it is destroyed.

RIGHT The nun at her ironing is a member of the Order of the Poor Clares, founded by St Francis and St Clare 1212–14. The Poor Clares is a contemplative Order, and most of its members lead an austere life devoted to prayer and manual work. Like the Franciscans, the Poor Clares regard poverty as a way to become brothers and sisters of all, and instruments of God's peace.

LEFT *Mevlevi Dervishes in Konya, Turkey. The Dervishes (or Darwishes) are found within the Sufi movement of Islam. Sufism emphasizes and encourages religious experience, and is found within both Sunni and Shi'ah branches of Islam. Sufis adopted various techniques of mystical practice, including the constant repetition of the name of Allah (dhikr) to induce a trance-like state of a heightened awareness of God's presence. The Dervishes developed ecstatic dance to cultivate trance and deepen religious experience. Sufis were once banned in secular Turkey, but Dervishes have clearly survived that period.*

RIGHT *Monks at St Catherine's Monastery at Mount Sinai. The Church of Sinai, the smallest independent Church among the Orthodox, is under the direct jurisdiction of the Archbishop of Mount Sinai. The monastery was established in 527 CE. Withdrawal into a life of testing and contemplation in the desert became widespread among Christians from the late third century; this sometimes resulted in the formation of monastic communities. The picture shows monks distributing bread to Muslim visitors. Contact between Christian communities and Muslims in the desert areas of the Middle East goes back to the earliest days of Islam.*

BELOW *An open-air Mass in Brazil. The chequered history of the Roman Catholic Church in South America has attracted much attention, particularly the connections between Spanish and Portuguese colonialism and Christian missions. Today the religious scene is crowded with different images. There are traditional Catholics; there is the new strain of radical Catholicism; and there is the increasing influence of some Protestant, and notably Pentecostal, movements. This picture focuses on the mixing of the traditional rite of the Catholic Mass with the religious observance and devotion of ordinary people in everyday surroundings.*

The annual Shembe pilgrimage of the Zulu Independent Church, founded by Isaiah Shembe in 1911, illustrates the strength and liveliness of African independent Churches. Christianity in Africa has been growing rapidly over the past fifty years – in contrast with the numerical decline in many of the old European heartlands of Christianity – and the fastest growing element within that has been of the African Independent Churches. These Churches substantially accept Christian teaching, but reinterpret it in ways that relate it closely to the culture, music, and religious experience of traditional African society. The amaNazaretha, or Zulu Independent Church, has its pilgrimage to its own holy mountain, Nhlangakazi, celebrates specific Zulu festivals, and uses its own Zulu Christian hymns.

this inner sanctuary is an indication of some piece of magical or religious ritual. If the figure is of some kind of sorcerer performing a sacred act, was the painting intended to do more than commemorate what the sorcerer could do in person at any time? Was the purpose, as Brandon suggests, to preserve the magical efficacy of the rite when the dance was over? Interpreting evidence of this kind is inevitably speculative. Cave art tells us that early man was capable of imaginative and abstract thought. It may also suggest that he was seeking through art and ritual the means of coming to terms with his environment in ways that were essentially religious.

The Sacred and the Holy

If The Dancing Sorcerer was a representation of a sacred person, then he was the forerunner of a type that is a common feature of religion. An early example of the 'sacred person', almost certainly existing from Palaeolithic times but still found in some areas today, is the shaman. The word 'shaman' is of Siberian origin, and it is in Siberia and northern and western America that some of the clearest examples of shamanism have been studied in recent times. The shaman is believed to have special contact with the supernatural and so to be able to secure good fortune and to avert evil. His power is thought to derive from direct contact with the supernatural: he is a person possessed by a god or by the soul of a dead person. Part of the shaman's authority comes from the ability to enter trance, and in this condition it is believed that his soul can leave the body and travel freely. It is in this disembodied state that he is thought to meet with supernatural powers and so to obtain their help.

Cave art may also contain references to shamanistic practices. In the caves at Lascaux there is a painting of a bison wounded by a lance. A man with the head of a bird has fallen before the bison, his hooked weapon pressed against the animal, and the bison's horns are pointed threateningly towards him. Nearby is a bird's head on a pole. The painting may be commemorative, or it may have been a piece of sympathetic magic intended to bring about the death of a hunter. But it has also been interpreted as the portrayal of a shaman in a trance before a sacrificial bison. The shaman's soul would then be free to travel to the gods in order to ask for success in the hunt. The bird's head on its perch or pole has been a symbol in Siberian shamanism until recent times.

The shaman's special place, particularly in hunting and nomadic societies, depends upon the ability to enter into states of trance and ecstasy, and this is regarded as evidence of being chosen by supernatural powers. Robert Lowrie has suggested that there is a useful analytical distinction in the comparative study of religious organizations between the shaman and the priest. The shaman represents a type which is regarded as speaking from God, or the supernatural, to people, while the priest derives his authority from a religious organization and sometimes also from skill in using texts, and so may be seen as speaking from, or for, the community to God. The distinction has its uses in analysing prophetic and priestly roles, but we have to remember that there are examples of types other than the shamanistic in which religious authority is based upon a perceived level of spiritual experience, including trance-like states. Some of the gurus of India would come into this category. And the understanding of priesthood often carries with it the connotation of a person sacred because he (and only very rarely she) is the vehicle through which God has chosen to communicate.

Sacred persons and sacred objects bear about them the marks of holiness. Holiness might be said to possess two chief characteristics: one is the idea of the separation of what is holy or sacred from the secular or profane order of things; the other is a sense of special power. In primitive societies examples of some of the qualities that later come to be associated with holiness have been identified as 'mana' and 'taboo'. Mana is a Melanesian word which is used to refer to the mysterious power possessed by special people

(medicine men, for example) and thought also to be the means by which spirits and gods are able to perform their superhuman feats. Mana is an elusive concept, but may be thought of as the kind of additional gift possessed by the exorcist, the spiritual healer, or even the person with exceptional powers of leadership or dominance. Taboo is a Polynesian word for objects or people that are considered to be too dangerous to touch or associate with. In some societies and among certain religious groups certain foods may be regarded as taboo, and in some cases this may reflect a people's experience of foods which have been found harmful or potentially dangerous. Certain people may be regarded as taboo during certain periods, perhaps of service in a sanctuary, and so will be isolated from normal human affairs, from family and sexual relations, for a time. This no doubt reflects the sense of otherness which is part of the concept of the sacred. Negatively, groups of people or individuals may be regarded as taboo because close association with them is thought to be defiling or polluting. Again, it is possible that religious sanction is here given to conduct that originally had to do with concern about hygiene. The most obvious example of this kind of taboo is the physical isolation which has been imposed traditionally upon the outcastes of Hindu India.

In more developed concepts of the holy and the sacred the positive ideas of mana and the largely negative notion of taboo still may be found. What is holy has a dual quality: it is both immensely beneficial and dangerous. The sacred, therefore, has to be approached with care after due preparation and often in accordance with special rites.

The sense of the holy as awesome and dangerous is conveyed in the story of Uzzah, in the Hebrew Bible (2 Samuel 6). The Ark (an elaborate rectangular box containing inscriptions of the Torah, regarded as a powerful symbol of the divine presence) was being carried back to Jerusalem after falling into the hands of the Philistines. On the journey 'the oxen stumbled, and Uzzah reached out to the Ark of God and took hold of it. The Lord was angry with Uzzah and struck him down there for his rash act'. To touch the sacred object, the focus of the divine presence, was to encounter the threatening nature of the holy. The sacred object represents the separation of the divine from the secular, and conveys the sense of spiritual power which is also part of the nature of what is regarded as holy. By derivation, what belongs especially to God is also thought to possess some of these same characteristics. The sanctuary is a special place where great benefits can be secured but in which the awesome and even dangerous aspects of the sacred may be encountered. The priest, too, is seen as separated in some sense from the secular world, with the derived authority to mediate the power and benefits of the holy, but also in certain cases with the ability to transmit some of the more ambiguous qualities of the sacred to those who are in contact with him. But the idea of holiness can be applied much more widely. In early Judaism, for example, the whole people of Israel came to be seen as belonging in a special sense to God, differentiated from other people by a relationship defined by cultic laws but which the prophets told them was also to be manifested in high ethical standards. In most religions similar connections can be traced. The holy is what belongs to God, or the supernatural, or the transcendent; but the worshippers regard themselves as separated from other people by their special commitment, and they too are in some sense 'holy'. It then comes to be recognized that ritual and cultic acts are not of themselves sufficient to express what it means to belong to a holy and righteous God or to follow a sacred teaching, and so ethical standards also come to be seen as important indicators of a people's commitment and a sign of personal holiness.

In looking in detail at a particular religious tradition, however, it will become apparent that there is constant conflict between the ideals of holiness and high ethical conduct on the one hand and the realities of everyday practice on the other. There is always a temptation for the believer to emphasize the cultic or ritual parts of a religious code – making an offering at the temple, attending mass, observing dietary laws, or whatever it may be – at the expense of the ethical. These are the clearly defined and easily performed religious acts; and they often provide essential frameworks without which religions would lose their distinctive characters and meaning. They do not contradict the ethical demands of religions, but they can become substitutes for them. Religious reformers are often found to be recalling people to what they regard as the true intentions of a religious tradition, demanding that they see through the outward forms to the inner meaning, and that religious profession should be matched by high ethical conduct. Inevitably, in all religious traditions, ideals are professed which are only imperfectly fulfilled in practice. This conflict is one of the fascinating areas that the student of religion can observe, and that the practitioner of religion is constantly challenged to try to reconcile.

METHODOLOGY

The study of religions, as is by now quite apparent, cannot be pursued by the methods of a single discipline. This may seem to pose problems for religious studies as an academic subject, although it is by no means unique in this regard. There are certainly examples of other subjects on the academic curriculum which also require a combination of discipline methods to do justice to them. And a too rigorous and jealous view of academic disciplines is in any case retrogressive in our complex and rapidly changing world. Area studies and other necessarily multi-disciplinary subjects have found their ways increasingly into curricula, and in many cases the multi-disciplinary approach will be better suited to exploring the questions of the modern world than the narrower approach of the academic purist.

Much religious study is concerned with history, and the history of religions constitutes one of the most frequently used approaches to the study of religious phenomena. This method has often

SOME RELIGIOUS FIGURES, WRITINGS AND EVENTS

HISTORY	APPROXIMATE DATES BCE	WRITINGS
CIVILIZATIONS OF EGYPT, MESOPOTAMIA, INDIA, CHINA	3000---	
INDO-EUROPEANS (ARYANS) TO INDIA	1500	
MOSES LEADS HEBREWS	1250	BOOK OF THE COVENANT
DEVELOPMENT OF 'BRAHMANISM'	1500-800	VEDIC HYMNS
ZOROASTER/ZARATHUSHTRA	1200-1000	FIRST AVESTA HYMNS
HINDU SAGES	800-300	UPANISHADS
HEBREW PROPHETS	850-400	PROPHETIC BOOKS
CONFUCIUS AND LAO-TZU	600-450	CHINESE CLASSICS
GAUTAMA THE BUDDHA	563-483	TIPITAKA
VARDHAMANA (MAHAVIRA) TEACHES THE JAINAS	540-468	JAINA ANGAS
SOCRATES, PLATO, ARISTOTLE	469-322	GREEK PHILOSOPHICAL WRITINGS
ASHOKA SPREADS BUDDHISM	250---	
HINDU HEROES AND TEACHERS	200-200 CE	MAHABHARATA AND RAMAYANA
	APPROXIMATE DATES CE	
JESUS CHRIST	6 BCE-27-30 CE	
CHURCH IN ROMAN EMPIRE	55---	NEW TESTAMENT WRITINGS BEGIN
BUDDHISM IN CHINA	64---	CHINESE BUDDHIST SUTRAS AND SHASTRAS
JEWISH DISPERSION	70---	
WRITING OF JEWISH LAW AND ETHICS	200	MISHNAH
CANON OF THE NEW TESTAMENT FIXED	367	NEW TESTAMENT
CHURCH IN ENGLAND	300---	
CH'AN (ZEN) BUDDHISM IN CHINA	520	
BUDDHISM IN JAPAN	538	
MUHAMMAD	570-632	QUR'AN BEGUN
BUDDHISM IN TIBET	625---	
ISLAM SPREADS TO SPAIN AND INDIA	632-732	
FIRST PRINTED SCRIPTURES, IN CHINA	868	BUDDHIST DIAMOND SUTRA
EAST AND WEST CHURCHES SEPARATE	1054	
NANAK AND THE SIKH GURUS	1469-1699	GURU GRANTH SAHIB
REFORMATION AND CATHOLIC REFORMATION	1520-1565	
ANGLICANS AND INDEPENDENTS SEPARATE	1662	
METHODIST REVIVAL	1738---	
BAB MARTYRED, BAHA'I FOUNDED	1850---	BAHA'I WRITINGS
SALVATION ARMY	1865---	
WORLD PARLIAMENT OF RELIGIONS, CHICAGO	1893	
RAMAKRISHNA MISSION FOUNDED	1897	
ISLAMIC KHALIFATE ABOLISHED	1924	
WORLD COUNCIL OF CHURCHES	1948---	
ISLAMIC REVIVAL IN THE MIDDLE EAST	1960---	
SECOND VATICAN COUNCIL	1962-1965	

been concerned with the distant past, with attempting to discern the religious significance of archaeological discoveries and with the translation of ancient texts. The intending historian of religion is faced, therefore, with the task of learning one or more of the languages in which the major texts of the great world religions are written. For a study of Jewish biblical texts he or she will need to know Hebrew; for the New Testament, Greek; for the Qur'an, Arabic; for Hindu texts, Sanskrit and perhaps at least one other Indian language; for Buddhist texts, Pali; and so on. This obviously requires a great investment of time and energy, and yet it is essential for anyone who wishes to penetrate beyond superficial judgements of traditions. A text in translation is inevitably different in some degree from the original and the language of a religion also provides insight into the thought-forms and concepts of a particular tradition. However, part of the task of the historian of religion will be to interpret as faithfully and clearly as possible the messages and insights of one religion to those who do not stand within the tradition. The historical method in religion is not confined to the examination of texts or the study of sources of considerable antiquity. Like all history, it can be modern, early modern or medieval, as well as ancient, and so is used for studies of particular periods and issues in the past, including the immediate past. What distinguishes the historical from other methods here is the use of the methodology of history, with its concern for the careful examination and evaluation of primary and other sources.

Historians of religion may have personal beliefs of their own, but clearly their belief or lack of it is not essential to the method. It is possible to record and analyse the development of religious movements or to examine the texts without sharing in the beliefs that have inspired them. The method of theology is different in this respect. The word theology has been used most often in Christian circles, and in Europe the study of religion was dominated for centuries by theology. University departments devoted to the study of religion were often designated as departments of theology, and this reflected the assumption that at the heart of the subject was a reflection upon *theos*, or God, and that theistic, and indeed Christian, religion was the norm. The method of theology also requires a knowledge of language, because theology is much concerned with the interpretation of texts. This reflects not simply an historical interest, but commonly an acceptance of revelation. The belief that true religion is primarily a matter of God reaching out to human beings, rather than people seeking for God, is an important one in many traditions, and it leads naturally to the conviction that revelation becomes enshrined in a text.

The word of revelation, embodied in a person, communicated to a special messenger, or spoken through the mouths of prophets, comes to be written down, and study of the written word is then seen to be the most direct way of apprehending the original revelation. The belief that the word of God was spoken directly to Muhammad and then recorded in the Qur'an is an important article of faith among Muslims; Jews and Christians regard their biblical texts as records which contain the word of God, although only a minority among them would regard every part of the texts as equally the word of God. Sikhs believe their holy book, the Guru Granth Sahib, to contain the divine word which was revealed through the leaders, or Gurus, of Sikhism, from Guru Nanak to Guru Gobind Singh. The interpretation of texts as the embodiment of the faith of a religious community and as divine revelation is therefore central to the theologian's task. The theological method proceeds on the basis of assumption or belief which most often includes belief in the existence of *theos* and of God's revelation of himself or of his will to people, although theologians have made, and continue to make, claims for the proof of the existence of God upon a rational basis. But a foundation of belief does not much restrict the room for argument and varieties of interpretation which are left to the theologian. It is one thing to say 'I believe in God', but quite another then to explain what is meant by such a belief and what the consequences of it might be. The layperson sometimes appears to be surprised by ways in which apparently fundamental tenets of faith can be interpreted and reinterpreted, often allegorically or symbolically.

Another methodological approach employed in the study of religions is the philosophical method. Philosophy is used extensively as a tool which can refine and clarify thought in a wide variety of disciplines, and this is one of its major uses in religious studies. But philosophy has a very long association with religion, and it is not always easy to distinguish philosophical from religious concerns. Plato clearly was a great philosopher, and his work a major contribution to the discipline of philosophy; yet his reflections on the nature of the soul and the possibility of life after death are also part of Greek religious thought, and grist to the mill of anyone concerned with the development of the religion of ancient Greece. In India, philosophy has often been regarded as one of the most important parts of religious expression. The Upanishads are replete with philosophical discussion (by contrast with the more declamatory nature of texts in the earlier Vedic period), and the six major schools of Hindu philosophy figure largely in Hindu religious teaching. Some of the greatest figures of modern Hinduism who have done much to defend Hindu

beliefs and practice against critics and to commend them to the West (Swami Vivekananda and S. Radhakrishnan, for example) have identified essential Hinduism with the philosophy of *advaita vedanta*. And in India it is not uncommon to find philosophers who maintain that the proper end of philosophy is some kind of religious understanding or commitment.

In the West, however, in recent times the discipline of philosophy has served chiefly as an analytical tool when applied to the study of religions. In this capacity it has drawn attention to problems of the use of language. Specialists in religion, accustomed to handling mythological and symbolic language, are not always as careful as they might be to distinguish between what are matters of belief or commitment and what are matters of fact. Philosophers remind them of the importance of exact language, help them to apply logic to their analysis of religion, and transmit the findings of the philosophical analysis of religious belief which has been so important in the re-assessment of religion in the western world over the last three hundred years or so.

The methods of sociology are also widely used in assessing the nature of religion, and especially of religious practice, and reference has been made above to this in elaborating upon the sociological dimension of religion. The institutional forms of religion are of great importance, and so a methodology which is designed to analyse forms of social life, reasons why people respond in certain ways to social pressures, the structures of institutions and their increase or decrease in appeal, is particularly useful. Differences between religion in different cultural contexts are evident in sociological enquiry. In western Europe the dominant religion is one to which people often attach themselves, or from which they detach themselves, by conscious choice, and so the analysis of patterns of membership and adherence over a period of time helps us to see what is happening to the formal institutions of religion. In other cultural contexts such measurement may be impossible or inappropriate. Muslims in Syria or Pakistan, or Hindus in village India, are unlikely to think of religion as an area of life that can be separated clearly from the secular world. Other aspects of social organization, however, such as caste in India, may be fruitful areas of study. In a European and American context especially sociologists have directed much attention to the question of 'secularization', a term which is itself open to a variety of interpretations, but which is often used to refer to a decline in the authority of religious institutions and, although much more difficult to measure, of religious belief in the face of secular (that is, this-worldly or materialistic)

A Hindu prayer meeting in North London led by a guru, or teacher. Six schools of Hindu philosophy figure in Hindu religious teaching. Unlike Western philosophy, which has served chiefly as an analytical tool when applied to the study of religion, essential Hinduism has been identified with the philosophy of advaita vedanta. *This Vedanta philosophy is based on the Upanishads which are themselves central to the Hindu religion.*

modes of thought and practice. The debate about secularization makes it clear that the strength of religious institutions and levels of church attendance differ widely between countries which share the same general background of thought and appear to be similarly placed in terms of their level of industrial development, and theories of secularization are advanced in attempts to account for such differences.

The related discipline of social anthropology is also of great importance for the understanding of religion. Social anthropologists have engaged in much careful and patient work, living alongside people whose backgrounds and culture may be quite different from their own in order to assess the nature of their beliefs and practices. Religion has been a major subject of enquiry for social anthropologists, and distinguished specialists (Radcliffe-Brown, Malinowski, Durkheim, Evans Pritchard and others) have produced theoretical explanations of religious practice and behaviour as well as amassing invaluable material from many different societies. One important contribution of social anthropologists has been to refine and challenge the theories of armchair scholars whose expositions of particular religions were based solely upon texts. The fact that texts may say one thing while believers say and do something else is one of the fascinations of the study of religions, and it has been heavily underlined by the work of social anthropologists.

Psychology appears to be used by religious studies specialists less than the other disciplines mentioned, but it has its part to play. Two of the great figures of psychology, Freud and Jung, have made a considerable impact upon thinking about religion. Freud's work is very critical of religion. In *Totem and Taboo*, Freud explained away religion as something that began with the Oedipus complex, and saw God as essentially an exalted father-figure. Religion was described by Freud as the expression of 'a universal obsessional neurosis', which might be thought a curious phrase since neurosis is normally taken to refer to abnormal rather than to 'universal' behaviour. Freud's views have had a considerable influence, although he has also been strongly criticized (for example by his one-time pupil, Theodore Reich) for constructing a speculative theory that is little supported by research into religious practice and history. Jung, however, took a very different view from Freud. Although critical of western forms of religion, and especially of Christianity, Jung believed that religion had an important part to play in developing a healthy and balanced personality. Whilst Freud saw religion as a symptom of disease, Jung regarded the absence of religion as an important source of psychological problems. In *Modern Man in Search of a Soul*, Jung claimed that psychiatric disorders among his adult patients

were 'never really healed' unless the patients regained a religious outlook on life. Jung was particularly attracted by eastern religions which coincided more clearly with some of his ideas than did Christianity. He thought that the dualism of good and evil in Christian thought was dangerous and less healthy than the integration of the lower side of human nature into religious symbols in the ways found in some eastern religions. He also believed that objectivized divinities are simply projections of the self, and was sympathetic to the view that religion is more concerned with self-discovery than with a relationship with an external, transcendent God. He developed the theory of a 'collective unconscious' in which are present ideas similar to those found in folklore and mythology, ideas to which he gave the name 'archetypes'.

Aside from the theoretical concerns of Freud and Jung, psychology makes a methodological contribution to the study of religions. Religion represents a significant area of human behaviour, and psychology helps to provide explanations for that. Questions about how processes of conversion work, whether some personality types are likely to be more amenable than others to sudden conversion, and why authoritarian patterns of religious life have a special appeal for some, are all questions addressed by psychology. The discipline also has its contribution to make to the study of religious experience, prayer and mysticism.

Finally, it is appropriate here to mention an approach to the study of religions which is not in itself a subject discipline, but which is often referred to in discussion of methodology, and that is the phenomenological approach. The abstruseness of the word is complicated further by the fact that it appears to be used in two different ways in religious studies. The word is sometimes used (especially by Scandinavian scholars) to describe a comparative approach, in which material drawn from the history of religions and other appropriate sources is arranged thematically. In this use of the word, 'phenomenological' refers to attempts to arrange material on themes which appear to be common to different religious traditions, and so to identify types of religion. The second, and more common, use corresponds to the use of the word in other social sciences. In this sense, a phenomenological approach is one in which the student or observer of a religious tradition attempts to enter into the thought-forms of the believers; to develop an empathy with those who believe and practise the religion being observed. The method involves the withholding of value judgements, and aims to enhance understanding of religion by adding a grasp of the subjective view of the believer to the more objective data gathered by the various discipline approaches. The intention of phenomenology clearly is important. The method encourages the student to do more than note and analyse the practices, rituals and festivals of a religious tradition, or to record and criticize the statements of belief agreed by adherents. Phenomenology encourages the view that such objective study, much encouraged in the nineteenth century when scholars were attempting to establish the academic respectability of the 'science of religion', may be deficient in an important way, namely in that it may overlook factors thought to be most important in religious traditions by their own adherents. Religious believers do not normally see their own traditions as a collection of objective phenomena, but as a living faith to which institutions, buildings and sometimes even history and writings are incidental. There is great difficulty in attempting to penetrate the inwardness of any religious tradition and to reach even a modest understanding of what it means to its adherents. But phenomenology suggests that the attempt be made.

Religion, then, is a complex subject, and may be studied in a variety of ways. In what follows the reader will discern the approaches that have been used in this book. It will be clear that the historical approach is important; that sociology is widely used; that some theology appears; and it is hoped that the sympathetic treatment of the phenomenological approach will also be evident.

For purposes of clarity and consistency, most of the articles follow a common structure, with material grouped under the headings of: History and Distribution; Belief; Writings; Ritual and Worship; Organization. The nature of the subject sometimes makes this inappropriate, however, and readers will notice that the section on Mahayana Buddhism is the most obvious exception to the overall pattern. In that section the gradual development of different forms of Mahayana is traced, and the implications for belief and worship are examined in the course of that development.

In a work of this kind there is bound to be considerable selectivity in the material that is presented, and the bibliography is provided partly in order to indicate possible further reading for those who wish to explore the religions in greater detail.

Not every religion of the world, past and present, is dealt with here. Such a treatment would require a considerably larger volume, or set of volumes. This book deals with the major religious traditions of East and West: most of these are living religions, although some are now little represented in their area of origin (Zoroastrianism and Theravada Buddhism), and some have ceased to be a major force in the civilization with which they are historically connected (Confucianism and Taoism). But all of them have been, and most still are, influential in the formation of religious thought and religious practice, and this seems sufficient ground for their inclusion. And, since religious thought and practice are constantly changing, attention is paid not only to the great traditions but also to examples of relatively recent movements, some of which have developed out of or in reaction against the major religious traditions.

From the great variety of religious beliefs and practices described and illustrated here it is hoped that the reader will be helped to develop a sympathetic understanding of the religions and perhaps a deeper insight into the issues with which religions have always been concerned.

JUDAISM

HISTORICAL OUTLINE

Judaism is centred on a people, the Jews, of whom in the second half of the twentieth century there are around twelve million, residing mainly in the USA and Canada, the State of Israel, the Soviet Union, South Africa, Australia and New Zealand, the United Kingdom, France, and other European countries.

A key concept in Judaism is that of the Torah, a word denoting 'teaching', 'law' or 'rule'. In its narrowest connotation the term refers to the Five Books of Moses (the Pentateuch, the first five books of the 'Old Testament' of the Bible, the sacred scriptures of the Jews). These books form the body of the teachings, the history, laws and doctrines from which is derived everything else in Judaism. Consequently, in its wider meaning, the Torah embraces the whole of authentic Jewish teaching, both that which is seen as implied in the five books and that which was added throughout the ages by way of commentary, elaboration and application of the original doctrines. The Torah is not an object of worship in Judaism, but it is through the Torah that God conveys His will to the Jewish people, and through them to the whole of mankind. The triad that constitutes Judaism thus consists of God, the Torah, and Israel.

Israel

'Israel' is another and older name for the Jews, derived from the patriarch Jacob, called Israel ('Prince of God', Genesis 32:28). The words 'Jew' and 'Judaism' are both derived from Judah, the name of one of Jacob's sons and therefore also of the tribe that son was associated with. The tribe of Judah was located in the south of ancient Palestine, and it is from this tribe that the majority of Jews are believed to be descended.

The traditional picture

The old Jewish tradition presents a clear picture of how Judaism originated and of its meaning and significance, a picture based on the biblical accounts and the later narratives as told by Jews from generation to generation. From the point of view of modern historical investigation the traditional picture is too simplistic, leaving many questions unanswered and even in some areas actually contradicting the evidence now available of how Judaism really did come about. But the traditional scheme possesses a grandeur of its own, and is in any event essential for an understanding of the impetus and historical dynamic of the ancient faith.

According to this traditional scheme, then, God created the world out of nothing and, as the highest of His creative acts, He made man in the image of Himself, the lord of creation. Adam, the first man, and his wife, Eve, were placed in the Garden of Eden where they were given free access to everything in the garden – everything, that is, except the Tree of Knowledge of Good and Evil. When Adam disobeyed God's command by eating fruit from this tree, he and his wife were driven out of Eden.

There were ten generations from Adam through his son Seth (although no indication is given of whom Seth married) down to Noah, each generation headed by a man who lived for hundreds of years (although none of them lived to reach a thousand years of age). In the days of Noah, humankind had become corrupt; God therefore decided to destroy the human race in a great deluge. Noah was instructed to build a huge boat-like vessel (Noah's 'ark') into which he was to bring his family and pairs of all the animals in the world in order to save them from the flood and re-populate the earth afterwards. After the deluge had destroyed all the rest of humankind Noah, his three sons, Shem, Ham and Japhet, and their wives came out of the ark and procreated to become the new ancestors of the human race. But God's plan remained unfulfilled. The worship of false gods instead of the one true God became so rife that eventually all men were won over to idolatry. This further fall from the truth took place during the ten generations between Noah and Abraham.

Abraham's father was an idolater but Abraham, by his own efforts, came to acknowledge the true God, who made a personal covenant with him and on behalf of his successors. At God's command, Abraham left his father's house to journey to the land of Canaan, which God promised to his descendants. Because Abraham and his wife Sarah were childless, Abraham took Hagar – Sarah's handmaid – as a second wife and she bore him a son, Ishmael. When Abraham was one hundred years old and Sarah ninety, their youth was miraculously renewed: a son, Isaac, was born to them too. It was as a sign of God's covenant with Abraham that he was instructed by God to circumcise himself and his sons.

Of Abraham's two sons it was Isaac who was chosen to be the second party to the covenant after Abraham and, in turn, of Isaac's two sons it was Jacob who was chosen for this role. Jacob had twelve sons, all faithful to the covenant, and they became the founders of the twelves tribes who eventually settled in the 'holy land', the land of Israel, promised to Abraham's descendants. Joseph, the favourite son, was sold into slavery in Egypt by his brothers who were stirred to jealousy by his prophetic dreams. But through Joseph's advice to the Egyptian pharaoh at a time of famine, Joseph rose to a rank second only to the ruler himself. During the famine years Joseph brought his father and brothers to Egypt where they settled and multiplied. A new pharaoh came to power in Egypt, however, and enslaved the 'Children of Israel', as the descendants of Jacob were then called.

Eventually God sent a leader, Moses, to redeem the Children of Israel from their Egyptian bondage. In his infancy Moses – a great-grandson of Levi (another of Jacob's sons) – was adopted by the pharaoh's daughter, who brought him up as an Egyptian prince. Moses knew, all the same, of his Israelite origin and when the Israelites petitioned to be allowed to leave the country, and were refused, he sided with his brethren against their oppressors. Finally, afttter God visited him and his people with severe plagues, the pharaoh did release the slaves, only to repent of his charity shortly afterwards and to pursue them until they were hemmed in at the edge of the Sea of Reeds. A tremendous miracle then occurred. The waters of the sea were divided and the Israelites walked to safety across dry land. The waters of the sea then returned to engulf the pursuing Egyptian warriors, causing the Israelites to sing a song of thanksgiving to the God of their deliverance.

Moses led his people to the foot of Mount Sinai in the wilderness of present-day north-east Egypt. Here Moses was told by God to prepare the people for His descent on to the mountain, where He would deliver to Moses the Ten Commandments. Accordingly Moses went up the mountain by

Hasidic Jews reading the Torah, the Five Books of Moses. These form the body of the teachings, the history, laws and doctrines from which is derived everything in Judaism. In a wider meaning the Torah embraces all authentic Jewish teaching including commentaries of the original doctrines. It is through the Torah that God conveys His will to the Jewish people.

himself for a period of forty days during which God taught him the Torah so that he might in turn teach it to the people. God's plan was now near its fulfilment: the newly-formed nation, equipped with the Torah, was about to become a 'kingdom of priests and a holy nation' (Exodus 19:6), living by God's laws as revealed in the Torah, and serving as a model of obedience to God's word for all the families of the earth. But during Moses' stay on the mountain, the people waiting below had taken to worshipping a golden calf. As Moses came down from the mountain, bearing the two tablets of stone upon which God had engraved the Ten Commandments, he witnessed the people dancing round the calf, at which scene he became so enraged that he hurled the tablets from him and they were shattered. In His own wrath, God considered destroying the faithless people and raising up a new, faithful nation from Moses' seed. Out of love for his people, Moses pleaded on their behalf . . . and God pardoned them. Moses again ascended the Mount to bring down two new tablets of stone. And during Moses' sojourn on the mountain God taught him both the written Torah, as recorded in the Pentateuch, and the oral Torah, the explanations and elaborations of the scriptural texts.

The children of Israel journeyed through the wilderness for forty years, during which period all the generation that originally took to the wilderness gradually died. As the people came to the threshold of the land of Canaan, the Promised Land, Moses climbed Mount Nebo where he, too, died and was buried, although his place of burial is not known. Before Moses took his last leave of his people he warned them that if they were to follow the abominable practices of the Egyptians and the Canaanites, God would drive them out of the land – their holy land – which was no place for settlement by an unholy people. He then laid his hands on his disciple Joshua, who was to take his place as leader and teacher of the children of Israel and act as their general in the conquest of the land promised to them by God. The tribes duly conquered the land and settled there, each tribe being allocated a portion.

Led by a succession of leaders and 'judges' after Joshua, the people eventually decided to appoint a king. The first was the warrior Saul. Saul was succeeded by David, the youthful general who was also 'sweet psalmist in Israel', to whom the Book of Psalms is traditionally attributed. It was David who made the city of Jerusalem his capital, in which David's son Solomon built the great Temple where sacrifices were offered to the true God not only by the Israelites but also by foreign visitors to the land. After Solomon's death, Jeroboam, son of Nebat of the tribe of Ephraim, set up a rival kingdom in the north of the country so that at that point there were two kingdoms: Judah (Judaea), headed by David's descendants, in the south, and Ephraim or Israel in the north.

The northern kingdom fell in 722 BCE to the Assyrian king Sennacherib, who transported all the northern tribespeople to other places, resulting later in considerable speculation about what had became of 'the lost ten tribes'. The southern kingdom of Judaea fell in 586 BCE to the Babylonian king Nebuchadnezzar, who destroyed the Temple and took the Judaeans (thus the 'Jews') into exile in Babylon. There they remained for seventy years until the Persian king Cyrus the Great, the new ruler of the Babylonian Empire, granted them permission to return. Those Jews who returned (for many remained in Babylon), under Ezra the Scribe and Nehemiah, rebuilt the Temple. They renewed the ancient covenant with God and swore undying loyalty to the Torah. Ezra and his associates, the spiritual leaders at the beginning of the Second Commonwealth, are known as 'the Men of the Great Assembly'.

During some of these political events, for a period of about 150 years from the eighth century BCE, a succession of remarkable men, the literary prophets, were prominent in both the northern and southern kingdoms. These prophets were given a message from God to the people of their day with implications for posterity. Because they believed that God had spoken to them, the usual preface to their proclamations was 'Thus saith the Lord'. The prophecies were later recorded to form the prophetic books of the Hebrew Bible. Although each of the prophets had his own particular emphasis and his own literary style, the general prophetic teaching is that God demands of His people that they practise justice, righteousness and charity, and show compassion.

The prophets warned, as Moses had, that if the people were faithless to God's word they would suffer exile from the land. Yet, throughout the period of the prophets, a faithful remnant was always to be found who kept the Torah alive by handing down its teachings from generation to generation. In fact, the prophets themselves were not so much innovators as teachers of the Torah given to Moses. An early Jewish work, *Ethics of the Fathers*, thus remarks with regard to the chain of tradition: 'Moses received the Torah at Sinai. He handed it down to Joshua, Joshua to the Elders, the Elders to the Prophets, and the Prophets to the Men of the Great Assembly.'

The Second Temple stood for more than 400 years, during which time Palestine (the name later given to the land of Israel) was ruled over successively by the Persians, the Greeks and then the Romans. In 70 CE the Romans destroyed the Second Temple, scattering the Jews among many peoples while allowing a Jewish population to continue to survive in Palestine. Even in exile – in the 'Diaspora' – many Jews held fast to the

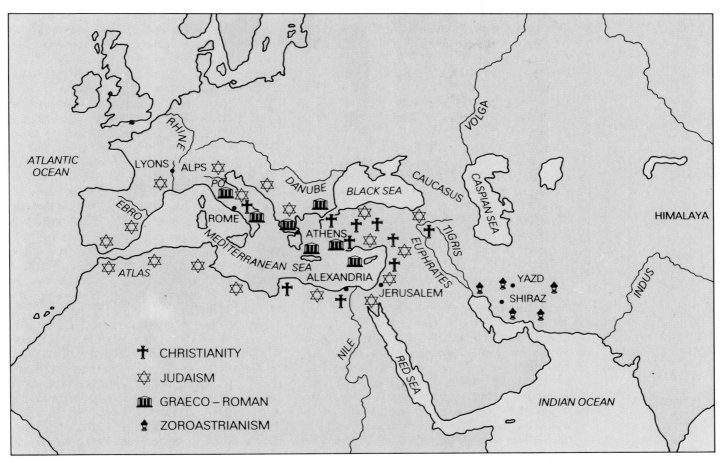

Areas of activity among differing religions in the 2nd century. After the destruction of Jerusalem by the Romans in 70 CE Jewish communities of the Diaspora, the exile, sprang up all along the North African coast and spread into Spain as well as merging into Turkey and Greece.

teachings of the Torah, looking forward to the day when God would send them a redeemer, the Messiah (the 'anointed one'), who would lead them back to the holy land, where the Temple would be rebuilt, never again to be destroyed.

This Third Temple will be a house of prayer and worship for all the people on earth, and the Kingdom of God will be established on earth. All people will acknowledge God as Sovereign and will obey His Word. In this culmination of human history, God's original plan will at last find its fulfilment.

Revision of the traditional picture

Modern scholarship has succeeded in convincing many Jews, no matter how committed to their religious beliefs, that the conventional scheme cited above requires qualification. For instance, it is now held to be far from certain that the biblical sources are always accurate about what really happened in what was even to them the distant past – and some of these sources were in any case not even intended to convey historical information. From this point of view the Adam and Eve narratives are best seen as mythical, that is, as the expression of ideas in which some truth is perceived but not necessarily a historical truth. The story of Noah's ark should similarly be seen as part of a widespread ancient Near-Eastern myth, parallel-

led (even in detail) by the Babylonian Epic of Gilgamesh and used by the biblical writers but transformed in the service of monotheism. In contrast to the other ancient tales in which divine beings lived for ever because they became gods, the antediluvians of Israelite narrations are all recorded as suffering death. Utanapishtim, the hero of the Babylonian epic, was spared from the deluge as a favourite of the gods; Noah is spared because he is the only righteous man in his generation, and when he is delivered he makes a covenant with the God who desires righteousness and justice.

Similarly, although it is not denied that the patriarchs are historical figures, it has become plausible to see them also as prototypes, many of the descriptions of whose lives are not factual but representations of how the lives of their descendants should be lived in obedience to the covenant.

Martin Buber has described this process as the 'mythization of history'. The historical facts have been worked over repeatedly as the ancient saga was told and recited through the ages; the result is a biblical record that is the end product of a lengthy process. Biblical criticism has endeavoured to detect various traditions coming together in the Pentateuch. The figure of Moses, the lawgiver, attracted to itself all the subsequent attempts at working out the Torah, God's will for His people, and it is in this sense that the whole of the Torah, written and oral, is the Torah of Moses – just as the figure of David attracted to itself psalm composition, so that David became the 'author' of the Book of Psalms.

Modernist Jews, who accept that the traditional picture requires revision in the light of critical research, nevertheless maintain that the traditional view of how Judaism came into being retains its force because in its essentials the truth by which Jews are expected to live remains unaffected. Whether monotheism erupted spontaneously in ancient Israel, or whether, as many scholars have argued, a gradual development can be discerned from polytheism through henotheism to pure monotheism, does not obscure the fact that monotheism did eventually emerge as the fundamental idea upon which Judaism is based.

The same applies to the two other concepts, Jewish nationhood and its special providential role, and the Torah as revealing God's will. It is certain that long before the Christian era these main themes had assumed a definite form which they have retained ever since. Judaism affirms that God, the Creator of the world and all that is in it, has chosen the Jewish people to live according to His will as revealed through the Torah and eventually to lead all humankind to His service.

The particularist elements in Judaism must be kept in proportion. Jewish peoplehood is basic to Judaism, in that there can be no Judaism without Jews, yet Judaism is a world religion in addition to being the source of two other world religions, Christianity and Islam. Special duties, obligations and responsibilities are felt by the Jews to devolve upon themselves – but the Torah, albeit with less severe demands, is addressed to all human beings. In later Jewish literature there are thus many references to 'the seven laws of the sons of Noah', principles by which all humankind is expected to live. These principles involve decent human conduct and include the need for a society to have just laws, and for all human beings to be honest in their dealings with one another and to avoid murder, theft, adultery and incest. The Gentile (non-Jew) who keeps these laws is said to belong to 'the righteous of the nations of the world', and such a person has, in the language of tradition, 'a share in the World to Come' – that is, the person merits the enjoyment of eternal bliss in the hereafter.

As a religion centring around the Jewish people, Judaism has been influenced by the cultural, social and political conditions under which Jews have lived. The various civilizations that have formed the background to Jewish life in different epochs and in diverse communities have produced varying emphases in the interpretation and application of the religion. In the Middle Ages,

for instance, the Jews of Muslim Spain absorbed Greek thought in its Arabic garb and came under the powerful influence of general Arabic culture, so that Spanish Jewry placed the emphasis on rational inquiry, showed a keen interest in poetry and other literary activities, and had a fondness for systematic presentation of Jewish ideas. The Franco-German Jewries, in the same period, in a Christian environment, were far less systematic and outward-looking but compensated for that by a more profound concentration on the tradition and its classical sources. Similarly, the Jews of Palestine in the early centuries of the Christian era, confronted with the challenges presented by Roman civilization and by Christianity, produced their own particular responses in the rabbinical traditions and writings of the Palestinian Talmud. The Jews of Babylon, meanwhile, against a background of Persian culture and the Zoroastrian religion, produced a different monument to their life and thought, the Babylonian Talmud.

For this reason Judaism did not develop as a monolithic structure. In all periods tensions are found between universalism and particularism, rationalism and faith, this-worldliness and other-worldliness, loyalty to the tradition and the desire for change and reform. It is not surprising that on many issues Jewish teachers have held differing views and that in theoretical – though not to the same degree in practical – matters considerable individual freedom was tolerated. Nevertheless, a kind of consensus did emerge among the faithful as to which beliefs could deviate permissibly from the norm and which so departed from that norm as to render those who held them to be apostates. It was possible, for example, for the fourteenth-century teacher Gersonides, without forfeiting his right to be called a Jew and a teacher of Judaism, to hold that God does not know the future activities of individuals (a severe compromise of the doctrine of divine omniscience). But no representative Jewish teacher could, or ever did, suggest that adherence to Christian or Islamic beliefs is compatible with Judaism. It was not that the issue was settled by a synod or great council in which questions of belief were debated and decided. It was rather the power of the consensus, operating with all the insights that Jewish historical experience afforded, which resulted in an attitude of inclusion in the one instance and exclusion in the other.

What Jews believe

It has sometimes been suggested that Judaism has no dogmas. It is certainly true, as noted above, that there has never been a series of propositions, drawn up by a representative body of Jewish sages convened for the purpose and belief in which is incumbent upon every Jew. But this does not mean that Judaism has no fundamental beliefs. A dogma-less religion has no identity as a separate system of faith. Because the beliefs are defined by the consensus at work among Jews, their precise formulation is bound to be flexible; some Jewish teachers stress one belief, other teachers a different belief. What is really significant is the question of exactly which beliefs are essential.

The search for the essence of Judaism has engaged the minds of many Jewish thinkers. The old tale is told in the Talmud of how one prospective convert to Judaism requested the sage Hillel to teach him the whole of the Torah while standing on one leg. Hillel is reported to have replied: 'That which is hateful unto thee do not do unto thy neighbour. This is the whole of the Torah. All the rest is commentary. Now go forth and study.' Some have tried to detect the essence of Judaism in the Ten Commandments, but only the first two of these – 'I am the Lord thy God' and 'Thou shalt have no other gods' – have to do with belief; the others comprise rules of conduct. Further passages in the sources which have been understood as conveying the essence of Judaism are open to the same objection. One of these passages is from the book of the prophet Micah (Micah 6:8):

It hath been told thee, O man, what is good,
And what the Lord doth require of thee;
Only to do justly, and to love mercy, and
To walk humbly with thy God.

Another passage often referred to in this context is Psalm 15:

Lord, who shall sojourn in Thy tabernacle?
Who shall dwell upon Thy holy mountain?
He that walketh uprightly, and worketh
*   righteousness,*
And speaketh truth in his heart.
That hath no slander upon his tongue,
Nor doeth evil to his fellow,
Nor taketh up a reproach against his neighbour;
In whose eyes a vile person is despised;
But he honoureth them that fear the Lord;
He that sweareth to his own hurt, and changeth
*   not;*
He that putteth not out his money on interest,
Nor taketh a bribe against the innocent.
He that doeth these things shall never be moved.

Noble summaries such as these can qualify as succinct statements of the essence of Judaism in practice, although beliefs are implied. It was not until the Middle Ages that a more or less authoritative list of fundamental beliefs was drawn up by the Egyptian Jewish sage Maimonides (1135–1204).

Maimonides himself evidently stressed these particular beliefs as essential because it was these that were at risk of challenge by some of his contemporaries, both Jewish and non-Jewish. His Thirteen Principles of the Faith have won wide acceptance, though the interpretation of each may differ from that specified by him.

1   Belief in the existence of God
2   Belief in the unity of God
3   Belief in the incorporeality of God
4   Belief that God is eternal
5   Belief that God alone is to be worshipped
6   Belief in prophecy
7   Belief that Moses was the greatest of the prophets
8   Belief that the Torah is from God
9   Belief that the Torah is unchanging
10 Belief that God knows the thoughts and deeds of man
11 Belief that the righteous are rewarded and the wicked punished
12 Belief in the coming of the Messiah
13 Belief in the resurrection of the dead

A 14th-century edition of Maimonides' 'Guide for the Perplexed'. The seated figure in the picture is Aristotle to whom Maimonides owed many of his ideas. Originally written in Arabic the Guide was an attempt to reconcile Judaism and philosophy.

Maimonides does not list the belief that humans have free will, a concept basic to Judaism, no doubt because this concept is implied in the eleventh principle. Nor does he list the doctrine that the people of Israel were chosen by God, probably because no challenge was presented to this idea in Maimonides' day (both Christianity and Islam believed in the original choice). Maimonides' ninth principle, the immutability of the Torah, is almost certainly directed against the claim of both Christianity and Islam that a new religion had superseded the religion based on the Torah. The seventh principle seems similarly to be directed against Christianity's claims for Jesus and, especially since Maimonides was writing in an Islamic environment, Islam's claims for Muhammad.

Maimonides' principles are concerned with three basic ideas. Principles 1 to 5 are concerned with the nature of God; principles 6 to 9 with revelation; and the last four principles with the doctrine of divine providence.

The first five principles have generally been accepted as they stand by the majority of Jewish believers. During the Middle Ages there was considerable debate on whether the ideal was to believe in the existence of God because such a belief was handed down by a sure tradition, or whether it was preferable for the Jew (if he or she had the ability) to prove by natural reason that there is a God. The arguments for God's existence among the thinkers who preferred the second option were chiefly cosmological and teleological; the ontological argument is hardly ever found among these thinkers. On the question of God's unity there was no compromise – all believers accepted only pure monotheism as the authentic Jewish belief. Nor was there any dissent from the principles of God's incorporeality and eternity or the principle that God alone is to be worshipped. There were, however, a few Jewish authors in the Middle Ages who believed, on the basis of anthropomorphic passages in scripture, that God could assume a form for a particular purpose and that He really did sit on a throne surrounded by His angels. Eventually, however, the Maimonidean principle won out. Even the most unsophisticated of present-day Jews considers the idea that God has or can assume a corporeal shape or form to be rank heresy.

Belief in revelation is constant in Judaism, although both the manner of revelation and its scope have been understood variously; from the view that God created a special voice by means of which He communicated His will, to the view that the prophet saw his message in the recesses of his own psyche; from the opinion that every word of the Pentateuch is Mosaic and a direct, verbal communication from God, to the opinion that the Pentateuch and the other parts of the Bible are the record, in a variety of versions, of the divine-human encounter rather than containing the actual words of the Almighty. All believing Jews accept the principle of the immutability of the Torah in the sense that Judaism has not been superseded by any other religion. Whether the principle also implies that the Torah suffers neither change nor development is a more complicated question around which there has been much debate, especially after the rise of the Reform movement in the early nineteenth century.

The principles of the doctrine of divine providence are also subject to debate. The interpretation of reward and punishment, for example, ranges from a general belief that righteousness will eventually win out and wickedness fail, to a tidy tit-for-tat belief that every particular good deed merits its particular reward either in this world or the next, and every evil deed its immediate punishment or the postponement of that punishment to the Hereafter. Maimonides' own eschatology follows closely on the ideas found in the earlier sources. The doctrine of the World to Come is understood by him, however, as referring to the eternal bliss the soul will enjoy. Although he records belief in a resurrection of the dead as his thirteenth principle, he is silent on this theme in his writings and was accused by his opponents of denying the physical resurrection. In an essay written towards the end of his life, Maimonides affirmed that he did believe in a physical resurrection but also that this state will not be eternal. After a lengthy period, the body will again return to dust with the soul alone enjoying immortality. Other thinkers tend to speak of a physical resurrection but qualify this doctrine by postulating a resurrection to what is in effect a more refined body, partaking more of the spiritual than the physical.

Jewish thinkers have been divided on whether there is eternal punishment in Hell for the most wicked. Some thinkers accept the doctrine; others limit the stay of the wicked in Hell to a comparatively short period. Maimonides is ambiguous on the question but has been accused of denying that there is a real hell. Hell to him, his critics have maintained, seemed to mean that the thoroughly wicked soul will be annihilated without suffering torment.

Although the doctrine of *creatio ex nihilo* is generally accepted by believers, some thinkers have seen no objection to a belief in the prior existence of a formless substance out of which God created the world. In modern times even some Orthodox thinkers have seen no incompatibility between the belief in God as Creator and the theory of evolution.

There has been considerable debate on the question of individual versus general providence. Maimonides limited individual providence to the human species, maintaining that providence extends only to animal species in general. God does decree that there should be the species of spiders and flies, for example, and He guarantees their continued existence, but it is by chance alone that any particular spider catches any particular fly.

The problem of evil in creation is generally approached through the idea that, so far as human beings are concerned, evil must exist in the universe for it to be an arena in which humans must struggle in order to make the good their own and merit the nearness of God for ever. And as far as evil in the animal creation is concerned, the tendency is to see the problem as beyond the scope of man's limited mind. Saadia (882–942) believed in a heaven for animals, but Maimonides ridiculed the notion. On reincarnation, Saadia considered that this belief, although held by some Jews, was a foreign importation into Judaism, whereas the majority of the Jewish mystics believed in the doctrine.

Among the biblical authors, some speak of a golden age in the future when war and enmity among men will have been banished and when the kingdom of God will be firmly established. Others speak of a person, a descendant of King David, ushering in that age. With the exception of a single rabbi in the Talmud, the traditional view of a personal Messiah prevailed and still does among Orthodox Jews. Reform Jews prefer to speak of a Messianic age rather than of a personal Messiah. And in spite of the teaching that these matters must be left to God, speculation on the date of the Messiah's coming has been rife.

In every version of the doctrine the Messiah is a human figure with no divine powers. Many Orthodox Jews hail the establishment of the State of Israel as heralding the advent of the Messiah in that it has caused many thousands of Jews to return to the holy land in something approaching the fulfilment of the prophetic vision. None holds, however, that the Messiah has actually come and the Messianic Age dawned. A term now much used for the contemporary situation is 'the beginning of the Messianic redemption'.

WRITINGS

The Hebrew Bible, the fountainhead of Judaism, is known as the Tanakh, a word formed from the initial letters of Torah (the Pentateuch), Neviim (the prophets, including the historical books) and Ketuvim (the writings, the Hagiographa). The Bible was produced over an extremely long time; some of its books were not declared sacred by the Jewish sages until the first centuries of the Christian era. From that time, however, the Tanakh has consisted of twenty-four books comprising the sacred scriptures of Judaism.

In the traditional scheme the sanctity of the three sections is in descending order, corresponding to the belief that they were composed under different degrees of divine inspiration. A devout Jew accordingly never places a book of the third division on top of a book of the first or second division, and so on. The twenty-four books of the Tanakh are:

The Torah (in its original sense)
Genesis Exodus Leviticus Numbers Deuteronomy

The Neviim
Joshua Judges Samuel Kings Isaiah Jeremiah Ezekiel The Book of the Twelve Prophets

The Ketuvim
Psalms Proverbs Job The Song of Songs Ruth Lamentations Ecclesiastes Esther Daniel Ezra and Nehemiah Chronicles

The Ark, which stands in the Eastern hall of the synagogue, is here opened to display the scrolls of the Torah. These scrolls are of parchment and handwritten. Emphasizing the importance of the Torah a scroll is taken from the Ark and paraded round the synagogue before being opened.

The Book of the Twelve Prophets itself comprises twelve small books which, because of their relatively small individual size, were written on a single scroll to prevent their being lost; they thus now constitute a unified book, in which are recorded the prophetic works of Hosea, Joel, Amos, Obadiah, Jonah, Micah, Nahum, Habakkuk, Zephaniah, Haggai, Zechariah and Malachi.

Typical of Rabbinic Judaism is the doctrine of the oral Torah, supplementing the written Torah of the Pentateuch and the other two sections of the Tanakh. The oral Torah consists of the earliest traditional explanations of the written text (in the Orthodox view, the oral Torah in this sense was also delivered to Moses) in addition to the subsequent 'enactments' of the sages, their discussions and elaborations of the laws and teachings. The oral Torah was eventually recorded in writing – the Mishnah, the Talmud and the Midrashim – and came to be held to be the sole authentic explanation of the biblical texts. For the Orthodox Jew, the final source of authoritative teaching is thus not the bare text of the Bible but the Bible as interpreted in the oral law. For instance, the biblical injunction to rest and do no work on the Sabbath provides little information regarding the nature of the work that is forbidden. The definition of 'work' is described in great detail in the Talmud and it is this definition which became binding on Jews.

This very issue of the authority of the oral law constituted the great divide between the Pharisees and the Sadducees towards the end of the Second Temple period. The Sadducees (and, in the Middle Ages, the Karaites) denied any value to an oral Torah, taking their stand on the written texts of scripture. The rabbis ('teachers') of the Mishnah, Talmud and Midrashim considered themselves to be the heirs of the Pharisees.

From the historical point of view, the oral Torah is the product of sustained reflection, through many generations, on the meaning of the original biblical texts. The Hebrew word *midrash* (from a root meaning 'to search', 'to inquire') is the word used to denote this process, the results of which are found in the Mishnah and Talmud and in the many collections of these reflections known as the Midrashim.

During the first two centuries of the present era in Palestine the Jewish sages engaged in interminable discussions and debates on the application of the laws of the Torah. Rabbi Judah the Prince collected this material at the end of the second century in the Mishnah ('Teaching'). Arranged in six Orders, this collection then took its place at the side of the Bible as a sacred work. The rabbis in Palestine and in the second great centre of Jewish life, Babylon, thereafter devoted their energies to the elucidation of the Mishnah just as their predecessors had done with regard to the Bible. The language of the Mishnah is the Hebrew used in scholarly circles during the first centuries CE (Mishnaic Hebrew) but the subsequent debates were conducted in the sister-language of Hebrew, Aramaic.

The deliberations in the Palestinian schools were edited at the end of the fourth century to form the Palestinian Talmud; those in the Babylonian schools, a century later, to form the Babylonian Talmud (the word 'Talmud' can also be translated roughly as 'Teaching'). The Babylonian Talmud became the more authoritative work for Jewish observance. A gigantic work of around 2500 folio pages, it attracted over the years a vast number of commentaries and super-commentaries. For centuries scholarly Jews devoted practically all their intellectual efforts to the elucidation of the Talmud – and all subsequent codification of the laws is based on this work. There are two types of material found in the Talmudic literature: *Halakhah* (from a root meaning 'to walk' so conveying the sense of 'the Jewish way') and *Aggadah* (from a root meaning 'to relate'). Halakhah comprises the laws, observances and rituals, and represents the legal side of Judaism. Aggadah comprises all the non-legal material: ethics, medicine, science, history, legends, folklore, tales of the saints and pious homilies.

In post-Talmudic times a number of Codes of Jewish law were compiled. These were based on the Talmud but took into account post-Talmudic developments. Long before the sixteenth century two communal groupings – each with its own particular customs, interpretations and applications of the Halakhah – had become distinguishable. These were the Sephardim (the communities of the Spanish peninsula and other communities influenced by them) and the Ashkenazim (the Franco-German communities and others influenced by them). The most authoritative Code of Jewish law, the Shulhan Arukh ('Arranged Table'), was compiled to meet the Halakhic requirements of these two groupings. The Shulhan Arukh, in its final form, consists of the main text by Joseph Karo (1488-1575), in which the Sephardi Halakhah is recorded, together with the glosses of Moses Isserles (1510–72) incorporating the Ashkenazi Halakhah. This work came to enjoy the highest authority for observant Jews (sometimes known as 'Shulhan Arukh Jews'). Nevertheless, new conditions in Jewish life frequently demanded a fresh approach, and the work of codification was undertaken anew by the post-Shulhan Arukh teachers of the law. In addition, questions in law were addressed to famous rabbis, whose replies were published in many collections. The vast 'Responsa' literature became an additional source of the Halakhah – and this too was given expression in later Codes.

Philosophical inquiry developed late in Judaism. Philo of Alexandria's attempt to reconcile the Bible with Greek thought was an isolated exercise in systematic thinking. Neither in the Bible nor in the Talmudic literature is there to be found anything comparable to the Socratic-type discussions on the nature of justice in the abstract. The situation changed radically in the Middle Ages. The challenges presented to Judaism by Christianity and Islam; the need to defend rabbinic teachings about the oral Torah against the Karaites; above all, the influence of Greek philosophy, which came to the Jews through Arabic translations of the Greek thinkers – these demanded a response in which Judaism was presented systematically. Especially in Spain, the Jewish teachers were very much at home in the world of Greek thought and aware of the theological discussions by Muslims of problems which were acute for Jews as well. And a large number of Jewish philosophical writings was accordingly produced.

Saadia wrote his *Beliefs and Opinions* in 933. This work – like the majority of the philosophical Jewish works – was written in Arabic, the language of philosophical discourse at the time. Others followed his lead. Bahya Ibn Pakudah (eleventh century), wrote *Duties of the Heart*, a work with a marked Sufi influence; Judah Ha-Levi (d. after 1140) produced *Kuzari*, a philosophical dialogue between a Jewish sage and a Gentile king; Gersonides (1288–1344) was the author of *The Wars of the Lord*; Crescas (1340–1416) of *The Light of the Lord*; Crescas' disciple Albo produced a *Book of the Principles*; and Don Isaac Abarbanel (1437-1508) wrote a number of philosophical commentaries. But Maimonides' *Guide for the Perplexed* remains the major achievement of the philosophical school.

The main aim of all these works was to demonstrate that rational inquiry, far from being detrimental, lent conviction to faith. The biblical injunctions to 'know God' (meaning, in the context, to practise justice and righteousness) were understood by the medieval thinkers as a command to 'research into' God, to discover as much about His nature as is possible for the finite mind. Although the result of the investigation might turn out to be that God is unknowable, this in itself is an important part of knowledge about the divine, far removed from ignorance and a lack of theological sophistication. Because reason was so important to them, the tendency among the medieval philosophers was to seek reasons for all the *mitzvot* ('commands'). What value is there in the sacrificial system? Why does the Torah forbid the meat of certain animals? Why should circumcision have been ordained as the sign of the covenant? This was the kind of question they asked, refusing to be content with the reply 'It is the will of God'. They wished to discover *why* it should be the will of God.

From the earliest times, on the other hand, there existed a mystical tradition in Judaism. It assumed many forms through the ages, but the best known is that of the Kabbalah. 'Kabbalah' means 'Tradition', and was so called because the Kabbalists refused to look upon themselves as innovators, seeing themselves rather as transmitters of the ancient tradition. In point of fact, however, the Kabbalah arose in Provence in the twelfth century and introduced many new ideas into Judaism, some of which involved a complete transformation of ideas about God. Influenced by philosophers who tended to dismiss all aspects of God's essence, the Kabbalists postulated two aspects of the Deity. God as He-in-Himself is the impersonal Ground of Being, known as *En Sof* ('The Limitless'). *En Sof* becomes manifest in creation by means of ten emanations, the powers or potencies in the Godhead through which the finite universe and its creatures are sustained. These are known as the *Sefirot* ('Numbers'), and it is to various combinations of these that the Bible refers whenever it speaks of God.

Detail from the broadsheet of the Christian Kabbalist Guillaume Postel c 1548. It shows the Sefirot world in the form of a menorah, a seven-branched candlestick. The Sefirot are the ten divine emanations through which adherents to this mystical tradition believe the finite universe and its creatures are sustained.

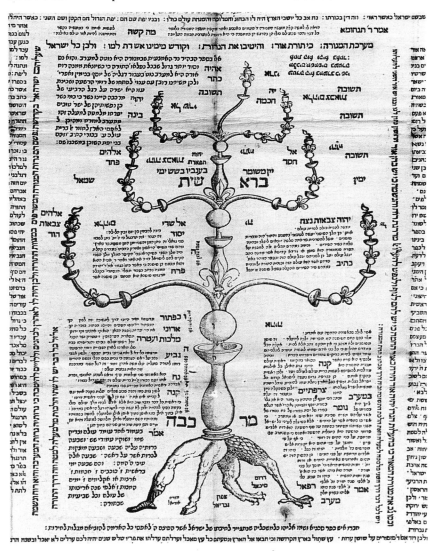

The Kabbalists were monotheists, but a central problem for them was to avoid the slightest suggestion that there were ten deities, as the doctrine of the *Sefirot* might have been understood to imply. They carefully explained that *En Sof* and the *Sefirot* form a unity much as colourless water, when poured into bottles of various hues, temporarily adopts the colour of the bottles into which it is poured. The whole of the Bible is seen by the Kabbalists as having an esoteric meaning with reference to the dynamic life of the Godhead.

The classical Kabbalistic work, the *Zohar* ('Illumination'), was brought to public attention in Spain, at the end of the thirteenth century, by Moses De Leon. It purports to be a series of revelations to Rabbi Simeon ben Yohai, a Talmudic saint of the second century. Modern scholarship is virtually unanimous that De Leon is, in fact, the author of the book he 'discovered', although many of its ideas go back to much earlier times. The work has been an essential guide to Jews with mystical aspirations. Isaac Luria (1534–72) taught a new version of the Kabbalah in Safed, which was recorded in writing by his chief disciples. The *Zohar* and the Lurianic writings, together with the commentaries on them, form the Jewish library of mysticism. It should be remarked, however, that the Jewish mystics have always been extremely reticent about recording their own, personal mystical experience. Few and far between are Jewish mystical writings of the type of St John of the Cross, Saint Theresa, Ekhart or Rumi.

ETHICS

The basis of Jewish ethics is the doctrine of *Imitatio Dei*. Man, created in God's image, is obliged to be God-like in showing compassion and mercy, practising justice and performing acts of charity and benevolence to all God's creatures. A key text in this connection is 'Speak unto all the congregation of the children of Israel, and say unto them: Ye shall be holy; for I the Lord your God am holy' (Leviticus 19:2). A Talmudic saying has it: 'Just as God is compassionate, be thou compassionate; just as God is merciful, be thou merciful.' Another Talmudic passage describes the special characteristics of a Jew as 'merciful, retiring and benevolent'. The imitation of God is to be expressed in almsgiving, visiting the sick, comforting mourners, burying the dead, clothing the naked, feeding the hungry and saving people from aggression and oppression. The Jew is enjoined to act benevolently to all men, not only to his co-religionists. It is forbidden to cause unnecessary pain, an injunction which applies to animals as well as human beings.

There is thus a strong social emphasis in Jewish ethics. Jewish communities are expected to provide relief organizations for the poor, suitable care for the aged and infirm, societies to help unfortunates, proper conditions of employment for workers, and educational facilities for every age group. The study of the Torah is held to be of particularly high religious value. In addition to the synagogue, the traditional community had a house of learning, well equipped with a good library of Jewish books. It is typical of the Jewish scale of values that, traditionally, the house of learning possesses greater sanctity than the synagogue: a synagogue may be sold in order to purchase a house of learning, but not vice versa.

The communal leaders were empowered to introduce special legislation for their community in order to promote communal welfare. If, for instance, the sellers of fish or meat for the Sabbath were deemed to be charging exorbitant prices, a communal edict was issued that these commodities should not be bought until the prices came down. The money for the upkeep of communal organizations was raised by individual taxation. No one was exempt from almsgiving and even today the devout Jew follows the biblical system of 'tithing' in giving to charity ten per cent of his income.

Peace, and the pursuit of peace, ranks high in the scale of Jewish values. War is held to be an abomination permissible only in defence of life. Moreover, not only is the word *shalom* ('peace') always used in greeting but the rabbis of the Talmud declare Shalom to be one of the names of God. All the more important prayers conclude with a prayer for peace on earth.

Although Judaism places stress on correct behaviour, on action, to the extent of encouraging a good deed even if the motive for performing that deed is self-seeking, the ideal is inwardness, in the sense both that the motive should be pure and that there should be awareness of what is being done. Mere mechanical observance is decried by all the Jewish moralists. A favourite prayer is 'Purify our hearts to serve Thee in truth'.

Humility is another high virtue, and pride correspondingly a severe sin. As the Talmud puts it, God says: 'I cannot be in the same world with the proud and arrogant.' The greater the man, the more humble should he be in the presence of the Almighty – which is why Moses is described as the most humble of men. People should not always insist on their rights but should be prepared to bow to the wishes of others if this will promote peace and harmony. Be of those who are insulted and not of those who insult others, say the Talmudic rabbis; be a victim rather than a victimizer. The ideal is to see the image of God in all people.

In the early traditional work *Ethics of the Fathers* it is taught:

There is a strong social emphasis in Jewish ethics. Jewish communities provide relief organizations for the poor, care for the aged, and educational facilities. This is particularly pronounced among the extremely orthodox Hasidic sects. Here a row of telephones is set up to enable followers of the Lubavitcher Rebbe in New York to listen to the live broadcasts of their rabbi. The Lubavitcher movement is a group within Hasidic Jewry which originated in Russia. In common with other Hasidim profound study of the Talmudic law is a guiding aim, but the rabbinic leadership is almost dynastic in its succession.

The wise man is he who learns from all men. The hero is the man who exercises self-control. The respectable man is he who respects all God's creatures. The rich man is he who is content with what he possesses.

These and a good many other ethical sayings were collected and elaborated on in the rich ethical and devotional literature. Whereas the study of the difficult Halakhic material was possible only for the scholar, the ethical and devotional literature brought living religion into the lives of the ordinary folk. In addition to Bahya and Maimonides, popular ethical works were compiled by Nahmanides (1195–1270), Jonah Gerondi (d. 1263) in Spain, and Moses Hayyim Luzzatto (1707–47).

It is an error, though, to see Judaism as necessarily opposed to asceticism. A group of German pietists in the twelfth and thirteenth centuries produced the *Sefer Hasidim* ('Book of Saints'), a primer for holy living. In this work and in the work of the Kabbalists a strong mystical tinge is evident; the whole of life's conduct is to be directed towards nearness to God. In addition, many of the ethical works actively advocate asceticism, although it was never suggested in the form of rejection of sex since, following the Jewish tradition, marriage is a divinely ordained institution. (But restraint is advocated by the moralists even in marriage, and all extramarital sex is forbidden.) Both in the Talmud and among the later moralists, there is debate on whether one who fasts is a holy man or a sinner (because he rejects God's gifts); the outcome has never been decided, and the matter is left to individual discretion.

Alcohol is certainly not proscribed – many of the benedictions are recited over a cup of wine – but drunkenness is seen as a vice. A folk-maxim has it that a Jew who drinks to excess is no real Jew.

INSTITUTIONS AND RITUALS

The observant Jew recites three standard prayers each day, in the morning, the afternoon and at night. These prayers may be recited in private, but it is held to be highly meritorious for them to be recited in public, that is, when at least ten male Jews are present. Women, in the Orthodox view, cannot help to make up the quorum for prayer because women are exempt from the strict obligation to recite the three prayers daily. In addition to the prayers, in the morning and at night the *Shema* ('Hear') is recited; this comes from the Book of Deuteronomy and reads:

Hear O Israel: the Lord our God, the Lord is One. And thou shalt love the Lord thy God with all thine heart and with all thy soul, and with all thy might. And these words, which I commanded thee this day, shall be upon thy thine heart; and thou shalt teach them diligently unto thy children, and shalt talk of them when thou sittest in thine house, and when thou walkest by the way, and when thou liest down, and when thou risest up. And thou shalt bind them for a sign upon thine hand, and they shall be for frontlets between thine eyes. And thou shalt write them upon the door posts of thy house and upon thy gates.

A Jewish marriage ceremony generally takes place in a synagogue, though in fact neither synagogue or rabbi is required for a marriage to be valid. Here Hasidic Jews celebrate a wedding. In Hasidism any service of God is a joyous occasion because members of this sect cultivate an awareness of the immanence of God in all existence. This leads to ever greater communion with God and true worship relates to all the activities of life, even the partaking of food.

Taking the last verses literally, the *Shema* is inscribed on parchment and placed into leather boxes – the *tefillin* (phylacteries) – to be worn during prayer on the head and the arm. The *Shema* is also placed in a case on the doorposts of the house, at which site this sign is known as the *mezuzah* (doorpost).

The synagogue, the Jewish house of prayer, has no particular architectural style. Provided that there is an Ark in the eastern wall to contain the Torah scrolls, and a platform from which the Torah may be read, the synagogue can have any shape, size or form that the congregants desire. A Torah scroll consists of the Pentateuch written by hand on parchment. The scrolls are adorned with silver bells and other ornaments, and are wrapped in embroidered mantles. A central feature of the synagogue service, on Sabbaths, festivals and certain other days, is the reading of the Torah. A scroll is taken ceremonially from the Ark and paraded round the synagogue, after which it is opened for reading. Each Sabbath a weekly portion is chanted, for which seven members of the congregation are nominally responsible, having been 'called up' for the reading. In ancient times the reading was carried out by the seven themselves; now, however, in the absence of skill in reading the Torah on the part of many Jews, a special reader is elected to read on their behalf. After the Torah reading there is a further reading from one of the works of the prophets, not from a scroll but from a printed text.

A *tallit* (shawl), to which *tzitzit* (fringes) are attached in obedience to the scriptural verses that speak of fringes in garments as a reminder of the commands of the Lord (Numbers 15:37–41), is worn by the male worshippers during prayers (and *tefillin* too, on weekdays). In the traditional synagogue the sexes are separated; the women sit in a special gallery. In Reform synagogues, and in some other synagogues as well, the practice of segregating the sexes has been abandoned. In these synagogues there is often a mixed choir as well as mixed seating – and in some, women too are called to the reading of the Torah.

Any congregant familiar with the Hebrew and acquainted with the melodies can lead the congregation in prayer, but in the larger synagogues it is customary to have a professional cantor. On the great occasions of the year a sermon is delivered by the rabbi. Neither the cantor nor the rabbi is a 'priest' with special priestly functions; indeed, until the fourteenth century there were no professional rabbis and, in any case, the rabbi's function traditionally is to teach the Torah and render decisions on Jewish law. The modern type of rabbi as preacher, pastor and counsellor is a product of the nineteenth century, in whose new role it is not difficult to discern the influence of the Christian priest or minister. Nevertheless, congregations, even the Orthodox, have adopted the new role for the rabbi. In recent years in progressive congregations, women rabbis have been appointed.

A boy who reaches the age of thirteen becomes *Bar Mitzvah* ('son of the Commandments'), at that time taking on the religious duties and responsibilities devolving upon all adult Jewish males. The *Bar Mitzvah* reads his own portion from the Torah and there is a family celebration to mark the occasion. Thereafter he may be one of the seven members of the congregation called to the reading of the Torah. A girl attains her religious majority to become *Bat Mitzvah* ('daughter of the Commandments') at the earlier age of twelve, but until recently there was no special ceremony for a girl and no celebrations. In more recent years, even in some traditional congregations, girls are similarly honoured. Such a move towards equality of the sexes finds some support in tradition; there have been occasions on which a determined attempt was made to remove some of the disabilities under which women suffered in the older law. At an early period, the authorities weakened the husband's power in marriage by introducing the marriage settlement: when divorcing his wife, the husband became obliged to provide for her maintenance. In the Ashkenazi world, divorce without the wife's consent was banned and polygamy proscribed.

Judaism sets great store by family life. Parents have responsibilities to their children: they must care for them, provide them with a proper education, and train them in the Jewish way. The fifth commandment, 'Honour thy father and thy mother', was extended to embrace step-parents, grandparents and older siblings. But there are limits to filial piety. According to many authorities, the wishes of parents may be disregarded if they object to a son's or a daughter's choice of a particular partner in marriage.

The Jewish marriage ceremony these days generally takes place in the synagogue although, strictly speaking, neither a synagogue nor a rabbi is required for the marriage to be valid. Bride and groom stand together under a canopy; the groom places the ring on the finger of the bride and declares, 'Behold thou art consecrated unto me by this ring, according to the law of Moses and of Israel'. A number of benedictions are recited, among them:

Blessed art Thou, O Lord our God, King of the universe, who hast hallowed us by Thy commandments, and hast given us command concerning forbidden unions, who hast disallowed unto us those that are betrothed, but hast sanctioned unto us such as are wedded to us by the rite of the canopy and the sacred covenant of wedlock.

If he is capable of doing so, a man at the point of death confesses his sins and recites the *Shema*, declaring his belief and trust in God to whom he commends his spirit. The body is bathed, wrapped in plain linen shrouds, and interred with a simple burial service. In many communities all this is attended to by a 'holy brotherhood', a society to which it is considered to be a high honour to

Passover falls in March–April and commemorates the Exodus from Egypt. In common with all Jewish practice it is a family occasion and the observance provides children with a training in the Jewish way of life. The youngest child present asks for an explanation of the ceremony and during the meal the story of the Exodus is read aloud. The toast is always 'Next year in Jerusalem'. Ritual food is eaten including the bitter herbs, an egg and salt.

belong. For seven days after the burial the near relatives, in mourning, sit on low stools in their houses. During this time they are visited by friends who recite prayers for the departed and extend their comforts to the bereaved. The sons (and, in some communities, the daughters) attend the synagogue for eleven months after the burial to recite the *Kaddish* (Sanctification). This is not a prayer for the dead but, as its name implies, a hymn of praise to God that His Kingdom may speedily be established on earth. It is seen as the children affirming that, like their parent before them, they will live so as to give glory to God's name.

Saturday, the seventh day of the week, is the Jewish Sabbath, a day of rest and spiritual refreshment. The Sabbath is described in the tradition as a 'bride' and a 'queen', to be welcomed in the home to a festive table with light, song and joy. The traditional definition of 'work' is that it embraces every kind of creative activity, such as writing, kindling fire, driving an automobile, or carrying objects in the street. The intention is that by resting from creative activity on the Sabbath, the Jew acknowledges God as Creator of the universe. Orthodoxy insists on strict observance of the Sabbath; Reform Judaism accepts that under the conditions of life in the modern world a less strict standard is called for. The Sabbath, like the festivals, begins at nightfall and ends at nightfall, that is, from Friday night to Saturday night.

There are five major and two minor festivals in the Jewish calendar. Passover falls in March-April, commemorating the Exodus from Egypt.

GREGORIAN CALENDAR	JEWISH CALENDAR	MAIN HOLY DAYS AND FESTIVALS OF THE JEWISH YEAR
SEPTEMBER	TISHRI	New Year (Rosh Hashanah) Day of Atonement (Yom Kippur) 1st and 2nd Days of Tabernacles Solemn Assembly Rejoicing of the Law
OCTOBER		
	MARCHESVAN	
NOVEMBER		
	CHISLEV	1st Day of Festival of Dedication (Hanukkah)
DECEMBER		
	TEBETH	8th Day of Festival of Dedication
JANUARY		
	SHEBAT	
FEBRUARY		
	ADAR	Festival of Esther (Purim)
MARCH		
	NISAN	1st Day of Passover 2nd Day of Passover
APRIL		
	TYYAR	
MAY		
	SIVAN	1st Day of Weeks 2nd Day of Weeks
JUNE		
	TAMMUZ	
JULY		
	AB	
AUGUST		
	ELUL	

The Jewish ritual year is a lunar year of twelve months containing three hundred and fifty-four days. The names of the months were taken from the Babylonian. Tammuz, for instance, which falls between June and July was the god of springtime and signifies the awakening land.

On the first night of Passover a home celebration is held, known as the Seder ('Order'), at which all present partake of four cups of wine. The Haggadah ('Telling'), an anthology of scriptural verses and later texts about the Exodus, is recited on this occasion. During the seven days of Passover no leavened bread is eaten, following the account in the book of Exodus of how, when the children of Israel went out of Egypt, in their haste to escape, they had insufficient time to bake their bread fully. At the Seder unleavened bread (matzah) and bitter herbs are eaten, the latter as a symbol of the bitterness the Israelites suffered during their bondage.

Pentecost falls exactly fifty days after Passover and commemorates the giving of the Torah. The practice of counting these fifty days, day by day, has been explained as linking the celebration of freedom with the celebration of the Torah: the Jew is glad to be free to practise his religion.

Tabernacles is an autumn festival during which meals are not eaten in the house but in a specially erected hut or 'tabernacle' as a reminder of the tabernacles in which the Israelites encamped during their forty years' journey through the wilderness. Tabernacles is also a harvest festival. During the synagogue service four plants – a palm branch, a citron, myrtles and willows – are waved in the hand and taken in procession around the synagogue with joyous singing.

The Jewish New Year falls in late September or early October. The festival on this day, Rosh Ha-Shanah ('Beginning of the Year'), is a solemn occasion as well as a feast. The central feature of the festival is the blowing of the ram's horn, the *shofar*. Among the meanings that have been read into this rite are: that the trumpet is sounded as God is crowned King; that it recalls the trumpet sound when the Torah was given; that it is a herald of the great trumpet that is to sound when the Messiah comes; and that it is an alarm call to awaken mankind from sleep in worldly vanity to lead the ultimately good life.

The great fast of Yom Kippur ('Day of Atonement'), which falls ten days after Rosh Ha-shanah, is a day devoted entirely to prayer and worship. The major part of the day is spent in the synagogue oblivious to all worldly concerns. During the twenty-four hours of the fast, no food or drink passes the lips. Confession of sin is repeated throughout the day, and pardon is sought of God who is merciful to forgive His children. For this forgiveness Yom Kippur is counted among the festivals. It is a day of great solemnity, but also a day of joy and trust in God who grants pardon to sinners. Yom Kippur has always exercised a powerful fascination over Jews. Even non-observant Jews feel impelled to fast and pray in synagogue on this day.

The two minor festivals are Hanukkah ('Dedication') and Purim ('Lots'). Hanukkah, commemorating the victory of the Maccabees over the army of Antiochus IV in the second century BCE, is the Feast of Lights, representing the victory of light over darkness, monotheism over idolatry. On each of the eight days of the festival, candles are kindled in home and synagogue. Purim is a boisterous one-day festival, commemorating the events told in the book of Esther when Haman cast 'lots' to determine on which day he would have the Jews destroyed. As the book of Esther enjoins, in celebration of the deliverance presents are sent to friends and the poor are not forgotten.

In addition to the festivals there are a number of fast-days, the most important of which is that of the ninth day of the month Av, traditionally the date on which both the First and Second Temples were destroyed. After the Nazi Holocaust in which some six million Jews were killed, this day has also come to be one of remembrance for the victims of a catastrophe more terrible than any other in Jewish history.

The dietary laws are strictly observed by Orthodox Jews, but with less strictness by Reform Jews. Corresponding to the biblical injunctions, it is forbidden to eat the meat of animals which do not chew the cud and have no cloven hooves: the meat of the pig, the camel, the horse and so on. Only fish which have scales and fins are permitted as food, and only birds which are not birds of prey. Meat and dairy dishes must be kept separately and not eaten together. In observant Jewish homes there are separate dishes and cutlery for meat and milk. Moreover, only the meat of animals killed by the method known as *shehitah* may be eaten. It is believed by Jews that this is the most painless method of slaughtering animals for food.

Various reasons have been advanced for the dietary laws, such as the hygienic – the pig is a 'dirty animal' and it is 'unwholesome' to eat meat cooked in butter – but the general view among observant Jews is that the discipline provided by abstaining from certain foods is spiritually sound, in that it brings the appetite for food into close association with the word of God, making such everyday activities as eating meals a means of divine worship. Grace is recited before and after meals. A special benediction is recited thanking God for His gifts whenever the Jew enjoys the good things of life.

MOVEMENTS IN JUDAISM

The Jewish historian Leopold Zunz observed that the Jewish Middle Ages lasted until the end of the eighteenth century in that the currents of thought and life which followed the Renaissance and shattered the medieval world picture largely passed by the Jews. Confined in the ghetto, the Jews cultivated their traditional way of life until the western world and its culture was opened to them after the French Revolution and Jewish emancipation.

There is much truth in Zunz's observation, yet a ferment of new ideas *was* introduced to Judaism in the eighteenth century. The foremost figure in this connection is that of Moses Mendelssohn (1729–86), a philosopher of the German Enlightenment and pioneer of the Haskalah ('Enlightenment') movement in Judaism. With followers in western and later in eastern Europe, Haskalah had as its aim certainly not the disavowal of traditional Judaism but the encouragement of the new science and learning among the Jews, of openness to western ideas and norms that might bring a rationalist approach to the Jewish tradition, and of a general widening of Jewish horizons. The adherents of Haskalah urged Jews to learn European languages, dress in European styles, move away from the narrow concentration on traditional learning alone to become, as one of the Russian followers of the Haskalah put it, Jews in their homes but men in the world at large.

Haskalah did not necessarily imply that Jewish observance should be abandoned. Many of its initial adherents, the Maskilim, were totally observant Jews. Nevertheless, the traditionalists were bitterly opposed to the movement, fighting it with every means at their disposal. And the Maskilim were not content with the introduction of the new learning into the Jewish schools; the traditional methods of Torah study, with its complete emphasis on the Talmud and the Codes and without any systematic approach to education, came under their attack. They urged a return to study of the Bible in its plain meaning, and Mendelssohn himself with his disciples produced a translation of the whole Bible into German (in Hebrew characters) with the aim of acquainting the intelligent Jew both with the hitherto neglected riches of the Bible and with the language of culture, German.

Allied to the Haskalah, but with an even more academic aim directed chiefly towards scholars, was the Jüdische Wissenschaft (Jewish Science) movement in the early nineteenth century. Its pioneers were Zunz in Germany, Nahman Krochmal and Solomon Judah Rapoport in Galicia, and Samuel David Luzzatto in Italy. These scholars and their followers sought to place the study of the Jewish sources on a sound 'scientific' basis, that is, to pursue Jewish learning through objective methods of scholarship without many presuppositions, and through investigation using the normal canons of historical research. In the early days of the movement, this critical method was applied to all the classical writings of the tradition with the exception of the Pentateuch. But as the movement developed, it was seen that the new Higher Criticism of the Bible must be given its head, and gradually this analytical approach became thoroughly accepted – although its Jewish practitioners failed to consider, to any serious extent, the implications of Pentateuchal Criticism towards belief in the Torah as the very word of God conveyed in its entirety to Moses.

In eastern Europe a new movement arose within the tradition; with strong revivalist tendencies it presented an internal challenge to the traditionalist leadership. Hasidism (from the Hebrew *hasid*, 'saint') centred around the charismatic personality of Israel ben Eliezer (1700–60), known as the Baal Shem Tov ('Master of the Divine Name'), who taught that religious devotion was more important even than the study of the Torah – a severe reversal of the traditional scale of values. Drawing on the Kabbalah, Hasidism was a mystical movement aimed as much at the ordinary, devout Jew as the scholar. Its main precept

Preparations for a children's party to celebrate Lag b'Omer. This lesser Jewish holiday, a joyful interlude during a traditional period of semi-mourning, falls on the 33rd day of the 49 days before Shavuot (Pentecost). The origin of the festival is obscure, but medieval sources relate it to the ending of a plague among the followers of Rabbi Akiba, an influential teacher in the 2nd century.

The Baal Shem Tov gathered around him a band of followers, some of them distinguished rabbis and Talmudists, who in turn became the leaders of Hasidic groups. The movement succeeded in bringing joy, enthusiasm and religious faith into otherwise drab lives, harrowed by the poverty in which Jews were living in eastern Europe and religiously unsatisfied with the dry legalistic fare offered by the traditionalists. Eventually, dynasties of Zaddikim were established; the saint bequeathed his spiritual gifts – or so it was believed – to his sons and they to their sons. In a little less than one century Hasidism succeeded in being adopted by about half of the Jewries of eastern Europe. After the Second World War, Hasidic dynasties were established in the USA and in the State of Israel, and the movement still has many thousands of adherents, each venerating one particular Zaddik as the saint who provides the link between him- or herself and the Creator.

For a century eastern European Jewry was divided between the Hasidim and the Mitnaggedim ('Opponents'). The latter hurled anathemas at the Hasidim, considering the movement heretical, claiming that it tended to denigrate mere Talmudic learning; that it taught that God was actually present in all things; that it encouraged singing, dancing and jollity instead of the sombre attitudes appropriate to a people in exile and with their Temple destroyed; and that it held the Zaddik in a veneration bordering on the idolatrous. Eventually, in the face of the threat from the Haskalah, the two united to defend the tradition.

Martin Buber (1878–1965) has since popularized Hasidism, telling the inspiring Hasidic tales in a style and language suitable for western society. But it cannot be maintained that Buber's neo-Hasidism has managed to win many followers (although its influence on Christian religious thought should not be underestimated).

The severest challenge to the traditional way of life was presented by the Reform Movement in early nineteenth-century Germany. It was in Germany, in the first instance, that the Jew who had recently emerged from the ghetto to take his place in western society experienced the tension between the traditional way of life and the lure of the new ways. Some of the more intellectual and wealthy Jews were so attracted to German culture that they cast off the tradition entirely, to become completely assimilated even to the extent that they converted to the Christian faith. Early Reform in Germany had the positive aim of stemming the tide of apostasy from Judaism, declaring that Judaism still had the power of its truth to hold its adherents if only some of the Jewish institutions were recast and the religion reformed so as to make less marked the differences between the Jew and his Gentile neighbours.

described the aim of the religious life as for man to be attached in his mind and his heart to God at all times, even when he eats and drinks, is engaged in business or in conversation with his fellows. The Kabbalistic doctrine that there are 'holy sparks' scattered throughout creation waiting to be redeemed from the powers of evil was used by Hasidism to encourage its adherents to enjoy the world, not in a worldly spirit, but for the purpose of elevating the 'sparks of holiness' to their source in God. Man, they proclaimed, should serve God with joy at seeing the whole universe sustained by His divine power, the light of which illumines all things. A new type of spiritual leader emerged, the Zaddik ('Righteous One'), a guru-like guide and spiritual mentor in Hasidism, whose prayers on behalf of his followers were bound to be answered by God.

At first, the Reformers introduced comparatively minor changes in the liturgy: they removed some of the less inspiring prayers from the prayer book, introduced some new hymns in the vernacular, brought in an organ accompaniment to the prayers, and inculcated a greater sense of decorum in the western style. Sermons in the vernacular were also introduced. The most far-reaching of the early reforms was the abolition of prayers for the restoration of the sacrificial system and for the restoration of the Jewish people to their ancient homeland. This of course involved a complete reinterpretation of the Messianic hope. The supernatural elements in Messianism were disregarded, as were the more pronounced particularist elements in the Jewish faith. The Messianic vision, to which they were faithful, for the Reformers meant the emergence of a better world in which liberal ideals would triumph. The prophetic theme that Israel would be a light to the nations was understood by the Reformers to refer not to a Jewish people in the Holy Land spreading abroad the truth about God and His relationship with man, but rather the mission of Israel among the nations of western Europe who had themselves been influenced, through Christianity, by the Jewish values of peace, justice and freedom. The Reformers understood Judaism as ethical monotheism, with its institutions not as divine laws but as human means of furthering ethical monotheism until it became the religion of all men. From this viewpoint it followed that the dietary laws, for example, had played an important role in assuring Jewish survival in the past but could now be a hindrance in that they frustrated social relationships between Jews and Gentiles.

The polemics between the Orthodox, as the traditionalists came to be called, and the Reformers, were fierce. The Orthodox treated Reform as rank heresy, no more than a religion of convenience which, if followed, would lead Jews out of Judaism altogether. The Reformers retorted that, on the contrary, the danger to Jewish survival was occasioned by the Orthodox who through obscurantism failed to see the new challenges which Judaism was facing consciously in the present, just as Judaism had done unconsciously in the past.

From Germany the Reform Movement spread. It became particularly active in the New World, where the most influential and wealthy American Jewish communities adopted Reform.

The Reform Movement had its moderates for whom the changes required were minimal. It also had its extremists who observed the Sabbath on Sunday, used very little Hebrew in the synagogue, did not fast on Yom Kippur, and frowned on circumcision as a barbaric rite. Since the Second World War, however, in many Reform circles a greater awareness of traditional values and in-

stitutions has become evident: Reform rabbis still stress the prophetic, ethical side of Judaism but recognize that there is much wisdom in the Halakhah, the traditional Jewish way of life. Especially after the Nazi Holocaust and the emergence of the State of Israel (resulting in a strong desire on the part of many Jews to return to the tradition), Reform thinkers have tended to argue that the selective process, by which the permanent values are extracted from their temporal expression, should be extended to the Rabbinic–Halakhic literature with its own wisdom and insights.

The reaction to Reform by the Orthodox took two different forms. The first was to deny that the western world had anything of real value to offer to Jews. Only in external matters of little ultimate consequence was the Jew obliged to conform to western mores anyway. Spiritual needs could be catered for entirely by the rich tradition inherited. Hasidism went its own way, in any event, concerned only with the joy of drawing nearer to God. The Mitnaggedim, particularly in their stronghold in the intellectually-oriented community of Lithuania, rose to the challenge of the new by establishing a network of colleges (Yeshivot) where the Talmud was studied with unparalleled assiduity by young men of the keenest intellect and indifferent to worldly success. The study of the Torah 'for its own sake', not as a means to a rabbinical career, was the ideal to which these Yeshivot and their successors in the State of Israel and the USA were committed, producing a galaxy of the most able Talmudists. Partly as a counterblast to Haskalah (Reform made no inroads into Lithuanian Jewry) the Yeshivot introduced the idea of the Musar ('Ethical and Religious Instruction') movement into their curriculum. This movement was founded by Israel Salanter (1810–83) who believed that only by intense concentration on ethical and devotional ideas could human nature rise in perfection. Unlike Hasidism, the Musar movement was not so much for the masses as for the scholarly elite. In the Yeshivah world, as it is now known, loyalty to the Torah was to be achieved by the application of the mind to Talmudic studies and the dedication of the heart through devotional exercises.

The second type of Orthodox response to the challenge was that of Samson Raphael Hirsch (1808–88) of Frankfurt. Hirsch advocated complete loyalty to the Torah in its traditional formulation but recognized that the Jew can learn much from western civilization. There was no need, in Hirschean neo-Orthodoxy, for the believing Jew either to opt out of western culture, as the traditionalists had argued, or to surrender any of the practices of the Torah which, Hirsch declared, are divinely ordained and immutable. Followers of the Hirschean school were to be found occupying positions in the highest echelons of western society – university professors, physicians, bankers, artists, writers, musicians and businessmen, no different in dress or in many of their ideas from their Gentile friends and neighbours but staunchly and proudly adhering to the Orthodox way of life in all its details.

The emergence of Nazism in Germany and the Holocaust which followed led many of the Hirscheans to be thoroughly disillusioned with Hirsch's regard for German culture. A significant number of his followers began to argue that Hirsch did not advocate his neo-Orthodoxy as in any way ideal, but the argument was only temporarily successful in stemming the tide of apostasy and assimilation. Consequently, many of them preferred to embrace Hasidism or to enter the Yeshivah world with its basic indifference to the outside world and its values. Modern Orthodoxy in the USA, however, has an ideal not very far removed from Hirschean neo-Orthodoxy.

A third religious movement, Conservative Judaism – particularly strong in the USA but with adherents elsewhere in the Jewish world – seeks a balance between Orthodoxy and Reform, taking issue with Orthodoxy in its theory and with Reform in its practice. Conservative Judaism affirms the validity of the traditional observances of Judaism, accepting the Halakhic scheme in its entirety, yet more open to change than Ortho-

doxy. The movement claims that historical investigation has shown the inadequacies of Orthodox theory. The Torah did not simply drop down from Heaven in its entirety but is the product of the historical experiences of the Jewish people in their quest for God. In the Conservative view, Jewish observances are binding on the Jew because they are the means by which the Jew gives expression to his religion. Divine inspiration is seen in a dynamic sense in which the human element is present to understand, adapt and further the divine element. Accordingly, the devout Jew can allow himself to be completely open on the question of origins: this is a question of scholarship, not of faith. But it is not origins which matter in religion. What matters is the development of ideas and institutions so as to serve the Jewish quest for nearness to God. For instance, the Conservative Jew is not disturbed at the suggestion that the dietary laws have their origin in primitive taboos, nor that the Sabbath may have originated in ancient Babylon. The fact is that the dietary laws and the Sabbath have become powerful vehicles for the survival of Judaism and for holy living. The precepts of the Torah provide the Jew with his way to God, and that is all the justification they require.

In the opinion of the later Jewish mystics, there is a triad in Judaism: God, the Torah and the Jew-

Children at a Hasidic Jewish school. These boys will always wear a cap, or yarmulkah, as a sign of respect for God, within whose presence they are at all times. Hasidic Jews retain an archaic style of dress which reflects their orthodox stance and displays their origins in 17th-century Eastern Europe. Many women hide their hair by wearing wigs.

ish people. It has been said, with some justice, that with reference to the three movements in contemporary Judaism, Reform places the stress on God, Orthodoxy on the Torah, and Conservative Judaism on Jewish peoplehood.

Zionism, as a secular, political movement, naturally places its emphasis on Jewish peoplehood. The Zionist movement has definite implications for the Jewish religion in calling attention to the tensions between Judaism as a religion and Judaism as nationalism. In the early days of the movement it was opposed by many of the Orthodox both because of its interpretation of Judaism in nationalist terms and because it seemed to compromise the Messianic hope, seen in terms of direct divine intervention rather than human endeavour to secure the return of the Jews to Palestine. Nevertheless, the Mizrahi movement believed in the possibility of a religious Zionism, embracing the slogan 'The Land of Israel for the people of Israel according to the Torah of Israel'.

Many of the Reformers were also in opposition to Zionism because it seemed to be in contradiction to the Reform idea of the mission of Israel among the nations, according to which the Jews were not in exile. On the contrary, the mission of the Jews could be carried out only if Jews remained in the Diaspora. On the other hand, some Reformers argued also that for Reform to be true to its nature, acknowledging change in response to changing circumstances, a revision of the mission of Israel was called for in which a Jewish State would be the best method of fostering the Torah that would go out from Zion and the word of the Lord from Jerusalem. Precisely because Conservative Judaism stressed the idea of peoplehood, this movement had no difficulties in embracing the Zionist idea.

The depletion in the number of Jews worldwide during the Second World War and the eventual establishment of the State of Israel made many of the debates about Zionism academic. Few Jews, Orthodox or Reform, see the emergence of the State of Israel in anything but positive terms. Jewish thinkers are not unanimous, however, on whether the establishment of a Jewish State demands a re-thinking of the role of peoplehood in Judaism. Perhaps the dominant tendency is to see the State of Israel as a centre for Jews and Judaism without rejecting the role that Diaspora Jews play both in supporting Israel and in their understanding and furtherance of Judaism in the world at large. From time to time the spectre of dual loyalties is raised, but here too it has become generally accepted that Jews as citizens of their own countries can help and support the State of Israel without having their loyalty to their countries impugned, since there is no conflict between the two loyalties.

ORGANIZATION OF PRESENT-DAY JUDAISM

There is nothing comparable to an organized 'Church' in Judaism, and there is no representative body of world Jewry. Nor does there exist anything like a 'synod' of rabbis with the power to define Judaism or to promulgate binding laws. Voices have been raised in favour of reconvening the ancient Sanhedrin, but the suggestion has won little support. If such a body were indeed to be reconstituted, it would enjoy authority only for the Orthodox, and the legality of its reconstitution in the pre-Messianic age is extremely dubious even according to Orthodoxy.

There are communal organizations in parts of the Jewish world, such as the Board of Deputies of British Jews, the American Jewish Committee and the American Jewish Congress, but these are very loose organizations with no legislative powers. There are also Reform, Orthodox and Conservative synagogical organizations, but these too exist purely for the purpose of furthering the ideas of the particular group and are similarly very loosely structured.

The majority of religious Jews are affiliated to a synagogue in their locality, whether it be an Orthodox or a Conservative synagogue or a Reform Temple (the Reform Movement generally prefers the term 'temple' in that it sees the synagogue as a substitute for the Temple of old). The local rabbi enjoys a degree of authority as a spokesman for his congregation's particular brand of Judaism; his views are normally treated with respect by his congregation – but their acceptance is purely voluntary. Even Orthodox rabbis who, out of their knowledge of the Halakhah, render decisions binding in Jewish law may not claim any kind of infallibility, and it is open to other Orthodox rabbis to argue against any decision.

Religious organization in the State of Israel is in a category of its own. Laws of personal status can be administered only by Orthodox rabbis who, in this respect, are judges and officials of the State. There is no civil marriage in Israel: all marriages – and divorces and conversions to Judaism – are valid only if conducted by the rabbis in accordance with the Halakhah. These rabbis – sages learned in the Torah, with neither preaching nor pastoral functions – follow the traditional view of the rabbinate as judicial, and are democratically elected by Rabbinic Councils composed of religious Jews in specific localities. Representatives on these councils may be rabbis but this is by no means essential.

In every community, rabbis are elected by the congregation in accordance with the traditional pattern. There are two chief rabbis, one Sephardi, one Ashkenazi, each enjoying authority for his

own section of the populace. This is because in some comparatively minor matters the law as administered by the Sephardim differs from that administered by the Ashkenazim. The chief rabbis are also democratically elected by a Chief Rabbinate Council, usually for a period of five years. There are no doctrinal aspects to the office of chief rabbi: neither in Israel nor in the other communities where this office is known is the office of chief rabbi anything more than of a purely administrative nature.

The many synagogues in Israel are supported not by the State but, as in the Diaspora communities, by individual contributions. The religious parties have seats in the Knesset, the Israeli parliament, and thus an influence on the religious directions of the State – in connection with Sabbath observances, for example. In addition to the official Orthodox rabbinate, Reform rabbis officiate in a few communities for their own congregations, but in response to private demands: the rabbis enjoy no official recognition. A Reform rabbi, for instance, cannot preside at a marriage of his own congregants if he wishes the marriage to be recognized as valid in Israeli law. The same applies in large measure to Conservative rabbis. Such restrictions have been the occasion for complaints of religious discrimination. The Conservative Movement in Israel has a number of congregations affiliated to it, known by the Hebrew for 'Conservative' or 'Traditional'.

The American Jewish community of more than five million is the largest Jewish community in the world. Orthodoxy in the USA is represented by the Yeshivah World, the Hasidim – under individual rebbes (a 'rebbe' is a Hasidic Zaddik, thus distinguished from a non-Hasidic rabbi) – and the Modern Orthodox.

The majority of the Yeshivot are of the Lithuanian type, who have established themselves in the New World with astonishing vitality. Although they avail themselves of American methods of organization, fund-raising and publicity, the Yeshivot seek to preserve the full Orthodox tradition of exclusive Torah study. Hasidism has also been revitalized in the USA, and the more important rebbes have thousands of followers. The Rebbe of Lubavitch (after the present-day Soviet town in which his predecessors resided) encourages his followers to engage in a kind of missionary activity among Jews, seeking to reclaim the non-observant to a fully observant life in the belief that there is a divine spark in every Jewish soul waiting to be awakened. (There is hardly any missionary activity directed towards non-Jews, even though Judaism does accept sincere converts.

This is partly because of the unhappy experiences Jews have themselves suffered through Christian missionaries in the past, and partly because of the official Jewish teaching that the righteous Gentile can find salvation just as effectively through his or her own religion.) Modern Orthodoxy is much more open to the outside world and to western ideas and culture. The main seminary for the training of Modern Orthodox rabbis is Yeshivah University in New York; the graduates of the university usually leave with a degree as well as rabbinic ordination.

Reform Judaism is strong in the USA, with a pronounced stress on social justice and a powerful voice in general American life. The main seminary for the training of American Reform rabbis is the Hebrew Union College in Cincinnati, which follows the pattern of western European Jewish academic institutions in which Jewish learning is characterized by strictly objective scholarship.

The movement with the largest number of affiliated congregations in the USA is the Conservative Movement, which has as its main seminary for the training of rabbis the Jewish Theological Seminary of America. Here too the highest standards of scholarship are maintained.

Jews have ever prided themselves, as 'the people of the Book', in reading and producing books. In the contemporary world, the spate of books in Hebrew, English and other languages, on every aspect of Judaism, continues unabated. The postwar period in Jewish publishing has witnessed the publication of a number of encyclopedic works. The massive *Encyclopedia Judaica*, in English, in sixteen volumes (with additional Yearbooks), is a complete survey of the whole range of studies on Judaism and the Jews. The work was published in Jerusalem, as other works of a similar nature have also been — notably the multi-volume digest of Jewish marriage laws, *Otzar Ha-Posekim*, and the extensive survey of the Talmud and the Codes, *Encyclopedia Talmudit*, both in Hebrew. Scholarly editions of the Jewish classics from every period are published every year; many of these have been translated into English. The quarterly *Judaism*, published in the USA, contains articles on the Jewish religion and related topics, opening its pages to authors belonging to Orthodox, Reform and Conservative Judaism. The monthly *Commentary*, also published in the USA, does not limit itself to Jewish topics but in each issue includes discussions and reviews of books of Jewish interest. The London *Jewish Chronicle*, a weekly that has appeared regularly for well over a century, is the most widely-disseminated newspaper devoted to Judaism and general Jewish concerns.

A feature of Jewish life that has become pronounced in the post-war period is that of Christian–Jewish dialogue. Although some Jewish leaders have said that there can be no significant dialogue between the two faiths, and that therefore to speak of a Judaic–Christian tradition is misconceived, several conferences have taken place at which Jews and Christians have exchanged views. There are also regular meetings of bodies that have the aim of furthering those ideals which Jews and Christians have in common; the Council of Christians and Jews in the United Kingdom, for example, enjoys the patronage of the Queen and has as its Presidents the Archbishop of Canterbury, the Cardinal Archbishop of Westminster and the Chief Rabbi.

The arts feature extensively in contemporary Jewish life. Architects, both Jewish and non-Jewish, have been engaged in the major centres of Jewish population to build synagogues in a variety of styles, some of them exciting and inspiring, although the only synagogue which might be thought to have ambitions to be a cathedral-like centre for worship for all Jews, is the Hekhal Shelomo synagogue in Jerusalem.

There are of course many Jewish artists – but it is a moot point whether there is any such thing as Jewish art. Nevertheless, some paintings by Jewish artists and the work of some Jewish photographers have succeeded in portraying Jewish life and Jewish ideals. The cinema, theatre, radio and television are all media currently finding increasing popularity for such portrayals. In Jewish music, a definite move can be discerned away from the old cantoral styles originating in Germany in the last century. There are now a number of highly successful compositions of sacred music for use in the synagogue. Hasidic melodies have become especially popular; many records of them have been produced, and there are even Hasidic pop-groups. The closest to an official Jewish system of melody in worship is to be found in the traditional chants for the prayers and, especially, for the cantillation (incantation) of the Torah reading; the Sephardim and Ashkenazim have their own traditions in this. The claim that these chants go back to the singing of the Levites in the Temple cannot be substantiated, but there is no doubt that many of them do serve to maintain an ancient traditional mode.

ZOROASTRIANISM

THE SOCIAL AND RELIGIOUS BACKGROUND

The period between 1400 and 1200 BCE was a time when the Iranians, as pastoralists, inhabited the southern Russian steppes east of the Volga. It seems that their society was divided traditionally into two main groups, priests and warrior-herdsmen, but that this pattern was then breaking down as the Stone Age yielded to the Bronze Age, and as roving bands of charioteers plundered and slaughtered their more peaceful and materially less advanced neighbours.

The Iranians conceived their gods as cosmic divinities, and apprehended a universal principle of 'that which ought to be' – *asha*, variously rendered as 'order', 'truth', 'justice' or 'righteousness' – which should govern everything, from the workings of nature to human laws and conduct. *Asha* was guarded, they held, by three ethical deities, the Ahuras or Lords. At their head was Ahura Mazda, the Lord of Wisdom, and below him were Mithra and Varuna, the Lords of Loyalty and Truth. Another powerful divinity, Indra, was worshipped as an amoral war-god, and there were many lesser divine beings. Together, it was evidently thought, the gods had created this world in seven stages: the sky, water, earth, plants, animals, mankind, and fire – the vital force that gave warmth and life to the rest and, through the sun, was the regulator of Nature. Then by sacrifice they set the world in motion: death was followed by new life, and the cycle of the seasons began. This process, it seems, was thought of as unending and would continue to be so, as long as men fulfilled their part through sacrifice and prayer.

Accordingly, priests solemnized a daily act of worship, the *yasna*, at which they blessed the seven creations (all represented physically there) and honoured the gods. As wandering pastoralists they had no temples and worshipped mainly in the open, without altars, and with natural phenomena for icons. The essential rituals of the *yasna* were the preparation and making of threefold offerings to fire and water, the givers of light, warmth and life. Fire received dry wood, incense and fat from the sacrifice; water a libation made from the *haoma* plant (Sanskrit *soma*), mixed with the sap of another plant and milk.

At death, it was believed, most souls passed as shadows to an underground realm, yet there was hope for some privileged beings that their souls would mount upwards and, if they succeeded in crossing the perilous Chinvat Bridge, would join the gods in Paradise. With this belief went the concept of a resurrection of the body, re-created from the dry bones a year or so after death, and reunited them with the soul, which thereafter enjoyed again in Paradise all the pleasures of this earthly existence.

Zarathushtra

It is not possible to assign a precise date and place to the great Iranian prophet Zarathushtra, but evidence from his own hymns – the Gathas – makes it probable that he lived between 1200 and 1000 BCE. He was himself a priest, and would have been trained from early boyhood in the beliefs and observances of his ancestral faith.

Zarathushtra saw the stable, age-old society which had evolved these beliefs being rent by bloodshed and lawlessness, and this led him to meditate profoundly on good and evil, and the goal of this earthly life. Finally he was able to offer his people, as revealed truth, a majestic vision of cosmic unity and purpose.

BELIEF

Zarathushtra taught that Ahura Mazda was God, the one eternal uncreated Being, wholly good, wise and beneficent. Opposed to him was Angra Mainyu, the Hostile or Evil Spirit – wholly evil, ignorant and maleficent, likewise uncreated but not eternal, indeed doomed in the end to perish. God, Zarathushtra taught, had created this sevenfold world as a place in which he could encounter this evil being and overcome him. To help him in this task he emanated the six great Amesha Spentas, 'Holy Immortals', who are at once aspects of God and independent divinities, one with him and yet distinct. He and they each took to themselves one of the seven creations as an especial charge: Desirable Dominion (Kshathra Vairya) took the sky; Wholeness or Health (Haurvatat) took water; Holy Devotion (Spenta Armaiti) earth; Immortality (Ameretat) plants; Good Purpose (Vohu Manah) animals; Ahura Mazda himself took humankind, in whom, if they are just, God's Holy Spirit – Spenta Mainyu – dwells; and lastly, Best Truth or Righteousness (Asha Vahishta, the embodiment of the principle of Asha) took fire. This doctrine, together with radical dualism, is at the heart of Zoroastrian theology, and links in a remarkable way the moral, spiritual and physical worlds.

It is the individual's duty to strive to bring all members of the Heptad into his or her own consciousness, and while seeking to attain moral and physical well-being for him- or herself, who is Ahura Mazda's special creation, to care as steward for the physical creations of the other six.

The Amesha Spentas emanated other, lesser divinities (corresponding generally to beneficent gods of the old religion). Angra Mainyu in turn produced a counter-evocation of evil beings, including the Daevas, ancient amoral gods, among them Indra.

Ahura Mazda, through his Holy Spirit, created this world perfectly good, but – as he had foreseen – Angra Mainyu maliciously attacked and polluted it, bringing corruption on all things, and the final blow of death. All seven creations should strive instinctively, or in the case of humankind consciously, to combat him and his forces and so achieve Frasho-kereti, the 'Making Wonderful', which implies the restoration of the world and the total eradication of evil.

Seeing little justice in this present world, Zarathushtra held that it would be meted out hereafter. When an individual dies, the soul, he taught, after lingering three days on earth (a traditional belief) goes up to the Chinvat Bridge to be judged. There its thoughts, words and deeds are weighed in the scales of justice, the good on one side, the bad on the other. If the former weigh more heavily, the soul ascends to the 'Best Existence' – Heaven; if the latter, the Bridge contracts to the thickness of a blade's edge, and the wicked soul plunges down into the 'Worst Existence', into Hell, a place of torment hollowed out by Angra Mainyu in the earth below. If good and evil weigh equally, the soul goes to a place where it feels neither joy nor pain but simply exists until Frasho-kereti. Only when this is brought about will the resurrection of the bodies of the dead take place: the Last Judgement will be enacted by which the blessed are separated from the damned. A torrent of molten metal will cover the

THE SIX HOLY IMMORTALS

AMESHA SPENTA	(ROUGHLY TRANSLATED)	CREATION
KHSHATHRA VAIRYA	(POWER)	SKY
HAURVATAT	(HEALTH)	WATER
SPENTA ARMAITI	(PIETY)	EARTH
AMERETAT	(IMMORTALITY)	PLANTS
VOHU MANAH	(GOOD INTENT)	CATTLE
SPENTA MAINYU	HOLY SPIRIT	MAN
ASHA VAHISHTA	RIGHTEOUSNESS	FIRE

Zoroaster taught that Ahura Mazda, the one and only eternal God, created the world as a battleground in which he could meet and overcome the Evil Spirit, Angra Mainyu. The creation was accomplished through his Holy Spirit Spenta Mainyu and the six Holy Immortals (Amesha Spenta), each of whom now dwells in and protects his creation.

earth, purifying it, and will flow down into Hell to destroy the last vestiges of evil. Humankind will have to pass through this torrent; to the just it will feel like warm milk, but sinners will perish. The kingdom of God will come on an earth made level again and as beautiful as a garden (Persian 'paradise') in spring, and the blessed will rejoice in God's presence for ever.

Zarathushtra appears to have believed that Frasho-kereti was not far off, but his prediction of a saviour to come after him, the *Saoshyant*, has still to be realized.

WRITINGS

The Avesta
The Zoroastrian holy texts are known collectively as the Avesta. They are composed in two stages of an otherwise unrecorded eastern Iranian language: 'Gathic Avestan' – which is close to the language of the Hindu Rig Veda – and 'Younger Avestan'. The former takes its name from the chief texts in this ancient dialect, the prophet's seventeen hymns. Although only this part of the Avesta is directly attributable to him, the whole Avesta is held to be inspired by his teachings and hence revealed by God.

Not only were the ancient Iranians unfamiliar with writing, the alien art was long regarded by them as unfit for sacred works. All their holy texts were accordingly transmitted orally until probably the fifth or sixth century CE, when they were at last set down in an admirably clear alphabet evolved especially for the purpose. The oldest extant manuscript is dated 1323 CE.

The Gathas of Zarathushtra
These short, difficult verse-texts are cast largely in the form of utterances addressed by the prophet to Ahura Mazda. They convey through inspired poetry visions of God and his purposes, and prophecies of things to come, here and hereafter; the prophet's ardently-felt beliefs are condensed into intricate, richly allusive verses. Arranged in five groups according to metre, they are set in the *yasna* liturgy before and after Yasna Haptanhaiti, the 'Worship of the Seven Chapters'. This, also in Gathic Avestan, consists of what appear to be essentially even more ancient texts, composed to accompany the traditional offerings to fire and water.

The Younger Avesta
Only the Gathic texts were strictly memorized by the priests. Others were partly learnt by heart, partly composed afresh by each generation of priestly poets and scholars, so that their language evolved with the spoken tongue, and new matter was interwoven with old. Younger Avestan texts are accordingly composite works, and anonymous. The *yashts* – hymns to individual divine beings – contain some matter which is older even than the Gathas; some were used to extend the *yasna* liturgy, which grew finally to have seventy-two sections.

Still today priests recite the whole *yasna* liturgy by heart. At one special service, solemnized at night, they read in addition the entire *Vendidad*, a work 'Against the Daevas'. This is a mixed collection of prose texts, compiled probably during the Parthian period and largely concerned with the purity laws as a means of combating evil.

After the holy texts had been written down, a book of common prayer was compiled, called the Khorda ('Little') Avesta, which consists of short devotional works in common use.

Pahlavi Writings
The Great Avesta, arranged in twenty-one books, contained all the devotional books already mentioned and many more. It was held to embody 'all knowledge', and its contents included the life and legend of the prophet, expositions of the doctrine, apocalyptic works, traditions of the faith, and treatises on law, cosmology and scholastic science. All these texts were accompanied by their Zand or 'interpretation', a translation into Middle Persian (also called Pahlavi), with glossaries and commentaries. All copies of the Great Avesta were destroyed during the Islamic period. Its contents are largely known, however, through Pahlavi summaries and extensive passages surviving from the Zand.

Some Pahlavi texts belong essentially to the Sasanian period. Other compilations begun then were added to substantially during the succeeding centuries right down to the ninth or even early tenth centuries CE. Yet others are original compositions of the Islamic period. Most Pahlavi material is, however, undatable (except in terms of its latest redaction) for it remains essentially an oral literature set down later in writing, with the general characteristics of anonymity, free borrowing from text to text, and interweaving of contemporary with traditional passages.

The chief works containing material from the Zand are the *Bundahishn*, 'Creation', and the *Wizidagiha*, 'Selections'. Both are concerned with creation and its purposes, and with eschatology, and the latter also contains material about the legend of Zarathushtra. Similar material is to be found in the *Denkard*, 'Acts of the Religion', the largest surviving Pahlavi work, which contains an enormous amount of diverse material. Unfortunately its style tends to be tortuous and obscure, adding to the normal difficulties presented by the Pahlavi script which has too few letters for clarity and uses fossilized Aramaic words as ideograms.

RELIGIOUS LEADERS, PROPHETS AND TEACHERS

Religious leaders and teachers are often professionals who are especially trained in the interpretation of a tradition, and who therefore exercise much influence in the development and understanding of religious thought and practice. Sometimes the role of the teacher may be endowed with particular authority as is, for example, the office of the Pope, the bishop of Rome, who is believed by Catholics to speak on certain occasions with infallibility. In other cases religious teachers may understand their role as one that has to do with re-interpreting ancient traditions in creative ways in order to enable a religious message to speak to modern people. The prophet is also a figure that is understood in a variety of ways. He may be regarded as a person through whom God's word is spoken

A painting by du Jardin of The Conversion of St Paul. *Paul's conversion on the road to Damascus (Acts 9) came to be seen as a critical event in early Christianity as well as a model of sudden and dramatic conversion. Paul played a leading part in the early spread of the Church outside Palestine and in the development of Christian theology.*

and a unique revelation declared, as in the case of Muhammad. Such a major figure may then be the actual founder of a religion, honoured and revered as much as those who are believed to have divine status. But the prophet may be a more ordinary person, who responds to what he or she discerns as the will of God by recalling people to the essentials of their faith, or challenging them with new insights.

LEFT Muhammad and 'Ali (both faceless) with the Companions, from Nizam's History of Muhammad. Muhammad is believed by Muslims to be the last of the prophets and the messenger through whom Allah's message of the Qu'ran was transmitted. His cousin and son-in-law 'Ali was Caliph from 656 until his assassination in 661, which marked the beginning of the break between Sunni and Sh'ite Islam. The Companions are esteemed as those who accepted Islam during Muhammad's life and accompanied him for some time.

ABOVE A boy is guided in his reading from the Torah during his Bar Mitzvah, held by the Western Wall in Jerusalem. The Torah is a major source of authority and teaching, and together with the Mishnah and the Talmud provides the basis for the teaching of divine law. Those who study and expound Torah and Talmud, therefore, whether as rabbis or as Yeshivot graduates or students, play a vital role in the transmission of the traditions and teachings of Judaism.

BELOW Young Parsis training to be priests wear a cloth over mouth and nose to prevent their breath polluting the sacred flame, and white to symbolize purity. Fire is present at all Zoroastrian rites. There are three grades of fire, and the highest two (Atash Bahram and adaran) must be tended by priests. Parsi priesthood is hereditary, although the line lapses if three succeeding generations fail to proceed to at least the first stage of initiation.

LEFT Buddhist bhikkhus (monks) in Thailand. The Sangha, or community of monks, is an important part of Buddhist life. In Theravada Buddhism especially it is the bhikkhu who is regarded as the serious seeker after enlightenment. Traditionally the bhikkhu is allowed few possessions. In addition to his robes he should have a bowl for food, a filter for water, a razor, a toothpick, a needle, a stick, and a fan. Here the bhikkhus go in silent and meditative procession to receive their daily gift of food from lay people, for whom it is a religious duty to support the Sangha.

BELOW A group of Jaina nuns of the Shvetambara sect, which admits women to the full monastic vows. The Shvetambara, or 'white clad', are concentrated in north India and especially in Gujarat. The nuns live a strict ascetic life, and wander from place to place relying on lay supporters for food. They are expected to apply Jaina teaching about ahimsa, or non-violence, very strictly, and to avoid harm not only to people but also to animals and insects. A mask is worn to prevent small insects being breathed in, and they often carry a brush to sweep the road before them in order to avoid killing unseen creatures. As a religion Jainism is numerically small, but some of its teaching has greatly influenced Hinduism.

ABOVE The Sikh sacred scripture, the Adi Granth, occupies an important place in the worship of the gurdwara and in Sikh life. The Adi Granth is also known as the Guru Granth Sahib, a title which reflects the decision of the last of the ten human Gurus, Guru Gobind Singh, to abolish the line of succession and to install the Adi Granth as the religious teacher of Sikhs. Thus the scripture has taken over the role formerly filled by the inspired teachers and prophets who were the human Gurus.

RIGHT A Greek Orthodox abbot, or hegumenos, in full regalia at the Chrysorroyiatissa monastery on Mount Troodos. An abbot is the superior of a religious house or monastery, and exercises some episcopal functions within his own domain. Christianity in Cyprus has a long history; the island was evangelized by St Paul and Barnabas (Acts 13). There is a close relationship between religious and national identity in Cyprus, marked when Archbishop Makarios became the first President of the new Republic of Cyprus in 1960.

FAR LEFT *An imam at a mosque near Samarkand, Uzbekskaya, USSR. An imam is essentially a leader of worship in the mosque, a task that any adult male Muslim of good character may perform, although in many cases teaching becomes part of the imam's duties. An imam is not a priest, and only in larger mosques is he likely to be salaried. Expansion to the borders of Afghanistan in the nineteenth century incorporated substantial Muslim populations into the USSR.*

LEFT *Young deacons wearing filigree crowns and carrying crosses as they take part in a procession to celebrate the Coptic feast of the Epiphany at Lalibela, Ethiopia. Deacons are a separate order of ministry from bishops and priests, and originally one which performed service to the community. In later times the diaconate became simply a stepping-stone to the priesthood, although there are moves to restore it to its earlier purpose. The Ethiopian Church, now much diminished, originated in the Coptic Church of Egypt.*

ABOVE LEFT *A cardinal and bishop in Rome. Of the three orders of ministry in the Christian Church (bishop, priest and deacon) the bishop is the highest. He has authority to ordain priests and usually has the oversight of a diocese. Cardinals in the Roman Catholic Church are bishops who are appointed to special duties and privileges, particularly as advisers to the Pope.*

ABOVE *Shinto priests at the Kitano shrine in Kyoto. The costume of the Shinto priest dates from the Heian period (ninth to eleventh centuries CE), a time when priests were recruited from a special hereditary class or from ritual families who served the court. Full-time priests have usually been employed for the larger shrines. Land reform after the Second World War removed land from many shrines and so increased the tendency, already evident in smaller shrines, for priests to have part-time employment.*

A stained-glass window by Gabriel Loire, illustrating the words of Jesus in Matthew 16.18, 19: 'You are Peter, and on this rock I will build my church. . . . I will give you the keys of the kingdom of Heaven.' The meaning of this text is much disputed. The traditional Roman Catholic interpretation is that the verse indicates an intention on the part of Jesus to give Peter a special authority as head of the Church. The conferring of this authority on both Peter and his successors has led to the belief that they hold a unique commission in the Church.

An extensive apocalyptic literature evidently once existed in Avestan. The longest work of this kind still extant is the *Zand i Vahman Yasht*. Old materials are also rehandled in the *Arda Viraz Namag*, which tells how the righteous Viraz was persuaded for the common good to enter a drug-induced trance in order to visit the other world and confirm the teachings about Heaven and Hell. The tale of his spirit-journey has been shown to be the ultimate source of Dante's *Divine Comedy*.

The *Shkand-gumanig Vizar*, 'Doubt-dispelling Exposition', is an enquiry into Zoroastrianism and other religions, in terms of comparison. This, and a number of other Pahlavi works containing expositions of doctrine, ancient legends, 'wisdom' texts, ritual injunctions, niceties of the purity laws and ethical homilies, survived the remorseless destruction of Zoroastrian texts in Muslim Iran only by being sent to India. There, from the latter part of the nineteenth century, they were published by Parsi priestly scholars, sometimes in collaboration with Europeans. The whole extant Avesta was also edited and printed.

WORSHIP

Zarathushtra retained the traditional priestly act of worship, the *yasna*, but gave it new spiritual and moral dimensions. At it, his followers were now to seek through communion with the divine Heptad to bring them into their own lives in order to attain the virtues or qualities which they embody, and to make room in their hearts for the indwelling of God's Holy Spirit. The *yasna* liturgy includes the Gathas, which have been recited daily by the priests for more than three thousand years.

The ancient Iranians had three traditional times for prayer: sunrise, noon and sunset. Zarathushtra increased these to five, requiring his followers to rise and pray also at midnight and before dawn.

Men and women alike wear a seamless white shirt, the *sedra*, and tie over it a sacred cord, the *kusti*. This they untie and retie while praying standing in the presence of fire (sun, moon or hearth fire), the creation of Asha. The *kusti* is tied three times round the waist, a constant reminder of the threefold ethic of good thought, word and deed by which alone an individual can attain salvation for himself and the world. The prescribed prayers include verses from the Gathas as well as from the Ahunvar, a short, very sacred prayer also composed by Zarathushtra himself.

For communal observance there were appointed seven holy days of obligation, to be spent in corporate worship followed by feasting and merrymaking. (Zoroastrian doctrine is that grief belongs to Angra Mainyu, and that fasting is a sin since it weakens the good body created by Ahura Mazda. All holy days are therefore observed joyously.) The seven great festivals are dedicated to the Heptad and their creations. The sixth, devoted to Ahura Mazda and humankind, celebrates the last night of the old year through the traditional festival of All Souls, Hamaspath-maedaya; and the next day is celebrated as the seventh festival, in honour of Asha and fire. This festival, known as 'New Day' (Persian 'No Ruz') is the holiest in the Zoroastrian year, an annual prefiguring of the Last Day and Frasho-kereti. In historical times it has been held in spring, with the revival of nature symbolizing the future resurrection to eternal life.

Early observances included the keeping of certain strict purity laws. Some were evidently traditional, but these received a firm doctrinal basis through Zarathushtra's dualism, by which pollution of all kinds was attributed to Angra Mainyu; they were accordingly greatly extended by later generations of priests. Few are retained to this day, however.

Because the physical creations also had to be kept as pure as possible, the dead were disposed of not by burial or burning (a contamination to earth or fire) but by exposure in barren places, to be swiftly devoured by birds or wild beasts. Later, funerary towers (*dakhmas*, 'towers of silence') were constructed for the purpose.

In Iran there are sacred fires of unknown antiquity. The oldest Parsi sacred fire has been burning since the tenth century. Such fires are cared for communally. Many fires founded more recently by pious individuals have trustees who appoint their own priests and manage the endowments. There are three grades of sacred fire, all sustained by wood: the Atash Bahram, which is kept burning brightly night and day, and requires the attendance of at least four priests; the Atash Adaran, which is allowed to 'sleep' under a blanket of hot ash between the five times of prayer, and can be served by two priests; and the Dadgah, which, when necessary, may be tended by a ritually clean lay man or woman. Most village fires are Dadgah.

Persecution and poverty long prevented Zoroastrians from maintaining imposing edifices, and no building housing an Atash Bahram is older than the nineteenth century.

THE SPREAD OF ZOROASTRIANISM

Zarathushtra succeeded in converting Vishtaspa (Hystaspes), an Iranian king, and his faith took root. From around 1200 BCE Iranians began to move south to conquer and settle the land now known as Iran; eastern Iranians evidently carried his teaching with them. Their hope in the coming saviour, the *Saoshyant*, became linked with devotion to Zarathushtra through a myth, according to which the *Saoshyant* will be born of the prophet's seed, miraculously preserved in a lake. When the time comes, a virgin will bathe there and become with child, and that child will be the World Saviour. This myth apparently took shape before the religion became established also in western Iran at the time of Cyrus the Great (around 550–30 BCE), who founded the Persian Achaemenid Empire. The priests of the Medes and the Persians – the *magi* – became thereafter the best-known Zoroastrian priests.

Under the Achaemenids Zoroastrianism enjoyed enormous power and prestige. The Per-

sians' subjects included Babylonians and Egyptians, Jews and Ionian Greeks, and Zoroastrian doctrines became widely known. Certain parts of the Hebrew Bible show traces of what appear to be Zoroastrian influence, for example the belief in a resurrection of the dead ascribed to Zarathushtra by the Greek scholar Theopompos in the first half of the fourth century BCE which appears as a late development in Jewish biblical thought (for example, Isaiah 26:19 and, more specifically, Daniel 12:2), and the myth of the creation of the world in seven stages which is probably reflected in the creation story set in Genesis 1 before the ancient Jewish story of Adam and Eve. Zoroastrian influences have also been detected among Ionian philosophers in the sixth and fifth centuries BCE, and later among Plato and his school. Conversely, some of the *magi* introduced Babylonian astrological lore into Zoroastrianism and also, under alien inspiration, evolved the only considerable Zoroastrian heresy, Zurvanism. This was a monism (based on a re-interpretation of a Gathic verse) which postulated a common father for Ahura Mazda and Angra Mainyu, namely the remote god Zurvan, 'Time'. Zurvanism developed its own myths and gained considerable support and influence, only to disappear entirely after the tenth century CE. In the late Achaemenid period a temple cult of fire was established by which sacred fires were tended in strict purity in consecrated buildings as a communal focus for devotion.

Alexander's conquest of Iran (from 334 to 326 BCE) brought considerable destruction to the faith, and slaughter of its priests. After a period of Hellenic rule, Iranian sovereignty was restored by the Parthians (from north-eastern Iran) whose empire lasted from about 141 BCE to 224 CE. Zoroastrianism thus became once more an imperial faith. It was at this time that major Zoroastrian teachings – concerning Heaven and Hell, the Evil One, individual judgement and the Last Judgement, resurrection of the body and eternal bliss for the saved – appeared also among the Jews, to become (despite rejection by some) established doctrine in both Judaism and Christianity.

Zoroastrianism remained the state religion of the third Iranian empire, that of the Sasanians (from 224 to 651 CE). Its doctrines reached the Arabs both through Judaism and directly: one of Muhammad's 'Companions' was a Persian-born Zoroastrian. Together with certain fundamental doctrines Muhammad is held to have taken from the Iranian faith the five times of daily prayers.

In the seventh century the Arabs conquered Iran and gradually imposed Islam throughout the land. Zoroastrians remained a considerable part of the population until the ninth century. Thereafter, successive conquests of Iran by Muslim Turks and the Mongols hastened their reduction

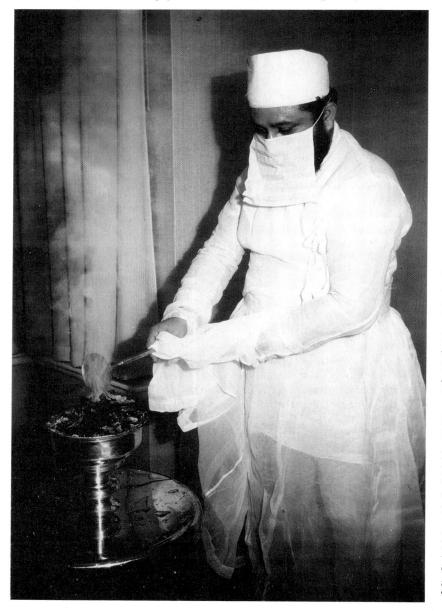

A Parsi priest attends the sacred fire. He wears a cloth over his mouth to prevent his breath from polluting the purity of the flame. The Parsi Panchayat, or association of Zoroastrians, in Bombay is the largest and most influential group of Zoroastrians today. The name Parsi marks the Persian origin of the religion in what is today Iran, where it has been almost entirely eradicated.

there until, by the late thirteenth century, only a persecuted minority survived mainly around the desert cities of Yazd and Kerman. Early in the tenth century a group sailed from Iran to India, seeking religious freedom, and settled in Gujarat, where they became known as the Parsis (or Persians).

Zoroastrians are still today divided accordingly into two branches, the Iranis and the Parsis. Although the Parsis adopted the Gujarati language and various Indian customs, the two communities have remained close in their religious beliefs and observances. The Parsis particularly flourished in British India. In recent decades there has been considerable emigration by members of both communities, chiefly to the UK and to Canada and the USA.

ORGANIZATION

The priesthood is hereditary, and has two main grades. A candidate first becomes a *herbad* at around the age of fifteen or a little older, then two or three years later he may become a *mobad*. A *herbad* is qualified to perform 'outer' ceremonies, such as the initiation of a child by investiture with the sacred cord and shirt (called *sedra-pushun* by the Iranis, *naojot* by the Parsis), or marriage, or *jashans* (short services of thanksgiving, supplication, or simply of worship). Such ceremonies may be performed in any 'clean' place, such as a Zoroastrian house. Only a *mobad*, however, may solemnize 'inner' ceremonies, which must be performed in a consecrated place (now always within the complex of a fire temple); these ceremonies include the *yasna*.

The need to know all the prayers and much of the liturgy by heart demands some considerable time spent in training, and priests tend to form a slightly separate part of the community. Family priests have no fixed incomes but receive a present of money for every religious ceremony at which they officiate. Temple priests are supported either through endowments or offerings by worshippers.

Priests form their own local associations, led by a *dastur*, a high priest, whose position is sometimes elective, sometimes hereditary. In Sasanian times the Persian high priest was head of the whole priesthood, and until the twentieth century he was represented in Iran by the *Dasturan dastur* of Yazd, to whom precedence was accorded by the high priest of Kerman. Both these dignities have now lapsed with the modern importance of Tehran for the Irani community. In Gujarat, the Parsi priests organized themselves geographically into five independent *panths*, each with its own *dastur*. This system has also now largely broken down, partly through the emergence of Bombay to the south of Gujarat as the chief centre of Parsi population.

The lack of a single ecclesiastical authority has been keenly felt since the abrupt impact in the nineteenth century of western scientific knowledge, which together with severe attacks on Zoroastrian dualism by Christian missionaries, led to a breakdown of traditional orthodoxy. Contemporary Zoroastrians are divided into traditionalists and reformists, theosophists, theists, mystics and rationalists, and the small community is rent by controversy for which as yet there is no real possibility of resolution.

Nevertheless, the community remains broadly united through adherence to Zarathushtra's teaching that each individual must earn his or her own salvation through good thoughts, words and deeds. This ethic has led Zoroastrians to be notable philanthropists, and active in communal and political life. There were Zoroastrian Members of the British Parliament in the nineteenth century, and of the Iranian *Majles* and the Indian Parliament in the twentieth.

The Zoroastrian community today has no political affiliations but expects its members to be loyal citizens of whatever country they inhabit. Wherever there is a group of Zoroastrians, a local association (an *anjoman* or *panchayat*) is usually formed to establish a place for meeting and worship and to collect and distribute charitable funds. The largest and most influential of such associations is the Parsi Panchayat of Bombay. Several federated organizations exist, notably the Association of Zoroastrian Anjomans of India and the Zoroastrian Associations of Europe and North America. A succession of World Zoroastrian Congresses has been held, at which religious and communal problems are discussed and common bonds maintained.

CHRISTIANITY

TO THE ELEVENTH CENTURY

HISTORICAL OUTLINE

Origins

Christianity originated in Palestine, in the homelands of Judaism. Although Palestine had been part of the Roman Empire since 63 BCE, the culture accompanying the imperial presence was Hellenistic or Greek-speaking. Accordingly the world from which Christianity emerged was partly Semitic and Jewish, partly Roman, and partly Hellenistic.

Christianity ensued from the career of a Palestinian Jew, Jesus. Due to the unique nature of accounts preserved in the New Testament, a full biography of Jesus is impossible. Information about him is what his followers considered to be significant.

Born about 6 BCE in Bethlehem in Judaea, Jesus grew up at Nazareth in Galilee. In his last three years, 27–30(?) CE, he became a public figure. He joined the radical Jewish spiritual movement led by John the Baptist. John was a repentance-preacher proclaiming forgiveness of sins in preparation for God's imminent direct rule. This readiness was symbolized by the ritual purification of baptism in water. Jesus of Nazareth was baptized and received at his baptism his messianic calling to deliver God's people from the powers of Satan.

Accompanied by twelve disciples, Jesus became an itinerant teacher. For about two years he worked in Galilee, proceeding then to the Jewish capital, Jerusalem. Although Jesus was comparatively unorthodox he was not schismatic; he continued to worship in the synagogue and to adhere to normal Jewish observances. In contrast to John the Baptist, he declared that God's kingdom was already present, in a hidden way, but that all would be revealed in glory at his future return (Second Coming). This was his 'gospel'.

To authenticate his message Jesus performed various miracles and acts of healing. To show that it is God's will to save sinners he fraternized with social and religious outcasts offering mercy and compassion, while at the same time he summoned his listeners to the highest ethical standards of Judaism. But it was a new morality of the heart that he preached, based on repentance, gratitude, love and freedom rather than mere outward observance of the Divine Law, the source of hypocrisy.

In his lifetime Jesus was designated variously. Some titles were controversial – 'Prophet', 'Son of Man', 'Lamb of God', 'Son of God', 'Messiah'. Jewish expectations of a Redeemer, a Saviour, a Deliverer, a Messiah help to explain this. Jesus was normally reticent on the matter and counselled his disciples to be discreet, wanting to eschew political messianism. The name 'Jesus Christ' means 'Jesus the Messiah'. Hellenistic Jews were to translate Messiah as 'Christos,' meaning the One anointed by God to deliver his people.

Jesus' ministry was not welcomed by the Jewish authorities. His presence in Jerusalem was considered provocative. At the Passover Feast of about 30 CE he was arrested and charged with being a false prophet claiming to be the Messiah and the Son of God, in other words, with blasphemy. Abandoned by his disciples, Jesus was tried respectively by the Jewish Sanhedrin and by the Roman magistrate, Pontius Pilate – being also suspected of agitating against the Roman government. He was convicted on uncertain grounds and crucified. The Romans designated him mockingly as the 'King of the Jews.'

Had matters ended there, Jesus might never have become more than a footnote in history. But on the Sunday after his execution, women-associates of Jesus found that his grave was empty. Following what some reported as an appearance to them by Jesus, they came to believe that he had been resurrected. A similar appearance to the fugitive disciples fulfilled his prophecy of resurrection made to them at his Transfiguration, when he momentarily revealed his divine glory. The Risen Christ now commissioned the disciples to be his apostles, telling the world what he had taught them. They returned to Jerusalem where at Pentecost, fifty days after the Passover, they received the gift of the Holy Spirit. The apostles then began to proclaim their experience of Jesus Christ.

The Crucifixion, the central panel from the Isenheim altarpiece by Matthias Grünewald (1515). The cross, a barbarous form of execution in Roman times, is perhaps the single most potent symbol of Christianity. The death of Jesus is believed to have sealed the New Covenant between God and Man. The Old Covenant with Israel is superseded and as bearer of the burden of mankind's guilt Jesus Christ, through his death, makes believers 'Sons of God': God's promise of mercy is fulfilled.

Jesus' life, death, resurrection, ascension into Heaven, and the imparting of the Spirit to those who repent and have faith in him, constitute the Christian faith and Church. But Jesus had no intention of founding a new sect or religion. Rather his aim was to consummate the faith of Israel for the benefit of the world by fulfilling the promises God had made to the Hebrews.

Mission

The course of Christianity in the first millenium was one of both expansion and contraction. Initially through its own momentum, and later aided by the entire apparatus of the State, Christianity spread within the confines of what was or used to be the Roman Empire. The setback following the collapse of the Empire in the West in 476 CE was temporary. But the Arab invasions from the seventh century entailed the loss of Christian lands to Islam, notably Syria, Palestine, Egypt, Libya, North Africa, South-east Europe and Spain. Thereafter Christianity was confined chiefly to north of the Mediterranean. Compensation for losses to Islam was provided by the progressive Christianization of the Germanic, Celtic and Slavonic indigenous peoples of Europe in the western post-Imperial epoch.

Initially the Apostles had confined evangelization to the Jews. That the mission became universal was due to the conversion and work of a Pharisaic Jew from Asia Minor, Paul. He helped establish the first non-Jewish or Gentile Church, in Syrian Antioch. There the name 'Christians' appears first. Paul convinced the other Apostles of the validity of the mission to non-Jews. His missionary journeys laid the foundations of Christianity in the Empire.

Christianity's growth was facilitated by the infrastructure of the Empire. Further, the bridge to the Gentiles was provided by the Jewish *diaspora*, which constituted about 7 per cent of the Empire's population. In a pluralistic and polytheistic society Christianity expanded from the bottom upwards, often in the face of hostility. The conversion of Emperor Constantine in 312 to the monotheistic faith precipitated a situation whereby by the end of that century the Empire was officially Christian and the Church was a state Church. In post-Imperial barbarian Europe, Christianity's most significant step forward was the conversion in 496 of Clovis, King of the Franks – although a heterodox form of Christianity, Arianism, had by then already spread among southern Germanic tribes.

A grave slab from the 4th century CE commemorating the martyrs Simplicius and Faustinus. Above the inscription is the Chi Rho symbol, the first Greek letters in the name of Christ. Before Constantine's adoption of Christianity in 313 many early Christians were martyred by the Roman authorities, the most notorious persecutions being those of Nero, Decius and Diocletian.

The later centuries of the first millenium are marked by two features. First, the entrenchment of a contracted and conservative Eastern Christianity which was centred in Constantinople (Byzantium) but which largely evangelized the Slavs. Second, the expansion of Western Christianity under the theoretical control of the Church of Rome to form a creative mixture of Germanic, Romance and Celtic elements united by a Latin Christian culture and theology.

Church and society

Christianity's expansion was due to its distinctive combination of monotheism; the notion that salvation by personal or institutional effort is superseded by the redeeming grace of God through Christ; and the ethics of love. But much hostility was encountered in a society which knew of Jesus as an executed criminal. Jewish animosity was inevitable (the Christian proto-martyr, Stephen, was killed by the Jews in Jerusalem) while pagan intellectual opposition peaked in the second century with the attempts of Celsus to expose Christianity as a fraud. Popular opposition is explained by the transference of endemic antisemitism on to Christians and by Christian nonconformism.

Then, between 64 and 311 CE, while religious pluralism obtained in the Empire, there occurred intermittent persecutions of Christians by emperors, the most notorious being those of Nero, Decius and Diocletian. While Christianity was never a crime, the refusal of emperor-worship was considered a treason. Moreover, the uncertain relationship between Christ and Caesar made Christians politically suspect, although in fact they pledged practical loyalty in the interim existence. The Church's organization also created resentment by resembling a state within a state.

Until 313, when legal toleration was granted, the Church was a confessional and voluntary community, edified by the martyrs. On becoming the sole imperial religion, the Church changed its character, a transformation best demonstrated in the sixth century when imperial sovereignty in the Church was enshrined in the law-code of the Emperor Justinian.

In Western post-Imperial Christianity, the State also dominated the Church, despite the claim of supremacy of the Bishops of Rome, and the view of Augustine that the City of God cannot be identified with the State, however Christian the State may be. As in the East, the Church was an agent of national or imperial unity. Civil existence apart from the Church became unthinkable; Augustine too had legitimized the notion of coercive Christianization. A quasi-Byzantine theocratic politico-religious entity of 'Christendom' under the Emperor was the ideal of Charlemagne in the ninth century. Similarly, the German monarch Otto established in 962 the 'Holy Roman Empire of the German Nation'. But a Church reform movement emanating from Cluny revived the determination of the Roman Popes to reclaim authority in the Church, resulting in the later 'Investiture Contest' between Rome and the secular rulers for ecclesiastical control.

The emergence of the Early Catholic Church

Originally the Church was a visible community of believers understood as the Body of Christ, guided and edified informally by a collective Ministry which was regarded as the expression of the diffused gifts and offices of the Spirit. Such a ministry was not so much professionally vocational as pneumatic, charismatic, and *ad hoc*. By the fourth century the Church had evolved to become an equally visible, but now statutory and institutional, organism staffed by a hierarchical ecclesiastical ministry. This emerging institution was governed by specific irreducible norms, and was to be called the 'Catholic' Church. Objectively Catholic meant Universal, General, or Ecumenical. Subjectively it meant true and orthodox compared to what was schismatic, heterodox or heretical. The norms constituting Catholic Christianity were threefold: the canon of Scripture, the Rule of Faith, and monarchical episcopacy.

The first identifies the authenticity of documents purporting to contain the record of revelation in Jesus Christ and its proclamation by the Apostles. This became the New Testament, the original Christian writings, which were added to the Old Testament inherited from Judaism. The second refers to the substance of traditional belief: it is the operative principle determining the canon and its interpretation. The rule of faith became formally embodied in the Apostles' and Nicene Creeds. The third meant that the monarchical bishop is the guarantor – individually and collectively – of the true faith and its correct transmission. Bishops were perceived as successors of the Apostles. This meant that where there is a valid bishop, there is the true Church. He embodies authoritatively the antiquity, consensus and universality of Christian belief. Apart from him and the Church Catholic, there is no salvation.

This development was the product of historical necessity. The second century had seen the Church in a struggle for its uniqueness. It had to expose accounts of Jesus which were apocryphal. It had to avoid the vortex of eclectic and syncretic Gnosticism. It was forced to vindicate Creation as God's and the genuine humanity of Jesus Christ against schismatic Marcionitism. And it had to affirm the priority of scriptural revelation against the enthusiastic spiritualism of Montanism. Out of these conflicts, Early Catholicism formed itself.

Evolution of the Roman papacy

Roman papacy refers to the claim of the See of Rome to both episcopal primacy and universal ecclesiastical supremacy. It became normative for later Catholicism in the sense of the statement 'no pope, no Church'. In the latter part of the first millenium, the claim extended to embrace at least formal secular as well as ecclesiastical authority. Only in western Christianity did these claims achieve any significant degree of realization. Papal power and authority evolved with time, aided by certain historical, political and ecclesiastical contingencies, although Papal apologists also claim that such authority is biblically grounded.

Bishop Callixtus in the third century was the first to enunciate the Petrine claim: the power Christ gave to Peter over the Apostles is inherited by his successors as bishops of Rome. This underlined Rome's precedence over the other ancient patriarchiates of Antioch and Alexandria. But the emerging see of Constantinople, the New Rome, claimed such primacy. In the face of this challenge Roman pretensions were advanced further by forceful popes in the fifth and sixth centuries, notably by Leo I and Gregory I. For them, the bishop of Rome is the Vicar of Christ, universal Bishop and Minister of God's ministers. Roman bishops have succeeded the Caesars, the glory that was Rome is now that of the Roman Church.

Only later in the millenium did Rome's authority begin to have real administrative and juridical significance in the West, though her doctrinal, moral and evangelical authority had been widely accepted. Furthermore, Roman claims became in addition territorial and political. The former led to the creation of the Papal States. The latter meant countering the imperial theocracies of the Carolingian and German empires, but with papal theocracy. Forged documentation in the Donation of Constantine and the Pseudo-Isidorian Decretals lent authority to these claims. But the original concern of the Papacy and the episcopate in this confrontation was to liberate the Church from secular control. Progress was made in this respect in the mid-eleventh century by a German pope, Leo IX. He was forerunner and mentor of the papal reformer and champion of ecclesiastical autonomy, Pope Gregory VII.

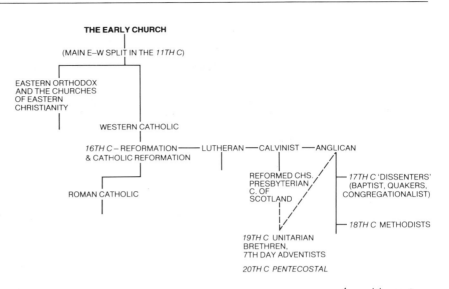

THE EARLY CHURCH

(MAIN E–W SPLIT IN THE *11TH C*)

EASTERN ORTHODOX AND THE CHURCHES OF EASTERN CHRISTIANITY

WESTERN CATHOLIC

16TH C – REFORMATION —— LUTHERAN —— CALVINIST —— ANGLICAN
& CATHOLIC REFORMATION

ROMAN CATHOLIC

REFORMED CHS. PRESBYTERIAN C. OF SCOTLAND

17TH C 'DISSENTERS' (BAPTIST, QUAKERS, CONGREGATIONALIST)

18TH C METHODISTS

19TH C UNITARIAN BRETHREN, 7TH DAY ADVENTISTS

20TH C PENTECOSTAL

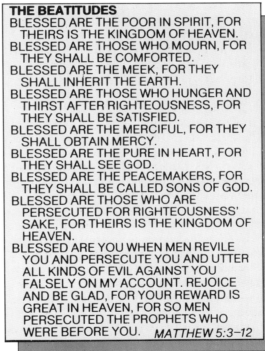

THE BEATITUDES
BLESSED ARE THE POOR IN SPIRIT, FOR THEIRS IS THE KINGDOM OF HEAVEN.
BLESSED ARE THOSE WHO MOURN, FOR THEY SHALL BE COMFORTED.
BLESSED ARE THE MEEK, FOR THEY SHALL INHERIT THE EARTH.
BLESSED ARE THOSE WHO HUNGER AND THIRST AFTER RIGHTEOUSNESS, FOR THEY SHALL BE SATISFIED.
BLESSED ARE THE MERCIFUL, FOR THEY SHALL OBTAIN MERCY.
BLESSED ARE THE PURE IN HEART, FOR THEY SHALL SEE GOD.
BLESSED ARE THE PEACEMAKERS, FOR THEY SHALL BE CALLED SONS OF GOD.
BLESSED ARE THOSE WHO ARE PERSECUTED FOR RIGHTEOUSNESS' SAKE, FOR THEIRS IS THE KINGDOM OF HEAVEN.
BLESSED ARE YOU WHEN MEN REVILE YOU AND PERSECUTE YOU AND UTTER ALL KINDS OF EVIL AGAINST YOU FALSELY ON MY ACCOUNT. REJOICE AND BE GLAD, FOR YOUR REWARD IS GREAT IN HEAVEN, FOR SO MEN PERSECUTED THE PROPHETS WHO WERE BEFORE YOU. *MATTHEW 5:3–12*

LEFT As an itinerant teacher in Galilee Jesus declared that God's Kingdom was already present on Earth, though hidden as yet. This was his gospel, or good news. In one recorded body of teaching, the Sermon on the Mount, Jesus's eight beatitudes outline the basis of Christian attitudes inherent in God's Kingdom.

East–West schism

In 1054 mainstream Christianity's universal unity came to a permanent end. The Church was juridically divided into the Eastern, Byzantine, Greek and Orthodox Communion, and the Western, Roman, Latin and Catholic Communion. Fertile ground for dissension was provided by differences of culture, experience, ideology, piety and theology. To the Hellenistic Easterners, the chief architects of Christian doctrine, Western Christianity was inevitably parvenu. Further, the relocation of the imperial capital in Constantinople and the Empire's collapse in the West created a spirit of autonomy in the See of Rome unknown in the East. And Rome's claims to primacy and supremacy antagonized the East. Besides, the Eastern Church had lost more to Islam than the West;

Christ in Majesty, from the Stavelot Bible. In this manuscript illustration Christ is portrayed as the cosmic twin emperor, supreme in power and authority. In post-Imperial Christianity however the State dominated the Church. By the 3rd century the Church had become an institution and was to be called the Catholic, or Universal, Church.

this engendered a siege mentality resulting in traditionalism and introspection reinforced by the Eastern Church's autocephalous structure. Its piety was that of conservative dogma, mysticism and liturgical sacramentalism. Lastly, the theological aspiration was different. Easterners were concerned with physical redemption and immortality, Westerners more with moral redemption and justification of the sinner.

In contesting imperial theocratic pretensions, Easterners often sought aid from Rome. But the spirit of Rome's interventions often provoked antagonism, as in the Monothelite controversy which occasioned a schism from 649 to 681; the Iconoclastic controversy 729–842; and the Photian schism 867–870. Relations suffered an irretrievable breakdown in the eleventh century when the Constantinopolitan patriarch, Michael Cerularius, pilloried Western Christianity for its theological and ecclesiastical novelties such as affirming the double procession of the Spirit (Filioque), clerical celibacy, eucharistic use of unleavened bread, and Saturday fasting. The West's champion polemicist was Cardinal Humbert. The outcome was a Papal Bull excommunicating the Eastern Ecumenical Patriarch, who in turn anathematized the Roman Church. It would be wrong to consider the schism as historically inevitable; but that it did happen was hardly surprising. In Europe the division was to be underlined by the Slavonic conversion to Orthodoxy.

BELIEF AND DOCTRINE

New Testament

The New Testament is a book witnessing to Jesus Christ (Gospels) and testifying to the life and thought of the first Christians (Acts of the Apostles, Epistles, etc). It is a book of faith validated by Jesus' resurrection. Although the Gospels reflect different interests, the core of Christ's teaching is common to them all: as Prophet, Redeemer and Messiah, he is the Gospel. In him, God's reign has started. God's promises of forgiveness and mercy for sinners are being fulfilled in Christ. The old Covenant God had made with Israel has been superseded by a new Covenant, sealed by Christ's death. Salvation and entry to God's Kingdom is only via Jesus Christ. By virtue of his work the condemnation of humankind following its incapacity perfectly to observe the Law of God is lifted. As fulfiller of the Law, and as bearer of the burden of mankind's guilt, Jesus Christ makes believers 'sons of God'.

For Paul, the symbol of God's work for humankind in Christ is the Cross. It is faith in the redemptive sacrifice of Christ which 'justifies', bringing grace and salvation from God. Believers are the Body of Christ. Their good works follow from the recognition of the reconciliation between God and man achieved by Christ. Christian love is Christ at work in believers. John stresses the cosmological significance of Jesus by identifying him with the Logos, that is God's Word, or Reason or Activity. Because Jesus is the Word made Flesh, he is God Incarnate and therefore God. James, in contrast to Paul, seems to stress justification by works and so reintroduces a moralistic tone to Christian belief, a tone that was soon to become dominant.

Most New Testament literature is eschatological in flavour. It was believed that Christ's Second Coming ushering in God's Kingdom in complete glory would occur very soon. The most extreme example of this expectation is the book of Revelation.

Doctrinal development

The core of New Testament belief and proclamation is found in the earliest Christian baptismal affirmations of faith. But the gradual resignation of Christians to the indefinite postponement of Christ's Second Coming together with the need for Christianity to explain itself to interested or hostile pagans encouraged the development of explained faith, that is, doctrine, dogma or theology. Since Christian self-explanation was not always uniform, internal authenticating organs of norms emerged: the scriptural Canon, the rule of faith (or tradition) and the episcopacy. Right belief was 'orthodoxy', wrong belief 'heresy'. The religious implication was that one's salvation depended on correct doctrine. In establishing orthodox doctrine the Church had to steer a path between popular piety, Scripture, Tradition and natural human speculation.

By 451, the fundamental dogma of Christianity had been formulated. This is summed up in the key doctrine of the Trinity: there is one God, but in the divine substance there are three co-equal and co-eternal Persons, the Father, the Son and the Holy Spirit. The Son, Jesus Christ, is without qualification both true God and true man. This doctrine was worked out at the Ecumenical Councils of Nicaea, Constantinople and Chalcedon 325–45. The language used is subordinate to the concern of the Church that Christianity offers the redemption of the world and mankind. The word 'trinity' is not biblical, but the Church believed that it corresponded to scriptural witness.

The path to this final formulation was strewn with controversy over key issues: 1. *Christ's humanity*. Christ's real humanity was asserted against the view that he was no more than pseudo-human (Docetism, Gnosticism, Marcionitism). 2. *The Spirit*. The views that the Spirit could operate independently (Montanism), or that it was not fully divine (Macedonianism) were resisted. 3. *God's unity*. Some felt that Christ's divinity could mean that there were two Gods, and so Jesus was just uniquely endowed (Adoptianism); or the one God operates in modes or disguises, as Logos, Son and Spirit (Modalistic Monarchianism, Sabellianism). Such theories were refuted. 4. *Christ's divinity*. The view that though Jesus was more than man he was not God (Arianism) was opposed by the view of the orthodox champion, Athanasius, that Jesus was God. Also opposed was a middle view that though Jesus was divine, he was subordinate (Origenism). The Nicene Council affirmed the belief that Jesus does not just resemble God, he is of the same substance as God (homoousios). He is God who saves humanity. 5. *The Trinity*. The operation of the Trinity came to be understood differently in the East and West. In the East the Spirit proceeded in a line from the Father through the Son. In the West, due to Augustine, the image was a triangle, the Spirit proceeding from Father and Son. This led to the future, unresolved 'Filioque' dispute. 6. The definitive acceptance of the Trinity doctrine depended on the outcome of the related *Christological* controversy, the problem of how divinity and humanity relate to each other in Christ's person. Orthodox concern was to exclude certain views, notably that Jesus Christ is a conjunction (Nestorianism), not a union of two separate persons or natures; that in Christ there is a single divine nature (Monophysitism, Eutychianism); and that the man Jesus is God but with a divine and not a human spirit (Apollinarianism).

Against these the Church affirmed that Jesus has a fully divine and a fully human nature united substantially (Hypostatic union) in one person; these natures are distinct, but not separable, confused, divisible, or changeable. These dogmas – articles of faith – were completed in 680 when it was agreed that Christ had two wills, and not one only (Monothelitism). Therafter, the only doctrinal issues to disturb the whole of Christianity were the Filioque dispute, and the question of the use of images or icons, an issue which was resolved in favour of qualified use.

There were further developments, however, which were unique to the West. Against the denial of original sin and the affirmation of unrestricted free will (Pelagianism), Augustine opposed the reality of congenital sin, the limitation of free will by predestination, and the necessity of grace. This grace is mediated exclusively through the sacraments of the Church as instituted by Christ. The Western Church condemned Pelagianism and its variations, though Augustine's views on predestination and grace were only accepted with reservations (Synod of Orange, 529). Against the belief that the Church must be a wholly pure and sanctified community (Donatism), Augustine vindicated the doctrine that the Church on earth must necessarily be a mixed body of perfection and imperfection, grace and sin.

The Council of Nicaea (325) produced the Nicene Creed which was eventually accepted by the Catholic Church as defining the doctrines which concerned the Trinity, the three co-equal and co-eternal Persons of God the Father, Son and Holy Spirit. Detail from a wall painting by Symenon Axenti (1513) in Galata, Cyprus.

For the rest of the millenium in the West the only other matters of note were the condemnation of double predestination (Gottschalk) and of excessive spiritualizing of Christ's sacramental presence (Ratramnus and Berengar of Tours).

WRITINGS

Christian writings are of two formal categories: the sacred canonical writings, known as the Bible, which are regarded as uniquely inspired and vehicles of divine revelation; and the vast corpus of Christian literature, understood ultimately as the interpretation of scriptural revelation.

The canon

This is the Old and New Testaments (or Covenants). In Christianity the Jewish Bible, interpreted in the light of Christ, became known as the Old Testament. Consisting of the 'Law, Prophets and Writings', it was not canonically fixed for both Jews and Christians until about 100 CE. Although originally in Hebrew, the most familiar version, the 'Septuagint', was in Greek. Hellenistic Jews reckoned some other writings as canonical – to be called the 'Apocrypha' – but Christians were never able to achieve a common mind as to their authenticity.

The Christian New Testament evolved out of orally-transmitted sayings and accounts of Jesus as well as letters written by apostles such as Paul. Everything that survived came to be committed to writing and invested with authority. The criteria used in determining this canon were apostolic authorship and compatibility with the Rule of Faith.

Factors that accelerated this process were: the demise of the original protagonists and witnesses; the popularity of apocryphal accounts of Jesus; the dissemination of Gnostic scriptures; provocation occasioned by a fixed but highly tendentious canon by Marcion; and the Montanist claim that the Spirit was transmitting supplementary Revelation.

A number of independent second century literary witnesses suggest strongly that by c. 200 the bulk of the present canon was *de facto* fixed. The earliest testimony to the New Testament as now known is Athanasius in 367. And in 382, a Roman synod published a list of canonical books equivalent to the present Old and New Testaments, the latter consisting of twenty-seven writings. The canon was not the product of an ecclesiastical act of canonization, but rather of evolving consensus. Written originally in Greek, although partly derived from lost Aramaic originals, the dominant version in the West was to be the Latin 'Vulgate', translated by Jerome c. 400.

Christian authors and works

Besides the Bible, there is a vast quantity of Christian literature and a great variety of genres depending on the specific purpose of any given work and on the intended readership. Only a general picture can be given here, highlighting broad phases and significant landmarks.

The period up to about 700 is usually called that of the 'Church Fathers', that is, the progenitors of fundamental Christian doctrine and ethics. The study of this era is called 'patristics' or 'patrology'. The end of the patristic period in the East is usually marked with the work of John of Damascus (d. 749), and in the West with the work of Isidore of Seville (d. 636). Traditionally the patristic period itself is divided into eras before and after the Nicene Council of 325. Our survey therefore falls into three parts: pre-Nicene Fathers, post-Nicene Fathers, and post-patristic and early medieval writers.

PRE-NICENE FATHERS 1. *The Apostolic Fathers* Alongside the New Testament, these are the earliest Christian writings, deriving from the period c. 60–155. They were reckoned to reflect the teaching and practice of the Apostles. Their value lies chiefly in the insights which they give into infant Christianity. Notable among them is a manual of Christian life and worship, the *Didache*; a letter of Clement, bishop of Rome to a sister Church at Corinth; letters from Ignatius of Antioch written on his way to execution; and a letter of the martyred Polycarp of Smyrna. 2. *The Apologists* This refers to authors in the period c. 120–220 who were concerned to defend Christianity from charges made by pagan and Jewish opponents by asserting Christianity's superiority. Chief among these are the Apologies of Justin Martyr as well as his 'Dialogue with Trypho'. The Apologists represent an acceleration of Christian accommodation to Hellenistic philosophy, especially in the positive adoption of the Logos doctrine. 3. *Early Catholic writers* These are authors from the period c. 180–250 who represent the growing maturity of Christian theology. They reaffirmed Christianity as a faith of redemption as distinct from a religious philosophy; they built up a stock of ammunition in the battle with heresies and rival ideologies such as Gnosticism; they helped to elicit and establish the three norms of early catholicism, that is, the scriptural canon, the Rule of Faith (tradition), and an exclusively episcopal ecclesiology. Three writers stand out: Irenaeus, and two African Latin theologians, Tertullian and Cyprian. 4. *The Alexandrians in Egypt* These sought rather to advance Christian truth with the aid of Platonist philosophy and of scholarly erudition. Clement attempted to demonstrate the superiority of Christian Gnosis. Origen was the first great Christian polymath. His versatility and range endowed his writings, especially in the area of biblical exegesis, with profoundly seminal significance.

Before 325 an important landmark was created by Eusebius of Caesarea. His *Ecclesiastical History* was the first work of church history.

POST-NICENE FATHERS This was very much the golden age of Christian theology which produced many prodigious theologians and churchmen. To confine ourselves to the most eminent: Athanasius of Alexandria – already famous for writing on the incarnation – was the principal mouthpiece of evangelical orthodoxy against Arianism. A more philosophical Christian orthodoxy is represented by the works of the Cappadocian Fathers, Basil of Caesarea, Gregory Nazianzus and Gregory of Nyssa. An influential systematic presentation of the Church's thinking on the Trinity and christology was the achievement of Cyril of Alexandria. A theological and philosophical approach in contrast to that of Alexandria was found in Antioch. Typical of this was the exegetical work of Theodore of Mopsuestia, who rejected allegorical methods in favour of literal, historical and philological methods. In the area of church life, much fame was attached to the sermons of John Chrysostom and his tract on the priesthood. Also influential were the lectures by Cyril of Jerusalem on the sacraments.

Significant for the future of theology was the appearance in c. 500 of a pseudonymous work entitled *The writings of Dionysius the Areopagite*. This offered a synthesis of neo-Platonism and Christianity. Eastern theology acquired its definitive and comprehensive presentation in the work of John of Damascus, *On the Orthodox Faith*. John also wrote a number of important tracts against the Iconoclasts.

In the West, the champion of Nicene orthodoxy against Arianism was Hilary of Poitiers in his writing on the Trinity. The four classical 'Doctors' of the Western Church are considered to be Ambrose of Milan, Jerome, Augustine of Hippo and Pope Gregory the Great. Ambrose was more of a practical than a dogmatic theologian, but he bequeathed to the West the example of a marriage between classical culture and Christianity. In the area of biblical exegesis and textual work, Jerome was the Origen of the West. His creation of the Latin Bible was based on genuine linguistic competence. Augustine is regarded as one of the greatest theologians of Christianity, although his influence was confined largely to the West. His *City of God* helped to prevent the Western Church collapsing along with the Roman Empire. His *Confessions* contributed much to Christian psychology. His anti-Pelagian and anti-Donatist writings were decisive in the shaping of Western Christianity. Gregory the Great did much to shape the future of Roman Catholicism, its churchmanship and piety. His writings on the episcopate and on liturgy were to be very influential, as were his hagiographical works. The patristic era in the West closes traditionally with Isidore of Seville. His significance was as an encyclopedist, and his book of *Sentences*, a manual of doctrine and Christian living, became a model in the West.

POST-PATRISTIC AND EARLY MEDIEVAL WRITERS This period is remarkable for its sterility compared to the patristic era. This was in part due to the Arab and barbarian invasions, forcing Christianity on to the defensive or into the field of mission and basic education. But the Carolingian Renaissance resulted in the re-awakening of some critical philosophical and theological discussion in the ninth century in the West. Involved in this were John Scot Eriugena, Gottschalk, Rabanus Maurus, Radbertus and Ratramnus. A notable reform-writing in the eleventh century was that against simony by Humbert of Silva Candida. In the East, mystical spirituality received a boost from the works of Symeon, the 'new theologian' (962–1040).

ORGANIZATION

Church polity and order

'Polity' refers to the form of church government, 'order' to the structure of ministry. The former provides the means by which the Church makes authoritative decisions in doctrine, administration, liturgy and discipline. The latter is the means by which the Church performs its spiritual and pastoral tasks. Order and polity are in practice inextricably linked.

Original and Apostolic Christianity was not furnished with a ready-made polity, but the Apostles had unique authority. When the issue of circumcision and mission to the gentiles became urgent, the Apostles assembled at a council in Jerusalem. This became the prototype of future church councils. Further, primitive Christianity did not have a statutory, uniform and fixed ecclesiastical ministry. Rather the gifts or offices of the Spirit were diffused throughout the church community and exercised somewhat informally as 'ministry' or 'service'. This comprised the functions of speaking in tongues (charismatism), interpretation, exposition of scripture or prophecy, administration, proclamation, leadership, social work, etc. Designations for these various offices were: apostle, evangelist, prophet, teacher, presbyter (elder), deacon, bishop (overseer) and pastor.

Within about a hundred years there had evolved out of this loose and informal order (at least so it appears in extant evidence) a more visible, regular, uniform and hierarchical ministerial order. It became the basis of the future accentuation of the distinction between clergy or ministry and laity. In essence, the order that evolved was three-fold: bishop, presbyter (or priest) and deacon. Since exclusive immediate authority resided in the bishop, the system of order and government is called 'monarchical episcopacy'. Above we have seen how it was one of the three norms of Early Catholicism. The earliest testimony (c. 107) to this emergent order is from the martyred Ignatius, bishop of Antioch. His claim or implication that such order was instituted by the Apostles and so by Christ was to be accepted everywhere at the expense of parallel collegial-presbyterial proclivities in some churches. If at first bishops were elective, chosen by presbyters or congregational acclamation, they were later appointed by figures higher up the ecclesiastical hierachy, notably patriarchs. There were to be five patriarchal episcopal sees in Christianity: Antioch, Alexandria, Constantinople, Jerusalem and Rome. The success of the monarchical episcopacy was due to three factors: the potency of the model of the Old Testament priesthood; the gradual assimilation by the Church of imperial juridical structures, and its effectiveness in maintaining the unity of the Church.

Initially a bishop was the chairman or president of a group of presbyters in a church. With time, the conduct of worship, especially preaching and celebration of the sacraments, was confined to him. As numbers increased with the expansion of Christianity, particularly in the fourth century, the local 'Church' meant groups of congregations organized in a district or 'parish' with the bishop at their head; he delegated powers and duties to presbyters or priests, who in turn were aided by deacons. Later, these parishes were brought together in larger 'dioceses', of which the bishop was now head. Groups of dioceses were created and called 'Provinces', with an archbishop or Metropolitan at their head. In turn, these were subject to the patriarch. An important element in this episcopal system is that the valid ordination of priests and the confirmation of those who have made professions of faith at baptism can only be carried out by a bishop.

In matters of doctrine and ethics, no bishop was in possession of inviolate autonomy. Uncertainties or matters of concern to the Church at large were resolved in a conciliar fashion, by bishops in a council. These councils or synods could be either provincial, or ecumenical. Ultimate authority lay with the Ecumenical or General Church Councils. In early Christianity there were seven of these: Nicaea 325, Constantinople 381, Ephesus 431, Chalcedon 451, Constantinople 553, Constantinople 680/681, Nicaea 787.

The decisions of these councils were accepted by the universal Church.

In practice and in theory the principle of the ultimate authority of a General Church Council has been limited by both the pretensions of emperors or kings to authority in the Church, in the sense of national state Churches, and by the claims of the bishops of Rome to ecclesiastical and spiritual supremacy as outlined above.

Canon law

The Church's development as a juridical and administrative institution, organized along hierarchical lines, like a state within a state, meant that it became necessary to arrange and codify its beliefs, laws and regulations. The outcome of this process was the corpus of canon law. In the end, that gave rise to a new class of cleric, namely canon lawyers or canonists.

Canon law was to comprehend ecclesiastical enactments and decisions in matters of dogma, morals, discipline, order and liturgy. It evolved from three sources: from decisions of provincial or general church councils, for example the 20 canons of the Nicene Council, or the enactments of the regular African church councils; from episcopal letters as practised in particular by Basil of Caesarea, for example; and from papal decretals, authoritative answers to a specific question, as initiated by Bishop Siricius of Rome in 385.

In the fourth and fifth centuries various canonical collections were made and cited as having real authority. These were known as the 'Apostolic Canons', the 'Apostolic Tradition of Hippolytus' (Bishop of Rome), the 'Canons of Hippolytus', and the 'Apostolic Constitutions'. But in the sixth century two important private collections were to have much influence on the development of canon law. In the West, the collection of Dionysius Exiguus was significant in that he included papal decretals. And in the East, the collection of Patriarch John Scholasticus included, not papal decretals, but legislation of the Emperor Justinian. This helped to determine the nature of future East–West differences.

In the remainder of the first millenium the most important step in the evolution of canon law in the West was the False Decretals, alternatively known as the Pseudo-Isidorian Decretals. These came to light in the ninth century, probably in France. They embody forged letters of ante-Nicene bishops of Rome, genuine conciliar canons and spurious correspondence of post-Nicene popes. The context which gave rise to these documents was the desire of the papacy to produce legal authority for its claim to ecclesiastical supremacy against the theocratic pretensions of the Carolingian emperors.

As canon law embedded itself in ecclesiastical government, the apparent fusion of divine and human law made it increasingly difficult to differentiate between the two.

WORSHIP AND RITUAL

In Christian worship or liturgy, there are two major rituals called sacraments. Sacrament means mystery, relating to the divine presence. These sacraments are baptism and the Eucharist (or Holy Communion, Mass, the Lord's Supper). The first is a rite of initiation or admission, the second of full membership of the Church. Worship is intended to be public, but until 313 services were largely secret and private due to the Church's non-legal status. To some extent Christian liturgical development was influenced by Jewish precedents, similar rites in the Mystery religions, and concepts of Neo-Platonism.

Baptism
Ideas linked to baptism with water were: repentance, conversion, cleansing from sin, promise of eternal life, regeneration, illumination, reception of the Spirit, union with Christ, and admission to the Church. Since it was held that Jesus commanded baptism, it was regarded as constitutive of the visible Church. Initially baptism was in Jesus' name, but later it became threefold, in the name of the Father, Son and Holy Spirit.

In the West, Augustine held that baptism removes the stain of original sin, the human condition meriting damnation. Baptism initiates the process of rehabilitation; the soul is marked with an indelible character indicating that it is owned by the Trinity, who will ultimately reclaim it.

As a result of controversies, the Church maintained the independent and inherent virtue and efficacy of sacraments which came to be understood as 'vehicles of grace'. Discernible here is the Stoic Neo-Platonic concept of Divinity, whereby God is not so much spirit as invisible substance. In baptism, then, the water is impregnated with this substance, becoming a holy and heavenly substance conveying divine grace.

Originally baptism was mainly for adults, so that the confessional element in the rite was evident. By 600, infant baptism was the norm, so that the objective virtue of the sacrament was highlighted. This engendered the practice that in an emergency any Christian may baptize. When adult baptism prevailed, its chief features were: renunciation of the devil, instruction or catechizing, fasting, total or partial immersion (though sometimes sprinkling), reception of milk and honey, anointing with oil, laying on of hands, and sponsoring by other Christians. It was followed by the Eucharist. Easter and Pentecost were the times of such joint sacramental occasions. Because of its solemnity and seriousness, as well as

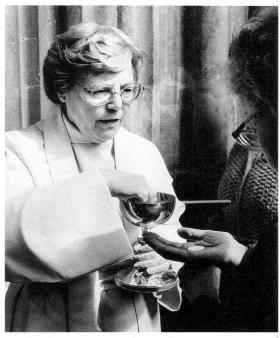

A woman priest giving communion. The position of the worldwide Anglican church on women priests differs from country to country. Originally a private service of prayer and the breaking of bread, the communion service or Eucharist came to be seen in the second century as a vehicle of grace and one of the sacraments.

original uncertainty about the consequence of post-baptismal sin, baptism was often deferred until the death-bed. When infant baptism became widespread and a legal obligation, the sacrament came to lose its liturgical centrality.

The Eucharist
Against the background of the Synagogue, the Passover and the Kiddush (the blessing at an informal religious meal), the first Christians in Palestine also held private services of prayer, mutual exhortation, 'breaking of bread' (Agape or love-feast), speaking in tongues, and a thanksgiving ceremony (eucharist) in remembrance of Jesus. This involved the expectation of his imminent return and fellowship expressed by material support of the needy. The thinking was that just as the ordinary evening meal of bread and wine restores the body, so the religious meal of the Eucharist, in which the bread and wine are images of Christ's body and blood, brings true life; Christ's body is perceived, eaten and enjoyed by faith. The significance of the Eucharist is that by means of it the same Christ who on the Cross redeemed humanity is offered to all and is received by believers as their salvation.

As later Christians reflected on the Eucharist, their thinking was influenced by Hellenistic religious culture – particularly the notion that sharing a meal with a god means partaking of the divine nature. The Eucharist then was seen as providing heavenly food to achieve immortality, it was a foretaste of the Divine banquet in Heaven. Like the water in baptism, the holy bread, impregnated with the invisible divine substance, is a vehicle of grace. The bread is not just a sign, but conveys the reality of Christ's body. This aspect of the sacra-

Pilgrims climb the hill of Craogh Phadraig, Co. Mayo, Eire. Pilgrimage first developed as a means of grace when the veneration of saints and relics associated with them grew. However in the course of time such activities sometimes came to be abused and misunderstood. The pilgrimage up Craogh Phadraig however is often undertaken in the nature of a penance. Some pilgrims will make the journey to the top bare foot and once there will repeat a stated number of prayers. Such penitential practice was once seen as a solution to the problem of post-baptismal sin. When a penance had been fulfilled the sinner was restored to full membership of the church once more.

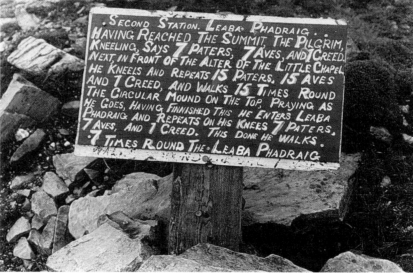

ment underlined the belief that Christ's humanity was not imaginary. Towards the end of the millenium some western theologians warned against excessive sacramental realism.

The notion of sacrifice in the Eucharist refers partly to Christ's sacrifice and partly to the sacrifice of the Christian life by believers. Western tradition stressed the 'sacrifice of the Mass', seeing the sacrament as prerequisite for redeeming sin. The Mass is a sacrifice offered to God by a priest on behalf of the Church; it is a propitiatory re-enactment of Christ's crucifixion. Fundamental to this way of thinking is the idea of inclining God to be gracious through the merits of worship and good works.

By the second century the normative structure of the Eucharist had been established: divorced from the evening meal, it was now the main element in the Sunday morning service which involved scriptural readings, psalmody, prayers, the kiss of peace, consecration of the bread and wine, Communion, and a collection of offerings and their distribution to the poor. It was a service of Word and Sacrament.

There was no universal uniformity of actual ceremonial procedures in the Eucharist. The three dominant traditions derived from Antioch, Alexandria and Rome. The earliest known complete Eastern liturgy is the Clementine Liturgy. But in the Byzantine Church, the Liturgy of John

Chrysostom became established. The Egyptian Church retained the Alexandrian Liturgy of St Mark. In the West, the earliest Roman liturgy, which was Greek, is that in the Church Order of Hippolytus. Further Roman development can be traced in the Leonine, Gelasian and Gregorian Sacramentaries. Roman usage did not begin to become universal in the West until the ninth century. Before that Gallican, that is, non-Roman usages prevailed, for example the Celtic and Ambrosian rites. All were to be superseded by the less elaborate and more solemn Roman Mass.

Other cultic practices

It was natural that martyrs – whose blood was regarded as the seed of the Church – should be recalled and venerated as intercessors with God. The veneration of saints and relics associated with them was based on the belief that the bodies of the saints were especially temples of the Holy Spirit. In 431 the veneration of Jesus' mother, Mary, was encouraged by the Church's affirmation that she was the mother of God, and so participated in the redemption of humanity. Later, and after much controversy, the use of icons and statues was permitted as an aid to devotion. Alongside these practices there developed litanies, processions and pilgrimages. In time such activities came to be abused and misunderstood.

CHRISTIAN LIFE

Sanctification

Very early in Christianity the Church was understood as a communion of saints characterized by moral purity. By the end of the first millenium the Church had become a juridical institution dispensing forgiveness and grace to petitioning and penitent sinners. This resulted from the history of the tense relationship between Law and Gospel, Sin and Forgiveness.

Possibly in reaction to antinomian misinterpretations of the writings of Paul, later New Testament epistles affirmed that holiness and righteousness meant ethical rigour and abstemiousness. Christians were bound to obey the Ten Commandments. Since Christ and sin were incompatible, being Christian meant striving for Christ-like perfect obedience to the law, and so sinlessness. Accordingly ethical failures after baptism could lead to disciplinary excommunication. This practice was related to notions that the baptismal forgiveness of sins cannot be repeated and that post-baptismal sin results in the loss of redemption.

Time was to show that these exacting demands were not sustainable. Either lapses were to be forgiven or the demands were to be scaled down.

Already in the late New Testament Epistles there is the idea that not all sin is mortal. This led to the later distinction between mortal and venial sin. For a period, mortal and unforgivable sin was confined to murder, fornication and idolatry, although by the fourth century even these were no longer regarded as unforgivable. This trend is not to be understood simply as accommodating laxity, for the Church was to devise means for making amends for sin and working for absolution in the Institution of Penance. Penitential practice was therefore a solution to the problem of post-baptismal sin. Works of atonement included prayer, fasting and almsgiving. When such requirements were fulfilled, full membersip of the Church was restored to those who had temporarily belonged to the 'order' of penitents.

The phenomenon of increasing laxity accompanied by increasing penitential practice was necessitated by the great changes in the Church which occurred from the early fourth century onwards. Previously the Church had been a voluntary and confessional community, attracting those of authentic conviction. Thereafter, the Church's status as the imperial religion led to mass accessions to Christianity making the feasibility of collective sanctification impracticable if it involved insisting on post-baptismal sinlessness. Various protest and schismatic movements in the early Church are in part explained by the desire of some Christians to restore the original moral rigour and purity; examples of these are Novatianism, Montanism, Marcionitism, and especially Donatism in North Africa. Against this, a definition was worked out whereby the Church is to be seen as a mixed body of perfection and imperfection, sin and grace.

There was also an evolution in penitential thinking and practice. Early penitential practice was found to be unworkable because: absolution acquired by this means was only offered once; the penance was public; and the enjoined continence was meant to be life-long. This inflexibility was overcome in later penitential development by a system introduced to the Western Church by Iro-Scottish missionary monks on the Continent. Though this system was severe, it was more realistic and less humiliating. The confession of sin and penance were private, and people were not restricted to one penance and absolution only. On the other hand, re-admission to the Church was not to be seen as a guarantee of salvation.

The ultimate consequence of this development was that what was considered holy and sanctified in the Church was not so much the people as the means of grace and sanctification. These states could be initiated only in this life, to be completed in purgatory. Christian piety therefore became characterized by the hope, rather than by the assurance, of salvation.

LEFT Believing that reunion with God could be accelerated by subjecting the body to deprivation and chastisement, celibacy, fasting and the wearing of hair cloth garments and heavy chains were common among ascetics who chose to withdraw from the world.

RIGHT This manuscript is the oldest example of the Benedictine Rule, which regulated the lives of the monks at the monastery of Monte Cassino, and later became the basis of all Western monastic discipline.

Asceticism and monasticism

The early establishment of Christianity in sophisticated urban centres opened up the problem of compromise and secularization among Christian communities. The desire of some zealous Christians to realize literally the ideals of sanctification, perfection and purity led them to opt for ascetic withdrawal from the world which was seen as no place for effective spiritual development. Such a practice was accompanied by poverty, chastity, obedience to the law and extraordinary penitential feats occasioned by even minor lapses. Christianity inherited this tendency from Judaism, but it was also very much reinforced and vindicated by contemporary Hellenistic philosophical notions. Platonic metaphysical dualism held that the material world and the body are a prison for the immaterial and invisible soul which seeks release and reunion with God. This could be accelerated by withdrawal from secular preoccupations and by self-inflicted bodily chastisement.

In the third century a wealthy Egyptian, Antony, rejected the world and withdrew to the desert to lead a life of prayer and devotion. With this the Christian eremitical tradition was established, that is, Christian witness by the solitary life of a hermit. Such 'desert fathers' were venerated by other Christians as 'bearers of the Spirit'. Out of this emerged coenobitic monasticism, in which groups of ascetics lived in a community practising a common rule and combining withdrawal from the world with practical involvement in the economic life of the surrounding area.

From the East, monasticism spread to the West and instrumental in its spread were Ambrose of Milan, Augustine, and John Cassian in South Gaul. In the Celtic Church of Ireland and Scotland a potent and creative but very austere monasticism developed. Western monasticism was however to develop along more moderate lines as formulated by Benedict of Nursia, the founder of the influential Benedictine Order, which made a remarkable contribution to the Christian culture and civilization of Europe.

Further development followed. In the ninth century it was the work of Benedict of Aniane to co-ordinate and standardize various monastic rules. In the tenth and eleventh centuries the Benedictine monastery of Cluny in Burgundy was the inspiration of a reform movement within the wider Church. The key to the success of monasticism in the fields of education, agriculture, pastoral care and scholarship was that, despite embodying the notion of Christian élitism, it was an organism which was integrated with the Church at large to its immeasurable benefit.

THE CHURCH OF THE EAST

The Eastern Orthodox Churches

HISTORY AND PRESENT-DAY DISTRIBUTION

The Eastern Orthodox Churches are a family of self-governing (autocephalous) Churches. They include the ancient Patriarchates of Antioch, Alexandria, Jerusalem and Constantinople – all now sadly diminished – and the Churches of Greece, Cyprus and Sinai. These are largely Greek-speaking, with some use of Arabic in the Middle East. Their presence in the countries where the Christian gospel was first preached highlights the continuity of Orthodoxy with the Church of the apostles and early Christians. From the fourth century the Church of Constantinople – as the Church of the new capital of the Roman (later Byzantine) Empire – ranked second in honour to the Church of Rome, and its leader, or Patriarch, came to be given the title 'Ecumenical'. The Church of Georgia, now in the Soviet Union, was founded in the fourth century, and is one of the oldest national Churches.

The Churches of the Slav peoples – the Russians, Bulgarians and Serbs – owe their existence to the missionary activity of the Byzantine Church from the ninth century; their heads have the title Patriarch. Smaller Slav Churches are the Polish and Czechoslovak Orthodox Churches. These all use Church Slavonic (a form of old Bulgarian) in their worship. The Romanian Orthodox Church, also a Patriarchate, is the only one whose people are of Latin origin and which uses a Latin language. Orthodox missionary activity in more recent times has led to the formation of small Churches in Japan and China: too small to be fully self-governing, they are nevertheless autonomous within the family of Orthodox Churches, as are the Orthodox Church in Finland, and the Macedonian Orthodox Church (which separated from the Serbian Orthodox Church in 1959 and remains unrecognized).

Emigration in modern times has resulted in the spread of Eastern Orthodox Christians to Western Europe, North America, Australia and other parts of the world. Their church organizations have usually remained dependent on their mother Church; originally closely identified with the culture and language of their country of origin, such Churches have increasingly adopted in worship the language of the country to which they have transferred, and have attracted converts. It is more accurate now to speak of the Orthodox, rather than the Eastern Orthodox, Churches.

BELIEF

One of the meanings of Orthodoxy is 'right belief'. All the Orthodox Churches are united in upholding the Christian faith as it was taught by the Church before the division between Eastern and Western Christians. The creed of Nicaea–Constantinople is regarded as the ecumenical creed, approved by the Council of Constantinople in 381 and upheld by subsequent Councils. The dogmatic definitions of Orthodoxy are those of the seven Ecumenical Councils recognized by

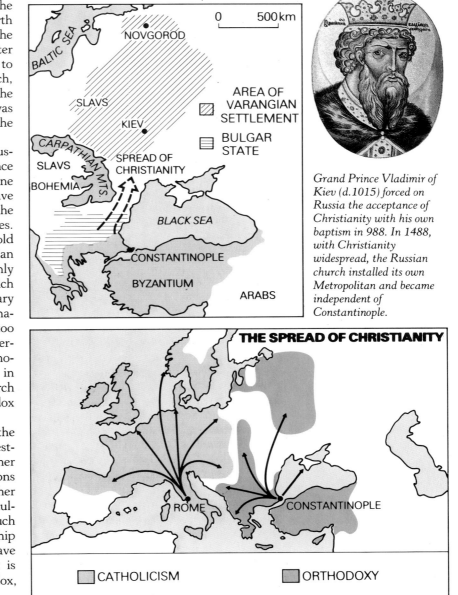

Grand Prince Vladimir of Kiev (d.1015) forced on Russia the acceptance of Christianity with his own baptism in 988. In 1488, with Christianity widespread, the Russian church installed its own Metropolitan and became independent of Constantinople.

81

East and West alike: Nicaea in 325, Constantinople in 381, Ephesus 431, Chalcedon 451, Constantinople 553, Constantinople 680–681, and Nicaea again in 787. The first two Councils were concerned primarily with the doctrine of God as Trinity, the subsequent five with the doctrine of the person of Jesus Christ as true God and true Man. The seventh Council was preoccupied with the doctrine of icons, regarded as intimately related to the doctrine of the incarnation of God the Son in Jesus Christ.

The Orthodox Church teaches the faith in the terms of these definitions, and accepts as fully authoritative the doctrine of the great theologians of the Christian East in the early centuries. No more dogmas have been added to those of the Councils, although theological controversy in later centuries has drawn out further precision in some areas of Orthodox teaching. The Orthodox Church finds unacceptable the later dogmatic definitions made by the Roman Catholic Church about the Immaculate Conception and Bodily Assumption of the Blessed Virgin Mary, and the infallibility of the Pope. These, together with the Western addition of the Filioque clause to the creed, constitute the major dogmatic differences between Orthodoxy and Roman Catholicism.

In the Orthodox Church, doctrine and worship are closely connected. Apart from the dogmatic definitions of the Councils, Orthodox teaching is contained in the service books of the Church. Rich in doctrinal content, the services for the great festivals and seasons of the Christian year set forth Orthodox teaching on the revelation of God as Father, Son and Holy Spirit; on the incarnation of God the Son in Jesus Christ; on the participation of the believer, through the Holy Spirit, in the life of God; on the role of Mary, the Mother of God, and of the saints, whose prayers are frequently invoked; and on the Christian life of repentance and ascetic discipline as the condition for growth in grace.

ORTHODOX WORSHIP

A second meaning of Orthodoxy is right worship. At the heart of Orthodox worship is the Divine Liturgy, the Eucharist, in which believers participate in the life of Christ through receiving his Body and Blood. They have already been united with Christ through baptism and chrismation (the equivalent of confirmation in the West), which are conferred together, normally on infants, although in modern situations it is not infrequently adults who ask to be admitted to the Church. Preparation for Holy Communion, which most Orthodox receive infrequently, traditionally includes private confession to a priest. Among the

other sacraments are marriage, ordination, and anointing of the sick. The full pattern of daily worship includes the services of matins, vespers and the lesser hours (as in the western tradition), although it is performed in its entirety only in monastic communities.

The church building is an integral part of Orthodox worship. Its characteristic plan is that of a cross-in-square, of which the central space is surmounted by a dome. The sanctuary at the east end is separated from the nave by the iconostasis, a solid screen pierced by doors in the centre and at either side and carrying icons of Christ, the Mother of God, angels and saints, and the great festivals. Often an image of Christ, the All-ruler, looks down from the central dome. The walls are covered with frescoes or icons, before which burn lamps. Believers pray in front of the icons, lighting candles and venerating the images by kissing them and prostrating themselves before them. The church itself represents heaven on earth, and its furnishing and decoration are carefully planned in accordance with a tradition which goes back many centuries to enable worshippers to realize their participation, as members of the communion of saints, in the worship of heaven.

Orthodox services are always sung, for the most part by clergy and choir or chanters. The congregation rarely participates vocally. But the singing and chanting, the icons and their lamps and candles, the incense, the priest's vestments and the ceremonial, invite the participation of all other senses. The frequent use of the sign of the cross and of prostration and bowing involve the body as well as the mind and spirit in Orthodox worship. In principle the vernacular is always used, although often the liturgical language represents an older form than that currently spoken.

MONASTICISM

The Orthodox Church values highly the monastic life, which appeared first in the Christian East in the late third and fourth centuries. Monasteries have always played an important part in the theological and spiritual life of the Church, whose present forms of worship owe much to the influence of the monastic tradition. There are no orders, in the western sense, in the Orthodox Church: the influence of the rule of St Basil the Great has been predominant, but within a common tradition each monastery has its own pattern of life. There is no distinction between active and contemplative communities: work, and prayer in church and cell, are equally important aspects of the life of monks and nuns.

The Orthodox spiritual tradition has been practised and handed on to a great extent in the monasteries. From this tradition comes the *Philokalia*, a late eighteenth-century collection of writings from the fourth to the fifteenth century on the life of prayer. Many of them relate to the 'prayer of the heart', best known as the 'Jesus Prayer'. Russian and Romanian versions of the Greek *Philokalia* have been made, and an English translation is being published.

The heart of Orthodox monasticism is Mount Athos, a peninsula off northern Greece, which from the tenth century has been the exclusive home of thousands of monks. All the larger national churches are represented there, although the majority of the monks are Greek. In recent years, after a period of serious decline, Athos has experienced a renewal of monastic life, to which significant numbers of young, often well-educated, men are being attracted.

In the traditionally Orthodox countries of eastern Europe, monastic life is now generally restricted, and entry into those monasteries which remain open is usually limited. But wherever they continue to exist, monasteries are still sources of spiritual strength and places of pilgrimage for Orthodox believers.

ORGANIZATION

The basic unit of the Orthodox Church is the parish. Parishes are grouped in dioceses, headed by a bishop. In the larger Churches dioceses may be grouped into larger areas, presided over – as in Russia and Romania – by a metropolitan, a title given in Greece and other Churches to all diocesan bishops. The boundaries of an autocephalous or autonomous Church usually coincide with national frontiers, except among Orthodox members who have emigrated, for whom Church organizations normally follow ethnic lines. The larger national Churches are headed by patriarchs, the smaller by archbishops.

The national character of the Orthodox Churches has been largely determined by history. In countries ruled for centuries by Arabs, Turks or Mongols, the Orthodox Church was the sole expression of national identity and cohesion for the conquered Christians. As a consequence it became deeply rooted in the life of the Greek, Bulgarian, Serbian and Russian peoples. The national, ethnic principle of organization is however accidental rather than fundamental: the Churches of Greece, Cyprus and Sinai, and most of the ancient Patriarchates, are Greek in culture and language but remain independent Churches. In the USA, where there are many Orthodox Christians belonging to different national Churches, there is a movement towards the formation of an American Orthodox Church.

The Patriarch of Constantinople is recognized as the focus of unity of the Orthodox Churches. He has no jurisdiction over Churches other than his own, and in this respect his office resembles that of the Archbishop of Canterbury in the Anglican Communion rather than that of the Pope in the Roman Catholic Church. The highest authority in the Orthodox Church, the ecumenical council, has not met since the Council of Nicaea in 787. Local councils have sometimes been recognized as having given expression to authentic Orthodox teaching. In the present divided state of Christianity it is doubtful if an ecumenical council could be held. But preparations are in hand for holding a Pan-Orthodox Synod to deal with a number of practical issues in contemporary Orthodox Church life.

A Russian icon, or image, of the Virgin and Child. In a wider sense an icon can be any form of representation of holy persons or scenes but such portraits as this are more usual. Very early 6th-century icons are to be found in the Monastery of St Catherine on Mount Sinai, in Kiev and at St Francesca Romana in Rome. These small portraits are painted on wood. Later icons of the 12th and 13th centuries are works of great spirituality and show a subtle use of colour.

CHURCH AND STATE

In the East Roman or Byzantine Empire there was a close link between Christian Church and

A Greek Orthodox nun studies the scriptures. The Orthodox Church is the established church of Greece, but in other European countries the majority of Orthodox Churches live under atheist governments. In fact Albania has outlawed all religious bodies. The exception is Romania where the Orthodox Church still plays a substantial part in the life of the people and is recognized as the church of the nation.

Church and State in traditionally Orthodox countries. In modern times their governments have delegated to specific departments the responsibility for church affairs.

In Europe the majority of the Orthodox Churches now live under atheist governments. The principle of the separation of Church and State has been put into operation in most of the socialist states, except in Romania where the Orthodox Church is recognized as the Church of the nation. In Albania all religious bodies have been outlawed. Although most of their constitutions guarantee freedom of worship, these states impose restrictions, sometimes severe, on the Church, whose activity is largely confined to acts of worship in church buildings. The Church may not teach, except to train its clergy, or become involved in any social action. Publications are limited.

The long tradition of association with the State, and often the long experience of subjection to rulers of another faith, have accustomed Orthodox bishops to guiding their Churches with discretion. There has been little tradition of active resistance to the State, although the Church played an important part in liberating Russia from the Mongols, and the south-east European peoples from Turkish rule.

Christian State. The Ecumenical Councils were summoned by the emperor, and Patriarch and emperor in Constantinople normally worked closely together. Within the Ottoman Empire the Turks made church leaders responsible for the civic life of their communities. The conversion of the Russian and other Slav peoples was by the decision of their prince or ruler. All these historical circumstances forged a powerful link between

The Independent Churches Of Eastern Christianity

Several Eastern Churches, some of whose foundations date from the time of the apostles, acknowledge the authority of neither the Roman pontiff nor the Ecumenical patriarch of Constantinople. The 'separate identity' of these Churches arose out of the Nestorian and Monophysite controversies which racked the Christian Church in the fifth century.

Although Nestorianism was condemned by the decrees of Ephesus, as was Monophysitism by those of Chalcedon, dissenters to the decisions of the two Councils remained a potent force, eventually assuming the leadership of the greater part of the Egyptian, Ethiopian, Syrian and Armenian Christian communities and effectively severing themselves from both Rome and Constantinople.

Both these Churches have endured great persecutions and diminution at the hands of both western and eastern Christians, as well as those of Zoroastrian and Islamic overlords. With the destruction of the Ottoman Empire early this century, the Nestorians faced a large-scale expulsion from their traditional homes in Kurdistan in which great numbers perished. In recent decades the Nestorian churches have often come into conflict with the governments of Iraq and Iran. Although the Nestorians have had little involvement with ecumenical endeavours, the World Council of Churches has been attempting to open up new channels of communication.

The Nestorian Churches

HISTORY AND DISTRIBUTION

The two main Nestorian Churches are the Assyrian or East Syrian Church, with about 170,000 adherents, more than half of whom live in Iraq, the rest being scattered throughout the Middle East, the Malabar coast of India and the USA; and the Chaldean Church, with almost 100,000 believers in Iraq, Syria and Iran.

BELIEF

Holding to the major tenets of the Christian faith, the major issue which separates Nestorian Christians from other eastern and western Christian Churches concerns the precise nature of the union of God and Man in the person of Jesus Christ. Nestorians maintain that although there is both a human and a divine nature which is 'morally united' in the person of Christ, these two natures nevertheless remain separate and distinct entities.

This view was championed in the fifth century by the then Bishop of Constantinople, Nestorius (381–451), although the Nestorian Church was not officially established until 486 at the Synod of Selucia-Ctesiphon. At its head was a *catholicos* (or patriarch) who was independent of the Byzantine hierarchy. In addition to those of Nestorius, the faithful have looked to the writings of Diodorus of Tarsus (d. 390), Theodore of Mopsuestia (350–428) and the dogmatic formulations of Babai the Great (d. 628) as doctrinal authorities. The Nestorian canon of the New Testament excludes the General Epistles and the Book of Revelation (the Apocalypse) and so retains a form which is very similar to the earliest compilations of Christian writings.

WORSHIP

The liturgical life of the Nestorians is similar to that of the other Eastern Churches (both Orthodox and Independent), although the liturgies themselves – attributed to Mār Addai and Mār Mari, Nestorius and Theodore of Mopsuestia – preserve many primitive Christian characteristics. An unusual feature of the Nestorian Eucharist is that each celebration is preceded by an elaborate preparation of the eucharistic bread, making use of 'holy leaven' which has been passed down through generations. The clergy, who are ordered in an episcopal, hierarchical pattern similar to that of the Orthodox Church, make use of intricate vestments in worship. Nestorian churches, however, are devoid of the pictures and icons which are normally associated with Eastern Christians.

The Monophysite Churches

HISTORICAL OUTLINE AND PRESENT-DAY DISTRIBUTION

Soon after the condemnation of Nestorius by the Council of Ephesus in 431 another Christological controversy arose in the church. In reaction to the Nestorians' complete separation of Christ's divine and human natures, other Christians put forward the belief that Christ was possessed of only one nature ('monophysite'). According to the Monophysites, Christ's humanity was completely absorbed by his divinity, just as 'a drop of wine melts into the ocean'. Although Monophysitism was condemned by the Council of Chalcedon in 451, this doctrinal position continued to enjoy a great deal of support both within the monasteries and among the rural masses. Moreover, in Syria and Egypt the Patriarchates of Antioch and Alexandria had long resented Constantinople's increasing hegemony – and their eventual repudiation of Chalcedon in favour of Monophysitism seems to have had political as well as doctrinal motivations. Ethiopia and Armenia soon followed the example of Egypt and Syria in turning against Chalcedon.

There are at present between 12 and 13 million Christians worldwide who have, to a lesser or greater extent, identified themselves with one or another of the many variant forms of Monophysitism. Generally it is possible to speak of four main Monophysite Churches: the Syrian Orthodox Church of Antioch (the West Syrian or 'Jacobite' Church), the Armenian Church, the Egyptian ('Coptic') Church, and the Ethiopian Church. Although each Church uses a different language and liturgy, and has its own particular history, there are also a number of similarities between the four. All four Churches maintain an episcopal, hierarchical, ecclesiastical structure which is similar to (and in some cases identical with) that of the Eastern Orthodox Churches. All have incurred large losses in members and property due to persecution, civil unrest, immigration, and through whole sections of their respective Churches seeking union with Rome ('Uniates') or with Constantinople. All have identified themselves, at various times, with the political and national aspirations of their regions and countries resulting, at least in the case of the Armenians, in widespread massacres and exile. All four Churches have, in recent decades, participated in a number of dialogues and discussions under the auspices of the World Council of Churches, aimed at renewed understanding and a re-examination of the Formula of Chalcedon.

THE WEST SYRIAN CHURCH

The West Syrian or Jacobite Church today numbers about 90,000 to 100,000 members located in Syria, Lebanon and Iraq as well as in numerous communities scattered throughout the Middle East and the United States. Although Monophysitism was introduced to Syria by Severus (465–538), Patriarch of Antioch, it became firmly established under Jacob (hence 'Jacobite') Būrd'āna (c. 500–78) who, assisted by large numbers of monks and ascetics, revitalized and reorganized the Syrian Church, ordaining thousands of priests and establishing a Monophysite hierarchy. Although treated well under the Islamic caliphate, the Syrians suffered under the Mongol invasions of the thirteenth and fourteenth centuries. Savagely persecuted by the Turks during the First World War, almost half perished.

The Eucharistic liturgy used by the Syrian Church – the Syriac Liturgy of St James – dates

The Armenian Church, which originated in northeast Turkey and what is now part of Russia, no longer has a homeland. This Armenian Cathedral is in Jerusalem. The ostrich eggs suspended from the roof serve as symbols of hope and resurrection. There are no statues in the churches and fewer icons than in Orthodox churches. This is the only Eastern Church to use unleavened bread in the Eucharist, and the bread is taken after it has been dipped in the wine. This form is known as communion by intinction.

The Armenian Church was founded in the late third century by Gregory the Illuminator (240–325) who effected the conversion of the Armenian king, Tiridates III. Armenia therefore might be considered the first Christian state. The Armenians rejected their original connection with the Church of Caesarea in 374, establishing their own hierarchy and making use of the Armenian vernacular in their literature and liturgy (a modification of the Liturgy of St Basil). Often in conflict with the Persian Empire, the Armenians were cut off from many of the doctrinal controversies that arose in other parts of the Christian Church in the fifth century. Eventually, however, although rejecting Monophysitism outright, the Armenians accepted the semi-Monophysite formulations now attributed to Cyril of Alexandria. A series of invasions and persecutions from the ninth century to the twentieth century has resulted in the death or exile of the majority of Armenians.

Armenian churches are simple in their decoration, apart from a number of ornaments placed upon the east-facing altar. A curious feature, however, is the suspension from the ceilings of their churches of ostrich eggs which seem to serve as symbols of hope and resurrection.

There are two classes of Armenian clergy: those who are married, and the celibate *vartabeds*, or 'doctors', from whom bishops are chosen. The clergy wear elaborate vestments; a special feature of their outdoor clothing is a pointed black cap, or *pakegh*, which monks wear with a veil. Most Armenians look for leadership to the *catholicos* of Sis whose seat, since 1921, has been located in Lebanon. The Armenians also possess Patriarchates in Jerusalem and Constantinople (Istanbul). Armenians in the USSR look to the *catholicos* of Echmiadzin in Soviet Armenia for spiritual direction.

from the fourth and fifth centuries and, although likened to other Eastern rites, contains an unusually large number of *anaphoras* (prayers for the consecration of the eucharistic elements) which may be used. The vestments used by the Syrian clergy are similar to, although not identical with, those used by other Byzantine Churches. This is also true of their church buildings, a major difference in which, however, is the sparseness of interior decorations and the absence of all but a few icons. The present Patriarch of the Church rules from Damascus, Syria, where the Patriarchate was moved in 1959.

THE ARMENIAN CHURCH

The plight of the Armenian Church today is that of a national religious body which no longer possesses a homeland. At the present time there are between 2 ½ and 3 million Armenian Christians with large communities in the Middle East, Europe, and North and South America.

THE COPTIC CHURCH

The Coptic Church today numbers about 2 to 2½ million followers. The vast majority of these are located in Egypt where they constitute the principal Christian Church. There are, however, small communities of Copts scattered about the Middle East and Africa.

Christianity in Egypt has by tradition looked on the apostolic mission of St Mark as its foundation. From the first part of the second century onwards there was a strong and thriving Christian Church in Egypt under the rule of the Bishop (or Patriarch) of Alexandria, who was considered one of the five pre-eminent leaders of the Christian Church. When, therefore, the popular Alexandrian Patriarch Dioscurus was condemned at the Council of Chalcedon in 451 for defending the

Monophysite position, and deposed from his See, the Egyptian Christians refused to recognize either his condemnation or the new 'orthodox' Patriarch of Alexandria who had been consecrated in Constantinople. Instead, the Egyptians (later known as Copts) chose a rival Monophysite patriarch: Timotheus Aelurus (d. 477). Encouraged by Coptic monks, the Egyptian Church had by the end of the fifth century completely broken its ties with Constantinople and had adopted a Monophysitism loosely based on the pre-Chalcedonian Christology of Cyril of Alexandria.

Following the Arab invasion of Egypt in 642, the Copts faced almost thirteen centuries of successive Islamic and western European rulers. Large numbers of Egyptian Christians converted to Islam for a variety of reasons, and the Coptic Church soon became a minority faith in a generally Muslim Egypt – as it still is today.

The church buildings and vestments used in the worship of the Coptic Church are very much like those used by other Byzantine Churches. Coptic art, on the other hand, is of a most singular and primitive style. The Coptic language today lives on only in the liturgies of the Egyptian Church (attributed to Basil, Gregory Nazianzus and St Mark). One unusual feature of the eucharistic liturgy is that it must be performed by the priest barefoot. The Copts are now guided by a patriarch (also called pope) who resides in Cairo and exercises jurisdiction over some nineteen bishops in Egypt as well as seven *diaspora* archbishoprics.

THE ETHIOPIAN CHURCH

Until the Marxist takeover of the country in the late 1970s the Ethiopian Church was the state Church of Ethiopia and boasted some 8 million members. No revised figures of any accuracy have become available since the revolution, but it is thought that the numbers of the faithful have been greatly reduced through famine, disease and persecution.

Christianity in Ethiopia dates from the time of Frumentius (fl. 356) who became Bishop of Axum under the jurisdiction of the patriarch of Alexandria in the fourth century. It was also through the Egyptian Church that Monophysitism was introduced to Ethiopia in the years that followed. Close ties between the two Churches have been retained to the present day, although in 1951 the Ethiopian Church received independent status from the Coptic patriarch – who has, however, retained a 'primacy of honour' over the Ethiopian bishops. Through the centuries Ethiopia has remained a 'bastion of Christianity', successfully repelling Muslim invasions which threatened the land.

The Ethiopian Church has remained unique among other Christian Churches in its individual customs, traditions, art and worship. The language of literature and of the liturgy is Ge'ez, an ancient Semitic dialect, although there has been a gradual introduction into Church life of Amharic, the dominant tongue of the country. The Ethiopian canon of holy scripture includes a large number of apocryphal books. Jewish customs such as circumcision, ritual purifications and the keeping of the sabbath are part of Ethiopian church life. Church buildings employ a three-fold division, similar to the ancient Jewish temple, and are often built in the round. The sanctuary, at the centre of the concentric circles, contains an altar upon which is a *tabot* (a replica in hardwood of the Jewish Ark of the Covenant). Vestments are of Byzantine and Coptic derivation, as is the liturgy which appears to be based upon that attributed to St Mark of Alexandria. Many aspects of national Church activity – including monastic life, once the mainstay of the Ethiopian Church – now seem to be under sustained attack by the government.

THE ROMAN CATHOLIC CHURCH

HISTORY AND DISTRIBUTION

The Roman Catholic Church constitutes the largest single Christian denomination and indeed is probably the largest form of religion in the world. The most recent full set of figures available, those for the end of 1983, indicate that there are 825,592,000 Roman Catholics, somewhat more than 17.5 per cent of the world's population. These statistics, however, are based upon the number of people known to have been baptized into the Church rather than upon the more realistic figure of those who, in some formal way, practise their faith. Though the number of Roman Catholics shows in some parts of the world a steady rise, as a proportion of the world's population Catholics are decreasing, and some absolute figures also show a fall. The number of clergy, for example, shows a distinct down-turn: at the end of 1983 there were over two thousand fewer priests serving the Catholics of Europe than there

The primacy of the Pope and his infallibility became a dogma of the Roman Catholic Church in 1870. The Second Vatican Council (1962–5) introduced the doctrine of collegiality, a theory of the responsibility of all bishops. As Bishop of Rome the Pope himself remains within the context of this doctrine. Pope John Paul II (a. 1978) is pictured here with Mother Theresa of Calcutta in the hospice where she and her nuns work among the poorest of the city's inhabitants.

were at the beginning of the same year, and the number of baptisms of children under seven and of Catholic marriages is also in decline.

These general statistics give no impression of the wide variation in the spread of Roman Catholicism. The Church claims that 90 per cent of the population of South America is Roman Catholic, while in the Far East that figure drops to 2 per cent, and no Catholics at all are recorded for the Republic of China though some are known to survive there. In Europe as a whole, 39 per cent of the people are claimed as Catholics, while in the United States of America they number just under a quarter.

Roman Catholicism claims to be the Church which Jesus Christ founded. It accepts that many of the Eastern Christian Churches may reasonably make a similar claim to apostolic succession. In its least sophisticated form, the notion of apostolic succession requires that bishops of the Church should be able to claim historical descent, by ordination, from the apostles. Many scholars regard this as unrealistic, but it is on these grounds that the Roman Catholic Church denies that the Churches of the Reformation have apostolic succession and, therefore, valid orders.

The history of pre-Reformation Christianity is related elsewhere, but some aspects of that history need to be highlighted if the present nature and structure of Roman Catholicism are to be understood. Recognition of the Bishop of Rome (the pope) as in some sense the head of the Church on earth is one of the distinguishing features of the Church. The exact nature of this primacy is a matter of debate and so, to some extent, is its history. There are apologists for the papacy who claim to find hints of the primacy in the First Letter of Clement, written at Rome before the end of the first century, but it is not until the second half of the fourth century that the claim is made explicit, based upon the text 'Thou art Peter and upon

this rock I will build my church' (Matthew 16:18). The most obvious way in which primacy showed itself was the steady growth of requests from bishops, particularly western bishops, for decisions from the pope about matters in dispute in their own dioceses, or between dioceses, or for interpretations of the law of the Church in relation to new situations.

Roman claims to primacy have varied in degree. Popes such as Damasus and his successor Siricius towards the end of the fourth century, Leo the Great in the middle of the fifth, Innocent III at the beginning of the thirteenth, and all popes since the middle of the nineteenth century have been able to exercise the primacy they claimed. Others, such as Gregory VII in the eleventh century and Boniface VIII at the end of the thirteenth, were unable to make their claims carry weight, in both cases because of conflict with secular authority. Other popes have been unwilling to, or uninterested in, urging their primacy over other bishops except, for financial reasons in the later middle ages, in the matter of episcopal appointments.

The primacy of the pope, together with his infallibility, became dogmas of Roman Catholic belief at the First Vatican Council of 1870. As they were defined, these two dogmas were hedged about with qualifications, but to some extent these qualifications were subsequently ignored by popes and their officials (known collectively as the Roman Curia). The Second Vatican Council (1962–5) attempted to set the authority of the bishop of Rome within the context of the reponsibility of all the bishops for the whole Church – the doctrine of collegiality. Since Vatican II, and especially since the accession of Pope John Paul II in 1978, there would appear to have been a whittling away of the practice of collegiality, even though lip-service still continues to be paid to the theory.

A second important aspect of Roman Catholic history which spans the Reformation is the survival of religious orders. Religious life, the commitment by men and women to a manner of life bounded by poverty, chastity and obedience, began in its present form in fourth-century Egypt, first of all as individual dedication to life as a hermit (the eremitical tradition), and then to life in a community (the coenobitic form). It is the latter which has made most impact upon the history of the Church in the West, particularly in the way of life which can be traced back to the Rule of St Benedict (c. 540). Individual monasteries followed the Rule in different ways, ultimately producing quite distinct families of monks such as the Carthusians, who combine living in communities with a degree of the eremitical form of life, or the Cistercians, who stress the value of manual labour.

Monasteries were, and are, usually to be found

in the countryside. In the eleventh century there emerged communities of priests living in towns and known generally as canons regular. Unlike monks or canons, whose life was restricted to one place, the friars such as Dominicans and Franciscans, both founded at the beginning of the thirteenth century, belonged to 'provinces' – fairly wide geographical areas within which they might move from house to house. Monks, canons and friars, and the equivalent orders of nuns, all maintained the practice of reciting the Divine Office, the Church's official prayer, in common. From the sixteenth century onwards there have been founded orders for both men and women which have not been bound to the common recitation of the Office. Chief among these is the Society of Jesus, better known perhaps as the Jesuits. They were given formal approval in 1540, and their missionary activity in Europe won over to Catholicism many areas of Europe which had converted to Protestantism. But the Jesuits were better known for their activities in India, China, Japan and South America, in all of which areas they showed remarkable skill in adapting the Roman faith to the *mores* of the people among whom they were working. Their success did not always find favour with other missionaries, especially it would seem with the Franciscans, nor with religious authorities in Europe. Rome eventually decided against the Jesuits in the controversy over Chinese rites, and this was only one blow in a long series in the eighteenth century which culminated in the suppression of the Society of Jesus by the Pope in 1773. Although the Society was restored in 1815 the Jesuits were able to regain the pre-eminence in the Church only in the present day. They are again to the fore in India, and especially in Latin America, in adapting traditional Roman Catholic beliefs to lives and needs of the people among whom they are working. Once again, their degree of success has generated tensions within the Church.

A third important element in the continuity of the Roman Church with medieval Christianity is that of law. From the second century onwards regulations governing the lives and worship of Christians were compiled by individuals and by councils or synods of bishops. Decisions taken by influential bishops, in particular the Bishop of Rome, were added to this 'Collection of Canon Law' (*Corpus Iuris Canonici*) in a very unsystematic fashion. In about 1140 Gratian, a monk teaching at Bologna, compiled his *Decretum*, an attempt to reconcile the differences between the canons contained in the *Corpus*. The correct title of his work was *Concordia discordantium canonum*. Further collections were added to the *Decretum*, in particular the canons of the Council of Trent (1545–63). These last not only reaffirmed the traditional beliefs of the Church against the criticism

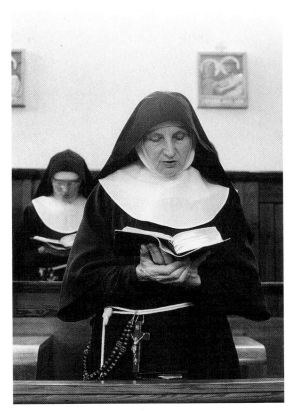

The religious orders of the Roman Catholic Church have made considerable impact on the history of the Church in the West. Their survival has spanned the Reformation and the way of life can be traced back to the Rule of St Benedict. Here a nun of the Poor Clares recites Divine Office or daily prayers. The hours of prayer, which many orders maintain in common, are lauds, prime, terce, sext, nones, vespers, compline and matins.

of the Reformers, but enhanced the authority of the Pope and of local bishops, and controlled the life of the clergy – it was Trent, for example, which insisted upon the establishment of seminaries for the training of priests. The *Corpus Iuris Canonici* was a very unwieldy tool. In the early years of the present century a commission was set up to reorganize it, and in 1917 was published the first Code of Canon Law (*Codex Iuris Canonici*) which reduced the Corpus to a more manageable form. A heavily revised version of the Code, bearing little resemblance to the original, was published by the Vatican in 1983.

BELIEF

There is no clear statement of Roman Catholic belief. In common with other Christians, Catholics commit themselves to the expressions of belief contained in the early creeds, particularly to the so-called Nicene Creed which is recited at Sunday worship and on other major liturgical occasions, but there is much more to Roman Catholic faith than can be found in these statements. No authoritative source for the range of beliefs exists. The best reference volume is *Enchiridion symbolorum, definitionum et declarationum de rebus fidei et morum* ('Handbook of creeds, definitions and statements on faith and morals') which is commonly known by the name of its first

The dogma of the Church was reaffirmed at the Council of Trent (1545–63) in the face of the criticisms of the Reformation. Roman Catholic dogma has continued to develop since that time though there is no authoritative source for the range of beliefs that now exist. Two Vatican Councils have pronounced clearly on Roman Catholic positions. The first in 1870 stated the infallibility of the Pope; the second, 1962–5, reasserted this dogma. Here Council Fathers attend a plenary meeting during Vatican II in St Peter's Basilica, Rome. In the foreground are the twelve cardinals of the Presidency.

compiler, Denzinger. This is a highly technical collection, both of statements about what Catholics are required to believe and of statements about what they are forbidden to believe, as these have been formulated down the ages by popes and councils. Denzinger exists only in Latin. The nearest English equivalent is *The Christian Faith in the Doctrinal Documents of the Catholic Church*, compiled by J. Neuner and J. Dupuis.

It was at the Council of Trent that what the Roman Catholic Church understood to be the traditional teaching of Christianity was reaffirmed against the criticism of the Reformers. In several instances the Lutheran (or other) view was rejected without there being any clear assertion of the Roman Catholic position. The central Lutheran doctrine of justification by faith alone was deemed to be unsatisfactory, but despite long debate there was no agreement on an alternative formulation. Luther's doctrine of 'consubstantiation' as an explanation for the presence of the body and blood of Christ in the eucharistic elements was thought to be inadequate. The common medieval view, known as 'transubstantiation', was however described by one of the canons of Trent only as 'a most apt way' of describing the Church's faith, and this doctrine did not become a

necessary matter of belief – a dogma – for Catholics. Likewise the bishops gathered at Trent (Triento in northern Italy) insisted against the Reformers that the Mass (as the eucharistic act of worship is known among Catholics) is a true sacrifice. But they did not determine how it might be so: this was left free to theological speculation.

Against the Reformers' reduction of the number of the sacraments, Trent insisted that there were seven, the first formal statement of a definite number in the history of the Church. Those recognized by Trent, and therefore part of Roman Catholic belief, are baptism, confirmation, the Eucharist, matrimony, holy orders, penance and extreme unction (last anointing). Since the Second Vatican Council the two last-named have been retitled the 'sacrament of reconciliation' and 'anointing of the sick' respectively.

A number of other matters upon which Trent pronounced divided sixteenth-century Roman Catholicism from the Churches of the Reform. Trent reasserted the propriety of the cult of the saints and their invocation in prayer. It insisted upon the value of prayers for the dead, and upon the existence of purgatory, a state which is not Hell but not yet Heaven, in which the soul is purged of any remaining guilt for sins committed during life. Many of these practices and beliefs, however, including prayer to the saints and especially to the Virgin Mary, have become part of the tradition of non-Roman Catholic Churches in the centuries since the Reformation. At the same time, discussions with other Churches, especially with the Lutheran and Anglican Churches, have brought the Roman Church to a greater appreciation of some of the insights of the Reformers.

Yet there have been developments within Roman Catholicism which have put up further barriers. In 1854 it was defined by Pope Pius IX as a dogma of faith that, from the first moment of her conception, the Virgin Mary was free of all original sin (the doctrine of 'the Immaculate Conception'). Though arguments can be adduced to defend the doctrine, it has no direct warrant in Scripture. On the other hand it has a long tradition in the history of the Church. In the Middle Ages it was a matter of much debate between the Franciscans who propounded the doctrine and the Dominicans who opposed it. Acceptance of the Franciscan point of view gradually grew until, in 1708, the feast of the Immaculate Conception was ordered to be observed throughout the Church. The 1854 definition was seen as a logical step, but it was one undoubtedly influenced by the desire of the pope and his advisors to exercise papal authority over the whole Church.

The Assumption of the Virgin, declared a dogma in 1950, asserts that after her death Mary was taken body and soul into Heaven. This, too, has no direct scriptural warrant, though it can be said to follow logically upon the doctrine of the Immaculate Conception and has an even longer history. Feasts of the Assumption seem to have been celebrated in Palestine as early as the fifth century, and elsewhere possibly even earlier. As a feast of the entire Church it appears to have been observed since the eighth century. It remains part of the liturgical calendar of the Orthodox Churches which do not celebrate the Immaculate Conception, largely because of a somewhat different doctrine of original sin from that of the Roman Catholic Church.

The same cannot be said for two dogmas which spring from Vatican I, the doctrines of the primacy and the infallibility of the pope. The doctrine of papal primacy insists that the Bishop of Rome, the pope, has full jurisdiction over the Church both in matters concerning faith and morals and in questions of ecclesiastical discipline and government. This authority is defined as 'ordinary' – it belongs naturally to the office of pope and is not something added on – and as 'immediate' – it is direct over all members of the Church and is not mediated by bishops. While this may seem to give the pope extraordinarily wide powers, it was accepted by Vatican I that papal primacy cannot detract from the divinely-imparted authority of the bishops within the Church, so in practice it remains somewhat ill-defined. The dogma was reasserted at Vatican II, but this Council associated all the bishops with the pope in his responsibility for the Church world wide. In recent years leaders of Churches springing from the Reform have found more problems with the practice of primacy than they have with the theory, seeing in the doctrine a way in which the unity of Christianity might be made manifest. That said, the formulation of the doctrine of papal primacy at Vatican I remains a distinctive feature of Roman Catholicism.

The same may be said about the doctrine of infallibility. Here there is much less sympathy with the Roman Catholic official position among the non-Roman Churches. Infallibility, the inability to err, is applied by Roman Catholics to the Church believing (the members of the Church at large), the Church teaching (the bishops as a body, though not singly), and to the pope personally. On the first two there is no great discussion. On papal infallibility there has been much debate. According to Vatican I the pope is preserved from error (which is not the same thing as to claim he is necessarily correct) when as teacher of the whole Church he declares some matter of faith or morals as a dogma to be held by all Catholics. The definition of infallibility requires that such a dogma be part, and recognized as part, of the Church's tradition, but that once the pope has declared some matter of faith (there is no example of a declaration on moral matters) to be a dogma, it has to be recognized as such by the very fact of the declaration itself. So the declaration does not depend for its validity upon acceptance by the Church at large. Two such definitions are: the declaration of the dogma of the Immaculate Conception, and of the Assumption.

Some have wished to claim papal rejection of artificial birth control as part of the infallible papal *magisterium*, or teaching. It is indeed often thought that Roman Catholic sexual ethics, including opposition to contraception, abortion and birth control, are a distinctive mark of the Church's faith. But these are precisely ethical or philosophic issues and cannot be regarded as part of the deposit of revelation. The Church may offer guidance on them from time to time but they are not strictly matters of faith.

WRITINGS

In common with other Christian Churches, the Roman Catholic Church recognizes in the Scriptures, both the Old and the New Testaments, its foundational documents. Unlike some Churches, however, it insists that it was the Church which produced the New Testament, not the New Testament which produced the Church. Between the 'Canon' of Scripture accepted by the Reformers and that accepted by Roman Catholicism there are a number of differences, and again it was Trent which determined which books of the Old Testament were to be regarded as canonical. (There is no disagreement over the New Testament.) Trent decided in favour of the Greek version of the Old Testament, known as the Septuagint, which contains seven books – Tobit, Judith, Wisdom, Sirach, Baruch and 1 and 2 Maccabees – generally included in non-Catholic bibles among the 'Apocrypha'. To distinguish these seven books from the very many other apocryphal writings purporting to belong to either Testament they are now called 'deutero-canonical'. The differences between the two canons of Scripture do not give rise to notable difficulties.

Again like many other Churches, in the matter of interpreting the faith Roman Catholicism gives a special place to the writings of the earliest Christian theologians, the 'fathers of the Church'. Among these a number who were outstanding both for holiness of life and for learning have been called 'Doctors of the Church', and they are regarded as having special authority. Originally there were four doctors of the Western Church, and four of the Eastern, but this number has been considerably added to, particularly in the West, and now includes, among many others, Teresa of Avila.

The era of the fathers of the Church, the 'patristic' period, is generally defined as ending by the beginning of the ninth century. Then began the period of the medieval 'schoolmen' to whom the Roman Catholic Church tends to give rather more prominence than do other Christian bodies. In particular the writings of Thomas Aquinas (c. 1225–74) have exercised considerable influence in the Church. His handbook of theology, the massive *Summa Theologica*, was much commented upon by subsequent scholars such as Cajetan and Suarez, and has formed part of Roman Catholic intellectual tradition down to the present day. Though from the sixteenth century onwards his works tended to be studied through the commentaries of others, Pope Leo XIII (1878–1903) revived the study of Thomas himself, and established a commission with the task of publishing definitive editions of all Thomas's many writings. This study of Thomas, and the development of a theological school based upon him and known as Thomism, very much improved the quality of Roman Catholic theological and philosophical learning in the nineteenth and twentieth centuries, but Thomas's medieval outlook and philosophy limited his value. A Jesuit priest, Karl Rahner (1904–84), has been credited above all others with moving Roman Catholic theology away from its dependence upon Thomas and exploiting the insights of modern philosophy. Thomism lingers on, especially among Dominicans (Thomas was a Dominican) and in the United States, but there is no longer a clear-cut school of Roman Catholic theology.

Unless they have been declared doctors of the Church none of the fathers, medieval schoolmen or recent theologians can claim to teach the faith authoritatively. Though much used, their writings have no special status. Papal documents, however, fall into a slightly different category. There are many different types of papal utterance, but those of particular significance in the present context are encyclicals, letters written by the pope to all Churches linked (or in communion with) his own on matters of faith and morals. Encyclicals have been much used by successive popes, for example for diffusing the teaching of the Church on social issues such as the world of work, or responsibility for development in the Third World. These letters do not of course claim to be infallible, but are regarded within the Church as authoritative and as giving guidance on major issues.

Documents produced by councils of the Church might also be regarded as authoritative, but in practice matters of importance were usually summed up in canons, or regulations, and the complete documents from which these canons were drawn have largely been ignored except by historians and theologians. The situation is somewhat different with the documents produced by Vatican II. It was not the intention of Pope John XXIII when he summoned the Council that it should issue canons or condemnations, and in keeping with Pope John's vision the bishops produced a number of statements of varying length on a variety of issues. These have served as a theological basis for a good deal of the development of Catholic theology since the Council closed. Vernacular editions of the documents of Vatican II were printed in very considerable numbers and have received wide diffusion throughout the Church and beyond. Since the Council there has been a number of gatherings (or synods) of bishops of the Church in Rome, and some of these synods have produced important documents, in particular perhaps the synod of 1971 with its statement on *Justice in the World*. Similar meetings have been held elsewhere on a regional basis, and again some have produced documents whose influence has extended far outside the area for which they were originally written. One might instance the letter by the bishops of the United Staes on nuclear warfare, and the statements produced by the bishops of Latin America at their conferences at Medellín in Colombia and Puebla in Mexico on the role of the Church in society and its responsibility towards the poor.

WORSHIP AND RITUAL

As in most Christian Churches, the central act of Roman Catholic worship is the Eucharist, usually called the Mass. The form in which Mass is celebrated is also part of the Church's tradition which survived the Reformation although, in keeping with the changes brought about by Trent, the service was somewhat simplified and made more uniform. A good number of different ways (rites) of saying Mass had become established by the sixteenth century, some associated with particular places or regions – the Sarum Rite was the form of service used in England, the Ambrosian Rite was used in Milan, and so on – and others with the older religious orders. Not all were abolished. The Mozarabic Rite survives in Seville, for example, and the order of a Dominican Mass remains distinctive. These exceptions were few. In the Western Church all rites were in Latin, but Eastern Churches in communion with Rome preserved other languages in their liturgies, some of them classical languages no longer in current use and others in the vernacular of the people those Churches served. One of the reforms which followed in the wake of Vatican II allowed the Western liturgy to be celebrated in the vernacular, and there were other changes to the rite established after Trent. The alterations in the liturgy have occasioned a good deal of resistance, and Rome has given permission for Mass to be celebrated, in special circumstances, according to the earlier rite of Trent. It may also be said in Latin, both in the older Tridentine rite and in the new version, but in practice a Latin liturgy or an approved Tridentine Mass are rare events.

Apart from variations among the rites there are, and from medieval times at least have always been, quite distinct styles of celebrating Mass, reflecting the degrees of solemnity of the occasion. In some churches a 'solemn high Mass' can be an almost operatic performance, with a professional choir singing baroque music and accompanied by a small orchestra, while in another church the same Mass might be accompanied by the sparse medieval tones of Gregorian chant. Increasingly Masses are sung to folk tunes played on guitars, despite ecclesiastical authorities' displeasure, or simply recited by the priest with no accompaniment of any sort. This last manner of saying Mass is frequently referred to as 'low Mass', in contrast with the 'solemn high' version.

A number of the sacraments are commonly bestowed within the context of Mass. This has always been the case for holy orders (the ordination of deacons, priests and bishops), but it is increasingly the case also for baptism, confirmation and matrimony. All of these are, of course, public acts involving initiation into, or change of status within, the Church. Penance, the confession of sin to a priest followed by absolution bestowed by the priest, is obviously a much more private affair. In recent years there has been a growth of penitential services, although insofar as confession of sin has been a part of these it has usually remained a private matter between priest and penitent. In some areas, however, there has grown up the practice of bestowing general absolution upon a congregation without prior confession being required. The sacrament of extreme unction, or last anointing, used to be given to those in danger of death from illness – it could not, for example, be given to soldiers before a battle, or to someone about to be executed. In its new guise it can be given to anyone who might be described as ill, even though not in danger of death. Consequently there has evolved the practice of holding services in churches for the anointing of the sick. But the sacrament is more often than not still administered privately. The minister of all sacraments except matrimony and holy orders is commonly a priest, although deacons frequently administer baptism and it is Roman Catholic teaching that, in an emergency, anyone may administer that particular sacrament. The minister of holy orders is a bishop. Matrimony is quite different. According to Roman Catholic belief, the two partners in a marriage service administer the sacrament to each other. The priest is a witness on behalf of the Church.

The modern emphasis on eucharistic worship observable in many Churches has, in the Roman Catholic Church, led to a decline in other forms of worship which used to be customary. At one time, for example, it used to be quite common to hold 'Benediction of the Blessed Sacrament' on Sunday evenings. At this service the Eucharist was displayed on the altar, hymns were sung and prayers said, and then a blessing given with the consecrated host. The 'exposition' of the sacrament, as it was called, was frequently preceded by the rosary, the recitation of prayers to the Virgin in five sequences or 'decades', interspersed with other prayers. Though no longer so regularly recited publicly in churches, the saying of the rosary has remained a common practice among Catholics.

One form of worship which survived the liturgical reforms and is perhaps even undergoing a revival, is the 'Stations of the Cross', a series of fourteen meditations on the sufferings of Christ from his condemnation to his burial. Most Catholic churches have fourteen crosses or, more commonly, fourteen pictures, portraying these scenes as an aid to meditation. Whoever is performing or leading this devotion walks from one picture to the other. The Stations of the Cross are frequently performed just before Easter as a form of public worship, but a visitor to a Catholic church might discover someone walking between the stations at any time during the year.

LEFT   At Doon Well, Co. Donegal, Eire, rosaries and pieces of cloth tied to the bushes represent thanksgiving. Rosary beads are a memory aid and consist of fifteen decades, each one of which denotes a recitation of the Lord's Prayer, ten Hail Marys and a Gloria.

RIGHT   Statues of the crucified Christ, of the Virgin and of a patron saint or other saints are a feature of Roman Catholic churches. This statue of Mary stands in a church in Palermo, Italy.

There can be few Roman Catholic churches which do not have statues within them as well as the figure of the crucified Christ above the altar. The statues most frequently to be found are of Christ (commonly in the form known as the 'Sacred Heart', a red-clad figure displaying a pierced heart as a symbol of God's love), of the Virgin Mary, of the church's patron saint and of other saints who have particular significance for the region or community. For example many churches have statues of St Patrick, the patron saint of Ireland, if there is a large Irish community in the parish. It is still common practice, and one which the Reformers rejected, to pray to the saints depicted in these images to ask that they intercede with God on behalf of the petitioner. Candles lit before statues remain a distinctive feature of Roman Catholic churches.

ORGANIZATION

The Roman Catholic Church is a union of local Churches (or dioceses) linked to each other by the bishop being in communion with the Bishop of Rome. As it is the role of the individual bishops to be the focal point of unity within each local Church or diocese, it is the role of the Bishop of Rome to be the focus of the world-wide Church.

It has to be said that the practice rather belies this theory, for it is Rome which moves bishops from one diocese to another, or appoints priests to vacant bishoprics, thereby destroying the autonomy of the local Churches. The independent authority of the bishop in his Church was affirmed by the Council of Trent and reasserted by Vatican II, but since Vatican II bishops of a country or region have often found it beneficial to work more closely together through synods or conferences. There are for example, a conference of bishops of England and Wales and a conference of European bishops. Likewise there are conferences of bishops in the individual countries of Latin America, in Central and South America and over the whole of the continent of Latin America. Though these conferences meet to tackle local problems, they have come to have considerable importance in the life of the Church and have occasioned considerable tension between the centralizing efforts of Rome and the independent existence of local Churches. Apart from these conferences of bishops, dioceses have traditionally been grouped into provinces, or geographical areas, under the general oversight of the bishop of one of the larger sees. This bishop is then the 'metropolitan', and is usually given the title of Archbishop. One diocese in a country is commonly recognized as the 'primatial' see. Its holder is frequently given the title of Cardinal.

Neither the title Cardinal nor that of Archbishop indicates a higher rank of clergyman. The Church recognizes only three grades of ordained ministry, each restricted to men: deacon, priest and bishop. The many other titles which exist in the Church indicate an office held or an honour conferred rather than status in the ministry. Thus canons, at least in theory, are priests who serve the local cathedral and serve as advisors to its bishop, while cardinals perform a similar function for the Bishop of Rome. At one time it was the role of the canons to select the next bishop, and it still remains the task of the cardinals to elect the pope in secret conclave. In practice all cardinals are bishops but they do not have to be, and technically could even be laymen though there has been no lay cardinal since the nineteenth century. Current legislation requires that though some deacons may be married, priests and bishops must be celibate except in unusual circumstances. There are married priests in some of the Eastern Churches in communion with Rome.

Another title frequently met with among the Roman Catholic clergy is that of 'monsignor'. It is awarded, rather in the manner of a knighthood, for service in the Church's bureaucracy. Though that bureaucracy in local Churches is often quite small – episcopal advisors, judges of marriage tribunals, finance officers and so on – in Rome it is enormous. The papal curia (the word means 'court') arose out of the advisors and functionaries who surrounded the pope both in his spiritual office and as ruler of the former papal states. The form which this administration now takes dates from the sixteenth century. There are a number of 'Sacred Congregations', each with a cardinal at its head, which look after different aspects of the Church's life. Though not called a congregation, the most important of them is the Secretariat of State, responsible for the organization of the papal curia itself as well as for relations between the Roman Catholic Church and other bodies. The Cardinal Secretary of State is the Pope's chief executive officer. The Congregation for the Doctrine of the Faith began in 1542 as the Universal Inquisition. It has the task both of promoting orthodoxy and of combating theological error. It is better known for the latter of these two functions. The Congregation for the Sacraments and Divine Worship is concerned with the Church's liturgy, while the Congregation for the Evangelization of Peoples, known at its foundation in 1622 as *De Propaganda Fide* (for Spreading the Faith), oversees the Church's missionary activity. Including the Secretariat of State, there are ten congregations. There are three tribunals or law courts of which the best known, because it is concerned with marriage cases, is the Rota, and there are three secretariats. Of these secretariats the most important is that for Christian Unity, estab-

lished in 1960. In addition to these there is a large number of councils, commissions, committees and other offices to undertake specific tasks. There is even a Vatican bank, the Institute for the Work of Religion, to handle funds for religious orders and for the Church's work in general. It acts as a clearing bank for Vatican officials and employees.

At the time of Vatican II there was much criticism that the Church's central administration was too dominated by Italians and too out of touch with those it was supposed to be assisting, namely the world's 2,500 or so bishops. Since that time, and particularly since the election of a non-Italian pope, the papal curia has been extensively internationalized and the three-yearly synod of bishops created to give first-hand advice to the Bishop of Rome on the situation of the Church in the world at large. The synods in this regard have not been notably successful, and have yet to

The many titles which exist in the Church indicate the office held rather than conferring status. There are three grades of ministry: deacon, priest and bishop. It is usual for one diocese in each country to be considered the first and its bishop is the primate. The primate of Poland is Monsignor Josef Glemp, seen above. The condition of the Church differs widely in communist countries. In Poland it must satisfy both the government and the outlawed Solidarity movement.

95

establish themselves, as the local conferences of bishops have done, as an integral part of the Church's organization.

The pope and his curia, representing the government of the Roman Catholic Church at an international level, are together known juridically as the Holy See. The Holy See is recognized in international law as a sovereign body and is analogous to an individual nation state. It is, for example, the Holy See which sends and receives ambassadors (full papal ambassadors are called apostolic nuncios). Mention is frequently made of the Vatican when talking of Roman Catholicism, but strictly speaking the Vatican is little more than a palace, the residence of the pope since the fall of the papal

states in 1870. The palace has given its name to the Vatican City State, an independent country only a third the size of Monaco, which was established in 1929. It is wholly surrounded by the city of Rome and is ruled by the pope as an absolute monarch. Though it has a number of offices located elsewhere in Rome, it is within the confines of the Vatican City State that most of the Church's central administration is undertaken. Though the Vatican is a term frequently used as a synonym for the Holy See, it has to be remembered that, legally, the two are quite distinct and perform different functions. And neither should be identified with the Roman Catholic Church worldwide.

THE REFORMATION

Antecedents To The Reformation

MORAL AND CIVIL REFORM

The Reformation was preceded by a renewal of the medieval Church in the West which took place between the reign of Pope Gregory VII (1073–85) and the forcible removal of the papacy from Rome to Avignon in 1309. These three centuries saw the expansion of the Church in almost every area of endeavour. It was to be the age of cathedral and crusade, of powerful popes and learned scholars. The reality of a secure and triumphant Church after the dark years of the tenth century was the result of three factors.

The first was a movement of reform which began in the great French monastery at Cluny. Later embraced by Gregory VII, the Cluniac reform stipulated moral and practical guidelines for the appointment and conduct of the clergy. It sought the enforcement of canon law concerning clerical celibacy and simony (the selling of church offices), as well as a prohibition of the practice of 'lay investiture' (the appointment of the higher clergy by secular rulers). To a large extent these aims were realized, and as a result Gregory VII made new claims for the papal office. Gregory asserted that because the Roman Church had been founded by God, only the pontiff of the Church had universal authority, and that he was, therefore, the final judge and arbiter in all matters, spiritual and secular. Although this view was opposed by successive emperors and kings, papal supremacy – reinforced by the calling of ecumenical councils – was generally exercised over the affairs of the West for almost two hundred years. The claims of supremacy, coupled

with the growth of the complex papal administration of its far-flung churches, made the papacy in the high Middle Ages the equal of any emerging nation in Europe.

A second factor which allowed for the flowering of the Western Church was a new political stability and security which had come to Europe. This was the result of a series of strong Holy Roman Emperors in Germany, beginning with Otto I (r. 936–73), and the development of feudalism as the basic structure of society. Feudalism arose in the eleventh and twelfth centuries and, in many respects, brought a solution to the anarchy of the Dark Ages.

Under the feudal system central power was vested in the king or emperor (or sometimes the pope) who then granted lands and privileges to his nobles or barons in return for certain services, mainly military. The nobles in turn granted estates to knights and the lesser families of the realm under similar oaths of obligation. Although not always a strict hierarchical system, feudalism did provide for defence against invaders, internal civil order, the systematic tilling of the land, and eventually resulted in a sense of regional and national loyalty that made possible the emergence of such kingdoms as France and England.

A third factor which brought about the revitalization of western Christendom was a resurgence of religious fervour which resulted in the founding of a number of new monastic orders. Although the Cluniac reforms had called for a stricter observance of the Benedictine Rule by those in monasteries, some felt the recommendations had not gone far enough. In 1084 a Carthusian house was founded which emphasized a life

DEATH AND THE AFTERLIFE

Toradja statues of the dead. The Toradjas live on the Indonesian island of Sulawesi. Despite conversion to Christianity, some of their previous tribal religious beliefs and practices persist. These statues are of carved wood, life size, and fully clothed, and serve as a reminder of the dead person's continued existence. Indonesian 'primal' religion included belief in an afterlife long before the arrival of Christianity and Islam.

All the great religions have been concerned with the mysteries that surround human experience of time and mortality (see 'The Nature of Religion', pp. 6ff). People appear always to have had hopes for some kind of survival beyond death, and to have cherished such hopes as part of a belief in the strength and vitality of the human spirit in a world of constant change, decay and disaster. Ideas about the afterlife have varied both within and between the great world faiths. Most Christians have believed in an eternal life made available through the saving power of Christ, and leading to the post-mortem enjoyment of communion with God. Muslims have believed in the power of Allah to overcome the apparent finality of death and to reward the faithful in paradise. Belief in the continuation of a human personality formed in one earthly existence is characteristic of Judaism, Christianity and Islam. The religions of India, by contrast, have generally taught reincarnation, and so have represented the 'afterlife' as a series of earthly rebirths to be followed eventually by liberation, through absorption into the ultimate reality of Brahman, the enjoyment of the peace and bliss of nibbana, or by communion with a personal God.

ABOVE Orthodox Jews read prayers around the grave of one of their dead. There are clear patterns of development in Jewish belief about an afterlife. In the early biblical period the concept of Sheol was of a shadowy world in which the spirits of the dead continued in existence, but with little pleasure or purpose. Later, in the Book of Daniel, there is evidence of belief in the resurrection of the righteous to a new life. Early rabbinical teaching included the immortality of the soul as a cardinal tenet, although the rabbis engaged in very little speculation about the condition of the afterlife.

ABOVE 'Holy Water', blessed by a priest, has long been used in connection with funerals. Here, a mourner sprinkles water on a coffin during a Roman Catholic funeral in Paris. Christian teaching has always included hope of eternal life. Teaching about the state of the soul at death has variously emphasized an immediate progress to a state symbolized by heaven or hell; a period of sleep followed by a resurrection; and a time in purgatory.

LEFT Funeral urns holding the bones of the dead in Hong Kong. The use of mortuary urns is very ancient in China, some having been found on Neolithic sites in Kansau Province and some reflecting more elaborate burials of the Shang period (1500–1000 BCE). The practice is assumed to indicate a belief in the continuing survival of the dead in some form. Attitudes to death in China have varied from the presumably agnostic view of Confucius, who asked, 'Not understanding life, how can you understand death?' (Lun Yu, Analects, XII,ii), to the particular attention paid by religious Taoism to the search for immortality.

LEFT *Hindu cremations by the river Bagmati in Nepal. Cremation is the normal means of disposing of the bodies of the dead in Hindu societies, a practice which goes back at least to the time of the Rig Veda. Cremation by a river is especially appropriate, and the most auspicious means of disposing of the ashes is to commit them to the Ganges. The eldest son has a duty to preside over the cremation rites. Death is a time of great ritual impurity, and those who deal with the bodies are regarded as impure and therefore traditionally have been low caste people.*

ABOVE *A Zoroastrian Tower of Silence, or* dokhma, *at Yuzd in Iran. In the Zoroastrian faith dead bodies are believed to be extremely polluting, partly because death itself is regarded as a victory of Evil. It is a pollution of the sacred element of fire to commit a body to the flames in cremation (although outside Iran and India Zoroastrians sometimes have to resort to cremation). The Tower of Silence allows for the disposal of bodies in a tranquil setting and with the minimum risk of pollution to the living. After washing and prayers the body is laid in the* dokhma, *where vultures devour it.*

RIGHT Bereaved brothers in south India say prayers for their mother. Sons, and especially eldest sons, have a special duty to attend to the last rites of their parents. Death in Hindu teaching is believed to be simply an incident in the cycle of existence. As a person discards clothes at night and puts on another set of clothes in the morning, so the soul is released from the body at death and will then assume the attire of another body in rebirth.

RIGHT An eleventh-century manuscript illustrates the resurrection of Christ. The resurrection is one of the most important doctrines of the Christian Church, although it has been interpreted in different ways. The first reference to the resurrection is in St Paul's letters, where he wrote that: 'Christ was raised to life on the third day . . . and appeared to Peter . . . to the Twelve . . . and to over five hundred of our brothers' (1 Corinthians 15.3–7). The Gospels, committed to writing later, included the stories of the empty tomb.

BELOW The death of Buddha depicted in a Thai temple. Although Gautama, the Buddha, is said to have achieved enlightenment at about the age of thirty-five, he then lived a long life before dying at eighty. The Mahaparinibbana Sutta tells of his death at Kusinara and his cremation. Buddhism accepts reincarnation, but has a different understanding of the nature of the soul that is reborn from that found in Hinduism. The popular Jataka stories teach the futility of grieving for the dead.

A Korean painting of an Immortal playing the flute in a Taoist paradise. Religious Taoism was much concerned with the pursuit of immortality. Taoists do not regard matter and spirit as essentially different, and so immortality is believed to be concerned with transformation through a balance of yin and yang rather than liberation by releasing the soul from the material world. Popular Taoist stories suggest magical ways of securing immortality. In this painting the Immortal, Han Hsiang-tzu, carries in his pocket a sacred mushroom. Mortals who took the drug produced from the mushroom were said to become immune to death.

of silent contemplation, manual labour and a total renunciation of the world. Another order that attempted a revision of the Benedictine Rule was founded in 1097; this became known as the Cistercian brotherhood, and it stressed simplicity in the construction of its abbeys, often built in remote and desolate regions, and strict self-denial in its members' life-style. Attracting large numbers of postulants, by the year 1200 more than 530 Cistercian houses had been established across Europe. The most famous Cistercian was Bernard of Clairvaux (1090–1153) who is remembered for his sermons, poetry, devotional writings and the preaching of the Second Crusade.

By the thirteenth century the rapid urbanization of Europe demanded a new type of monastic expression, one committed to popular preaching, teaching, and the serving of the poor and destitute on the fringes of society. Such an order was founded in 1209 by Francis of Assisi (1182–26). Brought up as one of a prosperous Italian family, Francis renounced his original intent to become a knight in order to devote his life to poverty and the service of Christ. Inspired by his example others followed, and by the beginning of the fourteenth century the Franciscans were the largest monastic order in the Western Church.

LEFT Under Pope Gregory VII (1073–85) a movement of reform began within the Roman Catholic Church. In this Benedictine window in Norwich Cathedral Gregory is seen in the centre of the left-hand panel. Originally the reforms concerned the appointment and conduct of clergy, but Pope Gregory also asserted the concept of papal supremacy.

BELOW In the period between the 10th and 14th centuries many new monastic orders were formed and spread through Europe in a resurgence of religious fervour which was to revitalize western Christianity.

- ■ BENEDICTINE MONASTERIES
- ♣ CLUNIAC MONASTERIES
- ✳ CISTERCIAN   ● OTHERS
- ✚ CARTHUSIAN   ♡ MILITARY ORDERS

TERRITORY OF THE TEUTONIC KNIGHTS

0   500 mls
0   800 kms

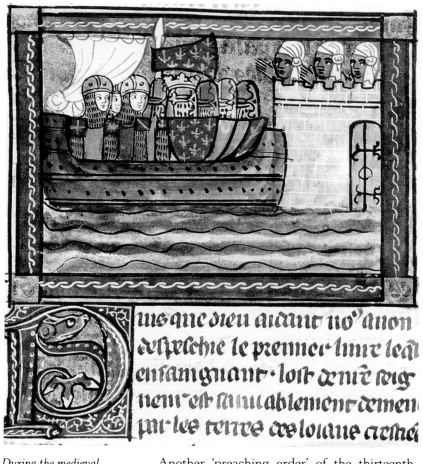

nople from the Muslim advance. The participants in the early crusades were drawn from all ranks of society, including women and children; later Crusaders were generally knights and their retinues. The Crusaders had initial successes in capturing Jerusalem (1099) and establishing a Latin Christian kingdom in its environs, but the occupying Crusaders lost the city less than a century later (1187), defeated by Muslim armies under the command of Salah ud-din (Saladin). Repeated efforts later to regain the holy land resulted only in further multiple disasters. Within two hundred years of the end of the crusading period Constantinople would also fall to Muslim forces (1453). In addition to the failure of their two stated aims, the Crusades also encouraged much of the religious intolerance·in Christian Europe. It was assumed that defeating the 'infidel' (as the Christian then described the Muslim) was a holy task, and one in which the constraints under which warfare between Christians was often conducted need not apply. The encouragement of such views also played a part in the severe persecution of Jews in many parts of Europe during that period.

MEDIEVAL LEARNING

The rise of the theological system known as Scholasticism took place in the West between the ninth and fourteenth centuries. A result of the monastic control of the schools and universities, the scholastics, or 'schoolmen', sought to present the Christian faith in terms of logical formulations based upon classical models of Greek thought. Assisted by the rediscovery in the West of Aristotle (whose writings had been kept alive by Muslim philosophers), the schoolmen developed a synthesis of Christian theology and classical philosophy. Early expressions of the scholastic system include the *Sentences* of Peter Lombard (c. 1100–60) which set forth the medieval concept of the seven sacraments, and the *Cur Deus Homo?* ('Why did God Become Man?') of Anselm of Canterbury (1033–1109) which explained the sacrifice of Christ in terms of 'divine satisfaction'. Peter Abelard (1079–1142), in his work *Sic et Non* ('Yes and No'), sought to reconcile faith and reason through a careful analysis of what constituted authority in Christian belief.

The 'Prince of the Schoolmen', however, was Thomas Aquinas (1225–74) a Dominican monk who had studied at the universities of Paris and Cologne under Albert the Great (c. 1200–80) before returning to his native Italy to pursue his literary labours. Aquinas eventually produced an exhaustive and systematic exposition of the Catholic faith in his two major works, the *Summa Theologica* and the *Summa contra Gentiles*. Writ-

During the medieval period of increased religious fervour European Christians became increasingly antagonistic to a Muslim presence in what they felt to be their own holy places. Defeating the infidels, the unfaithful, was seen as a holy task and kings and emperors encouraged their war-hungry knights to go on Crusade. This 14th-century French manuscript shows the King of France and his Crusaders on board ship approaching a fortress manned by Saracens. This name for the European Muslims comes from the Latin saraceni, nomadic arabs of the Syrian desert who harassed the borders of the Roman Empire.

Another 'preaching order' of the thirteenth century was founded in 1220 by Dominic de Guzman (1170–1221). The Dominicans were dedicated to the intellectual presentation and defence of the Christian faith. Known as 'friars' the Dominicans, and later also the Franciscans, came to dominate the emerging universities of western Europe.

THE CRUSADES

The combination of secular security, guaranteed by emperors and kings, and religious fervour, presided over by popes and bishops, produced an age rich in popular piety. Prince and peasant, craftsmen and cleric, worked side by side in the building of great cathedrals of first romanesque, and then gothic, splendour. Thousands embarked upon pilgrimages to points as distant as Jerusalem and Rome, Compostela and Canterbury.

There were many positive achievements in this age of faith, but there were also negative consequences, of which the most obvious were the Crusades. Eight separate crusades were called between 1095 and 1270, with the declared intentions of delivering the holy places in Palestine from Muslim control and preserving Constanti-

ten in the form of scholastic disputations, these works present a logical case for each doctrine of the Christian faith and attempt to answer all objections. With patient care and absolute thoroughness these writings cover the entire spectrum of Christian thought from basic belief in God to the complex sacramental theology of the medieval Church, including the thorny problem of transubstantiation. Although certain elements in Aquinas' system came under attack from later schoolmen like Duns Scotus (c. 1264–1308), it has, as a whole, remained a definitive statement of orthodox theology in the Roman Catholic Church to the present day.

SCHISM AND DISSENT

Although papal supremacy had reached its peak under Innocent III (1160–1216) in the early thirteenth century, within a hundred years the papal office once again succumbed to outside political pressure. In the early fourteenth century the kings of France succeeded in removing the papal office from Rome to Avignon where successive popes remained until 1377, when Pope Gregory XI (1329–78) made a final return to the 'Eternal City'. Following the death of Gregory, however, during the period known as the Great Western Schism, the Latin Church had two and then three rival popes. Each pope and anti-pope was supported by different national alliances in Europe. This inspired the calling of new ecumenical councils convening at such places as Constance (1414–18) and Basel (1431–49). These meetings of western Christendom, presided over by the emperor, with clergy and laity seated by 'nations', finally brought about an end to the scandal of a divided Western Church.

As a result of this 'crisis in Christendom' there were renewed calls for the reform of the Church. Civil and canon lawyers debated the basis for the exercise of power within both the ecclesiastical and the secular realms. Some advocated conciliarism, a system in which both pope and emperor would be responsible to councils of kings, bishops and nobles. Others, such as Marsiglio of Padua (1270–1342), envisaged a complete separation of Church and State. Dissent within the Church on religious grounds had already appeared in the thirteenth and fourteenth centuries in the form of men such as Peter Waldo (d. 1217) and John Wycliffe (c. 1330–84) who sought a return to earlier Christian values. By the fifteenth century this dissent grew to encompass whole communities, such as the Bohemians under the leadership of John (Jan) Hus (c. 1369–1415) and the Florentines under the guidance of Savonarola (1452–98).

Erasmus of Rotterdam (1466–1536) from an engraving by Dürer. The greatest of all the northern Humanists, Erasmus chose to write always in Latin. In common with other scholars of his day he disregarded the Middle Ages and studied Greek and Latin writers. He was a pure scholar, totally unpolitical in his outlook, believing that education and enlightened discussion would bring about moral improvement. He was not himself a reformer but for a man of his time he achieved surprising international repute. Influence of his thinking is to be seen in the works of all later reformers.

The desire for reform was given renewed impetus by the rise of two movements in the fifteenth and sixteenth centuries. The first of these was Christian mysticism. Personalities as varied as Thomas à Kempis (1380–1471), credited with the book *The Imitation of Christ*, and Dame Julian of Norwich (c. 1342–1414) advocated a personalized faith in which an individual could seek rapture with God. Other adherents of this 'new' devotion included the Brethren of the Common Life, a lay semi-monastic movement which became popular in northern Europe.

The second movement was humanism, which emphasized the 'new learning'. Often critical of the Church of their day, the humanists urged a renewed study of the scriptures in the original languages and a reappropriation of the classical and Christian Greek and Latin writers. Pre-eminent among the humanists was Desiderius Erasmus of Rotterdam (1467–1536). Educated by the Brethren of the Common Life, Erasmus became an Augustianian canon and was ordained a priest in 1492. Finding himself unable to live within the confines of a monastery, Erasmus went to study at the University of Paris in 1495 and later visited England, becoming friends with the English humanists John Colet (c. 1466–1519) and Thomas More (1478–1535). Erasmus was an unfailing advocate of the new learning and an unbending critic of clerical corruption in the Church, satirized in his book *In Praise of Folly*. In 1516 his greatest contribution, a critical edition of the Greek New Testament, was printed in Basle. Although Erasmus remained a Roman Catholic until his death, his writings and scholarship set the stage for the approaching Reformation.

The Reformation

The Reformation itself broke upon Europe in the sixteenth century. Originally begun as a movement of renewal within the Western Church, by the beginning of the seventeenth century the Reformation had resulted in a Europe divided along religious and confessional lines. In much of southern and central Europe (Italy, Spain, Austria and parts of France) a renewed and revitalized Roman Catholic Church emerged triumphant. Three other main traditions, however, separated from the Roman Church, also emerged during this century: the Lutheran, in Germany and Scandinavia; the Zwinglian and Calvinist, also known as 'Reformed', in Switzerland, Holland, Scotland and parts of France; and the autonomous Church of England. It is possible, in fact, to speak of three 'reformations' taking place in the sixteenth century: the Continental Reformation, the English Reformation and the Roman Catholic Reformation (also known as the 'Counter-Reformation').

THE LUTHERAN REFORMATION

The Continental Reformation began as a result of the writings and teachings of Martin Luther (1483–1546), an Augustinian monk, doctor of theology and professor of biblical studies at the University of Wittenberg. In 1517 he challenged the practice of selling papal 'indulgences'. An indulgence originally provided a remission from punishment after death for particular sins, but was granted only on condition of the sinner's sincere contrition and repentance. By the sixteenth century, however, indulgences were granted under papal authority for other activities, such as crusades, pilgrimages, or contributing funds towards the building of a church. The indulgences being sold in Germany at the time of Luther were providing finance for the construction of St Peter's Basilica in Rome. Although Luther's challenge began as an academic exercise, the central issues of the controversy soon shifted to questions of faith and authority.

Using Erasmus's edition of the Greek New Testament, Luther contended that an individual's salvation was the result of 'justification by faith alone' (*sola fide*) in the sacrificial death of Christ. Humankind received this 'justification' only as a result of God's grace (*sola gratia*) and without reference to prior good works or the exercise of papal authority which claimed to be able to 'shut the gates of hell and open the door to paradise'. All of these convictions were confirmed primarily not by popes or councils but by scripture alone (*sola scriptura*), which Luther believed all Christians should be able to read for themselves.

In 1520 Luther was excommunicated by the Pope and, following the Diet (synod) of Worms in 1521, he was declared an outlaw by the emperor, Charles V (1500–58). But through the use of the printing press Luther's ideas were spread throughout Europe. Protected by regional princes, Luther published dozens of books and broadsheets over the next twenty-five years. In perhaps his greatest literary accomplishment Luther translated the Bible into German. In 1529, at the Diet of Speyer, Charles V sought to impose his will in the curtailing of Lutheran activities. Certain of the German princes, however, protested – and thus bequeathed the title 'Protestant' to the Reformation movement outside the body which was to remain as the Roman Catholic Church.

The following year at the Diet of Augsburg (1530), the Protestants presented a statement of belief – the Augsburg Confession – prepared by Luther's closest colleague, Philip Melanchthon (1497–1560). Conservative and conciliatory in content, it was nonetheless rejected by the Roman Catholics at the conference. Unable in similar successive meetings to resolve the issue, both the emperor and the Protestant princes prepared for war, which finally came in 1547, the year after Luther's death. After years of conflict, a politico-religious settlement was achieved in 1555 at the Peace of Augsburg, which allowed each ruler the right to determine the religion of his own territory. By the time of the Peace of Augsburg, Lutheranism had spread through the greater portion of northern Germany and all of Scandinivia, as well as large sections of Poland and Hungary, and constituted a Christian community in size second only to Rome in the West.

THE SWISS REFORMATION

The Lutheran Reformation in Germany and Scandinavia had proved to be essentially conservative in nature and it retained many Catholic characteristics. The Swiss Reformation, however, although taking place at the same time, was largely independent of Luther's influence and adopted a somewhat different approach. Begun in Zurich by Huldreich (Ulrich) Zwingli (1484–1531), the Swiss Reformation quickly set aside previous Catholic customs and usages and instituted forms of church worship and discipline felt to be closer to the simplicity of the early Church. Often iconoclastic, and doctrinally divided from Luther on the question of the Eucharist, the Swiss did not enjoy the protection of the German princes, and at the Battle of Kappel (1531) Zwingli was killed in action against an invading Catholic army.

The Reformation in Switzerland continued under the leadership of French-born John Calvin (1509–64). Greatly influenced by the writings of Luther, Calvin had studied at Orleans, Bruges and the University of Paris before he broke with the Roman Catholic Church and left France to live as an exile in Basel (Basle). In 1536 he published the first edition of his famous work, *Institutes of the Christian Religion*, which set forth his own reformed theology. In the same year Calvin was invited to assist in the work of Reformation which had begun in Geneva. Although expelled by the citizens of that town in 1537, Calvin was invited to return in 1541; he was to remain in Geneva for the rest of his life, seeking to construct a truly 'Christian society'.

Similar to Luther in his theological outlook, Calvin emphasized the total sovereignty of God, the authority of the Bible, and the importance of the 'gospel' sacraments of Baptism and the Eucharist. Calvin also, however, asserted the doctrines of predestination and election – that some, and only some, are chosen by God from the first for salvation in eternity – and the absolute freedom of the Church from civil restrictions, although he meant the Church to assist the State in the building up of a Godly community.

Under Calvin's leadership Geneva became a centre for Protestants fleeing persecution. Refugees from France, Italy, Spain, the Low Countries and, for a time, the British Isles as well, came to Switzerland. Eventually all of them were to return to their home countries carrying with them Calvin's reformed ideals. By the early seventeenth century, Calvin's concept of the Reformation had been embraced by the Dutch Reformed in the Netherlands, the Huguenots in France, the Presbyterians in Scotland, and the Puritans in England.

THE RADICAL REFORMATION

Another result of the Reformation in Germany and Switzerland was the rise of an associated movement known as the Radical Reformation. Some felt that Luther, Zwingli and Calvin had not gone far enough in the restructuring of the Church's life and practice. Because of their use of baptism for adults ('believer's baptism') and their refusal to allow children to be baptized, many of these 'radicals' were called Anabaptists (from the Greek 'to baptize again'). In Germany the radicals, led by Thomas Munzer (1490–1525), found political expression in the Peasants' Revolt of 1525, which was vigorously opposed by Luther and brutally suppressed by the German princes.

ABOVE Vellum envelope containing John Calvin's Institutes of the Christian Religion published in Basel in 1536. Doctrines of Calvinism were established in this work, which was censored by the Roman Catholic Church.

LEFT This 16th-century engraving shows the sharing of goods by Anabaptists. Their belief in pacifism, and support of the separation of church and state led to intense persecution for many centuries.

In Switzerland the Swiss Brethren broke with Zwingli in 1525 and advocated pacifism and the complete separation of the Church from state affairs. Similar to the Swiss Brethren were the Hutterites of Moravia and the Mennonites of Holland. Many of these groups practised communalism of one variety or another. All of the Anabaptists were opposed by the main proponents of the 'conservative Reformation' as well as by the Roman Catholics, and suffered great persecution from both: in the sixteenth and seventeenth centuries, tens of thousands were put to death for their convictions.

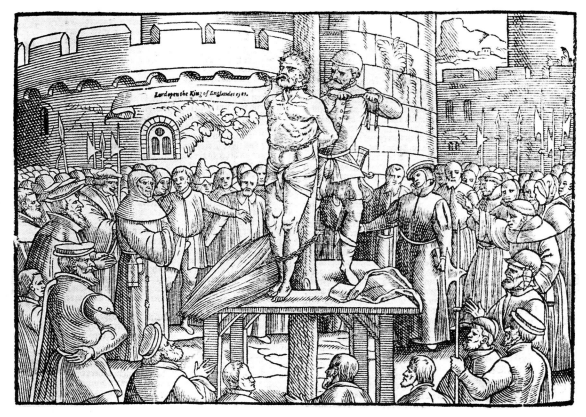

A woodcut from John Foxe's Book of Martyrs (1576) depicting Protestant reformer William Tyndale being burnt at the stake for heresy. Foxe was ordained deacon in 1550 and worked for the Reformation in England. With the accession of Mary he had to flee and settled in Basel in 1555. Here he worked on his 'martyrology', which was a history in Latin of the persecution of English reformers, from John Wycliffe to the death of Thomas Cranmer in 1556. He returned to London and continued to enlarge his book using registers and the accounts of eye witnesses.

THE ENGLISH REFORMATION

The English Reformation was the result of a diversity of factors which caused it to develop on a pattern different from that experienced in either Germany or Switzerland. For some two hundred years, since the time of John Wycliffe, there had been a genuine desire on the part of many in England for a reform of the Church which would result in freedom from papal authority. Such desires had been encouraged by Luther's writings and the success of the Reformation in Germany.

King Henry VIII (1491–1547), was initially opposed to Lutheran views and outlawed the sale of Luther's publications in England. A Renaissance prince, he had been given a broad education and had been deeply influenced by humanistic thought. A central concern of Henry's, however, was to provide a male heir to the throne of his country. His first wife, Catherine of Aragon (1485–1536), had failed to produce a prince. To marry Catherine at all Henry had needed a papal dispensation because she was the widow of his brother Arthur. Henry now sought another dispensation for the marriage to be annulled. When it appeared unlikely that such a dispensation would be forthcoming, Henry had the marriage dissolved by Thomas Cranmer (1489–1556), the Archbishop of Canterbury, and in 1534 Parliament passed the Act of Supremacy by which Henry and future sovereigns became 'Supreme Head' of the established English Church. The dissolution of the monasteries (all of whose orders were suddenly 'disestablished', and some of which had indulged in practices similar to those criticized by Luther) soon followed, and the destruction of papal power in England was complete. To the end of his life Henry nevertheless remained a Catholic in faith and practice. Protestant ideals were still not actively encouraged, apart from the order that an English translation of the Bible be placed in every church.

Under the reign of Henry's ailing son Edward VI (r. 1547–53), Reformation ideals from the Continent were welcomed in England. The leading English figure of the time, still Thomas Cranmer, saw to the compilation of two Prayer Books (1549 and 1552) which evidenced the growth of Protestant doctrine in the English Church. A time of religious reaction, however, followed the death of Edward when his eldest sister Mary Tudor (r. 1553–58), a convinced Roman Catholic, ascended the throne. Large numbers of adherents of the new Church were driven into exile, and more than three hundred – including Cranmer – were burned at the stake as heretics. The reintroduction of Roman Catholicism in England ended abruptly, after five years, with Mary's death. The subsequent reign of Mary's younger sister Elizabeth I (r. 1558–1603) saw an English Church – free of papal authority, Protestant in theology but Catholic in structure – restored and re-established.

THE RESPONSE OF THE ROMAN CATHOLIC CHURCH

The response of the Roman Catholic Church to the Continental and English Reformations was two-fold. Firstly it involved a renewed definition of Catholic faith and practice, which took place at the Council of Trent (1545–65) called by Pope Paul III (1468–1549). Earlier attempts at reconciliation with the Protestants, as had been encouraged by Cardinal Contarini (1483–1542), were rejected in favour of a positive assertion of the Catholic position, a statement of clarity that had been lacking in the early part of the century. The Council effectively ended the possibility of a rapprochement with the Lutherans, Calvinists and Anglicans who were now in control of the northern regions of Europe. A series of reforms were recommended, which were swiftly put into effect by a number of successive reform-minded popes.

Secondly, Rome responded with a spontaneous release of spiritual energy and power. This is evidenced by Ignatius Loyola (1491–1556) who founded a new monastic order, the Society of Jesus, which was approved by the Pope in 1540. The 'Jesuits' were bound not only by vows of poverty and chastity but also by a special vow of total obedience to the pope. Viewing themselves as the 'soldiers of Christ' the Jesuits served the Church throughout the world as missionaries, educators and diplomats. Great mystics also arose in the Roman Church at this time. Advocating a spirituality which emphasized both the personal and the sacramental, figures such as Teresa of Avila (1515–82) and John of the Cross (1542–91), a Spanish Carmelite monk, poet and mystic, brought new vitality to Roman Catholicism.

By the beginning of the seventeenth century both Roman Catholics and Protestants looked to their secular rulers to defend their respective faiths militarily. Religious confrontation led to both national and internecine war throughout the continent of Europe. Often political expediency dictated Catholic-Protestant alliances against their mutual co-religionists. Such was the case throughout the shifting course of the Thirty Years' War. The Treaty of Westphalia in 1648 ended the conflict and recognized the political and religious reality of a new Europe divided by differing confessions of faith and new regional and national alliances. Lutheranism ranged across northern Germany, Scandinavia and the Baltic states, but had lost much of its hold in Poland and Hungary. Calvinism was firmly established in Switzerland, the Netherlands and Scotland, but following the revoking of the Edict of Nantes in 1685 the Calvinists in France were driven into exile. The Church of England retained its position, despite an interim of curtailed power during the brief period of the Commonwealth following the English Civil War (1640–60). Roman Catholicism maintained its hold on France, Spain, Austria, Poland and Ireland. Missionaries of every faith were now making their way to the New World: the history of the Church was becoming the chronicle of the Churches and their denominations.

The Moravian Church

HISTORICAL OUTLINE AND PRESENT-DAY DISTRIBUTION

The Moravian Church (*Unitas Fratrum*, the 'Unity of the Brethren') was founded in 1457 in Bohemia by a group of the followers of the Czech reformer John Hus. Their emphasis was on Christian living within a fellowship of Christian people, rather than on doctrine and ecclesiastical organization. At the Synod of Lhota (1467), the Brethren agreed to establish their own ministry with the three orders of bishop, presbyter and deacon. To emphasize their link with the historic Church they obtained ordination from Bishop Stephen of the Waldensians.

From 1457 until 1620, periods of prosperity and growth alternated with periods of repression and persecution. The Church spread into Moravia and Poland. But at the Battle of the White Mountain (1620) the Brethren shared the defeat of the Protestant forces; the Unitas Fratrum continued to exist only as an underground movement. During these hidden years, Bishop John Amos Comenius, an original thinker and educator, gave courageous leadership, and kept alive the traditions of the Church.

In the early eighteenth century some descendants of the old Moravian families came into Saxony as religious refugees and were given a home on the estate of Count Zinzendorf, building in 1722 a little village which they called Herrnhut ('the Lord's Watch'). Within the next few years a Protestant religious community developed, under the guidance of Zinzendorf, with an extraordinary vision and commitment. During worship on 13 August 1727 the community shared a deep spiritual experience which resulted in a renewed sense of unity in Christ. Seeing themselves as true heirs of the old Unitas Fratrum, they came to feel that their particular calling was to be witnesses to Christ among people who did not yet know him.

Engraving showing the original Moravian settlement at Herrnhut in Saxony. Persecution of this Church in Moravia was such that it was almost destroyed, but its people continued to meet deep in the forests where they received encouragement from their exiled bishop Johann Amos Comenius. Some of these 'hidden' people escaped over the border and were given a home by Count Zinzendorf. Here they founded their village of Herrnhut. They were joined by German Lutherans and the Count himself came to live in the settlement. Such settlements were communal and have always had a strong musical tradition.

So from 1732 Moravian missionaries travelled to the Caribbean, to Africa, Greenland, Labrador, India, and to many other places. At the same time, other groups were settling in North America, establishing Moravian settlements there. In Britain, Moravians influenced John Wesley (the founder of Methodism) and played a part in the renewing of the Church in England in the eighteenth century.

The world Moravian Church today is made up of eighteen self-governing Provinces. Every seven years the International Unity Synod meets to agree the main principles of the Church's life, worship and doctrine. Co-operation between the Provinces remains close at all times.

BELIEF

The motto 'in essentials, unity; in non-essentials, liberty; in all things, charity' well reflects the spirit of the Moravian Church. There is no doctrinal test for membership, apart from acceptance of Jesus as Lord and Saviour. Entrance to the Church is through baptism and confirmation or, if the applicant is already a Church member, by reception. The two sacraments of baptism and Holy Communion are observed. The Bible is recognized as the ultimate source and rule of faith, doctrine and life. However, a broad tolerance in interpretation has been allowed, and this has made it possible to accommodate both those of theologically liberal and of conservative views.

WORSHIP

Again, freedom and flexibility is the norm. The ordinary Sunday service is Morning Service, for which there are various liturgical forms – although the local minister and congregation may arrange worship independently according to local needs. In Europe, Holy Communion is generally celebrated monthly; in North America, however, the practice of celebrating it only on special Church festivals has been retained from earlier times. Preceding the Holy Communion there may be an informal 'service' of hymn-singing and devotional discussion or teaching known as the 'Love Feast'.

ORGANIZATION

Although the Church preserves the three orders of ministry, Moravians accept the validity of other Churches' ministries whether episcopally ordained or not. Christ alone is recognized as the head of the Church. The bishop, elected by a Provincial synod, is a spiritual leader who ordains but has no administrative authority. Such authority is vested in the Provincial Elders' Conference, also elected by synod, which oversees the life of each Province.

By history and by spirit the Moravian Church is ecumenical in character and enjoys formal and informal fellowship with a number of Churches.

The Mennonite Church

HISTORICAL OUTLINE AND PRESENT-DAY DISTRIBUTION

Mennonites have their roots in sixteenth-century groups of radical reformers called Anabaptists. One of these groups originated in Switzerland, where disciples of the Zurich reformer Huldreich Zwingli (1484–1531) balked at his insistence that the City Council – not the Church's leaders – should determine the course of religious change. Contending that membership in a true Church is voluntary and sealed by the baptism of repentant believers (for which reason their enemies called them Anabaptists, 're-baptizers'), the radicals became modern pioneers of the believers' Churches whose identity is definitively distinct from that of the State and the general populace. As the Anabaptist movement spread, severe persecution – with torture and execution of thousands – ensued.

The movement survived in large part because of the effective leadership of a Dutch ex-priest, Menno Simons (d. 1561), after whom Mennonites came to be known. In the seventeenth and eighteenth centuries, Mennonites migrated to North America and Russia. And, after at least one century of isolationism, in the twentieth century they have spread rapidly too, through missionary and development activity. In 1984 there were 700,000 Mennonites in 52 countries.

BELIEF

Throughout their history the Mennonites have adhered to the major doctrines of Christian orthodoxy. They are not a people of creeds, but their sometimes unusual emphases and practices are a result of their attempt to be rigorously biblical. For them, both Old and New Testaments are the Word of God – but the New Testament, which records the life and teachings of Jesus, is the fulfilment of what is promised in the Old. Mennonites believe that Jesus was more concerned that people should follow him in practical ways than that they should give formal assent to his ideas. 'Discipleship' has therefore been a primary emphasis among Mennonites, and they have worked hard to give concrete expression to Jesus' teaching. 'No one can truly know Christ', one characteristic Anabaptist saying goes, 'unless he follow him in life.'

Mennonites also believe that through his death and resurrection Jesus freed them from the slavery of sin to enable them to live in a way that is radically new. This has led many Mennonites to adopt a lifestyle which has challenged accepted social norms particularly in areas of what they see as peace, justice and truth. At the heart of their tradition has been anti-militarism and commitment to enemy-loving; anti-materialism and a commitment to simplicity of living; opposition to swearing oaths; and a commitment to truth-telling under all circumstances. For understandable reasons they – despite their non-violence – have often been viewed as subversives.

WORSHIP

Following Jesus in these ways, Mennonites believe, is too strenuous for isolated individuals. It must be done corporately, by brothers and sisters who discover in congregations what it means to belong to God's family. There they support each other economically and spiritually, and help each other make major life decisions. Their congregations have generally had plural leadership, and although recently many congregations have called on full-time pastors, these do not constitute a spiritual elite. Early Mennonites held their meetings in forests, barns and domestic dwellings; typically today they gather in simple meeting-houses.

Huldreich Zwingli (1484–1531) by Hans Asper. Zwingli was convinced that the communion service should be celebrated in a manner as like as possible to that of the early Christians. In Zurich, following his teaching, images were removed from the churches and many festivals abolished. This caused opposition from surrounding cantons which led to civil war in 1531. Carrying his people's banner into battle Zwingli was killed and a rough stone marks the spot where he fell.

Mennonite worship has generally been non-liturgical and sermon-centred. From the earliest days of the movement, however, Mennonites were concerned to emphasize the corporate nature of the Church by giving freedom to all members to participate – sharing experiences, responding to the teaching, asking for prayer. The Lord's Supper has been an important part of Mennonite worship. As they eat bread and drink from the cup, Mennonites believe that Jesus is really present among them, his Body. Baptism is also a significant experience for Mennonite congregations, as they celebrate a person's new life in Christ, commitment to follow him, and entry into membership in the Body.

ORGANIZATION

Mennonite congregations are self-financing and self-governing. However, they often join together with other congregations in regional conferences which provide solidarity and, in times of difficulty, support and counsel. Every six years Mennonites from many countries gather for a World Conference, although the World Conference has no more jurisdictional authority than the regional conferences. But through the opportunity that it provides for fellowship and instruction, the World Conference has done much to give Mennonites the sense of belonging to a world-wide family.

Because of this international consciousness, as well as because of emphases which extend back to their earliest years, Mennonites repudiate a special connection with any government or nation. In most countries Mennonites have experienced the displeasure of regimes whom they have reminded that – in matters military, social and religious – there is a higher Authority. In every generation, therefore, persecution and migration have been the lot of Mennonites somewhere in the world, keeping them aware that they are a pilgrim people.

The Lutheran Churches

HISTORY AND PRESENT-DAY DISTRIBUTION

The Lutheran Churches constitute the largest of all Protestant bodies (more than 75,900,000 congregants) and are exceeded only by the Orthodox and Roman Catholic Churches in worldwide adherents in the Christian community. Their present-day numerical distribution by continents is: 60,400,000 in Europe; 8,900,000 in North America; 2,300,000 in Asia; 1,900,000 in South America; 1,900,000 in Africa; and 500,000 in Australasia. Lutherans are one of the three classic Protestant Churches of the Reformation, standing alongside the Reformed (Calvinist) and Anglican traditions.

There is no single date that marks the birth of the Lutheran Churches. They emerged in the various nations of northern Europe between 1517 and 1580, that is, between the time Martin Luther (1483–1546) published his Ninety-five Theses and the ratification of the Lutheran confessional writings in the *Book of Concord*. Although the early years of the Lutheran Churches are of course connected primarily with the writings and personalities of Luther and his friend and protege Phillip Melanchthon (1497–1560), there was by the end of the sixteenth century an independent, distinctive Lutheran confession entirely separate from and of no less significance than those of the Roman, Orthodox, Reformed, Anglican, and Dissenting traditions. This confession expressed itself in the formation of a number of national, territorial and minority Lutheran Churches.

In the West, second in size only to Rome, Lutheranism was practised initially, and to the greatest extent, in Germany, Scandinavia and the Baltic States. By 1618 Lutheranism numbered 15,000,000 followers who lived under a wide variety of circumstances yet shared the Augsburg Confession as a statement of faith. It was, however, only after the Treaty of Westphalia in 1648 that the expression 'Evangelical *Lutheran* Church' came into general use. Before this time the term 'Lutheran' was more often used by Luther's opponents in a derogatory sense. Those who followed Luther more often spoke of themselves as 'Catholic evangelicals' or 'adherents of the Confession of Augsburg' or by a national or territorial appellation such as 'the Church of Sweden' (to this day still not designated as 'Lutheran' in its official title).

BELIEF

The Lutheran Churches, to a greater or lesser extent, have sought to be three things: catholic, drawing on the common liturgical and didactic tradition of the Western Church; evangelical, judging that tradition by the Christian scriptures; and confessional, seeking to protect their catholic and evangelical character through shared declarations of faith.

Lutherans affirm the ancient creeds of the Church (the Apostles', the Nicene and the Athanasian creeds are included in the *Book of Concord),* although these are regarded as confessions of 'the Gospel' – the core of the Christian scriptures which affords salvation. Scripture alone (*sola scriptura)* is regarded as the final judge of doctrine and is seen as the primary and canonical attestation of the 'saving message' of the gospel. Lutheran confessions such as the Augsburg Confession (1530), the Articles of Schmalkalden (1537) and the Formula of Concord (1577) are considered to be the proper interpretation of this saving ('salvific') message contained in scripture.

The primary tenet of the Lutheran Churches is the doctrine of 'justification by faith alone' (*sola fide).* A response to Luther's question 'How can sinful Man find a gracious God?', the doctrine of justification provided a ground of assurance. The doctrine of justification teaches that the original righteousness possessed by Man at his creation was irretrievably lost in the Fall, leaving Man in bondage to sin and unable to do the good which God's law requires. Man's salvation is the result of faith in Christ, through whose sacrifice Man, although still sinful, is accounted righteous in the sight of God. This is thanks to God's grace alone (*sola gratia),* without co-operation on the part of Man. Luther saw justification by faith alone as the heart of the gospel, and it is this doctrine which provides the keystone of the Lutheran confessions. Modern Lutheran theologians such as Rudolf Bultmann and Paul Tillich have in the present century applied this doctrine to the problem of psychological guilt.

It was upon the tri-lateral base of 'scripture alone', 'faith alone' and 'grace alone' that Lutheran doctrinal and liturgical development was founded. The seven sacraments of the medieval Church were reduced to three – the Lord's Supper (Eucharist), Baptism and Absolution – which contained 'promises' in scripture and which were directly instituted by Christ. Through 'Word and Sacrament' faith was created and strengthened. As regards the Eucharist, the medieval doctrine of transubstantiation was set aside in favour of a 'physical' or 'real' presence of Christ's person 'in, with, and under the bread and wine' in the Lord's Supper, the Words of Institution in the consecration being regarded as a reaffirmation of the salvific message of the gospel. The result was to place the Lutheran concept of the Eucharist in the 'middle ground' between the Roman Catholics who held to an absolute physical transformation of the Eucharistic elements in the Mass and the reformed churches which regarded the Eucharist

as simply a memorial of Christ's death. In baptism (both infant and adult) the 'Word works with and in the water' (sprinkling, pouring, and immersion are all known in Lutheran Churches) for the cleansing of sin. Confirmation, usually between the ages of ten and thirteen, although not a sacrament, is connected with a reaffirmation of baptismal vows and admittance to participation in the Lord's Supper. Absolution, or the 'Office of the Keys', is normally connected with both baptism (daily repentance actualizing the baptismal vows) and the Lord's Supper (confession and absolution prior to communing).

Historically, the doctrinal attitude of the Lutheran Churches has passed through a number of phases over the centuries. The Lutheran Churches reflect the influences of Orthodoxy (seventeenth century), Pietism (seventeenth and eighteenth centuries), the Enlightenment (eighteenth century), Neo-confessionalism (nineteenth century), Liberalism (nineteenth and twentieth centuries), and Ecumenism (twentieth century). All of these approaches have left their marks upon the present-day Lutheran Churches and have added to their vitality and diversity.

Martin Luther (1483–1546) when a monk, by Cranach. Luther remained a monk of the Augustinian order for sixteen years, while preaching the need for reform in the Roman Catholic Church. Eventually he was excommunicated, but he had by this time become a leader of the evangelical movement for reformation, in which work he spent the rest of his life. In temperament he was highly-strung, emotional, and liable to fits of depression, for he had a sensitive conscience and a keen sense of sin which his life as a monk had only tended to intensify.

115

WORSHIP

Liturgical life is normative for the Lutheran Churches. In this they have taken their lead from Luther himself, who put forward a restructured Latin Mass, the *Formula missae et communionis* (FM) in 1523, which retained most of the substance and ceremonial of the medieval rite with only minor changes apart from the excision of the offertory and the canon. After commissioning 'German music' to 'fit' his native language, Luther issued a simplified vernacular rite, the *Deutsche Messe* (DM) in 1526. This service made use of metrical paraphrases to replace certain of the prose texts of the medieval Mass, and was to prove very popular with the laity. For the next three and a half centuries, Lutheran liturgies were largely based on either the FM or DM model.

The basic form of most Lutheran eucharistic liturgies is similar. The service consists of two main sections – Word and Sacrament – within which are placed traditional elements: the Introit, Kyrie, Gloria, Credo (creed) and Agnus Dei. Because of the Reformers' high regard for scripture, the sermon is given a central place in Lutheran liturgies. Most Lutheran Churches have also retained the Offices (orders of service) of Matins and Vespers, as well as forms for a number of occasional services such as marriage, burial, baptism, and confirmation. Historically, Lutherans have emphasized the didactic portion of the service over against the sacramental, although due to the liturgical movement of the present century there is now a greater sense of celebration in most Lutheran services.

Lutheran worship today, while moving towards greater uniformity, continues to exhibit great diversity. In almost every Lutheran denomination, there are both 'low' (relatively informal) and 'high'(relatively formal) Church parties, in addition to the broad mainstream of members. Vestments (ritual clothing) for the clergy range from the black ('Geneva') gown to cassock, surplice and stole, to alb and chasuble, to academic attire (gown and hood). Lutheran places of worship range from the gothic splendour of Ulm and Uppsala cathedrals, to the modern church architecture of Eero Saarinen; from the stave churches of Norway to the thatched chapels of the Batak Church in Indonesia.

ORGANIZATION

One of the peculiar features of the Lutheran Churches is their wide divergence of practice concerning church order, organization, and the office of the ministry. Luther advocated co-operation between the Church and the State – the 'two kingdoms'. The Christian ruler, acting in a 'godly manner', should govern the secular realm, and the Church should rule over spiritual matters. Each, in its respective sphere, would see to the well-being of the people under its care. Further, Luther's teaching concerning the 'universal priesthood of all believers' and the historical circumstances of the Lutheran Reformation and subsequent mission activity, have resulted in the polity of the Lutheran Churches varying from country to country. Despite the apparent differences in organization, however, Lutheran Churches generally regard the ministry as a 'Churchly office' of those who are 'rightly called' to a 'particular priesthood' which centres around public preaching· and the administration of the holy sacraments.

The church of Sweden maintains an unbroken apostolic succession, with a three-fold ministry of bishops, priests and deacons. Episcopal government (not in apostolic succession) has been the rule in Denmark and Norway and in their provinces. The Finnish Church, although supported by public funds, is free of state control and maintains an episcopal structure.

Until 1918 the German Churches, under secular authority, were administered by consistories (with lay and clerical representatives). Between the First and Second World Wars the Churches were organized into synods (some employing episcopal nomenclature for officials) independent of state control. In 1948 the majority of German Lutheran Churches joined together to form the United Evangelical Lutheran Church of Germany, which later became a component of the pan-Protestant Evangelical Church in Germany.

In North America the Lutheran churches function in the same way as other Free Church denominations. Both congregational and presbyterial polity are employed within regional and national synodal structures which have elected officials. There are three main Lutheran denominations (the American Lutheran Church, the Lutheran Church in America, and the Lutheran Church–Missouri Synod) as well as a number of smaller autonomous synods. There has been a new plan for a 'merged' Lutheran Church (ALC, LCA, AELC) in America by 1988, and interest in the employment of both episcopal polity and nomenclature in American Lutheranism.

Since 1947 the majority of Lutheran churches have belonged to the Lutheran World Federation (LWF). Founded as a co-operative organization (from the earlier Lutheran World Convention, 1923), the LWF has sought to foster communication and common policy among its members. An Institute for Ecumenical Research is maintained by the LWF in Strasbourg. Members of the LWF also belong to the World Council of Churches.

The Calvinist Churches

HISTORY AND DISTRIBUTION

Calvin was born in 1509 in France, at Noyon in Picardy, and received his early education in Paris. He first studied medieval theology with a view to the priesthood, and then he engaged in humanist studies at Orleans and Bourges with a view to the legal profession. A sudden conversion helped to bring him under the influence of the Reformation and Holy Scripture. He was forced to leave France. For a short time he was in Basel where in 1536 he published the first edition of the *Institute of the Christian Religion*. After a short first visit to Geneva along with William Farel and Peter Viret he spent over two years in Strasbourg as a colleague of Martin Bucer. He finally settled again in Geneva in 1542 and from then on his whole life's work was devoted to the reform of its Church and city life. His aim was to create a Christian commonwealth which did honour to the Word of God and the kingship of Christ. He held no office except that of pastor in the city and he concentrated on maintaining the spiritual independence of the Church in all important matters of its own doctrine and discipline. At the same time he acknowledged the divinely-given independent authority of the civil power in its secular affairs. He believed not only in the power of the Word of God but also in the imposition of religious and moral discipline freely accepted by a public educated to understand and value it. After years of bitter struggle he achieved astonishing success which can in fairness be attributed to his qualities of leadership, to the power of his preaching and convincing clarity of his thought, and to his moral integrity, patience, diplomatic skill, wisdom and organizing ability. Within the Reformation movement itself his most important contributions lay in defining more carefully than had been done before the new forms of Christian life and service and of church structure in which the movement should express itself, and in bringing order and clarity into its theological thought.

To Geneva religious refugees came from all over Europe and took away Calvin's doctrine and ideas on church organization. In Geneva the presbyterian form of government was developed which became a model for all Calvinist Churches, although it was later altered in the changed circumstances of national conditions. In France, although the Reformed cause was resisted by the Roman Catholic rulers, the University of Paris and the Roman heirarchy, many of the nobility, encouraged by Calvin and his pastors, supported the Protestant cause and the Huguenots grew in numbers and strength. Then war ensued and in 1572 thousands, including Admiral Coligny, died in the Massacre of St Bartholomew. Things improved with the accession of Henry of Navarre and the Huguenots were given some security by the Edict of Nantes of 1598 until the Edict was revoked by Louis XIV in 1695. Then vast numbers emigrated to Holland, Germany and England, leaving a small Reformed Church and a greatly weakened France. From Geneva Reformed ideas spread along the Danube to Hungary and then Poland and down the Rhine to the Palatinate and other parts of Germany and to Holland. In Holland, Calvinism gave strength to the drive for political and religious liberty under William the Silent; later the Dutch were the first to engage in mission work abroad, in Ceylon, the East Indies and South Africa.

In England Calvin's teaching had considerable influence on the development of theology in the Church of England and even more in the thinking and practice of the Puritans and Non-Conformists of later centuries (Presbyterians, Methodists, Congregationalists and Baptists). The Pilgrim Fathers sailed from England to Holland and then to the New World, and subsequently many thousands took the Christian faith in the Calvinist form wherever they went, including America, Canada, Australia and New Zealand. They were often joined by others from Scotland, where the Reformed Church had been established since 1560.

John Calvin (1509–64) wrote of his sudden conversion to Protestantism but did not clarify exactly when this took place. Clearly he was aware of the teaching of Luther as early as 1523, and may have been influenced by the burning of heretics at that time. In 1534 he refused ordination and took his stand with the Protestants.

The Nicene and Apostles' Creeds are short summaries, fixed in authorized language, of the essential beliefs of the Christian Church. They both evolved from the proclamation of belief of the early Christians, but with the passage of time it became necessary to crystallize these personal confessions of faith at baptism and in order to safeguard orthodoxy. The oldest is the Apostles' Creed, which came into being in the 3rd century; the Nicene Creed came later at the Council of Nicaea in 325. This latter is universally accepted, while the earlier version is not admitted by the Eastern Church.

THE NICENE CREED
WE BELIEVE IN ONE GOD, THE FATHER, THE ALMIGHTY, MAKER OF HEAVEN AND EARTH, OF ALL THAT IS, SEEN AND UNSEEN.
WE BELIEVE IN ONE LORD, JESUS CHRIST, THE ONLY SON OF GOD, ETERNALLY BEGOTTEN OF THE FATHER,
GOD FROM GOD, LIGHT FROM LIGHT
TRUE GOD FROM TRUE GOD, BEGOTTEN NOT MADE, OF ONE BEING WITH THE FATHER.
THROUGH HIM ALL THINGS WERE MADE.
FOR US PEOPLE AND FOR OUR SALVATION HE CAME DOWN FROM HEAVEN:
BY THE POWER OF THE HOLY SPIRIT HE BECAME INCARNATE FROM THE VIRGIN MARY, AND WAS MADE MAN.
FOR OUR SAKE HE WAS CRUCIFIED UNDER PONTIUS PILATE; HE SUFFERED DEATH AND WAS BURIED.
ON THE THIRD DAY HE ROSE AGAIN IN ACCORDANCE WITH THE SCRIPTURES;
HE ASCENDED INTO HEAVEN AND IS SEATED AT THE RIGHT HAND OF THE FATHER.
HE WILL COME AGAIN IN GLORY TO JUDGE THE LIVING AND THE DEAD,
AND HIS KINGDOM WILL HAVE NO END.

WE BELIEVE IN THE HOLY SPIRIT, THE LORD, THE GIVER OF LIFE,
WHO PROCEEDS FROM THE FATHER AND THE SON.
WITH THE FATHER AND THE SON HE IS WORSHIPPED AND GLORIFIED.
HE HAS SPOKEN THROUGH THE PROPHETS.

WE BELIEVE IN ONE HOLY CATHOLIC AND APOSTOLIC CHURCH.

WE ACKNOWLEDGE ONE BAPTISM FOR THE FORGIVENESS OF SINS.

WE LOOK FOR THE RESURRECTION OF THE DEAD AND THE LIFE OF THE WORLD TO COME.
AMEN

THE APOSTLES CREED
I BELIEVE IN GOD, THE FATHER ALMIGHTY, CREATOR OF HEAVEN AND EARTH.

I BELIEVE IN JESUS CHRIST, HIS ONLY SON, OUR LORD.
HE WAS CONCEIVED BY THE POWER OF THE HOLY SPIRIT AND BORN OF THE VIRGIN MARY.
HE SUFFERED UNDER PONTIUS PILATE, WAS CRUCIFIED, DIED, AND WAS BURIED.
HE DESCENDED TO THE DEAD.
ON THE THIRD DAY HE ROSE AGAIN.
HE ASCENDED INTO HEAVEN,
AND IS SEATED AT THE RIGHT HAND OF THE FATHER.
HE WILL COME AGAIN TO JUDGE THE LIVING AND THE DEAD.

I BELIEVE IN THE HOLY SPIRIT

THE HOLY CATHOLIC CHURCH,
THE COMMUNION OF SAINTS,
THE FORGIVENESS OF SINS,

THE RESURRECTION OF THE BODY,
AND THE LIFE EVERLASTING.
AMEN.

John Knox had been in Geneva and was greatly influenced by Calvin. He became the leading spirit in the Reforming movement in Scotland, where there had been martyrdoms at the behest of a demoralized Church and dissatisfaction with the political situation. The parliament approved the abolition of the papal power, a General Assembly met, and very soon the great majority of the population accepted the Calvinist understanding of the faith and the Genevan form of worship, although there had to be organizational extension to accommodate the change in context from city-state to whole nation. Kirk Sessions were set up and synods replaced dioceses. Later, presbyteries were formed round principal towns. For two periods in the seventeenth century the Church was forced to have episcopal rule, but since 1689 the Church of Scotland has been Presbyterian and most people consider themselves in some way related to the Reformed church.

Many Presbyterian Scots moved to Ulster, and from Ulster and Scotland many emigrants went overseas. In Scotland and in Holland the Reformed Churches were several times split by secession when standing for a principle seemed more important then retaining structural unity. In the twentieth century most wounds have been healed and many denominations reunited.

In the early years the Reformed Churches sought to provide for their members who moved abroad, but missionary work came only at the beginning of the nineteenth century. Reformed Churches had their own foreign missionary committees and boards and supported missionaries in Africa, India, China and indeed wherever a foothold could be found. Since the Edinburgh Conference in 1910 the Reformed Churches have co-operated with other Christian agencies in missionary activity.

In Europe the Reformed Church is strong in Switzerland, Holland and Scotland. In England the United Reformed Church, the union of Presbyterians and Congregationalists, is firmly in the Calvinist tradition. In Eastern Europe, Canada, Australia and New Zealand there is a strong presence. In South Korea, Indonesia and Brazil the Reformed Church is fast growing in strength. In the USA most denominations have felt the considerable influence of Calvinism and the Presbyterian Churches.

Most of the Calvinist Churches are members of The World Alliance of Reformed Churches which was formed in 1970 by the union of the World Presbyterian Alliance (1875) and the International Congregational Council (1891). At its full General Council in 1982 it was reported that scattered through 78 nations are 157 autonomous Churches holding the Reformed tradition of which 66 per cent are situated in Asia, Africa and Latin America. The communicant membership was over 70 million and this number would be greatly increased if adherents to the faith were also counted. The Alliance is one of the great federations which play their part in the broad ecumenical movement of the twentieth century, and most Reformed Churches have entered into that movement even though some have seen such action as disloyal to their fathers and to the purity of biblical truth.

BELIEF

The Reformed Churches, following Calvin, have accepted the major doctrines of the Apostolic age expressed in the Apostles', Nicene, and Chalcedonian Creeds with regard to the Holy Trinity and the Person of Christ, and claim to be part of the Holy Catholic (or Apostolic) Church. God is the Loving Father and the Kingdom of God is the gospel taught by the Son. However, Calvin believed that the Fall had made man's mind so perverse that he is unable to profit directly from any natural revelation of God in the world around him. He therefore requires the Holy Scriptures which are inspired and dictated by God and borne witness to by the Holy Spirit. Natural man has not only lost his freedom of will but has been deprived of all understanding of spiritual and eternal things. Yet by God's grace he has retained his admirable capacity to conduct temporal affairs and to pursue the liberal arts and science. Calvin's stress on this capacity of natural man, given to him by the natural grace of God, encouraged secular artistic expression and helped to contribute to the rise of modern science. Calvin stressed both religious and secular education and recognized that humanistic study can assist us to understand Holy Scripture.

Calvin believed that the natural man had no freedom even to decide his own destiny. He is saved only by pure electing grace. The place which he, following Augustine, gave to election in his discussion of justification by faith raised controversy even in his own day. His followers often applied even more rigid logic to the doctrine and they affirmed, without any qualification, that God had from all eternity predestined some to salvation and some to damnation. In reaction, man's free will was re-emphasized in Holland by Jacob Arminius, whose writings were condemned by the Calvinist Synod of Dort in 1618. It affirmed the total depravity of man, irresistable grace, and also the doctrine that Christ died only for the elect. The doctrine of limited atonement did not gain the universal approval of Calvinists since it is difficult to find it in Calvin's own writings or in the Bible itself. With the evangelical revival, Arminianism gained followers, especially among English Methodists. Calvin too had insisted that the Gospel should be freely preached to all men, and a strict doctrine of predestination is not now in the forefront of modern Reformed Church doctrine.

Very important for Calvin and the Reformed Churches has been the doctrine of the Church as the elect body of Christ the King. In its own sphere the Church is never to be subservient to any other authority. The civil magistrate, the State, has a duty to rule in justice and to uphold the Church and allow it to do its appointed tasks, and in return the Christian will be obedient to the civil magistrate in his sphere. In practice, however, the Church has often been in direct opposition to the State, either because of theocratic attempts by the Church or, more often, because of the State's interference with the Church's own life and freedom.

Calvin underlined the need for sanctification as well as justification by faith. He taught the need for obedience to the Ten Commandments interpreted in the light of the Gospel. For him the Christian life was a response to the call of Christ within contemporary society to deny self, take up the Cross of limitation and suffering and follow where He called each one within his own vocation. Such a vocation was possible through the mystery of the believers' living union with Christ. Calvin and the Reformed Churches have always stressed the very close bonds between religion and morals and the direct responsibility of each man to God, for all man's actions and life are under God's approval or judgement. There is stress on the values of integrity, sincerity and hard work. The emphasis on the individual's standing before God meant a new worth for the individual and new resistance to tyranny in Church and State. People in the Reformed tradition were strong in the cause of freedom, and Calvinism put iron into men's souls and made them and their nations strong. It had its part in the development of the enterprising spirit and of real democracy.

As time has passed, the insight of biblical scholars and change in social conditions have to varying degrees altered the working beliefs of most of the Reformed Churches, but the ordered system of Calvinist thought still guides the understanding of the faith of many millions of Christian people.

WRITINGS

Calvin's *Institutes* has never failed to gain widespread recognition, even beyond Presbyterian circles, as one of the greatest theological textbooks ever written. He also wrote Commentaries on nearly all the books of the Old and New Testaments which were desired everywhere in his own day and have continued to prove illuminating and useful. Among his numerous Tracts and Treatises his *Epistle to Sadeleto* is worth singling out as a remarkable defence of his Reformation movement. The national Reformed Churches themselves produced important confessions of faith, among them *The French Confession* (1559), *The Scots Confession* (1560), *The Belgic Confession* (1561), and *The Second Helvetic Confession* (1566). *The Heidelberg Catechism* (1563), prepared by two Reformed theologians of Calvin's time, also became very popular as a means of Christian instruction. Men of Calvinistic conviction among the Puritans, John Owen, Richard Baxter and others, produced a vast amount of homiletic and devotional literature and many political and theological treatises, all reflecting the Reformed outlook. The most important contribution of their times was *The Westminster Confession of Faith* (1647) with its accompanying *Larger* and *Shorter Catechisms*, which were accepted as standards of faith by the Church of Scotland and subsequently, often slightly modified, by many overseas Presbyterian Churches. Along with the Confession was also produced *The Westminster Directory of Public Worship*. *The Savoy Declaration* of 1658 was a modified form of the *Westminster Confession* to suit Congregational Church polity. Many modern attempts have been made to revise the old confessional standards. The United Presbyterian Church in the United States of America prepared and accepted a new Confession of Faith in 1967 which has been given a place alongside the older standards.

In the twentieth century there has been a renewal of Calvin study. Karl Barth owes much to Calvin's writings and those who have seemed to follow Barth in theological outlook have been called Neo-Calvinists. In many Presbyterian circles there has been a renewed interest in the scholastic Calvinism of the seventeenth century and many of the works of Calvinistic Puritans have been reprinted.

WORSHIP

Calvin and those who followed him sought to keep the order simple and relatively free from ritual. Only two sacraments were recognized, Baptism and the Lord's Supper: they alone were dominical and conveyed the promise of God. Musical instruments were at first not used because their sound could not be clearly interpreted, but the vocal singing of the psalms, to tunes which suited the words sung, was always important. Calvin regarded the sermon as the chief sacramental ordinance, God Himself being present to show His face and speak His Word through the human word of the preacher as he expounds Holy Scripture, repeating its promises and commands. Through the preached Word of God is created the faith which unites the believer to Christ, and the gifts which He won for His people are bestowed upon them. Calvin recognized that in the Lord's Supper, too, is the real presence of Christ to give Himself no less powerfully through the visible action of the Lord's table as through the preached Word. Since the Supper is Christ's gift, we may not neglect its celebration. Calvin wished to have it at every Sunday service, but the city men of his day, reacting from former superstition in the Mass, restricted its celebration to four times a year, although they sought to make such infrequent celebrations into very special occasions. One of Calvin's chief concerns in Geneva was that those who led scandalous lives would bring great dishonour to the name of the Lord if they were allowed freely and openly to continue both in participation in the Supper and in their own offensive practices. Therefore, prior to the distribution of the elements, there came the practice of openly forbidding those who were unrepentant of evil behaviour to partake. Church discipline would involve the temporary excommunication of people who persisted in flagrantly immoral behaviour. Unfortunately, the exercise of such discipline led to trivialization and hypocrisy. Calvin denied that the Lord's Supper was simply a visible exhibition to the mind of participants in order to stimulate their memory and faith. He disliked the Lutheran view that Christ was given, 'in, with and under' the elements. Calvin believed that everything that Christ has to give to us we must derive from his humanity which has ascended to heaven. Through our participation in the Sacrament by faith we are enabled by the Holy Spirit's marvellous power to enter into communion with the Ascended Christ and receive the gifts which are signified by the action at the table.

Calvin believed that though the New Testament must be a basic guide, nevertheless the forms of worship developed within the early Church during the first few centuries were closely in accordance with Apostolic teaching and he constructed his liturgy according to these ancient models. Later Puritanism tended to disallow anything not definitely prescribed in Scripture itself. Prayer in private and public worship was always important. As Christ is King and Prophet He is also Priest and it is through Him that God is truly worshipped. Calvin himself tended to use a fairly liturgical order, the Lord's Prayer and Apostles' Creed being included. John Knox prepared a *Book of Common Order* based on the book of Geneva. There was never a strict use of liturgy in the Reformed Churches, however, and much freedom in the order of worship has generally been allowed. *The Westminster Directory* has paved the way for most Presbyterians. For the sake of orderly discipline, Baptism and the Lord's Supper have nearly always been conducted by ordained ministers. Elders at Holy Communion, having themselves received the bread and wine, take them to the members of the congregation seated in their pews, and the bread and cups are passed from hand to hand. Sometimes white cloths have been laid along the pews, a relic of the days when the people came forward to sit at tables, to receive the elements. Often in the past there was an additional address at the time of distribution.

ORGANIZATION

The Reformed Churches, again following Calvin, have had no place for a personal hierarchy in church government. There was to be parity of ministry and the ministers had their special place because their primary duty was to handle the Word of God. They have an 'inner call', by the Holy Spirit, and also an outward call to minister, by the people. They are set apart, admitted or ordained, to work in a congregation. There are also 'doctors' set apart to teach the Word. In Geneva elders were appointed to assist in the 'Consistory' in church government with the ministers, and elders have played a significant part in Calvinist Churches since then. There has been some controversy as to whether the elder's office is purely lay or, since he is 'ordained', partly clerical. It is agreed however that he holds a spiritual office. He helps in the distribution of the elements at Holy Communion and is a member of the Kirk Session, the local congregational court in Presbyterian Churches. He may also be chosen to represent the Session in higher courts.

Presbyterian church government is conciliar, normally with equal representation of ministers and elders with a moderator (or chairman) usually a minister, appointed for a period. The highest court is the Synod or General Assembly which, through committees, administers missionary work and the Church's business and financial affairs. The court for a city or district is usually called a presbytery and it exercises local superintendence and discipline. It deals with overtures and appeals which may go to the General Assembly. It arranges ministerial inductions and its ministers ordain. In a congregation the session is responsible for spiritual matters and there is usually another body, a board or deacons' court, to be concerned with financial matters and upkeep of buildings. In Geneva Calvin provided for 'deacons' to be appointed for the care of the poor, and education; Reformed Churches have appointed deacons for similar purposes. Meetings of the whole congregation have to be held for specific purposes.

In Congregational Churches the congregational meeting exercises local church government, each congregation being independent. However there has been development in the creation of consultative councils in areas and at the national level. Likewise there is other variation in government to meet changing needs in Churches where Calvin's influence has been strong.

The Church of England and The Anglican Communion

HISTORICAL OUTLINE AND PRESENT-DAY DISTRIBUTION

The Church of England as the state-established, reformed church of the English people, independent of the see of Rome, dates from the sixteenth century, when Henry VIII's 'Reformation parliament' renounced the papal jurisdiction. However, as *ecclesia anglicana*, its origins go back to the earliest establishment of Christianity in the British Isles. The Reformation movement in England was to some extent anticipated by the teachings of John Wycliffe (c. 1330–84) and his followers, in particular their emphasis on the Bible as the sole criterion of saving doctrine, to which no ecclesiastical authority might lawfully add, and their denial that the papacy has any firm basis in scripture.

The movement was marked by two phases. The first was a constitutional revolution severing the Church's historic connection with Rome. The second was both more complex and more radical. From 1547 until Mary's retoration of papal authority, the influence of continental Reformers, especially the Swiss Zwingli, was strong. A reformed liturgy in the vernacular, largely the work of Thomas Cranmer (1489–1556), the first non-papist archbishop of Canterbury, was introduced in which characteristic Reformation teaching was clearly presupposed, as well as a series of forty-two 'Articles of Religion' purporting to set out the Reformed Church's doctrinal position. This trend was terminated by Mary in 1553, but resumed on Elizabeth's accession in 1558. The aim of the new monarch's ecclesiastical policy was to secure stability and comprehensiveness in a country whose

The title page from Cranmer's Great Bible which Henry VIII caused to be placed in all churches in his kingdom. The translation of the Bible and the holding of services in the vernacular were important tenets of all Reformation Churches. In England this was very largely the work of Thomas Cranmer (1489–1556), the first non-papist Archbishop of Canterbury.

religious tradition had become fragmented. Henry's anti-papal legislation was restored, with the queen herself as 'Supreme Governor' of the national Church. The 'Elizabethan Settlement', in which the queen's personal authority played a decisive part, thus sought to maintain the historic faith of western Christendom, subject only to such modifications as might be judged necessary in the light of biblical teaching. The liturgy was again revised, if with only relatively minor changes, as were the Articles, now reduced to thirty-nine. Moreover, of vital importance to the Church's claim to historic continuity, as also to the subsequent growth of what has come to be known as the Anglican Communion, was the retention of episcopacy as the requisite form of ministry. In this the Church of England has differed from that of Scotland, which opted for the presbyterian system, and most continental Protestant bodies.

The Elizabethan church had to defend itself against both Rome, a powerful external opponent then in process of self-reformation following the Council of Trent (1545–63), and the Puritan party within, which desired the abolition of episcopacy and the introduction of a new and more Calvinistic service-book. Its most able apologist was Richard Hooker (c. 1554–1600). His *Laws of Ecclesiastical Polity* (1594–7) presented not only the case for episcopal government but a broadly based religious philosophy as the ground of the whole Anglican system. The seventeenth century, despite the Puritan threat which climaxed in the Civil War, is sometimes referred to as the Golden Age of the Church of England, even though episcopacy was abolished during the Commonwealth and the use of the Elizabethan prayerbook prohibited. But with the restoration of the monarchy in 1660 the previous order was reverted to and the Book of Common Prayer (1661–2) adopted by Convocation and Parliament. The latter remained the sole legally recognized liturgy until recent years, when the Alternative Service Book was authorized.

The eighteenth century was not for the most part a time of spiritual vitality, and the established Church's failure to take full advantage of the revivalist missionary work of John Wesley and his brother Charles meant both a spiritual and an institutional loss when the preacher's 'Methodist' followers went into open schism, a division which the abortive reunion discussions of recent years (1958–71) between Anglicans and Methodists have left unhealed. But the evangelical movement in a wider sense did affect the established Church, and the Evangelical party, with its strong scripturalism, eventually acquired a position of influence such as to enable it to become a main force in the Church's life. But the next century witnessed the arrival of new and potent influences. Of these the first was the Oxford or Tractarian movement (1833–45), whose leaders were John Keble, Edward Bouverie Pusey and, above all, John Henry Newman who joined the Roman Catholic Church in 1845. The aim and achievement of the movement, which later gave rise to the Anglo-Catholic party, was to stress the Catholic heritage of the English Church in both doctrine and practice. The second influence was intellectual, resulting from the impact of science and historical criticism, which together were to have a far-reaching effect on the interpretation of the Bible and thus of the entire scheme of inherited Christian belief. The controversies to which it gave rise in the middle decades of the century were at times embittered, but the gradual assimilation by the Church's leadership of these new influences, along with the evangelicalism which linked it to its Reformation past, has produced the characteristic twentieth-century Church ethos of a liberal-

ized Christianity which is at the same time ambivalently Protestant and Catholic. In view of this development Anglicanism may be thought to hold the key to the future advance of the ecumenical interest which now concerns Christendom in general.

Within the last fifty years active membership of the Church of England has declined considerably in relation to the population as a whole, the names on the parish electoral rolls now numbering some 2.75 million. Even so, there is little or no evident demand for disestablishment.

The Anglican communion may be described as the worldwide fellowship of Churches in communication with, and recognizing the leadership of, the see of Canterbury. In addition to the Church of England, it is made up of the Church of Ireland, the Church in Wales, the Episcopal Church in Scotland, the Protestant Episcopal Church in the USA, the Anglican Church of Canada, the Church of England in Australia, and the Churches of the provinces of New Zealand, the West Indies, South Africa and various other parts of the African continent, and parts of China and Japan, as well as some small ecclesiastical groupings elsewhere. The constituent parts of the Anglican Communion outside the British Isles were thus largely the result of colonization and overseas missionary effort. The first overseas bishop was Samuel Seabury, consecrated in 1784 as bishop for the American Church. Later came consecrations for Nova Scotia (1787) and elsewhere in Canada, and in 1814 the first bishop of Calcutta was appointed. The first Australian bishop was consecrated in 1836, and five years la-

ter the diocese of New Zealand was established. South Africa was organized as a separate province in 1853, New Zealand in 1858 and Canada in 1860. Gradually complete independence of both the state and the see of Canterbury was gained by those dioceses that were provincially organized. The Anglican bishops meet periodically as a body at the Lambeth Conference, instituted by Archbishop Longley in 1867.

BELIEF

It was said of the Church of England by a recent archbishop of Canterbury – and in this he could have been speaking for the entire Anglican Communion – that 'we have no doctrine of our own. We only possess the Catholic doctrine of the Catholic Church enshrined in the Catholic Creeds, and these Creeds we hold without addition or diminution'. Despite the Church's 'reformed' character and the circumstances of its chequered history during the Reformation period, this claim has been continuously asserted. Although the Thirty-Nine Articles served at the time of their compilation as a 'platform' to identify the English Church's doctrinal position in relation to other Christian bodies, and more particularly the Roman Catholic Church, it has never fulfilled the role of a 'confession' in the sense that the Confession of Augsburg (1530) or the Second Helvetic Confession (1566), or even the Westminster Confession ratified by the Scottish Church's General Assembly in 1647, have done for Lutherans, Calvinists and Scottish presbyterians respectively. Not that the Articles do not bear clear marks of the controversies of their day: their tone is at times sharply anti-Roman; but they were never intended for use as a creed or as an explanation of some previously accepted theological principle. The doctrines to which the Church understood itself to be committed were those allegedly to be found in scripture and formulated in the decrees of the first four General Councils. On such matters as justification by faith alone or predestination its statements are guarded if not ambiguous. But the infallibility of the Church is questioned and both transubstantiation and – apparently – Zwinglian eucharistic doctrine are excluded, as also are certain Anabaptist teachings, among them pacifism and withdrawal from civic responsibility. Although episcopacy as a form of church polity is vital to Anglicanism inasmuch as no Church not having it could form part of the Anglican Communion, any specific interpretation of it – for example that a Church which lacks it is no real Church at all – has never been authoritatively enjoined, and opinion on the subject is free. Indeed, it is a characteristic of Anglicanism in general, as part of its tradition of comprehensiveness, that it does not demand that doctrines which it holds to be integral to the faith are yet incapable of diverse theological interpretation. This latitude has often no doubt given rise to concern among those who stand for a stricter view of orthodoxy and has at times caused lively dispute. But prosecutions for heresy have been very rare and their outcome invariably the upholding of liberty of interpretation.

WRITINGS

As the Church of England is not a 'confessional' Church, so too is it without a body of writings, such as Calvin's *Institutes of the Christian Religion* or the more famous of Luther's Reformation treatises, which could be said to have had a consistently normative influence upon its teaching. It certainly has had no *summa theologica*, and indeed Anglicanism has never shown itself to be a very favourable soil for the growth of doctrinal systems: Hooker's *Ecclesiastical Polity*, although it has always been accounted a 'classic' of Anglican divinity, is really no exception. Hooker has been read with great interest and respect, but never taken for an oracle. And the same is true of the outstanding Anglican authors of the seventeenth century: Andrewes, Donne, Laud, Thorndike, Taylor, Bramhall, Cosin, Ken and others on what roughly may be termed the 'high church' side, or men like Richard Baxter or the Cambridge Platonists on the Puritan or Latitudinarian. The for-

mer group especially are esteemed as admirably expressive of the Anglican 'mind', but as no more than that. The writings of the leaders of the Oxford movement, Newman in particular, are also representative for their re-emphasis of the Catholic strain in Anglicanism already referred to. But if the Church of England has been little given to systemic theologizing it has not despised 'sound learning', notably in the fields of biblical and patristic study and on the borderline of theology and philosophy, of which the eighteenth-century Bishop Butler's *Analogy of Religion* (1736) is a signal example. For it is of the nature of Anglicanism, with its disinclination to locate the seat of religious authority in either scripture or ecclesiastical tradition exclusively, to assign an important role to reason in its critical and discriminatory function, and its cherished freedom of interpretation is a token of its conviction that private judgement has a necessary place in responsible faith. This may also explain the Anglican aptitude for exploratory thinking, such as has found utterance in a succession of composite volumes: *Essays and Reviews* (1860), *Lux Mundi* (1889), *Foundations* (1912), *Essays Catholic and Critical* (1926) and *Soundings* (1962). In the nineteenth and the early years of the twentieth century the publications of F. D. Maurice, B. F. Westcott, Charles Gore and William Temple were widely influential in broadening the church's outlook, especially on social matters.

RITUAL AND WORSHIP

Apart from the episcopate it is arguably the tradition of worship that provides the cohesive force of Anglicanism, the *lex orandi* being in effect the determining element in the *lex credendi*. In other words, the Anglican liturgy itself furnishes a standard of doctrine, and until the recent liturgical changes were introduced the Church of England's prayerbook stood as a virtual memorial to Thomas Cranmer, whose first English service-book appeared in 1549. The latter was not far removed from the medieval forms of worship, but its successor of 1552 was decidedly more Protestant in tone, although the Elizabethan book of 1559, which replaced it, to some extent corrected the balance. The Book of Common Prayer endorsed by Parliament in 1662 was largely a re-publication of this. The service of Holy Communion is the central rite, with forms for morning and evening prayer daily and various 'occasional' services such as those of baptism and the solemnization of marriage. In the present century liturgical revision was widely felt to be necessary, but an attempt to introduce a revised service-book in 1927–8 proved abortive, since Parliament refused to sanction it, although some of the actual forms given in the book were very commonly used with episcopal sanction. After the Second World War the work was taken up again, using an experimental method of permitting various forms to be tested in practice before deciding on those for which full legal sanction would be sought. This process achieved its goal with the publication of the Alternative Service Book in 1980, since when the 1662 book, the use of which was still to be allowed, has fallen increasingly into abeyance. The new forms have generally, it seems, been welcomed in the parishes, but they have also been criticized on literary grounds and for what many feel to be their lack of spiritual depth, qualities for which the old book was much valued. But the aim of the revision was both to adapt modern idiomatic English for public worship and to enable the congregation to take a more active part in the Church's services.

Elsewhere in the Anglican Communion the original Book of Common Prayer has undergone numerous revisions, the first of which was that of the Scottish prayerbook of 1637. Each Church or province therefore now has its own particular liturgy reflecting its special circumstances, needs and preferences.

ORGANIZATION

The Church of England, with a parish electoral roll membership of about 1.5 million, consists of the two ancient provinces of Canterbury and York, each of which formerly had its own, purely clerical, assembly, known as Convocation. Originally the means by which the clergy taxed themselves, Convocation possessed legislative powers which were retained after the Reformation, although the laity were not represented, their representation, under the state establishment, being held to be in Parliament. The two assemblies still exist, but today, in consequence of the Synodical Government Measure passed in 1969, very nearly all the functions of Convocation, including the power to legislate by canon, were transferred to the General Synod which consists of the three 'houses' of bishops, clergy and laity sitting together, the representatives of the clergy and of the laity being elected. The purpose of the Measure was not only to achieve a more unified form of church government – albeit still subject in certain regards to the ultimate decision of Parliament – but to enable the laity to assume a more direct role in Church government. Synod is required to meet at least twice a year, but can deal with doctrinal and liturgical matters only on the terms proposed by the bishops. Similarly all other parts of the Anglican Communion have their own

representative bodies with appropriate legislative powers. As has already been said, the Anglican bishops meet in conference at Lambeth every ten years. Their decrees have no binding force, but as an expression of the common mind of the episcopate the world over they carry much moral weight.

THE FESTIVALS OF CHRISTIANITY

ADVENT, THE SEASON OF PREPARATION FOR CHRISTMAS, BEGINS THE CHRISTIAN YEAR ON THE NEAREST SUNDAY TO ST ANDREW'S DAY (30 NOVEMBER), AND INCLUDES THE FOUR SUNDAYS BEFORE CHRISTMAS.

CHRISTMAS CELEBRATES THE BIRTH OF JESUS, ON 25 DECEMBER IN THE WESTERN CHURCH AND ON 6 JANUARY IN THE EASTERN CHURCH.

LENT IS THE FORTY-DAY PERIOD IN PREPARATION FOR EASTER, STILL OBSERVED BY MANY CHRISTIANS AS A PERIOD OF FASTING, ABSTINENCE, OR SPECIAL DEVOTION.

GOOD FRIDAY COMMEMORATES JESUS'S DEATH BY CRUCIFIXION.

EASTER SUNDAY CELEBRATES THE RESURRECTION OF JESUS AND, FORTY DAYS LATER, **ASCENSION DAY** HIS ASCENSION TO HEAVEN.

PENTECOST (WHITSUNTIDE), TEN DAYS AFTER ASCENSION DAY, CELEBRATES THE GIFT OF THE HOLY SPIRIT TO THE APOSTLES.

The festivals of Christianity are forms of ritual, some of which the Church has usurped from earlier pagan festivals. For instance the celebration of the Winter Solstice, with its praise of the return of light, became Christmas and so a celebration of the birth of light into the world.

LEFT *Legislation in the Church of England rests with the General Synod which meets twice a year. Here the Archbishop of Canterbury is speaking during a Synod debate on the ordination of women. In 1987, after long deliberation, the Synod voted to accept women into the priesthood, though the first ordination could not be before 1991. In February 1987 the first women were ordained deacons, an office which enables them only to officiate at baptisms and funerals.*

OTHER PROTESTANT CHURCHES AND CHRISTIAN-RELATED MOVEMENTS

The Church Of Scotland

HISTORY AND DISTRIBUTION

The territory that is now Scotland was evangelized in the fifth and sixth centuries, first by St Ninian and his monks from their base at Candida Casa in Galloway, and then by the wave of Irish missionaries led by St Columba who made Iona one of the great centres of western Christianity. Initially Christianity in Scotland largely followed the Irish Celtic mode of organization and understanding. By the mid eleventh century, partly under the influence of King Malcolm Canmore's queen, Margaret, the Scottish Church adopted the customs and practices characteristic of the main western Churches in communion with Rome. By the end of the fifteenth century the Church in Scotland was wealthy and corrupt and widely felt to be oppressive and decadent. The Scottish Reformation was accordingly a far more popular movement than the English Reformation. Its leaders, among whom the most notable was John Knox, appealed to the common people and to the nobility for support against the Crown in their struggle to reform the Church, and the Reformation which was established in 1560 was carried through in the teeth of opposition from the Queen. A century and a half of tempestuous upheavals in Church and State led to the formal establishment of the Church of Scotland as a presbyterian Kirk in 1690. The relationship with the State was still a frequent point of tension which contributed to several secessions in the seventeenth century and in particular to the Disruption of 1843 when nearly half the Church seceded in protest against the political interference in the life of the Church and formed the Free Church of Scotland. In 1929 the main strands of Scottish Presbyterianism were reunited in a Church of Scotland which saw itself as a national Church 'representative of the Christian faith of the Scottish people' with a 'distinctive call and duty to bring the ordinances of religion to the people in every parish in Scotland through a territorial ministry' (*Articles Declaratory* 1929).

As a national Church, the Church of Scotland claims to have responsibilities towards all the people of Scotland, and there was a time when the vast majority of the population were baptized in the Kirk and identified with it. In the present century, and particularly since 1956, there has been a significant decline in the number of baptisms and in the membership of the Church. The adult communicant membership of the Church of Scotland in 1985 was about 900,000 out of an adult population of more than 3½ million. Although membership statistics and church attendance figures are significantly higher in Scotland than in England, the downward trend in both countries is similar. Outside Scotland the Church of Scotland has particularly close relationships with Presbyterian Churches in countries such as the United States, Canada, Australia and New Zealand which were established largely by Scottish emigrants; and the Church of Scotland's involvement in missionary work has led to continuing partnership relations with many Presbyterian or United Churches in Africa and Asia.

BELIEF

Like most of the Churches of the Reformation, the church of Scotland is a confessional Church in the sense that it requires of its ministers and office-bearers some form of subscription to a confession. The fine *Scots Confession* of 1560 was largely superseded by the *Westminster Confession* of 1649, which remains the 'subordinate standard' of the Church. Both confessions are Calvinist in theology, the *Westminster Confession* being a typical product of federal Calvinism. The belief of the Church is still commonly expressed in largely Calvinist terms, but a more liberal age has led to greater respect for freedom of conscience and a looser form of subscription to the *Westminster Confession*.

WRITINGS

In a Church whose life and worship is centred on the Book, the Bible, it is not surprising that most of the influential writings have to do with the Bible. An unbroken stream of published sermons flows, from the remarkable sermons on the Eucharist, *The Mystery of the Lord's Supper*, preached in the High Kirk of Edinburgh by Robert Bruce in the last decade of the sixteenth century, to the many volumes of published sermons by Professor James S. Stewart, the most distinguished of contemporary Scottish preachers. Scottish theological writing has been for the most part biblical and dogmatic and in both areas Scottish theologians have made major contributions. But there is also a strain of passionate devotional writing – excellent examples are Robert Leighton's *Practice of the Presence of God* and Samuel Rutherford's *Letters*.

WORSHIP

The Church of Scotland cherishes freedom in worship combined with shape and dignity. It has no mandatory prayerbook but recognizes the *Westminster Directory of Public Worship* as having some shadowy authority in matters of worship, and from time to time books of guidance for ministers in the conduct of worship, giving models for the various services, are issued. The most notable of these books are the *Book of Common Order, 1940* and the *Book of Common Order 1979*. Traditionally the worship of the Church of Scotland has taken two forms: family worship in the home, conducted daily by the head of the family and consisting of psalm singing, reading of Scripture and extempore prayer; and Sunday worship of the whole congregation in the church, following a simple form and reaching its peak in the sermon. Much Scottish worship was heavily didactic and non-participative, but the Church of Scotland, like other Churches, has been helpfully influenced by the liturgical movement and a movement for the renewal of worship continues. The Eucharist or Holy Communion, commonly called the Lord's Supper, was celebrated infrequently – in most parishes no more than four times a year – but was regarded with great solemnity as the peak of the Church's life.

ORGANIZATION

The Church of Scotland is Presbyterian, that is, it is ruled by courts rather than individuals. In each parish the minister is assisted in pastoral care, leadership and responsibility for the life of the congregation by Elders, men and women ordained to the office for life, who look after a district and meet under the presidency of the minister in the Kirk Session. A Presbytery, consisting of all the ordained ministers and an equal number of elders, has oversight over the parishes in an area roughly equivalent to a diocese and is presided over by a Moderator who holds office for a year. Provincial Synods continue to have a shadowy existence, but the central authority in the Church is the General Assembly, a body of some thirteen hundred ministers and elders. The General Assembly meets for a week each year, presided over by the Moderator who for his year of office acts as a representative of the Church of Scotland but does not have any kind of personal jurisdiction. All the committees of the Church report to the General Assembly which also acts as a court of appeal from the lower courts and sometimes makes pronouncements on issues of the day, being regarded by some as a kind of residual Scottish parliament.

The Baptist Churches

HISTORICAL OUTLINE

The Baptist Churches trace their historical roots to the Anabaptist movement in the sixteenth-century Protestant Reformation. These 'radicals' were fiercely opposed by the 'magisterial' reformers, such as Martin Luther and John Calvin, who were firmly committed to different expressions of the 'state Church' principle: Anabaptists believed in the idea of 'free' Churches, able to order their corporate life, worship and discipline utterly free from state control.

The movement spread though Europe despite increasing persecution which arose largely because of its baptismal doctrine. Opposed to the baptism of infants, seeing it in particular as a sign of incorporation into state Churches, these groups taught and practised the baptism of adult believers as an outward expression of personal commitment to Christ. Initially their baptismal practice was by affusion (pouring over), but this was soon replaced by the more meaningful symbolism of total immersion as an outward and visible sign of identification with Christ in his death and resurrection.

The Baptist movement entered England in the early seventeenth century through exiles returning from Amsterdam who had been influenced by Mennonites (see p. 000); the exiles, led by Thomas Helwys, were Arminian in theology (refuting the notion of predestination and maintaining that Christ's death was fully effective for the salvation of all who believe) and became known as General Baptists. At approximately the same time, some members of a London Independent congregation abandoned their earlier child-baptismal views in favour of believers' baptism, and became known as Particular Baptists because of their Calvinistic conviction that Christ's redemptive work was intended only for an elect.

Concerned about religious liberty since the publication of Helwys's *Mystery of Iniquity* (1612), some early seventeenth-century English Baptists sought freedom in America. In 1639, at Rhode Island, Roger Williams initiated Baptist work which, after early difficulties, spread rapidly throughout the USA from the mid-eighteenth century onwards. Baptist life in Europe was established by J. G. Oncken in Hamburg (1834), but soon extended to other parts of the continent. Baptist Churches were formed in Australia and New Zealand in the early nineteenth century, and in the twentieth century the denomination's work has expanded throughout Asia, Africa and Latin America. World membership figures exceed 31 million.

BELIEF AND WORSHIP

The range of theological views in the Baptist Churches is wide. Each local church is expected to make every aspect of its corporate life subservient to the Lordship of Christ, whose will must be sought by the entire membership. The membership itself is composed specifically of believers who actively wish to be so, in a voluntary – and thus 'pure' – congregation.

Worship services among Baptists have always given central importance to biblical preaching and communion (the Lord's Supper) – in fact, in many churches this is symbolized in visual form in that both the pulpit and the communion table are sited centrally. Moreover, the place of baptism (the baptistery) in most older churches is also central, though ordinarily kept covered; those of newer churches may be located at one side and allowed to remain open.

The usual services on a Sunday are Morning and Evening Service, which consist of the singing of hymns, prayer (sometimes, although not always, extempore), scripture readings and a sermon. Communion is most generally celebrated fortnightly, alternately in the morning and in the evening. Hymns are important at all services. The ordination of ministers takes place in local churches through the imposition of hands.

ORGANIZATION

Each 'gathered' Baptist Church is autonomous: its leaders, minister or pastor, elders or deacons, are all appointed by, and are responsible to, the total membership periodically gathered in 'Church Meeting'. Appreciating their autonomy, Baptist Churches have, at their best, nevertheless consistently opposed self-centred congregational insularity. Their conviction that each Church has a responsibility to help other Churches has been given expression in the life of county or regional Associations – a title that goes back to the mid-seventeenth century.

Each local church is self-financing, its members pledging their support for a full-time ministry. Many small churches, unable themselves to meet the cost of a minister's salary, are supported by funds voluntarily subscribed by other Baptist Churches in order to provide pastoral oversight.

Baptist Churches are affiliated to national Unions (as in the Baptist Union of Great Britain and Ireland) or Conventions (as in the Southern Baptist Convention of America). The forum for international co-operation is the Baptist World Alliance, formed in 1905, which has several Commissions to deal with a variety of denominational concerns.

The Methodist Church

HISTORICAL OUTLINE

Methodism originated through the activity of John Wesley (1703–91), a priest of the Church of England. While he was teaching at Lincoln College, Oxford, he belonged to a religious society the members of which, because of their methodi-cal devotion, were nicknamed 'Methodists'. A longing for a deeper religious experience led him to work in the new American colony of Georgia, but he returned to England still unsatisfied. Then, partly under Moravian influence, he sought 'justifying', saving faith, and on 24 May 1738 attained it at a meeting in Aldersgate Street, London. In his *Journal* he wrote: 'I felt my heart strangely warmed. I felt I did trust in Christ, Christ alone for salvation; and an assurance was given me that He had taken away *my* sins, even *mine*, and saved *me* from the law of sin and death.'

His ministry then became effective, and he soon began open-air preaching. The rest of his life was spent in constant travelling, preaching throughout Great Britain and Ireland and gathering his followers into societies. Preachers, mostly laymen, were sent 'in connexion with Mr Wesley' to preach throughout the land, and some eventually went overseas. From 1744 onwards, the preachers met with him annually in conference; forty years later, by a legal deed, he arranged for the continuation of the conference after his death.

It was in that same year, 1784, in response to an appeal from his followers in North America, that Wesley finally broke from the customs of the Church of England, in which only bishops may ordain, by ordaining two men as deacons, and next day as elders, for the work in America; Dr Thomas Coke, who was already a priest in the Church of England, he ordained to be superintendent there. Later he also ordained men for Scotland, England and other parts of the world.

Wesley did not regard himself as having separated from the Church of England. The 'people called Methodists', as they came to be known, had simple preaching-services at times different from regular church hours, and their societies met in groups known as bands and classes, but all these 'means of grace' were regarded as supplementary to the services of the Church of England. Wesley's brother Charles (1707–88) wrote thousands of hymns for Methodist use, now known and enjoyed by many other denominations.

The word 'Methodist' was used to describe various bodies only loosely connected with the Wesleys, especially the Calvinistic Methodists of Wales, now called the Presbyterian Church of Wales; the term is best restricted to those more directly linked with John Wesley.

After his death a gradual separation from the Church of England took place, which became virtually complete in 1795, after which the travelling preachers – who were distinguished from unpaid local preachers – assumed the right to administer the sacraments, and thus fulfilled the role of Christian Ministers of word and sacraments in charge of congregations. This body came to be known as the Wesleyan Methodist Church.

From 1836 onwards, all the travelling preachers were ordained by prayer and the imposition of hands. Other bodies broke from it on various grounds, notably the Primitive Methodists in 1811, and several smaller bodies, most of whom in 1907 formed the United Methodist Church. The three bodies, Wesleyan, Primitive and United joined in 1932 to form the Methodist Church.

Sunday service in a Methodist chapel: the minister receives the offering box. There are no rules about what the preacher should wear: some favour the gown with cassock and bands but for others a dark suit suffices. Methodist hymns are well known, many having been written by Charles Wesley, brother of the founder.

BELIEF

Methodists claim that they hold no doctrines other than the common faith of all Christians, but that they have distinctive emphases; all need to be saved; all can be saved by grace through faith (the free will of Arminianism as opposed to the predestination of Calvinism); all can know that they are saved (the witness of the Spirit); all can be saved to the uttermost (perfect love).

The doctrinal standards of British Methodism state that the Methodist Church claims and cherishes its place in the holy catholic Church which is the Body of Christ. It accepts the fundamental principles of the historic creeds and of the Protestant Reformation. The doctrines of the evangelical faith are based upon the divine revelation recorded in holy scripture. These doctrines are contained in Wesley's *Notes on the New Testament* and the first forty-four of his *Sermons*.

WORSHIP

The authorized services are in *The Methodist Service Book* (1975), and the official hymnbook is *Hymns and Psalms* (1983). Methodism observes the gospel sacraments, baptism and the Lord's Supper, and still has fairly simple preaching services, and other meetings for fellowship.

HOW THE METHODIST CHURCH IS GOVERNED IN BRITAIN

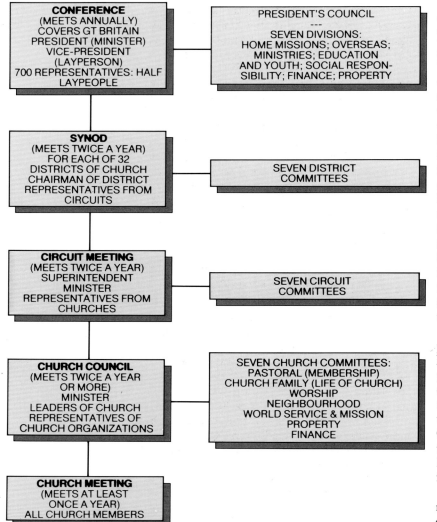

ORGANIZATION

The governing body in (for example) British Methodism is still the annual conference, with its ministerial president and lay vice-president. The 'connexion', as it is called, is divided into districts, each with its synod and a chairman; and then into circuits, usually with several ministers, one of whom is superintendent; and then into local churches. There is a complex constitutional structure in which lay people have a considerable part. Seven divisions organize the central activities of the Church. The ordained ministers are theologically regarded as 'presbyters', (a word which, based on the Greek word *presbyteros*, literally translated 'elder', was used in the New Testament (e.g. Acts 14:23) as a description of Christian ministers in pastoral charge of local churches, and is now widely used as a technical term to describe those ordained to preach the word and administer the sacraments). There are also deaconesses who are ordained, local preachers, class-leaders, stewards, Sunday-school teachers, and so on.

There are now Methodist Churches in many parts of the world. Nowhere, however, is a Methodist Church 'established' (with state support); each therefore has to be financed almost entirely by the voluntary contributions of its members. Nevertheless, all do much charity work. They also belong to the World Council of Churches. Much the largest Methodist Church is the United Methodist Church of America which, like most of the Churches which have sprung from it, is episcopal.

The World Methodist Council comprises more than sixty autonomous or semi-autonomous conferences, and a total community of about 50 million people.

The United Reformed Church

HISTORY AND DISTRIBUTION

The United Reformed Church in England and Wales (often known as the URC) was formed in 1972 from the union of a large majority of congregations of the Congregational Church in England and Wales and the Presbyterian Church of England – the first union across denominational lines in these countries since the Reformation. In 1981 it became the URC in the United Kingdom, following a further union with the Re-Formed Association of Churches of Christ (better known in North America as the Disciples), some congregations of which were in Scotland. It has thus inherited three Reformation tendencies: the classical Reformed tradition of Calvin, the more radical separatist and independent movement, and the revival of believer Baptist teaching in eighteenth century Scotland and nineteenth-century America.

The URC belongs to the British Council of Churches, the World Alliance of Reformed Churches and the World Council of Churches, and sees its life as a part of the search for the visible unity of all God's people to which it is pledged. In British terms it is a small denomination. In 1984 it had about 140,000 members and 55,000 children in nearly 2000 congregations served by some 1250 ministers, 10,000 teachers and 1000 lay preachers. Some congregations are part of local ecumenical united churches. The

URC has close links with other Reformed Churches in the British Isles, Europe and other parts of the world; sister Churches in North America include the United Church of Canada, the United Church of Christ, the Disciples of Christ, and Congregational and Presbyterian Churches in the USA. Through the Council for World Mission, the successor to the older missionary societies, it shares in a partnership of mostly English-speaking Churches from a Congregational and Presbyterian background, and both sends people to work abroad and also welcomes into its own life workers from the younger Churches.

BELIEF AND WRITINGS

The URC confesses itself to be part of the Church Catholic and Reformed and shares its faith in one God, Father, Son and Holy Spirit. It acknowledges the Word of God in the Old and New Testaments, discerned under the guidance of the Holy Spirit, as the supreme authority for the faith and conduct of all God's people. It receives with thanksgiving the witness to the Catholic faith of the Apostles' and Nicene Creeds, as also the declarations of faith of its own particular heritage: among Presbyterians, the Westminster Confession (1649) and *A Statement of the Christian Faith* (1956); among Congregationalists, the Savoy Declaration (1658) and *A Declaration of Faith* (1967); among Churches of Christ, Thomas Campbell's *Declaration and Address* (1806). These declarations and confessions serve to define the tradition in which the URC stands, but they are not used to impose a standard of credal orthodoxy upon ministers or people. The URC stands in the mainstream of Reformed belief and practice, though liberal, evangelical and neo-orthodox theology and liturgical and charismatic renewal have all been influential.

Because if its recent formation, there has not been time for a tradition of writings characterizing the thought and life of the Church to emerge. Alongside liturgical material, the main official publications are *The Manual* (second edition, London 1984), which contains the Scheme of Union and other documents governing the procedures of the Church, and the annual Year Book. Many shorter booklets, study guides and discussion papers are also produced.

WORSHIP

The ordering of worship rests with the local congregation, though much in practice devolves on to the minister. The commonest pattern is, as in other Free Churches, a preaching service with hymns, readings and prayers. Both infant and believers' baptism are practised; the lectionary is followed in some churches; the Eucharist is celebrated with varying (but increasing) frequency, weekly or quarterly in some congregations, once or twice a month in most. Freer forms of worship are used in some places, and family services have become popular. Worship tends to be simple but orderly and dignified, and hymn-singing is the chief means of congregational participation. Hymnody remains important. Watts and Doddridge were Congregationalists, metrical psalms came from Presbyterianism, and several modern hymn-writers have come from the URC (for example Erik Routley, Albert Bayly and Fred Kaan). *A Book of Services* in the URC's official liturgical publication.

ORGANIZATION

Church order represents a joining of elements from the uniting traditions. Church Meeting, the gathering of all members of the local congregation, exercizes authority over its life at the local level. From it elders are elected to take collegial responsibility with the minister(s) for pastoral, spiritual and administrative work. It calls ministers, though District Council must concur with the call. Elders are ordained for life but serve for specific periods, often with groups of members in their care. District Council has a wider authority, and the Districts are grouped in twelve Provinces which are each presided over by a Moderator appointed by General Assembly. Moderators share a ministry or *episkope* with the conciliar bodies, oversee ministerial movements, offer pastoral care to the ministry and preside at ordinations. The final court of the Church is General Assembly, the decisions of which are authoritative. Only General Assembly can rule on doctrinal matters. Each year it elects a Moderator, an office open to men and women, lay and ordained.

Most ministers are trained in one of the three theological colleges, in Cambridge, Manchester and Oxford, though the recent development of a non-stipendiary auxiliary ministry has modified traditional patterns of training and work. The ordained ministry is open to men and women: the first woman Congregational minister, Constance Mary Coltman, was ordained as long ago as 1917. The URC also commissions a number of Church-related Community Workers. At the national level Assembly appoints specialist committees to serve different areas of the Church's life. These work within five central departments: Faith and Life; Ministries; World Church and Mission; Church and Society; Finance and Administration.

The Brethren

HISTORICAL OUTLINE

The Brethren, often called – except by themselves – the Plymouth Brethren, are a Protestant denomination originating about 1825 in an informal group of young men in Dublin who were impatient with the ecclesiastical barriers which prevented them from enjoying the full intercommunion they believed to be desirable. About three years later they were joined by a clergyman of the Church of Ireland, John Nelson Darby (1800–1882), a godson of Admiral Nelson and a man of powerful personality. His energy caused the movement to spread widely in Great Britain and Ireland and on the continent of Europe. His tendency to impose his own 'High Church' judgements on others, however, led in 1848 to a division between those who accepted his discipline, commonly called Exclusive Brethren, and those who rejected it, commonly called Open Brethren.

Exclusive Brethren form a tightly knit and centrally controlled community; Open Brethren, on the other hand, hold and practise the autonomy of each local congregation.

BELIEF

In doctrine the Brethren are orthodox and evangelical. Apart from one Exclusive party they accept the traditional Christology of the Councils of Nicaea and Chalcedon, believing it to be in accord with the teaching of scripture. They believe in Christ as the incarnate Son of God, born of the Virgin Mary, who by his death opened up the way of salvation for all believers; they believe in his bodily resurrection, his present high-priestly ministry, and his Second Coming.

Traditionally the Brethren have shared the Puritan attitude to popular entertainments common to the majority of Protestant evangelicals in the English-speaking world, although this has been much modified in the television age.

Energetically applying themselves to the propagation of the gospel, they engage in a thriving foreign missionary enterprise.

WORSHIP

Holy Communion (the Lord's Supper) is normally celebrated weekly; Sunday morning worship centres around it, and it is open to all Christians to share it. It is a completely open service; some might consider it unstructured, as it is conducted according to no fixed order. The offering of thanks for the bread and the cup is not confined to specific persons, and the members pass the bread and cup from hand to hand.

Baptism (among Open Brethren) is normally administered by total immersion or personal confession of faith.

ORGANIZATION

The Brethren have no ordained ministry in the customary sense. Local congregations are guided by elders and served by deacons. Those who are manifestly gifted for an evangelistic or teaching ministry are encouraged to develop these gifts; many of those who do so exercise their ministry over a wide area, not confining it to one congregation. This shared ministry helps to provide a theological infrastructure; in addition, the social infrastructure is strong enough to foster and maintain a world-wide sense of fellowship.

Organized in this way, along strictly congregational lines, the Open Brethren have no federal mechanism to co-ordinate even local Churches. But individual congregations readily join with others on an *ad hoc* basis for various purposes – united evangelism, Bible study and so on – and for these purposes they are as likely to join with neighbouring Churches of other denominations as with other Brethren congregations.

Each congregation is financed by voluntary and systematic gifts from members. Both congregations and individual members contribute to foreign missions and other charitable causes. The Brethren's foreign missionary work is administered by a committee comprising the editors of the monthly periodical *Echoes of Service*, based in Bath, England.

The Pentecostal Churches

HISTORICAL OUTLINE AND PRESENT-DAY DISTRIBUTION

The roots of the Pentecostal Churches are found both in the nineteenth-century Holiness Movement (which itself developed out of John Wesley's doctrine of sanctification) and in the oral spirituality of the former slaves in the USA. In fact, most Pentecostal historians consider the main root of their Churches to have been the 1906 evangelical revival in Los Angeles, led by one of the most remarkable 'saints' of this century, black ecumenist William J. Seymour (1870–1922). He was the initiator of this inter-racial and inter-cultural movement. Soon, however, the emerging Pentecostal Churches came under heavy pressure from the established Churches to conform to what was considered at the time to be decent Christian behaviour – namely, to separate themselves into segregated congregations, black and white. This they did, and today the most important Churches on the white side are the different denominations of the Churches of God and the Assemblies of God (of about 1,500,000 adherents), and on the black side the Church of God in Christ (some 1,600,000).

The segregation, however, did not hinder the Pentecostal Churches from spreading across the world. All the same, their relationship to the independent non-white indigenous Churches now emerging in the Third World (of about 80 million adherents) is somewhat ambiguous. Many of these independent Churches in India and Africa have had contacts in the past with Western Pentecostal missionaries, and the majority of them show phenomenological parallels to the early Pentecostalism of Los Angeles.

Of the total of about 30 million adherents of Pentecostal Churches, the largest number in any one country is in Brazil where one Church alone, the Assembléias de Deus, counts four million members, and where the Igreja Evangélica Pentecostal – a member-Church of the World Council of Churches – counts one million. In Chile, some 10 per cent of the total population are Pentecostals. And there are large numbers of adherents also in Central America and Caribbean countries, Indonesia, Korea, the Soviet Union, and many countries in Africa. In Western Europe – apart from in Norway, Sweden and Italy – Pentecostals are numerically weak. (In the UK, for example, the Assemblies of God numbers 70,000 members, Elim Pentecostal Church 45,000.) Statistics and research on Pentecostalism are still in their infancy because the picture is changing from year to year. Furthermore, many Third World Pentecostal Churches do not have a centralized organization, and there are differences between the Churches as to exactly who may be counted as a member.

BELIEFS AND WORSHIP

The reason for the fast growth of the Pentecostal Churches in the Third World does not lie in any particular Pentecostal doctrine – doctrinally, the Pentecostal Churches do not in fact form a consistent whole, nor can they therefore have a representative international organization.

The reason for their growth lies in their simple and popular appeal, founded again on the absolute naturalness and faith of their black roots, and can be summarized accordingly: a liturgy that is almost entirely oral; theology and witness that are virtually all-narrative; maximum participation at the levels of reflection, prayer and decision-making, and therefore a community which is interdependent and communicative; the inclusion of dreams and visions into personal and public forms of worship, functioning in some fashion as icons for the individual and the community; and an understanding of the body-mind relationship that is informed by experiences of the correspondence between body and mind – the most striking application of which is the ministry of healing by prayer.

In Europe and North America, on the other hand, the Pentecostal Churches are fast developing into an evangelical middle-class religion. Many of the elements vital for its rise and expansion in the Third World are inapplicable to the West; they are being replaced by efficient fund-raising structures, a stream-lined ecclesiastical bureaucracy and a Pentecostal conceptual theology. In Europe and North America this theology follows the evangelical traditions, to which is added the belief in a 'baptism of the Spirit', generally (but not always) characterized by the 'initial sign' of speaking in tongues.

To list the several hundred Pentecostal denominations would be beyond the scope of this entry. Among them, however, one finds trinitarian and non-trinitarian, infant- and adult-baptizing Churches. In the Third World many of them have gone far in incorporating indigenous African, Indian or Latin American cultural traditions and religious rituals into their belief-system and practice. And as much as these Churches are thoroughly indigenous, most of their literature (if indeed they produce any literature) never reaches the West. That is the reason for the false impression that most Pentecostal Churches have a theology and a spirituality akin to the American Assemblies of God: from a worldwide point of view this is a minority stance within the Pentecostal Churches.

The Pentecostal Churches believe that the outpouring recorded in chapter 2 of the New Testament book The Acts of the Apostles, has been repeated in their Churches with the accompanying signs of speaking in tongues, prophecy, visions, healing the sick, and – in the case of many black and Third World Churches – a reconciliatory ministry between the races and classes.

The most challenging question with which Pentecostal Churches are faced is what the difference is between a Pentecostal experience of the Holy Spirit and similar experiences in the secular world and in non-Christian religions. Pentecostals answer that the difference lies in the 'fruit', by which they usually understand the acceptance of specific ethical or cultural behaviour patterns which are (or are thought to be) typically Christian. But this position rests on flimsy foundations, for it is very difficult for Pentecostals to reach a common agreement on these behaviour patterns. Some would include certain food taboos, others would not. Some think that the principle of non-violence is a *sine qua non* for a Pentecostal. Others, particularly in the Western tradition, see as a duty the support they give to the power politics of their government. Even if they could agree on these behaviour patterns, it would still be difficult to see them as a distinguishing feature, because many of the ethical and cultural 'fruits' of Pentecostal Churches (neighbourly love, care for the poor, honesty, and purity) appear also in non-Christian persons and societies, both religious and non-religious.

The Society of Friends ('The Quakers')

HISTORICAL OUTLINE AND PRESENT-DAY DISTRIBUTION

The Society of Friends, whose nickname the 'Quakers' – originally intended to be derogatory – has persisted, came into being in England in the mid-seventeenth century. Men and women dissatisfied with the religious life of the various Reformed Churches responded to the preaching of George Fox (1624–91), son of a Leicestershire weaver, coming to share his sense of Christ as inward teacher, and to feel that they had recaptured authentic early Christian experience. Fox and some sixty fellow evangelists, mainly farmers, quickly established worshipping groups (meetings) throughout England. They met in silence to 'wait upon the Lord', the silence usually being broken at intervals by spontaneous messages or prayers. Various outward practices soon further distinguished Friends as a separate radical sect: plain clothes, plain speech (the use of 'thee' and 'thou' to all, irrespective of social status), refusal to remove the hat as a token of respect and, in obedience to what they held as Jesus's command, refusal to take oaths – practices that led to persecution under both the Commonwealth and the Restoration in England.

At present there are nearly 142,000 Friends in the Americas, approaching 43,000 in Africa, some 18,000 in Great Britain, and smaller groups in other areas including Australia and New Zealand, most of the countries of northern Europe, India, Taiwan and Japan.

BELIEF

Rejecting Calvinist concepts of depravity and election, Friends stressed 'the Light which lighteth every man'. Today they still speak of the 'inward Light' and of 'that of God in every one' which enables them to respond to the leadings of the Holy Spirit, felt as power making for righteousness and unity, and giving guidance. Experience of such leadings has been determinative of Friends' understanding of Christianity. The seventeenth-century Quaker theologian Robert Barclay thus saw the catholic Church as the company of those led by the Spirit, and affirmed that 'there may be members both among heathens, Turks and Jews and all the several sorts of Christians'. He saw the scriptures as 'a secondary rule, subordinate to the Spirit, from which all have their excellency', a view shared by most modern Friends. The central conviction of 'that of God' has led to a general confidence in working for the kingdom of God throughout the world. Particular emphasis is given to the relief of suffering and prison reform.

Friends do not ordain ministers or observe other outward sacraments. Men and women share equally in the life of the fellowship. Creeds are seen as divisive, and in mainstream Quakerism assent to credal statements is not required. This has led to some Christological diversity, yet most Friends in practice regard Jesus's death on the cross as a revelation of divine love rather than as an atoning sacrifice.

WORSHIP

In much of the world, Friends' worship has changed little in form since the seventeenth century, although meetings are shorter (lasting usually for about one hour). In the western United States, however, frontier conditions led meetings to appoint pastors who arranged 'programmed' non-conformist-style services. Such worship obtains also in East Africa, Latin America and other areas where missionaries from these meetings have worked.

Worship may be held in Friends' homes or in meeting-houses, which are simple unconsecrated buildings. Mid-week meetings and study and discussion groups are common.

In meetings for church affairs members seek to discern the will of God. A 'clerk' takes the 'sense of the meeting' (decisions are never made by voting). Two volumes of 'discipline' – *Christian Faith and Practice in the Experience of the Society of Friends* and *Church Government* – are important handbooks and are periodically revised.

ORGANIZATION

In Britain local meetings are grouped geographically into Monthly Meetings, which in turn convene under the aegis of the London Yearly Meeting and its anachronistically-named standing committee, the Meeting for Sufferings. There is no hierarchy; all members are free to attend Monthly and Yearly Meetings and to participate in decision-making. Elders and Overseers are appointed for three-yearly periods to take special responsibility for the meeting for worship and pastoral care. The work of the Society is financed mainly by voluntary donation, although there is some investment income.

Organization in other countries is similar, although not identical, for every Yearly Meeting is autonomous. In the USA most of the thirty-two Yearly Meetings are linked in four main groupings: Friends United Meeting and Evangelical Friends Alliance (especially mission-oriented); Friends General Conference (more service-oriented); and Conservative Friends.

Friends early on developed 'testimonies', concerning for instance simplicity of life, integrity in business, and opposition to war. As individuals and through committees they have sought to promote peace and social justice, and to relieve the victims of war.

What is seen as the credal basis on which most Councils of Churches are founded has made many Quaker groups unwilling to accept full membership, but there are Friends involved in the ecumenical movement at all levels. The Friends' own World Committee for Consultation fosters understanding and co-operation, and gives the Friends status as a non-governmental organization at the United Nations.

But my *Troubles* continued, and I was often under great Temptations; and I fasted much, and walked abroad in Solitary Places many Days, and often took my *Bible*, and went and fate in hollow Trees and lonefome Places, till Night came on

A modern etching by Robert Spence of George Fox, the founder of the Society of Friends. In his journal (1647) Fox wrote: 'when all my hopes in all men were gone, so that I had nothing outwardly to help me, nor could tell what to do, then, oh then I heard a voice which said "there is one, even Christ Jesus, that can speak to thy condition"'.

The Unitarians

The Unitarian symbol of the flaming chalice, representing the flame of living truth within the cup of shared faith.

HISTORICAL OUTLINE AND PRESENT-DAY DISTRIBUTION

Unitarianism is the name most usually given – since the end of the eighteenth century and in some places even earlier – to a very radical form of Protestant Christianity originating among some of the more extreme Anabaptists and a group of Spanish and Italian humanists, who from the time of the Reformation onwards began to query such basic doctrines as the Trinity (God as Father, Son and Spirit), the divinity of Christ, and Christ's atonement for the sins of the world. A typical early representative was the Spanish doctor Michael Servetus, author of *The Terrors of the Trinity* (1531), who was burned to death as a heretic at Geneva in 1553.

Unitarian communities were first established in Poland (1565) and in Transylvania (1568). In Transylvania, the Church founded by Francis David (Dávid Ferenc, 1520–79) – the first to use the name 'Unitarian' – survives to the present day, a well-established Hungarian-speaking movement with 120 congregations in Romania and ten in Hungary. From about 1580, the leadership of the Church in Poland was assumed by Faustus Socinus (1539–1604), who so stamped his personality upon it that those who later came under its influence were known as Socinians. At first influential, by 1660 it had been completely suppressed; nevertheless, refugees carried its ideals – especially its faith in reason and tolerance – to many parts of Europe, including Britain.

John Biddle (1615–62) has sometimes been called 'the Father of English Unitarianism', but the movement did not become established in Britain until the end of the eighteenth century, when some of the Dissenting congregations (notably the English Presbyterians) embraced Socinianism under the leadership of Joseph Priestley (1733–1804) and others. Unitarian views had also penetrated the Established Church, and in 1774 Theophilus Lindsey – having resigned Anglican orders – founded in London the first avowedly Unitarian Church in England. From this time the name Unitarian rather than Socinian was preferred. The movement grew extensively in the nineteenth century, and there were some accessions from General Baptists and Methodists. James Martineau (1805–1900) reduced its dependence on scriptural authority and increased its spiritual depth. In Ireland, a group of churches of Presbyterian origin had moved in a Unitarian direction. The formation in 1928 of the 'General Assembly of Unitarian and Free Christian Churches' marked the final establishment of a definite Unitarian denomination in the UK (where there are now some 200 active congregations).

In the USA, the first Unitarian congregation – at King's Chapel, Boston (1785) – had an Anglican background, but the main Unitarian movement emerged early in the nineteenth century among the New England Congregationalists under the influence of William E. Channing. The American Unitarian Association was founded at Boston in 1825. Thanks to Theodore Parker, R. W. Emerson and others, later American Unitarianism became increasingly radical. The Universalist Church of America, founded in 1793, had also by this time adopted a Unitarian theology. In 1961 the two bodies came together to form the Unitarian-Universalist Association, now a vigorous and influential denomination with some 1,000 congregations or groups.

BELIEF

Unitarians have always been suspicious of abstruse dogma, repudiating the Trinity, and placing supreme emphasis on the unity and benevolence of God. Jesus Christ is not thought of as a personal manifestation of the Deity, and although at first some could accept him as a heavenly messenger worthy of adoration, later Unitarians came to regard him primarily as a supremely gifted but unequivocally human religious teacher and prophet. Correspondingly, the basic assumptions of Christian 'salvation' are now generally rejected. Unitarians believe in the essential goodness of human nature and see something of God in all people. The death of Jesus is thought of as an inspiring example of dedication and self-sacrifice. The earlier Unitarians accepted the notion of a physical resurrection, but most of the story is now interpreted in a symbolic fashion.

Although most Unitarians nevertheless still regard themselves as Christians, some – particularly in the USA – have now espoused a non-theistic form of religious humanism, and among all Unitarians there is an increasing tendency to look to other world faiths and not merely to the Judaeo-Christian tradition.

The imposition of fixed creeds in religion is in any case regarded as unacceptable, and in the English-speaking Churches especially, no confession of faith is required of either ministers or members. This has resulted in a ready acceptance of a wide variety of differing beliefs, practices, church architecture and forms of worship.

GODS AND GURUS

In some religious traditions the notion of portraying God in painting or sculpture is regarded with repugnance. How can one depict the divine in human or animal terms? Other traditions see value in using visual analogies to help people to approach the majesty of God. So images or pictures are used to encourage meditation or to provide a focus for worship. The use of images may also reflect beliefs about ways in which a transcendent God is made known in the world, and so may represent the stories of

Shiva as Lord of the Dance (Nataraja), a south Indian bronze. The tongue of flame (upper left hand) symbolizes the destruction of the world; sound (the drum in the upper right hand) signifies creation. Dancing on the body of a demon, Shiva perfectly balances creation and destruction.

avatars or other manifestations among people of the divine power or presence. Not all the illustrations here are of gods. Some are of great teachers, founders of religions or spiritual guides, who, in some cases, are believed to embody God-like qualities in their own lives.

ABOVE *Susana-wo-no-Mikoto ('the impetuous male deity') was often represented in Shinto mythology as malevolent. This painting shows the climax to the story of his destruction of the rice fields of Amaterasu, the central figure of Shinto worship. Amaterasu retreated into a cave, leaving the world in darkness. She refused to come out until a divine dance enticed her to the cave's entrance, where she saw her face in a mirror that the gods had hung on a tree. Her light was thus restored to the world. Amaterasu's representation or dwelling-place is a mirror, the symbol of the sun.*

RIGHT *Surya, or Savitar, the sun-god of the Rig Veda, being drawn across the sky in his one-wheeled chariot, which represents the annual cycle. The chariot is drawn either by seven horses or, as here, by a seven-headed horse. Surya was one of the greatest gods of the Rig Veda, a distinction he shared with Indra and Agni. He is variously described as 'the eye of Varuna' (the sky), the husband of Usha (the dawn), and as Vivasvat, 'the brightly shining one'.*

FAR RIGHT *A nineteenth-century Nepalese Tantric mandala. A Buddhist mandala is a diagram which serves as an aid to meditation. At the centre there is normally a figure of a bodhisattva, surrounded by an entourage. A square enclosed by the wider circle indicates the especially sacred area of the mandala. Around the outer circle are illustrations of legends from the life of the central character, Avalokiteshvara, a bodhisattva of infinite compassion. Meditation upon the mandala invites gradual identification with the One represented at the centre.*

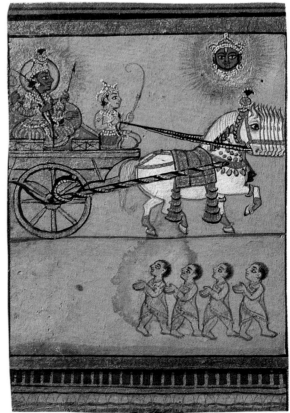

ABOVE Lord Vishnu reclining on the serpent Shesha in the act of creation. From his navel sprouts a lotus, from which the god Brahma appears to create the world. Symbols associated with Vishnu are shown here: a mace, a lotus, a conch, and a discus. The star-shaped jewel is a sign of Vishnu's immortality. At his feet sits his wife Lakshmi, goddess of good fortune and beauty. Vishnu became one of the two great gods of Hinduism (the other being Shiva), and is believed to have appeared on earth in a number of incarnations or avatars, the greatest of which were Rama and Krishna.

RIGHT A representation of the Prophet Zoroaster, or Zarathushtra, founder of the religion of Zoroastrianism. The fire that Zoroaster holds is an important symbol, signifying divine purity, presence and power. The star-like halo is derived from an early artistic convention in Zoroaster's native Iran. Zoroastrian teaching represents life as a battle between good and evil, and influenced Jewish and Christian ideas.

RIGHT An eleventh-century carving of the mother goddess Ambika from a Jaina temple in Orissa. Ambika is a nature goddess who features in the Hindu Puranas in stories of Shiva; but she was also regarded as the messenger of the Jaina Tirthankara Nemi, and so has a significant place in Jaina religion. She is associated with autumn and with the harvest.

LEFT A reclining-Buddha statue in Rangoon. Although the earliest forms of Buddhism avoided representations of the Buddha, images (or Buddha-rupa) are found from at least the second century CE in India and became widespread in Buddhist countries. Some particular features reflected teaching about the '32 characteristics of a great man', in which certain conventional signs (such as elongated ears and the mark on the forehead) were taken to indicate a future Buddha, and so were incorporated into images in order to aid meditation. Similarly, the size of the figure suggests that the Buddha fills the whole universe.

RIGHT A statue of Confucius in the Bamboo Temple, Kunming, China. Confucius, or Kong-fu-zi, has been regarded by Confucians and others as essentially a great man and teacher rather than as in any sense divine. In spite of this, many temples were erected in his honour and sacrifices offered in his name, including state sacrifices performed by the emperor. Many Confucians, however, regarded such sacrifices as ritualized occasions for instilling Confucian values rather than as ways of appeasing gods or spirits.

ABOVE LEFT A stone image of a fox guards the inari at Oinarinjinja, Gion, Kyoto. The fox-shrine is dedicated to the kami of the rice fields. Such inari, or fox-shrines as they are called, are common in rural Japan. The fox is regarded as a messenger of those kami who are connected with agriculture and fertility. Originally concerned with appeasing foxes and preventing damage to crops, the inari are now looked upon as fertility symbols.

ABOVE A statue of Lao-Tzu at Chun Pen Taoist temple near Chengon in Sichuan Province. Lao-Tzu (or Lao-zi) is traditionally the author of the Tao-tê Ching and an older contemporary of Confucius. He is an enigmatic figure, about whom little is known. Taoist temples flourished in China: some were great public temples which were also major monastic centres; others were hereditary temples, in which control was retained in the hands of a sect or sub-sect.

ABOVE *The ten Gurus of Sikhism. The Sikhs had ten great leaders, or Gurus, between 1499 and 1708. Guru Nanak (centre top, with attendant on his left) is revered as the founder of Sikhism, and his pre-eminence is illustrated here.*

RIGHT *Shri Sathya Sai Baba, a modern guru who is regarded as an avatar and a miracle-worker by his followers, here receives requests for help at his ashram in India.*

ORGANIZATION

A professional ministry is retained, largely on pragmatic grounds, since the movement fully accepts the implications of a 'priesthood of all believers'. Unitarians were among the first to admit women to the full ministry. Church polity for the most part is strictly congregational, although in some places (including Ireland) it is presbyterian. The Hungarian-speaking Churches have bishops, but the system is not truly episcopal. The movement has been generally noted for its strong commitment to radical social ideals.

Unitarians are excluded, on doctrinal grounds, from the World Council of Churches (although they are included as associate members in the British Council of Churches). The International Association for Religious Freedom, founded by American Unitarians in 1900, provides a basis for co-operation not only between the various independent Unitarian movements across the world, but also among a wide variety of religious liberals from other faiths.

The Salvation Army

HISTORICAL OUTLINE AND PRESENT-DAY DISTRIBUTION

The Salvation Army is a denomination in the mainstream of Christian faith and practice. Its founders, William and Catherine Booth, were both born in 1829, and married in London in 1855. William had become a minister in the Methodist New Connexion, but had very strong leanings towards itinerant revivalist preaching and a compulsion to reach the un-Churched masses with the gospel. When opportunities for this kind of ministry were denied him he left that de-nomination, in 1861, and on an independent basis preached in many places with considerable success.

In 1865 Booth became involved in a series of tent meetings in Whitechapel, East London, and it is to this mission that the Army traces its origins. Its expansion – at first mainly in the poorest city areas – was rapid. It was not originally intended to form a new denomination, but practical considerations led to the formation of what became known as The Christian Mission and later, in 1878, as The Salvation Army.

In the 1880s emigrants from Britain established offshoots in the USA, Australia and Cana-

One of the Salvation Army cycle brigades in East London c 1909. The Army has always used certain military features such as uniforms, flags and ranks as it sees itself engaged in spiritual warfare and these features help to bear witness to the world of a life consecrated to evangelism.
Government of the Army is autocratic and unquestioning obedience is expected. Members, or soldiers, must devote their whole time to Army work, must wear the uniform at all times and this uniform must in no way vary in any individual style, though the design is modified from time to time.

Music and singing form an important part of the Salvationist ethic. The rousing hymns and songs that are sung at times of worship and during service to the community reflect the Army's particular brand of militant evangelism.

THE ARMY IS COMING – AMEN, AMEN!
TO CONQUER THIS CITY FOR JESUS –
AMEN!
WE'LL SHOUT 'HALLELUJAH! AND PRAISE
HIS DEAR NAME,
WHO REDEEMED US TO GOD THROUGH
THE BLOOD OF THE LAMB.
THE SOUND OF ITS FOOTSTEPS IS
ROLLING ALONG;
THE KINGDOM OF SATAN, TRIUMPHANT
SO LONG,
IS SHAKING AND TOTT'RING, AND
DOWNWARD SHALL FALL
FOR JESUS, THE SAVIOUR, SHALL REIGN
OVER ALL.

da, and some planned expansion also took place in Europe. By the international congress of 1904, delegates represented 49 countries and colonies – well on the way to the present total of 86. The Army is thus a multi-racial and multi-cultural fellowship unified in an international structure. Salvationists preach the gospel in 121 languages, and there has been considerable missionary endeavour including substantial medical, educational and social welfare activity.

BELIEF

The Salvation Army's doctrinal basis is expressed in eleven articles which specify: that the divinely-inspired (but not verbally inerrant) Bible is the rule of Christian faith and practice; that there is one infinite God active in creation and the only proper object of worship; that there are three Persons in the Godhead, undivided in essence and co-equal in power and glory; that in Jesus the divine and human natures are united; that all humankind is sinful; that salvation is available to all through the death of Christ, and that it depends on God's grace, on repentance and faith in the sinner and on regeneration by the Holy Spirit; that those justified by faith may have assurance of salvation, but may fall from grace if obedience and faith are not maintained: that all believers may experience santification; and that there is an eternal destiny for all humankind, its nature for the individual depending on his or her response to God in this life.

WORSHIP

Salvationist worship is traditionally non-liturgical, and considerable variety is encouraged. It is primarily evangelistic, including free prayer and testimony and a strong musical content; it climaxes in preaching and opportunity for public decision for Christ. It is considered that the sacra-

The Salvation Army is known for much pioneering social work, such as employment bureaux, tracing missing persons, work for alcoholics and for single parents. Officers in the Army accept a degree of poverty, asking only for sufficient to supply their needs. However there are funds to provide for widows and orphans, and a retirement allowance.

ments are neither necessary to salvation, nor instituted by Christ for all time and all Christians; sacramental ceremonies are also thought to encourage the dangers of ritualism, and therefore are not practised.

SALVATIONIST CONCERNS

Other distinguishing features emerged early in the organization's history. For example, Catherine Booth had begun to preach as early as in 1860, and her thinking was an important factor in the development of the movement as well as in its public relations with the upper classes. Women have equality in status and ministry in The Salvation Army, and have often borne the brunt of grassroots evangelism – and of the considerable persecution that befell early Salvationists.

Social service as an expression of practical Christian concern also emerged at an early stage and found an organizational framework in The Darkest England Scheme in 1890. Besides providing institutional care for thousands, the Army pioneered social action in many spheres, for example in employment bureaus, the tracing of missing persons, the treatment of alcoholics, and the making of safety matches to protect workers' health.

Salvationists pledge themselves to abstain from alcohol, tobacco and non-medicinal drugs, to live morally upright lives, to seek growth in experience of personal holiness, and to be active in the spread of the gospel.

ORGANIZATION

The Army's form of government is quasi-military and theoretically autocratic, although more democratic processes are developing. Full-time ministers of religion (or 'officers' holding military rank) number about 17,000 worldwide, and are headed by a General elected by a High Council. There are more than 50,000 employees, and many of the lay 'soldiers' expend great effort in a variety of evangelistic, social, musical and other activities.

The Seventh-day Adventist Church

HISTORICAL OUTLINE AND PRESENT-DAY DISTRIBUTION

The Seventh-day Adventist Church was officially constituted in 1863, although the movement actually arose during the Great Advent Awakening of the 1830s and 1840s. In the early years, membership was confined to North America, but Adventism soon spread to Europe, Australasia and South Africa, thus taking on the characteristics of the world Church it was to become in the twentieth century. Present membership totals some 4.5 million in 184 countries.

Despite Adventism's localized origin in North America in the nineteenth century, many theologians and historians trace its roots back to the continental radical Reformation and to English Puritanism. Virtually every major doctrinal tenet of contemporary Seventh-day Adventist belief appeared first in these European movements, reappearing two centuries later in North America and coalescing in the Seventh-day Adventist Church. Adventism thus claims a historic continuity with the Protestant Reformation and, beyond that, with apostolic Christianity itself.

BELIEF

In harmony with the conservative Protestant position, Adventist theology is trinitarian and is grounded in the inspiration and authority of the Bible. Adventist doctrine is also strongly Christocentric, holding the traditional view of the Incarnation and the divine-human nature of Christ, emphasizing his exemplary life, his complete and sufficient substitutionary death on the Cross, his priestly ministry in heaven, and his literal and visible return to earth at the end of the age.

Seventh-day Adventists also emphasize the necessity of personal regeneration through the inward working of the Holy Spirit, and practise the baptism of believers by total immersion. They uphold the perpetuity of the moral law as contained in the Ten Commandments, and advocate a simple life-style based on the teachings of the Bible.

Adventism regards as particularly important its teaching on the nature of humanity, death and immortality, emphasizing the essential oneness of human personality and rejecting a dualistic view (of body and soul) as pre-Christian and non-biblical.

moral law given at Sinai; that it was observed by Christ himself and the apostles; and that it was kept by the early Church for several generations before Sunday began to be substituted for the seventh day on ecclesiastical authority towards the end of the second century. In this Adventists differ from most Christian Churches for whom Sunday, the first day of the week (observed as the day of resurrection from very early times), has commonly been kept as the weekly festival and a day of spiritual refreshment.

Seventh-day Adventist worship is free and non-liturgical, and is based on the understanding that worship is the response of the believer to the Creator. Worship centres around the Word, the sermon being the major feature of the service and having a strong biblical content, and is enhaced by congregational singing, choral or solo music (where possible), the reading of the Scriptures, and extempore prayer. The worship service is normally preceded by a service chiefly given to group Bible study and discussion.

ORGANIZATION

The Church is organized on a representative basis, which may be seen in effect as a blend of congregationalism and presbyterianism with an element of episcopacy. Each local congregation appoints its leaders (elders, deacons, deaconesses, and so on) and is responsible for its own life and activities, and the upkeep of its own church building (if any). Such congregations are linked together with a local (regional) 'conference' under the direction of a president and an executive committee composed of ministry and laity. Ministers, usually with a minimum of three years' full-time training, are appointed to local congregations by the conference executive committee.

Local conferences in turn are affiliated to union conferences which ordinarily correspond to a country, state, or other similar demographic area, and which are also administered by a president and an executive committee. Union conferences are then grouped in one of ten world divisions of the General Conference of Seventh-day Adventists, the main administrative body of the Church. Personnel are elected to office and committee membership at all administrative levels at regular intervals.

AFFILIATIONS AND ACTIVITIES

Although the Seventh-day Adventist Church does not hold full membership with any other religious organization, it has consultant observer

A Seventh-day Adventist baptism in the swimming pool of a California motel. The baptism is by total immersion. In this they are following directly the custom of the Early Christians who immersed new converts, usually three times.

People have a responsibility to care for their bodies in this present life. Guidelines for this are drawn from the Genesis account (which is taken to suggest an original vegetarian diet), the Old Testament food laws in general, and the New Testament teaching of the body as the temple of the Holy Spirit. Adventists consequently abstain from alcohol, tobacco, narcotics, the flesh of 'unclean' animals, and the irresponsible use of drugs.

The future life, in a re-created earth, is seen as a re-unification at the resurrection of the body and the spirit (breath) which are separated at death, rather than as the continuing existence of an immortal soul immediately after death. Adventists believe that this latter view is essentially a Greek philosphical belief superimposed in some parts of the Christian tradition on the biblical teaching (which portrays death as a sleep) and holds that men and women are called to judgement and eternal life through the resurrection of the body at the Second Coming of Christ.

WORSHIP

Seventh-day Adventists are distinctive in their observance of Saturday as the day of rest and Christian worship. This practice derives from the Adventist understanding that the seventh-day sabbath was instituted before the Fall for the benefit of humankind; that it was reiterated in the

status at the World Council of Churches and with several national Councils of Churches, and works closely at local level with similar councils and other Christian organizations.

The Church has from its earliest years fostered a strong publishing enterprise, printing today in 189 languages through fifty publishing houses; a strong educational enterprise, with 5,320 denominational schools from primary level to two fully accredited universities; and a strong medical enterprise, with 160 hospitals and sanitariums in virtually every part of the world. This worldwide programme is financed mainly by donations from members in the form of tithe contributions (10 per cent of income) and free-will offerings (additional to the tithe).

The motivation for this relatively extensive programme, and the financial commitment that is needed to maintain it, is the firm conviction – essential to the identity of the Seventh-day Adventist Church – that the human predicament can only be solved by the gospel of Jesus Christ, traditionally understood, and by his Second Coming and subsequent Kingdom on earth.

The Jehovah's Witnesses

HISTORICAL OUTLINE AND PRESENT-DAY DISTRIBUTION

Jehovah's Witnesses began in Pennsylvania, USA in the 1870s as a small group who met as Bible students to consider prophecies pointing to the Second Coming of Christ. The name is intended to distinguish people in all ages who have borne witness to Jehovah. This name is used by Jehovah's Witnesses as the most familiar pronounciation of the tetragrammaton, the Hebrew personal name for God, written in Hebrew texts only in consonants (YHWH or JHVH) and regarded by Jews as too sacred to be uttered. In Jewish readings *Adonai* ('Lord') is substituted for the sacred name, and it is the combination of the vowels of *Adonai* with the consonants of JHVH which give the name Jehovah.

The movement has expanded rapidly through energetic and dedicated evangelism and publication. More than 200 countries and island groups are cared for by branch offices of the Watch Tower Society under the direction of their world headquarters in New York. The translating and printing of Bibles, the periodicals *The Watchtower* and *Awake!* and other Bible-study aids is undertaken at these branch offices, known as Bethel homes. Worldwide, the number of Jehovah's Witnesses – all active preachers – is now approaching three million.

BELIEF

Jehovah's Witnesses believe that Christ's Second Coming took place in 1914, and that the 'last days' dawned then, so inaugurating the fulfilment of Jesus's prophecy (Matthew 24, 25) by which 'nation shall rage against nation'. God's war of Armageddon is to occur within this generation, after which millions now living will enter into everlasting life on earth under the rule of God's Kingdom (the Theocracy).

With regard to Jesus, Witnesses believe that the Christ redeemed the whole human family from the original sin of Adam at the cost of his own life; that he, the perfect man, was raised from the dead as an immortal spirit to open up the way to heavenly glory to be shared with him by his chosen congregation comprising faithful men and women who undergo a similar resurrection. During the Millennium the general resurrection will see the opportunity of everlasting life on earth extended to resurrected humankind under God's Kingdom government, at which time the earth will be restored as a Paradise home.

Jehovah's Witnesses do not hold to any national or political powers or parties; their first loyalty must be to the movement. They relate to scripture their strict ethical conduct and their opposition to blood transfusions. Moreover, Witnesses uphold the Bible as the infallible source of truth, accepting every detail as literally true.

WORSHIP

The aim of a Jehovah's Witness is to follow as closely as possible the example set by Jesus Christ, and to do good to all humankind. A Witness also follows Jesus's command actually to witness – to preach the 'good news of the kingdom' and 'make disciples of people of all the nations'. In 1983, the house-to-house ministry resulted in 1.8 million Bible studies being conducted each week in homes throughout the world.

Instead of 'celebrating services' in 'church', Jehovah's Witnesses have meetings in a Kingdom Hall. There are four types of meeting: for a Bible lecture; for study of a biblical theme or prophecy as published in the current issue of *The Watch-*

tower; as a school for training Witnesses to proclaim the 'good news'; or concerned with the care of the witnessing work in the local community. All are open to anyone. At the meetings, prayers are spoken aloud extemporaneously. In addition, once a week Witnesses meet in small groups in private homes for Bible study.

Jehovah's Witnesses celebrate no religious festivals other than one in commemoration of Jesus's death, the date of which is reckoned each year by the Hebrew calendar. On that day they meet and discuss the significance of Jesus's death. There are no other festivals because Jehovah's Witnesses believe that the Bible neither mentions nor commands them.

Baptism is a symbol of an individual's dedication to Jehovah God through Jesus Christ (it is not viewed as a sacrament). After a period of systematic Bible study, adult candidates meeting the strict scriptural requirements are considered for baptism by total immersion in water.

ORGANIZATION

Jehovah's Witnesses make no distinctions between clergy and laity. In the congregations dedicated men who meet the scriptural qualifications (1 Timothy 3:1–9) are appointed as elders or as ministerial servants. No special or distinctive clothing is worn.

The denomination is financed entirely by voluntary contributions: each Kingdom Hall has a contribution box for the maintenance of the building and for donations to support the worldwide work of evangelism. Collections are not taken.

In 1942 the Watch Tower Bible School of Gilead was established. Its missionaries concentrate on educating people in the Jehovah's Witnesses' understanding of the Christian way of life and in teaching the Bible as the authority for true Christian doctrine.

The Church Of Christ, Scientist (Christian Science)

HISTORICAL OUTLINE AND PRESENT-DAY DISTRIBUTION

The Church of Christ, Scientist, was founded upon the ideals of Mrs Mary Baker Eddy in Boston, Massachusetts, USA, in 1879. Some seventeen years earlier she had undergone a spiritual experience involving the healing of a serious injury, a healing which at the time she had attributed almost entirely to the doctrines of Phineas Quimby, at that time a well-known philosopher and a religious healer. But in 1866, after suffering further injury, she constructed her own metaphysical formulation and method of healing in Christian Science. Another nine years passed during which the teachings and principles of what was to be the Church gradually crystallized and were put together as an institution. In 1875 her *Science and Health* was published, later re-issued as *Science and Health With Key to the Scriptures*; she was also later to produce the 'constitution' and doctrines of faith in the *Church Manual*. One of her first students, Asa Gilbert Eddy, became her third husband in 1877. Mrs Eddy died in 1910 at the age of 89.

After some years of difficulty and a certain amount of suppression, the movement spread rapidly to become world wide – although since 1950 world membership is said to have declined. Nearly 3,000 Christian Science churches hold daily and weekly services. There are, however, two types of Christian Scientist: those inside the Church (formally listed in the *Christian Science Journal*), and those outside the Church who nevertheless adhere to the tenets, study the readings daily, and follow the way of life implicit in the beliefs.

BELIEF

Fundamental to Christian Science is the perception that matter and evil are unreal, that the only reality is God, described as 'Good' or 'Mind' and available to all in the practical form of healing. The Christ is God's Son, and the historical person of Jesus constituted the Christ to the greatest extent possible, not in any way by atoning for the sins of the world but by showing the way to salvation – that is, to cease sinning and be healed. In demonstration, Jesus healed the sick and himself overcame sin and death – sickness, sin and death did not exist for him – and it is in this example that the Christian Scientist is to find guidance. To believe that sickness or sin is real is itself punishable by God.

The notion of healing, of spiritual and bodily health, is thus central to Christian Science (although physical healing is only part of its ministry on earth).

Study of the Bible is regarded as essential, although biblical interpretation tends to be subjective, especially in detecting allegory and metaphor, as opposed to the fundamentalist notions or linguistic criticisms found in the exegesis of many other denominations. The Bible is considered a guide sufficient to lead any reader to eternal life.

Reliance upon the principles of physical healing – as practised by members specifically accredited by church authorities – is respected by most believers to the extent that any other kind of medical treatment may be refused.

WORSHIP

Worship is identical at all Christian Science churches in the world. Every Sunday, two elected readers read aloud to the congregation passages of the Bible chosen by the church authorities. This reading is followed by another of related interpretative texts from *Science and Health*. The same readings are studied during the week by the members either in groups or alone. At mid-week meetings, testimonies of healings are witnessed.

Members are expected to participate actively in both worship and church organization, particularly in attending or giving classes and lectures in Christian Science.

Members are also expected to live moral lives in the serenity afforded by the knowledge that evil is unreal, and in the health of those to whom healing is not only guaranteed but continual.

ORGANIZATION

The Church is governed by a Board of five Directors, as laid down in the *Church Manual*, in which all provisions and 'by-laws' are listed and detailed. The Directors are responsible ultimately for all the Church's work, including the publication of the periodicals the *Christian Science Journal*, the *Sentinel* and the daily *Christian Science Monitor*. Every local church likewise has its own Board of Directors (and indeed its own 'constitution', although in practice all are virtually identical). There is no priesthood as such.

The financing of the Church is almost entirely through voluntary donation by members of the congregation and endowment.

The Church Of Jesus Christ Of Latter-day Saints (The Mormon Church)

HISTORICAL OUTLINE

The 'Mormon' Church – more properly known as the Church of Jesus Christ of Latter-day Saints – was formally incorporated on 6 April 1830, in Palmyra, New York State (USA), under the leadership of Joseph Smith Jr, the first President and Prophet of the Church.

The incorporation was the culmination of events that had originated some fifteen years earlier, when Joseph Smith as a young boy claimed to have received a vision of God the Father and of Jesus Christ in response to a prayer. Later he said he had been told that none of the Churches then on earth acted with the full authority of God, and that although they had many of the teachings of the gospel, there was not one that had the message in its entirety. For this purpose Joseph was required to be the instrument of God in organizing His restored Church upon the earth.

In the interim, Joseph claimed to have received many heavenly visitors, one of whom (an angel named Moroni) delivered into his hands a set of

The Great Mormon Temple and Tabernacle at Salt Lake City, Utah, USA. It was built (1853–93) of grey granite, with walls six feet thick. On the top of the highest spire is a statue of the angel Moroni. The Mormons came to Utah to escape persecution in the east. When they first settled in 1847 they suffered many hardships. Over 6,000 of their number died in the winter migration. The Sea Gull monument which stands in the Temple Square commemorates the flock of gulls which saved their first crops from being eaten by a swarm of crickets.

gold plates on which was inscribed in cipher a history of the migration of an ancient Israelite family across the Atlantic to the American continent where he founded what became the American Indian peoples, and a record of their religious dealings. (The plates were afterwards handed back to Moroni and sealed away.) The translation of part of this history is in use within the Church as *The Book of Mormon*, and is held as scripture alongside the Bible and the *Doctrine and Covenants* – a collection of written revelations received by Joseph Smith and his successors.

Mormons is the observance of 'The Word of Wisdom', a revelation said to have been given to Joseph Smith in February 1833 advocating abstinence from alcohol, tobacco, tea and coffee, and promoting preparation of wholesome foods with moderation in meat.

Members contribute a tithe to the denomination and are also required to live by a strict moral code. The code precludes all extra-marital sexual relationships; polygamy is no longer practised among the members, having been forbidden by the President of the Church in 1890.

BELIEF

Central to the doctrine of the Church is the acceptance of Jesus Christ as the literal Son of God, without whose atoning sacrifice our existence on earth would be wasted. In commemoration of the sacrifice members accept the duty of putting their faith into working practice, of making the belief an active force. Any charitable act may thus be seen as an act of worship, but more specifically 'Mormons' are required to attend their local 'ward' (parish) each Sunday to partake of the sacrament administered by the priesthood. As a 'New Testament' Church, the members believe in divine gifts and revelation, which are accessible to all worthy men and women.

Distinct to Latter-day Saints is a belief in the eternal family unit: marriages may continue for eternity if the couple are 'sealed' in a temple, a special building designated for the purpose. Only members of good standing may enter such a building with a recommendation from their local leaders to perform work either on their own behalf or for their departed ancestors. Another distinguishing feature of the

ORGANIZATION

From its inception, the Church has maintained the same organization, led by a Prophet holding the gift of revelation from God and with the authority to direct the whole Church worldwide. The Church has a lay clergy (involving ordination of the priesthood for all worthy males aged twelve and above), and puts heavy emphasis on evangelical and missionary work.

A feature of the Church's practical work is seen in its welfare programme which advocates sufficient education of every individual to enable him or her to maintain independence. In addition, emergency resources are available for times of extreme hardship and disaster. Church schools are run primarily in Third World countries, particularly in South America and the Pacific, and health and hygiene missionaries are also in operation in the same areas.

The Church has no official political or religious affiliations, although members are encouraged to participate actively in local communities in whatever capacity conscience may dictate.

The Unification Church
('The Moonies')

HISTORICAL OUTLINE AND PRESENT-DAY DISTRIBUTION

The Holy Spirit Association for the Unification of World Christianity, now more widely known as the Unification Church (and its members as 'Moonies'), was founded in Seoul, Korea, in 1954 by the Reverend Sun Myung Moon. It spread to Japan, but had little success in the West until Moon moved to the USA in the early 1970s. Since then the public visibility of the movement has in-

creased rapidly, but in fact there have never been as many as 10,000 full-time members in the West at any one time. It is difficult to assess accurately the full-time membership for the rest of the world, but there are some tens of thousands in Asia (nearly all in Japan and South Korea) and perhaps a further thousand in Africa and South America.

One reason for the relatively small numbers of full-time adherents is that, despite allegations of 'brainwashing', more than 90 per cent of those who attend Unification 'workshops' do not in fact become members, and of those who do join the majority leave – of their own free will – within a couple of years.

BELIEF

Unification theology is to be found in the *Divine Principle*, which offers a special interpretation of the Judaeo-Christian Bible (Old and New Testaments), with additional revelations which, it is claimed, Moon received from God and from religious leaders of the past (Jesus, Buddha and Muhammad). The Fall is said to have been the result of the misuse of the most powerful of all forces: love. The Archangel Lucifer had a (spiritually) sexual relationship with Eve, who then had a (physically) sexual relationship with Adam before they had reached a state of sufficient maturity to be blessed by God in marriage. History is interpreted as the struggle to restore the world to the state originally intended by God. As part of this restoration process, Jesus was intended to marry and to establish the God-centred (as opposed to Lucifer-centred) family which should have been founded by Adam and Eve. But Jesus was killed before he was able to complete his mission, and was thus able to offer spiritual, but not physical, salvation to the world.

The Unification reading of history reveals that now is the time when the Lord of the Second Advent is upon the earth, when the Messiah – a sinless man, though born of human parents – can restore the kingdom of heaven on earth. The Church members believe Moon to be the Messiah, although he himself has made no public statement to the effect. As well as the *Divine Principle*, however, there also exists (for internal distribution) a large collection of speeches made by Moon. These tend to expound and expand upon Moon's messianic role and to exhort the members to work harder in their efforts to restore the kingdom of heaven on earth.

WORSHIP AND PRACTICE

The members typically join while in their early twenties, are well educated and from the middle classes. In the West, full-time members usually live in communal centres. The life-style is one of hard-working, 'sacrificial' concentration on restoring the world. Frequently, long hours are spent fund-raising on the streets and trying to recruit new members. Obedience to leaders and celibacy outside marriage is expected.

Moon himself suggests who should marry whom, and mass wedding ceremonies (Blessings) are held at intervals. In 1982 nearly 8,000 couples were blessed in two ceremonies, one in New York and the other in Seoul. The Blessing is the most important Unification rite, the movement having little else in the way of formal ritual apart from a weekly 'Pledge', a service held every Sunday morning. The pledge is repeated in unison, and forms a recommitment to the Unification Church.

ORGANIZATION

The organization is of a strictly hierarchical nature, with Moon at the apex of a complicated pyramid of command and communication. Those with most power tend to be the early Korean disciples, but the Japanese movement's success in recruitment and fund-raising has resulted in the appointment of several Japanese to important positions in the West.

The Unification Church owns several valuable properties and businesses. It publishes daily newspapers in Washington DC and Tokyo. It has a theological seminary in Barrytown, New York, and it runs the 'Little Angels' school in Seoul. It also sponsors a large number of conferences to which academics, theologians, journalists, clergy, the military and others of potential influence are invited. Various other organisations – such as the Collegiate Association for the Research of Principles (CARP), the International Cultural Foundation (ICF), the International Conference on the Unity of the Sciences (ICUS) and the Confederation of the Associations for the Unification of the Societies of the Americas (CAUSA) – are either affiliated to or closely connected with the Unification Church (which in the East is itself known as Tong Il).

In almost every country in which it has made an appearance, the Unification Church has received considerable hostility from members' parents, the media, the 'anti-cult' movement, and various other secular and religious bodies. The main accusations include brainwashing, connections with the Korean CIA, the splitting up of families, the use of deceptive practices, amassing great wealth for the leadership while exploiting the followers, and the manufacture of armaments. The Unification Church (together with several other new religious movements) has been the subject of a condemnatory resolution passed by the European Parliament; the Church's status as a charity has been questioned by the British Parliament; and from July 1984 to August 1985 Moon served a prison sentence in the USA for tax evasion. As the result of such actions the movement claims to be the victim of constant persecution, particularly when its members are illegally kidnapped and 'deprogrammed'.

ISLAM

The Arabic word *islam* means 'surrender', and the use of the term in various passages of the Qur'an shows that this is surrender to God. Thus Islam is the religion of surrender to God, and one might say that among the great religions Islam is characterized by its emphasis on the omnipotence and transcendence of God and humanity's servile or slave status before him. In a sense Islam goes back in history as far as Abraham, but in normal usage it means the religion derived from the teachings which Muhammad proclaimed on the basis of what he believed to have been revealed to him by God.

HISTORY

Origins

The religion of Islam had its origins in the small town of Mecca about the year 610 CE. Mecca at this date had recently become an important commercial centre controlling most of the trade between the Indian Ocean (the Yemen) and the Mediterranean (Syria). No agriculture was possible in the neighbourhood of Mecca, but at the heart of the town was a sacred edifice, the Ka'ba or 'cube', which had become the centre of an annual pilgrimage. The area around Mecca was regarded as sacred, as were also the month of pilgrimage and the surrounding months. This sanctity of place and time, in which fighting was forbidden, made possible the holding of trade fairs to which the desert tribes could come without fear of attack; and the fairs were the foundation of the commercial prosperity of Mecca. It is not altogether clear why there should have been a great commercial expansion round about the year 600, but it may have been due mainly to the protracted series of wars between the two great powers of the time, the Byzantine and Sasanian (Persian) empires, and the consequent difficulty of using the route through Iraq from the Persian Gulf to Aleppo. What is clear is that the great merchants of Mecca had become very prosperous. It is likely that most of the people of Mecca shared in this prosperity, and that there was no serious poverty; but there was increasing disparity of wealth, much discontent and social malaise.

An important feature of the situation was the breakdown of the traditional morality. Although Mecca was a small, settled community, a generation or two earlier its people had been nomads and the merchants still maintained close relations with desert tribes to ensure the safety of their caravans. Thus the traditional morality of Mecca was that of their nomadic ancestors. This promoted the tribal solidarity which had been necessary to make life possible in the harsh conditions of the desert and the honour of the tribe was all-important. In the very different conditions prevailing in Mecca around the beginning of the seventh century, however, the great merchants, who were usually the leading men in their clans, neglected the traditional duties of chiefs in looking after poor and unfortunate clan-members, and thought mainly of increasing their own wealth. As business associates they preferred competent operators from other clans to less competent kinsmen. They avoided public criticism by buying over the poets who had traditionally been the voice of the tribal conscience. Their commercial success seems to have gone to their heads, so that they considered that the course of events could be determined by the combination of their wealth and business expertise.

In the religious situation at the time, so far as we can know it, there was nothing to alleviate the social malaise felt at Mecca. The names have been preserved of many deities, but belief in these deities had little influence on conduct, whether in Mecca or among the desert tribes. Almost universal among the Arabs was a belief in Fate or Time, though this was not worshipped as a deity but rather regarded as an impersonal natural force, something like 'the course of events'; it determined not the whole of a person's life but only such matters as the provision of food he received and the date of his death.

From the Qur'an we further learn that there were people who believed in Allah as a 'high god', remote from the ordinary concerns of life but worth appealing to in dire emergencies. Other deities were often asked to intercede with Allah on behalf of their worshippers. There were usually a few Christians temporarily in Mecca, such as craftsmen from the Byzantine empire and slaves from Abyssinia, and there were settlements of Jews at Medina and elsewhere in the Hijaz (western Arabia). In all this, however, there was nothing to deter the wealthy merchants of Mecca from selfish exploitation of the situation. They are recorded as having used a variety of unscrupulous methods in order to ensure that all the trade to and from Mecca was in their own hands.

Muhammad was born about the year 570 as a posthumous child, his father having died on a trading journey to Syria. He was under the guardianship first of his grandfather 'Abd-al-Muttalib and then of an uncle Abu-Talib, and he himself travelled to Syria with the latter. By Arab custom, however, a minor could not inherit, and thus Muhammad received no property from his father or grandfather. About 595 a wealthy widow, Khadija, employed him as steward to handle her merchandise on a trip to Damascus. He acquitted himself so well that she made him an offer of marriage. Though she is said to have been forty when they married, she bore him several children, of whom only daughters survived. This marriage meant that he was in a position to engage actively in trade, though he was certainly not one of the major merchants. It was possibly his experiences as an orphan which made him reflect on the problems and needs of Mecca. He is said to have gone to a cave near town each summer to spend a month in meditation.

About the year 610, during his month's retreat, Muhammad experienced the call to be a prophet and received the first of the messages he was to transmit to his fellow townsmen. (In English he is mostly called 'prophet', for which the Arabic is *nabi*, but the more usual appellation in Arabic is *rasul Allah*, 'the Messenger of God'.) He continued to receive messages at frequent intervals for the rest of his life, apart from a gap near the beginning which worried him for a time. These messages often consisted of short passages. They were collected and formed into *suras* or chapters, partly by Muhammad himself and partly after his death (as will be described later). Muhammad believed that these messages were the words of God himself brought to him by an angel, and he was convinced that he could distinguish them from his own thoughts; in this the modern historian must adjudge him to have been sincere. It is therefore inappropriate to speak of Qur'anic teaching as if it were Muhammad's own, though he must be assumed to have believed in its truth. Muslims universally believe that the Qur'an is the very speech of god.

There are great difficulties in assigning a date for the revelation of each particular passage of the Qur'an. What follows is based on a dating of passages which would be accepted – in general, though not necessarily in detail – by many western and some Muslim scholars. In the earliest passages the main themes are: God is all-powerful and benevolent, and controls events in the interests of the human race; God will judge all humanity on the Last Day, assigning each person either to paradise (heaven) or hell; human beings are commanded to serve and worship God; they are also commanded to act in various ways, especially to be generous with their wealth; finally, Muhammad has been specially commissioned to be God's Messenger to his fellows. It will be seen that these themes are particularly relevant to the

A view of Mecca depicted on a tile from Asia Minor. In the centre is the Ka'ba, the shrine of the Black Stone which has from prehistoric times been a centre of pilgrimage. The building is draped in a holy carpet, the Kiswa, which is renewed each year.

بِالْغَيْرِتِ الْفَقِيرِ لَا بِهِ مِنْ لَاكُمْ صَلِّ عَلَيْهِ وَصَلَّوْا اَكْثُرِيْا وَلَهَ خَيْرِتَ الْمَارَ كَافِاعَلِ خَطِيرُ عَظِيمٍ مِنَ الْفَوْقِ فَخَتَّ اخَرُنِتَ اللَّيْسَ سَوُّ...

The Miraj, or night ride of the Prophet on the horse Burak: from the World History of Ra'shid al-Din. This event is only hinted at in the Qu'ran but became popular and very influential on Muslim thought and devotion. Muhammad made his ascent to the heavens from the high rock in Jerusalem now enshrined in the Dome of the Rock. It is believed that from there the Prophet went to the throne of Allah.

situation at Mecca. The command to be generous with one's wealth is a critique of the selfishness of most of the merchants. The judgement on the Last Day provides a new sanction for morality where the old sanctions had ceased to be effective. God's control of events is a denial of the pretensions of the merchants; and to worship him is to acknowledge his supremacy.

After the call to be a prophet and the receiving of messages Muhammad began to communicate these, first to his household, then to his immediate friends and then to a wider circle. Those who believed in the truth of the messages met together, discussed the meaning and implications of the messages and participated in common worship. Lists have been preserved of those who became Muslims while Muhammad was still at Mecca (though the name Muslim was not used until later), and from these lists an idea can be formed of the kinds of people to whom the Qur'anic message appealed. Some of them were sons or brothers of the wealthiest men in Mecca, belonging to the most powerful clans; others were older men from less powerful clans; and there were a few 'regarded as weak' (mustad'afun). The latter were not a proletariat but rather persons with little or no effective 'clan protection', presumably because they were from outside Mecca and only loosely attached to one of the local clans. Security of life and property in Mecca, as in many parts of the ancient world, depended on the lex talionis, by which a clan or other kinship group exacted vengeance for the injury or death of one of its members. Where there was no strong and impartial police force, this was an effective way of maintaining peace. The exacting of vengeance was regarded as a sacred duty, but clans were often unwilling to carry it out on behalf of one who was only 'attached' to them and not a full member.

The critique of the leading men of Mecca implicit in the Qur'anic messages meant that, as soon as they realized what views were being prop-

agated, they would adopt a hostile attitude. They tried to silence Muhammad by offering him opportunities for more lucrative trade. They tried to reach some sort of compromise with him and get him to recognize local deities, perhaps as a kind of angel. They spread abroad various lies, such as the allegation that he had human help in the producing of the Qur'an. When these failed, they turned to persecuting Muhammad and his followers, sometimes in petty, sometimes in more serious ways. Some of the believers are said to have fled to Abyssinia to escape this persecution. The climax was a boycott of Muhammad's clan of Hashim. Nearly all the clans of Quraysh, the dominant tribe of Mecca, entered into an agreement that they would have no commercial or marital relations with the clan of Hashim. The boycott is said to have lasted for nearly three years, but it apparently did not inflict undue hardship on Hashim. Although many of the members of Hashim, including the chief Abu-Talib, had not become Muslims, it would have been dishonourable for them not to 'protect' Muhammad, and so they put up with the boycott.

About the time the boycott ended (probably in 619) Abu-Talib died and was succeeded as chief by Abu-Lahab, another of Muhammad's uncles. Abu-Lahab soon found an excuse for ceasing to 'protect' Muhammad without being thought dishonourable: Muhammad had asserted that his own grandfather, 'Abd-al-Muttalib, was in hell; and this was denigrating a former chief of the clan. Abu-Lahab did not immediately withdraw 'protection', but probably threatened to do so if Muhammad continued to preach Islam. It is recorded that Muhammad went to the neighbouring town of at-Ta'if, which had been forced into commercial dependence on Mecca, but had no success in proclaiming his religion there. The significant point, however, is that before returning to Mecca he had to obtain the 'protection' of the chief of another clan, and this he did only with difficulty and presumably on condition that he did not continue to propagate Islam.

While the outlook for Muhammad and the Muslims was thus gloomy, a ray of hope came at the pilgrimage of 620. Here Muhammad met some men from Medina who were themselves interested in the Qur'anic message and thought others in Medina would also be. At the pilgrimage of 621 twelve representatives of the main clans of Medina met Muhammad and came to an agreement with him known as 'the pledge of women' by which they accepted Islam but did not go so far as to promise to support Muhammad by fighting. A Muslim from Mecca was sent to Medina to give instruction in Islam, and doubtless also to report back on local conditions. By the following pilgrimage (probably June 622) over seventy Muslims from Medina, including two women, came to Medina and took 'the pledge of war'. The essential point of this was that Muhammad was to go to Medina and that after he reached its territory his 'protection' would be the responsibility of various clans there. A document has been preserved by the historian Ibn-Hisham which is often known as 'the Constitution of Medina' and probably reproduces the main articles of the original agreement, though articles from similar later documents seem to have been added and some articles may have been omitted.

The conclusion of this agreement opened the way for the Hijra or 'Emigration' to Medina of Muhammad and his Meccan followers. As soon as the pilgrimage was over small groups of Muslims began to move to Medina. By September there were in Medina some seventy emigrants (*muhajirun*, as they came to be known) together with wives and children. There were still Muslims in Mecca who did not want to emigrate or who were prevented from doing so by their families, but apart from these only Muhammad, Abu-Bakr, 'Ali and their families were left. Muhammad and Abu-Bakr set out together secretly and avoided the normal routes because Muhammad could have been killed with impunity after abandoning his 'protection' in Mecca. The journey was without incident, however, and the two reached the outskirts of the oasis of Medina on 24 September 622. (Islamic chronology is based on the era of the Hijra – Annus Hegirae or AH – and this starts at the beginning of the Arabian year in which the Hijra took place, the equivalent of 16 July 622. The year is a lunar one of 354 days.)

With the opposition to Muhammad in Mecca, various new themes are found in the Qur'anic revelations. The most notable is the insistence that 'there is no deity but God' (*la ilaha illa Allahu*). This is probably to be linked with the attempt by the pagans of Mecca to get Muhammad to compromise by regarding their deities as angels who could intercede with Allah, the 'high god'. The Qur'an firmly rejected any such compromise, and from this time onward the oneness or unicity of God is particularly emphasized in Islam. The Qur'an also came to have many brief references to previous prophets. These include several Old Testament prophets and other notables such as Noah, Lot, Abraham, Moses and David; some prophets from Arabian tradition are also mentioned. The point of such references is often some parallel with the experience of Muhammad. Also emphasized is the punishment of those who reject prophetic messages.

Muhammad at Medina

Medina, quite unlike Mecca, was an oasis in which dates and cereals were grown. Most of the inhabitants were Arabs belonging to the related tribes of al-Aws and al-Khazraj, but for many purposes the effective units were subdivisions of these which may be called clans. Eight clans were participants in the Constitution of Medina, but many smaller groups also seem to have functioned as clans for some purposes. For the past century there had been feuds between single clans leading to violent clashes, then between groups of clans, and a climax had been reached a year or two before the Hijra in a battle in which most of the clans of Medina were involved. The peace following this battle was still somewhat fragile when Muhammad came to Medina. Indeed, the main reason why so many of the people of Medina joined in inviting Muhammad there was that they hoped his presence would help to keep the peace; and he was careful not to ally himself by marriage with any of the groups in Medina.

The acceptance of Islam by the Arabs of Medina was made easier by the attraction some of them had felt for the religion of the Jewish settlers in the oasis. There were three main clans of Jews and some smaller groups. It is not known how far they were of Hebrew descent and how far Arabs who had accepted Judaism. Apart from retaining some practice of the Jewish religion their culture was almost identical with that of the surrounding Arabs. They had been largely responsible for the development of agriculture in the oasis, and for a time had been dominant politically. Some minor Arab groups were still dependent allies, but when the main Arab tribes became stronger the Jews had to be content with second place. The Jewish groups were allied to different Arab clans, and could be involved on opposing sides of the struggles endemic in Medina.

Muhammad had expected the Jews of Medina to accept him as a prophet in the tradition of their own prophets, since he regarded the revelations he had received as identical in their essentials with those of the Old Testament (of which he knew virtually nothing). Only a mere handful of the Jews, however, accepted Islam. Most were rather inclined to make fun of Muhammad and taunt him with making mistakes about the teaching of the Old Testament. The Qur'an records some of the Jewish criticisms and gives instructions about appropriate replies. Early in 624 it became clear that the Jews as a whole would not co-operate whole-heartedly with the Muslims, and there occurred a series of events which modern scholars refer to as 'the break with the Jews'. One of these events was the change of *qibla* or direction to be faced in prayer. Hitherto at least some Muslims had been facing Jerusalem like the Jews, but now the Qur'an told them to face Mecca instead, and this has ever since been the Muslim *qibla*. Hitherto also the Muslims had been observing the Jewish fast of the 'Ashura' but, while the 'Ashura' remained optional for them, their own fast of Ramadan was made obligatory.

Shortly after these changes the Jewish clan of Qaynuqa' gave Muhammad grounds for besieging them in their strongholds – all the clans in Medina, Jewish and Arab, had strongholds or fortified houses – and, when they could hold out no longer, they accepted terms of surrender which included leaving Medina.

Something similar happened to the clan of an-Nadir a year later. Then, in 627, on the conclusion of the abortive siege of Medina by the Meccans, the clan of Qurayza was attacked: they had acted suspiciously during the siege, and had probably been ready to attack the Muslims in the rear if occasion offered. When they surrendered, their Arab ally, now a Muslim, passed the sentence that all the males should be killed and the women and children sold into slavery; this was carried out. Some small Jewish groups remained in Medina, living quietly and inconspicuously.

Muhammad's agreement with the clans of Medina, reflected in the Constitution, created an Islamic community which was both religious and political. In form the agreement was according to traditional Arab custom and did not speak of Islam as the religion of the community. However, the fact that the main contracting parties, the eight clans of Medina and Muhammad with his 'clan' of Emigrants, were all Muslims meant that it was in effect an Islamic community. Muhammad's basic position was that of one clan chief among nine, although it was also stated that disputes were to be referred to him for settlement. This continued to be his position for the first few years, but his power and authority gradually increased as a result of the expeditions he sent out, especially those in which he defeated the Meccans. His own 'clan' of Emigrants also increased in numbers relatively to the clans of Medina, since many Muslims from Mecca or from nomadic tribes settled in Medina and were added to it. By the end of his life Muhammad had become unquestioned ruler of Medina and leader of a large federation of tribes.

Before making the Hijra to Medina Muhammad must have considered how the Muslims from Mecca were to gain their living there. They were presumably not prepared to engage in agriculture, nor to remain permanent guests of the Muslims of Medina. Trade would certainly be attractive but, if they tried to trade with Syria, they would almost certainly come into conflict with the merchants of Mecca. It seems likely, then, that even if Muhammad contemplated some commercial activity he must also have decided to raid Meccan caravans. Raiding was almost a national sport in Arabia. For early Arab historians Muhammad's ten years at Medina are thought of as a series of *maghazi* or 'raiding expeditions', some seventy or eighty in all being listed. In some of these a mere handful of men

took part, whereas there was one in 630 in which 30,000 men were involved. Not all these were against Meccan caravans. Many were directed against nomadic tribes over a wide area to make a show of force, to forestall a concentration of hostile warriors, to punish some hostile act, or for a similar reason. It is convenient to look first at relations with the pagans of Mecca.

In the year after the Hijra one or two small expeditions of Emigrants went out to try to intercept Meccan caravans but none was successful. Presumably the Meccans had agents in Medina who kept them well informed of Muslim movements. Eventually, in January 624, Muhammad sent out eastwards a dozen men with sealed orders. When they opened the orders they found that they were to go south to the neighbourhood of Mecca and intercept a small caravan coming from the Yemen. This they achieved, killing one of the four Meccans who were with the caravan and taking another prisoner. In doing this they violated either the sacred territory of Mecca or the sacred month (there is some uncertainty) and when they reached Medina with the caravan their reception by some Muslims was cool. No doubt there was fear of Meccan reprisals. In the end, however, Muhammad accepted his share of the booty, and with it ultimate responsibility for what had happened. It was a clear challenge to the Meccans.

A few weeks later, in March 624, Muhammad led out a combined force of about 315 Emigrants and Ansar; the latter, literally 'helpers', were the Muslims of Medina. The aim was to intercept a rich caravan returning from Syria by the coastal route. The leader of the caravan received information about Muhammad's plans and eluded him, but a relief force of 800 to 900 men from Mecca encountered the Muslims at a place called Badr and were badly defeated, about seventy killed and seventy made prisoner in contrast to a Muslim loss of fourteen dead. Some of the leading merchants of Mecca were among those killed.

To retrieve the situation, in March 625 the Meccans advanced on Medina with 3000 men and camped on level ground in the north of the oasis. The Muslims took up a position north of the Meccan camp on the hill of Uhud where they could not be attacked by the Meccan cavalry. They themselves had only two horses. The Muslims at first routed the Meccan infantry but during the pursuit the Muslim archers, in their desire for booty, abandoned their posts and left open the way for a cavalry attack on the Muslim rear. This resulted in about seventy Muslims being killed, but Muhammad and most of his followers were able to regain a position on Mount Uhud. Despite the successful cavalry charge the Meccans were not able to follow up their advantage, and they set out for Mecca. Though this was not militarily a serious reverse for the Muslims it caused many to wonder if God was still supporting them, as they believed he had done at Badr. A Qur'anic revelation made it clear, however, that the reverse was the Muslims' own fault in that some of them had disobeyed orders.

The Meccans could not overlook their loss of face with its damaging effect on their trade, but it was two years before they could mount another major attack. In April 627 they marched on Medina with 10,000 men, including some allied nomadic tribes, but Muhammad had taken precautions which forced them to attempt a siege. After a fortnight of fruitless efforts to penetrate the defences, some of their allies began to drift away and the siege had to be called off. This was the depths of failure. Certain younger leaders tried to rally the Meccans and to find some way of dealing with Muhammad, but many had lost heart. In 628 the Meccans made a non-aggression treaty with Muhammad, but he was becoming stronger all the time and, after violations of the treaty by Meccan allies, he was able to march on Mecca with 10,000 men. Mecca surrendered almost without a blow being struck, and was generously treated. Indeed 2000 Meccans joined him a few days later for the battle of Hunayn, a little east of Mecca, where he decisively defeated a threatening concentration of nomads. Muhammad made arrangements for the administration of Mecca by a Muslim governor and then returned to Medina.

While Muhammad was thus experiencing a spectacular reversal of fortune in his relations with the pagan Meccans (nearly all of whom became Muslims sooner or later), he was also in either friendly or hostile relations with many nomadic tribes as a result of the numerous expeditions he had sent out from Medina. By the time Mecca submitted to him he had laid the foundation of a federation of tribes. With his successes at Mecca and Hunayn his prestige had soared, and for the remaining two years of his life tribes from all over Arabia were coming to him and asking to be accepted as allies. He made it a condition that those accepted into the federation should become Muslims, should observe Islamic worship and pay 'alms' (zakat), and should not fight against other Muslim groups. This last point had an important bearing on later developments. As already mentioned, the raiding of rival tribes was a widespread custom among the Arabs of the desert; but the more tribes there were in Muhammad's federation the less scope there was for raiding. It seems likely that Muhammad had realized this, perhaps soon after the abortive siege of Medina or even earlier, and had decided that it would be necessary to direct the energies of the nomadic tribes outwards, that is, into raiding surrounding countries. Some of his largest expeditions seem to have been reconnaissances of the

routes to Syria and Iraq. During his lifetime the expeditions did not advance beyond Arabia, but within a dozen years of his death the Muslim raiders had reached Iraq and Syria and from the latter had gone on to Egypt. It is difficult to give a precise figure, but it is likely that at the time of his death about two-thirds of the tribes of Arabia were members of the federation.

The changing political situation of Muhammad and the Muslims is reflected in the revelations he received at Medina. Many of the themes in the Meccan revelations were repeated with modifications, especially during the early years at Medina. In addition, there were references to current events, containing encouragement, instructions and interpretation. There were also many regulations for the life of the community in re-

During the seven circumambulations of the Ka'ba the pilgrims stop and kiss or touch the Black Stone. Five miles from the holy city the pilgrim must cover himself in a seamless garment and take off his shoes. This is because the area around the Black Stone had long been a sacred place and dedicated to peace.

spect of marriage, divorce and inheritance, homicide and theft, slavery, and various commercial matters. The regulations were chiefly concerned with points of pre-Islamic Arabian custom which were unsatisfactory in an urban community or where practice differed from one section of the community to another. Apart from such matters pre-Islamic custom was in general followed. At the same time Islamic ritual was taking a definite shape, though the details are not all made clear in the Qur'an and in later times were largely based on the records of Muhammad's practice (Hadith).

In the last two years or so of Muhammad's life he came into closer contact with Christians and found that they, like the Jews, were not going to accept his revelations. Earlier he had had good relations with Christians. He had received encouragement from one of Khadija's kinsmen who, if not a Christian, knew Christianity well. Then those who fled from Mecca to Abyssinia to avoid persecution were warmly welcomed by the Christian emperor. When Muhammad began to look at the route to Syria, however, he found that there were Christian tribes likely to oppose Muslim raiding parties. Criticisms of Christian belief and practice appear in the Qur'an, the same criticisms sometimes being applied to both Judaism and Christianity. On the last great expedition to the north (late 630) several small Christian and Jewish communities near the Gulf of Aqaba submitted to Muhammad and were given the status of 'protected minorities' (*ahl adh-dhimma* or *dhimmis*), and this provided a model for the later expansion of the Islamic state. This practice was based on the belief that Christians and Jews were 'People of the Book' (*ahl al-kitab*), that is, worshippers of the same God as the Muslims even if, as Muslims held, their faith had lost something of its original purity.

Muhammad himself conducted the pilgrimage to Mecca in March 632, but was seen to be in poor health when he returned to Medina. He died on 8 June after a short illness. After some discussion his chief lieutenant, Abu-Bakr, succeeded to his political position and took the title of 'caliph' (*khalifa*), that is, successor.

The expansion and distribution of Islam

In speaking of the expansion of Islam it is important to distinguish between the territorial expansion of the Islamic state and the expansion of the religion through numerous conversions of individuals and groups. In the century after Muhammad's death the Islamic State expanded amazingly to become an empire stretching from Spain to Pakistan, but this was primarily a military operation, in a sense continuing the Arab practice of raiding, and the objective was booty not conversions. In Arabia itself pagans were in effect given the choice of 'Islam or the sword', but in the con-

quered provinces Jews and Christians as 'people of the Book' normally became 'protected minorities', and this status was extended to Zoroastrians, Buddhists and Hindus. A 'protected minory' had internal autonomy under its religious head who was responsible for seeing that the taxes were paid to the provincial governor. On the whole these minorities were well treated, often better than by their previous rulers, and in most cases the taxes were not unduly onerous; but non-Muslims were excluded from certain spheres of life, such as politics, and tended to feel themselves second-class citizens. This feeling was probably increased by the unshakable confidence of the Muslims, especially the Arabs, in the superiority of Islam to other religions. Social pressures of this kind through the centuries led to a trickle of conversions from Judaism and Christianity. Shortly after the conquest of Iran there were many conversions from Zoroastrianism which had become so much an official cult that many people were disaffected. These facts show the falsity of the idea that Isalm was a religion which spread by the sword, an idea which is still part of the distorted image of Islam formed in medieval Europe.

The spread of the Islamic religon beyond the frontiers of Islamic states came about in a different way, being chiefly due to Muslim merchants and traders. Such men carrying goods across the Sahara to West Africa, for example, would marry local women and have their children brought up there as Muslims. After a time local business partners would find it useful to become co-religionists, being perhaps impressed also by the supreme self-confidence of the Muslims in their religion. When many African merchants had become Muslims, rulers found it expedient to become Muslims too. It was mainly in this way that Islam spread into East and West Africa, Malaysia and Indonesia. Many details of this expansion are given in *The Preaching of Islam, a History of the Propagation of the Muslim Faith* by Sir Thomas Arnold (London 1935).

After the rapid formation of the Islamic empire in the century after Muhammad there was little further territorial expansion until first the Seljuq Turks and then the Ottoman Turks occupied Asia Minor and south-eastern Europe. The heyday of Islamic political power was the sixteenth century when the Ottoman empire was at its height in the western Islamic world, the Safavid dynasty in control of Iran and the Mughal dynasty establishing its rule over much of the Indian subcontinent. The following centuries were marked by decline and stagnation as the Muslims experienced the growing power of the western European states. By 1960 or so most Muslims had recovered their political independence from the colonialists but were becoming acutely aware of the cultural and economic pressure of the West. It

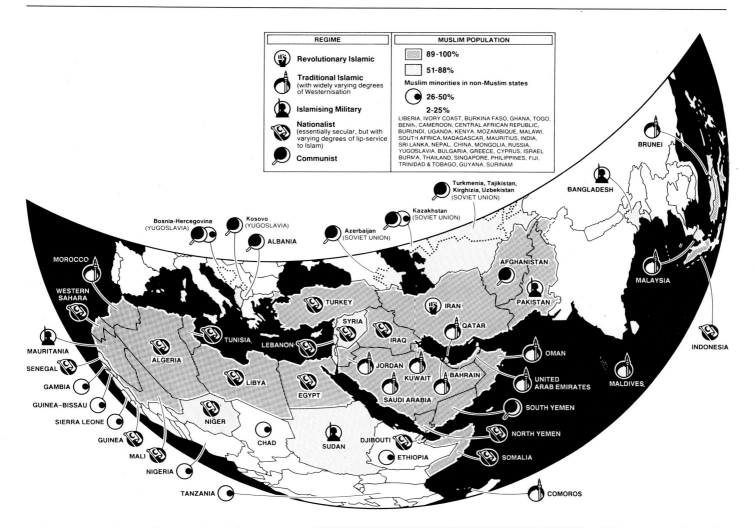

REGIME

 Revolutionary Islamic

Traditional Islamic
(with widely varying degrees
of Westernisation)

Islamising Military

Nationalist
(essentially secular, but with
varying degrees of lip-service
to Islam)

Communist

MUSLIM POPULATION

89-100%

51-88%

Muslim minorities in non-Muslim states

26-50%

2-25%

LIBERIA, IVORY COAST, BURKINA FASO, GHANA, TOGO,
BENIN, CAMEROON, CENTRAL AFRICAN REPUBLIC,
BURUNDI, UGANDA, KENYA, MOZAMBIQUE, MALAWI,
SOUTH AFRICA, MADAGASCAR, MAURITIUS, INDIA,
SRI LANKA, NEPAL, CHINA, MONGOLIA, RUSSIA,
YUGOSLAVIA, BULGARIA, GREECE, CYPRUS, ISRAEL
BURMA, THAILAND, SINGAPORE, PHILIPPINES, FIJI,
TRINIDAD & TOBAGO, GUYANA, SURINAM

is this pressure above all which has led to the resurgence or revival of Islam in the last two or three decades. The resurgence is to be seen as an attempt to reassert an Islamic identity which Muslims felt was being threatened by western culture. It is noteworthy that the resurgence has emphasized aspects which show them as different from westerners, notably the prohibition of alcohol and usury, and the veiling of women.

The total number of Muslims in the world is given as 555 millions by the *Encyclopaedia Britannica Book of the Year 1984*. There are, of course, no complete statistics available, and this estimate may be somewhat low, but the total is unlikely to be much more than 600 millions. The Muslims are concentrated in a wide sweep of territory from Morocco through North Africa and western Asia to parts of Soviet Central Asia and Pakistan. They also occupy the northern steppe regions of West Africa, some coastal regions of East Africa, Bangladesh, Malaysia and Indonesia. There is a large minority in India. Smaller numbers are found in many other countries including parts of southeastern Europe. In recent decades some ten million Muslims have migrated to western Europe and North America.

BELIEF

The centrality of the revealed law

Intellectually the central place in the Islamic faith is taken not by theology but by the Shari'a or 'revealed law' and the various disciplines associated with it. Theology was and is studied in Islam, but it is subordinate to jurisprudence. That this is so is doubtless due to the fact that from the Hijra the Muslims constituted a community that was both a religious and a political entity. Regulations for the life of the community occur in the Qur'an, but they cover explicitly only a fraction of the problems faced by Muslims as their State grew in size. After Muhammad's death concerned Muslims formed the habit of meeting in the mosque to discuss the proper praxis of their community. There was a danger that, if Qur'anic principles could not be seen to apply, the rulers would follow pre-Islamic Arab custom or some provincial practice.

In the course of the Umayyad period (661–750) the discussions became more formal, and in each city a few men came to be recognized as having a degree of expertise. One such would give what amounted to a series of lectures, sitting in a mos-

This map shows the main areas of Muslim population throughout the world. Although the last twenty or thirty years have seen a revival of Islam by Muslims who have felt increasing cultural and economic pressure from the West, the question of whether a Muslim state should be religious or secular continues to cause debate and conflict in many countries.

161

The Iranian holy city of Qom, home of the Ayatollah Khomeini. This spiritual and political leader of the Shi'ite Muslims has made Iran the home of fundamentalist reaction to Western culture. The Shi'ites have throughout their history looked to charismatic leaders who will teach the way of salvation. The first, they believe, was a cousin of Muhammad himself.

que with his disciples round him. By the end of the Umayyad period there was a measure of consensus in each of the main cities – Medina, Damascus, Kufa, Basra – but the cities differed from one another. The early 'Abbasids (from 750) favoured the legal schools more than the Umayyads had done and urged them to aim at greater uniformity, but this was only ever partially achieved.

The basic problem confronting the jurists, as they may now be called, was how to devise appropriate regulations for all the multifarious concerns of the Muslim citizens of the empire. The jurists were not thought of as themselves propounding new regulations, but as deciding how the principles implicit in the Qur'an applied to fresh cases. A crude example of this would be the question whether the Shari'a permits the drinking of whisky (which was of course unknown to Muhammad). The jurists argued: the Qur'an prohibits the drinking of wine (*khamr*) because it is intoxicating; whisky is intoxicating and so is also prohibited.

There were slight variations in the types of argument admitted in the different centres. The jurist ash-Shafi'i (d. 820) is reckoned to have established the discipline of 'the roots of law' or jurisprudence (*usul al-fiqh*). The roots in his view were four: Qur'an, Hadith, analogy and consensus. By Qur'an he meant the regulations found in the Qur'an itself. The Hadith were the anecdotes (formerly called 'traditions') about what Muhammad had said or done in various circumstances, so that this root amounted to the Sunna or 'example' of Muhammad. ash-Shafi'i quoted several verses of the Qur'an which said that God had given 'the Book and the wisdom' to Muhammad, and argued that because of this wisdom his sayings

and actions were divinely inspired. The root of analogy (*qiyas*) is exemplified by the above argument about whisky; but ash-Shafi'i insisted that only a strict analogy should be allowed. The root of consensus (*ijma'*) was sometimes taken to be that of the people as a whole, sometimes as that of only the jurists. Other roots sometimes invoked were *istihsan* and *istislah*, both meaning roughly 'finding good' and being methods of avoiding strict analogy.

Another term found in discussions of legal matters is *ijtihad*, which literally means 'expending effort' but was used to describe the exercise of independent judgement by a jurist who went back to first principles without referring to precedents. The opposite of *ijtihad* was *taqlid*, or the following of precedents. Gradually the right of *ijtihad* was restricted to a very few jurists, and then ceased to be exercised. This resulted in the formation of the *madhahib*, legal 'schools' or 'rites'. The latter term is in some ways preferable since each Muslim belonged to a 'rite' and this affected practical matters such as the precise rules for inheritance. Among the Sunnites four 'rites' or 'schools' came to be recognized as equally sound. The Hanafites, taking their name from Abu-Hanifa of Kufa (d. 767), made much use of rational methods and were latterly the official rite of the Ottoman empire. The Malikites followed Malik ibn-Anas of Medina (d. 795) and spread into North and West Africa. The Shafi'ites were the followers of ash-Shafi'i himself. Ahmad ibn-Hanbal (d. 855) gave his name to the Hanbalites who opposed rational methods, even the use of analogy. These four rites have continued to the present time, but some Islamic states, especially since they became independent, have tended to disregard them.

One of the features of Islamic jurisprudence is the absence of a final authority in legal matters. Rulers and governments have certain prerogatives. They can say that their subjects have all to follow a particular rite, and they can make arrangements for the practical application of the jurists' decisions (although the decisions themselves are final). Within each rite, however, there is usually a dominant view on any particular point and one or more variants. Moreover, the dominant view is not codified, and can only be discovered by consulting a dozen lengthy books – a cumbersome and time-consuming process. Since the nineteenth century reforming Muslims have clamoured for the reopening of the 'gate of *ijtihad*', but so far because of the conservatism of the majority of the jurists, no radical adaptation of the Shari'a to modern conditions has been achieved. In the Republic of Turkey Atatürk abolished the Shari'a in 1927 and replaced it by a code based on European models. Some other Islamic statesmen have partly disregarded the Shari'a and the jurists have enacted what seemed best for their country.

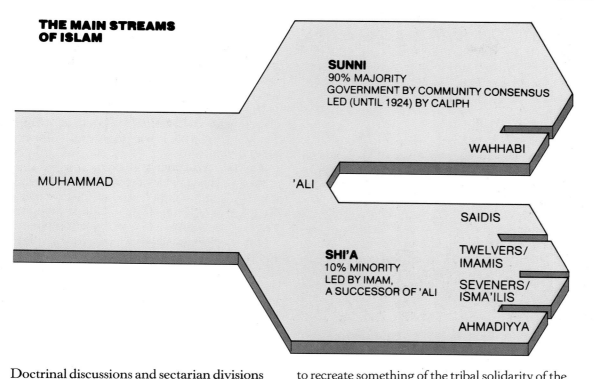

THE MAIN STREAMS OF ISLAM

MUHAMMAD

'ALI

SUNNI
90% MAJORITY
GOVERNMENT BY COMMUNITY CONSENSUS
LED (UNTIL 1924) BY CALIPH

WAHHABI

SAIDIS

TWELVERS/
IMAMIS

SHI'A
10% MINORITY
LED BY IMAM,
A SUCCESSOR OF 'ALI

SEVENERS/
ISMA'ILIS

AHMADIYYA

Doctrinal discussions and sectarian divisions

Muslims, like members of other religious communities, soon began to discuss what precisely their beliefs were. Because of the religio-political character of the Islamic community most of the early discussions of doctrine involved political questions. The event that was most debated for the first century and longer was whether those who killed the caliph 'Uthman in 656 were justified in so doing. The argument for their justification was that 'Uthman had acted sinfully and so deserved to die.

The principle involved here was taken up by a group of sects, collectively known as Kharijites. Their formulation of the principle was that the person who commits a grave sin is thereby excluded from the community (and so can be killed with impunity). The underlying thinking was probably that the community is the People of Paradise (that is, destined for Paradise), and that their hope of Paradise is threatened if among them is someone destined for Hell. Another of their principles was that there should be 'no judgement but God's', meaning that matters of social and political praxis should be decided in accordance with the principles of the Qur'an.

There were many revolts of small groups of Kharijites, first against 'Ali (656–61), then against the Umayyads (661–750). Some of those with extreme views were little better than terrorists, since by the principle that the grave sinner was excluded from the community they justified robbing or killing all who did not believe precisely as they did. They maintained that they themselves in their small group were the only true Muslims. In general the Kharijites seem to have been trying

to recreate something of the tribal solidarity of the pre-Islamic nomads, and to have felt that salvation came through the community (tribe). Their insistence that social and political praxis should be based on the Qur'an was an important contribution to the development of Islamic thought. In the eighth century some small settled communities adopted one or other form of moderate Kharijism but did not try to convert other Muslims to their views. One of these, the Ibadites, has survived into the present century in the sultanate of Oman and at Mzab in Algeria.

The contrasting position to Kharijism was taken by Shi'ism. Where the Kharijites had looked for salvation to the community of true believers, the Shi'ites looked to a charismatic leader. In particular they came to hold that Muhammad's cousin and son-in-law 'Ali ibn-Abi-Talib had been designated by Muhammad as his successor, and that the caliphs from 632 to 656, Abu-Bakr, 'Umar and 'Uthman, were usurpers. Later Shi'ites held that 'Ali's rightful successors were his sons, first al-Hasan and then al-Husayn. On the death of his father in 661 al-Hasan, after a feeble attempt to gain the caliphate by arms, submitted to Mu'awiya, the first Umayyad caliph, on generous terms. When Mu'awiya died in 680 al-Husayn made a similar attempt, but refused to surrender to a vastly superior force at Karbela in Iraq, and, as Shi'ites believe, died a martyr's death along with about a hundred of 'the family'. For the rest of the Umayyad period most persons of Shi'ite sympathies remained quiescent, and there was still some fluidity in their beliefs.

The most important surviving branch of Shi'ism is the Imamite, also known as the

Ithna'ashariyya or Twelvers. These hold that there was a series of divinely supported imams, each designating his successor: first 'Ali, al-Hasan, al-Husayn, and then going from father to son to the eleventh imam, al-Hasan al-'Askari, who died in 874 after designating his son Muhammad to succeed him. This son disappeared soon afterwards, but the Imamites claimed that he was not dead but in seclusion or 'occultation' (ghayba). Imamites still believe that this 'hidden imam' is alive and that at an appropriate moment he will return as the Mahdi or 'guided one' (a kind of Messiah) and will set everything right in the world.

It is difficult to know in what sense the imams were recognized in the period up to 874. If they had been plotting to overthrow the 'Abbasid caliphate, the secret police would have dealt with them. The aims of the Shi'ites must have been something less, but there was much diversity. More than a dozen different groups are mentioned after death of al-Hasan al-'Askari. Great political acumen seems to have been shown by those who, after 874, welded most of these groups into a coherent unity on the basis of imamite doctrine. Politically the Imamites supported 'Abbasid rule, but stood a little aloof from the government. In the following centuries Imamites seem to have remained a sizeable minority in the caliphate. A great change took place in 1501 when Shah Isma'il, the founder of the Safavid dynasty, made Imamism the official religion of his domains (Iran or Persia). It became the dominant religion there, but lost adherents elsewhere, apart from one or two pockets which remained solidly Imamite, such as those round the Imamite shrines in Iraq.

The other main branch of Shi'ism is the Isma'ilite. These claim that the true successor of the sixth imam, Ja'far as-Sadiq (d. 765), was his son Isma'il, not another son Musa al-Kazim as the Imamites say. There is also, however, a complete difference of doctrine and attitude. The Isma'ilites were activists and it was probably because of this that they separated from the other followers of Ja'far. They became an underground movement, and then in 909 suddenly made themselves masters of Tunisia under a leader who claimed to be a descendant of Isma'il. In 969 they conquered Egypt, and made it the centre of their rule with a new capital at Cairo. The Isma'ilite imams who ruled Egypt until 1171 are known as the Fatimid dynasty. They claimed to be rightful rulers of the whole Islamic world and for a time tried to foment revolt in the 'Abbasid domains, but later lost enthusiasm for propaganda. The subsequent history of Isma'ilism is complex because on several occasions different groups followed rival imams. For a time there was a strong body in Syria, apparently known as the Hashishiyyun or hashish-men, who originated the practice of political assassination and gave their name to it. The best known group of Isma'ilites today are the followers of the Agha Khan who have become a prosperous and peaceful community, scattered through many countries and devoting themselves mainly to commerce.

The Zaydites are usually reckoned a third form of Shi'ism, but differ from the previous two in that they accept as imam any member of the Prophet's family who by military force has asserted his right to rule. The 'Abbasid caliph al-Ma'mun (813–33) had some sympathy with Zaydite ideas, but after him Zaydism had little political influence. The Zaydite dynasty of the imams of Sanaa in the Yemen has continued into the present century.

Rather different from both the Kharijites and the Shi'ites was the sect of the Murji'ites. Indeed it was not really a sect but the word was a convenient blanket term for various groups of people who along with other doctrines held that of irja' or 'postponement'. The term was interpreted in various ways, but the basic and original meaning seems to have been the postponement of the decision whether the grave sinner was a believer or an unbeliever, leaving that for God to decide on the Last Day and meanwhile treating him as a believer. The Murji'ites wanted to preserve the solidarity of the community, including those members who had sinned, although of course punishing the latter appropriately. The Murji'ite position, here in strong contrast to that of the Kharijites, was finally adopted by the Sunnite Muslims in general, but the term irja' dropped out of use. One of the leading Murji'ites was Abu-Hanifa, the nominal founder of the Hanafite legal rite, but he was clearly not a heretic.

In the closing decades of the Umayyad period (up to 750) opponents of the régime appeared known as Qadarites. These based their opposition on the doctrine of free will, responding in this way to the assertion of the Umayyads that their succession to the caliphate and their governmental acts were predetermined by God, and that to disobey them was tantamount to sin. The Qadarites, though united by their opposition to the Umayyads, combined the doctrine of free will with various other views. When the 'Abbasids replaced the Umayyads and abandoned the form of legitimation employed by the latter, Qadarism lost much of its point and faded away as a distinct movement, although later upholders of free will were sometimes referred to as Qadarites by their opponents.

Belief in free will was in fact adopted by the sect of the Mu'tazilites who traced their beginnings to the first quarter of the eighth century, at which time they probably formulated their doctrine that the grave sinner was in an 'intermediate position' (manzila bayn al-manzilatayn). They thought that the Murji'ite attitude encouraged moral laxity. The historical importance of the Mu'tazilites, however, began about 800 when some outstanding thinkers, notably Abu-l-Hudhayl and an-Nazzam in Basra and Bishr ibn-al-Mu'tamir in Baghdad, introduced into their theological discussions a number of conceptions from Greek philosophy, and thus made theology more rational and intellectual. The caliph al-Ma'mun (813–33) was following Mu'tazilite teaching when he decreed that men in authority, such as judges, should publicly profess that they believed the Qur'an to be the created word of God, not the uncreated; this was the 'Inquisition' (*mihna*), and was continued until about 850. It was hoped that this doctrine, as a kind of *via media*, would bring about a reconciliation between those who looked to an inspired imam (people of Shi'ite sympathies) and those who relied on the Qur'an and the jurists' interpretations (those who may be called Sunnites, though the term was not yet in use). When the Inquisition was abandoned and the caliphate became definitely Sunnite, the Mu'tazilites became a school of academic theologians remote from public affairs.

The Falasifa or Islamic philosophers were distinct from the theologians. The Muslims found schools of Greek learning in the conquered provinces, especially Iraq, and became particularly interested in medicine and astronomy. Philosophy was taught alongside these, usually in Syriac and by Christians. In time some of these scholars became Muslims and brought their learning with them. Apart from those, like the Mu'tazilites, who adapted Greek philosophical conceptions to Islamic theology, there were a few who, while remaining Muslims, became whole-hearted enthusiasts for Greek philosophy. The translation of Greek books had been promoted by al-Ma'mun and others, and eventually original philosophical works in Arabic also appeared. The great names are al-Farabi (d. 950), Ibn-Sina or Avicenna (d. 1037), who was also an outstanding authority on medicine, and Ibn-Rushd or Averroes (d. 1198), who became better known in the Christian West than in the Islamic East.

The mainstream Islamic jurists and other scholars, the *ulema*, did not mix with the Falasifa, partly because they could not understand their arguments, and partly because they suspected them of heresy. After the first acceptance of philosophical ideas by theologians about 800, the Falasifa had little influence on theology until nearly three hundred years later when a brilliant scholar, al-Ghazali (d. 1111), made himself an expert in their disciplines. He wrote a refutation of some of their metaphysical (theological) doctrines; but he was also greatly impressed by Aristotelian logic, especially the syllogism, and was responsible for its acceptance into Islamic rational theology. Al-Farabi and Avicenna were Neoplatonic in outlook

THE FIVE PILLARS OF ISLAM
THE QUR'AN TEACHES FIVE PRINCIPLES TO BE BELIEVED AND OBEYED BY ALL MUSLIMS.
THE FIVE PILLARS OF BELIEF
1 BELIEF IN ONE GOD
FAITH, THE MAIN PILLAR OF ISLAM, IS BASED ON BELIEF IN ONE GOD.

2 BELIEF IN THE ANGELS
ANGELS ARE SPIRITUAL BEINGS TO WHICH GOD HAS ASSIGNED VARIOUS DUTIES.

3 BELIEF IN MANY PROPHETS BUT ONE MESSAGE
SINCE ADAM, THE FIRST MAN AND ALSO THE FIRST PROPHET, GOD HAS CHOSEN MANY MEN TO TRANSMIT HIS MESSAGE INCLUDING ABRAHAM, MOSES, JESUS AND MUHAMMAD.

4 BELIEF IN THE DAY OF JUDGEMENT

5 BELIEF IN THE QUDAR (THE TIMELESS KNOWLEDGE OF GOD)
WHILE MAN HAS BEEN GIVEN THE POWER OF CHOICE IN HIS ACTIONS, NOTHING IN THE UNIVERSE TAKES PLACE WITHOUT GOD'S PRE-KNOWLEDGE AND DETERMINATION.

THE FIVE PILLARS OF OBSERVANCE
1 SHAHADA (THE CREED)
'THERE IS NO GOD BUT ALLAH, AND MUHAMMAD IS HIS PROPHET'

2 SALAT (PRAYER)
THE FIVE COMPULSORY DAILY PRAYERS ARE SAID AT DAWN, MIDDAY, IN THE AFTERNOON, AFTER SUNSET AND AFTER NIGHTFALL.

3 ZAKAT (CHARITY)
THE GIVING OF 2½ PER CENT OF ONE'S INCOME AND OF THE VALUE OF CERTAIN PROPERTY IS REGARDED AS BOTH AN OBLIGATION AND AN ACT OF WORSHIP.

4 SIYAM (FASTING)
THE QUR'AN TEACHES THAT FASTING IS AN OPPORTUNITY TO PRACTISE SELF-DISCIPLINE AND RESTRAINT.

5 HAJJ (PILGRIMAGE)
EVERY MUSLIM MUST MAKE THE PILGRIMAGE TO MECCA ONCE IN HIS LIFETIME, ONLY THOSE PREVENTED BY ILLNESS OR POVERTY BEING EXCUSED THIS OBLIGATION.

and Averroes slightly more Aristotelian. This type of philosophy died out after these men, though forms of gnostic philosophical speculation have continued until the present century in the Iranian cultural context.

The foundation of the discipline of Kalam or 'rational theology' may be ascribed to the Mu'tazilites named above and a few like-minded persons. About a century later the Sunnite theological schools began to take shape. The Muslim historical accounts attach much importance to the 'conversion' of al-Ash'ari (d. 935). He was trained in the Mu'tazilite school in Basra, but at the age of forty abandoned Mu'tazilism for a mainstream Sunnite position which he defended by Mu'tazilite methods. The Ash'arite theological school, which took its name from him, was for centuries the dominant school in the central provinces of

The teaching of Muhammad was a result of divine revelation. All his teaching is believed to be recorded in the Qur'an and is defined as surrender to the will of God as so written. In addition five observances are expected of every Muslim. By these observances every believer hopes to earn salvation at the Day of Judgement.

A painting from the Mughal courts of India showing a gathering of ascetics. The Sufi, a sect of the Sunnite form of Islam, practised asceticism although this has no part in the main teaching of Muhammad who had in fact condemned the monastic celibacy of the Christian world.

the caliphate. Among its distinguished members was al-Ghazali, already mentioned, who has been found a most attractive personality by western readers of his spiritual autobiography *Al-Munqidh min ad-dalal* ('Deliverance from Error'). In this he tells how, after becoming the main professor at the prestigious Nizamiyya *madrasa* (college) in Baghdad at the early age of thirty-four, he decided four years later to abandon his professorship in order to become a *sufi* (mystic).

Al-Maturidi (d. 944), a contemporary of al-Ash 'ari, founded a somewhat similar school in Samarqand but, although boasting some famous names, it remained unknown at the centre of the Islamic world for centuries. The Maturidite theologians, however, were closely associated with the Hanafite legal school and, when the latter became the official rite of the Ottoman empire, al-Maturidi was placed on a level with al-Ash 'ari, and the two were said to be the joint founders of the discipline of Kalam in its Sunnite form.

Many Hanbalite jurists were interested in theological doctrine and wrote books on the subject, but these do not belong to Kalam since their authors disapproved of its rational methods. There were keen intellects among them, however, and eventually some of these used forms of argument not unlike those of Kalam. The most distinguished later Hanbalite was Ibn-Taymiyya (1263–1328), whose thinking covered not only doctrine but the whole socio-political field. The adherents of Hanbalism were fewer than those of the other legal rites, and their chief strength was originally among the populace of Baghdad. By 1300, however, Damascus had become the main centre, and Ibn-Taymiyya lived mostly there. His influence among the Hanbalites remained strong for centuries, and contributed to the thinking of Muhammad ibn-'Abn-al-Wahhab (1703–92), the founder of Wahhabism, now the official form of Sunnism in Saudi Arabia. Wahhabism claims to be pure Islam, freed from such accretions as the veneration of saints.

The Sunnites now constitute about 90 per cent of all Muslims, but there cannot be said to have been any Sunnite self-awareness until about the year 1000. More than a century earlier there were groups calling themselves Ahl as-Sunna wa-l-Jama'a, 'the People of the Sunna (example of Muhammad) and the Community', and similar names; but it seems to have been only after 1000 that they began to think of slightly different groups as fellow-Sunnites. Western writers are inclined to equate 'Sunnite' with 'orthodox', but the latter term is inappropriate in an Islamic context since correct doctrinal belief is not the primary issue, but acceptance of the Shari'a. Some such term as 'mainstream Islam' or 'standard Sunnism' is preferable.

Islamic Sufism or mysticism has some relevance to theological doctrine. The earliest sufis were chiefly interested in ascetic practices and moral discipline, but soon there were others whose aim was to attain experiences of ecstasy. Best known of these was al-Hallaj, who claimed to have experienced union or even unity with God – a claim which was held to be blasphemous by the jurists. He was executed by crucifixion in 922, apparently on the grounds that he professed heretical doctrines which were dangerous for the state. From this time on there were many groups or schools of sufis, most of which held more or less normal Sunnite views and did not offend the jurists. Indeed there were some jurists who were sufis. Nevertheless many jurists were suspicious of the sufis, since besides those who held heretical views there were some who were lax in observance of the daily prayers and other ritual obligations. The situation changed after the 'conversion' of al-Ghazali, (see above). His greatest work is *Ihya' 'ulum ad-din*, 'The Revival of the Sciences

(or Disciplines) of Religion', which consists of forty chapters or books, each of which makes a small volume in European translations. This work covers the whole field of Islamic praxis, and is particularly concerned to show how a scrupulous observance of the Shari'a can be the basis of a truly mystical life. In the closing years of his life al-Ghazali established a hostel or monastery at Tus in eastern Iran where disciples joined him in leading a life that accorded as closely as possible to the monastic discipline of his rule.

The twelfth century saw the beginning of the sufi or dervish orders, which in time became numerous and widespread. As well as sharing a common life in a monastery each order (*tariqa*) had its distinctive form of worship, or *dhikr*, which supplemented the observance of the Shari'a. Thus the Mevlevi dervishes, centred at Konya in Turkey, are famous for the whirling dance which is part of their *dhikr*. The word *dhikr* means 'mention' or 'remembrance', especially of the name of God, and for many orders the continuous repetition of *Allah* for a long period is an essential part of the *dhikr*. In recent times many orders, in addition to their full members have had ordinary people associated with them as a kind of 'third order' (in Christian terms); and in cities these people could attend the *dhikr* and to some extent share in it. It is difficult to assess the importance of the sufi orders at the present time. Some appear to flourish and to provide for the spiritual development of members and adherents, but others seem to have become degenerate, with the leading men living luxuriously at the expense of poor adherents.

The Islamic creed

Since there was nothing in Islam comparable to the Ecumenical Councils of the Christian Church, there was no possibility of an official creed. Many creeds were produced by jurists and theologians, however, and some of these found wide acceptance, especially within their authors' schools. There were some slight differences between Hanafites, Ash'arites and Hanbalites, and some slighter differences within each school. In the end, however, there came to be a broad consensus among Sunnites on the main doctrines, and these may be said to constitute the standard Sunnite creed. These doctrines are summarized here, with comments, although not in the precise form found in any particular creed.

1. 'There is no deity but God' (la ilaha illa 'llahu); he has no partner.
The Arabic word *Allah* is probably contracted from *al-ilah*, 'the god,' and, as is shown by the Qur'an, was used by Arab pagans before Islam to designate a supposed 'high god'; it is also used by Arabic-speaking Christians. The first clause above is the first part of the Shahada or confession of faith (see below) and is Qur'anic. The greatest sin in Muslim eyes is to 'ascribe partners to God' (*shirk*).

2. God has existed from all eternity and will exist to all eternity.
Since Arabic has no single word for 'eternal', but separate words for 'without beginning' (*qadim, azali*) and 'without end' (*baqi, abadi*), some misleading translations are occasionally found.

3. God is unlike all created things; he is incor-

poreal; he neither begets nor is begotten; the categories of substance and accident do not apply to him; he has no spatial location, and may not be said to be in any direction. This last point is not contradicted by the Qur'anic assertion (7.54, etc.) that he is seated on the throne.

The human terms applied to God in the Qur'an, such as 'hand' and 'face', were much discussed. To take these terms literally was often regarded as the heresy of *tashbih*, 'making (God) resemble (humanity)'. The Mu'tazilites and, in later times, some of the rational theologians held that the terms were to be understood metaphorically. A middle course favoured by Hanbalites was that these terms were to be understood neither literally nor metaphorically but 'amodally' (*bi-la kayf*, 'without [specifying] how').

4. God will be seen by the faithful in Paradise.

Since God is incorporeal there were discussions about how this is possible. The idea of the vision of God balances the more sensual pictures of Paradise found in the Qur'an.

5. God has many names (*asma'*), such as the Merciful, the Powerful (or Omnipotent), the Forgiving; the qualities indicated by these names are his attributes (*sifat*).

The names are found in the Qur'an, some of them frequently repeated. There is a form of devotion which uses 'the ninety-nine beautiful names'. The earlier rational theologians paid special attention to seven attributes: power, knowledge, will, life, hearing, seeing, speech. They held that these attributes are 'not God, yet not other than God' and are eternal. The Mu'tazilites maintained that there are no distinct attributes and that, for example, God knows by his essence (*dhat*), not by an attribute of knowledge.

6. The Qur'an is the uncreated and eternal speech of God, remembered in human hearts, uttered by human tongues, and written in the copies of it.

The Mu'tazilites maintained that the Qur'an, while being the speech of God, was created. This was the point at issue in the Inquisition begun by al-Ma'mun. The Arabic term *kalam*, here rendered 'speech', could be translated 'word' to bring out Christian parallels; but it so happens that the more precise term for 'word', *kalima*, is applied to Jesus in the Qur'an (4.171) in the phrase 'God's messenger and his word'.

7. God will judge all men on the Last Day and, according to their deeds, assign them to Paradise (Heaven) or Hell.

This point is prominent in the earlier passages of the Qur'an where the sensual delights of Paradise, the Garden, and the excruciating pains of Hell, the Fire, are also depicted. There were many popular beliefs about the period between death and Judgement and also about the exact details of the Judgement.

8. Muhammad had God's permission to make intercession on the Last Day on behalf of sinners of his community. Provided the sin was not *shirk*, 'ascribing partners to God', the sinners would not be in Hell eternally, though they might be punished there for a time.

The Mu'tazilites denied the possibility of intercession, and held that people were judged strictly according to their acts.

9. God has sent prophets (*anbiya'*) and messengers (*rusul*) as instruments to convey his messages to the human race.

According to one creed there are 120,000 prophets but only 313 messengers. It was held that prophets were preserved (*ma'sum*) by God from all sin, or at least all serious sin.

10. The best of men after Muhammad was Abu-Bakr, then 'Umar, then 'Uthman, then 'Ali.

This is an affirmation of the basic Sunnite position that the first four actual caliphs (sometimes called the Rashidun or 'rightly guided') were the legitimate heads of the community. It contradicts the Shi'ite assertion that 'Ali was best after Muhammad and should have succeeded him.

11. A believer who sins does not thereby become an unbeliever (*kafir*).

This is the denial of the Khārijite principle that the grave sinner is excluded from the community.

12. Faith (*iman*) consists in knowing, confessing publicly, and acting; it increases and decreases.

By faith is meant 'what makes a man a believer' (mu'min). The statement given is of the Ash'arite and Hanbalite position, whereas the Hanafites held that actions were not included and that faith did not increase or decrease.

Other religions are not usually mentioned in the creeds, but there is traditionally a wide consensus about them. Moses as the founder of Judaism and Jesus as the founder of Christianity are spoken of in the Qur'an as prophets and messengers to whom God revealed a message identical in essentials with that given to Muhammad, whose coming they also foretold. It is generally agreed, however, that the Jews and Christians have corrupted the scriptures given to their founders, though it is not agreed what this corruption (*tahrif*) of the scriptures consists in, whether alteration of the text or alteration of the interpretation, or something else. The effect of this belief is that traditionally-minded Muslims are not prepared to listen to arguments based on biblical texts. Islamic universities, however, are now beginning to teach comparative religion, and some of the younger liberal Muslims realize that the traditional doctrine of the corruption of the Christian and Jewish scriptures can hardly be maintained in the modern world. The scholar al-Biruni (d. 1048), who was an expert on Indian affairs, regarded Hinduism, because of its scholars, as a monotheistic religion with written scriptures, despite the obvious polytheism of the ordinary people.

WRITINGS

The Qur'an and subordinate studies

The primary document or scripture of Islam is the Qur'an. This consists of the revelations which came to Muhammad during the last twenty years or so of his life. These are now arranged in *suras* or chapters, varying in length from 286 verses to 3 verses. Each *sura* has a name (occasionally more than one) taken from a distinctive word in one of its verses, and this name is normally used by Muslims in references. In a number of places Muslim scholars had different views of the exact point at which a verse ended, and this has led to different systems of numbering the verses. The numbering used in the nineteenth-century European editions of the Qur'an, and by western scholars until 1950 or so, has now been replaced in the main by that of the 'Egyptian standard edition' of 1924. In the earlier passages the verses are short and rhythmic, and the last word of each verse has a rhyme or assonance. Thus what is usually regarded as the first revelation runs as follows in transcription:

iqra' bi-smi rabbi-ka ladhi khalaq
khalaqa l-insana min 'alaq
iqra' fa-inna rabba-ka l-akram
alladhi 'allama bi-l-qalam
'allama l-insana ma lam ya'lam

Recite in the name of your Lord who created,
created man from a blood-clot;
recite, since your Lord is most generous,
who taught by the pen,
taught man what he knew not.
(96.1–5)

As the years passed the verses tended to become longer, especially after the Hijra when they were often both long and prosaic, but still had rhyme or assonance.

Much of the Qur'an appears to have been revealed in short passages, though there may also have been some longer ones. The work of putting these together into *suras*, or 'collecting' the Qur'an, was begun by Muhammad, since *suras* are mentioned in the Qur'an. Many of the early Muslims remembered much of the Qur'an, and a few wrote some of it down. By about 650, since most of those who remembered it had died and the exact wording of some passages was disputed, the caliph 'Uthman appointed a commission which 'collected' the complete Qur'an and produced a definitive text. While this procedure eli-

minated the so-called pre-'Uthmanic variants, the script then used did not indicate vowels and did not clearly distinguish certain consonants, and so there continued to be variants. Eventually scholars agreed that the Qur'an had been revealed in seven *qira'at* or sets of readings, and that these were all acceptable, while a few scholars wanted to add even more. All the variants are of minimal importance theologically. The Egyptian standard edition gives the form of the text known as 'Hafs from 'Asim', that is, the set of readings of 'Asim as recorded by his pupil Hafs.

A scholarly discipline of great importance is *tafsir*, the interpretation or exegesis of the Qur'an. This was also first discussed in mosques by devout Muslims, and gradually became less informal. The most important of the views put forward until about 900 were collected in a great commentary by at-Tabari (d. 923), an outstanding historian. Another well-known commentary was that of az-Zamakhshari (d. 1144), who was noted for his excellent knowledge of the Arabic language. Although he was a Mu'tazilite in theology, this affected his interpretations at only one or two points. The standard Sunnite commentary is usually held to be that of al-Baydawi (d. 1286), who used az-Zamakhshari but brought all the interpretations into harmony with his own Ash'arite views. The compiling of commentaries has continued through the centuries. One of the most recent, the Urdu commentary of Mawlana Abul Kalam Azad (d. 1958), has been translated into English under the title *The Tarjuman alQur'an* (London 1962).

Hadith

It was only natural that the first Muslims should hand on to their families and others the stories of their contacts with Muhammad. When those interested in law discussed some matter not dealt with in the Qur'an, some one might remember a saying or act of Muhammad that seemed appropriate, and this would help to decide the

Islam forbids any portrayal of Muhammad or other figural representation in religious works and there can be no depiction of God in any form. Therefore the art of calligraphy became important and emphasizes the value of the written word of God in the Qur'an. The earliest form was the Arabic Kufic script. Here are two names, of Allah on the left, and of Muhammad on the right. In speaking the name of Muhammad Muslims by custom always add the phrase: 'Peace and blessings of God be upon him', as a mark of respect.

Prayers in the Al Azhar Mosque, Cairo. This mosque is attached to a 1,000-year old school or madiasa. Today the University (as it was designated in 1930) is one of the most important centres of Islamic study. The prayers occur at dawn, midday, afternoon, at sunset and at the close of the day. Each service is preceded by a form of washing, and the worshipper should remove his shoes. The service always includes the words: 'There is no deity but God'.

point of law. By the second Islamic century the preservation and study of such anecdotes about Muhammad had become a distinct discipline. The common Arabic term for such anecdotes is *Hadith*, which was formerly translated 'tradition', but scholars now realize that this can sometimes be misleading and are preferring to retain the Arabic word.

After the use of *Hadith* in juristic arguments became normal it was found that rival jurists could produce different *Hadith* (or different versions of the same *Hadith*) with contrasting applications. Obviously, too, a *Hadith* could have been invented in order to establish some point of law. A form of criticism of *Hadith* was therefore established in order to distinguish those which were 'sound'. The method was based on the *isnad* or chain of authorities. Someone recounting a *Hadith* would say: 'I received this from L, who received it from M, who was told by N that he was once present in such and such circumstances when the Messenger of God said . . .' The names L, M, N constitute the *isnad*, and N, the last name in the chain, must be that of a 'Companion', that is, someone who had been with and heard the Messenger of God. If all the persons in the *isnad* (and women could be included) were good Muslims of correct views and upright character, then the *Hadith* was adjudged 'sound' (*sahih*). Nineteenth-century western scholars mostly held that this critique of *Hadith* allowed the acceptance of many which were clearly false but, as many early collections become accessible, it is being realized that these scholars were unduly sceptical

and that many they rejected were at least partly sound. There was probably little sheer invention of *Hadith*, but details may often have been modified to alter the emphasis and implications; and the *isnad* could be in part invented. It has also to be remembered, however, that the concern of Muslim critics of Hadith was not pure historical objectivity but the establishment of an appropriate basis for the social fabric of Islam.

By the ninth century extensive collections of 'sound' *Hadith* were being made, and by a kind of informal consensus, six of these eventually came to be recognized as authoritative. The most important are the *Sahih* of al-Bukhari (d. 870) and that of Muslim (d. 875). Each contains about 10,000 entries, though there is some overlapping within each and between them.

A subordinate discipline was *'ilm ar-rijal*, 'knowledge of the men', that is the evaluation of the transmitters in vast biographical dictionaries.

RELIGIOUS OBSERVANCES

The chief religious observances of Islam are known as 'the five pillars' and are: the Confession of Faith or Witnessing (*Shahada*), Worship or Prayer (*Salat*), Almsgiving (*Zakat*), the Fast (*Sawm*) of Ramadan, and the Pilgrimage (*Hajj*).

The *Shahada*
The *Shahada*, the Confession of Faith or Witnessing, is 'I bear witness that there is no

deity but God, Muhammad is the Messenger of God'. The formal pronouncement of these words makes a person a Muslim. They are repeated in the formal acts of Worship.

The *Salat*

The performance five times a day of the *Salat*, or formal Worship, often referred to as the prayers, is an obligation on every Muslim. The times are: dawn (*fajr*), midday (*ẓuhr*), afternoon ('*asr*), sunset (*maghrib*), night ('*isha*'). The worship must always be preceded by ablutions to ensure ritual purity. Worshippers face towards Mecca, and mosques are usually built oriented in this way and have a niche in one side to indicate the *qibla* or direction to be faced. From the minaret of the mosque a man called the muezzin (*mu'adhdhin*) gives the call to prayer at appropriate times.

Each of the five acts of worship is preceded by an introduction consisting of: standing upright; expressing the intention (for example, 'I offer this act of worship in fulfilment of the obligation of the dawn prayer'); repeating the *takbir*, 'God is very great', at which point short private prayers may be added. Then follows the first *rak'a* or ritual cycle.

Each *rak'a* begins with the *qira'a* or recitation of the Fatiha (the opening *sura* of the Qur'an) and another short passage. Then comes the *ruku'* or 'bowing', hands on knees, accompanied by the words 'Praise be to God'. After briefly returning to the upright position (*i'tidal*), the worshipper then prostrates himself in the *sujud*, touching the ground with his forehead, palms, knees and toes, while saying the *takbir*. From this he changes to a sitting position on his heels, and says another *takbir* before making a second prostration in which he asks for God's mercy. This action concludes the first *rak'a*.

The dawn worship has two such *rak'as*, the sunset worship three and the others four. After the second prostration of the last *rak'a* the worshipper takes an 'upright sitting' position (*qu'ud*), hands on knees, while pronouncing greetings on God and the Prophet, then repeats the Shahada or Confession of Faith, followed by a prayer that God will bless and preserve Muhammad and a prayer for the peace of those on his right and his left. This completes the act of worship.

It will be seen that the *Salat* consists of a number of bodily movements accompanied by expressions of adoration and praise (which may be more numerous than those mentioned). The culmination is the prostration when the worshipper acknowledges the might and majesty of God and his own status of slave to God. It is not essential to go to a mosque for the *Salat*, though many do, but attendance at the main local mosque is expected for the Friday midday prayer, at which there is a sermon. Where there are numerous worshippers

they form lines facing the *qibla*, and a leader (*imam*) stands in front to give the timing for the various movements, which all perform together. An individual may perform the worship by himself, and usually does so on a prayer-mat which he lays down facing Mecca.

The *Salat* may also be performed at certain other times of day as a non-obligatory devotion, and there are special forms of *Salat* for occasions such as a funeral or a severe drought. Informal private prayer is *du'a*'. For the guidance of the faithful there are large numbers of prayer manuals, and these have been fully described by Constance E. Padwick in his book *Muslim Devotions* (London 1961).

Zakat

Almsgiving, or *Zakat*, was an obligation for Muslims from the earliest times. A Muslim was required each year to give a prescribed amount of his property to the poor and those in unfortunate circumstances. The amount varied for each type of property. For camels it was roughly one for every forty owned, for sheep and goats one for every hundred owned; on agricultural produce it was a tenth, except where irrigation was required, when it was a twentieth. Through the centuries the practice has varied considerably. Where rulers demanded a tax of a tenth on the annual produce, it was virtually impossible to pay *Zakat* as well. Now the implementation of the obligation of *Zakat* is a matter for the individual.

Sawm

The Fast (*Sawm*) of Ramadan is widely observed by Muslims despite the difficulties it creates in the circumstances of modern life. It consists of abstinence from food, drink, smoking, sex and the use of perfume from before dawn until after sunset during every day of the month of Ramadan. In practice those who observe the fast spend much of the nights in eating, though this is frowned on by the pious. Many engage in the reciting of the Qur'an and other devotions. Voluntary fasts may be observed at other times.

Hajj

To make the *Hajj* or pilgrimage to Mecca at least once in one's lifetime is an obligation for every Muslim who has the necessary means and the opportunity; and nowadays millions from all over the Islamic world fulfil the obligation. The person who does so becomes a *Hajji*. The *Hajj* consists of a number of ceremonies spread over several days of the pilgrimage month of Dhu-l-hijja. These include: the sevenfold circumambulation of the Ka'ba (the cubical building in the centre of the 'sacred mosque' of Mecca, with a black stone which is kissed built into one corner), which is performed several times during the ceremonies;

The Shi'ite Muslims of Iran have always been followers of imans who, they believe, are successors of the fourth caliph, 'Ali. From a political movement theirs became a religious force. Although for centuries the religion of the majority in Iran, much was done to destroy its traditions by the former Shah who endeavoured to westernize the country. Here an Iranian woman at a rally holds up a portrait of the country's spiritual leader, the Ayatollah Khomeini.

the 'running' (*sa'y*) seven times between as-Safa and al-Marwa, two points beside the mosque 400 metres apart; the 'waiting' (*wuquf*) on 'Arafat, a plain 15½ miles (25 kilometres) from Mecca, for most of the period between midday and sunset on the 9th day of the month, while listening to two addresses and possibly conversing with friends; the sacrifice of a sheep or goat, if one can afford it, at Mina (halfway back to Mecca) on the 10th of the month, the day known as *'id al-adha*, 'the festival of the sacrifice'; the throwing of 49 (or 70) pebbles at three heaps of stones in Mina, of which one is identified with 'the great demon'. Before entering the sacred territory of Mecca the pilgrim must put on the simple pilgrim garb (*ihram*) consisting of two lengths of white cloth. The ceremonies in Mecca itself constitute the 'lesser pilgrimage' or *'Umra*, and this may be performed at any time of the year.

ORGANIZATION

Though there is no priesthood in Islam, there is, from a sociological point of view, a religious 'institution' constituted by the jurists. Frequently this has been based mainly on informal agreement. In the Ottomon Empire, however, by the early nineteenth century the religious institution had become highly organized and controlled the administration of justice, the formulations of laws and all higher education. There was a hierarchy

with many grades, alternating between academic and judicial appointments, and at its head the Shaykh al-Islam. This structure continued until the early years of the Turkish republic, but even before the replacement of the Shari'a by a European-type law in 1927 the traditional jurists had lost much of their power. In the nineteenth century they showed themselves unwilling to adapt the Shari'a to the contemporary needs of the empire, and the sultans, disregarding them, began to promulgate codes of law for various spheres of activity such as maritime commerce. This led to new courts and new forms of legal training, which excluded the traditional jurists.

Something similar happened in many Islamic countries, so that by the 1920s the Shari'a courts were dealing with little beyond questions of marriage, divorce and inheritance. Since 1950 parts of the Shari'a have been revived in various Islamic states, but the traditional jurists are nowhere so highly organized as in the Ottoman Empire and have little share in higher education.

The jurists of Iran were in a different position, since the source of their authority was the 'hidden imam' rather than the shahs, and weak shahs had had to concede to them control of the finances of the religious institution. This made it possible for them in 1979 to gain supreme power and expel the shah. Among the Iranian jurists there might be said to be a fluid and informal hierarchy. The more senior of them have the grade of *mujtahid*, and a few of these are further dignified with the honorific title of *'ayatullah'* (sign of God).

BABISM AND THE BAHA'I FAITH

BABISM

Babism is a religious movement which originated in nineteenth century Iran as a powerful expression of messianic Shi'ism. Its founder was Sayyid 'Alí Muhammad Shírází (1819–50), a young merchant who in 1844 laid claim to be the Báb, the traditional intermediary between the Shi'i Hidden Imam and his faithful followers. Later he made the higher claims of being the Imam Mahdi and the 'point' (*nuqta*) of a new divine revelation.

Under the Báb's direction, his chief disciples – themselves clerics – undertook an intensive missionary campaign which soon led to the widespread diffusion of the movement throughout Iran. Many of these early followers were members of the Shaykhi sect, and there are evident continuities between the theosophical esotericism and charismatic leadership of the two movements. Indeed, during this early period the Babi movement remained strongly Shi'i in orientation and, despite its pronounced messianism, its followers conformed strictly to the requirements of Shi'i law. Nevertheless, its doctrines were evidently heterodox, and its rapid expansion alarmed the Shi'i ulama, and they began to oppose and persecute its missionaries. In response, some Babis tended towards militancy and, in 1848, fighting broke out between Babis and orthodox Shi'is in the northern city of Barfurush. This followed closely on the proclamation of the Báb's higher claims, and together these events serve to mark a decisive turning point in the movement's development. The claim to Mahdihood constituted a direct challenge to the entire existing political and religious order which could not be ignored. The doctrinal changes conveyed by the Báb in his book, the *Bayán*, were thus over-shadowed, and the new code of Babi law was not put into general effect.

The Babis' separation from civil society was underlined by events at Barfurush. The government had already intervened to imprison the Báb (1847). It now intervened in the local conflict, driving the Babis into total opposition to the regime. Further conflicts ensued (1850–1), and at government order the Báb was executed (8/9 July, 1850). Deprived of its religious focus, the movement began to fragment. One small group of Babis made an unsuccessful attempt to assassinate the Shah (August 1852). The government then completed its suppression of the movement and the Babi remnant effectively went underground until its revival in the late 1850s by Bahá'u'lláh, the founder of the Baha'i Faith (see below). This development engendered internal tensions within the movement. Bahá'u'lláh's younger half-brother, Subh-i Azal (Morn of Eternity) (1830/1–1912), was the Báb's appointed successor, but he had been ineffective as a leader. In 1866, a definite rift opened between the two brothers, and the Babi remnant divided between a Baha'i majority and a small Azali minority. In contrast to the pacific policies of Bahá'u'lláh, Subh-i Azal continued to advocate political militancy, several of his younger followers being prominently involved in the Iranian constitutional movement at the turn of the century. Azal died in exile in Famagusta, Cyprus, on 29 April 1912. A small and semi-secret community of Azali Babis still survives in Iran.

THE BAHA'I FAITH

The Baha'i Faith is a religion founded by Mírzá Husayn 'Alí Núrí (1817–92), known as Bahá'u-lláh (Glory or Splendour of God), who claimed to be a messenger of God and the promised redeemer of all religions.

HISTORY

The Baha'i Faith emerged out of Babism (see above). As the son of a leading Iranian landowner and courtier, Bahá'u'lláh was one of the most socially prominent Babi converts (1844), and was imprisoned for his involvement with the movement in 1852. According to his own account, this imprisonment – in the fearsome Black Pit of Tehran – marked the beginning of his religious mission, and he experienced a number of revelatory visions. Released from Tehran, he was exiled to Baghdad in Ottoman Iraq. Following a two-year period of ascetic withdrawal in Kurdistan (1854–6) he set about revivifying Babism, effectively displacing his half-brother, Subh-i Azal

'Abdu'l-Bahá, eldest son and successor of Bahá'u'lláh, designated as the 'Servant of Splendour' or 'Centre of the Covenant'. His missionary journeys in Europe and America during 1911–13 led to the setting up of Baha'i communities overseas.

(1830/1–1912) as leader of the movement. On the eve of his departure from Baghdad in 1863 he told his immediate followers of his claim to be a divine messenger. Subsequently exiled to Edirne (Adrianople) (1863–8), he made an open declaration of his claim (1866). This led to a definite breach between his followers (Baha'is) and those of Subh-i Azal (Azalis). In 1868 he was transferred to the prison-city of Akka (Acre) in Ottoman Syria, in and around which he remained until his death in 1892. During this period the Baha'i religion was consolidated, and by the 1870s most Babis had become Baha'is. An efficient missionary endeavour gained new converts in Iran, Egypt, Russian Turkestan and British India.

After Bahá'u'lláh's death, leadership of the Baha'is passed to his eldest son and appointed successor, Abbas Effendi (1844–1921), known as 'Abdu'l-Bahá (Servant of Bahá). Although initially challenged in his authority by his half-brother, Muhammad 'Alí, 'Abdu'l-Bahá soon gained the support of most of the Iranian Baha'is, guiding them through the years of political turmoil at the turn of the century. This period also saw the first conversions of Baha'is in North America and Europe, a development consolidated by 'Abdu'l-Bahá's own extensive travels in the West (1911–13). Although the western Baha'is were few in number a gradual process of 'Westernization' was set in train, a development accelerated under the leadership of 'Abdu'l-Bahá's appointed successor and eldest grandson, the Oxford-educated Shoghi Effendi Rabbani (1897–1957), the 'Guardian of the Cause of God' (*valí amru'lláh*).

Under Shoghi Effendi's leadership the system of elective assemblies which 'Abdu'l-Bahá had fostered was standardized, and these institutions were given responsibility for local and national Bahá'i administration. This bureaucratic form replaced earlier and more personalized forms of leadership and, in the West, there was prolonged opposition from those Baha'is who rejected the degree of control this represented. Opposition reached its peak in the late 1920s and early 1930s, but thereafter the attention of the Baha'i world was increasingly directed towards the systematic campaigns of expansion instituted by Shoghi Effendi. A series of national Baha'i plans (1937–53) was followed by an international ten-year crusade (1953–63) designed to secure the world-wide diffusion of the Faith. Further administrative developments occurred in the 1950s, so that when Shoghi Effendi died unexpectedly in 1957 without having appointed a successor, a group of leading Baha'is, the 'Hands of the Cause', were able to assume temporary authority. This 'interregnum' came to an end in 1963 with the election of the

Universal House of Justice as the supreme ruling body of the Baha'i Faith. Whilst the vast majority of Baha'is accepted these developments a small group, under the leadership of Charles Mason Remey, sought to continue the Guardianship. These soon broke into a number of antagonistic factions.

Under the direction of the Universal House of Justice, the Baha'i community has undergone further expansion in a series of systematic teaching campaigns. Increasing attention has also been directed towards the wider social role of the Baha'i Faith in areas such as education, socio-economic development and world peace. Existing contacts with the United Nations and its agencies have also been considerably strengthened in recent years.

DISTRIBUTION

With a strong emphasis on global diffusion, the Baha'is have established at least minimal representation in almost all the countries of the world. Baha'i literature has also been translated into all the world's major languages as well as many of its minor ones. Nevertheless, Baha'i distribution is highly uneven. In terms of the history of Baha'i expansion, the world may be divided into four cultural areas: the Islamic heartland; the West; the Third World; and the Communist bloc. The first three of these areas represent successive cultural breakthroughs in the religion's diffusion.

In the Islamic heartland, Baha'i originally derived from Iranian Shi'ism. Even though expansion was soon made beyond this cultural constituency it was limited in scope. The number of Sunni Muslim Arab or Levantine Christian converts has remained few. Only amongst Iranian Jews and Zoroastrians have significant numbers of conversions occurred. Thus, despite considerable persecution, the Iranian Baha'i community (c. 300,000) dwarfs all others in the Middle East and North Africa. The latest persecution (1979–) indicates both its tenacity and its beleaguered position in Iranian society.

Expansion in the West began in the 1890s, first in the United States and later in Europe, Canada, Australia, New Zealand and Hawaii. The United States remains the largest single western Baha'i community (c. 100,000), but a widespread diffusion has been achieved throughout the area. Until the late 1950s most western Baha'is were former lapsed or liberal Protestants, although there were also a small number of Jewish conversions. Since that date there has been a great expansion in numbers – partly reflecting the religious upsurge of the 1970s – and a corresponding diversification of membership. Particularly significant has been a massive influx of southern US blacks.

Expansion in the Third World was at first largely confined to Iranian and western oriented social groups, but from the 1950s onwards there was significant expansion amongst the indigenous rural populations. Larger Baha'i communites have thus begun to develop in various parts of Latin America, sub-Saharan Africa, Asia and Oceania. The largest single Baha'i community in the world is now in India, with approximately two million members and collectively the Third World Baha'i communities now constitute the demographic majority of the world's estimated four million Baha'is.

Expansion in the communist block has been extremely limited, even where minimal Baha'i activity has been permitted by the authorities. Formerly flourishing Baha'i communities, such as those in Russian Turkestan and Vietnam, have been effectively destroyed or disbanded.

WRITINGS

The primary sources of Baha'i doctrine and practice are the authenticated writings of Bahá'u'lláh and the authoritative interpretations of 'Abdu'l-Bahá and Shoghi Effendi. The directives of the Universal House of Justice are regarded as authoritative guidance for the conduct of Baha'i activities. The writings of other individual Baha'is may be influential, but they are not vested with authoritative status. The writings of the Báb (see p. 000) are also regarded as part of Baha'i scripture, but they are not a direct source of doctrine. The sacred books of other religions are revered.

The collected writings of Bahá'u'lláh, 'Abdu'l-Bahá and Shoghi Effendi comprise at least 60,000 items, the majority of them letters. Most of these remain unpublished. Even so, to date, nine volumes each of Bahá'u'lláh's writings and 'Abdu'l-Bahá's writings and talks have appeared in English translation. Fifteen volumes of Shoghi Effendi's letters in English have also been published, together with his book *God Passes By* (1944).

BELIEF

God is the all-powerful and all-knowing creator of all. He has created human beings that they might know and love him. As God is, in essence, completely transcendent, this knowledge is mediated by the 'Manifestations of God' (*mazáhir-i iláhí*). These individuals reflect and manifest God's attributes and reveal his specific purposes to humankind. This revelation varies in accord with the receptivity of the peoples of each particular

Always a missionary sect, Babism has many world-wide adherents. Its headquarters are in Haifa, Israel where there is a shrine of the Báb, an archives building and an administrative centre. Baha'is continue to spread their missionary work through education and publications; Baha'i literature has been translated into 230 languages. Their work is organized by local and national spiritual assemblies. In 1963 the National Assemblies elected the first Universal House of Justice which has administrative, judicial and legislative functions.

age. All the great religions of the world are part of a progressive revelation of a single 'religion of God.' Past revelators have included Abraham, Moses, Gautama Buddha, Jesus, Muhammad and the Báb. Bahá'u'lláh is the Manifestation of God for the present age. Other Manifestations will succeed him in the future.

The Baha'i Faith teaches that the individual human soul comes into being at the moment of conception. After death it may progress through the various 'worlds of God'. These are spiritual realms. There is no reincarnation. Again, 'heaven' and 'hell' are not places but states of soul. Spiritual progress results from recognition of the Manifestations of God, obedience to their commands, prayerfulness and well-motivated good deeds.

Evil does not exist as a positive force. The selfishness and wrongdoing of human beings stem from their lack of spiritual education and development. Human suffering represents both a challenge to human endeavour to devise means of mitigation and a reminder of the ultimate transcience and weakness of human life in this world.

Each Manifestation provides the teachings for social as well as individual development. At a societal level, the present age is unique. The unity of all the people and religions of the world is its destined hallmark. To this end governments and people must work to secure world peace; a world government; a world auxiliary language; political justice; the abolition of racial, national and religious prejudices; the ending of all forms of economic and chattel slavery; the abolition of extremes of wealth and poverty; the full emancipation of women; universal education and the development of human and natural resources.

The Baha'is believe that true religion is based on love and compassion for all the peoples of the world. Fanaticism and religious disputation erode this basis. Religion is complementary to science and reason and should be in harmony with them.

WORSHIP AND THE REGULATION OF SOCIAL LIFE

Religious life centres on individual acts of devotion and a communal 'Feast' held once every nineteen days. The specific acts of devotion comprise daily prayer, moral and spiritual self-accounting and reading of Baha'i scriptures, and an annual nineteen-day fast (2–20 March). Giving to the Baha'i fund, work in the spirit of service and missionary activity are also regarded as forms of worship. The Nineteen Day Feast is held at the beginning of each month in a specially devised Baha'i (Babi) calendar. It consists of devotional, consultative and social sections. Meditation is encouraged, but there are no set forms. Pilgrimage to the Baha'i shrines in Haifa and Akka is also encouraged.

Besides Feasts, Baha'i communities come together to commemorate various holy days, including the Baha'i New Year at the vernal equinox (usually 21 March) and the Ridván festival (21

FESTIVALS

A portrayal of Sita in the Ramlila festival. Sita is the wife of Rama and the daughter of king Janaka. Through the popular story of the Ramayana Sita reinforces traditional ideas of feminine virtue, especially those of loyalty, faithfulness and purity.

Festivals play an important part in all religions, although they also relate closely to cultural and social activities that are wider than religion. People are sometimes concerned that the religious message of Christmas, for example, is diluted or distorted by secular celebrations; yet to disentangle the secular and religious meaning of Christmas is difficult. The location of the festival close to the shortest day of the year in northern Europe is related more to ancient practices that had to do with persuading the sun and light to return than with certainty about the actual date of the birth of Jesus Christ. And Churches themselves have willingly embraced the pre-Christian symbolism of Christmas lights and fir trees, and might be thought to have baptized such symbols successfully into the context of a joyful and colourful Christian celebration. So it is with festivals in all religious traditions. By their very nature they tend to embrace secular as well as religious concerns, and to provide outlets for social and sometimes national celebrations, as well as for the more narrowly religious intentions to which purists often seek to recall them. Festivals serve to express the fundamental rhythms of life, and in this expression they are as essential to the secular world as they are to religion.

ABOVE & RIGHT The Ramlila festival celebrates the climax of the story of the Ramayana, one of the two great epics of Hinduism. The story tells of the exile of the great and good king Rama (who in the Vaishnavite tradition is the seventh avatar of Lord Vishnu), accompanied by his beautiful wife Sita and his brother Lakshmana. During their exile in the forests of south India the three were in conflict with demons, and especially with the king of the demons, Ravana. Ravana kidnapped Sita and took her to his kingdom of Sri Lanka, from where Rama, with the help of the monkey god Hanuman, rescued her and destroyed the demon king. In story form the Ramayana conveys important Hindu ideas of dharma, or duty, of the virtues of the good king and the faithful wife, and of God who comes as an avatar to deliver people from evil and to restore righteousness in the world. The festival of Ramlila is connected with the final day of the September/October festival of Navaratri (also called Durga Puja and Ayudha Puja). On this day the victory of Rama over Ravana is celebrated, and effigies of Ravana (right) and his lieutenants Meghanada and Kumbhakana are filled with fireworks and burned.

ABOVE *Durga, a consort of Shiva, is one of the two great gods of Hinduism. The character of Shiva is ambiguous, possibly symbolizing the reconciliation of opposites (asceticism and family life, for example), or reflecting the incorporation into orthodox tradition of pre-Aryan indigenous religion. Shiva is both creator and destroyer, and that paradox is expressed in the character of Durga, a Bengali goddess who is worshipped both as 'the Mother' and as a fierce warlike figure especially celebrated as a destroyer of demons, and so of all evil. Here, at the festival of Durga Puja, the goddess is seen carrying a variety of weapons in her arms.*

ABOVE *The elephant-headed Ganesha is a very popular Hindu god. The son of Shiva and Parvati, he symbolizes wisdom, good luck, prosperity and peace. The festival of Ganesha Chaturthi, celebrated in August/September, may originally have been a fertility festival among the Dravidian people. During the festival small clay images of Ganesha are kept in the house, and prayers for prosperity and good fortune offered before it. This large image of Ganesha, sitting astride the world, is being taken in procession for disposal in a river.*

ABOVE *This representation of the Nativity by Giotto reflects the birth story of Jesus according to St Luke's Gospel. Luke's story of the birth taking place in a manger, and of shepherds, told of the birth in a vision, hastening to see the baby, may represent a revelation of ordinary people, by contrast with St Matthew's account in which it is the wise men, or magi, who greet the child.*

LEFT In San Salvador, El Salvador, a Holy Week procession acts out the events recorded in the Gospel narratives of the last hours of the life of Jesus. Here a young boy plays the part of Jesus, wearing a crown of thorns (Matthew 27.29; Mark 15.17; John 19.1,2) and carrying a cross. In Christian, and especially Catholic, devotion, the re-enactment of the Passion ('suffering') of Jesus plays an important part, and portrayals of the last moments in the life of Christ have been part of Christian liturgical drama since the fourth century.

ABOVE A Roman Catholic Palm Sunday procession in Saltzburg, Austria. The carrying of branches reflects the tradition that when Jesus entered Jerusalem on the Sunday before the Passover (Pesach), 'the great body of pilgrims who had come to the festival, hearing that Jesus was on the way to Jerusalem, took palm branches and went out to meet him' (St John). In the Christian calendar Palm Sunday marks the beginning of Holy Week, in which Jesus' arrest, trial and death are commemorated. Holy Week culminates in the solemn recollection of the crucifixion on Good Friday, which is followed two days later by the joyous festival of Easter.

ABOVE *Muslims celebrate the feast of Id al Fitr, which occurs at the end of the month of fast called Ramadan. Five fundamental duties (din) are required of Muslims: one of these is to fast from sunrise to sunset throughout the month of Ramadan. The corporate fast widely observed among Muslims provides a period of self-examination, repentance, and heightened devotion, and enhances the sense of community. The end of the fast is marked by the celebration of Id al Fitr, which is an occasion for public worship, the exchange of gifts, and special meals.*

LEFT Unmarried amaNazaretha women perform a religious dance during their annual July festival. Zulu people from many parts of South Africa gather together for three weeks in July, erect temporary dwellings, and hold meetings for worship and fellowship. This dance, performed on the last day of the festival, lasts for many hours and is intended to renew spiritual power for the coming year. The umbrellas appear to have taken the place of traditional dancing sticks. The instruments reflect the mixture of biblical and Zulu concepts of the dance (see Psalm 150).

LEFT An image of the Buddha is paraded around the streets of Bangkok during the celebration of 'the Buddha Day', which occurs at the time of the full moon in May, and is the first festival in the Buddhist annual cycle. Although in Theravada Buddhism the Buddha is regarded as an enlightened man and not a God, the Buddha image has become a common object of worship in both Theravada and Mahayana countries, and a feature of this festival is the public processing of the Buddha image.

ABOVE Jews join in worship during the festival of Pesach (Passover) at Mea Shearim, a strongly orthodox quarter of Jerusalem; dress, beards, and sidelocks reflect the orthodoxy. Pesach, originally a spring agricultural festival, has for many centuries been a celebration of the Exodus of Hebrew slaves from Egypt. Part of the Passover Eve service is in fulfilment of the injunction that 'you shall tell your son, "This commemorates what the Lord did for me when I came out of Egypt"' (Exodus 13.8).

The dramatic Heron Dance at the Sensoji Shinto Temple, Asakua, Tokyo, takes place in April each year. The heron, or Japanese crane, is a symbol of happiness and longevity, and people in the local community are always eager to participate in the dance and to act out its symbolic meaning. The celebration probably reflects a Shinto tradition going back to the ninth century CE, although the present form of the dance appears to be the result of a sixteenth- or seventeenth-century revival. The dance reflects an important aspect of Shinto teaching, namely that the community is to be united through the celebration of its festivals with the kami, divine beings immanent in the world, who encourage vital and dynamic living as well as communal harmony.

April-2 May) marking the anniversary of Baha'u'lláh's first declaration of his mission (1863). There are also regular home-based teaching meetings ('firesides'). Baha'i meetings do not require special buildings, but there are Baha'i Houses of Worship (seven to date) in various parts of the world.

Apart from the set form of certain prayers, and simple ceremonies for marriage and burial, there are few distinctive Baha'i rituals. There are no specific forms of dress and no food prohibitions. Many Baha'is use the Baha'i greeting, *Alláh-u-Abhá* (God is Most Glorious), and wear a Baha'i ring, but these practices are not obligatory.

Great emphasis is placed on the importance of stable family life. Marriage is monogamous, and is conditional on the consent of both the bride and groom and their parents. Divorce is strongly discouraged, but is permitted after a set 'year of waiting'. The procreation of children is regarded as a primary purpose of marriage, but the planning of family size is regarded as a personal decision. All extra-marital sexual relations are forbidden.

Homosexual relationships, gambling, begging, the use of alcohol and narcotics, and involvement in partisan politics are also forbidden. Backbiting is morally condemned. Positive injunctions include loyalty to duly established governments, the valuing of education and work, and personal cleanliness. The importance of personal conscience is emphasized and much stress is placed on the principle of consultation as a means of resolving problems.

ORGANIZATION

There is no priesthood. Administrative authority rests with local and national Spiritual Assemblies. These are nine-member councils which are elected annually. Various individuals occupy advisory roles as Counsellors and Auxiliary Board Members. Supreme authority rests with the Universal House of Justice, a body which is elected every five years.

A calligraphic representation of the 'greatest name of God', ya baha' al-abra, ('O Splendour of the most Splendid'). This sign is found in most Baha'i homes. Another symbol is the name Baha', which is often found engraved on ringstones. Babism, like Shi'ism, is rich in magic, the use of talismans and incantations.

HINDUISM

HISTORICAL OUTLINE AND PRESENT-DAY DISTRIBUTION

Hinduism is the major religion of India and one of the world's oldest faiths. Of the 700 million inhabitants of the Republic of India in 1984 more than 547 million (or 79 per cent of the total population) were Hindus. Today Hindus are also found in many other countries of Asia, Africa and the West and the total number of Hindus in the world is estimated at over 647 million.

The term 'Hinduism' was coined by Europeans in relatively modern times to describe the Indian way of life. Hindus themselves originally had no word to describe their own religion, but now often refer to their religious beliefs and practices as *sanatana dharma*, the 'eternal law' or 'eternal order', for Hinduism is believed to be eternal and unchanging. All the same, Hinduism has evolved over a period of at least three millennia, and includes a great many different beliefs, from the most elementary to the most highly developed philosophical and theological ideas. 'Hinduism' is thus an umbrella-term referring to a conglomerate of different religions sharing essential characteristics.

The origins of Hinduism are lost in the distant past. It possesses no single founder, no central doctrine, no unified organization, hierarchy or transmission of teaching. Its essential carriers were the bonds of family, caste and village life. Until the late nineteenth century Hinduism was not a missionary religion but had primarily an ethnic character. In many ways, however, Hinduism is much more than a religion; it embraces an entire way of life and has shaped a whole civilization. Right action and right behaviour are more important than right beliefs and for this reason Hinduism is often described as an 'orthopraxis' rather than an 'orthodoxy'.

In spite of its complex internal diversity Hinduism can be considered as an integral whole embracing all areas of life. It covers religious, social, economic, literary and artistic aspects and represents a cultural heritage of enormous wealth and richness. Hinduism has a great tradition of learning and possesses a rich store of religious and philosophical literature which has been created and faithfully handed down through the centuries, largely by the Brahman class. The tradition of the Brahmans is sometimes referred to as 'Sanskritic' because much of it is embodied in texts written in the sacred language of Sanskrit. This Sanskritic, all-India tradition is accorded great prestige but most of Hinduism, as practised by the majority of Hindus, is based on local, regional or sectarian traditions which are immensely diverse. Over 80 per cent of Hindus live in villages of which there are more than 500,000 in India. Western knowledge of Hinduism was for a long time mainly based on the study of Sanskrit texts, but many scholars are now studying Hinduism in the villages and also pay attention to the distinct tradition of south Indian Tamil culture.

Whilst it would be wrong to speak of a separate village or popular Hinduism distinct from a higher, philosophical Hinduism, as earlier authors used to do, one must be aware that Hindu diversity is so great that it includes many different elements, from philosophical and theological thought to numerous folk beliefs and practices as well as distinct influences from tribal groups which were absorbed into Hindu society. The entire range of Hinduism from simple folk beliefs to sophisticated thought can be found both in Indian villages and cities, depending on the caste, sect and education of particular individuals. There are strong regional and sectarian differences in Hindu religious practice so that one can always find exceptions and contradictions to what is said about Hinduism in general.

The systematic, critical study of the Hindu religious tradition began only in the modern period with the pioneering efforts of western orientalists and missionaries and was soon furthered by the outstanding work of Hindu scholars and reformers of the nineteenth and twentieth centuries. Through this work the traditionally separate philosophical and religious teachings were presented in a more unified and coherent manner. As a result many general works on Hinduism and the

Hindu view of life exist today, but however much has been achieved by way of a better understanding in the West, many facets of the Hindu religious tradition and the deep religious resources of this ancient faith still await further exploration and appreciation. The major aspects of Hinduism can be only briefly characterized in what follows.

The earliest times

The history of Hinduism can be divided into several periods and the influences of earlier developments lie side by side with later ones. Before the emergence of Hinduism there was first the Vedism or Brahmanism of ancient India; earlier still there was the civilization in the Indus valley (3000–1700 BCE), of which archaeological remains have been known only since the 1920s through the excavations at Mohenjo Daro (in modern Pakistan) and several other sites far beyond the valley of the Indus. This highly developed urban civilization – usually referred to as Harappa culture – shows evidence of the cult of the Mother Goddess and the Bull, perhaps even of a prototype of the later Hindu god Shiva, of yoga, phallic emblems, the worship of sacred trees and animals, and of ritual bathing and purification rites. It is thought that certain Hindu beliefs may include archaic survivals going back to this prehistoric period, although since the language of the Indus valley civilization has not yet been deciphered many uncertainties remain.

During the early second millennium BCE the Indus valley civilization disappeared, for reasons not entirely clear. It was soon replaced by the culture of the invading Aryans, who entered India from the north and came from the steppes of southern Russia and central Asia. Before they invaded the Indian subcontinent (in about 1500 BCE) the Aryans had been in close contact with the ancestors of the ancient Iranians and with other branches of the same people who penetrated far westwards into Europe. The kinship of all these groups is evident from the Indo-European family of languages and from the similarity of certain religious ideas.

The Vedic period: the *Rig Veda*

The Aryans brought into India the Sanskrit language (akin to the classical languages of Europe), the horse and chariot, and a sacrificial system known as Brahmanism or Vedism. Whereas the earlier Harappa culture is known only through its archaeological finds, the Vedic period (1500–600 BCE) has hardly left any material remains at all: the little that is known about Vedic religion and society must be inferred from the literary heritage of the Aryans, especially from their earliest source, the *Rig Veda*, a collection of hymns in early Sanskrit, composed over several centuries and reaching its final form about 900 BCE.

Hinduism is the development of a synthesis of the early religions of the Harappa civilization and the sacrificial cults brought into India c 1500 BCE by the Aryan invaders. The Harappa culture shows evidence of worship of the Mother Goddess and also of the Bull. This seal is one of many of this type found during excavations at Mohenjo Daro.

IN THE VEDIC PERIOD OF HINDUISM, THE MAIN GODS WERE:

AGNI, THE LIFE-FORCE, GOD OF FIRE AND SACRIFICE
INDRA, GOD OF WAR AND STORM
VARUNA, SKY GOD: GOD OF THE DAY AND OF WATER
RUDRA, A MOUNTAIN GOD
DYAUSPITR, THE 'HEAVEN FATHER'
SURYA, THE SUN, DESCRIBED AS 'THE EYE OF VARUNA'
THESE, AND THE OTHER GODS REPRESENTING THE HEAVENLY BODIES AND THE ELEMENTS, LATER GAVE WAY TO A SECOND SET OF DIVINITIES:
BRAHMA, THE CREATOR
VISHNU, THE PRESERVER AND CONTROLLER OF HUMAN FATE
SHIVA, THE DESTROYER, SOURCE OF BOTH GOOD AND EVIL
SARASVATI, BRAHMA'S CONSORT AND GODDESS OF KNOWLEDGE AND TRUTH
LAKSHMI, VISHNU'S WIFE, GODDESS OF FORTUNE AND BEAUTY

The corpus of Vedic literature comprises four major collections, generally known as the four Vedas, and many later ritual and philosophical texts called *Brahmanas* and *Aranyakas* ('forest treatises') which culminated in the philosophical dialogue of the Upanishads. The Aryans were a martial and patriarchal people whose main divinities were male. The religion of the *Rig Veda* is a polytheism consisting of divinities associated with the sky, the atmosphere and other natural forces. Many of the most important Vedic gods are almost forgotten today. Indra was the great war god of the Aryans but later became mainly a rain god. Varuna, the guardian of the cosmic order, is rarely remembered today, whereas Surya, the sun god, and Agni, the god of fire and sacrifice, are still honoured.

The divinities were propitiated through an elaborate ritual of sacrifices that was thought indispensable in upholding the natural order of cosmos and society and gave the priestly Brahman class power and prestige.

The hymn 'The Sacrifice of Primal Man' (*Purusha-sukta*, *Rig Veda* X,90) describes how the whole world appeared out of the great sacrifice of a cosmic person (*purusha*) whose ritual dismemberment created all realities, including the Vedic social order of four classes which is headed by the Brahmans:

> *When they divided primal Man,*
> *Into how many parts did they divide him?*
> *What was his mouth? What his arms?*
> *What are his thighs called? What his feet?*
>
> *The Brahman was his mouth,*
> *The arms were made the Prince,*
> *His thighs the common people,*
> *And from his feet the serf was born.*

The *Brahmanas* and *Aranyakas*

The *Rig Vedas* seems to have been chiefly composed by people living in the Punjab; the later Vedas and *Brahmanas*, alternatively, are centred on the region around modern Delhi. During the period of the *Aranyakas* and Upanishads, Aryan culture penetrated further east into the plain at the Ganges and reached the borders of modern Bengal. New doctrines appeared during this time, perhaps borrowed from the indigenous inhabitants of the Ganges basin. The most important of these new teachings was the belief in transmigration. First there appeared the belief that death occurred even in Heaven; then the gods themselves were declared to be subject to death; and ultimately it was believed that all beings must be reborn again and again.

Together with this belief in transmigration appeared the need for a final release (*moksha*) from the bonds of earthly existence. To achieve this the best way was thought to be a life of asceticism, and so many Brahman youths – as well as people from other social groups – left their homes and went around as wanderers or lived in forest huts where they meditated, debated with each other, and underwent severe self-mortification.

From among these groups a number of heterodox teachers then appeared who denied the validity of the Vedas, denounced the supremacy of the Brahmans, and rejected the existing social order. These heretics included some of the greatest religious teachers of India, such as Vardhamana Mahavira of the Jainas and Siddharta Gautama, the Buddha. Other ascetics gradually found a place in the Brahmanic fold, and their philosophical discussions are recorded in the Upanishadic dialogues.

The rise of early Hinduism

The Vedic period was thus followed by a period of reaction and criticism of the beliefs and practices of Brahmanism. This led not only to the rise of the new religions of Jainism and Buddhism during the sixth century BCE, but also to the gradual emergence of early Hinduism (600 BCE–300 CE). Through a long process of assimilation and amalgamation the cult of the Vedic élite had thus been superseded by new religious traditions from both Aryan and indigenous non-Aryan sources, including possibly some Dravidian elements, today found largely in south India. Early Hinduism represents a new religious synthesis based on Indo-European, Indo-Iranian and indigenous sources from either the Indus valley or other areas.

During this period the rules for domestic and other rites, and for the general conduct of life, were worked out in great detail. To counteract the strong influence of asceticism, the Brahmans devised the teaching about the four *ashramas* (stages of life) and the concept of *varnashramadharma* (duty according to one's *varna* – 'class' – and stage in life), fully articulated in the *Laws of Manu*.

In addition to this codification of social and individual conduct, the worship of the major gods and the celebration of rituals underwent a change of emphasis. Two comparatively insignificant Vedic gods, Vishnu, connected with the sun and sacrifice, and Rudra, later known as Shiva ('the Auspicious'), superseded the Vedic nature-divinities and provided the central focus for the newly emerging religions of Vaishnavism and Shaivism. The nature of worship changed from public sacrifices to domestic ritual (*puja*) and personal devotion (*bhakti*). The major philosophical insights were formulated in *sutras* ('threads', or collections of aphoristic statements) which later provided the basis for the main philosophical schools of Indian thought. And, finally, at this time the two great epics, the *Mahabharata* and *Ramayana*, came into being.

From the puranic period to modern times

The development of most of Hinduism as we know it today was completed during the next stage (300–1200 CE), called the puranic period after the texts of the *Puranas* ('ancient stories') which reflect a new religious and social situation. They provide some of the major sources for Hindu mythology and tell us much about popular religious beliefs and practices. During this period brilliant religious thinkers developed a systematic elaboration of Hindu theological and philosophical doctrines, whilst important developments of *bhakta* devotionalism occurred at the popular level. This wave of devotionalism began in southern India from where it spread slowly northwards. It was later further intensified through contact with Islam which entered India before the end of the twelfth century and dominated many Indian developments, especially in the north, until the modern period which began around 1800.

The development of modern Hinduism has been much influenced by contact with the West. During the nineteenth and twentieth centuries many changes and reform movements arose to purify, reform and strengthen Hinduism, leading to what has been called 'neo-Hinduism', which has produced many apologetic, spiritual and philosophical works, often written in English. From the late nineteenth century onwards, Hindu missionaries became active in the West and preached a unified version of Hinduism. In India itself Hindu religious ideals provided the dynamic inspiration for much of the modern independence movement.

Today, Hinduism exists in many countries outside India. In addition to western converts to Hinduism there are now, for example, more than 300,000 ethnic Hindus living in the United Kingdom. They have emigrated mainly since the 1960s, either directly from India or via East Africa. The majority are Gujaratis, followed by Punjabis and a number of smaller ethnic groups. Hindu immigrants, like Hindus in India, are divided into many different religious groups and sects. The fastest growing group, with over 30,000 members, is the Swaminarayan sect founded as a reform movement in early nineteenth-century Gujarat, but now present wherever Gujaratis reside, whether in East Africa, Britain or the United States of America. Another well-known group with many members in India and abroad follows the teachings of the modern Indian guru Shri Sathya Sai Baba.

Overseas Hindus have brought with them their traditional religious beliefs and practices. They not only perform family *puja* but also observe temple ritual and festivals. In Britain, as an example, there are now more than a hundred Hindu temples, usually not purpose-built but adapted from private houses and disused churches. For the immigrant communities the temple provides a new focus for identity and cultural activities in a foreign environment.

BELIEF AND PRACTICE

Some essential characteristics

Hinduism is doctrinally tolerant and includes many different, even contradictory beliefs. But in spite of the immense regional and sectarian variations of religious beliefs and practices, there are certain essential characteristics that are typical of the Hindu view of life.

One of the most distinctive features is the belief in *samsara*, the round of birth, death and re-

birth, understood as a cycle of transmigration from one living form into another. This belief is not found in the Vedas but is first mentioned in the *Brihadaranyaka* Upanishad where it is said that after death a human being may be reborn in a higher or lower form of life. The belief in transmigration is closely related to a cyclical view of life and of the universe. It is also connected with the belief in *karma*, which denotes both an action and its good or bad effect. The *karma* accumulated through the acts done in a previous life is a determining factor towards the condition of the present life, which in turn affects the rebirth in the next life. Such an overall 'balance' in *karma* can help to explain injustices and suffering – as well as good fortune – in a person's life. The law of *karma* governs the universe and all beings within it; it acts impersonally and binds each individual soul (*atman*) to the world and in addition to the cycle of transmigration.

All worldly existence is subject to the cycle of *samsara*, which is thought of as having neither beginning nor end; many Indian stories illustrate how beings are caught up in it. One parable is shared by both Hindus and Jainas. It describes *samsara* as a terrible jungle full of wild beasts which seek to devour man. Trying to escape, man loses his way and falls into a deep pit covered with creepers. Luckily, he can hold on to these but at the bottom of the pit a gigantic serpent is awaiting his fall and at the mouth of the pit stands an elephant ready to trample him to death. At the edge of the pit stands a tree with a honeycomb which, through its dripping honey, gives man some sustenance. But this comfort is short-lived as the roots of the tree are being nibbled away by white and black mice, which are employed as a dramatic representation of the days and nights of all-devouring time.

Nine-day worship of Kali, whose name means the 'Black One'. Blood sacrifices are common in her temples; in the myths she becomes intoxicated by drinking the blood of her victims on the battlefield. In the 19th century an organization of assassins, the thugee, devotees of Kali, was finally suppressed. Now she is understood as the goddess of death.

This is a pessimistic story expressing the nature of *samsara,* an inescapable round from which liberation can be found only through gaining ultimate release (*Moksha*) is the highest ideal of Indian religion and philosophy. It describes an idea of absolute spiritual freedom which can only be understood in stark contrast to the complete bondage of *samsara.* There have been centuries of discussion as to how this ultimate goal may be reached, and different schools of thought point to different ways by which *moksha* may be attained.

Another important and pervasive belief is the doctrine about the universal Self (*atman*) and Ultimate Reality (*Brahman*) based on the teachings of the Upanishads. *Brahman* is the ground of all reality and existence. An uncreated, external, infinite and all-embracing principle, it is the ultimate cause and goal of all that exists. It is One and it is All. It has caused the universe and all beings to emanate from itself and all beings will return back to the same source. *Brahman* is in all things and it is the true Self (*atman*) of all beings.

The thinkers of the Upanishads believed that the ultimate ground of the universe is one with the ground of the thinker himself. One of the great sayings of the Upanishads is the celebrated *tat tvam asi* ('that art thou') of the *Chandogya* Upanishad, expressing the identity of *Brahman* and the Self (*atman*). It proclaims the insight that the human soul in its deepest essence is identical with the immortal *Brahman,* the changeless ground and unchanging source of all change which sustains the entire universe. Much of Indian thought is concerned with reflecting on this fundamental insight and with interpreting its implications for human life.

Brahman is conceived as impersonal – or better, as transpersonal – as Being itself, without attributes or qualities (*nirguna Brahman*). But on a lower plane it can manifest itself with attributes (*saguna Brahman*) and is then worshipped as personal God and Lord (*Ishwara*), often in the forms of either Vishnu or Shiva or one of their many manifestations. Already in the late Upanishads there are passages which point to a personal, theistic understanding of Ultimate Reality; but the monistic teaching, stressing the impersonal or transpersonal nature of the Absolute, has on the whole been in the foreground of Indian philosophical reflection.

The single-minded pursuit of the knowledge of *Brahman,* implying the attainment of *moksha,* has always been accorded an enormous prestige in the Indian tradition, yet it has remained the privilege of a small minority. The life of most Hindus is less directly concerned with seeking *moksha* than with conforming to the demands of *dharma* ('duty', 'order'), a fundamental notion with a number of different meanings referring to an order with cosmic, moral, social and individual dimensions.

Dharma is that which is established, a kind of sacred order; it also prescribes what people ought to do, and governs every aspect of human conduct, including the duties that are an essential part of everyday life.

The rules of conduct were defined in great detail in several treatises dealing with *dharma* (*Dharma Shastras*). The most important of these, the *Laws of Manu* (200 BCE–100 CE), describe human life in terms of *varnashramadharma*: there is no universal *dharma* for all; each individual's duty is dependent on his or her *varna* (class) and *ashrama* (stage in life).

The caste system

As Hinduism is an all-embracing social and religious order, it is important to understand the significance of *varna* in relation to the caste system which has provided both cohesion and flexibility to Indian society over the centuries. The origin of the caste system is unclear, but the idea of the four basic *varnas* (the word means originally 'colour') into which every Hindu is born goes back to Vedic times and is linked to four hierarchical divisions found among the Aryans. The earliest scriptural reference (in the *Rig Veda,* X,90) speaks of four social orders: the Brahmans or priests; the Kshatriyas or princes, rulers and warriors; the Vaishyas or traders and merchants; and the Shudras or serfs, the lowest caste who had no access to the Vedas. This fourfold *varna* order is a theoretical one and is linked to a strict ranking of ritual and social status. At the practical level, caste is understood as *jati* (birth or lineage) and is not divided into four groups but into several thousand linguistic and regional subgroups. Thus one must distinguish between the all-India *varna* system (for which the words 'group' or 'class' are appropriate) and the regional or local system of *jati* (caste). The caste system is a unique social order with such pervasive features that it has affected other religions in India besides Hinduism – even, for example, Islam and Christianity.

Underlying the caste system are a strong sense of hierarchy and important ideas about purity and pollution. The Brahman castes are at the top of the hierarchy and have to follow the strictest rules, for they must be pure to serve the gods. In turn, all other castes must serve the Brahmans. Caste is hereditary and traditionally linked to specific occupations passed down from father to son. The system is held in force by equally strong rules of endogamy (marriage within one's own caste) and of commensality (rules affecting the taking of food). Both the nature and the preparation of food are governed by complex rules of purity; for example, whilst raw food is immune from pollution and can be accepted from anyone, cooked food can easily become polluted through contact and will only be shared with certain castes but not

Brahman priest and his apprentice in West Bengal. The Brahman are among the twice-born castes, signified by the wearing of the thread given during initiation, and worn throughout life over the right shoulder. The Brahman caste is the highest status and clearly understood. The lower end of the caste system is also clear-cut, but for those in the middle the status is less precise.

with others. Other sources of pollution are natural phenomena such as bodily emissions (saliva, blood, especially menstrual blood, etc.) and life crises such as birth and death, all of which require elaborate rites of purification. The rules governing purity and pollution are instilled into people from their earliest years and severe violation of these rules, especially of caste endogamy, is punished by a caste council.

When a pure person comes into contact with an impure one, the latter communicates the impurity to the former and not vice versa. In general, the Brahman priests have to observe the rules of purity more scrupulously than any other caste because purity has a great deal to do with the high ritual status of the Brahman caste. So purity and impurity apply to whole castes as well as to individuals within them. Purity is not determined by one single factor but depends on different criteria such as occupation, dietary and marriage customs. Strict vegetarian castes are usually ranked higher in purity than meat-eating castes. Brahmans in different parts of India may adhere to widely different religious beliefs and practices, but they will all share a belief in the superiority of their caste and be considered among the purest caste in their area. However, the manner in which this superiority and purity manifests itself in a particular Brahman caste will depend on varying circumstances.

Purity rules could be strictly enforced in traditional village life but are much more difficult to maintain in an urban environment or even within contemporary villages where new economic opportunities have brought about profound changes.

Traditionally, the economic interdependence of castes in the village was expressed through a system of mutual obligations and services (the *jajmani* system) oriented towards serving the needs of the whole community. The *jajmani* system can be described as a patron-client relationship whereby each family of a farming caste had a permanent, hereditary relationship with families of different artisan and service castes, such as those of the potter, weaver, carpenter, barber, washerman or sweeper, who provided their regular specialized services in return for certain gifts and payments in kind, especially an annual share in the grain harvest. Although the higher and lower castes remained socially separate, they were economically closely bound together in a permanent, relatively stable, though somewhat unequal relationship.

Although the Brahman caste always enjoys the highest social and ritual status, it is not necessarily always the most powerful caste in the village. The families with the greatest wealth, which traditionally meant the ownership of land, dominated village life and were often found among non-Brahman agricultural castes. The upper and lower ends of the caste system were always clearly known and fixed, but in the middle range hierarchy was less precise and a certain amount of mobility was possible. Over the centuries the caste system also allowed for the absorption of many foreign and tribal groups into the Hindu social order. Within the *jati* (caste) system individual castes can move up or down whilst the position of a particular caste within the fourfold *varna* system is much less mobile.

There is no uniform process by which lower castes can improve their social and ritual status, but traditionally the ownership of land and power over other human beings were significant sources of social mobility. Lower, impurer castes tend to imitate the dietary and other rules observed by purer high caste groups in order to raise their own status. This imitation is sometimes referred to as a process of 'Sanskritization' as it is primarily concerned with adopting practices associated with Brahmans and other high castes who base their conduct on authoritative Sanskrit texts.

Outside the traditional *varna* system altogether are the outcastes or untouchables responsible for particularly polluting tasks such as the tanning of leather, doing the washing, performing cremation etc. The untouchables live in separate parts of the village with their own wells, shrines and religious specialists. Gandhi renamed the untouchables 'Harijans' or 'children of God'; his campaign on their behalf was an important factor in the outlawing of the concept of untouchability in modern India.

Many religious reformers of the past have criticized and challenged the caste system, but without success. Often, when a new religious sect came into being, it developed into a new, separate caste group. The caste system is always changing as new castes continue to appear and old ones disappear. Today especially castes enjoy an increasing mobility. Modern Hindu reformers have all taken the view that caste is a purely social phenomenon whereas in fact it is also strongly tied to religious aspects of Hinduism, particularly in the way purity and pollution affect ritual and social ranking.

The modern Indian legal system takes the individual and not the caste as its basic unit. Caste endogamy is no longer a prerequisite for a valid marriage and untouchability has been declared illegal whilst special provisions have been made to improve the position of the so-called scheduled castes and tribes. At the same time, caste allegiances have been reinforced through the power that castes wield in elections and in political life.

Legislation against caste restrictions, especially regarding the access to temples and wells, has been more successful in urban regions than in rural areas. Even today there still exists a large number of untouchables in India, which represent in some states more than 20 per cent of the population and, although outlawed, discrimination remains as prevalent as ever. In recent years, untouchables have organized themselves into a militant movement, particularly in the states of Karnataka, Andhra Pradesh and Maharashtra. This so-called 'Dalit Movement' is making increasingly strong political demands and fights for all untouchables to gain access to full social and educational equality.

The Brahmans, Kshatriyas and Vaishyas are also called the three upper or 'twice-born' (*dvija*) castes as they undergo initiation and are given the sacred thread in their youth. For the twice-born an ideal pattern of life was developed consisting of four successive stages (*ashramas*). These stages involved being: 1. a student (*brahmachari*) who leads a celibate life, and studies under the guidance of a guru to learn parts of the Veda as well as secular and ritual knowledge; 2. a married householder who brings up a family and contributes to the general welfare of society; 3. a 'forest-dweller' – someone who, with the arrival of grandchildren, may withdraw from family responsibilities in order to seek wisdom in the forests, as in the time of the Upanishads; and 4. a renouncer (*sannyasin*) who sheds all social ties and devotes himself exclusively to the pursuit of *moksha* by becoming a wandering ascetic. In this way ascetic renunciation occurs ideally in old age after a contribution has been made to society. But it remains possible in practice to by-pass the stage of the householder and become an ascetic at a young age. These stages provide an ideal structure, yet few pass through all four.

Other characteristics of the Hindu way of life

Another important concept underlying the Hindu attitude to life and daily conduct is that of the four aims of man (*purushartha*). The first and overriding one of these is right conduct (*dharma*) involving notions of righteousness, duty and virtue. But human beings may legitimately seek other aims too, such as material gain or wealth (*artha*), the second aim; or the satisfaction of desires and pleasure, including the pleasure of physical love (*kama*), the third aim.

The fourth and ultimate aim of life implies the renunciation of the three preceding ones and is concerned with complete release (*moksha*) from all wordly attachments and from the cycle of rebirths. The sages of the Upanishads considered that liberation from the miseries and continuous changes of this life could be reached through the knowledge (*jnana*) of the truth concerning the nature of the Self (*atman*) and of *Brahman*.

In later times, especially since the *Bhagavad Gita*, three ways (*marga*) or disciplines (*yoga*) for reaching liberation were distinguished. In addition to the way of knowledge or wisdom (*jnana yoga*), only accessible to a small brahmanical minority, the way of works (*karma yoga*) and the way of worship or devotion (*bhakti yoga*) were recommended. The way of works referred originally to the ritual acts relating to the sacrifices of the Vedic period and to instructions about the performance of worship, but in the *Gita* it also refers to works in a wider sense. The way of worship or devotion (*bhakti*) is exalted above all others in that it is open to all people (including Shudras and women who were excluded from the path of wisdom). By listing three different disciplines (*yogas*) for attaining *moksha*, the *Bhagavad Gita* accounts for three dominant trends of Indian religion, a *dharma*-based Brahmanism, a wisdom-based asceticism, and a devotion-based theism. The way of *bhakti yoga* is characteristic of the different forms of Hindu theism, and Hinduism developed in such a way over the centuries that much of it can be equated with popular *bhakti* religiosity.

The Hindu deities and their devotees

Perhaps no other classical language possesses so many different linguistic terms for Ultimate Reality as Sanskrit. Hindus have developed the lofty philosophical concept of *Brahman* as the One and the All, yet the visible manifestations of the Divine in the form of different gods and goddesses number millions.

The Ultimate is referred to as *Purushottoma* (Highest Spirit), *Parameshvara* (Highest Lord), *Bhagvan* (God) and many other terms. Sometimes the three gods Brahma (a personification of the impersonal *Brahman*), Vishnu and Shiva are grouped together in a triad called *Trimurti*, occasionally although wrongly described as a 'Hindu trinity'. In this representation of 'One God in three forms' Brahma is the creator, Vishnu the preserver and Shiva the destroyer. Well known from Indian sculpture, the triad has largely remained artificial and is unimportant to Hindu worship, which is much more strongly founded on the notion of *istadevata*, the idea that an individual or a family chooses a specific god as the main focus for devotion.

Hindus can be broadly divided into three groups according to the main god they worship: the Vaishnavas worship Vishnu, the Shaivites Shiva, and the Shaktas worship Shakti (the female aspect of Shiva). The god Brahma has a central place in Hindu mythology but is not important in worship; hardly any temples are dedicated to him.

Each god is accompanied by his consort. Brahma's wife is the goddess Sarasvati, patroness of learning and the creative arts. Lakshmi, also known as Sri, is Vishnu's consort and worshipped as goddess of beauty and good fortune. Shiva's wife is known as Parvati, Uma, Durga or Kali. Another characteristic feature of Hindu gods is an accompanying animal which serves as their 'vehicle': Brahma rides a goose, Shiva is accompanied by the white bull Nandi, and Vishnu by the bird Garuda, for example.

VAISHNAVISM Vaishnavism in one or other of its forms is the most popular and widespread Hindu religion. The Vedic god Vishnu is a solar and cosmic deity who excelled through his 'three steps' by which he measured the earth and heavens. In the epics Vishnu is equated with Prajapati, the creator

---

MANY HINDUS DEDICATE THEIR LIVES TO THE GOD VISHNU, THE INNER CAUSE OF ALL LIFE. ONE OF THE THREE CREATOR DEITIES, VISHNU IS SAID TO INCARNATE OR BECOME AN AVATARA (LITERALLY 'ONE WHO DESCENDS'), TEN TIMES TO SAVE THE WORLD FROM DESTRUCTION. THE TEN AVATARAS ARE:—

MATSYA (*THE FISH*) Vishnu is said to have taken this form in order to save a sage, Vaivaswata or Manu, from a great flood. The Bhagavata Purana adds to the story of the flood an incident in which a demon carried off the Veda which had come from the mouth of the sleeping god, Brahma. Matsya instructed Manu and the Rishis in the doctrines of the Veda, then slew the demon and restored the Veda to Brahma.

KURMA (*THE TORTOISE*) During another flood objects indispensable to the continuing work of creation were lost. Vishnu descended in the form of Kurma, a tortoise, and lent his back for a pivot on which Mount Mandara could be turned as a stick for churning the ocean. In the churning of the seas the lost objects were recovered.

VARAHA (*THE BOAR*) Vishnu took the form of a boar in order to raise up the earth from the bottom of the sea, to which it had been consigned by a demon.

NARASIMHA (*THE MAN-LION*) The story of Narasimha tells of a demon king who had become invulnerable to any harm from gods, men, or animals. When the wicked king's actions became intolerable, Vishnu took the form of a man-lion (neither man nor beast) in order to destroy the king.

VAMANA (*THE DWARF*) In this incarnation Vishnu reclaimed for the gods their kingdom from which they had been driven by the demon king Bali.

PARASURAMA (*THE RAMA WITH THE AXE*) When the warriors became so powerful that they even persecuted the Brahmins, Vishnu took human form and destroyed the warrior race.

RAMA Vishnu incarnated as Sri Rama to save the world from the tyrannous Ravana, the ten-headed demon king. The story is told in the Ramayana.

KRISHNA In this incarnation Vishnu came to earth to destroy the evil king, Kamsa. This and many other stories of Krishna are told in the Mahabharata and the Bhagavata Purana.

LORD BUDDHA As the Buddha, Vishnu brought teachings to reclaim the people who had gone astray.

KALKI It is believed that in this present age Vishnu will incarnate as Kalki, and that he will be waving a sword of destruction since the world will be so degenerate that salvation can only be through total destruction and the rebuilding of a new world.

---

and supreme god. Vishnu is also the cosmic ocean, Nara, which spread everywhere before the creation of the universe. As Vishnu Narayana he is represented in human form asleep on the coiled serpent Shesha or Ananta, floating on the cosmic waters with his wife, the goddess Lakshmi, seated at his feet while the god Brahma arises from a lotus growing out of Vishnu's navel.

Vishnu's abode is the Vaikuntha heaven from where he periodically descends in the form of an incarnation (*avatar*) to alleviate the plight of humankind. Vishnu's incarnations may be full or partial; it is generally believed that there have been nine such incarnations so far, and that there is one further yet to come.

The first six incarnations, well known through legends and temple carvings, are of little religious value today. These are the fish (*Matsya*), the tortoise (*Kurma*) and the boar (*Varaha*), sent to save the world from a flood; the man-lion (*Narasimha*)

Of the various cults following the worship of Vishnu that of Rama is particularly strong in Uttar Pradesh. The literature of this cult has a very high ethical content and the Ramayana is widely read by millions of Hindus of northern India. Krishna in many legends is a flute player and so symbolizes God calling to the human soul.

and the dwarf (*Vamana*) to rescue the world from destruction by demons; and *Parasurama*, Vishnu's incarnation as a hero, to destroy the arrogant warrior class (*Kshatriyas*) and establish the supremacy of the Brahmans.

Vishnu is mostly worshipped in one of his human incarnations, as Rama or Krishna who represent the seventh and eighth *avatars*. Both appear as heroes in the epics, but Krishna's story was much enlarged upon from other sources. He is often worshipped as a divine child whose pranks and miracle stories are widely known. As a youth Krishna dwelled among the cowherds of Vrindaban, near Mathura, and charmed the hearts of the *gopis*, the wives and daughters of the cowherds, who danced to the accompaniment of his flute. Krishna, the divine flute player, has been the subject of much exquisite poetry, painting, music and dance. His relationship with his favourite mistress Radha has been interpreted allegorically as the mystical relationship between God and the soul. Then there is Krishna, the divine charioteer of the *Mahabharata* and the preacher of the *Bhagavad Gita*. In all these different forms Krishna represents a divine-human model for action and worship. Devotees can see in him father, friend and elder brother, but also lover, husband and son, depending on what kind of *bhakti* relationship is emphasized.

Vishnu's ninth incarnation – added only in the Middle Ages and religiously not very important to Hindus – is the Buddha, a rather puzzling figure in the *avatar* series. One explanation for his inclusion is that Vishnu wanted to lead wicked men astray by denying the Vedas (as the Buddha did) and thus ensuring their destruction.

The final incarnation is known as *Kalkin*, a warrior on a white horse, a form in which Vishnu is to descend at the end of the present dark age to destroy the wicked and restore the golden age. This refers to the Hindu belief in the cyclical nature of the universe where each cycle is divided into four ages (*yuga*) descending from a golden to a dark age (*Kali yuga*), characteristic of the present, in which evil proliferates and *dharma* is almost extinct.

There are many different Vaishnava groups all over India. Some of the major ones are the Shrivaishnavas and Dvaitins of southern India, the followers of Vallabha in western India, and several groups following the teaching of Chaitanya in Bengal. The groups in the south mostly worship Vishnu, Rama or Vishnu's consort, whereas the groups in the north usually worship Krishna.

SHAIVISM   The second great god of Hinduism is Shiva. Whereas Vishnu is an entirely benevolent god, Shiva is ambivalent and has a dark, destructive side to his nature. His antecedent was the Vedic god Rudra, the fierce storm god of the mountains. Shiva is thought to haunt battlefields and cremation grounds; in the character of *Bhairava* his terrible, violent nature as destroyer is emphasized. Shiva is the great ascetic, the master yogin who sits wrapped in meditation on the slopes of the Himalayas, his body smeared with ashes and his head covered in matted hair. But Shiva is also known for his eroticism, as the bringer of fertility and the supreme lord of creation, *Mahadeva*. His creative power is celebrated in the worship of the *lingam*, a short cylindrical pillar with a rounded top, evidently phallic in origin, although it is said that the ordinary worshipper does not recognize it as such. The *lingam* is one of the most common objects of worship in temples and household cults. It is considered Shiva's 'fundamental form', and as a symbol of male creative energy it is often combined with its female counterpart (*yoni*) forming the base from which the *lingam* rises.

Shiva reconciles within himself opposite but complementary aspects by being both terrible and mild, creator and destroyer, eternal rest and ceaseless activity. The latter attribute is symbolized by the figure of *Shiva Nataraja*, the cosmic dancer surrounded by a circle of flames, who represents the eternal movement of the universe from creation to destruction to re-creation.

Shaivism is a more coherent entity than Vaishnavism, but there are several different schools with their own teachings, in particular the monistic school of Kashmir Shaivism and the south Indian school of *Shaiva Siddhanta* where the harsh elements of Shiva have practically disappeared. Shiva is here primarily celebrated as a god of love, grace and compassion; it is sometimes claimed that this Tamil Shaivism is the highest form of Hindu devotional religion with a fully developed theology of grace not unlike that found in Christianity. Another separate group is represented by the *Virashaivas* or *Lingayats* ('lingam-bearers') of Karnataka, founded in the twelfth century CE.

SHAKTI   The *Devi* or *Mahadevi* (Great Goddess), considered to be Shiva's active energy or *shakti*, is worshipped both as consort of Shiva and as a power in her own right with both auspicious and terrifying aspects. In her fierce form she is known as Durga or Kali, in her mild form as Parvati and Uma. Often she is simply referred to as 'the Mother'. She is worshipped as a secondary deity by most Hindus but of course represents the major divinity for the Shakta sects.

The fully developed cult of the Mother Goddess is only attested from the fifth century CE but it has very ancient, possibly non-Aryan roots. Shaktism believes that God as Ultimate Being is essentially inactive; his active energy (*shakti*) is 'personified' by his wife so that the divine 'creative energies' appear as female deities. Shaktism has been described as an amalgam of Shaivism and folk Mother Goddess cults. The different roles of Shakti depend on the religious systems involved: in some she may be the dynamic aspect of *Brahman* producing the universe through her *maya* (mysterious power), in others she may be the ruler of Nature in its destructive aspects, or a benign mother goddess. The *Markandeya Purana* is an important medieval Shakta text which glorifies the eternal Mother in its *Devimahatmya* ('Wondrous Essence of the Goddess') section.

TANTRISM   Shaktism is often interwoven with Tantrism, which appeared in both Buddhism and Hinduism from the fifth century CE onwards. It is based on mystic speculations concerning the divine creative energy. Essentially Tantrism may be described as a method of conquering transcendent powers and realizing oneness with the highest principle by yogic and ritual means, partly magical and orgiastic in character. Tantrics believe in a strong parallelism between macrocosm and microcosm. The macrocosm is conceived as a complex system of powers which can be activated within the body of a devotee who, through the performance of the relevant rites, transforms the normal, chaotic state of his body into a 'cosmos'.

Tantric worship is complicated. Devotees ascribe esoteric meanings to their texts and make wide use of *mantras* (one-word spells), the most potent of which are the *bija mantras* ('seed mantras') which embody the essence of divine power. Tantrism is divided into the so-called 'left-hand path', whose practices are secret and based on the breaking of normal Hindu taboos, and a 'right-hand path', which attaches great value to *yoga* and *bhakti*.

FOLK BELIEFS AND PRACTICES   Outside India more is generally known about the philosophical and religious thought of Brahmans and of Hindu Sanskrit texts than about the numerous folk beliefs and practices which characterize much of living Hinduism, especially in its village setting. In recent years, social anthropologists have undertaken a large number of village studies which have brought to light many fascinating aspects of Hinduism as practised by the masses.

It is difficult to disentangle the textual and non-textual layers of village religion neatly but, on the whole, villagers are far less concerned with ultimate metaphysical speculations about *Brahman* and *moksha* than with the immediate, practical needs and difficulties of everyday life. In coping with these they are guided by a strong awareness of the power and ambivalence of the supernatural. This finds expression in their belief in different deities, various ghosts, spirits and demons which may possess a person, bringing tangible signs of illness, misfortune or suffering.

Shiva is a more remote deity than Vishnu. In myths the god sits on a mountain peak in eternal meditation. He is thus seen as a tremendous spiritual force, and since he always has a two-fold aspect he is thus both eternal rest and ceaseless activity. This latter attribute is symbolized in the figure of the cosmic dancer encircled by flames. Shiva is also Lord of Creation, originally a fertility god.

Different kinds of deities are distinguished and worshipped in different ways. The great *devas* or major gods and goddesses of the all-Indian pantheon are only important in so far as they can be identified with a god of the regional or local tradition. But far more attention is paid to the village deities or *grama devatas*, a generic term which describes all the deities associated with a particular village. These possess their own, locally known names and are considered either guardian of the village or the bringer of rain and bountiful harvest or the source of all kinds of this-worldly benefits or misfortunes.

The divine pantheon is arranged into a hierarchy; the status of a particular deity depends in a way on the caste status of its devotees, but also on the nature of its offerings, that is whether a deity is vegetarian or meat-eating, requiring an impure animal sacrifice. The village pantheon thus appears like an upward extension of the caste system since the distinctions of pure and impure and of hierarchical status differences are applied to the realm of the supernatural. The relationship of human beings to the different deities is in certain respects not unlike that of low castes to high castes.

For many villagers one of the main motives of religious practice is the fear of ambivalent and powerful spiritual forces which demand constant attention and offerings. There exists a certain specialization between these different spiritual powers which is taken into account by the worshipper. The benevolent deities are mainly worshipped for acquiring merit or for specific ends while the malevolent and hostile forces have to be placated in order to avert their dangerous influence.

A particularly important type of village deity is called *mata*, 'mother', a being who in general is far from motherly but represents a rather bloodthirsty goddess who demands animal sacrifices as offerings. There are specialized *matas*, such as the cholera and smallpox goddesses (Sitalamata), but in general these goddesses are worshipped as local female village deities from whom all good and bad luck emanates and who are competent to deal with the facts of village life but not with larger, more universal issues. In south Indian villages the goddess Mariyamma is widely known while the male deity Aiyanar, considered a son of Shiva, is worshipped as watchman and patron of village life. As he is a vegetarian god, he ranks higher than the female village goddess.

Some goddesses may simply reside in a thornbush with rags tied to its branches, or they may be represented by sticks, clay figurines, a small brick shrine or a rough stone platform under a tree where offerings of rice, fruit and flowers are made. Other goddesses have temples, often located in the village quarter where the untouchables live, but there are also important regional centres of worship such as the famous temple of Ambajimata on Mount Abu.

Another aspect of the supernatural finds expression in the widespread belief in different kinds of ghosts, many of them female. The general term for ghosts is *bhut*, but there are many special kinds of ghosts, each with their own name. Ghosts are most feared when they inhabit open fields, but they can also enter houses or even possess their victims. The most powerful male ghost is that of a Brahman, and the most feared female ghost is that of a woman who died childless or in childbirth. Villagers also believe in various spirits dwelling variously in trees, wells, stones, water and the ground.

Yet another expression of the power of the supernatural is the belief in magic and the influence of the 'evil eye' associated with greed and envy. However poor and low in status a person may be, there is no one completely immune to misfortune resulting from the envy of others. People often fear that the 'evil eye' will affect the well-being of their children or other family members and go to great lengths to turn away these potentially harmful influences.

The use of divination, the reading of omens to determine auspiciousness, and the recourse to astrology are also an important part of living Hinduism. A horoscope is provided for a child at the time of birth, and before marriage an astrologer is consulted to ascertain whether the horoscopes of the future bride and bridegroom are compatible. Astrologers also determine which times of the day, week or year are auspicious or inauspicious for any major undertaking, be it a wedding, a journey, a business deal or sometimes even a political decision. Astrology exercises a widespread influence on Indian life in general, not only in villages.

For the Indian villager spiritual reality is complex and supernatural assistance is implored on every imaginable occasion. Local spirits, ghosts, family ancestors, disease goddesses and village deities all have to be worshipped in one way or another. Whilst the major gods (*devas*) are served by Brahman priests who also perform important, textually sanctioned lifecycle rites for the villagers, the village deities (*grama devatas*) can be worshipped without the help of a priest. However, if a priest is called upon, he is from a lower, non-Brahman caste, sometimes even an untouchable, who may also act as an exorcist or diviner. He may even become obsessed by the deity, enter a trance and speak as a divine oracle. Such non-Brahman religious specialists fulfil an important role in village life as they are frequently called upon to diagnose and cure ailments thought to be due to village deities or minor spirits and ghosts.

For the Indian villager religious life consists primarily of innumerable observances, fasts, feasts, visits to nearby shrines and temples, and occasional pilgrimages. In spite of modern reform movements, the spread of education and economic changes, Hinduism in the villages is only changing slowly. But social changes, such as the eradication of smallpox and cholera epidemics have had an effect on the cult of certain local village deities. Here, as in other areas, an increasing popularity and more widespread adoption of gods and rituals connected with the all-Indian Sanskritic tradition can be observed.

OTHER GODS Hinduism also worships a number of animal deities. One of the best known is Ganesha or Ganapati, the elephant-headed son of Shiva and Parvati, whose vehicle is a rat. He is one of the most popular Hindu deities, worshipped as the remover of obstacles, the god of wisdom and prudence, to be propitiated at the beginning of any undertaking. Another favourite deity is the monkey god Hanuman, renowned for his learning, agility and speed, and for his faithful service and devotion to Rama. The cow is worshipped as holy in her own right, but there is no specific cow-goddess.

WRITINGS

Hinduism has produced many sacred oral traditions and written texts bearing on every aspect of human experience and including much that is considered secular elsewhere. Its sacred literature is divided into basic categories: *Shruti*, 'hearing', and *Smriti*, 'memory' or 'recollection'. It was the

Shruti that was believed to be revealed at the beginning of creation as the eternal 'word' heard by the *Rishis* (sages of immemorial antiquity). Considered to be authorless, the *Shruti* thus embodies eternal truth and knowledge whereas the *Smriti* texts represent later, secondary traditions which bring out the hidden meaning of the *Shruti* and provide precise instructions concerning essential human conduct.

The term *Shruti* is therefore taken to refer to the corpus of Vedic literature which historically falls into three strata: the four *Samhitas*, or *Vedas* which are collections of hymns relating to the sacrifice, followed by the *Brahmanas,* which explain the meaning of the sacrificial rites, and the *Aranyakas* ('forest treatises'), which are concerned with philosophical speculations. The latter culminate in the Upanishads, themselves representing symbolic and mystical interpretations of the Vedic rites and their relationship to man and the universe. (The word 'Upanishad' refers to a pupil's sitting down at the feet of a teacher.)

The texts that have been 'remembered' from generation to generation count as *Smriti*. They have never been as rigorously defined as the *Shruti*, but in practice the *Smriti* texts are understood to comprise the *Sutras* (largely philosophical texts), the law books dealing with *dharma*, the two great epics – the *Ramyana* and the *Mahabharata* (which includes the *Bhagavad Gita*) – and the *Puranas*. To count as an orthodox Hindu one has to be born into a caste and accept the authority of the *Shruti*, but in practice the *Smriti* texts are much better known.

For many centuries the transmission of the Veda was entirely oral. Its sound was considered sacred and great emphasis was laid on correct pronunciation and recitation of the texts, handed down by Brahman families. Other castes were allowed to hear the words of the Veda only, if at all, at the performance of rituals.

The *Samhitas*

The four collections of hymns consist of the *Rig Veda* (*rig* means 'praise'), which contains by far the oldest material, the *Sama Veda, Yagur Veda* and *Atharva Veda*. The first three are directly connected with the sacrifice; the *Atharva Veda* contains much later, more popular material that includes spells and exorcist chants.

The *Rig Veda* consists of 1,028 hymns in early or Vedic Sanskrit which reflect the cosmic religion of the Aryans. The hymns contain some intriguing speculations about the origin of the universe, whether it stems from a cosmic sacrifice, a golden germ, a universal egg, or has simply evolved out of non-being. Heaven and earth are apprehended as divine parents; Varuna is the guardian of the cosmic order (*rita, dharma*) and of human mortality; Agni is present as terrestrial fire, as atmospheric lightning, and as celestial sun. Indra is the god most prominent in the *Rig Veda*, an atmospheric god often identified with thunder. His greatest feat is the slaying of the demon Vritra who represents cosmic chaos. Through his destruction Indra releases the essentials of life: water, heat and light.

For the later Vedic seers the plurality of gods became a scandal. They increasingly asked what constituted the underlying principle of the universe behind all its multiplicity. One verse of the *Rig Veda* reads:

> *They call it Indra, Mitra, Varuna and Agni*
> *And also heavenly delightful Garutman:*
> *The Real is one, though sages name it variously.*

A trans-polytheistic theism developed and eventually gave way to the pantheistic monism of the Upanishads, with their overriding emphasis on the exclusive oneness of *Brahman*.

The *Brahmanas* and *Aranyakas*

The *Brahmanas* give an account of the actual conduct of the sacrifices; they are the oldest source for the history of Indian ritual. The principal concern is with the power of the sacrifice which keeps the universe in motion. Parallels are devised between the elements of the sacrifice and the universe and its parts. A deity very different from the older gods apears: Prajapati, or the Lord of the Creatures, who is not so much worshipped as generated and regenerated by the sacrifice.

These cosmic-sacrificial speculations continue in the *Aranyakas* ('forest treatises') which contain discussion of rites not deemed suitable for the village and so are debated in the secrecy of the forest. In these texts the word *Brahman*, denoting the creative power of the sacred utterances of the sacrifice, is increasingly prominent and later assumes the general meaning of sacred power.

The Upanishads continue these speculations and bring them to their full development. The texts do not present a fully developed system of philosophical thought but are poetic utterances, mostly in the form of debates between different teachers and their disciples, including some women. As many as 108 different Upanishads are known, although the thirteen principal ones are usually grouped together. The two earliest are the *Brihadaranyaka* and the *Chandogya* Upanishads, possibly dating back to 600 BCE or earlier. As the culmination and end of the Vedas, the Upanishads are also called 'Vedanta' ('the end of the Vedas'), a term later applied to one of the schools of orthodox Hindu philosophy which is partly based on the Upanishads. Almost every idea expounded in the Upanishads has its antecedents in earlier Vedic texts, but the Upanishads probe more deeply to find new interpretations and obtain a more coherent view of the universe and the human beings within it.

The general teaching of the Upanishads is not that the phenomenal world is unreal but that it emanates from *Brahman* as sparks emanate from fire, or as a spider's web is woven out of the spider itself. The manifest and formed parts are as much part of *Brahman* as are the unmanifest, immortal and unformed. Complete monism is found in the relatively late *Mandukya* Upanishad, which describes four stages of consciousness: the waking stage of ordinary consciousness; the stage of dream consciousness during sleep; the stage of deep, dreamless sleep in which there is nothing but the One; beyond that is the 'fourth stage', devoid of all duality, where the ground of the objective universe and that of the human soul are absolutely and identically the same. The four stages are symbolically related to the sacred syllable 'Om', the most sacred sound of Hinduism, said to be the whole universe. In this absolute non-duality culminates one of the great streams of Hindu thought. Other utterances that refer to the Absolute in more personal terms as 'Inner Controller', Lord, King, or God are interpreted as approximations to this ultimate Oneness.

Smriti: the two great epics

The best-known *Smriti* texts – apart from the *Laws of Manu* – are probably the two epics, which are more concerned with practical than with ritual or philosophical issues. The *Mahabharata* and *Ramayana* are almost the sole documents of Hindu religion for the period 400 BCE to 200 CE.

The *Ramayana*, or 'story of Rama', is attributed to the poet Valmiki and may have been composed as early as the fourth century BCE. It tells the story of how Prince Rama was exiled from his kingdom, how his wife Sita was abducted by the demon king Ravana, and how the latter was eventually defeated at the hands of Rama and his monkey allies led by Hanuman, the monkey god, and how Rama's rule was rightfully restored.

This Sanskrit epic has been used to illustrate the highest moral virtues: Rama is the perfect king, Sita the ideal wife, Lakshmana the perfect brother; Rama's reign, *Ramaraja*, is the epitome of harmony and prosperity. The story of Rama travelled all over South-East Asia and was reworked during the Middle Ages. It was translated into Tamil, Bengali and Hindu. Although initially Rama was only a great hero, he is presented in the later versions of the epic as an *avatar*, or incarnation of Vishnu. Today the *Ramayana* is best known in the Hindi version created by Tulsidas, whose work was most important in spreading devotion to Rama (or Rama *bhakti*) all over northern India so that the name of Rama came to stand for the name of God. The continuous reading of the *Ramayana* is an act of great religious merit. Also, the popular re-enactment of the Rama story, or *Ramlila*, is an annual event that attracts large crowds. In Ramnagar, near Varanasi (Benares), performance of this drama takes a month.

The *Mahabharata*, or 'Great (Epic of the) Bharata (Dynasty)' has the distinction of being the longest epic in the world's literature. Traditionally said to have been composed by the sage Vyasa, it now consists of 100,000 Sanskrit *shlokas* (of two to four verses each), grouped into eighteen major sections and subdivided into many chapters. The nucleus of the *Mahabharata* is the story of a family feud between the two branches of King Bharata's dynasty, the Kauravas and the Pandavas. but the *Mahabharata* is much more than an epic poem: it has become the storehouse of Indian myths and legends, with tales of gods, heroes and sages, enlarged upon and told again and again by popular bards down the centuries, so that some material may have been inserted as late as in 400 CE.

The main concern of the heroes is with *dharma*. Offical religious practice takes the form of Vedic ritual, but much religious activity revolves around pilgrimages and the adoration of different gods. The Upanishadic *Brahman* is here 'personified' as the god Brahma. Shiva is present too, but most prominent is Vishnu and his incarnation Krishna – so that the epic is sometimes called the 'Veda of Krishna'.

Before the description of the main battle comes the short but important dialogue between Krishna and Arjuna, known as the *Bhagavad Gita*, the 'Lord's Song'. This Sanskirt poem of 700 verses, divided into eighteen chapters, has been inserted into the *Mahabharata (Book VI)* and has almost the status of *Shruti*.

When the opposing armies stand ready to begin battle, the warrior prince Arjuna despairs at the thought of having to kill his kinsmen and lays down his arms. His charioteer and friend, Krishna, argues that as a warrior it is Arjuna's duty to fight. The discussion soon evolves into a general philosophical debate about the nature of the Self (*atman*), *Brahman* and the different paths to *moksha*. Krishna's 'Sermon of the Gita', as it is often called in modern India, is concerned with upholding the stability of society through the performance of one's duty (*sva dharma*) and through the unquestioning acceptance of the social order of the four classes (*varnas*). In contrast to the Upanishadic ideal of renunciation, Krishna emphasizes the discipline of action (*karma yoga*) performed in a selfless spirit of detachment without desire for reward. It is not action as such but an attachment to the fruits of action which are seen as binding man to the cycle of rebirth.

Another important teaching concerns the role of devotion (*bhakti*), which finds its first literary expression in the *Bhagavad Gita* and is praised above all else as the way to come to God. One chapter describes a powerful theophany in which Krishna discloses himself in his universal form as the great god Vishnu in whom all beings converge. This is the vision and experience of a personal god beyond the impersonal *Brahman*, a god who expresses nearness and help to man. Whenever righteousness (*dharma*) is threatened, Krishna promises to incarnate himself, age after age, and assures man of his love and salvation:

> *Give ear to my all-highest Word,*
> *Of all the most mysterious:*
> *'I love thee well.'*
> *Therefore will I tell tee thy salvation.*
>
> *Bear Me in mind, love Me and worship Me,*
> *Sacrifice, prostrate thyself to Me:*
> *So shalt thou come to Me, I promise thee*
> *Truly, for thou art dear to Me.*
> BHAGAVAD GITA XVIII: 63–64

The *Bhagavad Gita* has always enjoyed a very special place in Hinduism. It was the first Sanskrit religious text ever to be translated into English (by Charles Wilkins in 1785, and again by Edwin Arnold in 1885 under the title *Song Celestial*), and is today found in millions of copies, translated and commented upon all over the world. It has often been compared with the Christian New Testament, and its teachings have exercised a profound influence on modern Hindu thought.

The *Puranas* and other writings

Also part of the *Smriti* texts are the *Puranas*, a general term for collections of Hindu myths and legends concerned with five major themes: creation, periodic re-creation, the genealogy of gods and sages, the description of eras, and the feats of particular dynasties. The *Puranas* deal with many religious and moral matters of popular importance, and document Hindu religious concerns from about 400 to 1000 CE.

There are said to be eighteen great *Puranas*. Whereas some have no sectarian affiliation, many are devoted specifically to one of the incarnations of Vishnu, or to Shiva or Shakti. The most popular text is the *Bhagavata Purana*, a southern creation dating from about the tenth century. Divided into twelve books, its best-known part is Book Ten which describes in great detail the life of Krishna, especially his youth among the cowherds of the village Gokula and his adventures with the *gopis* (cowherd girls). These stories have inspired many miniatures, songs and dances, an enormous amount of vernacular literature, and a strong love mysticism.

In many respects similar to the *Puranas* are the *Tantras* (literally 'looms'), which are divided along sectarian lines and reflect the religious be-

liefs and practices of medieval India. They deal with four different subjects: philosophy, yoga or concentration techniques, ritual (including the making of icons and the building of temples), and the conduct of religious worship and social practice. Each of the Hindu religious groups has its own tradition of sacred literature, and following the three major divisions the *Tantras* are divided into three classes, namely: Shaiva *Agamas*, Vaishnava *Samhitas* and Shakta *Tantras*.

There also exists a rich devotional literature in different regional languages. Numerous *bhakti* saints, poets and musicians have created many popular devotional songs still widely sung today. Among the earliest *bhakti* lyricists were those of Tamil South India. The *Alvars* ('divers', that is, into the depths of mystical experience) were passionately devoted to Vishnu, and the Nayanars to Shiva. In Bengal, Chaitanya was particularly important for the ecstatic worship of Krishna. In North India the lyrics of Ramananda and Kabir, of Princess Mira Bai and of Surdas are well known. Tukaram is considered the greatest poet of Marathi.

Unlike the restrained intellectual *bhakti* of the *Bhagavad Gita*, the later popular *bhakti* movement has expressed *bhakti* in strong emotional terms, with a passionate love and longing for God who reciprocates this feeling. The movement is far removed from an abstract *Brahman* and thus celebrates a more intimate and direct contact between man and God, an interpenetration of the different worlds of the human and the divine.

Hinduism has offered an enormously wide field of myth and legend for the artist. Its poets and musicians have created many popular devotional songs in different regional languages. Painting reached a most refined stage in Rajputana. This miniature, showing Shiva and his family, is of the mid 18th-century Kangra school. This was in some respects the most exquisite phase of Rajput painting. A fine collection of this type of work may be seen in Lahore Museum.

Om, *a sacred syllable used as a mantra in meditation. It symbolizes the three worlds, the three states of consciousness, the three vedas, the past, present and future.*

PHILOSOPHY AND THEOLOGY

Hindu philosophy cannot be sharply separated from religion. The ultimate aim of all philosophical reflection, as of much of religious practice, is the attainment of *moksha* (liberation). Philosophical and religious thought are deeply grounded in the speculations of the Upanishads, but these have always been open to divergent interpretations. Gradually, six different viewpoints (*darshanas*) or philosophical schools emerged, all of which were already in existence at the beginning of the Christian era. These schools base their teachings on philosophical texts or aphorisms (*Sutras*) in Sanskrit which serve as a starting-point for their special doctrines. However different in their interpretation of the Veda, they all accept it as authoritative and for this reason are called the orthodox (*astika*) schools of thought, as distinct from the unorthodox (*nastika*) ones which reject the Veda (such as the Buddhist schools, Jainism, materialists and others).

The six *darshanas* are usually grouped in these related pairs:

Nyaya and Vaisheshika;
Sankhya and Yoga;
Mimamsa and Vedanta.

Nyaya and Vaisheshika
Nyaya ('analysis') is the Indian school of logic based on the *Nyaya Sutra*, dating from somewhere between the second century BCE and the second century CE. It is primarily concerned with the nature of reasoning and induction, and thus more of generally philosophical than religious importance. There was originally little reference to a god, but Nyaya was later influenced by Shaivite thinking and became more theistic.

Vaisheshika ('school of individual characteristics'), sometimes also called 'atomism' because of its analysis of elements into atoms, is based on the *Vaisheshika Sutra* which originated at about the beginning of the Christian era. It teaches a dualism of matter and soul, and believes in a plurality of souls. The soul must free itself from matter and realize its complete independence and self-sufficient detachment. There is no union with a deity. In fact, Vaisheshika is essentially atheistic and its doctrines have much in common with Jainism (see page 208).

Sankhya and Yoga
Sankhya ('enumeration' or 'count') is also fundamentally atheistic and dualistic. It has been argued that Sankhya – like Yoga, Buddhism and Jainism – may have had its earliest origins in the Indus valley civilization. Although perhaps the oldest of the six philosophical schools, said to

have been founded as early as in the seventh century BCE, its earliest text is the *Sankhya-karika* of the third or fourth century CE. Sankhya ideas are mentioned in the late Upanishads and also in the *Bhagavad Gita*.

According to Sankhya teaching, reality is divided into two completely independent elements: matter or nature (*prakriti*) and innumerable souls (*purusha*). All other elements develop out of matter or *prakriti* in a series of evolutes. The souls are entangled in matter, and in order to gain release the soul must recognize the essential difference between itself and matter. The dualism of *prakriti* and *purusha* dominates Sankhya thought and there is little room for a god. But theism was introduced at a later stage. Another feature of Sankhya is the doctrine about the three qualities or *gunas*, likened to the three 'strands' of a rope: goodness or brightness (*sattva*), passion or energy (*rajas*), and darkness or dullness (*tamas*). The *gunas* are understood as both material forces and psychological types. Depending on which *guna* dominates, goodness, passion or darkness prevail. *Sattva* is nearest to the supreme spirit and leads to liberation. *Rajas* bind the soul to transmigration, and *tamas* keep it in sloth and darkness.

The doctrine of the three *gunas* occurs first in the *Bhagavad Gita*, but it has had a wide influence on Indian thought. Also, the originally atheistic doctrine of soul and matter was later taken up by the theistic sects who identified the inactive *purusha* or spirit with God, and *prakriti* or matter with the active female principle (a doctrine especially common among the Shakta sects).

The term 'Yoga' has both a specialized and a more general meaning. It refers to a separate philosophical school or *darshana* but it is also used in a wider sense to describe different methods of self-control and meditation in Hinduism. The word is related to the English 'yoke' and can mean both 'joining' and 'controlling'.

The Yoga school of thought relies on Sankhya metaphysics and uses as its basic text the *Yoga Sutra* of Patanjali, dating from the second century BCE. Yoga differs from Sankhya in that it emphasizes specific practices for the attainment of liberation and introduces the Lord, *Ishvara*, as an object of devotion. He is presented as a specially exalted soul which has never been enmeshed in matter, a methodical help and meditational focus for the seeker. The final goal of Yoga, however, is not union with him but isolation of the soul.

The practices of Yoga may be very ancient – a figure seated cross-legged can be seen on some of the Mohenjo Daro seals from the Indus valley. Patanjali in his famous *Yoga Sutra* set out the eight stages of Yoga, not unlike the eightfold path of Buddhism, including self-control, breath-control, physical postures, contemplation and deep meditation. The Yoga school has developed carefully graded physical and spiritual exercises which in modified form have become part of many schools of Hinduism.

Mimamsa and Vedanta

Mimamsa ('enquiry') developed as a systematic exegesis of the Vedic texts; it is also called *Purva Mimamsa* or 'earlier' Mimamsa to distinguish it from the later exegesis (*Uttara Mimamsa*) of Vedanta. The basic text is the *Mimamsa Sutra* of Jaimini, belonging to the early Christian centuries. It is largely concerned with the interpretation of Vedic ritual and the meaning of the statements of the *Shruti*. The Vedas are regarded as eternal, without reference to God, and the Vedic heaven is the goal of conduct. Later Mimamsa teachers admitted the reality of a Supreme Being, but the school lost much of its importance with the subsequent growth of Vedanta, by far the most significant of all Hindu philosophical schools.

Vedanta gave an organized and systematic form to the teaching of the Upanishads, basing itself on the *Vedanta Sutra* and *Brahma Sutra* of Badarayana, written in the early Christian era. It consists of 555 short, cryptic verses in Sanskrit, some of only two or three words. The first two run: 'Desire to know *Brahman*; from which origin is this.' To understand it, the *Brahma Sutra* requires the additional commentaries provided by all the major Vedanta philosophers.

Vedanta concentrates on the attainment of *moksha* through knowledge (*jnana*) of the unity of *Brahman* and *atman* as taught by the *Shruti* (scriptures). The subjects treated by Vedanta philosophers include the fundamental human condition of ignorance or nescience (*avidya*), the desire for true knowledge, the right conditions required for the seeker after truth, and the nature of *Brahman* and *atman*.

Vedanta philosophy is subdivided into three major schools, *Advaita Vedanta*, *Vishisht Advaita* and *Dvaita*. The first, *Advaita Vedanta*, refers to the strict non-dualism of the Kerala Brahman Shankara (also called Shankaracharya', the 'teacher Shankara') who taught in the early ninth century CE. A devotee of Shiva, he travelled widely, reformed Hinduism through the foundation of monastic orders and wrote long commentaries on the Upanishads, the *Brahma Sutra* and the *Bhagavad Gita*. Shankara took the existence of the Self (*atman*) as undoubted; it is both universal and infinite and in every way identical with *Brahman*.

Brahman is chiefly described in negative terms. It is without qualities, unbounded, without action, has no consciousness of 'I' or 'thou', is eternal and immutable. It is described as existence (*sat*), knowledge or consciousness (*cit*) and bliss (*ananda*), or simply as the combination, *Sacchidananda*. Yet in spite of its ultimate oneness there is a plurality of perceptions and objects in the world.

A Hindu ascetic. The practice of self-mortification has a long history in Hindu literature; it may act as a means of self-liberation, penance or for initiation purposes. It may be very old, for cross-legged figures can be seen on seals from Mohenjo Daro. The system embraces members of every caste and outcasts as well and may have derived initially from popular magic and hypnotism.

OF THE SIX SYSTEMS OF HINDU PHILOSOPHY, *YOGA* HAS BECOME MOST WIDELY KNOWN, PARTICULARLY IN THE FORM OF *HATHA YOGA. RAJA YOGA,* THE 'KING OF YOGAS', TEACHES THROUGH 8 STEPS, OR LIMBS, TECHNIQUES OF DEEP CONCENTRATED MEDITATION. THE FIRST, *YAMA* (SELF-RESTRAINT) INVOLVES THE OBSERVANCE OF FIVE RULES OF CONDUCT – NON-INJURY TO LIVING THINGS (*AHIMSA*); TRUTHFULNESS; NOT STEALING; CHASTITY; AND RESTRAINT OF COVETOUSNESS.

THE SECOND STAGE IS *NIYAMA* (LIMITATION, OR RESTRICTION TO FIXED RULES), AND INVOLVES RITUAL PURITY; CONTENTEDNESS; AUSTERITY, OR SELF-DENIAL; STUDY OF THE SCRIPTURES AND REFLECTION ON ONE'S OWN LIFE; AND SUBMISSION TO THE WILL OF GOD.

THE THIRD PART OF YOGA IS *ASANA,* THE POSTURES AND EXERCISES WHICH ARE DESIGNED TO INCREASE THE MIND'S CONTROL OF THE BODY, AND WHICH FORM THE BASIS OF HATHA YOGA; FOURTHLY THERE IS CONTROL OF BREATHING; THE FIFTH STAGE IS THE WITHDRAWAL OF THE MIND FROM OBJECTS OF SENSE EXPERIENCE, THE ISOLATION OF THE MIND FROM NORMAL DAILY PREOCCUPATIONS.

THE SIXTH STAGE IS CONCENTRATION, DEVELOPED THROUGH EXERCISES SUCH AS FIXING ATTENTION UPON A PARTICULAR OBJECT.

THE SEVENTH STAGE IS CONTEMPLATION (*DHYANA*) IN WHICH, FREE OF DISTRACTIONS, THE YOGI DEVELOPS HIS OR HER AWARENESS OF REALITY.

THE FINAL STEP OR *SAMADHI* IS A STATE OF TRANCE OR MYSTICAL AWARENESS IN WHICH THERE IS CONSCIOUSNESS ONLY OF THE OBJECT OF MEDITATION AND NOT OF THE MIND ITSELF.

To account for these, Shankara developed a two-level theory of truth. At the lower, pragmatic level the world has a relative reality; at the ultimate level nothing is real but *Brahman*. The world is but the sport (*lila*) of the divine; ultimately it is unreal or *maya* (illusion, transience). At the lower level of reality the soul is surrounded by a series of sheaths, conditioned by *karma*, the outermost one being the physical body of the individual. But at the ultimate level the idea of individuality and of separate beings in the world is an illusion. Liberation consists in the overcoming of our nescience by recognizing the true being we are already. Personal liberation from the phenomenal and illusory worlds is thus gained through true knowledge that 'I am *Brahman*'. Shankara was a brilliant dialectician, but his system, however admirable and coherent, did not go unchallenged, and many sub-schools of Vedanta reject his strict monism.

One of the greatest challenges came from Ramanuja, a Tamil Brahman who taught during the eleventh century CE. Unlike Shankara, who emphasized the way of knowledge (*jnana marga*) in reaching *moksha*, Ramanuja developed a strongly theistic theology and claimed the way of *bhakti marga*, of intense devotion to a personal God, as the way of salvation. Ramanuja's teaching is known as qualified non-dualism, or *Vishisht Advaita*, for it maintains that the ultimate oneness of God is qualified and internally complex through containing within it the world and the 'selves', considered as God's body but having also a reality of their own. Salvation is not obtained through identification with *Brahman* but through devotion to Vishnu. Hence there is a place for the *avatars* or various divine descents who reveal to people the grace of God. Whereas Shankara's teaching seems to be destructive of true theism and religious worship, Ramanuja gives the devotional *bhakti* cults philosophical respectability and provides the basis for a theology of grace.

Later, in the thirteenth century, the theologian Madhva went even further than Ramanuja by teaching a doctrine of complete dualism or *Dvaita*. According to him, God, soul and matter are eternally distinct and God saves people entirely by his grace.

There were a number of other important Vedanta teachers in medieval India who established schools with a following of their own. The devotional theism of Ramanuja has been particularly influential in the south, whereas the intellectual monism of Shankara is widely revered all over India and perhaps of all the Hindu religious systems is the best known abroad, although only a small minority of Indians adhere to it.

Since the nineteenth century the teachings of Vedanta, especially in their strictly monistic form, have become known in the West. The quite distinct doctrines of the various Vedanta schools are sometimes presented as an organic whole in an overall synthesis. This modern reinterpretation is really a 'neo-Vedanta' and has exercised a strong attraction for some western intellectuals who are particularly drawn to the deep philosophical insights of Indian thought.

WORSHIP

There exists a wide variety of religious rites in Hinduism which differ considerably according to sects and regions. The publicly performed sacrifices of Vedism were replaced in Hinduism by image worship (*puja*), mental adoration, and private acts of devotion that are largely home- and family-centred. One distinguishes between both home and temple worship but the latter is also largely private in that it is performed by a *pujari* (or temple attendant), who may or may not be a Brahman, on behalf of individuals.

The Hindu temple is like the palace of a king, the abode of one or several divinities. Temple *puja* resembles a royal hospitality ritual and has a daily and a seasonal cycle. The god dwells in the holiest place at the heart of the temple palace and is rendered personal services by his attendant subjects, from being awakened and dressed in the morning to receiving ablutions, food and refreshments, and finally to being laid to rest at night. During the day worshippers come to do *puja* by paying their respects and making their requests; in turn they share the god's food (*prasada*) as a special blessing. The worshippers may bring gifts of flowers, incense, food or money; their main ritual action consists in circumambulating the shrine, keeping it always on their right.

Hindu worship is not so much the worship of images as a worship in images (*murti*): statues cannot be used for worship until they have undergone an elaborate consecration ceremony through which the living god is believed to take residence in them. Hindu *puja* consists of sixteen carefully graded actions which represent the invocation, reception and entertainment of a god as royal guest. The *puja* rites are completed by the beautiful *arti* ceremony, the waving of burning lights around the statue and then around the worshippers, an act of purification and sanctification.

The diversity of Hindu *murtis* embodies a rich visual theology. The anthropomorphic statues express a particular aspect of a god's nature and considerable use is made of various gestures (*mudras*) that denote divine activities. In addition to the use of *murtis*, worship also includes the use of abstract symbols such as *yantras* or ritual diagrams, and *mandalas* or sacred circles, representing a geometric projection of the universe.

There is no obligation to take part in temple *puja* – indeed, a number of Hindu reform movements have castigated image worship as 'idolatrous'. Many Hindus pay regular visits to a temple, however, and in addition to the many ancient temples often visited on pilgrimage, many new temples have been built in modern urban centres.

Daily *puja* is performed at the family shrine, usually found in the corner of a room. High-caste families may even have a special room set aside for *puja*, much of which is performed by women. The various religious duties depend on the individual's caste *dharma*, but for the orthodox there are five daily obligations: to revere the gods (by fire), the Rishis or Brahmans by recitation of the Vedas, the ancestors (by offering water), all beings (by scattering some food), and all men (by offering hospitality).

Daily worship is offered to the five protecting deities Vishnu, Shiva, Parvati, Ganesha and Surya, the sun god. Morning and evening rites consist of a mixture of Vedic, puranic and tantric elements, with variations according to whether the worshipper is a Vaishnavite or Shaivite. The daily prayers of a Brahman also include several recitations of the brief *Gayatri Mantra*, the most sacred verse of the *Rig Veda*, addressed to the sun god under the name of Savitri.

The major life-cycle rites (*samskaras*), sometimes called 'Hindu sacraments' by analogy with Christian rite, are traditionally sixteen in number. But most have fallen into disuse except for the four most important ones relating to birth, initiation, marriage, and death. The initiation rite (*upanayana*) applies to upper-caste boys only who, between the age of eight and twelve, are invested with the sacred thread and thereby become 'twice-born' and able to perform religious rites. In the past, this was also the beginning of a long period of Vedic study under the guidance of a teacher (*guru*).

Most important is the wedding ceremony which has remained elaborate and expensive. The marriage date is usually fixed after careful astrological calculation, and the central part of the rite consists in the bridegroom's conducting the bride around the sacrificial fire in seven steps that solemnize the marriage.

The traditional funeral rite centres on cremation. Following death, the corpse is carried to a sacred spot, usually by a river, to be burnt on a funeral pyre. It is considered particularly auspicious to die on the banks of a sacred river, especially of the Ganges at Varanasi. Burial is reserved for those who have not been sufficiently purified by *samskaras*, specifically children, but also for ascetics who have renounced all earthly concerns. The nearest relatives of a dead person are considered ritually impure for a time following death. Offerings are made to assist the deceased in their

LEFT An iconic representation of a lingam. Shiva, as Lord of Creation, is worshipped in this form which recalls the phallus of earlier fertility rites.

BELOW Funeral rites centre on cremation since death causes massive pollution. After cremation the ashes may be thrown on a river, especially the Ganges or another sacred stream.

These women are taking part in a Hindu New Year Festival. This lasts for a period of four days and is associated with Vishnu and his wife Lakshmi. Festivals of this sort are occasions of great rejoicing and are often linked to music, drama and dance performances and the coming together of extended families. Other well-known festivals are Holi, which ushers in Spring; Divali, the ceremony of lights; and Durga Puja, which is especially celebrated by Bengalis.

journey to the beyond. An important annual rite is the *shradda* ceremony offered by all Hindu males to their forefathers reaching back three generations, carried out on the death anniversary of each ancestor in question.

Although generally speaking there is no congregational worship in Hinduism, certain communal forms of *bhakti* have developed, especially in the form of *kirtan* and *bhajan* singing accompanied by musical instruments. *Bhajan* gatherings are particularly popular among urban Hindus and many sects overseas. They may take place in private houses or at public gatherings.

FESTIVALS

The Hindu religious year is marked by many important and colourful festivals which vary according to region and calendar. Because both the solar and lunar calendars are used in India, there is no single New Year's Day. Some festivals celebrate the harvest season, others the coming of the new year, others again events in the life of gods and goddesses. Festivals are occasions of great rejoicing, and include not only religious ceremonies such as *puja* and processions but are often linked to music, drama and dance performances and the coming together of extended families. Whilst important festivals are common to a particular region or known throughout India, there are also innumerable, purely local festivals with widely varying religious practices connected with particular village deities.

A well-known festival, primarily celebrated in northern India, is *Holi*, which ushers in spring. It is not only associated with Kama, the god of love and sexual desire, but also with the boy Prahlada who, contrary to his father's wishes, worshipped Vishnu and was carried into the fire by the female demon Holika, the embodiment of evil, who believed herself immune against the flames. However, through Vishnu's intervention, Prahlada was saved even as Holika was burnt to ashes, an event widely commemorated by bonfires. People also throw coloured water at each other and play practical jokes. It is a joyous occasion marked by a carefree atmosphere.

The new year begins immediately after *Holi*, but according to another calendar it starts with *Divali* (or *Dipavali*) celebrated in about October with worship and ceremonial lights in honour of Lakshmi, the goddess of wealth and good fortune. This is the most widely celebrated festival all over India. People paint their houses, open new accounts and start everything afresh. Fireworks are lit in the streets, houses are illuminated and sweets, make of thickened milk and sugar, are widely distributed.

Another popular festival is the nine-day *Durga Puja*, especially celebrated among Bengalis in honour of the goddess Durga. Among Gujaratis the Mother Goddess is honoured by the *Navaratri* festival. *Pongal* is a south Indian harvest festival. *Onam* takes the place of *Divali* in Kerala. Also much celebrated is *Janamashtami*, the birthday of Krishna at the end of August. *Ganapati Puja* is the most important festival in Maharashtra, held in honour of the god Ganesha.

An extraordinary religious festival is the *Kumbha Mela*, a kind of religious fair, held about every twelve years at four sacred places in northern India. It is primarily a ritual bathing festival associated with the holy river Ganges. The city of Allahabad, where the Ganges and Jumna rivers join, is the site for one of the largest *Kumbha Melas*, where as many as ten million pilgrims meet.

PILGRIMAGES AND OTHER PRACTICES

Pilgrimages are an important religious activity in Hinduism. The practice of visiting holy rivers and other sacred places was already known in Vedic and epic times. Many sections of the *Puranas* praise the sacredness of particular temples and isolated places, especially in the Himalaya mountains. Although the whole of India, and especially Kurukshetra (where the battle of the *Mahabharata* is said to have taken place), is considered holy ground, a great number of places are especially sacred: Vrindaban (associated with the life of Krishna), Hardwar, Kashi or Varanasi, Kanchipuram in the south, Ujain and Dwarka. There are local, regional and all-India sites of pilgrimage (*tirtha*). Many places are particularly sacred to specific groups and sects so that almost daily pilgrimages take place somewhere in India. People go on pilgrimage for a wide variety of motives: they may fulfil a vow, they may hope for a special blessing, such as a good marriage or the birth of a child, or they may seek general prosperity, release from misfortune and absolution from sin, or they come to offer worship and thanksgiving to a particular deity and desire to gain merit and salvation. Sometimes several families or even a whole village decide to go on pilgrimage together. Important pilgrimage sites are well organized with guides and priests to receive the pilgrims and instruct them in the rites to be performed at specific places and shrines.

Throughout the centuries, pilgrimages have been an important factor in the spread of religious ideas and the cultural unification of India. Modern means of communication and travel have brought about a great increase in the number of pilgrimages, also made possible by greater affluence and the availability of an economic surplus for religious activities.

Other Hindu practices include regular fasts and vows, vegetarianism, belief in non-violence (*ahimsa*) and a general respect for all life, practices that are widespread and yet have never found full acceptance everywhere.

An important social and religious role has always been performed by the ascetic or renouncer who abandons all worldly attachments in pursuit of *moksha* and undergoes some form of initiation (*diksha*). The authority to intitiate belongs to a qualified spiritual guide (*guru*) who is often regarded as representing God himself. Ascetics, known as *sadhus* or *sannyasins*, follow different forms of initiation and religious observances, fitting into the pattern of either Vaishnava or Shaiva practices. Shaivites are more inclined towards individual asceticism; Vaishnava ascetics are more closely organized into communities.

HINDUISM AND THE MODERN WORLD

The emergence of a 'Hindu Renaissance' during the nineteenth and twentieth centuries is closely linked to the history of modern colonialism (see 'Religion in the Modern World', pp. 312 *ff*). Intensive contact with western ideas about education, science and technology, and with Christian missionary activity, led to a reform and strengthening of Hinduism. Central in this modernization process was Bengal, especially Calcutta, from where many of the reform movements started. They begin with Rammohun Roy (1772–1883) who in 1828 founded the *Brahmo Samaj* as a strictly monotheistic group which rejected image worship and introduced religious services on a Christian model. The *Brahmo Samaj* was rather rationalist in outlook and much influenced by Unitarian theology. But although its members have always remained few, it made a deep impact on many Indian intellectuals.

Quite different and with a wider popular following was the *Arya Samaj* founded in 1875 by Dayanand Sarasvati (1824–83). He preached an aggressive Vedic fundamentalism which rejected all post-Vedic accretions to Hinduism and attempted to convert adherents of Islam and Christianity back to Hinduism.

Many Hindu ideas were first mediated to the West through the work of the Theosophical Society, also founded in 1875, but in New York. The Society later set up its headquarters in Adyar (Madras) from where Annie Besant in particular exercised a powerful influence on the modern Hindu revival.

Most important in bringing Hinduism to the West was Swami Vivekananda (1862–1902), a disciple of the Hindu saint Ramakrishna (1836–86) who had been a temple priest in Calcutta devoted to the worship of the Mother Goddess but who had also experimented with the spiritual disciplines of different faiths; he taught that all religions are one in leading to the same Universal Spirit. Ramakrishna left no writings but his sayings were later published as *The Gospel of Sri Ramakrishna*.

A holy man using a spinning wheel. Spinning in this way became a symbol of self-rule at Gandhi's ashram at Sevagram. The Mahatma saw this as a way by which India might escape the burden of industrialism. Although widely celebrated as 'Father of the Nation' Gandhi's practical influence is limited in present-day India. His ideals of non-violence however have found many admirers abroad. Other modern Hindu leaders include the poet Rabindranath Tagore, and Sri Aurobindo Ghose.

Vivekananda vigorously devoted himself to the propagation of Ramakrishna's teachings. In 1893 he visited the United States and made a great impression at the World Parliament of Religions in Chicago. This stay in the West also helped him to formulate his ideas about 'practical Vedanta', fusing ideas about Indian spirituality with those of education and social service. On his return to India he founded the Ramakrishna Order in 1897, now widely known for its educational and social work and for its Ramakrishna Mission Centres established in many countries overseas. Since 1945 an independent female branch, inspired by the example of Ramakrishna's wife, has been developed, called *Sri Sarada Devi Math*. Like the Ramakrishna Mission it has social and educational objectives and is active in the propagation of Indian spirituality.

The nineteenth-century reforms of Hinduism provided the necessary spiritual resources for a vigorous Hindu nationalism which inspired the political independence movement. The internationally best known Indian figures of the twentieth century are probably the poet Rabindranath Tagore (1861–1941) who received the Nobel prize for literature for his religious poem *Gitanjali*; the philosopher-mystic Sri Aurobindo Ghose (1872–1950) who reinterpreted Hinduism in the light of modern evolution and founded an influential ashram in Pondicherry; the philosopher-statesman Sarvepalli Radhakrishnan (1888–1975) and, more than any other, Mahatma Gandhi (1869–1948), the great political leader with deep religious convictions, especially regarding non-violence (*ahimsa*), the understanding of God as truth (*sat*) and the application of truth as a soul-force (*satyagraha*) in practical life.

Gandhi always saw himself as an orthodox Hindu, yet he was one of the most vigorous reformers of modern Hinduism, criticizing caste distinctions, untouchability and ritual pollution. His views were so revolutionary that he was assassinated by a fanatical member of an orthodox Hindu movement. But although he is widely celebrated as the 'father of the nation' and even considered an *avatar* by some, his ideas remain praised, yet his practical influence is minimal in present-day India. His political ideals of non-violence have found many admirers and even followers abroad (especially Martin Luther King in the United States of America). In India itself Gandhi's work has been continued by the social reforms of Vinoba Bhave.

From the 1960s there has been a considerable interest in Hinduism in the West. Several Indian gurus have been very active in recruiting western disciples to selective ideas of Hindu spirituality, as opposed to Hinduism as a whole. A number of neo-Hindu missionary movements are now well established in western countries, of which the best known ones are probably the Hare Krishna Movement or 'International Society for Krishna Consciousness'; the Bhagwan Shree Rajneesh Centres; and Transcendental Meditation (TM).

The Hare Krishna Movement is closely related to the teachings of the sixteenth-century Bengali *bhakti* saint Chaitanya, as reformulated by A. C. Bhaktivedanta Swami Prabhupada who in 1965, at an advanced age, came to New York to establish the movement in the West. From there it has spread throughout the world and today, for example, there are between nine and ten thousand Hare Krishna members of various categories in Britain where the movement has several temples of its own. A fast-growing group among Gujaratis in the West is the Swaminarayan sect founded as a reform movement in early nineteenth-century Gujarat by Sahajanand (1781–1830), later called Swaminarayan. His message of social and religious reform first attracted members of the lower castes and was much admired by the British administration of the time for the order and peace it created. Swaminarayan soon gained a wide following throughout the whole of Gujarat. In its essentials his teachings adhere to the *Vishisht Advaita* tradition of Ramanuja, but at the same time he adopted many of the rituals of the medieval Vallabhacharya sect whilst rules on non-violence and strict vegetarianism are shared with the Jainas.

All the rules and observances for the different categories of devotees are laid down in Swaminarayan's Sanskrit work *Shikshapatri*, written in 1826. He also established his succession through a line of married teachers (*acharyas*) taken from among members of his family and created different groups of ascetics.

After his death Swaminarayan became an object of worship and was considered the highest manifestation of divinity in human form. His followers split into different factions with their respective organizations centred on temples in Ahmedabad, Vadtal and Gadhada in Gujarat. Whilst Gujarat remains the chief centre of pilgrimage for Swaminarayan devotees, Gujaratis emigrating overseas have carried their faith wherever they went and built numerous temples elsewhere.

In East Africa, the Swaminarayan religion was firmly established in 1950 and active temples remain today in several cities of Kenya and Tanzania. Following the Africanization policy of several states from the mid-1960s, East African Gujaratis, like other Indian groups, emigrated to Britain and brought the Swaminarayan religion with them. The sect now counts more than 30,000 members in Britain and owns a growing number of temples in different British cities. In the United States of America, the first Swaminarayan organization was founded in 1970, and the first temple opened in 1977. It is estimated now that there are about five million Gujaratis worldwide affiliated to the Swaminarayan sect.

Another well-known modern Hindu group is the Shri Sathya Sai Baba Fellowship with many members in India and abroad. It is based on a contemporary guru, Shri Sathya Sai Baba, born in 1926 in Andhra Pradesh and considered to be a reincarnation of Sai Baba of Shirdi, a widely revered saint who lived earlier this century. Shri Sathya Sai Baba is worshipped as a living *avatar* and referred to as 'Bhagwan' or 'God' by his devotees. His syncretistic, eclectic teaching incorporates elements from different religions but possesses strong Shaivite learnings. Members of the Shri Sathya Sai Baba Fellowship have their own temples where they regularly meet for worship and the singing of *bhajans*. Their major places of pilgrimage, not far from Bangalore in south India, are associated with the life and activities of their founder. Devotees from all over the world regularly gather at these to obtain the *darshan* of their guru or to see him perform one of his extraordinary miracles for which he is perhaps best known of all. In Britain alone, the number of Shri Sathya Sai centres has grown to over 50 since the early 1970s.

The Indian Republic was founded as a secular state but the majority of its inhabitants are Hindus. The planned economic development and rapid modernization of Indian society may eventually have deep repercussions on the Hindu religious tradition which are as yet difficult to assess. As has been the experience of religious faiths elsewhere, Hinduism in its modern setting is bound to meet secularizing influences leading to a crisis of belief. Hinduism is perhaps more vulnerable to change as it lacks the organization of, for example, either Christianity or Islam. At present there exists a tension between certain Hindu fundamentalist movements which are strongly reactionary and nationalistic in character and modern Hindu universalism which sees itself as having a spiritual message for the entire world. It is difficult to say what the future of Hinduism will be, but its resources are certainly deep and strong enough to maintain an important place among the religions of the world.

JAINISM

HISTORICAL OUTLINE AND PRESENT-DAY DISTRIBUTION

Jainism, with Hinduism, Buddhism and Sikhism, is one of the major religions which originated in India. The name derives from *Jina* ('conqueror' or 'victor') meaning someone who has achieved the highest spiritual liberation. It is applied especially to twenty-four religious figures called *Tirthankaras* ('ford-providers'), on whose example the religion is based – human teachers who have attained infinite knowledge and bliss, and who preached salvation (*moksha*).

Like Buddhism, Jainism originated mainly during the sixth century BCE, but whereas Buddhism spread far beyond India, Jainism has remained largely confined to its country of origin. There, it continues to be a living faith with more than 3 million adherents today. It is found in nearly all Indian states but is concentrated mostly in western India, Uttar Pradesh, Mysore, Madhya Pradesh and Maharashtra.

According to a survey, in 1984 there were about 5,620 Jaina ascetics – monks and nuns – the majority belonging to the Shvetambara sect (1,200 monks and 3,400 nuns), followed by the Sthanakavasis (325 monks and 520 nuns), and then the Digambaras (65 monks, 60 'lay brothers' and 50 'lay sisters'). However, the vast majority of Jainas are lay people who are now also increasingly found abroad, outside their country of origin.

In India itself, Jainism has achieved a social and economic importance quite out of proportion to the number of its adherents. Gandhian thought owes much to Jainism, especially to the teaching on non-violence (*ahimsa*) and non-possesion (*aparigraha*), and the Jaina insistence on strict *ahimsa* has made a lasting impact on modern India. Today, Jainism presents itself as a rational, scientific body of beliefs, fully compatible with twentieth-century progress and able to lead people to salvation through their own efforts.

Sadly, the study of Jainism has been relatively neglected in the West in comparison with that of other Indian religions. During the nineteenth century Jainism was often considered a mere branch of Buddhism; even today it is sometimes mistakenly described as 'an offshoot of Hinduism', whereas it is in fact an independent religion with roots older than the origins of Buddhism. Yet it is undeniably true that during its long history Jainism has undergone a considerable process of 'Hinduization'.

Origins

Jainism as it is known today is based mainly on the teachings of an ascetic, Vardhamana Mahavira, who probably lived between 540 and 468 BCE and is mentioned in the Buddhist scriptures as one of the Buddha's chief opponents. Mahavira and Buddha were contemporaries preaching in the same area, but there is no tradition recording their ever having met. Like the Buddha, Mahavira protested against Vedic ritualism, caste and the exclusiveness of Brahman ascetics. Both Jainas and Buddhists recruited mainly from among the Kshatriyas – the powerful upper-middle class – and rejected Hindu scriptural authority and the idea of a creator god. The Hindus later described both religions as unorthodox in relation to their own orthodox teachings based on the Vedas.

Jainas do not consider Mahavira to be the founder of their religion but as the last in a long line of teachers. Mahavira's teaching is closely related to that of a predecessor, Parshvanatha, who lived some 250 years earlier and is considered a historical figure. He was himself preceded by twenty-two other enlightened beings or *Tirthankaras*. The first, thousands of years previously, was Rishabhanatha; the nineteenth was a woman, Princess Mallinatha. Jainas also believe that the twenty-four *Tirthankaras* are significant only for the present age; because the universe is cyclic, each cosmic age has its own particular series of *Tirthankaras*.

The belief in twenty-four *Tirthankaras* evolved gradually. Their biographies are found in a canonical text of the fourth century CE, the *Kalpa Sutra*, which is still held in the highest esteem. It describes in some detail the lives of the first and the three last *Tirthankaras*, who are the most

Images such as this are the focal point of Jaina temples. This depicts a Tirthankara or ford-provider, one who builds a ford across the ocean of human suffering. In Jainism there were twenty-three such saints who preceded Mahavira, the founder, who was a contemporary of the Buddha. Following the teaching of their leader Jainas became dissenters from Hinduism. In the temples celibate monks and nuns remain to teach and study.

prominent in worship; the remaining twenty are covered in a brief form of little historical value.

Vardhamana

Vardhamana – later called 'Mahavira' (great hero) – was, like the Buddha, the son of a chief ruling one of the powerful tribes north of the river Ganges. Many legends are told about him, yet hardly any solid historical information survives. As a minimum it is accepted that Vardhamana was brought up as a prince, married and had a daughter, and at the age of thirty, after the death of his parents, left home in quest of salvation from the cycle of births, deaths and rebirths. He joined a group of ascetics founded some 200 years earlier by Parshvanatha – and for this reason the latter ought perhaps to be considered the real founder of Jainism, for Mahavira seems to have reformed his teachings.

For twelve years, then, Vardhamana wandered from place to place, begging, meditating and practising severe austerities. At first he wore one single garment; later he discarded even that and went naked. He also plucked out his hair 'in five handfuls' – a rite still followed by Jaina monks today. In the thirteenth year of his asceticism, Vardhamana obtained perfect knowledge and achieved full enlightenment or *nirvana*, although tradition is silent about the particular truths he discovered. He then became Mahavira, a *Jina* or conqueror of self, and a *Tirthankara* or ford-provider – that is, one who builds a ford across the ocean of human suffering. He soon acquired a great reputation and a large following of ascetics and lay devotees, many of whom were women.

After teaching for a further thirty years, Mahavira died at the age of seventy-two (through a rite of self-starvation) and became a *siddha*, a free soul of the greatest perfection, omniscient and detached from the cycle of rebirths. The place of his death, Pava – a village not far from modern Patna – is a great centre of Jaina pilgrimage. It is sometimes thought that the similarities between the life-stories of Mahavira and the Buddha may indicate a common pre-existing source, but there is no firm evidence of this.

Mahavira held two convictions: first, that absolute asceticism is essential to save one's soul from evil and purge it from all contaminating matter; secondly, that to maintain the purity of one's soul involves the ceaseless practice of non-injury to all living beings (*ahimsa*).

Mahavira then set up the organization of his followers, instituting a fourfold order (*chatursangha*) of monks, nuns, lay men and women, into which Jainas are divided to this day. The life of the monks was modelled largely on that of the ancient Brahman ascetics, as can be seen from the similarity of their rules. But the laity, unlike the Buddhist laity, is accorded a fair measure of religious significance in its own right.

Little is known about the early history of the order except that a certain Jamali, later said to be Mahavira's son-in-law, led the first schism during the *Jina*'s lifetime. Seven further schisms are reported, the last one during the third century BCE when a famine in the Ganges valley forced many Jaina monks to emigrate to the area known as the Deccan, where they established important religious centres. It was out of this separation that the two principal sects of Jainism – the *Shvetambaras* ('white-robed') and the *Digambaras* ('sky-robed', or naked) – eventually evolved, but the break did not become final until the first century CE.

The ancient Indian sign of the swastika (sv = good, asti = being). It is adopted by the Jain religion for the four possible levels of rebirth: divine, human, netherworld and animal.

BELIEF

Jainism reflects very ancient metaphysical and cosmological speculations not unlike those of the Yoga and Sankhya schools of Hindu thought. Jainas believe that the universe is infinite and uncreated, there is no creator god, but there are lesser deities somewhat similar to those of Hindu mythology. These gods may be objects of meditation but cannot themselves obtain liberation without first becoming human.

There is an infinite number of souls in the universe. The individual consists of a soul closely enmeshed in matter from which it must free itself by its own efforts to gain salvation (*moksha* or *nirvana*). Time is imagined as an eternally revolving wheel with an upward and downward course, indicating improvement and decline; at present we are living in a declining phase. The eternal universe is divided into an infinite number of cycles, each with its own *Tirthankaras* who are propagators of truth not given by divine revelation but reached by themselves. Anyone – irrespective of caste, creed or sex – can attain this truth provided that the path of the *Jinas* is followed, although many births and deaths may have to be undergone. Mahavira himself is said to have experienced twenty-seven births before finally attaining liberation.

Jainism is basically dualistic. It classifies everything into one of two categories: *ajiva*, which consists of all that is lifeless (i.e. matter, apprehended as atomic in structure), and *jiva*, which refers to anything alive including the soul. There exists not only a life-soul in plants but even in the elements, yet there is no universal world-soul as in Hinduism. Jainas divide all living things according to the number of senses they possess. The highest group – with five senses – consists of human beings, gods, higher animals, and beings in Hell. These are the four categories into which beings are born and reborn according to their merit during the continuous cycle of transmigration (*samsara*). Below these beings a descending hierarchy of life, with many subgroups down to one-sense beings, has been developed. The whole world is thus alive in a more extended sense than in Buddhism or in Hinduism. Every living being has a spirit or soul, however imperfect its body, even if it possesses only one sense.

This complex theory of living beings has important consequences for Jaina ethics. It is the highest duty of a Jaina not to kill any living being; the avoidance of injury to all life-forms (*ahimsa*) is therefore of the utmost importance for all practical behaviour.

All souls are fundamentally equal, but they differ according to the amount of *karma* adhering to them. Jainism, unlike other Indian religions, understands *karma* materialistically. *Karma*, although subtle, is matter that accumulates and adheres to the soul in successive layers. The naturally bright, all-knowing and blissful *jiva* becomes dulled by karmic matter and thus acquires first a spiritual and then a material body. The *karma* acquired leads to the acquisition of further *karma*, with the result that transmigration continues indefinitely.

Jainas distinguish many different kinds of *karma*. There is *karma* which determines one's family and length of life; there is *karma* that clouds knowledge and faith, or produces delusions, or emotions of pleasure and pain, and so forth. Through this association with karmic matter the *jiva* is held in bondage. To obtain liberation requires complete dissociation of the soul from matter through the elimination of all karmic matter already in the soul, achieved by penance and purification, and by preventing a further influx of *karma*, possible through disciplined conduct.

The complex theory of *karma* is central to Jaina ethics. Strict rules of asceticism are required to prevent the formation of new *karma*. The same purpose is served by the pursuit of austerities (*tapas*) and contemplation (*dhyana*). The necessary condition for reaching *moksha* is the possesion of the 'three jewels' (*triratna*) of right faith, right knowledge and right conduct. These become manifest on the removal of *karma* and shine like jewels in a good life.

Right faith can only arise when *karma* which obscures it is eliminated; it implies respect for and belief in the teachings of the *Tirthankaras*.

Right faith is thus based on the right knowledge of the essentials of Jainism, which implies the removal of ignorance.

Right conduct means refraining from what is harmful and doing what is beneficial in order to get rid of the *karmas* that produce bondage and suffering. Central to right conduct are the five vows: not to do violence (*ahimsa*), not to lie, not to steal, not to have sexual intercourse, and detachment from material things, or not coveting (*aparigraha*). Ascetics keep these five as 'great vows' (*mahavrata*) in a very strict sense; lay people, on the other hand, observe them as far as their conditions permit as the 'small vows', strengthened by seven further rules to guide their ordinary behaviour.

Along with the immense respect for life goes the respect for the opinion of others articulated in the philosophical doctrines of Jainism. In contrast to the (Hindu) Upanishadic view that the ground of reality is one and without change, Jainas maintain that reality is always subject to production, continuation and destruction: reality is not one but many-faceted – a view expressed in the doctrine of the 'indefiniteness of being' (*anekantavada*). It is supplemented by a sophisticated theory

THE JAIN CONCEPTION OF THE UNIVERSE

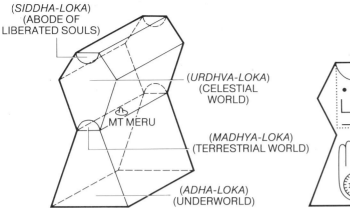

(*SIDDHA-LOKA*)
(ABODE OF
LIBERATED SOULS)

(*URDHVA-LOKA*)
(CELESTIAL
WORLD)

MT MERU

(*MADHYA-LOKA*)
(TERRESTRIAL WORLD)

(*ADHA-LOKA*)
(UNDERWORLD)

(*THE ARCHAIC VIEW OF THE UNIVERSE, REPRESENTING IN ROUGH OUTLINE THE HUMAN FORM, AND ITS FOUR LEVELS OF ABODE.*)
HUMANS DWELL IN THE *MADHYA-LOKA*. THE CELESTIAL WORLD AND UNDERWORLD COMPRISE MANY INTERNAL LEVELS CORRESPONDING TO THE TYPE OF CELESTIAL OR INFERNAL BEING.

(*JAIN PRATIKA, SYMBOL OF JAIN FAITH, OFFICIALLY ADOPTED IN 1975 AT CELEBRATION OF THE 2,500TH ANNIVERSARY OF MAHAVIRA'S NIRVANA.*)

THE SYMBOL CLEARLY REFLECTS THE ARCHAIC VIEW OF THE UNIVERSE (SEE LEFT).

THE PORTION SHOWN INSIDE THE DOTTED RECTANGLE IS A SIGN COMMONLY MADE DURING *PUJA*. THE PALM OF THE HAND CARRIES A STYLIZED VERSION OF THE WORD *AHIMSA:*

of judgement known as *syadvada* which was developed by the great Jaina scholar Hemachandra (1088–1172 CE). As several judgements about the same reality may be true, each judgement is relative and should be qualified by 'perhaps', 'maybe' or 'somehow' (*syat*).

This doctrine of epistemological and metaphysical relativity, together with the Jaina cosmological views about space and time, is sometimes compared to the modern world-view of relativity physics. Jaina philosophy is not to be equated with scepticism. It only emphasizes with much conceptual subtlety the conditional or relative character of knowledge available to the limited minds of human beings.

THE SECTS

The last schism, from which the two principal sects of Jainism emerged, was due to a difference over a point of monastic discipline. The leader of the emigrants to the south insisted on retaining Mahavira's rule of nakedness (and his followers were therefore described as 'sky-robed', *Digambaras*), whereas the northern leader allowed his people to wear white garments more suited to the local climate (and were thus 'white-robed', *Shvetambaras*). The separation is sometimes also explained by the fact that isolated groups, such as those living in the Deccan, remained more conservative and less open to change.

There are no fundamental doctrinal differences between the two sects, but they accord different emphases to the interpretation of Jaina history and religious practices. Although most *Digambara* monks later took to wearing robes in public, they maintain that anyone who owns property (and thus who wears clothes) cannot reach *nirvana*. *Shvetambaras*, conversely, contend that white robes – unlike all other possessions – do not impede liberation. Among the *Digambaras*, women are rigorously excluded from attaining salvation because they are not allowed to go around naked. *Digambaras* also do not believe that Mahavira ever married. Each sect has its own tradition of spiritual leaders, different religious ceremonies and different scriptures.

After Mahavira's death, his followers spread from the ancient kingdoms of north-eastern India to western, central and southern India, so that eventually Jainas became more numerous in those regions than in their homeland, Magadha. Like the Buddhists, the Jainas enjoyed the patronage of various kings, among them the grandson of the Emperor Ashoka who supported Jaina influence in southern India. As early as in the late second century BCE, a king from Kalinga (modern Orissa) professed Jainism and set up Jaina images in cave temples. Kings and wealthy merchants supported poets, writers and Jaina building activities throughout the Middle Ages. According to some traditions, Jainas have also been severely persecuted at various times in Indian history.

The *Digambaras* are now found mainly in the Deccan and Mysore, and comprise several communities or *sanghas*. The *Shvetambaras*, who gained ascendancy in Rajasthan and Gujarat, eventually divided into as many as eighty-four subgroups or *gacchas*, but only a few of these survive today.

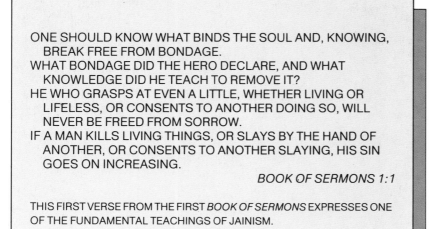

ONE SHOULD KNOW WHAT BINDS THE SOUL AND, KNOWING,
    BREAK FREE FROM BONDAGE.
WHAT BONDAGE DID THE HERO DECLARE, AND WHAT
    KNOWLEDGE DID HE TEACH TO REMOVE IT?
HE WHO GRASPS AT EVEN A LITTLE, WHETHER LIVING OR
    LIFELESS, OR CONSENTS TO ANOTHER DOING SO, WILL
    NEVER BE FREED FROM SORROW.
IF A MAN KILLS LIVING THINGS, OR SLAYS BY THE HAND OF
    ANOTHER, OR CONSENTS TO ANOTHER SLAYING, HIS SIN
    GOES ON INCREASING.

BOOK OF SERMONS 1:1

THIS FIRST VERSE FROM THE FIRST *BOOK OF SERMONS* EXPRESSES ONE
OF THE FUNDAMENTAL TEACHINGS OF JAINISM.

achievements in the secular sciences. The Jaina scriptures, although not well known in the West, are thus of great significance in studying the history of Indian languages (despite often being described as dull and tedious), for the Jainas helped to develop Tamil, Telugu and Kannada; Jaina scribes also wrote a considerable amount in Gujarati and in Hindi.

Among Jainas, the copying of manuscripts, even secular ones, was considered a work of religious merit. The Jaina monasteries of western India have preserved many rare and otherwise unknown texts of both Jaina and non-Jaina origin, often beautifully illustrated. In recent times there was initially some opposition to putting Jaina sacred books into print, but a modern *Shvetambara* leader has planned critical editions of all the Jaina canonical works.

WORSHIP

Ascetics: Monks and nuns

Jaina ascetics, male or female, are spiritually advanced people who dedicate themselves exclusively to the pursuit of *moksha*. When a lay person is ready for further advancement on the path to liberation, he or she renounces name and wordly possessions, assumes the five great vows in an initiation ceremony (*diksha*), and takes on the lineage name of a teacher. Today, novices are chiefly recruited when young. *Shvetambaras* accept people from eight years old onwards; *Digambara* renouncers, however, usually join at an advanced age.

A monk is allowed only the barest necessities: clothes, a blanket, a begging-bowl, a stick, a broom to sweep insects from his path, a piece of cloth to cover the mouth so that nothing living can enter when speaking. Nuns are similarly equipped, but are permitted more clothes. Monks also shave or remove their hair by plucking it out.

Jaina ascetics formerly led a wandering life, staying in one place only during the rainy season. Gradually, permanent monastic buildings (*upashraya*) were introduced, and *Shvetambara* ascetics now reside in these. Monastic life is organized on a strictly hierarchical pattern with several junior and senior positions. Monks and nuns have a daily round of duties including meditation, study, begging for alms, careful inspection of clothes for the removal of any insects, religious ceremonies and vows.

Lay worship

Lay people are fully recognised members of the Jaina order; their close relationship with the ascetics has always to date provided the necessary stability and support for the survival of Jainism.

During the sixteenth century a further sect, the *Sthanakavasis*, developed in western India out of the *Shvetambara* order. Their chief feature is the rejection of image worship and temple services, which they claim is not sanctioned by the scriptures – although this attitude may also be due to Islamic influence. Image worship is also repudiated by one of the subgroups of the *Digambaras*.

WRITINGS

Some Jainas believe that Mahavira's teachings were handed down orally in fourteen *Purvas* ('former texts') although others trace these right back to the first *Tirthankara*, Rishabhanatha. However, both *Shvetambaras* and *Digambaras* accept that the *Purvas* were irretrievably lost and the scriptures had to be reconstructed in twelve *Angas* ('sections') of which only eleven have survived. These represent the oldest available source material on Jainism, and consist of both prose and verse written in the spoken language of the day, Ardhamagadhi, also called Jaina Prakrit. New material was later added in the form of twelve *Upangas* ('minor sections') and other works. The total canon of scriptures – of which the final form evolved comparatively late and was committed to writing only in the fifth century CE – now consists of forty-five texts. The canon is, however, accepted only by the *Shvetambaras*; the *Digambaras* claim that the old canon was hoplessly lost and they therefore devised completely new scriptures for themselves.

During the Middle Ages many commentaries were written in Prakrit, Sanskrit and the vernacular languages. The Jainas, more than the Buddhists, extended their literary activities far beyond religious subjects and attained remarkable

Nevertheless, the ascetic life remains the highest ideal to which the laity can approach only to a limited extent. But they are encouraged to take up periodic retreats with stricter ascetic practices so as to benefit temporarily from monastic life. Jainas distinguish eleven stages of ascending spiritual progress (*pratima*) for the ordinary person, involving the observance of six daily duties:

1   worship of the *Tirthankaras*
2   venerating and listening to the gurus
3   study of the scriptures
4   self-control, including the observance of the 'twelve rules of conduct' (which include a modified form of the five vows of the monk)
5   austerities, especially fasting on holy days
6   charity, including provision for the ascetics and the needy

The ascetics do not themselves engage in worship (*puja*). The religious duties of the laity include daily morning and evening attendance at a Jaina temple where the *Tirthankaras* and lesser deities are worshipped. Almost every town or village inhabited by Jainas has a Jaina temple; many Jainas, especially wealthy ones, also have a domestic shrine. The Jainas community appoints a temple priest (*pujari*), generally a Hindu Brahman among the *Shvetambaras*. Considerable Hindu influence is apparent in the consecration and worship of Jaina statues, and in celebrating life-cycle rites and festivals. Brahmans also perform marriage ceremonies and funeral rites.

The principal festivals are connected with the five auspicious events in the *Tirthankaras'* lives: descent from heaven, birth, renunciation, attainment of omniscience, and death and the final emancipation. Especially important are the festivals connected with Rishabhanatha, Parshvanatha and Mahavira (whose birth, *Mahavira Jayanti,* is celebrated all over India).

The most popular festival is *Paryushan* (August-September), an eight-day period of penance which includes a ceremony of general confession and pardon (*pratikramana*) and commemorates the giving of the *Kalpa Sutra*. The festival marks the end of the Jaina ecclesiastical year, and on the last day alms are distributed and a *Jina* image is taken out in procession.

A number of other festivals are celebrated, including Hindu festivals such as *Holi*, the spring festival, *Pongal* and *Navaratri*.

The building of temples is an act of religious merit. Image worship was introduced at an early stage, perhaps even during the first century after Mahavira's death, and the sites relating to the lives of the *Tirthankaras* are important places of pilgrimage. Early cave temples exist in Orissa, Maharashtra and Tamil Nadu; some contain beautiful wall-paintings. In Ellora and Khajuraho,

Jaina temples were built alongside those of Buddhists and Hindus. Some of the finest Jaina temples were built on Mount Abu in Rajasthan (eleventh to thirteenth century CE). Equally famous is the giant statue of Gommateshvara, son of the first *Tirthankara,* carved in the tenth century CE out of solid rock on top of a hill at Sravana Belgola (Mysore) and solemnly anointed by Jaina worshippers every twenty-five years. The variety and beauty of Jaina temples is evidence of the great piety and wealth of medieval Jaina merchants. Palitana (Gujarat) is a famous temple city where 863 temples have been built on a hill; it is a popular focal point for pilgrimages.

Worship includes five other daily duties. While ascetics do not themselves engage in worship every Jaina town or village has a temple. Under attack by Muslim invaders in the 15th century Jainas often blended the style of their temples with Mughal features.

RELIGIOUS ART

The most distinctive contribution of Jainism to Indian religious art lies in the realm of sculpture. Innumerable statues have been created in practically all mediums and sizes, but their expression is almost invariably the same. At first *Tirthankaras* were represented naked, but statues with a lower garment appeared in the fifth century CE. During the same period, a distinctive animal symbol and colour was assigned to each *Tirthankara* by which the similar-looking statues can now be differentiated. Parshvanatha was given a seven-hooded cobra, connected with the ancient Indian serpent cult, Rishabhanatha a bull, and Mahavira a lion. *Tirthankara* statues are found in sitting or standing poses, often carved from white or black marble, with the eyes encrusted with precious metals. These figures seem neither animate nor inanimate but radiate a strange and timeless calm, ex-

A Jaina pilgrim wears a mask and sweeps his path in order that he may preserve ahimsa *or non-violence by prohibiting any possibility of destroying life through inhalation or under his own feet. Jainas who move into business or teaching activities are identified by their rigorous asceticism which ironically has led to extreme wealth.*

living beings. Over the many centuries, Jainas have moved from agriculture into business and trading activities, and many now work as bankers, money-lenders, jewellers, cloth merchants, grocers or industrialists. Their business attitude, based on absolute honesty and frugality, has generally meant that the Jainas – with their rigorous asceticism – have also become well known for their wealth. Although initially opposed to caste, Jainas today have a number of *jatis* (castes) of diverse rank and occupation, and some times intermarry within corresponding Hindu *jatis*.

Jainism is additionally well known for its charitable institutions, such as rest houses (*dharmasala*) and pilgrimage centres in large towns, homes for lame or aged animals (*panjarpola*), dispensaries, hospitals, libraries (*grantha bandhara*), religious schools (*pathasala*) and monastery halls (*upashraya*). Modern Indian reform movements that have affected Hinduism, Buddhism and Sikhism have also inspired the Jaina order to pursue reform and educational objectives from the late nineteenth century onwards. The All-India *Digambara* Jaina Conference was founded in 1893, followed by an all-India organization of the *Shvetambaras* (1903) and *Sthanakavasis* (1906). The young men of all three sects formed the Jain Young Men's Organization 1894.

Much emphasis is laid on adequate education, especially for monks, with an eye to countering Hindu and Christian criticism. Several Jaina educational institutions and newspapers have been founded; libraries are maintained; a training college for monks has been set up in Benares; and the restoration of temples is undertaken. The education of women has also been championed.

At a later stage, the three sects felt the need for greater unity and established the All-India Jain Association, of which the aim is the unification and progress of the Jaina community and the propagation of Jainism. An International Jain Literature Society was founded in London in 1910, and a Jaina World Mission, especially concerned with vegetarianism, has existed since 1949. More recently, a European Jain *Samaj* has been formed, a focal point for some 25,000 Jainas now living in Europe; its headquarters are in Leicester (UK), where a centre for all Jaina sects is being set up consisting of a temple, an *upashraya,* a library and other facilities. It is also to contain a separate room for the special needs of each sect, and will be the first fully consecrated Jaina temple in Europe, decorated with traditional Jaina carvings made in India, including three marble statues of *Tirthankaras*.

pressing the translucence of a body purified from all matter and symbolizing the isolation and non-particularity of released beings who lack all individual features. The most frequently represented *Tirthankaras* are the first and the last three, but temples of the others can also be found.

MODERN JAINISM

The vow of *ahimsa* naturally means that Jainas may not engage in such trades as fishing, butchery or any other activity in which violence is done to

BUDDHISM

THE BUDDHA

HISTORICAL OUTLINE

The man who was to be known as the Buddha, the 'Enlightened One', was born into the ruling family of a small principality in north-eastern India in about the year 560 BCE; his family name was Gautama, his personal name Siddharta, 'the accomplisher.' Later he was nicknamed Sakyamuni, the 'sage of the Sakyas'. As often with remarkable people, miraculous stories were later told about his birth – that, for example, his mother Maya conceived by a divine white elephant provided by a Bodhisattva (an earlier incarnation of a Buddha) who wanted, in compassion, to produce his own reflection on earth; or that at his birth there was a shower of blossoms from the sky and the sound of heavenly music, and the infant emerged already filled with wisdom.

He was brought up to privilege, married young, and had a son. But a seer predicted that a parting of the ways lay before him: he would either be a world ruler or, were he ever to see individually or together a decrepit old man, a diseased man, a corpse and a monk 'carefully and decently dressed', he would become a homeless wanderer. His father tried to protect him from seeing such sights, but in vain. From the first three spectacles he learned the vanity of earthly things; the fourth offered him a way forward through renunciation. Thereupon, in his 'great renunciation', he renounced his wife and family, power, privilege, military might and earthly glory, and went in search of Truth. He was aged twenty-nine. The prevailing faith around him at this time was largely polytheistic, reflecting a stage of early Hinduism now commonly referred to as Brahmanism. The contemporary Brahman priests proclaimed a doctrine of reincarnation according to the laws of *karma*, and the quest for *Brahman*, the ultimate reality or primordial power manifested in *Atman*, or the self. But there was already some questioning of traditional beliefs and practices, partly through philosophical reflection which led to reinterpretations of sacrificial practice in ways that suggested, for example, that non-violence, chastity and truthfulness may make appropriate offerings at the sacrifice (Brihadaranyaka Upanishad 3.17.4). Another important movement of reaction against Brahmanism was Jainism, with its strong emphasis upon ascetic practice and rules of conduct similar to those that developed in Buddhism.

Indian philosophy was also passing through a productive period, and Siddharta would have encountered a form of Sankhya philosophy which was to play an important part in developments of Hindu traditions (see Hinduism, p. 186). In these philosophies, in mysticism and in ascetic practices he was unable to find the liberating truth for which he was striving; and although he practised terrifying mortification of the flesh, he found no ultimate satisfaction in these extreme expressions of renunciation.

One day as he wandered, he stopped to meditate under a bo-tree (or pipal-tree, *Ficus religiosa*), sitting cross-legged in the lotus position, his tongue touching his palate, one hand in contact with the earth. Mara, the lord of sensory pleasures, sent him one distraction after another; he met and mastered them all. Storm and danger could not disturb his ecstasy. Lust, restlessness and greed had no power to move his mind. All day he sat in meditation. And in the dark he received the great enlightenment.

The first watch of the night acquainted him with all his earlier lives. The middle watch revealed the present condition of the universe. The third watch unfolded the whole chain of cause and effect. Thus did Siddharta arrive at the great truth: that all suffering is rooted in desire (*tanha*), in the will to live and to possess, and in attachment to this world. The sole release from suffering is to completely destroy desire.

Now came the final temptation, fully to enter *nibbana (nirvana)*, the heaven-haven of the Buddhists which consists in the total annihilation of desire, freed from the weary wheel of death and birth. He looked over the world with the all-perceiving eye of the Enlightened One and saw men whose eyes were darkened. He was the lotus-flower which had sprung to blossom above the water while others remained beneath the surface. For these he felt an infinite compassion. So the Enlightened One remained on earth for a further forty-five years, and devoted the rest of his life to proclaiming the gospel of salvation.

THE BUDDHA'S TEACHING: THE *DHAMMA*

The gospel he proclaimed was the *Dhamma*, or doctrine. Its general purport is clear, although it does not translate easily into English: it consists of four Noble Truths.

The first is the Noble Truth about suffering: that all life is suffering – there are more tears in the world than water in the ocean.

The second is the Noble Truth about the origin of suffering: that it derives from *tanha*, desire, the will to live, attachment to this world.

The third is the Noble Truth about the cessation of suffering: that the means to the cessation of suffering is the extirpation of desire.

The fourth is the Noble Truth about the way to the cessation of suffering: that it consists in

ABOVE   A pilgrim prays at the site of the Lord Buddha's enlightenment, Bodh Gaya, India. Here is venerated the night that the Buddha spent in meditation waiting for that enlightenment.

RIGHT   This sculpture from Gandhara (second to fourth century CE) depicts the Buddha's first sermon to his disciples. They became the nucleus of what was to be the Sangha (community) of Buddhist monks.

MYTHS
AND LEGENDS

Krishna playing the flute to the cowgirls of Vrindaban. Stories of Krishna in the Puranas tell of his attractiveness to women and the way in which their desire was heightened by his playing the flute. The stories are taken to be an analogy of divine – human love.

Religious teaching cannot always be communicated through ordinary language. The mysteries of religion require more if they are to connect with the lives of ordinary people. So ritual is used to dramatize worship and channel emotions, and mythology has an essential role in conveying beliefs and teaching which matter-of-fact descriptions may not be able to explain adequately. Myth has a particular meaning in religious discourse (see 'The Nature of Religion', pp. 6ff). The word does not signify, as so often in common usage, stories which are simply untrue. It refers rather to the expression of beliefs held to be true and important by large numbers of people and expressed in the form of stories. To understand mythological material one must penetrate beyond the outward form of the story – although no doubt enjoying that along the way – to the essential belief or idea which the story is intended to convey. Myths are a vital part of the fabric of most cultures and civilizations. The illustrations in this section visualize what people have believed about the origins, nature and destiny of humankind; about the relationship between good and evil; and about the power of the human spirit.

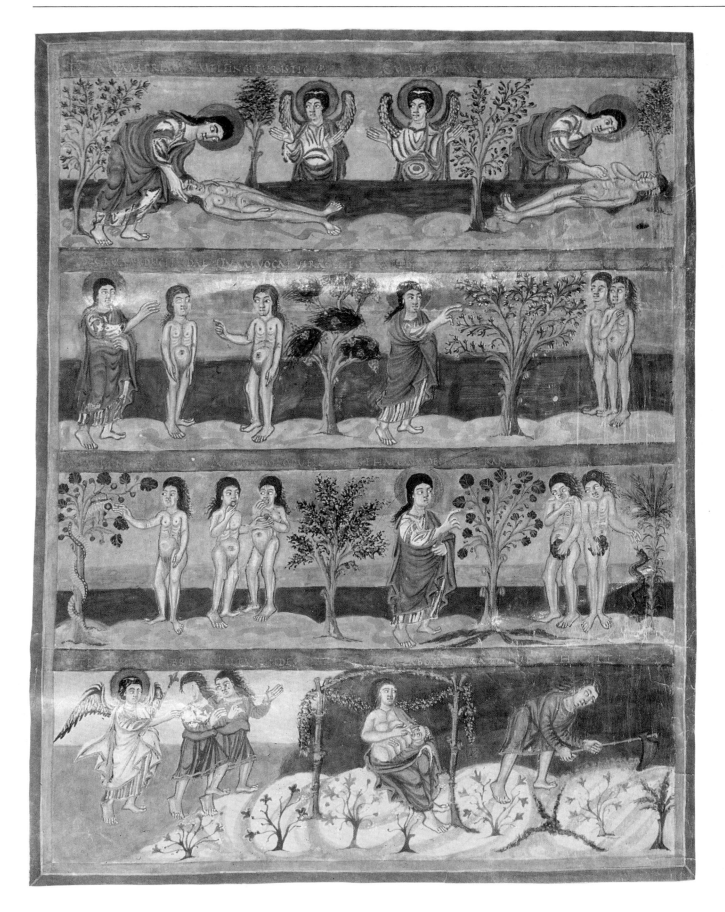

LEFT *This illustration of the creation and fall of man is taken from the Moutier-Grandval Bible written and illuminated at the abbey of St Martin at Tours, France. The illustrations largely follow the story contained in the second chapter of Genesis. The top picture shows Adam being formed 'from the dust of the ground' and woman taken from the rib of the man. The illustration moves on to the warning not to eat from 'the tree of the knowledge of good and evil', and in line three shows the serpent tempting Eve, and Eve sharing the apple with Adam. The final line shows the consequence of the Fall in an aetiological myth (that is, a myth that suggests a cause for facts of human experience) as Eve gives birth in pain and Adam gains bread by the sweat of his brow (Genesis 3.19).*

LEFT *A representation of a Taoist immortal, Ho Hsien-ku, the only female among the 'eight immortals' of Taoism. Religious texts that pre-date the earliest Taoist religious movements indicate a belief in immortal beings and the conviction that humans can achieve immortality. The immortals were believed to appear disguised among people to confer their magical powers and immortality on chosen subjects. Ho Hsien-ku, whose emblem is the lotus and sometimes also a bamboo ladle, was herself believed to have been mortal, but by dietary and other disciplines to have restored to her body the 'pure energies' which were natural to it.*

BELOW *Popular Chinese belief about death and the afterlife was the result of a mixing of ancient ideas with Buddhist teaching about* karma *and rebirth and Taoist teaching about immortality. It was generally believed that after death spirits went to one of ten courts presided over by a judge, and from there the soul could progress or regress. The intercession of Buddhist or Taoist priests was believed to be efficacious for the progress of the soul. Here the wicked souls descend in fetters, while the good souls, carrying scrolls and (top right) a Buddha figure, ascend to a new existence.*

RIGHT In addition to more philosophical writing Jainas produced a collection of literature that included stories explaining the origins of people and things. This illustration is of a story explaining the wondrous nature of the birth of Vardhamana (Mahavira), the reformer and propagator of Jaina teaching in the sixth century BCE. Trishala, Vardhamana's mother, is said to have had a series of dreams which foretold the birth of a great emperor or Tirthankara. Shortly after the dreams Shakra (Indra) arranged for an unborn child in the womb of Devanada, a Brahman's wife, to be transferred to Trishala's womb, and as a result Trishala gave birth to Vardhamana.

ABOVE This sixteenth-century manuscript in the Topkapi Palace Museum, Istanbul, shows the Prophet Muhammad (whose face is not represented) at the Battle of Uhud. Soldiers at the battle were without water, so the Prophet held out his hand and water flowed from his fingers. Islamic teaching proscribed the depiction of human or animal forms, lest they be identified with Allah and so encourage the sin of shirk. So mosques are usually decorated with calligraphy and geometric and floral designs, although figurative art was important in manuscript illustration, especially in the Ottoman and Mughal empires.

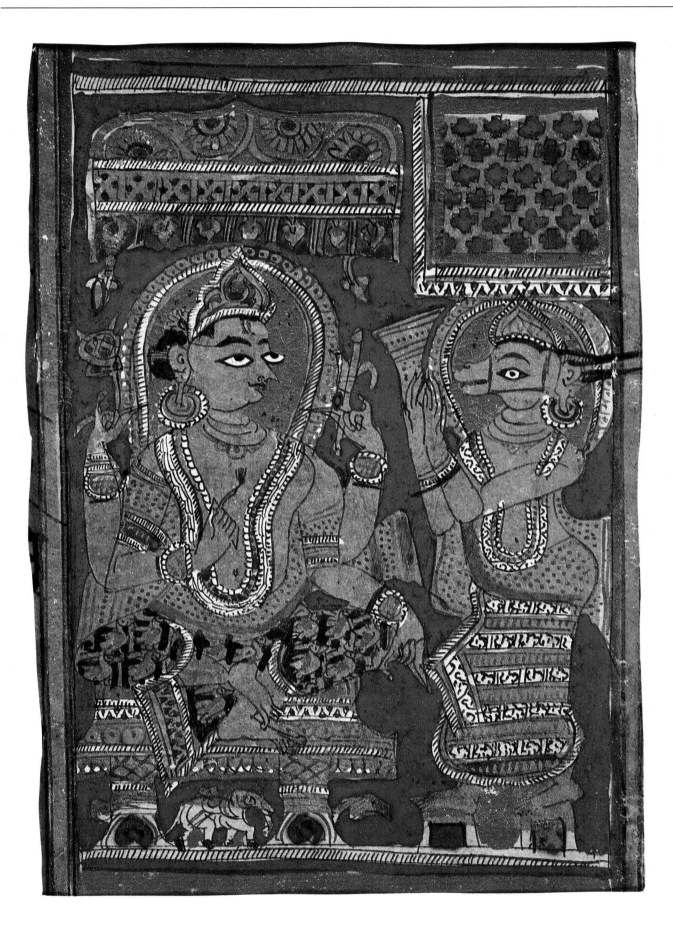

FAR LEFT This Ethiopian manuscript illustrates the story of Noah's Ark. Stories of great floods (no doubt reflecting experience) are found in many religious traditions and form a significant part of religious mythology. In this story Noah, a righteous man, is warned by God of an impending flood which will destroy the wicked and lead to a new beginning for humankind. Noah and his helpers build the Ark, stock it with animals and people, and so ensure the continuation of life after the flood.

LEFT A bronze statue of Garuda, also called Tarkshya, a mythical Hindu figure with human body and head but with the beak and talons of a predatory bird. Garuda, of whom there are many stories in the Mahabharata and the Puranas, was associated with the sun, and regarded as the destroyer of snakes and serpents. He appears in some extended lists of avataras of Lord Vishnu, but is probably pre-Aryan in origin. Garuda is both a remover of obstacles and an antidote to snake bites.

BELOW The Shinto shrine of the 'wedded rocks' at Isé, Japan, joined by ropes which indicate their sacred nature. The shrine is associated with the temple of the sun goddess Amaterasu at the national shrine at Ise. Amaterasu ('Heavenly shining deity'), after her creation in a primal act of purification, was said to have fled to a rock cave because of a quarrel with her brother. She sent Ninigi-no-Mikoto to rule on earth, and through him the imperial line of Japan was established.

RIGHT *A Japanese painting showing the seven Gods of Good Fortune (Shichi Fukujin), who are essentially household guardians or deities. The seven are believed to travel together on the Treasure Ship (Takarabune) which symbolizes some of the blessings they bestow; each God represents a different blessing. Their names are Bishamonton (riches); Benten, a goddess of music; Ebisu (good fortune); Daikoku (wealth); Fukurokuju (long life); Hotei (prosperity); and Jurojin (longevity). Small representations of the group are often kept around the house.*

LEFT *Rama destroys the ten-headed demon king, Ravana. The story of Rama, who is both an ideal king and the seventh avatar of Lord Vishnu, provides the theme for one of India's great epic poems, the Ramayana. With the other epic, the* Mahabharata, *the story is well known in India at all levels of society, conveying important Hindu philosophical and social teaching. In this scene from the* Ramayana, *Rama, the epitome of duty, truth and goodness, overcomes the great power of the evil king Ravana and so ushers in a new kingdom of righteousness.*

morality, meditation and the attainment of wisdom. This may be expanded under eight headings, making the familiar 'eightfold path':

1 Right understanding: to see life as it is, characterized by impermanence, suffering and 'no-soul'

2 Right thought: a mind pure, free from lusts, ill-will and cruelty

3 Right speech: avoiding lying, backbiting, harsh words, idle gossip

4 Right action: not to kill, not to take what is not given, not to commit sexual misconduct, not to use false speech, not to take intoxicants; the positive side of these is constituted by non-violent love, charity and generosity, purity, honesty and truthfulness, and self-discipline

5 Right vocation: an occupation that does not harm others, and is consistent with Buddhist principles

6 Right effort: preventing new evils, expelling old evils, encouraging new good, and fostering existing good

7 Right mindfulness: constant awareness of the truth about the body and its feelings, the mind and its ideas

8 Right concentration: the direction of the mind to a wholesome object in disciplined meditation.

It should be noticed that the gods play no part in the *Dhamma*. They were no doubt there as part of the backcloth of existence, but not as ultimate or permanent. In that sense early Buddhism may be thought to be oddly categorized as a religion – in the teaching of the Buddha it appears more as a way of life involving 'ultimate concern', and perhaps also as a revolt against contemporary religious practice.

The Buddha accepted Indian belief in *karma*, that is that the individual's destiny is governed by the way the person lives and by the working out of the consequences of moral and religious practice through a wearisome succession of births and deaths. But the idea of reincarnation in the Buddha's teaching is different from the Hindu idea in at least two respects. Firstly, in Buddhist teaching the self is regarded not as an entity that passes largely unchanged from one life to another but as an aggregate of constantly changing factors (the five *khandha*), so that the self that is reborn is not quite the same self as the one that died. Secondly in Buddhism caste-related *dharma* (in the Hindu sense), with its emphasis upon ritual purity, was not believed to play a significant part in the accumulation of *karma*.

THE BUDDHA'S PROCLAMATION

The Buddha had had five disciples, but they had left him. Now, in his enlightened state, he went to see them in Varanasi (Benares) and found them there in a deer park. To them he said 'I am the Saint, the Perfect One, the Fully Enlightened. Give ear, O monks: the Way is found. Hear me.' They prostrated themselves before this apparition of light. Then came the Sermon at Benares, also known as the Discourse (*sutta* or *sutra*) Setting in Motion the Wheel of Doctrine.

Learn, monks, that all existence is nothing but pain, inasmuch as death, contact with anything unpleasant, separation from that which you love, inability to satisfy your desires, are all painful . . . The origin of this universal pain is the craving to exist, the craving for the pleasures of the five external senses and the internal sense, and even the craving to die.

The Buddha remained in Benares for four months, making more converts. According to one tradition a young man named Yasa, of wealthy family, ran away from home in distress at the sordid side of life. 'Come, Yasa,' said the Buddha, 'here you will find neither distress nor danger,' and he spent the day teaching him. Yasa's father, coming in pursuit of his wayward son, also came under the spell and became the Buddha's first lay follower. He invited the Buddha to his home the next day, and Yasa's mother and a friend became his first women lay followers. Four of Yasa's friends joined, and these five, with the original five disciples, formed the nucleus of the *Sangha*.

So for forty-five years the Buddha travelled through north-eastern India, preaching and proselytizing, hailed not as Mystic, Sage or Pilgrim, but as Saviour, Perfect Master, Tathagata (the 'Truly Arrived'). He proclaimed a life between sensuality and mortification of the flesh; and the values of love and compassion.

His celebrated Fire Sermon was directed at a proud Brahman:

The fire of life must be put out. For everything in the world is on fire with the fire of lust, the fire of hatred, and the fire of illusion. Birth, old age, death, care, lamentation, pain, sorrow and despair are so many flames . . . . Illusion devours you like a flame.

Finally he came to the 'great decease'. His parting words were 'All compound things are subject to decay: strive with earnestness.' Then through a series of ecstasies he escaped from the wheel of birth and death, and entered *nirvana*.

NIRVANA

Nirvana or *nibbana* is the ultimate goal for the Buddhist, the absolute which transcends the empirical world, freedom from all constraints, the cessation of passion and desire, a condition of emptiness and peace. It is not to be defined; it is hardly to be spoken of without paradox. A remarkable parable conveys something of it. Disciples set out from the land of *samsara* (illusion, constant change) to reach *nirvana* by boat. As they set foot on the far shore, the land they have left disappears, the sea disappears, the boat disappears – *and the land they have reached disappears.* Positively, *nirvana* suggests the peace that accompanies the extinction of selfishness and craving for material things, and as such it has been described as the 'harbour of refuge', 'the supreme bliss', 'the immortal'.

THE TEN PRECEPTS

THE PRECEPTS ARE SET OUT AS GUIDES TO CONDUCT: THE FIRST APPLY TO ALL BUDDHISTS; THE FOLLOWING THREE APPLY TO BHIKKHUS (MONKS) AND SOME PIOUS LAYPEOPLE; AND THE FINAL TWO APPLY ONLY TO BHIKKHUS.

ABSTINENCE FROM DESTROYING LIFE

ABSTINENCE FROM STEALING

ABSTINENCE FROM IMPURITY

ABSTINENCE FROM LYING

ABSTINENCE FROM STRONG DRINKS AND INTOXICATING LIQUOR, WHICH CAUSE STUPIDITY

ABSTINENCE FROM EATING AT FORBIDDEN TIMES (THAT IS, NOT EATING AFTER NOON)

ABSTINENCE FROM DANCING, SINGING AND SEEING SPECTACLES

ABSTINENCE FROM GARLANDS, SCENTS, UNGUENTS, ORNAMENTS AND FINERY

ABSTINENCE FROM HIGH OR BROAD BEDS

ABSTINENCE FROM ACCEPTING GOLD OR SILVER

From the MAHAVAGGA, 1:56

THE SANGHA

The Buddhist proclaims the efficacy of three Jewels or Refuges:

I go to the Buddha for refuge.
I go to the *Dhamma* (doctrine) for refuge.
I go to the *Sangha* (community) for refuge.

Before the 'great decease', the Buddha said to his favourite disciple:

> It may be, Ananda, that in some of you the thought may arise: 'The word of the Master is ended; we have no Teacher any more!' But it is not so, Ananda, that you should look at it. Let the truths and rules of the Order which I have set out and laid down for you all be your Teacher after I am gone.

The Buddha's preaching, then, led to the establishment in Benares of a Community or Order of his disciples, the *Sangha*: this was normal for any teacher in India (as in ancient Greece or Palestine). His followers at first would have included some who were curious, some who were hostile, some in need and not knowing what they wanted, some clearly seeking for truth. For them the alternatives were the Brahman *gurus* or the ascetics. The Buddha offered something these lacked.

The Master's most effective word was '*Ehi*', 'Come'. Or the word might issue from one of the other preachers, or from a Community.

Those who followed fully became monks, or *bhikkhus*, but there were others, both women and men, who remained in the world as disciples. They were expected to observe the basic moral rules, to avoid violence, theft, lying, sexual impropriety and alcohol; to provide the monks with food and clothing; and to practise devotional exercises which, in later times, included venerating the Master's relics, visiting temples for meditation, and listening to the words of the Buddha. It is important to stress that the Buddha's teaching was directed not at an esoteric élite but to ordinary men and women.

The *Sangha* is composed of *bhikkhus*. Each *bhikkhu* renounces all worldly goods and his own identity as an individual. He is expected to be celibate and continent. His aim is to destroy desire, and through meditation to attain that enlightenment which leads to liberation from suffering. He shaves head and beard, and wears a yellow robe. The rules require him to abstain from: destroying life, stealing, impurity, lying, strong drinks and intoxicating liquors which cause stupidity, eating at forbidden times, dancing, singing and seeing spectacles, garlands, scents, unguents, ornaments and finery, high or broad beds, and accepting gold or silver. In modern times, however, these rules are not always applied with equal rigour. His only possesions are a begging bowl, water filter, tooth-pick, razor, needle, stick and fan, all returned to the Community after his death. He lives on beg-ged food, mostly balls of rice, which must be con-sumed by midday. As a novice he has a spiritual master. He rises early and leads a carefully disci-plined day, with time for meditation and spiritual instruction.

COUNCILS AND SECTS

A few weeks after the passing of the Blessed One, 500 adepts, or *arhats*, met at Rajagaha in the First Buddhist Council to determine the content of the *Dhamma*, which was thereafter handed down in three *Pitakas*, or 'Baskets': the Rules of the Disci-pline of the Order (*Vinaya-pitaka*), the Dis-courses (*Sutta-pitaka*), and the metaphysics, psychology and philosophy (*Abhi-dhamma*).

Within about a century a Second Council had to be held, at which a progressive party argued that the Rules were too rigid and should be re-laxed. Buddhahood was internal and should be allowed to grow naturally. The Orthodox held that Buddhahood came from observing the Rules. They won – and the progressives seceded. This was the beginning of the sects within Buddhism. (Subsequent Councils have been infrequent, and always designed for the purifying of the records; the sixth was held in Rangoon in 1956.)

The greatest division took place in the later centuries BCE, between the Theravada – part of the 'Little Vehicle' (bearing humankind across the ocean of suffering to salvation) – with its orthodox concern for the Teaching of the Elders, and the Mahayana or 'Great Vehicle', with its greater accommodation to local practices and beliefs.

THERAVADA BUDDHISM

HISTORICAL OUTLINE AND PRESENT-DAY DISTRIBUTION

Theravada, the Teaching of the Elders, is an orthodox form of Buddhism claiming to conform to the interpretation of the Buddha's teachings by the senior monks of the Sangha, the monastic Order founded by the Buddha. Today it is preva-lent in Burma, Kampuchea, Laos, Sri Lanka and Thailand. With the exception of Vietnam, Buddhist countries of South-East Asia practise mostly Theravada Buddhism.

Theravada constitutes one of the schools (and for the time being, the only extant school) of Hinayana Buddhism, as distinct from the Mahayana Buddhism of China, Japan, Mongolia and Tibet.

In the fourth century BCE, the Buddhist monas-tic order split into two sects called the Sthavira and the Mahasanghika respectively. The Sthavira claimed a stricter adherence to the original teaching and monastic discipline; from it there developed several schools, one of which is the Theravada, its origins in fact going back to the Third Buddhist Council, held during the reign of the Emperor Ashoka (d. 232 BCE) in India.

Among the earliest Theravada communities were those that flourished in southern India and in Sri Lanka, where it was introduced by mis-sionaries sent by Asoka in the third century BCE, and where it has been the dominant religion ever since. In Burma the Theravada, or an allied form of Buddhism, was practised as early as the fifth century of the Common Era, and in Thailand from the sixth century. But the actual and active predominance of the Theravada in these coun-tries dates from later times – the eleventh century in Burma and the fourteenth century in Thailand. And at about the same time as the influence of Sri Lankan Theravada was firmly establishing itself in Thailand, Thai influence in turn was simul-taneously converting the inhabitants of Kam-puchea and Laos to Theravada.

It is often claimed on behalf of Buddhists in Burma, Sri Lanka or Thailand that their specific form of the belief has preserved – and continues to preserve – the pure form of Theravada Buddh-ism. Certainly it is true that these countries have maintained a devotion to the study of the Ther-avada canon and have retained a religious practice of which the origins stem from the Elders' teachings found in the ancient commentaries of the canon. But each religious practice also con-tains many syncretistic features or adaptations of local observances. Nowhere did Theravada sup-plant completely the observances of other cults. Thus astrological concepts, the ritual propitiation of various deities and so forth, are widely preva-lent in the Theravada countries, mostly in con-nection with matters of health, personal well being and material success. Underlying these observances are concepts and ideologies that have little to do with the original teachings of Buddh-

This map shows the distribution of Buddhism in India and south-east Asia c *1300* CE.

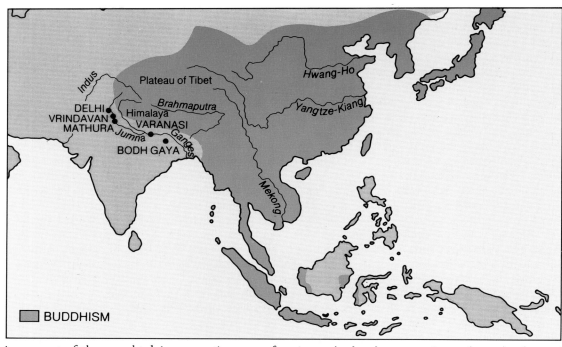

BUDDHISM

ism, most of them embodying a continuance of the ancient culture of these lands. By incorporating some elements of such cultures, Theravada practice has in each country developed features that are unique to itself, and in this sense it is legitimate to speak of Burmese, Thai or Sinhala (i.e. Sri Lankan) Buddhism.

BELIEF

Philosophically Theravada subscribes to a qualified realism. Phenomena exist 'objectively', but there are worlds and beings beyond the normal experience. In the Abhi-dhamma the Theravada teaches the doctrine that all mind and matter is reducible to eighty-one distinct elements; what is real are those elements and not their configurations as objects and beings. Things are also radically 'impermanent' – but death is not the end of living beings – yet there is the Ultimate Reality of *nibbana* which is not amenable to description and totally different from phenomena both objective and subjective.

An important teaching of Theravada, as indeed of all Buddhist schools, is that of the 'three characteristics' which mark phenomenal existence. These 'characteristics' are impermanence (*anicca*), unsatisfactoriness (*dukkha*) and 'absence of self' (*anatta*).

According to the teaching of *anatta* or 'no-self', the common assumption of an enduring personal core is a mistaken belief resulting from ignorance. All the factors that constitute the so-called individual can be summed up as five aggregates (*khandha*), namely physical form (*rupa*) sensa-

tions (*vedana*) perceptions (*sanna*), 'mental formations' or volitional activities (*sankhara*) and consciousness (*vinnana*). All of these are subject to constant change and modification (*anicca*), which is their first characteristic. Not one of them, either singly or in any combination, perdures through time as an unchanging self or ego (*atta*).

Theravada does however admit within its teachings the fact of the continuance of individual *consciousness*. This 'consciousness of self' has its origin in ignorance and its continuance is by way of a causal process. This is the process of 'dependent origination' or, literally, 'conditioned co-arising' (*paticca samuppada*). The doctrine is presented in this traditional formulation:

> Conditioned by ignorance, there arise mental formations
> Contined by mental formations, there arises consciousness
> Conditioned by consciousness, there arises name-and-form
> Conditioned by name-and-form, there arise the six bases (senses of sight, hearing, smell, taste, touch and thinking)
> Conditioned by the six bases, there arises contact
> Conditioned by contact, there arises sensation
> Conditioned by sensation, there arises craving
> Conditioned by craving, there arises attachment
> Conditioned by attachment, there arises 'becoming' (strong sense of continuing self)
> Conditioned by 'becoming' there arises birth
> Conditioned by birth there arises decay (old age), death, pain and sorrow, lament and despair

for the purpose of explaining rebirth and continuance of the ego-consciousness without assuming an enduring self.

Psychologically Theravada propounds a theory of mind and 'mental states' that recognizes the existence of residual (unconscious) forces stemming from prior experiences and constituting a block or fetter that holds the individual in a field of operations that are libidinal, greedy, malevolent, violent, and inwardly ignorant (*raga, dosa, moha*).

Within the totality of Buddhist teachings, called the *Dhamma*, Theravada thought also deals with the other major Buddhist themes, including *samsara*, the cycle of births and deaths; the four Noble Truths; the eightfold path; the liberation of mind from its bonds – which is co-equal with the realization of *nibbana* – and so on. Specifically, it propounds the notion of a graduated religious enterprise to which the ultimate end is this liberation. A central place is occupied by the three concepts of the middle path (the avoidance of extremes), 'dependent origination', and *karma* (that deeds wilfully done condition the consciousness and bring their own repercussions).

WRITINGS

These and other doctrines are found expressed in the Canon of the Three Baskets (*Tipitaka*), the compilation of the first two of which is traditionally ascribed to the First Buddhist Council held at Rajagaha in 483 BCE, soon after the death of the Buddha. The Canon is thought to have been agreed in a final form at the Third Council held in the time of the Emperor Ashoka.

The First group of scriptures, or 'baskets', includes the *Vinaya* ('discipline'). Its main concern is the corpus of monastic rules for *bhikkhus*.

The second basket of texts is the *Sutta Pitaka* ('collection of discourses'). The Sutta Pitaka is made up of five *nikaya* (collections). The first four *nikaya* are regarded as the chief source for knowledge of the teaching of the Buddha, or the *Dhamma*. They are: *Digha Nikāya* (the long collection); *Majjhima Nikāya* (the middle collection); *Samyutta Nikāya* (the grouped collection); *Anguttara Nikāya* ('an additonal limb' collection).

The fifth *nikaya* of the Sutta Pitaka is a collection of fifteen works of varying length. These include some of the most important texts of the school such as the Dhammapada, Sutta Nipata, Thera- and Theri- gatha as well as the Jataka. The last-named work is a collection of verses which formed the basis of the later Jataka Commentary which purports to narrate the past lives of the Buddha. Many of these Jataka stories are undoubtedly folk stories pressed into Buddhist use. Their importance lies in the fact that they deal with major Buddhist themes in a way that is eminently adapted for conveying the Buddhist teachings to the common people.

The third basket, the Abhidhamma ('the further *dhamma*', meaning perhaps '*dhamma* of higher level' as distinct from *dhamma* taught to every person. i.e, the Sutta Pitaka) is assigned by modern scholarship to a later date. It is based on scholastic elaborations of lists called *matikas* which are summaries of the teachings found at different places in the Sutta Pitaka. The characteristic concern of the Abhidhamma is to explain all phenomena in terms of certain irreducible impersonal elements or *dhammas* (see 'Belief').

All the major works of the school, including its version of the Three Baskets, are in Pali, the religious language of the Theravada, which is a literary language based on an as yet unknown vernacular of India at (or shortly after) the time of the Buddha, having a simpler structure than the Sanskrit of the Hindu texts.

WORSHIP

Buddha, *Dhamma* and Sangha constitute for Theravada (as for other schools) the 'threefold Refuge' – and the least that is expected by tradition of a Theravada Buddhist is the acceptance of this refuge and the observance of the five precepts: not to kill, not to steal, not to indulge in sexual misconduct, not to lie, not to take intoxicants.

Active religious observance is more complex, and is grounded in the theory of *kusala kamma* ('wholesome deeds'). Any act that strengthens greed, ill-will and ignorance is unwholesome. On the other hand, any act that tends to dissolve or counteract these unwholesome roots is a religiously good deed. The teaching is that the individual must 'internalize' the wholesome act by genuinely wanting to do it: formal performance is not sufficient. Such works of religious merit (*kusala* or *punna*) constitute the beginning or first part of the religious enterprise. Its higher purposes are achieved by dedication to the second part, of which the aim is to deepen the understanding of the truths of the teaching and, through self-knowledge and meditation, to realize the nature and workings of the mind and thereby transcend its limitations, and to awaken to a selfless awareness of the truth. Underlying this view is the notion of the final emergence of a radically different dimension of awareness, an insight 'empty' of the normal contents of consciousness.

It is in terms of this theoretical scheme that teachers of Theravada recommend to followers an extensive 'worship' and a routine round of 'good works' which generally involves and accommodates a number of social, ethical and religious activities. 'Good acts' comprise not only the active (and financial) support of monks and religious institutions, but also the wider tasks of looking after parents, the aged, the sick and the needy; religious praxis ideally fosters the social ethic at the same time.

Such 'wholesome' or 'meritorious' deeds are usually indicated under the threefold classification of *dana* ('giving'), *sila* ('right conduct') and *bhavana* ('meditation'). But a more extensive tenfold classification gives a truer insight of what the traditional praxis emphasized:

1 Gifts to the worthy
2 The observance of precepts
3 Meditational practices
4 Offerings at shrines and elsewhere
5 Attending to the sick and encouraging the virtuous
6 Gifts to the religious community, for the express purpose that deceased relatives and friends many benefit by these acts
7 Enjoining others to a sense of sharing in one's religious merit
8 Hearing *dhamma*
9 Teaching *dhamma*
10 'Straightening' one's true perceptions, for example by praising wholesome deeds, by recollecting good deeds done, by taking refuge in Buddha, and so on.

In this scheme, 1, 2 and 10 are items that ensure the continuance of the religious tradition and its basic concepts and institutions; 3, 8 and 9 tend to foster a broader religious understanding; 6 and 7 accommodate popular practices amid which are aspects of funeral cults, now presented in a Buddhist setting: gifts are given not to the spirits of the dead but to monks – the dead (and this involves aspects of rebirth too) are expected to become aware of these acts, and be induced 'to a happy and morally wholesome state of mind'. The idea behind 1 is that ideally, monks are the ones who live the *Dhamma*: to maintain them is to foster the highest good. Under 4, offerings to persons or to symbolic objects that deserve veneration are envisaged; this is to remind the donor of the good that they represent – in practice this means the Buddhas and their disciples, represented symbolically by their images and their relics (sometimes in shrines or *stupas*), or by the bo-tree which recalls the Buddha's enlightenment (see page 215). Food, drink, flowers, incense and lights are all considered to be appropriate offerings to the Buddha.

In this scheme one can also see the accommodative effort that has gone into evolving a broad system of religious acts, a spectrum extending from the popular – for example, 4 – to the austere – for example 3. In the system even 8,

hearing *dhamma*, is capable of having its own ceremonial mode, especially in the form of recitation of the Buddha's discourses in a stylized chant, a very popular practice deemed to be conducive to a soothing frame of mind and an auspicious atmosphere.

Variations in the observance of the Buddhist 'sabbath', the *uposatha* – which falls on the 1st, 8th, 15th and 23rd days of the lunar month – also illustrate how some of these 'meritorious acts' have popularly been performed. The most devout observe the *uposatha* as a day of retreat and meditation, perhaps in the precincts of a temple. Others may listen to religious sermons and chants or go on pilgrimage to a special shrine. Most, however, devote offerings (generally of flowers) and worship at the shrine-room, *stupa* and bo-tree of the local temple, at which the monks organize 'services' of congregational rites with accompanying music, processions, and at times even pageants and firework displays.

BUDDHIST BUILDINGS

Socially and religiously, then, the temple is the most important building of the entire community. A complete Theravada temple typically has residential quarters for the monks; a sacred area for their *Vinaya* rites; a shrine for worship containing Buddha images and altar, and walls and ceiling painted with scenes from religious legends; a *stupa* enshrining relics of the Buddha and the great disciples; a bo-tree; and a preaching hall for monks to deliver sermons on days of religious observance.

In a special category of their own are historic structures like the great *stupas* – the Shwe Dagon in Rangoon, Burma, for instance, or Ruvan-vali in Anuradhapura, Sri Lanka – or the Temple of the Tooth, dedicated to the worship of the Buddha's tooth relic in Kandy, Sri Lanka, the centre of a colourful annual pageant steeped in the traditions of the feudal past.

ORGANIZATION

Central to the organization of Theravada is its monastic order, the Sangha. Its members, the celibate *bhikkhus*, are ideally expected to lead a life of simplicity. A comparable order of nuns (*bhikkhunîs*) existed in the past but is now defunct in Theravada countries. The monks are obliged strictly to follow the disciplinary code called the *Vinaya*, part of which is the fortnightly *uposatha* ceremony at which the monks of each local Sangha are expected to confess transgressions.

In theory, the Buddhist Sangha is indivisible and, after the death of the Buddha, without an overall head. In practice, however, in each country it is split into several sects that nominally correspond to a hierarchical structure, comprising *nayaka* (chief) and *anunayaka* (deputy chief) monks chosen by electoral committees. But for the purposes of daily administration, the basis for the division between sects is neither doctrinal nor functional; rather, it is – at least in Sri Lanka – sociological and the result of history: the temples affiliated to the various sects are administered with considerable autonomy by their own incumbent chiefs whose promotion to office generally follows traditional rules of accession.

The chief monk of each temple fulfils a very important role in the religious life of the community both inside and outside the temple buildings. His stature and competence is crucial to the success of the temple's internal organization of religious activities as well as of its external fundraising efforts. Such close links with the surrounding community are imperative: the religious services the monks perform are highly regarded by the local populace, who in turn take it as their duty to look after the temple and the monks. Throughout history the laity have supported the Sangha; kings and local chiefs have seen to the construction of religious buildings, donated large tracts of productive land, and assigned numbers of workers to serve the temple authorities in a feudatory relationship. This tradition of state support continues, but now in the form of financial aid through departments of religious affairs.

But of course the most enduring source of support for the Sangha and the places of worship it maintains is the local laity, organized into maintenance committees (*dayaka sabhas*) for each temple, seeing to the day-to-day requirements of the monks, and acting as fund-raisers for special events.

Larger lay organizations are a comparatively recent development. Now of international structure is the World Fellowship of Buddhists of which all Theravada countries are members. The various missions to foreign countries, such as the Mahabodhi Society, are also international in both function and outlook. Other large organizations have social and educational objectives, among them the Young Men's Buddhist Associations, the Buddhist Congress and the Buddhist Publications Society.

POLITICAL AFFILIATIONS

The sense of Buddhist identity is strong in Theravada countries. The widespread emotional attachment among the people to the continuance

and well-being of the institutions of the religion can bring about situations charged with considerable political significance, as was demonstrated for example in Sri Lanka in 1956 when a relatively popular governing party was ousted from power after having been given an anti-Buddhist image by the triumphant opposition.

Another example of political significance is the repeated failure of Marxist parties in electoral politics in at least one Theravada Buddhist country. And it is possibly due to an appreciation of the hold of Buddhism on the mass mind that successive regimes in Burma, Sri Lanka and Thailand have throughout modern history made strenuous efforts to be perceived as benefactors and protectors of the religion, even to the extent of supporting the ideological aspirations of Buddhists where they may conflict with the broader interests of a multi-religious society.

Strangely, perhaps, there are no specifically Buddhist political parties in Theravada lands. The reason is presumably that enough major political groups are already sensitive and responsive to Buddhist opinion. But the result is that it is not possible to identify Theravada with any actual political stance or doctrine, although scholars would generally agree that Buddhist ideals, by their very nature, are compatible only with democratic social structures.

A Buddhist worshipper makes an offering of a flower. Every day simple offerings such as this are made in Buddhist homes in Sri Lanka before the small household shrine. Traditionally a flower, water and a little rice are the appropriate gifts. Lay people also support the Sangha, the community of monks, who in return perform religious services.

MAHAYANA BUDDHISM

ORIGINS AND DISTRIBUTION

Mahayana Buddhism is one of the most influential movements in history. Arising in India at about the time of Christ, it expanded in a series of ripples which had consequences that were far removed from its place and time of origin. First it added a new dimension to Buddhism itself. Second, it had profound effects on the Indian religious tradition generally. Third, it travelled to Tibet (and hence to Mongolia) and China (and from there to Korea, Vietnam and Japan) and fundamentally transformed the world-views of those countries. Our task is to explain how all this could have happened.

The word 'Mahayana' means 'great vehicle' or 'way'. It is a term that the Mahayanists themselves invented and they contrasted it with the Hinayana or small vehicle/way of the traditional Buddhism that had preceded them. They gave two reasons why the Mahayana is great: it carries over more beings; and its aspiration is higher than that of traditional Buddhism: nothing less than to become Buddha. It did not take long for the Mahayana to combine these two and thereby formulate one of its more startling tenets: eventually, all beings will become Buddhas.

Traditional Buddhism had never said this. It taught that certain disciples of the Buddha could become enlightened, but not that they would have the full majesty and grandeur of the Buddha himself. The Mahayana teaching that not only can a disciple became a Buddha, but that all living creatures, whether human or animal (including amoebas and bacteria), can become Buddhas, is exceedingly radical. In fact, it adds a new dimension to Buddhism altogether.

How did this new departure come about? To answer this question, it is necessary to give an account of the origin of the Mahayana. There are three factors that have to be borne in mind in giving this account. First, the Mahayana relies exclusively on its own *sutras*. A *sutra* is a record of the words of the Buddha. These words are regarded as precious, holy and unique and it is unthinkable that any Buddhist, however pious, would *invent* a *sutra*. Yet the Mahayana does claim that the works which contain its teaching are the words of the Buddha, even though it is quite clear that they are different from the *sutras* of traditional Buddhism which are accepted by all Buddhists as the actual utterances of the historical Buddha. There are problems concerning the transmission of the traditional Buddhist *sutras* and it is not at all

necessary to accept that they *are* the unalloyed words of the historical Buddha. But the essential point is this: traditional *sutras could* be the words of the historical Buddha, but Mahayana *sutras* could not. Yet the Mahayana insists that they are the Buddha's teaching. This is an enormous and far-reaching claim. How could it be justified?

The answer is to be found in the Mahayana *sutras* themselves and it is essentially quite simple: the Buddha has appeared in a non-physical form and has personally founded the Mahayana himself. There are many passages that indicate that this is how the Mahayana began. The Buddha is said to manifest his brightly shining body to those who are engaged in spiritual practice (*Lotus Sutra*, ch. 10, v. 28); elsewhere, the Buddha's body is described as golden, shining like the sun, and filling the beholder with delight. The sight of the Buddha (*buddha-darshana*) removes suffering and craving, and is purifying.

This visionary encounter with the Buddha is the second factor in our account of the origins of the Mahayana. And it has another facet to it: the buddha not only appears, he also speaks. This speaking, of course, is the Mahayana justification for its insistence on its own *sutras* – they are only recording the actual words of the *real* Buddha (i.e. the Buddha who has appeared to them.) The Buddha's voice (*buddha-shabda*) is described in the new *sutras* as sweet, deep and resounding; those who hear it are related and overjoyed, yet calm and detached. And, of course, the words that the Buddha speaks are, by definition, true.

It is not difficult to realise the devastating impact that encountering the Buddha in this way must have had, and it helps us to understand the relation that the Mahayana has with the Buddhism that preceded it, the Hinayana (see p. 227), though this term is somewhat disparaging and scholars try not to use it. Entering the Mahayana was a powerful and transformative experience. Although the majority of those who did so were probably Buddhists (whether members of the *sangha* or lay followers), there was no special reason why they had to be. Essentially, the Mahayana stood on its own feet, since it had an independent source of truth via its own *sutras* (themselves received directly from the Buddha). It therefore tended to have a very casual attitude to the traditional Buddhist *sutras*. Undoubtedly, many Mahayanists were well acquainted with them and we do find the occasional passage in Mahayana *sutras* that can be identfied from a earlier tradition. But although most Mahayanists are clearly

THE MAIN STREAMS OF BUDDHISM

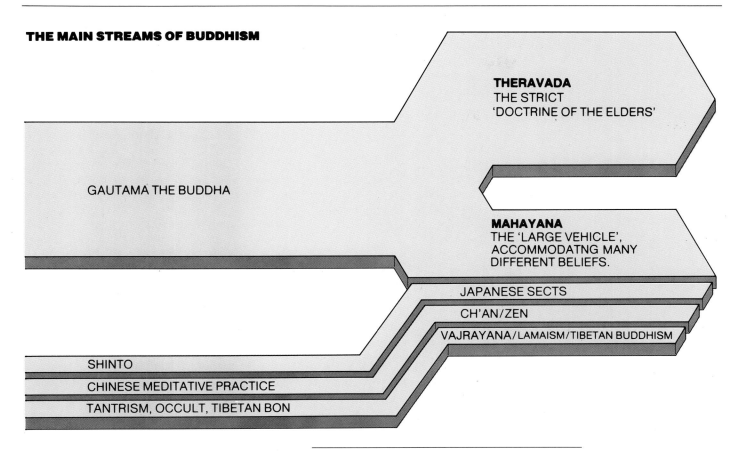

GAUTAMA THE BUDDHA

THERAVADA
THE STRICT
'DOCTRINE OF THE ELDERS'

MAHAYANA
THE 'LARGE VEHICLE',
ACCOMMODATNG MANY
DIFFERENT BELIEFS.

JAPANESE SECTS

CH'AN/ZEN

VAJRAYANA/LAMAISM/TIBETAN BUDDHISM

SHINTO

CHINESE MEDITATIVE PRACTICE

TANTRISM, OCCULT, TIBETAN BON

at home in the traditional Buddhism, it is apparent from the Mahayana *sutras* that they pay little attention to it. There is hardly any mention of the four noble truths, the principle of causation, or even the eightfold path. Instead, what we find is that the Mahayana either heavily reinterprets the tenets of traditional Buddhism or adds completely new teachings of its own. Although it is often difficult to distinguish between these two, it is probably fair to say that 5 per cent of Mahayana *sutras* is a restatement of traditional Buddhism; 30 per cent is reinterpretation; and 65 per cent is completely new.

The relation that Mahayana has to traditional Buddhism is the third factor in our account of Mahayana origins. It can be summarized as follows. Suddenly, about the time of the beginning of the Christian era, some Buddhists had a visionary encounter with a non-physical, glorious Buddha and received teachings from him. These teachings are recorded in the Mahayana *sutras* which, while they do not ignore traditional Buddhism completely, are still essentially a new departure and contain many ideas that are not found in the earlier tradition. And, although the teachings of the Mahayana are its abiding legacy, the essential feature of the founding of the new Buddhism was the astounding transformative experience of being in direct contact with the Buddha – an experience that was open to everyone regardless of religious or social background.

TEACHINGS

In order to find out what the Mahayana taught, we have to look at its *sutras*. And when we do so, we immediately discover two things: there are enormous numbers of them, and they vary considerably. Our account of the origin of the Mahayana helps to explain why. The Mahayana is the shared experience of its practitioners – namely, those who have seen or heard the Buddha. But this does not mean that the experience, though shared, has to be the same for everyone. The Buddha may reveal one thing to a monk with forty years of solitary meditation behind him, and another to a young woman who knows little or nothing about Buddhism. The very nature of the Mahayana allows different teaching for different people according to their circumstances.

The subtlety and richness of the Mahayana *sutra* is without parallel in the spiritual literature of the world. We shall try to do justice to it, while yet making it comprehensible, concentrating on these interacting ideas:

1   The *person* of the Buddha and the Bodhisattva
2   The *concepts* of emptiness (*shunyata*) and thought or mind (*chitta*)
3   The *attributes* of wisdom (*prajna*), compassion (*karuna*) and skill-in-means (*upaya-kaushalya*)

233

Mahayana Buddhism allows the existence of Bodhisattvas. These are believed to be beings who have vowed to become a Buddha but delay doing so through their great compassion for others. Maitreya represents the oldest notion of a Bodhisattva of the present era. Maitreya waits in the Tusita heaven for the time to leave and enter the realm of humankind. In Mahayana Buddhism Maitreya is a deity of light and an inspiration to teaching masters.

The Buddha and skill-in-means

As we would expect, given the visionary origins of the Mahayana itself, the central teaching of the Buddha is that he is unlimited or unrestricted. There are two ways in which this idea is expressed, both of which are found in the *Lotus Sutra*, one of the earliest and most influential works in the Mahayana canon. On the one hand, the Buddha is said to be able to take on a form that is suitable for leading beings to enlightenment; on the other, he gives forth a teaching that is adapted to the spiritual needs of beings. Both of these are instances of skill-in-means or *upaya-kaushalya* (often called *upaya* for short). The word *upaya* means 'device', 'method', 'means'.

In chapter 15 of the *Lotus Sutra*, the Buddha says that his physical body is only skill-in-means. That is, he manifests it so that people should think that if he, Gautama Buddha, can attain enlightenment, so can they. But really the Buddha is not restricted to the physical form and is always teaching the *Dharma* whether or not he is in the body. The Buddha says that he was already enlightened before he was even born, and that his search for, and attainment of, enlightenment was only apparent. In short, everything that we know of the historical Buddha is only a device to benefit beings. There is nothing ultimate in any of it.

This leads us to the other sense of skill-in-means: that the Buddha gives different teachings to different people. This idea is contained in

chapter 3 of the *Lotus Sutra*, the famous parable of the burning house. A man, seated outside his house, sees that it is on fire, but that his sons are busy playing with their toys unaware of the danger. He tries to warn them but they take no notice. So he tells them that he has some splendid carts for them: some pulled by goats, some by deer and some by bullocks. The children rush out of the house in order to have the cart of their choice. But the father gives each of them the best kind of cart, the ones pulled by bullocks.

The interpretation of this parable is as follows. The burning house is *samsara*, the world of suffering, and the man is the Buddha, the father of the world. He is resolved to save all beings (his children) from suffering. But when he tells them about suffering, they do not heed him – so he uses a device (*upaya*). He promises them happiness (the carts) that is greater than any in *samsara*, making sure to vary what he says to suit the different predilections of beings. Yet in the end, he gives them all the same liberation. This is the liberation of the best cart, the Mahayana, the great vehicle. The chapter ends by asking: 'Is the Buddha guilty of a falsehood by promising many carts but giving only one, the best? No. Even if he had given no cart at all, he would not have been guilty, for he has liberated beings by his skill-in-means.'

These two meanings of *upaya* – the form that the Buddha takes and what he manifests in order to save beings – were quickly developed by the Mahayana to an extraordinary degree. First, the Buddha can take on any form. He does not limit himself to the occasional human body who searches for and attains enlightenment. He can appear in any part of *samsara* – as a god, or an animal, or among the hills. And when he does he is indistinguishable from other gods, other animals, other inhabitants of the hills. In other words, the Buddha is the perfect master of disguise. It follows from this that we can never know who is an ordinary being and who is a Buddha pretending to be an ordinary being. Indeed, the distinction between the two phenomena collapses. There are innumerable Buddhas and they can take innumerable forms. Thus it follows in logical conclusion that absolutely any being can be a Buddha in disguise.

Secondly, the Buddha can *manifest* any form: he can slip into the world, as it were, perfect counterfeits of what *samsara* ordinarily contains, in order to aid beings in their search for enlightenment. And the same principle applies here as with the forms that he takes himself – there is no restriction on what and where he manifests these forms. Hence the Mahayana quickly went from saying that anything *could* be manifest by the Buddha's skill-in-means to saying that everything *is* manifest by him. One cannot tell the difference between something that is as it is in itself and something that has been introduced by the Buddha. And the reason for this is that, since the Buddha is unlimited, there can be nothing, however insignificant, that is separate from him or outside his sphere of influence. In fact, the Buddha controls all space and time and he can create whole worlds. Nothing approaching this idea is found in traditional Buddhism and it is a good example of how much further the Mahayana goes beyond the earlier tradition.

Skill-in-means and compassion

But why should the Buddha manifest all these forms? The answer is: out of compassion (*karuna*). The Buddha sees suffering and wishes to alleviate it. Being unrestricted, he has infinite resources and he draws on them in order to benefit beings. This wish to lead others to the same state that he is in – so that they become Buddhas – is natural because the Buddha, having no craving or needs of his own, is able to respond to the needs of others. This response is compassion, for it is always the result of seeing things as they are, undistorted by selfish desires or attachments. The ability to see things as they are is called wisdom (*prajna*). There is therefore a close relation between wisdom and compassion – indeed, they are two sides of the same infinitely thin coin.

Emptiness, mind and wisdom

The Mahayana teaching on the nature of wisdom is inextricably tied up with the doctrine of emptiness (*shunyata*). In essence, it is very simple but it has ramifications that are exceedingly radical and challenge all our assumptions about the nature of reality. In order to make this doctrine clear, it is first necessary to give a technical definition of emptiness and then explain the principles that lie behind it.

The technical definition is: all *dhammas* are empty of own-being. The word *dharma* here should not be confused with exactly the same term with a different meaning, namely, the Buddha's teaching or truth (for which the Pali spelling, 'dhamma' is used here). In the context of emptiness, *dharma* means whatever can be held before the mind, or the object of the sixth sense, *manas* or mind. (Sometimes *chitta* 'thought' is used instead of *manas*, and since it is preferred by the Mahayana we shall refer to *chitta* from now on.)

A basic principle of Buddhism is involved here which may be summarized as follows. There is no act of awareness that does not involve the turning of the mind in a certain direction or, to put it in different words, that does not require the mind to focus in a *particular* way. This is true whether I am looking at a dog or hearing it bark; whether I am just thinking about a dog, or considering an abstract argument concerning the importance of dogs in human civilization. This art of focussing is

a *skill*. A person who is frightened of dogs will not perceive them (or think about them) in the same way as someone who is fond of them. It is a cardinal tenet of Buddhism (whether traditional or Mahayana) that unskilful use of the mind leads to craving and attachment – in short, to suffering. This is because an unskilful mind is obsessive, and an obsessive mind continuously fantasizes about the objects that come before it and distorts them.

And here we come to another central idea of Buddhism: the forms that the mind (*chitta*) generates will eventually appear in reality. This is not an easy idea to understand and it runs counter to the commonsense assumptions of western empiricism: namely, that the world is given and as it is in itself, and human beings have to adjust to it. The Buddhist teaching is in fact the opposite of this: all beings (human or otherwise) create their own reality or world (*loka*) by the persistent generation of forms by the mind or consciousness. This is the law of *karma*.

The Mahayana version of this law is the doctrine of emptiness (*shunyata*), As was stated above, the technical definition of emptiness is that all *dharmas* are empty of own-being. 'Dharmas' here means 'forms that can come before the mind', and the definition is meant to include *any* object of awareness, however minute or abstruse. To say that all forms are empty of own-being is to say that these forms have no essence or inherent unity – and for the simple reason that they are the result of the mind's obsession, and obsession is by definition always unsatisfied and always restless. Hence no form (or *dharma*) can remain stable; it must always dissolve. So the doctrine of emptiness comes to this: there is nothing at all – no object of experience – that we can *have*. All *dharmas* are empty.

Put like this, the emptiness teaching can appear stark and unappealing. But the Mahayana is quick to point out the necessary corollary to it: if there is nothing we can have, then equally there is nothing that can hold us. As Chogyam Trungpa has put it, emptiness is really openness. All forms are open and can be *trans*formed. Nothing can tie us down. We are, like the Buddha, unlimited.

There is, however, a crucial move here that must be understood. If there is nothing that we can have, then we cannot 'have' enlightenment. We cannot 'have' Buddhahood. This can be put paradoxically as follows: enlightenment can only be when the desire to 'have' it is given up. A Mahayana slogan makes the same point: *nirvana that is grasped is samsara; samsara that is not grasped in nirvana.*

The ramifications of the doctrine of emptiness are enormous. If all *dharmas* are empty, then Buddhahood itself is empty. So there cannot be a real, essential distinction between a dog and a Buddha. The Mahayana *sutras* say this in so many words.

If an empty *dharma* is unlimited, then it follows a) that everything, however tiny and insignificant, is unlimited; b) that the Buddha, however unlimited, is empty; and c) that there cannot be two classes of things, limited and unlimited, but only one class: the unlimited or empty.

The realization of this truth is what the Mahayana means by wisdom (*prajna*). The Buddha, of course, 'has' this realization (though this statement must be immediately qualified because such a realization cannot be 'had', even by a Buddha). And this is because he is empty or open. To him anything is possible.

Emptiness, compassion and skill-in-means

It should now be possible to understand why wisdom (*prajna*) and compassion (*karuna*) are so intimately linked. That which is full is closed and excludes everything else. (This is, in fact, a definition of ego or self.) That which is empty is open and can include everything. Therefore the Buddha has unlimited compassion, because, being empty (that is, not full of himself), he can respond to the needs of beings. And this response is not passive but dynamic and active and it manifests itself as skill-in-means. All this can be summarized in an equation:

emptiness + compassion = skill-in-means
(= openness (= response) (= contriving
 or the means to
unrestrictedness) lead beings to
 Buddhahood)

This, of course, is a paradox. Wisdom, which knows that all *dharmas* are empty, that all forms are insubstantial and like foam, is yet able to give rise to an inexhaustible energy that acts without ceasing for the benefit of all beings in all worlds. This paradox can be restated as follows. On the one hand, there is nothing to be done (because nothing *can* be done). This is the emptiness side of things. On the other hand *anything* can be done (because there are no inherent restrictions that can prevent anything being done). This is the skill-in-means side of things. Both are true simultaneously. That reality can be like this is completely accepted by the Mahayana and they use the term *achintya*, literally 'unthinkable' or 'inconceivable', to describe it. What is truly so (sometimes called *tathata* or suchness) cannot be the *object* of the attention of the mind (*chitta*). That is why it is called *achintya*. (The words *chitta* and *achintya* are both derived from the same Sanskrit root.)

Skill-in-means and mind

We have already looked at the Buddha's skill-in-means in an earlier section. We have also examined the notion of *karma*, which was defined as

the universal law that mind gives rise to the forms on which it dwells. The next step is to bring these two ideas together and see how they fit. The doctrine of emptiness has as one of its consequences that there is no real distinction between the enlightened one (the Buddha) and all other unenlightened beings. If these beings are constantly giving rise to various forms by the obsessive operation of their mind, must this not be true in some sense of the Buddha also? The short answer is: yes, in principle, but not in practice.

This needs to be explained. It is perfectly true that the Buddha does constantly give rise to forms, and in this he is exactly like all other beings. But because, in his wisdom, he knows that whatever is produced by the mind is empty, he is open, unattached and non-obsessive. In other words, the Buddha creates forms consciously (that is, with wisdom) while ignorant beings do so unconsciously. Now, when a form that has been created unconsciously is encountered (by an ignorant being) it is always experienced as being *other* than oneself and is therefore restrictive and limiting. But the opposite is also true: a form that is consciously created is recognized as one's own creation and does not restrict the creator of it. On the contrary, it is seen as a means (*upaya*) of liberation.

This principle may be stated succinctly as follows. Unconscious creation of forms is *karma* and binds; conscious creation of forms is magic and liberates. So the Buddhas play the game (and there is only one game and you can never stop playing it), but they do so for the benefit of others. The use of the term 'magic' may be somewhat startling, but the Mahayana fully accepts it. According to their world view, reality *is* magical because anything that exists is the creation of mind. So the world (indeed, all the worlds in their unlimited profusion) is inherently transformable. To know this is to participate in the magic by skill-in-means; to be ignorant of it is to be bound by *karma* (which is one's own creation that one does not recognize).

Naturally a Buddha, because of his compassion, cannot help creating forms for the benefit of beings. (And this does not limit his freedom, because there is only one game and the only question is whether it is played consciously or unconsciously.) Perhaps the best known example of this is the pure land (*vishuddha-kshetra*) of the Buddha Amitabha (meaning 'measureless light'), called Sukhavati-vyuha. The word *vyuha* is best translated 'magnificent display or manifestation' and in effect it means a whole world or reality that has been consciously (and therefore magically) created for the benefit of beings. *Sukhavati-vyuha* thus means 'a marvellous world (*vyuha*) that is endowed with happiness (*sukhavati*)'. This is the supreme skill-in-means.

The description of this pure land is contained in the *Sukhavati-vyuha Sutra*, one of the earliest Mahayana works. Dharmakara (literally, 'Dharma-mine') is a monk who takes a vow to become a Buddha. This vow is, of course, a conscious shaping of the mind (*chitta*) and must therefore, by the universal law that we have already mentioned, give rise to those forms that fulfil (or make manifest) that vow. In fact, the vow is made up of a number of declarations which establish the qualities of the world that Dharmakara wishes to create. He accomplishes his vow – which means that he both becomes the Buddha Amitabha and creates Sukhavati-vyuha. (In fact, these two are really the same thing.) And anyone who brings Amitabha to mind will benefit by being reborn in Sukhavati, the world or reality that Amitabha has created.

In sum, there is no limit to what a Buddha will do in order to bring beings closer to himself. His activity is unceasing and all-embracing. This is another instance of a Mahayana doctrine that is unthinkable (*achintya*) because it goes beyond the limits of the mind.

The Buddha and the mind

There is a second, parallel doctrine that is the exact opposite. (We should be expecting these Mahayana paradoxes by now.) This is that the Buddha does not need to create anything or do anything because he is already at the centre of all creation and action. One Mahayana text encapsulates this doctrine thus:

> *The body of the perfect Buddha irradiates everything; its suchness is undifferentiated and the road to Buddhahood is open to all. At all times have all beings the seed of Buddhahood in them.*

Whereas the unthinkable skill-in-means doctrine says that everything needs to be done (and the Buddha can do it), this teaching of the undifferentiated Buddha says that nothing needs to be done. Or, to put it another way, that everything has already been done. This is because the Buddha, being empty and therefore unlimited, is not separate from any being or from any *dharma* (i.e. any state of mind). In other words, the Buddha is contained within all *dharmas*.

The Mahayana uses four kinds of terminology to express this idea. The first is that of irradiation. The Buddha is like space. Just as all forms must by definition exist in space, so all beings and all *dharmas* are pervaded both within and without. Similarly, if there is matter there must be gravity. Gravity is not produced *by* matter; gravity *is* the way that matter exists. Analogously, beings cannot be separate from the Buddha, nor can he be separate from them. The condition of beings is inseparable from the Buddha's existence.

The second kind of terminology is that of the *tathagata-garbha*. *Tathagata* is another word for Buddha; and *garbha* means both 'embryo' and 'womb'. Hence *tathagata-garbha* has two (opposite) meanings: 'embryonic Buddha' and 'the Buddha womb'. The first of these has the sense that all beings have within them the seed of Buddhahood. Sometimes this idea is expressed by the metaphor of a precious jewel (Buddhahood, the *tathagata-garbha*) hidden in mud (the physical body that is the result of obsession and ignorance). The second meaning is akin to the idea of the Buddha as being like space. Everything is contained within the womb of the Buddha and all beings are nurtured by it. In the *Lankavatara Sutra* this sense of *tathagata-garbha* is allied with the *alaya-vijnana* or 'store consciousness'. That is, whatever exists is an emanation from the inexhaustible storehouse of Buddha consciousness which holds all things effortlessly.

The third way of talking about the Buddha contained within all beings is in terms of *buddhata*, a word that can be translated 'Buddhahood' or 'Buddhanature'. It is not that beings are on the way to Buddhahood, but rather that they already have the Buddha-nature within them. In other words, nothing has to be accomplished because the goal (Buddhahood, which is Buddha-nature) has already been achieved. Indeed, Buddhanature is a necessary precondition for there to be an aspiration towards becoming a Buddha – an aspiration that 'in the end' is seen to be self-contradictory because Buddha-nature is the true nature of all beings (though this nature is not a particular nature and therefore cannot be possessed or 'had'). One cannot become a Buddha because one already is a Buddha.

The Mahayana constantly juggles with two ways of presenting the truth. On the one hand, there is a task to be accomplished and the Buddha helps us to accomplish it. This is the way of skill-in-means, of transformation and magic which is reflected in the interpretation of *tathagata-garbha* as the womb of the Buddha (from which everything comes) and *buddhata* as Buddhahood (to which all beings are eventually led). On the other hand, there is no task to accomplish and the Buddha has to do nothing in order to help us. This is the way that we are considering now: that we are already embryonic Buddhas (the first interpretation of *tathagata-garbha*) and already 'possess' the Buddha-nature (the second interpretation of *buddhata*).

This leads us to the fourth kind of terminology that is used to express the idea that the Buddha is not separate from any being: that the mind of all beings is pure (*vishuddha*) and brightly shining (*prabhasvara*). Or to put it another way, the real nature of beings is the mind, or thought, of enlightenment (*bodhichitta*). This *bodhichitta* or enlightenment mind has no beginning or end and cannot be defiled. It is *buddhata*. It is the embryonic Buddha yet without limits; it irradiates everything. It is the Buddha. In short, the true nature of consciousness is enlightenment (*bodhi*).

The Buddha and the Bodhisattva

It is a natural progression to step from the *bodhichitta* to the Bodhisattva, who is the central pivot of the Mahayana and to whom the paradoxes raised above naturally apply. On the one hand, he takes upon himself (or herself – the Mahayana accepts that there can be female Bodhisattvas) a task that is as great as can be conceived – indeed, it is inconceivable (*achintya*); on the other, there is no task and he has nothing to do – this is also inconceivable. The union of these two constitutes the Mahayana, the vehicle that can carry all beings and which aspires to Buddhahood. And the Mahayana is the Bodhisattva path, so if we understand one we understand the other.

The word 'Bodhisattva' means 'enlightenment being' – that is, one who wishes to attain enlightenment or to be a Buddha. As has just been shown, the paradox of the Mahayana is that one cannot attain or 'get' enlightenment or become a Buddha (since one already is a Buddha) – but the traditional way of presenting the Bodhisattva path is in fact in terms of attainment. It is necessary to adopt this way of expressing it to begin with and then turn it inside out (as the Mahayana itself does).

There are four stages on the Bodhisattva path. The first is the arising of the thought of enlightenment or enlightenment mind. There are two ways of understanding what this arising of the *bodhichitta* involves. One way is to see it as referring to a certain level of spiritual aspiration – and this can either be an advanced or an elementary level. That is, it may be that the arising of the *bodhichitta* is very, very rare; or it may be that it is relatively common. The latter view is taken by the *Lotus Sutra* (ch. 2, v. 81) which says that even a small boy who piles up a heap of sand with the intention of dedicating it to the Buddha – even he will reach enlightenment. (That is, his intention is the arising of the thought of enlightenment.) The other way of understanding the meaning of *bodhichitta* is from the other side of the Mahayana paradox: every act of awareness, without exception, is the arising of the *bodhichitta*, because there can be no consciousness that is separate from enlightenment.

It is easy to see how the interpretation of the meaning of *bodhichitta* (see above) affects our understanding of what a Bodhisattva is. On the first interpretation there is one class of beings who are Bodhisattvas and another who are not; and then the class of Bodhisattvas is either very small (because the arising of the thought of enlighten-ment is very advanced) or reasonably large (because the *bodhichitta* arises reasonably often or easily). On the second interpretation, *all* beings are Bodhisattvas (because the *bodhichitta* arises in every act of awareness).

Having established the paradox at the very beginning of the Bodhisattva path, we will now go on to look at the next three stages. The second stage is the Bodhisattva vow (*pranidhana*; a word that literally means 'fixation' and refers to the principle already discussed, that what the mind fixes upon becomes real). This vow is twofold. First, to become a Buddha. Second, to save all beings and lead them to *nirvana* before he himself enters *nirvana*. It is easy to see that those two vows contradict themselves, since how can the Bodhisattva save beings unless he himself is saved? We shall return to this paradox later.

The third stage of the Bodhisattva path is the actual practice of it (called the *Bodhisattva-charya*, 'the course of the Bodhisattva') and consists of six (or ten) levels (*bhumi*) or perfections (*paramita*). The six perfections are:

1 The perfection of giving: a generosity that gives without expecting reward
2 The perfection of morality: a purity of thought, word and deed that shines like gold because it is based on a fundamental respect and love for all beings
3 The perfection of patience: an absence of the obsessive need for people to be a certain way; a realistic (not fatalistic) acceptance of things as they are
4 The perfection of energy: a never-ceasing movement towards the benefit of all beings, but one that is natural and unstrained
5 The perfection of meditation: constant clarity and sharpness of mind that allows the Bodhisattva to perceive all situations in their totality
6 The perfection of wisdom (*prajna*): insight into the true nature of all *dharmas* and all beings – that they are empty and open and free.

The consequence of the successful practice of the *Bodhisattva-charya* is the fourth stage – the attainment of Buddhahood. The Bodhisattva becomes a Buddha.

We saw at the beginning that the definition of the Mahayana is that all beings will become Buddhas. Here we see that those on the way to this goal are the Bodhisattvas. We have also seen that the Mahayana is irreducibly paradoxical and uses two ways of talking: that there is a great task to be done, and there is nothing to be done. And, finally, we have seen that the Bodhisattva takes a vow that is self-contradictory: he will become a Buddha, but he will not finish his task until he has led all other beings to become Buddhas.

We find, then, that the nature of the Bodhisattva is at the core of the Mahayana. What are we to make of it and how can we reconcile the paradoxes that themselves exist in the very centre of his nature and his path? The simple answer to this is that a Bodhisattva never in fact finishes his task; the very idea that there is a final resting place, where there is nothing more to be done, is false. To begin with, a Bodhisattva cannot believe this, but his vow is such that it forces him to attempt it 'in the end' (though there cannot be an end, of course). In other words, a Buddha is simply a Bodhisattva who has realized the full implications of his vow. He will always be a Bodhisattva: one who works continuously for the benefit of beings. To put it another way: there are no Buddhas because a Buddha would be someone who had finished his task and this is impossible.

This is certainly a startling view, yet such is the profundity and subtlety of Mahayana that it is not the only one. The same insight can be put in other ways. Here are four more interpretations of the Bodhisattva path (which in effect is the essence of the Mahayana).

1 The path is very difficult and takes a very long time. This is only a provisional view and must be transcended.

2 The path is impossible and takes an infinite time. We have just discussed this view.

3 The path is easy and takes no time at all. This view is based on a certain understanding of emptiness. Since all *dharmas* (i.e. conditions of mind) are empty, there is no real distinction between them. Hence the arising of the enlightened mind (*bodhichitta*) which is the beginning of the Bodhisattva path, and the 'attainment' of Buddhahood (*buddhata*), at the end are not separate at all. They are the same *dharma*, and all states of awareness are simultaneously *bodhichitta* and *buddhata*.

4 The path is neither difficult nor easy, and it takes as long as it takes. In other words, it is a mistake to try and establish what the task is, for it just is what it is. Categorizing it doesn't change it at all.

THE THREE BODIES OF THE BUDDHA

We have now been through all the major facets of the Mahayana mentioned on p. 233. We have seen how they interweave, such that from any one all the others can be derived; and also that all of them are paradoxical. This complicated state of affairs may be summarized as follows:

Personalized Mahayana	Universalized Mahayana
The Buddha is born to save beings	The Buddha is not born
The Buddha can take on any form	The Buddha is beyond form
The Buddha can do anything	There is no need for the Buddha to do anything
The Buddha saves us	The Buddha does not need to save us; we are already saved; indeed we were never lost
Turning the mind to the Buddha benefits beings	Beings cannot turn their minds to the Buddha because the Buddha *is* the mind
All beings will become Buddhas	All beings are already Buddhas
The Buddha is glorious like the sun	The Buddha is without qualities like space
The Buddha is infinite	The Buddha has no dimensions
The Buddha can produce anything out of emptiness	Nothing is ever produced out of emptiness
The Bodhisattva path is infinitely long	There is no Bodhisattva path

Around 300 CE, this division was explicitly stated in the Mahayana itself in the doctrine of the three bodies (*trikaya*) of the Buddha.

The Buddha's form body
(*rupa-kaya*)

The conjured-up body
(*Nirmana-kaya*)

The body of blissful encounter
(*Sambhoga-kaya*)

The Buddha's formless body
(*arupa-kaya*)

The body of truth or reality
(*Dharma-kaya*)

Tibetan literature contains a wide variety of Buddhist works; it is not the collection of a single school but is the product of many sources collected over time. This 18th-century Tibetan statue (below left) shows Adibuddha with his shakti Prainaparamita. This is a concept of the Tantric school which regards this as the primordial Buddha, the original Buddha-essence.

239

The *Nirmana-kaya* refers to the physical body which the Buddha uses in order to bring the *Dharma* to human beings. But reality is not restricted to the physical. In meditation or in visionary encounter, other higher forms are seen and the Buddha also manifests himself at these levels in his *Sambhoga-kaya*. So it could be said that the physical form of the Buddha is only a special (though necessary) instance of the blissful body. Finally, there is the *Dharma-kaya* which is beyond form. It is synonymous with emptiness: always present but never changing. It is the silence within which all the sounds of the world arise and fall. The point to remember is that the Mahayana held all these positions simultaneously. We shall find versions of them when we come later to examine Mahayana in China and Tibet (see page 243).

THE MADHYAMAKA AND YOGACHARA SCHOOLS

Everything that we have said so far has been based on the Mahayana *sutras* – that is, those works which are regarded as the words of the Buddha. But there were other works called *shastras* (literally 'teaching'). These were the product of specific doctrinal schools within the Mahayana and were their textbooks. They were not books at all to begin with, however, being memorized and recited for the teacher's use when he was teaching and they therefore tend to be extremely compact because the teacher would explain them as he went along. We will briefly summarize here the two most influential schools.

The Madhyamakas

Madhyamaka means 'middle', and the school was so called because it taught a middle way between two extremes: that of saying that there is an unchanging reality, and that of saying that there is nothing real at all. Its most famous exponent was Nagarjuna (born c. 150 CE) and this account of the Madhyamaka teaching is taken from his work, the *Mula-Madhyamaka-Karika* ('Stanzas concerning the fundamentals of the middle way'). Nagarjuna's single aim is to demonstrate that there is no alternative to the doctrine of emptiness (*shunyata*). He does this by showing that any other position is self-contradictory. Since his writings are extremely formalized and abstruse I shall give a simple example in order to demonstrate his method more clearly.

Suppose that I am sitting quietly in the jungle and I hear a tree crash to the ground. What is actually happening in this incident and how does the teaching of emptiness help me to understand it? First of all, say Nagarjuna, to say that a sound is a tree falling is only a label. There is nothing wrong with labels in themselves, but they are only conventions; they can be incorrectly applied and there is nothing about them that is inherently connected to reality. And what is the reality? The sound. Let us assume that what I can hear is in fact three sounds: an initial crack, a rushing sound and a final thud. Nagarjuna wants to ask two questions (which are intimately related). When does one sound start and finish? And how do I distinguish between the sounds? In the first split second when I hear the crack what is there about it that enables me to say what it is? Certainly I could not say after a ten-thousandth of a second that it was a tree (falling or not falling). It isn't at all obvious that I could even say it was a crack – because 'crack' is itself a label. And do I actually hear it as it is? If we represent the sound by a line so: ∿∿ perhaps what I hear is not so detailed and jagged but only like this: ∕⌐ Moreover, maybe I don't hear it when it actually begins, but only when my attention is caught by it – and my attention could be wandering or distorted or weak. So although it looks as if there is nothing problematic about saying that I hear that initial sound, in fact there is nothing definite about it at all. And 'definite' here means 'nothing that is real in itself'. Nagarjuna does not deny that the conventional description of this incident – namely that I hear the crack of a tree beginning to fall – is acceptable in certain circumstances. What he does deny is that there is *anything* in the incident that one can fix or pin down and say 'that is definite'.

We can now generalize this example and see how the doctrine of emptiness applies to it. First, there are no distinguishing marks that any object of awareness (or *dharma*) 'has' in itself – they are ascribed by convention. Hence if we say that a *dharma* begins here and ends there we cannot claim that there is a definite point at which it begins and ends. This does not mean that it does not begin or end – only that our certainty about its real beginning or end is misplaced. We can use measurement as an analogy here. When I say that a line is a yard long, what I mean is that it fits the marks on a measuring instrument give or take a certain margin of error. And this margin of error can never be completely eliminated – it can only be reduced to the point where it is no longer significant for a particular purpose. This is purely conventional – absolute accuracy is impossible.

This leads to the second point to be derived from Nagarjuna's analysis: to assume absolute knowledge is self-contradictory. If I know absolutely that I am hearing a crack, I cannot know later (even a ten-thousandth of a second later) that I *heard* it, because now I'm not hearing that bit of the crack but another bit. And so on and so on. Therefore the only explanation of the world of our experience, according to Nagarjuna, is that all *dharmas* are empty. That is, there is nothing absolute or fixed about *any* object of experience.

The consequences of this argument, which may look fairly innocuous, are in fact extremely radical. For example, causation as we normally understand it (and as traditional Buddhism understood it) is undermined. If I say that A causes B, am I perceiving A or B when I make this assertion? If I am perceiving A, then I am not perceiving B, and I cannot say what B is. And vice versa. And I cannot perceive both A and B simultaneously because the mind can only be aware of one thought at a time. In short, causation is a label that is applied to the relation between A and B; it is never actually perceived.

Samsara is the name given by Buddhism to the collection of causal relations. But Nagarjuna denies that these are real. He also denies that any object of awareness 'has' distinguishing marks in itself. And the reason is that all *dharmas* are empty. It therefore follows that *samsara* itself is empty. But so is *nirvana* – it also cannot have any distinguishing mark that 'makes' it what it is. From this double conclusion Nagarjuna arrives at perhaps his most famous assertion: there is no (real) distinction between *samsara* and *nirvana*.

We have already come across this idea before from the *sutras: nirvana* that is grasped is *samsara; samsara* that is not grasped is *nirvana*. There it was simply asserted. Nagarjuna, on the other hand, argues for it (or, more accurately, shows that any alternative is self-contradictory). We can see therefore that the Madhyamaka *shastras* are designed to complement by rational means the truth that is revealed in the *sutras*.

The Yogacharins

Much the same can be said about the Yogacharin school, which also has its own *shastras*. The founders of this school were the brothers Asanga and Vasubandhu (who lived around 400 CE). 'Yogachara' literally means 'Yoga instruction', but the word 'yoga' here simply has the sense of discipline or practice. And since the fundamental tenet of the school is that the *chitta* (mind) must be used correctly in order to avoid false perception, the implication of the term 'yogachara' is: instruction concerning the practice of using the mind correctly.

The Yogacharin teaching has often been called idealism because it says that everything that exists (i.e. all *dharmas*) is based on *chitta*. But the label of idealism is somewhat misleading because in fact the school says two things about *chitta* which are inseparably connected even though they are opposite. On the one hand, *chitta* is synonymous with reality itself – that is, it is brightly shining (*prabhasvara*), perfectly pure (*vishuddha*), beginningless and endless, beyond all duality and con-

ceptualization. On the other hand (as we saw in our discussion of *chitta* in the Mahayana *sutras*), *chitta* constantly gives rise to forms which exist 'in' reality but do not disturb its essential unity (or non-duality, to be strictly accurate). In other words, both reality (in itself), and the forms that it gives rise to, exist – but there is no 'real' distinction between them. This reality is called *chitta*, and since all forms arise from this reality, they also are *chitta* or based on mind.

The Yogacharins then go on to develop their own particular version of the Mahayana. They make two basic moves. First, if there is grasping at any form in order to make it mine (and remember that the word 'form' here in fact means *dharma* in the sense of any object of awareness), then duality is introduced into a reality that in fact is non-dual, and suffering must result. Secondly, the solution

Tanka showing the Parinirvana of the Buddha. After entering a series of higher states of consciousness he attains final release, or Nirvana. Nirvana is believed to be that beatitude which is attained by the extinction of all individuality.

241

to this grasping/duality/suffering (and the Yogachara regards all three as synonymous) is wisdom (*prajna*), which is defined as the seeing of reality (*tattva-darshana*). And for the Yogacharins this seeing is an actual experience which happens to each practitioner (though of course it cannot be an experience like any other, for then it would be based on duality and therefore false). The term they use for this concept is transformation or *paravritti*. In order to render this term more fully comprehensible, we may translate it as 'turning back, reversion (of a sentence or judgement), rebounding, not taking effect'.

Now that we understand the principles of the Yogacharin position, we can tackle some of its technical terminology with some confidence. When Vasubandhu says that the world (*loka*, meaning *samsara*) is mind only (*chitta-matra*), he is simply saying that reality (*chitta*) gives rise to forms. But *samsara* is the world of bondage and suffering, or what the Yogacharins call a false reality (*abhuta-parikalpita*); literally 'imagination of what does not exist' – as a separate, graspable reality, that is). It is imagined or created by the distinction between me and mine. That is, the 'me' wants things to be mine, which they cannot be because nothing (no thing) can be 'had' or possessed.

One of the most distinctive terms used by Asanga is *alaya-vijnana*, 'store consciousness'. This is understood as the sum total of all false or dualistic awareness, which is naturally experienced by beings as independent and separate, with a reality of its own. In short, *alaya-vijnana* is *samsara*. But this is a false reality (*abhuta-parikalpita*). There are no separate things. Reality as it is (*tathata* or suchness) is perfectly pure (*vishuddha*).

Thus the *alaya-vijnana* is itself perfectly pure because it cannot be separate from reality. Therefore, since *alaya-vijnana* is *samsara*, *samsara* itself cannot be separate from reality. Now, that which is perfectly pure and non-dual is *nirvana* or emptiness (*shunyata*). Therefore, there is no 'real' distinction between *nirvana* and *samsara*.

This, of course, is exactly what Nagarjuna said in his *Mula-madhyamaka-karikas* (see p. 240). The only difference between the Madhyamakas and the Yogacharins is that the latter say that this realization comes about by transformation (*paravritti*), whereas the Madhyamakas say that this realization already exists and all that is required is not to obscure it.

However, since both schools agree that grasping is the 'cause' of all suffering, they are not so far apart even on this point. It can be fairly, argued, therefore, that the two schools agree on practically every fundamental issue, and both are concerned with providing a clear argument where the *sutras* give straightforward declaration.

SPIRITUAL PRACTICE IN THE MAHAYANA

One of the distinctive tenets of the Yogacharins is that enlightenment consists in *paravritti* or transformation of awareness. This leads naturally to a consideration of what Mahayanists actually did, since a teaching is useless if it does not have consequences in action and behaviour. Two significant kinds of spiritual practice in the Mahayana are *shila* and *samadhi*. In traditional Buddhism these terms meant 'ethical conduct' and 'concentration' respectively, and the Mahayana is certainly aware of this. But it also interprets them in its own way. *Shila* is open-heartedness in the sense that one is willing to receive; *samadhi* is flexibility of mind in the sense that one can send the attention in any direction and hold it in any shape. *Shila* is also associated with faith (*shraddha*) and worship (*puja*). There is nothing in the least un-Buddhist about these as far as the Mahayana is concerned. The Buddha out of his compassion responds to the needs of beings. Hence his very form (*rupa*) is a sign of this compassion. The *shila* attitude to the Buddha, therefore, delights in glorifying the Buddha, and this means to be receptive to everything, however tiny or insignificant, that reminds us of him. The technical name for such practice is *buddhanusmriti*, 'remembrance of the Buddha'. It can involve many different practices: chanting his name, making images of him, reciting stories of his heroic and compassionate deeds, visiting the *stupa* (a shrine built around the Buddha's bones or relics). All of this is no more than our response to the Buddha (since he is regarded as the one who responds to the needs of beings).

Closely allied with *shila* is *samadhi* – indeed, the two are reflections of each other. The essence of *samadhi* (according to the Mahayana and here it differs considerably from traditional Buddhism) is the ability to *project* a form or image. This is the inverse of *shila*, which is the ability to *receive* a form or image (and see it for what it is – a gift from the Buddha). *Samadhi*, therefore, is simply the conscious use of *chitta* or mind; it is the deliberate fashioning of a form into which will be poured, as it were, the presence of the Buddha himself. *Samadhi* is therefore a discipline – but a creative one. The aim is to free one's mind from its obsessive habits and make it so flexible that it can easily create those forms that outline the essential attributes of the Buddha. When the mind is in this state, it constantly perceives that reality is a constant show of marvellous transformation. And this is exactly what the Mahayana teaching on the Buddha's and Bodhisattvas' skill-in-means says: everything we see is the result of magic, the conscious creation of forms by the mind.

The third kind of spiritual practice in the Mahayana is that of wisdom (*prajna*). It is associated with emptiness (*shunyata*) and non-duality (*advaya*). It does not reject forms but neither does it glorify them (like the practice of *shila*) nor create them (like *samadhi*). In a way, then, wisdom is a non-practice. And the justification of this is that enlightenment already exists. It does not therefore have to be received as a gift (which is the attitude of *shila*) nor participated in by conscious action (which is the *samadhi* attitude). Our true nature *is* Buddha-nature and so there is nothing to be accomplished.

In summary, then, we can say that Mahayana practice, like Mahayana teaching, is enormously varied. It allows people to bow before a statue of the Buddha; to practise a discipline so that consciousness goes beyond the physical world; and just to observe without moving in any direction at all. In this, it reflects the multi-faceted nature of reality which the Mahayana declared from the beginning and to which it remained true throughout all its phases.

Having established the main contours of the Mahayana in India, we shall now look at the form that it took in the two countries which took it most to their hearts: China and Tibet.

The Mahayana in China

The first mention of Buddhism in China is in 64 CE but we do not know if this was a form of Mahayana or not. It took another 350 years for the Chinese to reach the point where Buddhist teachings were reasonably accessible to them and another 200 before the Chinese genius fused with the Mahayana so completely as to give rise to a genuinely Chinese Buddhism.

A period of over 500 years is a very long time for any religion to gain ground, but the fact that it happened at all is even more remarkable. We shall briefly examine why this should be so and then look at the three main phases of Buddhism in China in the light of the Chinese world-view and temperament, which influenced Buddhism at every conceivable turn.

There were two reasons why the success of the Mahayana in China was unlikely. First, China is a long way from India, and it is very difficult indeed to go from one country to the other. Neither the silk route over the top of Tibet nor the sea route round Burma and Malaya are attractive and the number of Indians or Chinese who used them was tiny. So there was no natural day-to-day contact between the Indian and Chinese people.

But the second difficulty is even more striking: the fact that Indian and Chinese civilizations were opposite in nearly every way. These differences can be gathered under three heads: cosmological, social and linguistic.

Cosmology means the account of the nature of the world and its laws. The Chinese starting-point was one of primary harmony, a harmony that it was simply assumed must be maintained. By contrast, the Indian mind was quite at home with the idea that the universe may be chaotic (or, at least, quixotic) and that things are never quite what they seem. Thus the Chinese saw religion as an organic relationship between heaven (*t'ien*) and earth (*ti*) and man (*jen*); while the Indians were more drawn to the spiritual path as a means of alteration or transformation. To put it simply: the Chinese valued order and gentleness, while the Indians valued changeability and energy. (And we have seen how central these two latter values are to the Mahayana.)

The differences between the Chinese and Indian cosmologies come out most dramatically if we look at their concepts of space and time. The Chinese unit of time is human and social: the life-span of a human being or a dynasty. And the Chinese regard both space and time as workable modes of reality – they are natural and to be used wisely.

By contrast, the Indian mind tends to see both these modes as vast and overpowering. The Buddhists were perhaps the first to present a cosmology in terms of huge size and almost limitless aeons, and the Mahayana delights in algebraic analogies that serve to bring home the vastness of the universe. There are even Sanskrit words for every power of ten from 100 (10^2) to 100,000,000,000,000,000,000,000,000,000,000,000,000,000,000,000,000 (10^{50}).

The Indians, therefore, were quite at home with abstract numbers, whereas the Chinese were not. Hence the Indians (and in particular the Mahayanists) had no difficulty with the idea of infinity nor with that of a series of universes (and were quite happy to combine the two to form the notion of an infinite series of universes or even an infinite series of infinite universes).

The Chinese found such notions difficult, or even downright ridiculous. On the other hand, the Chinese, who believed in taking time seriously, meticulously dated their manuscripts, sometimes to within an accuracy of a few hours. Indians, by contrast, rarely bothered to date their manuscripts at all.

As for social relations, the Chinese ideal was this-worldly: man should live in harmony with heaven and earth. The family was sacrosanct; the imperial law, regarded as an edict from heaven, was applicable to everyone; and there was little analysis of the individual, because the individual derives his reality from the larger social dimension of which he is part. The Indian model was almost the exact opposite of this. The world was treated with suspicion – to be escaped or transformed. Buddhism was centred round the *sangha*, a collection of men and women who had renounced family ties and had their own monastic rules and laws. There was a highly developed psychology which served to remove the individual from dependence on any structure, social or cosmic. The Chinese found such a conception almost incomprehensible.

Finally, the Chinese and Indian languages are completely different. Chinese is written in ideograms, all of which are monosyllables or diphthongs. It is uninflected (that is, it does not modify the form of words to change the meaning – for example 'going' is an inflected form of 'go' – but adds extra words instead – for example 'will go') and extremely unpredictable phonetically. What this means is that if you can pronounce a Chinese word, you may not know the ideogram which represents it, and if you see an ideogram, you may not know how to pronounce it.

By contrast, Sanscrit is alphabetical and polysyllabic. It is highly inflected and new words and compounds can be created with ease – some Mahayana *sutras* contain words that are long enough to extend over two lines. Moreover, it is phonetically perfect. If you know a word, you can always write it down, and if you see one, you always know how to pronounce it.

Chinese, therefore, is tight and controlled, whilst Sanskrit is much freer. These characteristics are reflected in the literature of the two languages. Chinese favours the terse, using metaphors from familiar objects and concrete images; Sanskrit is discursive, hyperbolic and abstract.

Given these striking differences it is astounding that Buddhism made any inroads into China at all, let alone that it completely dominated it for centuries. The simple explanation for its success is that the Mahayana, being built on a paradoxical union of opposites, was so remarkably flexible that it could adapt to the extremely heavy and extended demands that the Chinese made of it. The story of the Mahayana in China is essentially that of Chinese ideals being expressed in Buddhist terms.

These ideals are twofold and are themselves somewhat in conflict with one another. They are harmony and integration on the one hand, and simplicity and directness on the other. It is no accident that such conflicting values should both find expression within the Mahayana, the epitome of the reconciliation of opposites. We shall investigate Chinese Mahayana by looking at its development in the three main historical periods that followed that first mention of Buddhism in 64 CE: the earliest centuries up until the end of the period of disunity, the T'ang dynasty and Sung dynasty.

THE EARLY CENTURIES (64–581): A FRAGMENTED BUDDHISM

The first 500 years of Buddhism in China are extremely complex. There are three reasons for this. First, China went through a period of social upheaval. The Han dynasty which had ruled a united country from 206 BCE finally collapsed in 220 CE but it had been fading for a century or so before that time. Thereafter, during what is called the period of disunity – which only ended in 581 with the Sui (pronounced 'Sway') dynasty that once more ruled a united China – there were various forces at work in a divided China. Of these, the most intrusive was the Hun invasion of North China in 316, and the most familiar was the aristocratic literati who fled south to avoid that invasion. This division of the country, however, meant that no indigenous Chinese patterns of thought or social organization were to be found everywhere. What was found everywhere was Buddhism.

Yet though Buddhism was ubiquitous, it was not homogeneous. And this is the second reason for the complexity of the early centuries – different forms of Buddhism were being digested in different ways and at various speeds by separate groups of Chinese. It never occurred to the Chinese that the assorted teachings they encountered were not all equally the teachings of the Buddha. And, of course, the *sutras* and *shastras* did not arrive in chronological order but completely out of sequence. Given that the Chinese assumed that this great inchoate mass of literature must somehow be consistent, while it still continued to grow and change as it spread from India to China, it is only natural that it took the Chinese a very long time to make full sense of it. And this whole process, of course, was made more difficult by the great difference between the Indian and Chinese minds that we have already discussed. (This is the third factor in the early complexity.)

Throughout the period of disunity, therefore, Buddhism developed very unevenly. Sometimes it was favoured by the ruling power of the time and prospered; sometimes it was persecuted and faltered. In certain parts of the country there would be one kind of Buddhism, but elsewhere there would be another kind. In fact, it was the very profusion and diversity of Buddhism that enabled it to survive such a changeable environment. In contrast, the exactitude of Confucianism and the unworldliness of Taosim were not well suited to the circumstances. Yet even though the development of Buddhism was uneven, it was undeniable – so much so that what began as a decidedly foreign religion in 64 CE had become a pan-Chinese phenomenon by about 450.

Amidst all this complexity, we can isolate four main trends which were the most influential teachings that Buddhism introduced to China during this long period.

1   The notions of wisdom (*prajna*) and emptiness (*shunyata*). These had certain similarities with some Taoist ideas and appealed to the Chinese love of simplicity.
2   The worship of the Buddha Amitabha (and to a lesser extent, the next Buddha, Maitreya). This is a purely Indian import since China really had nothing similar of its own to act as a foundation. The success of this form of Buddhism is probably best explained by the Chinese love of directness (if you appeal to Amitabha, he will help you), augmented by the political and social uncertainty of the time.
3   The practice of meditation. Again this is an Indian import. Although it is true that there were contemplative Taoist practices, the influence of Buddhist methods far outstripped those of Taoism.
4   The idea (found in the *Lotus Sutra*, the *Mahaparinirvana Sutra* and the *Avatamsaka Sutra*) that there is room for everything and that all conflict is illusory. This naturally appealed to the Chinese love of harmony and integration, both intellectual and social.

These four aspects of Buddhism are very varied. As we have said, this very variety explains the endurance and eventual success of Buddhism. But there was another dimension yet to come: the realization by the Chinese that Mahayana actually *allowed* this variety as part of its central teaching. That is, the diversity of Buddhism, which was originally a result of fragmentation of Chinese society throughout the early centuries, was subsequently seen as an expression of its essential unity. What was required for the Chinese to see this was the one factor that had been lacking for 500 years: a unified country. This was provided in 581 by the Sui dynasty and immediately afterwards by the T'ang dynasty.

THE T'ANG DYNASTY (618–907): THE DEVELOPMENT OF THE CLASSIC SCHOOLS

The T'ang period is the flowering of Chinese Buddhism. The country was united, peaceful and prosperous; Buddhism was firmly established but still somewhat fragmented; the Chinese could now digest it completely. They certainly did so, and infused it with their own genius in the process. The best examples of this are the four most influential schools of Chinese Buddhism: T'ien T'ai, Hua Yen, Ching T'u and Ch'an. We should also mention that there were Chinese versions of the Madhyamaka and Yogacharin schools (called San Lun or Three Treatises, and Fa Hsiang or Characteristics of *Dharmas*, respectively). It would be wrong to say that they were unimportant but the fact remains that neither was entirely suited to the Chinese temperament. The four schools that were had no counterpart in India. They are genuinely Chinese and they reflect the two ideals that are mentioned at the beginning of this section. T'ien and T'ai and Hua Yen represent the Chinese love of harmony and integration; and Chin T'u and Ch'an represent their love of simplicity and directness.

Before going on to discuss them, two points are worth noting. The first is that all of them (and the San Lun and Fa Hsiang) are Mahayana schools. There were pre-Mahayana schools also, but they were far less influential. The reason for this is that the Mahayana was far more flexible than the Buddhism that had preceded it in India. The second point is that the Chinese were far more dependent on schools than Mahayanists in India. This is probably because the Chinese had struggled for centuries to make sense of the profusion of *sutra* material, whereas in India it had evolved gradually and naturally, so schools were not necessary to understand it. In China they were.

The T'ien T'ai and Hua Yen schools
Although these schools were quite distinct, both historically and in their organization, they do share some common features. Both of them have as their central doctrine the idea that reality is a harmonic *structure*. But whereas T'ien T'ai says that everything has its place, Hua Yen goes a little further and says that everything is reflected in everything else. In addition, both schools have a scheme for classifying the teachings of the various *sutras* (both Mahayana and pre-Mahayana) so that the Buddha's words can be presented as an integrated whole. The T'ien T'ai has five periods of the *Dharma*:

1   The first 3 weeks: ecstatic inspiration (which no one understood)
2   The next 12 years: elementary teachings – pre-Mahayana
3   The next 8 years: preliminary Mahayana
4   The next 22 years: advanced Mahayana (the emptiness doctrine – no distinctions exist)
5   The final 8 years: the perfect teaching (all distinctions exist but do not exclude each other)

This list is a good instance of the fusion between Mahayana and Chinese thought. On the one hand, this is clearly a version of the skill-in-means doctrine, and an ingenious one at that. On the other, the doctrine of emptiness is relegated to fourth position and is superseded by the Chinese ideal of natural, harmonious existence – yet this idea is far subtler and richer than any form of it that preceded the Mahayana in China.

The T'ien T'ai school (which means 'Heavenly Terrace' and takes its name from a mountain near its place of origin) is based on the *Lotus Sutra*, though in fact it goes considerably beyond that text. It teaches that there is one absolute reality called *ju-lai tsang* or 'Buddha womb' (the Sanskrit equivalent is *tathagata-garbha* – see p.000). This reality is a perfectly harmonious, undivided whole and contains all possible states of existence or *dharmas*, which exist side by side at all times without any interference or disharmony. Not only that, but this totality of *dharmas* is immanent in a single instant of thought. Thus whatever one is aware of, however seemingly insignificant, *is* the one reality. This is because what the T'ien T'ai calls essence (*t'i*) or true nature (*hsing*) necessarily coexists with function (*yung*) or concrete particularity (*shih*). The former needs the latter to express itself, and the latter needs the former in order to be comprehensible.

This is a very Chinese way of putting things, but we can see how it reflects Mahayana ideas – for example, the formless *dharma*-body of the Buddha never exists without his form body (the *Nirmana-kaya* or *Sambhoga-kaya*). And T'ien T'ai parallels this metaphysical distinction (which is really no-distinction) with two equivalent aspects of mind. On the one hand, *chih* (cessation) is aware of the pure undivided mind or essence (*t'i*); on the other, *kuan* (insight) is aware of the manifestations of mind or particulars (*shih*).

T'ien T'ai is exceedingly subtle – yet its neatly interwoven teachings can be summed up in two very simple doctrines, both of which follow from the idea that the absolute reality is never separate from any state of existence. The first is that even inanimate objects, indeed every particle of dust, contain the Buddha-nature. The second is summed up in the beautiful sentence 'Every colour or fragrance is none other than the middle path'.

The Hua Yen school (pronounced 'Hwa Yen' and meaning 'Flower Garland', a literal translation of the Indian *sutra* from which it takes its name, the *Avatamsaka-sutra*) also stresses the harmonious coexistance of all *dharmas*, but in the sense that all *dharmas* interpenetrate each other. That is, every *dharma* contains every other *dharma* and is itself contained in every other *dharma*. Or as Hua Yen itself put it: every *dharma* is simultaneously a mirror and a reflection.

Both T'ien Tai and Hua Yen call their teaching the round or perfect doctrine (the same Chinese character has both meanings). Although neither contains anything which Indian Mahayana would find difficulty with, they are presented with a de-

licacy and precision which is delightfully Chinese yet lacks the exuberance and outright wildness of the Indian original. In short, they are truly Chinese Mahayana.

The Ching T'u or Pure Land school

Whereas T'ien T'ai and Hua Yen solved the problem of the profusion of Buddhist teachings by harmonizing them all, the Ching T'u and Ch'an schools took the opposite tack: they concentrated on one source and ignored all the others. 'Ching T'u' means 'pure land' and refers to Sukhavati, the world created by the Buddha Amitabha as part of his Bodhisattva vow (see p. 237). But athough the *Sukhavati-vyuha-sutra* was well known in Indian, we have no evidence that worship of Amitabha ever reached the proportions that it did in China. The reason for this may be that the Chinese skilfully combined the many-sidedness of worship (which includes art, sculpture, shrines – often on an exceedingly elaborate scale) with its essential simplicity.

Unlike T'ien T'ai and Hua Yen, the Pure Land school is not concerned with balance and totality. Instead, it wishes to focus on the object of worship – Amitabha (known as Amida in China). In effect, then, Pure Land is a school of practice. There were two sub-schools within the sect. One taught two levels of practice: auxiliary and primary. The auxiliary practices consisted of chanting the *sutras*, meditating on the Buddha or bringing him to mind (*buddhanusmriti*), worshipping images of the Buddha, and singing his praises. But the primary practice is uttering the name of Amida – for in the name resides the essence of Amida himself and it descends, like grace, on anyone who has a fervent wish for it. In essence, therefore, this form of Pure Land is a teaching of faith. But it stresses that faith is not easy – hence constant practice is required to inculcate it.

The other form of Pure Land is much more radical. It teaches that the power of salvation does not reside in faith but in the name of Amida itself. In other words, just to utter the name is enough. This is strikingly brought out in a story about Shao-k'ang, a wealthy man who held this view. He would give a penny to anyone who would call out the name of Amida; and, as a consequence, the moment he appeared in a thoroughfare of the city the whole street would ring as everyone earned their penny. The motive, of course, is irrelevant; it is only the act that counts.

Eventually this doctrine became yet more refined. Even if one thinks of Amida for a single instant of thought, that is sufficient to gain his blessing. We see here both a similarity and a difference with the T'ien T'ai and Hua Yen schools. They also taught that everything is available in a single instant of thought. But the difference is that for those schools 'everything' means a complete

Raking the sand of a dry landscape garden. These meditational gardens play an important part in the Zen Buddhist tradition; their emptiness serves to affirm the nature of Being itself. In Zen Buddhism there are three features of truth: it is direct, instant and ordinary. These gardens, now a part of Japanese culture, exemplify these features. In their simplicity they are ordinary, yet their composition in black and white makes an impact that is both instant and direct.

totality, whereas for Ching T'u, 'everything' means Amida, pure and simple. There is no need for anything else, whereas for the two 'totality' schools, one cannot actually have one thing *without* everything else.

The Ch'an or Zen School

The Ch'an school manages to combine both these positions. It is a quintessential form of Chinese Buddhism and is worth considering in some detail. The word *Ch'an* has no meaning; it is a contraction of *ch'an-na*, which was the nearest the Chinese could get to the Sanskrit word *dhyana* which means 'meditation'. But in fact Ch'an is only a meditation school in the most idiosyncratic sense. (It is better known as *Zen*, the Japanese form; *zen* is the Japanese pronunciation of the Chinese character *Ch'an*.)

The first important figure in Ch'an Buddhism is Bodhidharma, an Indian who, according to tradition, brought Ch'an to China (in 520) and became the first Chinese patriarch. He is regarded as in direct line with the very first Ch'an master of all, a disciple of the Buddha called Mahakashyapa. One day, the Buddha was asked to teach the Dharma. Buddha simply picked up a flower and held it up, smiling. In the whole audience only Mahakashyapa understood and was immediately enlightened. This famous story contains three features of Ch'an (as we find it in China – there is no record of an Indian school): truth is direct, instant and ordinary.

Bodhidharma himself exemplifies these qualities. He is depicted in Ch'an paintings as fierce and uncompromising. He is said to have meditated for nine years facing a wall, a demonstration of the fact that everything is within us so that we need never go into the world to find satisfaction. Bodhidharma did not seek disciples but one did come to him. He had to wait a long time before Bodhidharma would take any notice of him. Then he said: 'My mind is not at peace; how may it be pacified?' Bodhidharma replied: 'Bring it to me and I will pacify it.' The disciple said: 'Because it is not at peace, I cannot bring it to you.' 'There,' replied Bodhidharma, 'I have pacified it!'

This story is typical of Ch'an in two ways. First, it is a teaching, but not one that is formally laid out. The truth is seen as existing in everyday situations and is brought out by the Ch'an teacher as part of life. Secondly, the teaching itself is simple yet radical. A restless mind obscures truth only so long as you let it. It can never be pinned down and made to stop. But there is no need to do so, because ordinary mind is Buddha mind. Truth is nothing special; it is eating when you are hungry and sleeping when you are tired.

Bodhidharma died in about 530. He was succeeded by a line of patriarchs of whom the most important was the sixth, Hui-neng (pronounced Hway-nung), who lived from 637–715. Ch'an at this time had become rather quietistic, and Ch'an

247

KOANS

IF I HAVE NOTHING, WHAT SHOULD I DO?
ANSWER: THROW IT AWAY!

YOU ARE NOT ALLOWED TO TRAVEL AT NIGHT, BUT YOU MUST ARRIVE BEFORE DAY-BREAK

THE BRIDGE FLOWS, THE WATER DOES NOT

WHAT IS THE SOUND OF ONE HAND CLAPPING?

IF YOU RUN AWAY FROM THE VOID, YOU CAN NEVER BE FREE OF IT
IF YOU SEARCH FOR THE VOID, YOU CAN NEVER REACH IT

WHAT IS THE PURE DHARMAKAYA?
THE BLOSSOMING HEDGE AROUND THE PRIVY

WHAT IS THE MEANING OF BODHIDHARMA'S COMING FROM THE WEST?
THE CYPRESS TREE IN THE GARDEN

monks spent long hours in silent meditation. Hui-neng taught that this was unnecessary.

Enlightenment is your own nature;
Originally it was entirely pure.
Only avail yourselves of this mind
And you will immediately become a Buddha.

We see here a perfect fusion of Indian Mahayana and Chinese simplicity. The terminology is entirely Buddhist but the conclusion that Ch'an draws is entirely Chinese. It is not just that our original nature or mind is the Buddha-nature (or Buddha mind); this original nature is our *ordinary* nature. It is not amazing or unexpected; it is here and now; immediately within reach.

It is the supreme paradox, perhaps, that the very simplicity of this teaching makes it difficult to understand. Ch'an teachers were well aware of this and one of its sub-schools, the Lin-chi (named after its founder who died in 867), developed a technique to prevent complacency and simultaneously release the ordinary mind that is enlightenment. This technique is called *kung-an* (better known in its Japanese form *ko'an*; literally, it means a 'magistrate's table', a place where cases are argued in court – in other words, a test of what is true). A *kung-an* was a question or problem that could not be solved by rational means; that is, a structure was presented to the mind, but the 'solution' had to go beyond structure. In short, it had to be direct, immediate and ordinary.

Naturally, there could be no definite, fixed answer to a *kung-an*. One of the most famous is: 'What is the sound of one hand clapping?' A lot of

ideas can be generated by this question: that the sound is silence; that silence is not a sound in itself, yet there can be no sound that is not surrounded by silence; hence to hear a sound one must also be aware of silence; that silence has no beginning or end. And so on and so on. But, of course, the *kung-an* is designed to stop ideas and release Buddha mind. So the answer might be: 'With no bird singing, the mountain is yet more still'; or: 'Rice in the bowl, water in the bucket'; or, instead of a verbal answer one might silently cup one's hands, or just laugh. The Lin-chi version of Ch'an (the most influential throughout the T'ang dynasty) also made use of shouts and blows. Again we find the essential Ch'an features: directness, instantaneousness, ordinariness.

There is a well-known Ch'an saying, 'Before Ch'an, mountains are mountains and rivers are rivers; during Ch'an, mountains are no longer mountains and rivers are no longer rivers; after Ch'an, mountains are mountains and rivers are rivers.' Or, as one teacher put it, 'There's nothing much to this Buddhism.' And another said: 'Now than I am enlightened, I'm just as miserable as I was before.'

There is something shocking about this to the Indian Mahayana mind. Ch'an has no regard for the elaborate and subtly abstruse. Ch'an masters tore up the *sutras* or used a blank scroll instead. They referred to the Buddha as an old reprobate. And since Ch'an cut itself off from its roots by its denial of tradition, it is arguable whether it is a form of Buddhism at all. Yet at the same time, we can see that it is entirely true to the spirit of Mahayana. If the Buddha (or Buddha-nature) really is inseparable from everything, then it can never tie itself down to a religious tradition – it must grow as the grass grows.

THE SUNG DYNASTY (960 ONWARDS): THE COLLAPSE OF CLASSICAL BUDDHISM

In 845, during the T'ang dynasty, the emperor approved measures against the Buddhist *sangha* which virtually destroyed it as an inflential force in the land. Some of these measures were justified. Buddhist monasteries had grown very wealthy and owned huge tracts of land which were exempt from imperial taxes. Many monks and nuns were extremely lax in their behaviour and were openly living a pampered existence without fulfilling any obligations to the community at large. But the persecution was extreme. Practically every Buddhist building was destroyed; nearly all Buddhist land was confiscated; the golden statues and iron bells were melted down for coinage; and the monks and nuns were forced to return to lay life. In all, over 250,000 members of the *sangha* were once again placed under imperial law (and therefore imperial taxation) and over 40,000 temples and shrines destroyed.

Although the persecution was short-lived it was effective, and Buddhism never completely recovered. The T'ang dynasty itself became weak and collapsed in 907, followed by fifty years of civil war. And though the Sung dynasty reunited the country in 960 and was favourably disposed towards Buddhism, the latter was already a spent force. T'ien T'ai and Hua Yen were particularly hard hit. Both of them relied heavily on their *sutras* and the long and difficult training that was required to master their intricate and subtle doctrines. The persecution of 845 removed their support in terms of money, seclusion and training and they could not survive without it.

The only two schools that did survive with any vigour were the Pure Land and Ch'an, both of which emphasized simplicity over subtlety, and neither of which needed an elaborate back-up system in order to function. Yet both suffered from over-reliance on themselves; they lost much of their freshness and vitality which, during the classic T'ang centuries, had been stimulated by the sheer variety of the different Buddhist schools. In the Sung dynasty, this stimulation was lost and the Pure Land and Ch'an schools became isolated and somewhat dull, both living off former glories.

What we find, then, is that a thousand years after entering China, Buddhism is represented by two distinct groups – one chanting the name of Amida and the other with little regard for traditional Buddhism in any form. In effect, this is the triumph of the Chinese need for simplicity over the Mahayana ideal of unlimited profusion.

The Vajrayana

ORIGINS

Indian Buddhism did not finish with the Mahayana. Around 600 CE another form of Buddhism began to make its presence felt. It was regarded by its practitioners as a new *yana* (way or vehicle), as different from the Mahayana as the Mahayana had been from the Buddhism that preceded it. This new form of Buddhism is called the Vajrayana (Diamond Vehicle). It is also known as Tantra because its teachings are found in texts called *tantras* The word *tantra* is derived from another that means 'to spin, weave', and it never lost this connotation of interwovenness. Its essential meaning is 'an interconnected system/doctrine/teaching'.

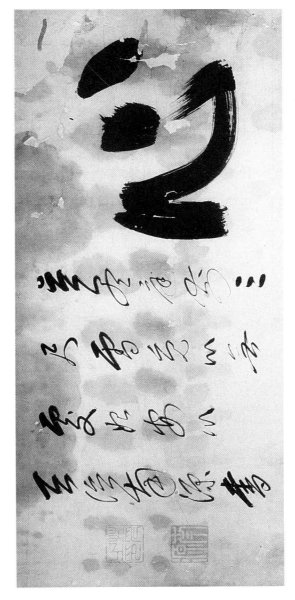

Zen priest calligraphy is regarded as highly as painting. An art in itself, Zen calligraphy depends on the free and assured movement of arm and hand.

Very little is known about the origins of the Vajrayana or the dates of the earliest *tantras*. This is simply because tantric practitioners regarded their teachings as secret – in two related senses. First the subject matter of the *tantras* is a level of experience that is beyond the ordinary and they are written in an esoteric language; and secondly, one can only reach this supermundane level if one is initiated by a teacher who has already attained it. It is therefore quite senseless for tantric teachings to be made public because an uninitiated person cannot make use of them. Even if he can interpret the esoteric language (and that would be very difficult if he has no experience to guide him), without a teacher he has no means of access to the level of reality with which Vajrayana is concerned.

It may well be, therefore, that Tantra was transmitted from teacher to teacher, in small groups, centuries before there is any reference to it that can be dated. The earliest Buddhist *tantras* may have been composed as early as 350 CE The influential teacher Saraha has been dated by some scholars in the early seventh century and Vajrayana as a movement was certainly well known by about 780 when Padmasambhava was invited to Tibet. The date of Naropa, to whom the famous six *yogas* are attributed, is approximately 1000 CE. All these individuals are included among the 84 Siddhas (meaning 'accomplished ones') who span the period from the seventh to the eleventh centuries.

TEACHING AND PRACTICE

The underlying principles of Vajrayana are familiar from the Mahayana that preceded it. Reality is empty (*shunya*) – that is, it is open and unrestricted (see p.235–236). And the mind (*chitta*) is pure or brightly shining (see p.237), and is capable of unlimited transformation (see p.242). From this dual premiss, Vajrayana draws a simple but radical conclusion: the mind can transform *anything* into Buddhahood.

The Tantric texts teach that emptiness is indivisible and impenetrable; it is therefore referred to as *vajra*, 'diamond'. Because it can contain no distinctions, there cannot be any real difference between *samsara* and *nirvana*. Apart from the novel use of the word *vajra* this is mainstream Mahayana. But the Vajrayana wants to push this truth as far as it will go. The defiled states of *chitta* such as lust, anger, hatred, etc. must also be nondistinct from its pure state which is Buddhahood. Therefore, passions do not have to be set aside in order to attain enlightenment; they must be transformed *into* enlightenment. The Vajrayana uses the very apt analogy of homoeopathic medicine. To give just one example: a fever that resembles arsenic poisoning is cured by taking a minute quantity of arsenic. In other words, poison is cured by the same poison. Similarly, passion is cured by passion. Or, to put it another way, the very things that bind us to *samsara* can be used to free us from *samsara*.

The direct and indirect paths

This is the central Vajrayana insight – and it has two applications. The first is the direct or instantaneous path (if 'path' is the correct word to use), often called the teaching of the innate (*sahaja*) or Mahamudra. 'Mahamudra' is often translated 'Great Seal/Symbol', but as with most tantric terms, a literal translation tells us practically nothing. *Mudra* can also mean 'passport' and hence the meaning could be: the great passport (to enlightenment). And since *mudra* comes from a

word meaning 'to delight', and Vajrayana sees enlightenment as bliss, the full esoteric meaning might be: the great passport (to the bliss of enlightenment). This teaching simply states that every form of experience, if it is not clung to but is left free, will naturally lead one to its source – which is the blissful, radiant reality of Buddhahood. There is no particular form (*rupa*) that need be given up, and nothing that need be striven for. Mahamudra is therefore strikingly similar to Ch'an (see p. 247).

The second application is the indirect path – the progressive transformation of *chitta* (using all the forms of *samsara*), culminating in Buddhahood. At least 90 per cent of all *tantras* are concerned with it, and there are huge numbers of them containing a staggering variety of complex and esoteric details. These *tantras* also contain those instructions for spiritual practice that have made the Vajrayana notorious – specifically, practices that are regarded as repugnant or morally reprehensible, on the one hand; and as strange or downright incomprehensible, on the other.

Some *tantras* (and they seem to be the earliest ones) make explicit reference to bodily impurities (urine, faeces) and to sexual intercourse. Although authorities such as Tucci and Govinda (see bibliography) claim that these references are only symbolic, it is difficult to read, say, the *Chandamaharoshana Tantra* without taking them literally. There are two possible explanations of why such practices were enjoined. It may be that they represent the two extremes of disgust (urine, faeces) and pleasure (sex), and that only a mind that can remain steady in the face of both is capable of going beyond both to enlightenment. In reality, bodily impurities are not disgusting and sexual intercourse is not pleasurable, such ascriptions are the labels of ignorance. But when a disciple realizes this *by practice*, then there arises *within the body* the bliss of enlightenment. And this bliss, of course, is identical with emptiness and therefore cannot be clung to.

Subtle levels of reality and visualization

But this cannot be the whole story because it omits the central practice of the indirect path: visualization. What is involved here is a particular application of a basic Buddhist tenet – that the mind gives rise to forms (*rupa*). And as was pointed out earlier this is the principle of magic. But *conscious* creation of forms by the mind is a means of liberation. The Vajrayana has its own version of what this means.

Visualization is based on three principles. The first is that reality consists of a series of levels, with the higher levels existing *within* the lower ones. By 'higher level' is meant three things: that the forms at this level are more concentrated; that they are more powerful; and that they are conscious. In other words, they are manifestations of a purer level of mind (*chitta*). All levels of reality are the creation of *chitta* and hence the forms that are encountered at higher, subtler levels are not *mere* forms – they are also beings. And because they *are* higher, Vajrayana calls them gods (*deva* or *devata*). In short, there exist beings or gods that have a natural 'place' at the subtle levels of *chitta* – and they are powerful. And since the gradual purification of mundane *chitta* requires the practitioner to go through these subtle levels (in order to arrive at the 'original point' of radiant, empty *chitta* which is Buddhahood), Vajrayana teaches that the gods should be made use of.

The second principle is that of homology – namely, that whatever exists in the world (*loka* or *samsara*) also exists within each human being. In other words, all the levels of reality – and therefore all the gods – exist within the body. The nature of *chitta* is enlightenment. The practitioner has to purify his *chitta* or consciousness in order to become a Buddha. Hence he will find within himself all the manifestations of *chitta*. To put it in Vajrayana terms: the precious jewel of Buddhahood resides within us all, but it is guarded by the gods.

The third element in the practice of visualization is the teacher or *guru* (sometimes called *siddha* in the Vajrayana). He has already made the journey and knows the path through the subtle levels of *chitta*. He also knows what forms or shapes the mind of the practitioner must adopt if it is to be able to engage with the powerful forces that already exist, in a dormant state, within. Hence the teacher gives instructions that allow the practitioner to create a certain shape in his mind into which can enter, as it were, the beings or gods that 'live' at these subtle levels. (Such instructions are not merely a transmission of information about techniques, however; a transmission of power is also given.)

These three elements combine to make sense of the practice of visualization. The practitioner is in the hands of the teacher (in much the same way as someone who is lost in a forest is in the hands of one who knows the hidden pathways and dangers). The teacher prepares the disciple for the journey through the subtle levels by giving him instructions in visualization. There are four stages in this journey. To begin with, at the level of gross mind, the disciple knows that he is projecting a form from his own *chitta*. Then, at the subtle level, there are two developments. First, when the form begins to live (for it does have its own place in the scheme of things, just as the practitioner himself does), the disciple cannot but believe that this 'being' is separate from himself – it is, after all, extremely 'real' and powerful. Secondly, the practitioner, by more intense visualization, merges into this separate, living being and be-

comes identical with him. That is, the disciple becomes a god. Finally, at the ultimate level (which is the level where *chitta* is realized to be empty), the being that has been visualized dissolves into emptiness – which means, of course, that the disciple himself dissolves into emptiness. For in truth *all* forms created by *chitta* only arise and fall in emptiness.

The sequence, then, is: conscious visualization; encounter with a higher, subtler being; the taking on of a divine form: and realization of emptiness. Or to put it another way: The forms/beings that are visualized are the practitioner's own 'divine' forms, but ultimately they are unreal (as all forms are). The Vajrayana teaching is that, unless one by-passes the subtle level of reality altogether by practising the direct path, then one must encounter these beings or gods. Hence the need for a teacher and the instructions he gives.

An image of Padmasambhava, the supposed founder of Vajrayana Buddhism. The image is to be seen in the Bodnath Temple, Kathmandu where this same form of Tantric Buddhism is dominant. It was a late Indian form of Buddhism which reached Nepal in the 8th century CE.

A pilgrim turns a row of prayer wheels while walking round the great stupa at Suayambhunath, Nepal. The cylinders are inscribed with mantras and contain prayers written on scrolls whose rotation brings merit to those who perform the action.

Visualization in the *Hevajra Tantra*

It cannot be denied that most of these instructions are bizarre and flagrantly flout common sense (and only those who have begun to doubt the wisdom of common sense will find the Vajrayana even remotely plausible). They are also extremely varied but they can be divided into three traditional categories: the subtle body, *mantras* and *mandalas*. All of these are regarded as related types of visualization by the Vajrayana – and they can all be combined, too.

For example, in the *Hevajra Tantra* (which can be dated in the eighth century), we find the following sequence. The subtle body of the practiioner is visualized as a luminous form which is higher than, and therefore contains more power than, the physical body. Within it is conjured up (that is, visualized) the *mantra* RAM (pronounced 'rung'). This sound is regarded as the essential seed (*bija*) from which develops or emerges an inner light that the text likens to the circle (*mandala*) of the sun; and out of that emerges another seed *mantra*, HUM (pronounced 'hoong').

This *mantra*, because it exists at the subtle level, has its own life and power. The text says that it is fearful and that it should be transformed by the disciple into the form of that inner being or god who is the focus of the practice: Hevajra, 'whose nature is wrath'. Hevajra should be wor-

shipped (*pujayet*) in the company of eight goddesses (*devi*), one of whom is seen as engaged in sexual intercourse with him. (The text actually says that she is 'clinging to his neck and impassioned by great passion'.) The whole group of nine has emerged from the circle (*mandala*) of the 'sun', and is itself regarded as a *mandala* or great power. And because it is found within the body, the body is viewed as a *mandala* (or centre) which contains all things.

'All things' here in fact means three types of reality: the so-called bodily impurities or defilements (including sexual desire); the *mandala* of gods and goddesses, with all their attributes (including the *mantras* that 'contain' them, because *mantras* are the seeds of the divine forms); and the pure, brightly shining mind which is formless and identical to enlightenment/emptiness/Buddhahood.

'Enlightenment is within the body'

It should now be possible to see how the references to bodily impurities and sexual intercourse that were mentioned earlier in the *Chandamaharoshana Tantra* can be understood. The physical body is not a distinct, self-sufficient entity. It has the form and the functions that it has because it is derived from the subtle body (which is its seed). But the subtle body contains divine power. Hence *all* aspects of the physical body must participate in that divine reality. So the impurities are not 'really' impure, and sexual intercourse is not merely a physical act. They are reflections of, or precipitations of, a higher, subtler, more powerful level of reality.

For the Vajrayana, therefore, it is perfectly natural that they should be used as a way of opening out the awareness to the source (or seed) from which they come. The same goes for emotions such as wrath. These are defilements in the gross state, but they have their subtle or divine origin. Hence Hevajra is encountered as a wrathful god. This does not mean, however, that he is to be feared. On the contrary, he is to be worshipped, for what binds at the gross level is a means of liberation at the subtle level. The reason for this is that, while at the gross level there is attachment (which is the consequence of unconscious visualization), at the subtle level there is realization (as a result of conscious visualization).

Ultimately, of course, enlightenment is beyond all opposites: impure and pure, passion and even-mindedness, wrath and peace, male and female. And that, too, is within the body. But the indirect path of Vajrayana – the path of transformation – is inclusive not exclusive. Everything is made use of; for nothing is separate from the Buddha. As we said earlier, this is a central Mahayana teaching – but the Vajrayana application of it is so radical that it completely transforms Buddhism.

The Vajrayana in Tibet

The first reference to Buddhism in Tibet is about 625 CE when the Chinese wife of a Tibetan ruler founded a monastery. It is extremely unlikely, however, that this had anything to do with Vajrayana, which did not arrive from India until the eighth century, when the famous teacher Padmasambhava was invited to Tibet by King Trisong Detsen. In 779 the first ordinations were carried out and Buddhism became the state religion. Monasteries were established by royal decree, supported by the wealthy aristocracy. Buddhist texts were meticulously translated into Tibetan. However, the new religion only flourished for two generations, for in 842 an extremely rigorous persecution was carried out by King Langdarma which took back all monastic property and virtually eliminated Buddhism from central Tibet. But it appears to have clung on in the outlying provinces throughout the next 150 years, during which Tibet was a divided country, with different families ruling different areas.

Then, around 950 CE, the rulers of western Tibet began to become more powerful, and simultaneously grew more interested in Buddhism. The links with India were renewed and in 1042 Atisha, one of the most prestigious figures in Indian Buddhism, was invited to Tibet. From this point on, Buddhism was the dominant force in Tibetan history, notwithstanding frequent interference from China and Mongolia. Nor was this foreign influence purely one-sided. The Mongols were converted to Buddhism by the Tibetans during the thirteenth century. Then, when the Mongols invaded China and established the Yuan dynasty in 1260, they took Vajrayana with them. And even though seminal *tantras* had been known in China since the early eighth century, it had little impact there until it received the patronage of the ruling Mongols.

The distinctiveness of Tibetan Buddhism

For fifty years after Atisha's arrival in 1042, large numbers of monasteries were established in Tibet; and Atisha himself founded the Kadam pa (literally, 'instruction, ordinance') school. The other important schools in Tibet are: Kagyu pa ('the lineage of the [Buddha's] word'), founded by Marpa (died 1098); the Nyingma pa ('ancient, old [-style]'), which is associated with Padmasambhava (see above); the Sakya pa ('grey earth' – referring to the soil around its main monastery, which was established in 1073); and the Geluk pa ('virtuous'), founded by Tsongkhapa (1357–1419), a reorganized form of the Kadam pa (which it eventually supplanted).

The relationship between these schools and the reason that they have the form that they do, cannot be seen without first understanding the special circumstances that led to the establishment of Buddhism in Tibet. There were four factors that combined to give Tibetan Buddhism its distinctiveness. First, Buddhism was a cultural as well as a religious import; its artistic and literary forms were far superior to anything that the Tibetans already had. Even the Tibetan script is modelled on an Indian orginal. In addition, the Tibetan language contained practically no words that could be regarded as the equivalents of the fundamental terms of the Buddhist teaching. So even the basic vocabulary of Buddhism had to be imported.

Secondly, the very structure of the Buddhist way of life – its reliance upon the community of monks and nuns, the abandonment of the householder life and all worldly ties, and the importance of the monastery as the centre of spiritual excellence – was completely new to the Tibetans. It therefore required considerable social reorganization to establish it. This was achieved by royal patronage, in which the aristocratic families were inevitably involved. They gave land on which the monasteries were built and money to support the monks. And as part of their conversion to Buddhism, prominent members of these families also became monks. Naturally, therefore, they had considerable influence in all the activities of the monasteries, especially in the appointment of the abbots.

Musician in the orchestra of a Tibetan temple. Ceremony and ritual play an important part in Tibetan Buddhism since it was of cultural as well as religious import. During China's cultural revolution wholesale attempts were made to destroy Tibetan religion but in recent years Chinese policy has become more moderate and some temples are being rebuilt.

Thirdly, because Vajrayana relies so heavily on the person of the teacher as *guru*, its development in Tibet could not be successful unless a transmission of teaching could be clearly established. And this meant two things. First, that the details of ritual and instruction had to be brought from India and exactly preserved in Tibet. And second, that there had to be a lineage of teachers. This second requirement explains the supreme importance of the figure of the *lama* (literally, 'the higher one') who is the Tibetan equivalent of the Indian Vajrayana *guru* in one (or both) of the senses of that term – as a transmitter of the teaching or as a transmitter of spiritual power. But since the importance of the *lama* as a religious figure was combined in Tibet with the wholesale adoption of new social forms involving prominent political families, it is not difficult to see that he took on functions that were much more extensive even than those of his Indian original, the tantric *guru*.

Lastly, as a matter of historical fact, Buddhism always made ground in Tibet at a time when the country was moving from a condition of political instability or fragmentation to one of greater order and harmony. There were four obvious examples of this: the establishment of Buddhism during the reign of King Trisong Detsen; its re-establishment when the rulers of western Tibet gained control of the whole country in the eleventh century; the predominance of the Sakya pa school during the thirteenth century as a result of its pact with the Mongols; and the creation of the office of Dalai Lama (again as a result of Mongol influence) in the sixteenth century, which gave rise to the theocracy that lasted until the Chinese invasion in 1959. Each of these events marked a greater consolidation of Tibet as a unified country, and, in each case, a profound change in the political order went hand in hand with spread of Buddhism. In short, the development of Tibetan Buddhism over many centuries was simultaneously a cultural, a political and a religious phenomenon.

The contrast with China is instructive. There, too, Buddhism was a foreign import. But China had its own highly developed culture with established standards of literary excellence and philosophical profundity. The Buddhist texts had to compete with the Chinese classics; but at the same time Chinese Buddhists used indigenous terms like *tao* ('way', 'truth', 'reality') and *wu-wei* ('non-action') to translate Indian words such as *dharma* or *nirvana*. Neither of these options was available to the Tibetans. Moreover, it is fair to say that Buddhism would never have been successful in China if the empire had not been divided and social norms in disarray after the fall of the Han dynasty (see p.244). The opposite is true of Tibet: Buddhism needed to align itself with

political expansion and consolidation. Thus some non-Buddhist Chinese always viewed the order of monks and its denial of worldly ties with suspicion, whereas in Tibet, monastic organization was accepted without question as the highest form of social good. Lastly, in China it was the Mahayana with its unlimited profusion and flexibilty that was successful, and it is doubtful if any other form of Buddhism would have been. By contrast, the precise instructions of the Vajrayana, so dependent on personal transmission, were more suited to the special circumstances in which Tibet became Buddhist – namely, the wholesale importation of a complete world view *and* a set of practices to go with it.

THE FUSION OF SPIRITUAL AND TEMPORAL POWER IN TIBET

Brief mention was made above of the four main stages in the consolidation of political power in Tibet and its simultaneous fusion with Buddhism. The last two are worth giving in detail. In 1239, the Mongols attacked Tibet and the Tibetans sent their most able representative to negotiate with them: the head *lama* of the main Sakya monastery. The result of these negotiations was that while the Tibetans accepted the suzerainty of the Mongols, the Mongols in their turn appointed the Sakya *lama* as the *de facto* ruler of Tibet. Since the Sakya pa school allowed their members to marry and have children, the effect of this incident was to create a simultaneously religious and secular dynasty. It lasted for only a century, however, before the Sakya pa domination was usurped by another family. But the seeds of theocracy had been sown.

This brings us to perhaps the most significant event in Tibet's religious history: the founding of the Geluk pa school by Tsongkhapa (1357–1419) and its eventual emergence as the dominant power in the country, via the office of the Dalai Lama. Tsongkhapa was a superb organizer; he transformed the Kadam pa school and gave it new life in the form of the Geluk pa. Many monasteries were established in all parts of Tibet. This social consolidation, however, was combined with a religious innovation – perhaps the only one that Tibet has unequivocally introduced into Buddhism. This is the idea of the *tulku*.

The word can be translated as 'apparent/ illusory/magical/transformation body'. And the idea is linked to one that is found in the Mahayana – namely, that the Buddha can manifest a body through his skill-in-means in order to benefit beings (see p.234). The Tibetans have their own version of this idea, however. An advanced *lama* can if he wishes (or is compelled by his compas-

In this Tibetan wheel of life passion, the cock; hatred, the snake; and stupidity, the pig appear in the centre. There are six spheres of existence and the demon holding the wheel symbolizes death or impermanence. The Buddhism which passed into the mountainous regions of Tibet became mixed with the indigenous religion. This was a form of nature worship accepting hostile and kindly spirits and allowing both human and animal sacrifice. These combined to produce the complex religion of Tibet.

sion to) reincarnate deliberately so that he can continue his spiritual mission. This is not strictly speaking a personal decision, however. Rather each *tulku* is regarded as manifesting a quality or facet of enlightenment. The usual interpretation of *tulkus* as living Buddhas is therefore somewhat misleading. It would be more accurate to say that the lineage of *tulkus* is the constant presence in the world of an aspect of the Buddha.

All the schools make use of the idea and it was known before the advent of the Geluk pa. What made it significant in Tibetan *history*, however, was the combination of a spiritual lineage with political power. The first Geluk pa *tulku* was Gendutrup (1391–1475), a pupil of Tsongkhapa. He was the head of the school (known by the title *Gyelwa Rinpoche* – the final syllable is pronounced 'chay') and has in effect successively reincarnated as the Gyelwa Rinpoche from his death until the present day. That is, every head of the Geluk pa school has been the same 'person'. The importance of this, of course, is that the activity of the *tulku* is tied to an *office. Tulkus* are 'found' at a very early age and trained to take on the office that they had in their previous birth. They do not reincarnate randomly; they are always part of the Buddhist organization.

Then, in the sixteenth century, the third Gyelwa Rinpoche sought help from the Mongols in his political struggles with influential families in Tibet (who had themselves formed an alliance with another of the Tibetan schools). He visited Mongolia in 1578 and Altan Khan conferred on him the title of Dalai Lama (*dalai* is a Mongolian word meaning 'sea'; the implication is that of the depth and vastness of the ocean). This title was applied retrospectively to the two previous incarnations. It is plain that the political and religious strands of Buddhism are now inseparable. The lineage of the Geluk pa school is established as a series of *tulkus*, but their activity is incontrovertibly political. Thus when the 'new' Dalai Lama died in Mongolia in 1588, his incarnation was 'found' to be Altan Khan's grandson. And over the next century, the Mongols actively interfered in Tibetan politics, handing over their conquests to the Geluk pa school. By the mid-1600s the Dalai Lama was the effective ruler of a unified country. Tibet had become a theocracy.

THE NATURE OF THE TIBETAN SCHOOLS

It is necessary to trace the development of Buddhism in Tibet in order to understand the significance of the different schools (see p.253 for the names of the principal ones). They are primarily units of transmission and their doctrinal differences are quite secondary. That is, the schools do not define themselves by the doctrines that they hold but by the lineage of lamas which they recognize. But along with this lineage goes an array of other ingredients in the spiritual life: the texts that are accepted as authoritative; the commentaries that are used to explain the texts; the details of ritual, liturgy and dress; the initiations that can be bestowed.

Each school offers a complete package that allows its adherents to follow the path to enlightenment. What distinguishes them is history, method and the salvific instruments that are used rather than metaphysics. In fact, all the important figures in Tibetan Buddhism (with the possible exception of Milarepa – see below) are individuals who either established a school (like Atisha or Marpa) or significantly reorganized one (like Tsongkhapa) or, like Buton (pronounced 'Bootern') (1290–1364), rearranged the Buddhists' texts into a form which all the other schools, except the Nyingma pa, use (though they may

select different texts within it). In other words, Tibetan Buddhism regards individuals as significant only as part of a school. This is true even of the fourteen Dalai Lamas, none of whom made major contributions to Buddhist thought. But they were never expected to – rather, they guaranteed the transmission of the teaching.

This teaching is, of course, Vajrayana Buddhism, imported wholesale from India. It would be wrong, however, to suggest that the Tibetan contribution was negligible or second-rate. It is worth looking at two examples: the *Tibetan Book of the Dead* and the songs of Milarepa. They represent the indirect and direct paths, respectively (see p. 250).

THE TIBETAN BOOK OF THE DEAD

The *Book of the Dead* is a somewhat free rendering of the Tibetan *bardo thodoll*, meaning 'being set free while hearing in the *bardo*'. *Bardo* is the intermediate state between physical death and reincarnation in another body. And the text has two aims: to explain what happens in this intermediate state; and to give the explanation in such a form that when a person has died, he can profit from hearing the text read while he is still in the vicinity of his dead body. Although the work is often attributed to the Nyingma pa school, in fact all the schools use it, and the various versions are not really very different. It is the Nyingma pa recension that is followed here.

According to the text, there are three stages in the *bardo*. The first occurs immediately at death, when everyone without exception experiences the clear light of the true nature of *chitta*, which is enlightenment. But for most people, who have had no training in visualization, this experience is very short-lived.

It is followed by the second stage of *bardo* which is called 'reality'. It consists of the manifestations of all the forms and beings which exist at the subtle level of existence (according to the fundamental tenets of Vajrayana – see p.250). The dead person now has what the text calls a 'thought body'. For seven days, various Buddhas manifest themselves, emerging out of lights of different colours. If the dead person can merge his mind into any of these forms, he obtains Buddhahood. But if not, then he passes on to the next Buddha. At the end of seven days another cycle of seven begins, in which the Buddhas appear in their wrathful forms (called Heruka, which is identified with Hevajra – see p. 252). The text says that these are only 'the peaceful Buddhas in changed aspect'. It is stressed that they are also manifestations of the clear light, but appear

WORSHIP

The Crystal Cathedral in Los Angeles, California. Many religious buildings present an aura of other-worldliness and provide a sense of continuity with the past. Others, like the Crystal Cathedral, adopt contemporary architectural styles to relate their message to their own age.

Worship is another universal feature of religion, and one which attempts to bring abstruse ideas within the grasp of ordinary people. One intention of worship is to mediate the mysteries of the sacred and the holy through sight and sound. Worship itself is full of apparent paradox, for how else may profound mysteries be contemplated than in ways that seem to the uninitiated to be incongruous? Do Buddhists worship the Buddha, or do they believe him to be simply a great teacher? What part do the saints and the Virgin Mary play in Christian worship? What is a Hindu doing when she or he bows before an image of a god? There are no precise answers to these questions, because the same images (and even words are images) will mean different things to different people. What an act of worship 'means' may be widely different for different participants. There are, of course, different styles of worship. Worship may be congregational or individual. It may require a special building or it may be performed in the open air – but all will be designed to enhance experience and to deepen devotion and commitment.

TOP A worshipper at the Shwe Dagon Pagoda, Rangoon, before a statue of the Buddha. The practice of worshipping before an image, and especially of washing an image, is often thought of as a Hindu practice, yet here a similar action is found in the worship of an ostensibly Theravada country.

ABOVE A wayside shrine at Sakopane, Poland. Wayside shrines, where a traveller can say a prayer or make an offering, asking for protection for a journey or a blessing from a local saint or god, are common in the popular practice of many different religions throughout the world.

LEFT This neighbourhood shrine in the Higashiyama district of Kyoto is composed of primitive Buddhist images, or Sekibutsu. The Buddhas are wrapped to protect them from the cold. The covering sometimes commemorates a dead child, and is thought to protect the child from the cold also.

LEFT An Arab Muslim at the ablution fountain outside the Dome of the Rock, Jerusalem. The Dome commemorates the story of Muhammad's night journey to Jerusalem and his ascent to heaven from the rock, which is also associated with Abraham. Muslims are expected to be in a state of ritual and physical purity before prayer and when visiting a holy place.

RIGHT The gateway, or torii, to the Itsukushima Shrine, Japan. The torii, which is partially submerged by the sea at high tide, is dedicated to Itsukushima-Hima, daughter of Susa-no-wo-no-Mikoto. He is the rain and storm god of Shinto, and has an ambiguous character, both destructive and beneficient. In Shinto mythology he is depicted as a trouble-maker.

LEFT The interior of Santa Sophia, Istanbul. This famous place of worship was built as a Christian church between 532 and 537 CE, and dedicated to the 'Holy Wisdom'. It is regarded as an exceptional example of Byzantine architecture, and is particularly celebrated for the great dome, part of which is seen here and which contains forty windows. In 1453, following a successful invasion of Constantinople, as it then was, by Turkish Muslims, the church was converted into a mosque. Original Christian mosaics were covered up, but are now partly restored, providing a mixture of Christian and Islamic styles of church and mosque design.

RIGHT The exterior of the Shwe Dagon, the Golden Pagoda, at Rangoon, Burma. The building of pagodas has long been regarded as an act of religious merit, and much care and wealth have been lavished upon them. The central stupa, pictured here, is covered entirely with gold leaf. The style is typical of south-east Asian Buddhism, reflecting the mixture of local cultural forms with a wider Buddhist culture. This and other great pagodas are important centres of devotion, attracting worshippers and visitors from considerable distances, and providing images and symbols to encourage meditation on the teaching and lives of the Buddha.

RIGHT *A Hindu woman praying in a temple in the great Hindu city of Varanasi (Benares), India. Temple worship among Hindus is usually a practice of independent devotion, worshippers approaching the shrine or image separately to make offerings and prayers. Congregational worship is less common, although it is found increasingly in forms of Hinduism practised in the West.*

RIGHT *Worshippers in a Jaina temple in Calcutta. Here offerings are being made in celebration of the birth of the twenty-second of the twenty-four Tirthankaras. The Tirthankaras are theoretically regarded as 'great souls' who have attained liberation, but the worship and literature of some Jaina temples suggests a correspondence between them and God in popular practice.*

LEFT *Prayer flags in Sikkim. Prayer flags are one of the expressions of popular devotion found especially in Tibetan Buddhism. Flags, as well as streamers, scrolls and prayer-wheels carry invocations and petitions which are believed to be conveyed to the Buddhas and bodhisattvas who are objects of worship.*

BELOW Muslims at prayer in Jordan. As one of the essential duties of Islam, the times of prayer (salat) are observed faithfully by devout Muslims around the world. The formal requirement is that prayer should be offered five times a day, during which periods the Muslim, having washed, turns to face Mecca and repeats set prayers which are accompanied by physical movements.

These unusual pictures of the Nanzenji shrine in Kyoto, Japan, illustrate a number of important matters connected with worship. The novelty of Nanzenji is that visitors and worshippers approach the window in the wall (left). Looking through, they see the scene pictured below, designed to enhance the sense of mystery and wonder which is an essential part of genuine worship. The use of images, whether of the Buddha or a bodhisattva, a Hindu god, or a Christian saint, is intended to provide a window through which the worshipper can catch a glimpse of the mystery signified by the image. In Japan there has been a considerable sharing of religious ideas, especially between the various forms of Shinto and Buddhism found in the country. One result of this is that the shrines or ceremonies of one religion may on occasion serve the devotees of another. The religious allegiance of the two people pictured left is not clear. They may be devout Buddhists, adherents of a Shinto sect, or simply tourists interested in the novelty of this shrine. Places of worship may, and often do, serve the needs of people other than those for whom they are designed.

wrathful because of the mental disposition of the dead person. It is therefore doubly difficult to merge one's mind into them – but if it can be done, liberation will be achieved.

If the dead person is carried beyond the fourteenth day by his inability to recognize the forms that he sees as products of his own *chitta*, then the third stage of *bardo* is entered: the creation of a desire-body, which seeks out that place which is best suited to the person's attachments and cravings. The individual sees, as if from a distance, the world that he is about to inhabit. Even at this stage, the text says, visualization will prevent rebirth – but the path is very slippery and it is very difficult not to re-enter *samsara* – that is, to reincarnate in another body.

MILAREPA

The principle behind all these details is that, even though *chitta* is capable of amazing and unlimited transformations, skilful use of that same *chitta* will enable the practitioner to become detached from the forms and thus 'see' the clear light of enlightenment. And it is this clear light that is the focus of the teaching of Milarepa (1040–1123). He was a pupil of Marpa, founder of the Kagyu pa school, who himself received initiation in India from the great Vajrayana teacher, Naropa.

With Milarepa, transmission of teachings and transmission of power are inseparable. He had to undergo great hardships before Marpa would accept him, and his songs constantly emphasize the need for a *guru*. He was not a monk but an enlightened solitary, living in a remote cave without possessions of any kind. He had no time for book learning and was critical of those who, even at this early juncture in Tibetan Buddhism, when the links with India were still strong, thought that mere intellectual knowledge was sufficient to follow the path. His songs are refreshingly simple and contain beautiful descriptions of the joys of the unattached life in the mountains. 'At my feet, wild flowers bloom, vibrant and profuse . . . in the sky, the eagles circle freely.' In another song, Milarepa says: 'In such a lovely place as this, I am joyous in the clear light of the realization of emptiness.'

This realization is of the nature of the mind, which is Buddhahood. It is bliss and wisdom simultaneously. From this radiant emptiness many forms arise. Ignorant of this, one is bound by them; knowing it, one may enjoy them. But it is not merely a matter of knowledge, for wisdom also bestows power. Milarepa is credited with magical abilities and he certainly taught that they existed. But they have to be kept in their place. They are a natural consequence of diving deep

into the mind, but they must be abandoned just like all other manifestations. For, as we have seen, all forms are empty.

This insight is fundamental to both the Mahayana and the Vajrayana, and indeed it could be argued that it is the central teaching of Buddhism itself. Although there is a great gap, both in culture and time, between Gautama Buddha and Milarepa, this verse of Milarepa's crystallizes a truth which the Enlightened One himself would have had no difficulty in accepting:

In this desolate valley, this place where no men dwell,
The Yogin's joyful song resounds like thunder.
On all sides falls sweet-sounding rain
And the flower of compassion spreads out its petals.
The fruit of pure mind has ripened to the full
And the action of enlightenment now pervades all things.

The Dalai Lama, spiritual head of Tibetan Buddhism, has been reincarnated in an identifiable series since the 16th century. With the help of the Mongols they ruled Tibet from 1642, but the present Dalai Lama, whose Tibetan name means 'Precious Conqueror', has been in exile from Tibet since the Chinese invasion in 1959.

265

SIKHISM

HISTORICAL BACKGROUND AND PRESENT-DAY DISTRIBUTION

In the second half of the fifteenth century CE, the area of north-western India known as the Punjab had for some time been under Muslim rule. The population, however, was historically Hindu. How much, and in what way, these two antecedent religious elements actually contributed to the foundation and philosophies of the Sikh religion is in dispute. The strong monotheism of Islam and its rejection of the Hindu caste system could have exerted an influence on Sikhism, which on these aspects shares Islamic views. The Hindu bhakti movement of northern India, with which Sikhism has strong affinities, may or may not have developed in response to Muslim criticism of Hinduism. Certainly Sikhism is not a Hindu-Islamic synthesis aimed at reconciling the two religions. Islam cannot compromise on the Qur'an; non-Islamic doctrines such as *karma* and *samsara*, central to Sikh teaching, must make it unacceptable to Muslims, as must the assertion that through Guru Nanak God made a revelation later than that through Muhammad.

For several centuries by this time, in northern India, a number of nominally Hindu teachers had already proclaimed a belief in a single God and in salvation through his grace, available to all people regardless of caste, class and sex. Most used the vernacular (rather than Sanskrit) and rejected the rituals of brahmanic Hinduism and the authority of the Vedas; many were themselves from the lower castes of Hindu society. Prominent among such teachers were Namdev, Ravidas and Kabir, now considered to have constituted the 'Sant' tradition of northern India although they did not consciously make up a specific religious movement or group – indeed, they were probably unaware of each other's activities and teachings. Certainly all claimed to have received individual inspiration from a divine source, and none acknowledged any human teacher (guru). Followers of some of these teachers still exist as groups within Hinduism. Only the disciples of Guru Nanak have assumed such a separate identity that they have emerged as a distinct religion.

Guru Nanak

It was into this background that Nanak was born in 1469. He grew up to be critical of the formal and ritualistic expressions of both Hinduism and Islam that he saw around him. In 1499, after a spiritual experience that he regarded as a commission to begin his work, he took to preaching his message throughout the Punjab and beyond, and continued until about 1521 when he settled in a village he had himself founded, called Kartarpur. There he lived until his death in 1539, practising and preaching his ideals. And before he died he appointed a successor.

Nanak was thus the first spiritual leader, or Guru, of the Sikhs. It is upon his work and teaching that Sikhism has remained solidly grounded to this day, and it was at his initiative that the leadership of the religion became a sort of succession, although not necessarily a hereditary one. In fact, however, after Nanak there were to be nine more Gurus, the last one being Guru Gobind Singh who died in 1708. It is because of this same succession of leaders, together with the unity and solidarity of their message and its generally increasing dissimilarity from Hinduism, that Sikhism has developed its own identity and become a distinct religion.

Another reason must be its strong reaction to external pressures.

The Hindu challenge

Sikhism has always been regarded by Hindus as a movement within Hinduism, although it has resisted pressure to be reabsorbed from early times. The Gurus fostered distinctiveness in a number of ways – through the line of succession, by establishing their own rituals (especially of initiation and marriage), by creating a corpus of scripture, by instituting their own holy days and assemblies, and particularly by the forming of the Khalsa (the body of the initiated Sikhs) which possessed a distinctive appearance and life-style.

Separation from Hinduism began in Guru

Nanak's lifetime, at Kartarpur, and continued thereafter for about two centuries – but it was in the late nineteenth century that the Hindu challenge became critical. Renascent Hinduism, to some extent reformed as a response to the Christian missionary impetus which threatened both Hinduism and Sikhism, attempted to absorb the Sikhs into itself once again. The Sikh response was to emphasize its separateness by accentuating further the differences that had emerged during the period of the Gurus. It was at this time that many Sikh rituals and ceremonies, whatever their actual origins, assumed the form they have today. The chief instigator of this reaction was the Singh Sabha movement. (The 'threat' of Hinduism is even now not regarded as ended. Sikhs explain the agitation in the Punjab of the 1980s as a continued and revived attempt to deny them separate recognition, challenge their existence, and reabsorb them once and for all.)

The Islamic challenge

In contrast to the Hindu challenge was the challenge which came from Islam, and which started just as early in the religion's life. In 1526, centuries of intermittent invasions and dynastic rivalries that had created instability in the Punjab were finally replaced by settled government when the latest invader, Babur, established himself in Delhi and inaugurated the Mughal Empire. Early Mughals, especially Akbar (r. 1556–1605), permitted a considerable degree of religious freedom, even if preference was given to Muslim subjects. During Akbar's reign the Sikhs prospered and perhaps aspired towards their faith's becoming the third accepted religion – the one which the Emperor could use to reconcile his Hindu and Muslim subjects. Interpretations of Sikhism as a synthesis of Hinduism and Islam are thought possibly to have been purposively formed for the first time during this period, and from a modern viewpoint, many Sikhs now regard the Gurus as precursors of Gandhi, bringing a message of brotherhood to Hindus and Muslims, trying to weld them together in a united India.

In 1606 Guru Arjan became the first Sikh martyr, dying after torture and imprisonment by the successor of Akbar, the Emperor Jehangir. During the following century, relations between the Sikhs and the Mughal rulers varied but never, not even in the time of Guru Gobind Singh (1666–1708) – whose father, the ninth Guru, Tegh Bahadur, also suffered martyrdom – was the attitude of the Gurus one of out-and-out hostility. The reign of Emperor Aurangzeb (1658–1707) witnessed the introduction of a policy of 'Islamization', in the course of which many Hindu temples were destroyed and replaced with mosques.

Yet it was in the seventy years after his death that the Sikh struggle for survival really took

place. A price was placed upon the heads of Sikhs who were hunted down in their thousands and killed. They resisted, and only won respite when one of their number, Maharajah Ranjit Singh, established himself as ruler of Lahore in 1799 and gradually extended his influence over the geographical region of Punjab.

Revitalization

In some respects, Sikhism seems to thrive in adversity. The freedom which Sikhs enjoyed under Maharajah Ranjit Singh (1799–1839) threatened Sikh existence more than the oppression of Mughals and Afghans. Some slipped back into Hinduism. Places of worship – the gurdwaras – together with the considerable incomes they enjoyed from attached property donated to them, passed into the ownership of Hindu families. It was only another threat – that of Christian missionaries in the Punjab and the Hindu Arya Samaj reform movement – that stirred the Sikhs from

The Golden Temple, Amritsar, India. Beyond the Pool of Nectar is the Akal Takht, Throne of the Timeless God. This is the principal Sikh shrine where daily readings of the Guru Granth Sahib are performed. Guru Gobind Singh instructed that the collected writings were to be his successor, that there should be no further human gurus.

The brotherhood of Sikhs bound by a common uniform, discipline and allegiance to the Guru, is called the Khalsa, the Pure, and was instituted by Guru Gobind Singh in 1699. These five Khalsa members attend a Sikh rally in London held to call for the establishment of a Sikh state, Khalistan, in India. Sikhs are to be found throughout India but have long demanded home rule in the Punjab where 85 per cent of the Sikh population live.

their apathy. The Singh Sabha movement founded educational institutions. Pressure was exerted for the reclamation of gurdwaras and the recognition of Sikh ceremonies. In 1909 the Anand Marriage Act recognized the legality of weddings performed in the presence of Sikh scripture. In 1925 the Sikh Gurdwara Act placed Punjab gurdwaras in the hands of a committee, the Shiromani Gurdwara Parbandhak Committee (SGPC) which had actually existed since 1920. In 1962 the Indian government at last acceded to demands for a degree of home rule in the Punjab; the Punjabi Suba was established, boundaries were redrawn, and within four years 85 per cent of the Sikh population of India was gathered together in the new Punjab state.

Political wranglings, however, have led them to further assertions. At one extreme, Sikh reaction has been to agitate for a totally independent Sikh state, Khalistan; at the other, a minority of Sikhs would prefer not to link the future of Sikhism with any political aspirations at all. But most Sikhs regard political safeguards as important because of their historical experiences and because in secular India, Hindus constitute the vast majority of the population.

The total world population of Sikhs is probably about 13 million, most of whom live in the Punjab. Outside India, some 350,000 live in the UK and another 100,000 in North America. Sikhs are also to be found in most of the countries once ruled by Britain (with the exception of the Caribbean) and in other parts of South-East Asia. Sikhism is not a missionary religion; so most members of the Sikh dispersion are of Punjabi origin.

THE GURUS AND THEIR TEACHING

Sikhism owes its existence and form more to its Gurus than to any other influence. The Sikh affirmation is that the light of revelation shone through each of them equally, in that none was more important than any other. As two Sikh bards put it, in the time of the fifth Guru:

The divine light is the same, the life form is the same. The king has merely changed the body.
(AG 966)

The ten Gurus were:

Guru Nanak, 1469–1539
Guru Angad, *b.* 1504, Guru 1539–1552
Guru Amar Das, *b.* 1479, Guru 1552–1574
Guru Ram Das, *b.* 1534, Guru 1574–1581
Guru Arjan, *b.* 1563, Guru 1581–1606
Guru Hargobind, *b.* 1595, Guru 1606–1644
Guru Har Rai, *b.* 1630, Guru 1644–1661
Guru Har Krishan, *b.* 1656, Guru 1661–1664
Guru Tegh Bahadur, *b.* 1621, Guru 1664–1675
Guru Gobind Singh, *b.* 1666, Guru 1675–1708

The first four Gurus were unrelated but all were members of the Kshatriya varna (the relatively well off 'warrior' class) of Hinduism, although belonging to different groups within it. The last six were also Kshatriyas, members of the same Sodhi family. Succession was always to the most suitable candidate nevertheless, not automatically from father to eldest son.

Guru Nanak was born at Talwindi, now in Pakistan. His ecstatic experience at the age of thirty he described as 'being taken to God's court' where he was entrusted with a divine message and commissioned to proclaim it to all humankind. His greatest impact was upon those who could find little in formal Hinduism and Islam to give them hope or satisfaction. His success resulted in a movement for which he then felt obliged to provide a leader in succession to himself.

Guru Angad consolidated the achievements of Guru Nanak.

Guru Amar Das organized the Sikhs into administrative units (manjis) and introduced the custom of summoning them to appear before the Guru on three annual occasions, at the *Baisakhi*, *Diwali* and *Magha* festivals, which contributed greatly towards the development of a sense of Sikh identity.

Guru Ram Das founded the city of Amritsar and composed the wedding hymn (*lavan*); the Sikh form of marriage is attributed to him. He denounced the practice of *sati* and the veiling of women, and permitted the remarriage of widows.

Guru Arjan built at Amritsar the Harimandir or Darbar Sahib, the centre of worship and pilgrimage known to westerners as the Golden Temple. One of the most famous lines he composed reads:

I neither keep the Hindu fast nor the Muslim Ramadan.

It should be remembered that the following lines continue:

I serve him alone who, in the end, will save me.
My Lord is both the Muslim Allah and the Hindu Gosain.

(AG 1136)

Instead of rejecting either of the two religions he was commending a path he hoped the Emperor Akbar might find attractive in reconciling Hindu and Muslim. He collected his hymns and those of the earlier Gurus, with compositions also by Hindu and Muslim poet-saints, in a volume called the Adi Granth, which was installed in the Harimandir in 1604. Under him, Sikh aspirations reached their zenith – yet under Akbar's successor he became Sikhism's first martyr.

Guru Hargobind's name, 'world lord', may be indicative of Guru Arjan's hopes for the Sikh movement. His relationship with the Mughal court varied from his being imprisoned to his taking part in its hunting expeditions, and conversely again to his opposing Mughal power in military campaigns. The tradition of Sikh resistance to the Mughal Empire dates from his reign (which had a distinct temporal as well as a spiritual dimension).

THE FIVE Ks

THE FIVE Ks, TRADITIONAL SINCE GURU GOBIND SINGH FIRST ESTABLISHED THE KHALSA, ARE WORN BY ALL MEN AND WOMEN AT THEIR INITIATION INTO THE BROTHERHOOD.

KESH	LONG, UNCUT HAIR (SYMBOLIZING SPIRITUALITY)
KANGHA	A COMB (KEEPING THE HAIR IN PLACE, THUS SYMBOLIZING ORDER AND DISCIPLINE IN SPIRITUALITY)
KIRPAN	A SWORD, FROM A FEW INCHES TO TWO OR THREE FEET IN LENGTH (SIGNIFYING DIGNITY, COURAGE AND SELF SACRIFICE)
KARA	A STEEL BRACELET, WORN ON THE RIGHT WRIST (SYMBOLIZING UNITY WITH GOD AND ALLEGIANCE TO THE KHALSA)
KACH	SHORTS, WORN AS UNDERWEAR, AND INTRODUCED BY THE GURU AS MORE PRACTICAL IN BATTLE THAN THE *DHOTI* AND, IN EVERYDAY LIFE, MORE MODEST (WORN TO REPRESENT MORAL RESTRAINT)

Guru Har Rai reverted to the spiritual emphasis of the fifth and earlier Gurus, although he held court after the manner of his predecessor.

Guru Har Krishan spent much of his time as Guru under house arrest in Delhi, where he died of smallpox.

Guru Tegh Bahadur the son of Guru Hargobind, was twice passed over when a new leader was being chosen because his reflective nature did not accord with his father's style of primacy. He supported Hindu rights, and was arrested and executed in Delhi after being accused of possible complicity in a rising against the Emperor Aurangzeb, so becoming the second martyr Guru.

Guru Gobind Singh was the most influential of the Gurus after Guru Nanak. Sikh tradition often portrays him as a relentless opponent of Mughal rule, but relations even with Aurangzeb were not always hostile. He died while leading his army in the Deccan, campaigning alongside Emperor Bahadur Shah. It was Gobind Singh who instituted the Khalsa in 1699, a brotherhood of Sikhs bound by a common uniform, discipline and allegiance to the Guru. The uniform comprises the

।। ੴ ਸਤਿ ਨਾਮੁ ਕਰਤਾ ਪੁਰਖੁ ਨਿਰਭਉ ਨਿਰਵੈਰੁ ਅਕਾਲ ਮੂਰਤਿ ਅਜੂਨੀ ਸੈਭੰ ਗੁਰ ਪ੍ਰਸਾਦਿ ।।

THE 'MOOL MANTRA' IS OFTEN WRITTEN, IN ABBREVIATED FORM, ON THE CANOPY OVER THE THRONE OF THE ADI GRANT (ABOVE). KNOWN TO ALL SIKHS, THE VERSE EXPRESSES GURU NANAK'S MOST IMPORTANT TEACHING, THE SIKH DOCTRINE OF GOD:

There is one God, his name is truth eternal.
He is creator of all things, the all-pervading spirit.
Fearless and without hatred, timeless and formless.
Beyond birth and death, he is self-enlightened.
He is known by the Guru's grace.

'five Ks': uncut hair (*kesh*), a comb (*kangha*), a band on the right wrist (*kara*), a sword (*kirpan*), and short trousers (*kachha*). To these the men added the turban in respectful imitation of the Guru. Members are initiated by means of a procedure using *amrit*, a mixture of sugar and water which five Sikhs – representing the original five Khalsa members – sprinkle on the eyes and hair of initiates and give to them to drink.

It was also Guru Gobind Singh who, in 1708, instructed that the Adi Granth, the collected writings, was to be his successor, and that there were to be no further human Gurus. Accordingly, the book is now called the Guru Granth Sahib. He included it in some of his father's compositions but none of his own; his work is instead to be found in the Dasam Granth, compiled after his assassination in 1708.

The formation of the Khalsa and the conferring of the status of a Guru upon it and the scripture completed the process of establishing a separate Sikh community which had begun at Kartarpur under the first Guru.

There was one further serious influence on Sikhism dating from the age of the Gurus. Guru Arjan built three towns in an area dominated by Jats, a land-owning agrarian caste characterized by both democratic spirit and military enterprise. This group was therefore strongly represented in the Sikh membership from at least the time of Guru Arjan, and the militancy of the community in the seventeenth century – as well as its emphasis upon egalitarianism – may well owe something to the presence of the Jat members. The principle influence in Sikh development has, however, always been the Gurus.

The Guru Granth Sahib

In addition to the hymns of six Gurus, The Guru Granth Sahib contains compositions by such saints and poet-saints as Kabir, the Muslim Sheikh Farid, Ramananda, Namdev, Ravidas, and a number of lesser-known people from a variety of castes. No passages from the Vedas or other Hindu scriptures, or of the Qur'an, are included: their presence might have been seen as a denial of the claim that the teachings of the Gurus and other saints received individual divine revelation. Sikhs insist that the Adi Granth (*Adi* means 'first' in the sense of both 'primal' and 'original') is revelation quite equal to other scriptures, not dependent on any for its authenticity. It is in itself an assertion of the egalitarian and universalist message of Sikhism.

BELIEF

The principal belief of Sikhism is that God is one. 'He is the eternal giver and there is no other' (AG 933). The essential tenets of the Sikh concept of God are encapsulated in the Mool Mantra, a terse statement enunciated by Guru Nanak which appears at the beginning of the Guru Granth Sahib at the head of one of his major compositions, the Japji, and is used to introduce divisions and subdivisions. Explained to initiates during the *amrit* ceremony, it begins with the figure One, and may be paraphrased:

This being is One, the True One, eternal, immanent in all things and their sole sustainer. He is the creator, immanent in his creation. He is without fear or enmity, not subject to time and beyond birth and death. He manifests himself solely when and as he wills. He makes himself known by his, the Guru's grace.

God the only eternal reality is ineffable but reveals himself as Guru, by grace. For Sikhs, then, God is the supreme Guru who discloses himself as guide and teacher through his word. The ten human Gurus, born not as a result of *karma* but by God's will, received and passed on this word. It is now contained in the sacred book of the Sikhs (the Guru Granth Sahib). The physical volume is treated with immense respect because of the word (*shabad* or *bani*) it contains.

God as Guru is the self-revealing and humanity-saving dimension of the divine. Humankind is by nature ignorant and misguided; life is consequently characterized by illusion and the pursuit of material substance and goals, and dominated by five evils: lust, covetousness, attachment to worldly things, wrath and pride. A person of such a kind is the victim of *haumai* (self-reliance or egotism). The consequence of this is the cycle of birth and rebirth until, ultimately, God's grace effects a liberating transformation which finally ends the cycle.

In this unregenerate state a person is *manmukh*: attitudes and actions are determined by the individual will. The solution to the human predicament is to become *gurmukh*, God-centred, so that the thoughts and actions are guided by the Guru. Sikhism is a religion of grace. Only when God reveals himself through grace can the *manmukh* become *gurmukh* – although human effort may produce the conditions in which grace becomes effective.

Sikhism accepts the Hindu concept of *karma*, so it is possible to achieve a better birth in the next life through effort in this life. Final liberation, however, depends upon grace, for ultimately God is a sovereign being. Sikhism, like many another religion, recognizes a tension between human free will and divine omnipotence.

Liberation need not wait upon death. It is possible to become *jivanmukt* – liberated – while in the body, at which time the individual's outlook and life-purpose becomes transformed. Effort is no longer an attempt to seek liberation, it is an eagerness to serve God. Life becomes characterized by five virtues or blessings: truth, contentment, compassion, patience and *dharma*, the humble service of God and humanity. To quote Guru Nanak:

Truth is the highest of all virtues, but higher still is truthful living.

(AG 62)

The Sikh Gurus greatly emphasized practical religion and ethics. They exalted the despised peasant life to a virtue. They rejected the four *ashramas* (stages) of Hinduism which ended in that of *sannyasin* (renunciation), when a man left his family and devoted himself to the pursuit of the fourth and ultimate goal of *moksha* ('liberation'). All stages become one, that of *grihastha* ('householder'). The four goals of wealth, pleasure, duty and liberation become concurrent rather than consecutive. As Guru Tegh Bahadur said:

Why go to the forest to seek God? He is to be found at home.

(AG 684)

Three fundamental concepts provide a basis for Sikh life and conduct: *kirt karo, nam japo* and *vand cako* – work, worship and charity.

The householder who gives all he can afford to charity is as pure as the water of the Ganges.

(AG 952)

Begging is rejected. The virtues of honest labour, voluntary service to the community and the world at large (*sewa*) and the traditional generosity of the Indian are seen to be manifestations of religious devotion.

WORSHIP

Sikhism is a community religion stressing corporate worship focused upon the Guru Granth Sahib. It consists mainly of the singing of hymns to instrumental accompaniment, taken from the book, and talks, lectures and sermons based upon its teachings. There is no priesthood, although many gurdwaras have a *granthi* who organizes and conducts services. Despite the emphasis on the grace of God there are no rituals which can be described as 'sacraments' in the sense that they are especially grace-conferring. Listening to the *gurbani* – the words of the Guru Granth Sahib – is the commended way of attaining grace. There is no regular or weekly holy day; the nearest to it is the practice of some gurdwaras of emphasizing the first day of the lunar month, but Sikhs visit gurdwaras at any time, often daily especially in the early morning and the evening. In such places as the Golden Temple at Amritsar the singing of hymns takes place for about eighteen hours every day, beginning before dawn. Except for the closing ceremony at the end of a service there is no formal liturgy. At the end of the day the scripture is respectfully carried from the room in which services are held and laid to rest. In the mornings it is formally installed again.

Diwan, the Sikh name for the act of worship, also provides the context for naming-ceremonies and marriages. A copy of the Guru Granth Sahib may be taken to the parents' home for a child to be given a name, or the baby may be taken to the gurdwara. The scripture is opened at random and a name given using a letter from the first new verse on the left-hand page. Weddings also take place in the presence of the Guru Granth Sahib which, in India, is usually taken to the bride's home or to a piece of open ground on which awnings have been set up to protect the guests from the sun. The ceremony is brief, consisting only of the reading and then the singing of each of the four verses of the *lavan* (wedding hymn) followed by a clockwise circumambulation of the Guru Granth Sahib after each verse. The service is protracted by the singing of other hymns as guests assemble and after the ceremony, and by the making of speeches. The reception is informal, given to eating and friendly conversation.

After a death the Guru Granth Sahib is not taken to the cremation ground but its hymns are sung by the mourners who, instead of lamenting,

Sikhs are to be found worldwide though there is as yet no World Council of Sikhs. Here a priest leads prayers at a Sikh gurdwara in East London. On the table are offerings of money. Public worship is not held on any particular day though there is some emphasis on the first day of the lunar month. The business of each gurdwara is run by an elected committee but doctrinal matters are referred to Amritsar.

give thanks for the deceased's life and his repose with God.

Initiation (*amrit pahul*) also takes place in the presence of the Guru Granth Sahib. It is performed by five already initiated Sikhs. Someone who has received *amrit* and then broken the initiation vows may undergo the ceremony a second time if his repentance is considered genuine.

Sikh festivals are limited to *Baisakhi, Diwali, Hola Mohalla* and *gupurbs* (anniversaries associated with the births or deaths of the Gurus). Central to each celebration is a continuous, complete reading of the Guru Granth Sahib (*akhand path*) lasting about forty-eight hours.

All Sikhs are required to repeat and meditate upon the *gurbani* daily, especially after bathing early in the morning and in the evening. This act is known as *Nam Simran*, 'calling God to mind' or 'God-remembrance'. Often a *gutka*, a small anthology of the main Sikh hymns, is used.

ORGANIZATION

The Shiromani Gurdwara Parbandhak Committee (SGPC) was initially established to manage gurdwaras in the Punjab. It now exerts a greater influence and may be regarded as the nearest that Sikhism has at present that approaches to a committee or Council of Sikh affairs. It is elected by registered voters in the Punjab. As yet there is no World Council of Sikhs.

Issues involving doctrine and practice are de-

cided by the head *granthi* of the Akal Takht in Amritsar, and the *granthis* of gurdwaras at Anandpur Sahib, Nanded and Patna Sahib, to all of whom he is senior. The Rehat Maryada, a Guide to the Sikh Way of Life approved by the SGPC in 1945, names the Akal Takht as the final arbiter in doctrinal and ritual matters. At local level, each gurdwara elects its own committee, usually annually.

SIKHS IN SOCIETY

Between the teachings of the Gurus and the practices of the Sikhs there is an inconsistency of the kind found in many other religions. Ritualism has crept in and become institutionalized. Caste distinctions have never been successfully excluded, although the Punjab is a region less caste-conscious than some other parts of India. Inter-caste marriages, however, are not common. In Britain and in North America, separate gurdwaras have been established to meet the needs of different castes. The difference between precept and practice lies in the nature of Indian society, and the place of Sikhism as a minority religion in a predominantly Hindu culture. These factors make individual and even group reactions against the norm difficult. Religious tolerance is strongly emphasized.

Although a military career has traditionally attracted Sikhs, they are to be found in all other walks of life and in most major cities in India.

CONFUCIANISM

HISTORICAL OUTLINE

Many leading scholars, both western and Chinese, maintain that Confucianism is not a religion but rather a socio-political ethical system concerned not so much with theological beliefs and questions regarding humankind's origin and ultimate destiny as with the living of life in the here and now. Its attitude to belief in gods or in a meaningful afterlife is agnostic. It lacks many elements usually associated with a religion, such as a consecrated priesthood, codified creeds and dogmas, other-worldliness, and even a sharp division between those who are and those who are not adherents. Confucianism is primarily a way of life based on ethical teaching designed to produce a peaceful, harmonious and well ordered society in which each individual functions according to his or her capacity.

Confucianism has a religious dimension in that it incorporates the pre-Confucian religion of ancient China, a religion which was already well established before the beginning of the first millennium BCE. It held a belief in a supreme deity called Tian, usually translated as 'Heaven'. This deity presided over the cosmos and controlled the activities of a host of subsidiary gods and spirits. Elaborate rites were developed for their worship and for the worship of ancestor spirits. By means of prayers, divination, sacrifices, ritual music and mime it was believed possible to gain the benevolent support and assistance of a spiritual hierarchy and, at the same time, to appease the wrath of those deities who had been offended by human behaviour. Long before the time of Confucius there existed a class of specialists whose duty it was to assist the rulers in all matters by which contact was made with the spiritual world of the gods and the deceased ancestors.

Religious practices were an integral part of government, and those who assisted the ruler in secular affairs needed also to be experts in religion. They were known as *ru*, the scholars or literati, and what is now called Confucianism was known in China then as the Ru Jiao, or the Teaching of the Scholars.

Confucius

The name Confucius is the latinized form of Kong-fu-zi (sometimes spelled Kung-fu-tzu), which simply means Master Kong. His real name was Kong Qiu, and his cognomen was Zhong-ni. He is reputed to have lived from about 551 to 479 BCE. He lived and died in comparative obscurity in the small and relatively weak state of Lu, situated in present-day Shandong province. At that time the country was divided into a large number of independent states which, for ritual purposes and as a matter of decorum, recognized the tutelary overlordship of the great Zhou dynasty. Most of what has been written about Confucius is apocryphal and unreliable. The most reliable source is the *Lun-yu*, translated into English as the

An imaginary Chinese painting of Confucius. Very little is known of his early life and much that has been written is apochryphal. His name in Chinese, Kong-fu-zi, simply means 'Master Kong'. He and his followers taught self-cultivation, believing that through individual moral efforts would come political and social improvement. This is the Way of Jen, or Love.

CONFUCIUS IDENTIFIED IN HUMAN SOCIETY FIVE FORMS OF HUMAN RELATIONSHIP – THE RELATIONSHIP BETWEEN

RULER AND SUBJECT

FATHER AND SON

HUSBAND AND WIFE

THE ELDEST SON AND HIS BROTHERS

ELDERS AND JUNIORS OR FRIENDS

AND HE TAUGHT THAT IF, WITHIN THESE RELATIONSHIPS, EVERYONE LIVED BY *LI* – COURTESY, REVERENCE AND THE CORRECT FORM OF SOCIAL AND RELIGIOUS CEREMONY – THERE WOULD BE HARMONY WITHIN EVERY UNIT OF SOCIETY AND SOCIAL AND POLITICAL HARMONY WITHIN THE STATE.

'Annals of Confucius'. These saying and reminiscences were compiled from notes and jottings made not long after his death by disciples who loved and revered him.

It seems fairly certain that Confucius claimed descent from the royal house of Song (or Sung) which, like the state of Lu, although small was recognized as the repository of great cultural traditions. His great-grandfather moved to Lu, and the family gradually became impoverished. The father of Confucius was a military officer who died when his child was three years old, leaving him to be brought up in poverty by the widow who managed, however, to see that he was provided with a sound education. Confucius was married at nineteen, but practically nothing is known about his wife, his daughter, or the son who predeceased him. His education fitted him for government service. At first he held a minor post as keeper of granaries; later he was promoted to be in charge of public lands. But although he aspired to high office it is doubtful that he ever became a minister of state. Instead, he won recognition as a teacher.

He trained large numbers of young men for service in government, and seems to have been one of the first to take as pupils gifted young men from all ranks in society, not just from the aristocracy who could reward him with fees.

In 497 BCE, at the age of fifty-four, recognized as a great scholar and teacher – but disgusted at the internal politics of Lu – Confucius set out on thirteen years of travelling from state to state, hoping to find some ruler who would take to heart his teachings and accept his advice. In those days it was customary for princes to attract to their courts men of scholarship and learning, and to offer them lodgings and emoluments. It seems that Confucius was supported in this way, but there were also times in which he was in dire poverty and even danger. Finally he returned to Lu to spend the remaining three years of his life in study. He was buried near the present-day town of Qu-fu in Shandong. Long after his death, a magnificent temple was built there in his honour, and it became a place of pilgrimage.

BELIEF

The teachings of Confucius

Confucius was in no sense the founder of a religion. He accepted the religious belief and elaborate religious practices of his time, although he was sceptical in regard to magic and superstition. He was primarily, and superbly, a scholar and a teacher who devoted himself to the study of all aspects of the ancient wisdom. He sought – and believed that he had found – those principles of virtue which had motivated the lives and actions of holy and wise men in ancient times and particularly at the time of the founding of the Zhou dynasty more than 500 years previously. He believed with all his heart that if these virtues were inculcated and followed in his own day, the result would be true nobility of character, the greatest happiness and well-being of family and state, and the peaceful re-unification of the whole country under a wise and benevolent ruler. What he himself learned he taught to others by his example and precept.

Already by the time of Confucius there was in existence a large body of literature. Together with music it consisted of what in later times was to be expanded into the Confucian canon: the five great Confucian Classics. These were *The Odes, The Historical Documents, The Book of Rites, A Book of Divination*, and lastly the *Annals of the States*, which is more often known as *The Spring and Autumn Classic*.

In his use of these earlier documents Confucius was selective and discriminating, using them to illustrate his belief that individual and social life and all good government must be founded on morality. Believing that the attainment of true wisdom and saintliness is beyond the reach of ordinary mortals, Confucius set forth as an attainable ideal the *Jun-zi*. *Jun-zi* originally referred to a member of the nobility. But for Confucius, true nobility is nobility of character, and is not dependent on princely birth and privilege. Anyone who is bent on cultivating noble moral qualities can become a *Jun-zi*, but such cultivation needs constant application and development. A truly noble character must learn to be true to his inmost self, and loyal, faithful and considerate towards others. He must be moderate in all things, cultured in manner and meticulous in observing those rites and ceremonies which appertain to human behaviour and relationships. In addition he taught the need for wisdom and sincerity in speech and action. To produce men with these qualities was Confucius's aim as a teacher.

For Confucius the supreme virtue from which all other virtues stem is *ren*, variously translated as 'goodness', 'love', 'benevolence', 'human-heartedness' or 'humanity'. Political and social stability is only attained by following the Way (*Tao*, or *Dao*) of the ancient rulers, who governed not by fear and force but by *de*, which is a pervasive moral force that emanates from a wise and good ruler, influencing the lives of all his subjects and gaining the approval of Heaven.

Confucius and religion

Although Confucius did not found a religion he was a deeply religious man. This is evidenced in two respects. Firstly, he had a profound belief in, and reverence for, a supreme cosmic spiritual power called *Tian* which was ever working for good and was the author of the virtue within him. He was conscious of providential guidance and a Heaven-appointed mission. He believed that an individual's first duty is to strive for perfection in goodness and love. Although acutely conscious also of human weakness, failure and error, Confucius believed that through teaching, training and discipline they could be overcome. Secondly, he taught the necessity for the meticulous performance of those rites and ceremonies by which Heaven and the ancestor spirits were worshipped. He remained, however, a moral philosopher and was in no sense a theologian or a metaphysician.

THE SPREAD AND DEVELOPMENT OF CONFUCIANISM

Early developments after Confucius's death

Soon after his death the greatness of Confucius became recognized by an ever-widening circle. His disciples many of whom took up responsible positions in government, spread his teachings. The rulers of a number of independent states discovered that they could rely on such learned men of high moral character, who could advise on how to make land and people prosperous and who were skilful in inter-state diplomacy; and they found their own prestige to be much enhanced by attracting scholars to their courts and giving them patronage.

Consequently, during the period between the death of Confucius and the unification of China under the first emperor in 221 BCE, Confucianism grew in strength. What are now known as the Hundred Schools flourished, most of which were Confucian. Some were antagonistic – the Mohists, Taoists (Daoists), Legalists, Agronomists and others – which added to the great intellectual ferment. Great Confucian scholars arose to give varied interpretations of the Master's teachings. Tradition ascribes the 'Doctrine of the Mean' (*Zhong-yong*) to Zu-si, the grandson of Confucius, and 'The Great Learning' (*Da-Xue*) to Confucius's disciple Zeng-can. These, together with the 'Annals', and the writings of Mencius (c. 371–289 BCE) – ranked second only to Confucius – were later to become known as the Four Books, an essential study for all who aspired to scholarship and official recognition. Over the next few centuries the influence of Xun-zi (c. 298–238 BCE), and his doctrine that human nature is basically evil, was to rival the teachings of Mencius.

On the unification of China in 221 BCE and the establishment of a totalitarian empire under the ruthless ruler of the erstwhile state of Qin, Confucianism fell into disrepute. Confucian scholars were persecuted and the literature proscribed. But the early demise of the Qin empire and the founding of the great Han dynasty (206 BCE–225 CE) brought Confucianism into its own.

Confucianism during the Han dynasty

It was during this period that Confucianism came to full fruition. Diligent research was carried out into all aspects of the ancient learning, and the results were collated, edited and revised. The five great Confucian Classics were produced, substantially as they are today, together with all the historical, philosophical and literary material that could be found.

Dong Zhong-shu (179–104 BCE) was the most influential Confucian in the western Han period. He helped to found what is known as the New Text School, and was largely responsible for the exaltation of Confucius as 'unique sage' and 'uncrowned king', a superhuman being worthy of divine honours. By imperial decree Confucianism became the state cult. An imperial university was established in the capital, and state schools opened throughout the empire. An examination system based on knowledge of the Confucian Classics became the gateway to official employment and preferment. This emphasis on Confucian education has continued until the present century.

There is no doctrine of an afterlife in Confucianism. Nevertheless, archaeological evidence from the Han dynasty shows conclusively that there was an almost universal belief in some form of survival after death. Many Confucian scholars, however, were agnostic and carried on a tradition of rationalistic humanism which stemmed from the writings of Xun-zi. Yet it was Confucians who

THE CONFUCIAN CANON

THE FIVE CLASSICS AND THE FOUR BOOKS COMPRISE THE CONFUCIAN CANON OF LITERATURE.

THE FIVE CLASSICS, COMPILED AT THE TIME OF CONFUCIUS FROM EXISTING DOCUMENTS, CONSIST OF:

THE BOOK OF DIVINATION DEALING WITH RULES OF PERSONAL CONDUCT

THE HISTORICAL DOCUMENTS COVERING 17 CENTURIES OF CHINESE HISTORY AND CONTAINING MORAL AND RELIGIOUS TEACHINGS

THE ODES THE EARLIEST COLLECTION OF CHINESE POETRY

THE BOOK OF RITES GIVING GUIDANCE ON WORSHIP AND ON MORAL AND SOCIAL RELATIONSHIPS

THE SPRING AND AUTUMN CLASSIC A HISTORY OF THE PROVINCE OF LU

THE FOUR BOOKS, COMPILED BY CONFUCIUS' FOLLOWERS SOME 150 YEARS AFTER HIS DEATH, ARE:

THE DOCTRINE OF THE MEAN EXPOUNDING THE PRINCIPLE OF THE 'RIGHT WAY'

THE GREAT LEARNING WHICH PROVIDES A BASIS FOR A GOOD EDUCATION

THE ANNALS THE APHORISMS OF CONFUCIUS, CONCERNED WITH SOCIAL, POLITICAL AND RELIGIOUS DUTIES AND CODES OF BEHAVIOUR

THE BOOK OF MENCIUS THE TEACHINGS OF CONFUCIUS' DISCIPLE MENCIUS

became the custodians of the ancient learning, the experts in ritual and the instructors and guides of rulers. They were skilful in taking up into their system philosophical and cosmological ideas which had been taught by Taoist (Daoist) and *yin-yang* schools.

The relation of Confucianism with Buddhism and Taoism

At the collapse of the Han dynasty (*c.* 225 CE) there followed three and a half centuries of political disunion in which most of China was ruled by foreign governors. Taoism and Buddhism – the latter introduced from central Asia and India – became major religious forces, winning the allegiance of the majority of the population. Syncretism between Confucianism and philosophical Taoism had already occurred. Confucianism was now faced with the challenge of a foreign religion claiming an equal antiquity and a corpus of philosophical and religious literature which had a strong appeal to the scholar class. While still taking an active part in the state religion, many scholars became devout Buddhists. For the first time Confucianism was challenged, by both Taoism and Buddhism as religious organizations actively and successfully at work in winning over adherents who accepted these faiths by individual and voluntary choice.

Throughout the long centuries of political disunity and during the Tang dynasty (618–907 CE), famous Confucian scholars attacked Buddhism not only because of the gross superstitions associated with its popular expression but also because it was inimical to the interests of the state. It was a foreign religion, drawing thousands away from productive pursuits and family life into monasteries and nunneries. It was claimed to be destructive of traditional Chinese religion, morality and ancestor worship. In 819 CE the famous Confucian scholar Han Yu was disgraced for presenting a memorial attacking Buddhism. Yet by 845 a terrible persecution of Buddhism and other foreign religions broke out from which they never completely recovered. A strong revival of Confucianism was on its way, absorbing philosophical and psychological insights from Buddhism. This was to result in the great Neo-Confucian movement in the Song (Sung) dynasty (960–1279).

Neo-Confucianism

With Neo-Confucianism coming to fruition in the Song dynasty, Confucianism gained an unrivalled ascendancy in China both in state administration and in education, and inculcated Confucius's teachings regarding personal morality, filial piety, social responsibility and government. Five great Neo-Confucians of the eleventh century provided Confucianism with a firm metaphysical and cosmological basis. They were Zhou Dun-yi (1017–73), Shao Yong (1011–77), Zhang Zia (1020–77), Cheng Hao (1032–65) and Cheng Yi (1033–1107) and they were followed in the twelfth century by Zhu Xi (1130–1200) and Lu Xiang-shan (1139–93).

Although Zhou Dun-yi, the author of 'The Diagram of the Supreme Ultimate', is regarded as the brilliant founder of Neo-Confucianism, it is Zhu Xi who is universally recognized as the one who did more than any other to re-establish Confucianism in China, also greatly influencing the religious philosophy of Japan. By his prolific writings and his commentaries on the five great Classics he laid the foundation of an ethical and social philosophy which, with various modifications, was a determinative factor in both Chinese life and thought until the beginning of the twentieth century.

Zhu Xi taught that the Supreme Ultimate (*Tai Ji*), through the interaction of Principle (*Li*) and 'Ether' or Material Force (*Qi*), produced all phe-

Confucius was a moral philosopher and in no sense a theologian. Yet he was a deeply religious man and had a profound belief in a supreme cosmic spiritual power, the author of all good. Thus Confucius promoted the traditional worship and as a sacred duty the Emperor would attend the Hall of Annual Prayers in Peking, shown here. This is the principal hall of the Temple of Heaven complex built in 1368 during the Ming Dynasty.

nomena including humankind. Man's nature (*Xing*) is therefore wholly good. It must be distinguished from consciousness or mind (*Xin*) which, when it is activated, results in feelings, emotions and desires that lead to aberrations from the norm and to the obscuring of the Heaven-implanted nature. The aim of moral education is to foster in humankind those virtues of love, righteousness, propriety and wisdom which will allow the Heaven-bestowed nature to shine forth.

The realistic philosophy of Zhu Xi is contrasted with the more idealistic philosophy of his contemporary Lu Xiang-shan, a philosophy that was to find its greatest exponent in Wang Yang-ming, who lived three centuries later (1472–1529). He taught that all men possess an original mind, the underlying quality of which is love (*ren*). This mind possesses intuitive knowledge which it is the role of wisdom to uncover, develop, and bring into operation. Knowledge is the beginning of conduct, and conduct is the completion of knowledge. The Confucianism of Wang Yang-ming was to have a great influence on the movements towards reform in nineteenth-century Japan and twentieth-century China.

WORSHIP AND ORGANIZATION

Until the beginning of the twentieth century Chinese orthodoxy taught that the Confucian way of life, if sincerely followed, was as perfect as human society could hope to attain. It was possible by human reason and moral education to correct any aberration from the norm. A sacred duty devolved upon the emperor and all his functionaries to ensure the well-being of land and people by the correct performance of religious rites which had been handed down through the centuries in the Confucian tradition. In order to perform this duty to the best of their ability they were guided by the Board of Rites (Li Bu), the most important of the six departments of state.

The state sacrifices were categorized as great, medium and small. For the great sacrifices the emperor was expected to attend in person. The supreme expression of Confucian state religion was performed at the winter solstice at the Altar of Heaven. It would be difficult to find anywhere on earth a more impressive and awe-inspiring place of worship than this plain white marble altar rising in three concentric circles and open to the sky. There before sunrise each year at the winter solstice, in a deeply moving ceremony consisting of nine separate acts, and surrounded by all the dignitaries of state, the emperor of the most populous nation on earth humbled himself before the Supreme Deity on high and offered prayers and sacrifices on behalf of himself and the people of his domain.

At stated times in every county seat in the land the duly appointed magistrate at the head of his officials worshipped the protective gods of his district in the temple of the city god, and in all schools worship was offered to the spirits of Confucius and the great Confucian worthies.

CONFUCIANISM, THE WORLD AND THE FUTURE

Throughout the nineteenth century Confucianism faced the effects of serious rebellions, a revival of Buddhism, and an evangelizing Christianity which accompanied the aggressive expansionism of the West. More and more Chinese intellectuals were attracted by scientific materialism and western forms of democracy. The example of Japan made it abundantly clear that modernization and reform were necessary. Some Confucian scholar-statesmen, such as Kang You-wei (1858–1927), believed that Confucianism should be accepted as a national religion under a constitutional monarchy. Gradually, in a welter of ideologies, Confucianism lost its hold.

In 1905 the centuries-old examination system was abolished. In 1911 China became a republic bent on speedy modernization. Many younger scholars rejected Confucianism as conservative and a hindrance to progress and national salvation. More and more were attracted to scientific materialism, humanism, atheism and communism. In the universities Confucianism came under serious criticism which turned to vituperation under communism, being labelled as feudalistic, class-preserving, upholding privilege, wealth and social prestige, and teaching a slave morality designed to keep the masses in subjection. It was held to exalt the family at the expense of the individual, restrain women in subjection, and to glorify the past to the detriment of the present. Atheistic materialism had no use for the idea of an overruling Providence, and all religious expression was regarded as the mumbo-jumbo of crass superstition.

That phase of anti-Confucianism seems to be passing in China's effort to revive and preserve her great cultural heritage. The academic study of Confucianism has also revived, particularly in regard to its contribution to literature, music and the arts. Confucius is regarded as a great figure of the distant past – but no longer to be either idolized or disparaged.

Within the Chinese dispersion – Taiwan, Hong Kong, Indonesia, Malaysia and the West – the richness of the ethical and spiritual contribution of Confucianism has never ceased to be recognized. There is little, apart from worship of ancestors and the honours paid to great Confucians of the past, that can be called distinctively religious. Yet the teachings that have survived the vicissitudes of two and a half millennia still continue to inspire people to strive after that wisdom which springs from an inner integrity and a complete sincerity, and manifests itself in the virtues of love, justice, courtesy and faithfulness.

From the present to the future

The question remains as to how far Confucians will have a moral and religious influence over the Chinese people in the future. Because it has exerted such a profound influence on the lives of almost one quarter of the human race for more than two thousand years, Confucianism is usually counted among the major religions of mankind. The peoples of Korea, Japan and Vietnam found in Confucianism a source of moral and spiritual inspiration and of practical wisdom for the guidance of individual and social behaviour. But its resilience has been tested over the centuries, and may be again in China.

Confucianism's teachings and its enlightened humanistic form of religion, which have always emphasised that Heaven (*Tian*) is primarily concerned with the happiness and well-being of all the people, have affinities with those socialistic principles which declare that government should be *of* the people, *by* the people and *for* the people. And however far Confucianism has in the past strayed by its élitism – its illiberality and its lack of concern for peasants and women – the teachings of Confucius and his great disciple Mencius cannot fail to have a profound influence on all thoughtful and intelligent Chinese.

Innumerable sayings of Confucius have become proverbial, part of the moral and spiritual heritage of the Chinese people, and much quoted in the western world. Many Chinese scholars inwardly agree with Mencius who wrote:

All things are there within me. On self examination I find no greater joy than to be true to myself. We should do our best to treat others as we wish to be treated. Nothing is more apposite than to seek after goodness. [ren].

(Mencius 7a:4)

TAOISM

HISTORY AND DISTRIBUTION

Taoism is a term which is applied to a religion and to a number of schools of philosophy. The term 'Taoism' was not applied until the time of the first Han Dynasty in the second century CE, by when many of the main elements of the Taoist creed had merged. Yet the religion belongs to a much earlier period, possibly as a revival of religious beliefs of a magico-shamanistic character which were prominent in the period of the Shang dynasty (c. 1500–1100 BCE). However, the religion came to prominence during the period of the Warring States (481–221 BCE) as a powerful indigenous growth which had its influence in many areas of Chinese life, including medicine, politics and warfare, as well as in the field of philosophy. The growth of Taoist belief was no doubt encouraged by the rise of lower social groups and changes which took place in the structure of Chinese society.

The Shang and Han dynasties

During the period of the Shang dynasty, the worship of ancestors and sacrifices to the hills and streams as well as other aspects of nature were prominent. There was a profound belief in the connection between human affairs and natural events, with rules for divination as set forth in part of the book *Shu-ching*. Such rules presupposed not only guidance for the future but also the exercise of virtue to secure success. These beliefs are also apparent in the dynasty which followed, the Early Chou period. It is during the period of the Warring States, however, that there is more evidence of this tendency, especially in the reign of Shih-huang-ti, who issued a decree in 213 BCE that the books of the Confucian School were to be burnt but exempted books on medicine and divination. That emperor is said to have had great faith in charms to confer immortality. He sent expeditions to the islands of P'eng-lai, where the blessed were deemed to live in the eastern seas, to bring back the herb of immortality. Professors of magical arts were sought for advice. During the

Chin dynasty (221–206 BCE), the first Chin emperor sent a fleet of ships with young men and girls to find the islands of the blessed, thought to be located among P'eng-lai, Ying-chou, Fu-sang and other islands off the coast of Shantung. The abode of the blessed and immortality were also sought through medicine, a prominent feature of Taoism.

The concept of Tao as the unity behind the multiplicity of things became personified into a deity, the first and greatest god of Taoism. As the Greatest One he was introduced into the official worship during the first Han dynasty (206 BCE–8 CE) and placed above the five legendary emperors. The belief that another of the abodes of the immortals was on the summit of the K'un-lun mountain in the west of China may have been fostered by the Han rulers in their drive to the west. It was during the Han period, in 184 CE, that the biggest Taoist rebellion took place under the leadership of Chang Chio. As economic conditions became worse, he made use of the widespread discontent among the rural population and gathered very large numbers of followers. These followers were organized by missionaries and priests clad in yellow robes with yellow turbans who came to be known as the Yellow Turbans. Chang Chio claimed that the happy year of T'ai-p'ing (Universal Peace) would take place in the year 184 CE when the present Blue Heaven would be replaced by the Yellow Heaven, but that in the ten years leading up to the event, there would be political disasters and natural catastrophes including pestilence and plague. From all such disasters the magical powers of Chang Chio would protect believers who, in addition to believing, must confess their sins of misconduct against their fellows. The chief deity of this T'ai-p'ing belief was the Central Yellow-Old Ruler (Chung-yang Huang-lao-Chün) who had been worshipped in the rural Taoist communities since the third century BCE. This deity ruled the external world of natural phenomena; he also ruled the inner life of man (dwelling in the heavens and in the centre of the human head), hence his power over the human body, including the power of healing. As his

the Han river between Shensi and Szuchuan. It was administered by a Taoist hierarchy and appears to have been ruled with considerable probity and tolerance. For example, an offence against the law could be repeated three times before sentence was passed on the offender. Free hostelries were established for travellers, and food was made available to the poor. Misuse of such facilities, it was believed, would be punished by diseases inflicted by offended spirits.

To this period, too, belongs the main figure in Taoist religion, Chang Tao-ling (grandfather of Chang Lu), whose descendents claimed his magical powers and held the title of 'Tien Shih' (Master of Heaven). The title the Taoist 'pope' was conferred in the middle of the second century CE by the emperor Liu Chih on his family.

The T'ang dynasty

During the T'ang dynasty (618–906) Taoism was powerfully supported by the ruling house. A contributory factor to this support lay in the fact that the reigning house had the same surname, Li, as Li Erh (or Lao-tzu), supposedly the 'father' of Taoism and the putative author of the *Tao-tê Ching*. He appeared in a vision to the first emperor to inform him, and the name of the imperial house being thereby exalted, the T'ang rulers bestowed many honorific titles on him. A further contributory factor no doubt was the desire of the emperors to lessen the economic power of the Buddhists, which developed into acute rivalry and eventually led to a severe persecution of the Buddhists in 845 CE.

The influence of Taoism in this period has several facets. On the side of religion, there were two marked developments. On the one hand the Taoist monastic life became fashionable, to the extent that in 711 some imperial princesses became nuns. There is evidence of eighth-century Taoist monasteries and nunneries in Changan, the capital, although the Buddhists outnumbered them six to one in this regard. The rules for the monks were based on the Buddhist code of discipline, the Vinaya, including such precepts as not to kill, not to eat meat or drink alcohol, and to live in chastity; such rules increased in number with progress up the monastic hierarchy. On the other hand, there was during this period an attempt to reform the morality of the empire, for example by the leader Lü Yen or Lü Tung-pin (755–805) who prepared a form of moral account-keeping in which actions and attitudes were listed and accorded merits and demerits. Bearing with troublesome parents, for example received 100 merits, while not fixing one's eyes on a pretty girl received 5 merits. Other facets of Taoist influence are manifest in the fact that three, if not four, T'ang emperors died from poisonous drugs while searching for the elixir of life. In the field of poet-

A Taoist temple in the Tai Shan mountains of China. The temple offers rituals on all festival days, and services are also offered for the ancestors. Popular Taoism, as a religious influence, can be expressed in a variety of ways, through superstitious practices, through secret societies and by nature worship. Temple sites are now protected by the government.

prophet, Chang Chio was believed to have great power, and many people from the central part of the Han empire gave up their homes and livelihoods to follow him. There is reference in the *History of the Later Han Dynasty* (25–220 CE) that some Taoists distributed their property to the poor, established homes for orphans, built roads and bridges with voluntary labour and performed other such good works. Although Chang Chio's movement was originally intended to be a peaceful demonstration, the government attacked him and his followers at the end of 183 CE. Chang Chio died soon after, but the fight with his followers dragged on for twenty years.

There is evidence of other Taoist political activity in the same period, between 118 CE and 215 CE: the foundation by Chang Lu of a small Taoist state in the valley of the upper course of

ry, Taoism's imaginative fancy inspired such famous names as Li Tai-po, Tu Fu, Wang Wei and others.

Reference has been made to the T'ien Shih (Master of Heaven), a title and dignity which was confirmed in the Chang family, by Hsüan Tsung (748 CE) during the T'ang dynasty. The descendents of the Chang family received further recognition early in the eleventh century when the emperor Chen Tsung of the Sung dynasty gave them large tracts of land on the Lung-hu shan (Dragon-Tiger Mountain) in 1016 CE. The authority of this Taoist 'pope' continued until 1930 CE when the Red Army destroyed the pots in which the Heavenly Master had imprisoned evil spirits. It was believed, by a process of transmigration, the soul of Chang Tao-Ling passed into one of his descendents who was to succeed him in office.

The Sung dynasty

The emperors of the Sung dynasty (which succeeded the T'ang dynasty) ruled from 960 to 1127 CE and continued to support the Taoists. The religious impetus appears to have weakened during this period while the influence of Buddhism on Taoist practices became more marked. From the earlier desire to prolong life by breathing exercises and other means, the emphasis changed to a search for a paradise such as Buddhism offered. In fact, under the Sung emperors there was an attempt to revive interest in Taoist belief by borrowing from Buddhism. In imitation of Buddhism there appeared a new god, the Pure August One, introduced by Taoists with the support of the third Sung Emperor. This deity became the supreme god of official Taoism. Reference to the influence of Buddhism on Taoist practice is considered below.

Another facet in Taoist life during the Sung Dynasty was the production under imperial patronage of much literature. Some of this work was brought together into the *Tao-tsang*, the Taoist canon, published in the early fifteenth century. Like the Buddhist *Tipitaka*, it has three sections. These sections are presided over by the Three Pure Ones, namely, the Perfect Holy One, the Highest Holy One and the Greatest Holy One, in imitation of the Three Precious Ones of Buddhism known as the Three Jewels (The Buddha, the Law or Dharma, and the Community or Sangha) but transmuted in popular Mahayanist Buddhist thought to the Buddha, past, present and to come. The rapid spread of printing in the Sung period made Taoist and other literature more readily available. Whilst there was a flowering of Chinese poetry in the T'ang period, especially during the reign of the emperor Hsüan Tsung (also known as Ming Huang, 715–756), there was disaster at the close of his reign in the rebellion of An Lu-shan,

who partially destroyed the capital city and scattered the poets, painters and musicians who had enriched it. These artists, especially the poets, had sought to 'return to nature', and Taoism encouraged meditation on nature's mystical aspects as did Ch'an Buddhism. This was expressed in the Sung period by the great landscape painters whose works were outstanding artistic achievements as well as outpourings of philosophical belief, as may be seen in the work of the tenth-century painter Ching Hao who provides us with an account of the artist's mind as well as beauty in form. The emperors of the North Sung Dynasty took a keen interest in art: a catalogue of the emperor Hui Tsung has 6391 studies by 231 different masters, with biographical sketches. Leading principles of *ch'i* (inner essence) and *li* (form) are sought by these painters, principles which are important issues in Taoist thought. During the later years of the Sung period, Taoist philosophical thought tended to merge with Confucian thought to form Neo-Confucianism. Popular Taoism, as a religious influence, came to be expressed in a variety of ways, through a complex of superstitious practices, through secret societies and sects, for example, as well as in its appeal to nature-worship. This aspect of Taoism is discussed under 'Organization' on page 286.

BELIEF AND PHILOSOPHY

A number of different philosophical strands served to form the main Taoist philosophy of later times. Prominent among these are the teachings of Mo-tzu (Mo Ti) (c. 480–400 BCE), Yang-Chu (c. 300 BCE) and Tsou Yen of the Chi-gate school, prominent in the late fourth century BCE. Mo Ti taught that 'Heaven loves all the people in the world' and was opposed to elaborate court expenditure since it did not benefit the common people. He praised the worthy emperor of earlier times, Yü, who sacrificed himself for his people. In contrast, the school of Yang-Chu stressed the salvation of the individual by keeping out of harm's way and seeking means to prolong life. His teaching developed into a theory of 'fine parts' or inner elements of *ch'i* (air or breath) which were accumulated within a person's body to preserve life. If these fine parts, the imperishable elements in the body, were fostered, they might prolong life – an important Taoist tenet. The academy of Chi-gate (the gate of the god of agriculture) played an important part in the development of such theories. A leading figure was Tsou Yen, who sought to set forth a view of the universe which was based on two universal principles: *yin* (dark, female, passive) and *yang* (light, male, active), which were combined with the five

YIN-YANG: THE SYMBOL OF OPPOSITES

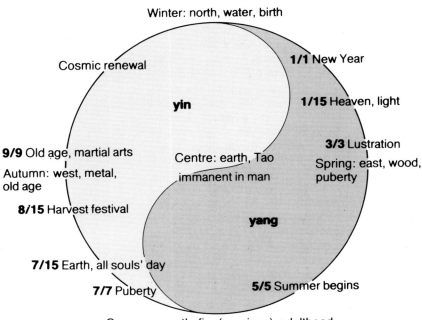

Winter: north, water, birth

Cosmic renewal

1/1 New Year

1/15 Heaven, light

yin

3/3 Lustration

9/9 Old age, martial arts
Autumn: west, metal,
old age

Centre: earth, Tao
immanent in man

Spring: east, wood,
puberty

8/15 Harvest festival

yang

7/15 Earth, all souls' day

7/7 Puberty

5/5 Summer begins

Summer: south, fire (marriage), adulthood

The balance and harmony of yin and yang are reflected in the Chinese view of the rhythmic cycle common to all life. Yang is born at the winter solstice, yin at the summer solstice. These two contrasting elements together form the whole, and are reflected in the seasons, the annual festivals and the life-cycle of man.

moving elements (*wu-shing*). Sung Hsing and Yin Wen were also leading members of this academy, and their teaching developed theories which came to hold an important place in Taoist thought. The problem of prolonging human life and securing co-operation with natural forces to safeguard life lay behind many Taoist beliefs and practices and resulted in the links with medicine, charity and social well-being which came to the fore in later periods. The leading Taoist writers – Lao-Tzu, Chuang-Tzu and Lieh-Tzu – sought to find an answer to this problem, in particular by their use of the concepts of *Tao* and *Tê*.

Tao

The concept of *Tao* as the fundamental basis of all being developed over a long period. In the *Tao-tê Ching*, the 'Classic Book of the Tao and the Te', (a classic text which served as a bridge between religion and philosophy) there is reference to 'the doorway of the dark female' as the base from which all things sprang (ch. 6). This may refer to an earlier belief in a water spirit or earth goddess who gave birth to all things and received them again at death. From the womb of this goddess there is apparently the passing from non-being to being and then the return of all beings to non-being. Later there arose the concept of a silent and unmoving base from which all existence and

movement spring and to which they will return. Motion is contrasted with objects at rest. (The Chinese delighted in making play with contrasts, for example: 'Everyone under heaven recognizes beauty as beauty and so ugliness is known' (*Tao-tê Ching*, ch. 2).

Since rest is deemed to be prior to movement and serenity to action, pre-eminence is given to the *Yin* element (of Earth, the female, the dark and the lowly). In nature, the valleys are 'nearer to *Tao*' than the hills, since the passive, female element is more open to access to *Tao*, mirrored in stillness. So it is with human action: 'the soft and the weak sit on high' (ch. 76), while the three treasures are 'pity, frugality and a refusal to be foremost of all things under heaven' (ch. 67). Such affirmation of the *yin* over the *yang* (male) element is seen also in the prominence given to water as the highest good: 'it does not scramble but is content with the places that all men disdain' (ch. 8). By taking the lowest place, water is nearest to the *Tao*. Such a view had important implications in the political as well as in the academic sphere and contrasts with the Confucian emphasis on the *yang*, the princely man, the scholar and the administrator taking a prominent part in affairs. For the Taoist thinker, 'the *Tao* (Way) of heaven is not to strive but nonetheless to conquer', and was expressed in civil affairs by non-interference. 'The people are difficult to control because those above them interfere' (ch. 75) and all 'can only be won by letting-alone' (ch. 57). The true scholar does not parade his knowledge but 'the sage wears haircloth on top but carries jade underneath his dress' (ch. 70), hiding his knowledge since 'true wisdom is different from much learning; much learning means little wisdom' (ch. 81). Thus, the Mysterious Female, 'the base from which Heaven and Earth sprang' (ch. 6), was replaced by the concept of the Nameless; the Incommunicable, 'something formless yet complete, that existed before Heaven and Earth . . . dependent on nothing, unchanging . . . the mother of all things under Heaven. Its true name we do not know; *Tao* is the by-name that we give it' (ch. 25). From such a conception there developed a form of quietism which had profound implications in many fields, including warfare, since 'in battle, he (the Taoist) is not touched by weapons of war'.

Tê (Power)

While *Tao* is ineffable, a state of non-action, it is not ineffective. Its efficacy is expressed by the term *Tê* (which Waley translates as 'Power' and others as 'Virtue'). *Tê* appears as a 'function' or force that animates all things in their primal spontaneity – a latent power inherent in all things, unimpeded by man-made impositions. It is also the efficacy acquired by the sage ('man of *Tao*'), who thus directs his stock of *ch'i* (vital energy). *Tê* is also seen as a criterion and guide to a person's inner conduct which is hidden as a precious gift, 'a piece of jade beneath the gown'. The function of *Tê* is seen as the manifestation in actual existence and in individual objects of *Tao*, so 'Tao gave them birth; the 'power' (*Tê*) of *Tao* reared them' (ch. 51). Herein *Tê* makes visible the *Tao*, the unity behind multiple phenomena. Existence means clinging to the *yang* (the light), so the true seeker turns to the *yin* (the dark), as in a saying adapted from Lan Tan in the *Tao-tê Ching*: 'He who knows the male, yet cleaves to what is female, becomes like a ravine, receiving all things under Heaven', since 'he who knows the white, yet cleaves to the black becomes the standard by which all things are tested' (ch. 28). To turn to the *yin* is to seek the dark hidden source of life, to 'return to the state of infancy ... to the Limitless'. The harmonious blending of the *yin* and the *yang* was recognized as necessary but much controversy took place over which 'breath' should have predominance. Eventually, by the end of the fourth century CE, the *yang* principle came to have the preference, but there continued to be two conflicting schools in Chinese medicine, one stressing the importance of the *yin* power and the other that of the *yang*.

TAOISM AND MEDICINE

The relationship between the *yin* and the *yang* in the field of medicine is a part of Taoism's continual search for life-preservation and life-prolongation. The belief that physical immortality, in which the mortal body could be changed into a durable form, was possible stems from beliefs found in the state of Ch'in north-east China which spread to various parts of China by the third century BCE. These beliefs held that as the snake sloughs off its old skin, so humans may do the same and go on to a paradise. In the state of Ch'in, the first emperor, Shih-huang-ti, (221–10 BCE) sought to become an immortal (*hsien*) and gathered many magicians in his court. It was believed that life-prolonging practices were related to the breath, and the *Tao-tê Ching* enquires: 'Can you, when concentrating your breath, make it soft like that of a little child?' (ch. 10). The reference to a child is significant, as the 'power' (*Tê*) is most potent in infancy (ch. 55). The endeavour to prolong life took a variety of forms, some of a directly physical nature, others derived from religion. The former – possibly borrowed in part from Buddhism – were sought by vegetarian diets, medicines, breathing methods and exercises to stimulate 'the finer parts'. The religious approach entailed adherence to commandments, good moral conduct, the use of incantations, amulets and charms.

The physical and the religious were often combined as means were sought by which the body's destructible elements might be replaced by indestructible ones. These could take strange forms: for example, as fire was deemed an essential element, some seekers threw themselves into a fire to ascend to the sky as a flame, which drew the sarcastic comment from the Manchu emperor K'ang Hsi, 'Who ever saw them fly up into the air in broad daylight? Their pretensions are a farce.'

It was believed that the body might be cleansed and made lighter by a diet of lighter materials, such as those which contained jade, cinnabar, gold and certain types of herbs and flowers. Above all, if one could live on air, by inhaling the fresh morning mist and the sun's rays, and combine this with gymnastic exercises, then such air might be stored in the body until one could rise into one of the stellar paradises, ride flying dragons as horses and become like the genii who inhabit the green forests and high mountains. Certain medicines, moreover, were thought to confer on the adept the ability to walk on and beneath the water.

Linked with the desire to prolong life was the desire to become an immortal, which in the third and fourth centuries CE took the form of a search for a wonder-drug, the arcanum, which could transform the body, produce feathers to enable its adepts to fly to heaven, avert disaster and even transform base materials into precious ones. A leading alchemist was Ko Hung (Pao-p'u tzu) who also advocated good works.

TAOISM AND POLITICAL THEORY

The fruits of *Tê* were deemed to be gentleness, frugality and humility, qualities which could take socio-political shape in government policies as non-violence and the avoidance of aggressive wars, a return to the earlier ways of the golden age of pre-history freed from the cultural accretions of later times. Such a doctrine may well appear as weakness – yet *Tao* reveals its strength in that, like water, it yields to the resistant rock yet quietly reduces it to powder: 'the yielding conquers the resistant' (*Tao-tê Ching*, ch. 78). Such a doctrine appealed to the powerless.

The tenets of Taoism came to have particular appeal to lower social groups in Chinese society, in contrast to Confucianism which was a reflection of and support for a feudal state of society and government. In the rural communities which abounded in China there were many religio-political leaders who practised various types of magic to secure the loyalty of their followers. The influence of Mo-tzu and his creed of universal love on the one hand, and the threat of spirits

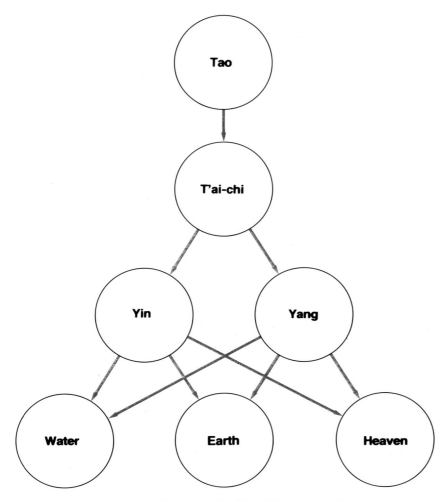

A structural view of the Chinese cosmos from the Tao-tê Ching. *The Tao gives birth to the One:* T'ai-chi *(primordial breath); the One gives birth to the Two: yin and yang; the Two give birth to the Three: watery underworld, earth and heaven; the Three give birth to myriad creatures.*

(good and bad) and demons on the other, led to a doctrine of rhythm in cosmic (including human) affairs. This rhythm was one in which times of disaster were followed by times of universal peace – according to the correlation of *yin* and *yang*. The latter periods of peace and prosperity were known as *T'ai-p'ing* (Universal Peace) and it was the task of religious leaders to use all their magical powers and bring their followers through dangers of fire, water, war and pestilence to reach the happy time of *T'ai-p'ing*. This time was regarded as a form of corporate salvation, in contrast to the individual salvation advocated by the Yang Chu school. Such belief in magical help was evident in contemporary history in the Boxer Rebellion of 1900, in which thousands of Chinese rebels believed that a Taoist charm could prevent harm from any weapon and could turn a bullet on its marksman.

Political protest against feudal society is evident in some descriptions of Taoist paradises. Lieh-tzu describes such an earlier state of bliss: 'This kingdom was without commanders or elders; it simply went on itself. Its people were without desires or cravings; they simply followed their natural instincts' (Lieh-tzu, ch. 2). There is a striking contrast between the Confucian ideal of the 'man of virtue and education' (*Chün-tzu*) who

was trained for tasks of government, and the Taoist 'true man' who was also portrayed as a model prospective administrator but whose aim was not to make a reputation for himself but to show humility and a spirit of 'yieldingness' – to abstain from activity (*wu-wei*). On this basis, the emperor was to refrain from governmental affairs and occupy himelf with meditation, leaving the government to the guidance of an old and wise prime minister. This view came to be endorsed later by Confucianist writers in support of mandarin advisers.

Women were given more place in Taoist sects, which were opposed to the drowning of female infants. Women followers were numerous and some groups also had women leaders, in complete contrast to Chinese society where women lacked status and wives were often the menial domestic servants of their mothers-in-law and husbands.

Some Taoist sects (especially those of the *T'ai-p'ing*) became lively centres of political opposition, bursting into open conflict over grievances, which might arise from maladministration or oppressive taxation or from natural disasters such as floods and famine. Reference has been made to the rebellion of the 'Yellow Turbans' (page 279). Many sects were peaceful, but political opposition to the Manchu dynasty (1644–1911) was strongly supported by Taoist secret societies which after the 1911 revolution had considerable power. In 1949 Mao Tze-tung took steps to exterminate such groups by arresting leaders, and members apostatized.

WRITINGS

The classic text of the *Tao-tê Ching* probably dates from about 240 BCE. Nothing is known of the author, but the work is traditionally ascribed to Lao-tzu, whose birth-date is given as 604 BCE, some fifty years before the birth of Confucius – according to the historian Ssu-ma Ch'ien (first century BCE). The two sages, Lao-tzu and Confucius, are said to have met. When Lao-tzu decided to retire from the world, through the pass of Hsien-ku, the warden of the pass (Yin Hsi) besought him to leave a record of his teachings, and this comprises the eighty-one chapters of the *Tao-tê Ching*. The emperor Ching (156–143 BCE) made the work a classic, and it is extensively quoted by Han Fei (d. 230 BCE) and Huai-nan (d. 122 BCE).

The leading ideas of the *Tao-tê Ching* have been set forth above (from Arthur Waley's translation) in regard to the concepts of the *Tao* (Way) and the *Tê* (Power) (page 282). The classic served as a bridge between the religion and the philosophy of Taoism as well as indicating a transition from one to the other. The brevity of its aphorisms as well as its appeal to the Chinese love of nature have contributed to its wide popularity. Its denunciation of war and its strong ethical tone have also contributed to its influence.

Lieh-Yu-k'ou (known as Lieh-tzu)

This writer appears to have lived shortly before 398 BCE, but his connection with 'The Book of Lieh-tzu' appears to be obscure. The work is divided into eight books and has reminders of or allusions to the *Tao-tê Ching*, as in the passage: 'The source of life is death; but that which produces life never comes to an end. The origin of form is matter; but that which imparts form has no material existence . . . All phenomena [of sound, sight, taste, etc.] are functions of the principle of inaction.' He emphasizes human ignorance and he regards the distinctions of morality as artificial and temporary. 'Death is the boundary-line of virtue.'

Chuang Chou (Chuang-tzu)

Chuang-tzu, the most brilliant of the Taoist writers, was a contemporary of Mencius and his influence was very prominent between 332–295 BCE. He died about 275 BCE. In the records of the Han dynasty fifty-two essays are ascribed to him, but only thirty-three have survived. These are divided into three classes – seven in the inner division, fifteen in the outer, and eleven designated 'miscellaneous'. When in 742 CE his birthplace was renamed Nan-hua by imperial decree, his book was designated *Nan-hua cheng-ching*, the 'True Classic of Nan-hua'.

Chuang-tzu does not give any systematic exposition of Taoism but uses a wealth of anecdote and allegory, in strong contrast to the *Tao-tê Ching* which is practically devoid of anecdote and has only veiled allusions in certain subjects, such as mental abstraction or death. His conception of *Tao* is substantially the same as that found in the *Tao-tê Ching*. He states that: 'Tao has its laws and evidences. It is its own source and root' (Essay 25). He stresses the illusoriness of knowledge based upon sense perception, and urges that there is no essential distinction between right and wrong since paths of approval and disapproval are inextricably confused. His view of the moral life is set forth in his 'two great sanctions' which are expressed as: 'One is the requirement implanted in the nature. The other is the conviction of what is right' (Essay 4). Love of parents is his example of the first; the duty of a minister towards his ruler of the second (Essay 4). The first is seen as 'natural'; the second as 'right'. Apart from love of parents, he deems desire for food and clothing as common to all human beings.

Chuang-tzu agrees with Lao-tzu that man and society have degenerated since the days of the primitive sages, Yao and Shün. He protests against the artificiality of civilization (Essay 9), claiming that the horse was happier unbroken by man and pointing out that the potter destroys the clay and the carpenter interferes with nature in cutting the tree. Government should be by non-interference. The theme of non-interference with the course of nature is developed in that there is seen the control over nature which is found in the *Tao-tê Ching*. He claims that the perfect man may find that 'the wide waters

A silk tapestry depicting the Seven Sages of the Bamboo Grove. These were a group of 3rd-century poets who opted for a life of hedonism and frivolity at the expense of public responsibility.

might boil but he would not feel heat. The great rivers might freeze but he would not be cold . . . storms throw up the ocean without making him afraid . . . he would chariot himself upon the wind . . . roam beyond this earthly sphere . . . where death and life do not affect him'. Since absence of bodily form is followed at birth by breath and life, and followed again by formlessness, he restrained himself, on his wife's death, from lamentation, since death is appointed for all. Vital powers need conservation.

Taoist tracts

Other Taoist writers include Han Fei-tzu who wrote a book of fifty-five chapters, two of which claim to 'explain *Tao*' and others which apparently quote the *Tao-tê Ching*. He died by his own hand in 230 BCE. Huai-nan-tzu, who died in 122 BCE, a more fanciful writer, was closer to Taoist tradition. Much of Chinese hortatory literature came from Buddhist and Taoist sources. Most popular was the tract entitled *Kan-ying-p'ien* (Book of Rewards and Punishments) which was widely distributed in temples. There is much dispute about its date but it apparently reflects Taoist morality of the Sung dynasty (960–1279 CE). In its introduction, the Most High (T'ai-shang) says: 'Woe and weal have no doors but come only at the call of men. As the shadow follows the form, so are good and evil requited.' Heaven and Earth have appointed spirits as ministers of justice who measure out the length of days in men's lives according to the degree of gravity of their crimes. Star deities record men's deeds. The Kitchen-god (Tsao-wang) hands in a report giving details of the family's deeds. A shorter tract, the 'Book of Secret Benefits' (*Yin-chih-wen*), lays particular emphasis on social obligations such as care for orphans and the importance of displaying hospitality and general care to the needy.

ORGANIZATION

The survival of many earlier beliefs of a shamanistic-magical character not far removed from animism served as a base from which later doctrines developed. There do not appear to have been temples and liturgies and forms of public worship until the arrival of Buddhism when practices along these lines apparently developed, hence the claim by Legge that Taoism is 'a degenerate appanage of Buddhism' and that 'it was begotten by Buddhism out of the old Chinese superstitions'. Prior to the arrival of Buddhism, Taoism does seem to be mainly a strange mixture of sacrifices and beliefs in a wide variety of spirits.

In course of time Taoism, like Confucianism, came to deify famous men and to establish other deities of its own such as the three whose large images are found at the entrance of Taoist temples – The three Pure Ones: the Perfect Holy One, the Highest Holy One and the Greatest Holy One. The first of these is P'an Ku, represented as a shaggy dwarf, breaking great rocks with hammer and chisel. The second is Lao-tzu, and the third is Yu Huang Shang-ti who was the most popular and who was identified with a member of the Chang clan deified by a Sung Emperor Hui Tsung in 1116 CE. Other deities, such as the gods of Wealth, Happiness, Official Rank and Old Age, were also prominent among the vast pantheon which developed.

Taoist sects came to have their own emphases. In the region south of the Yangtze, most prominent was the Principal One sect (Chêng-i). This was developed, from the early twelfth century, from the legend which grew around Chang Tao-ling (see page 280), the Master of Heaven, whose dignity and power won increasing imperial recognition. The claims that his sword could kill demons from a distance of thousands of miles and that he had many secret charms whose mystique had been passed on to members of his family gave scope to the claims of large numbers of magicians that he had given them diplomas in the art of magic. These Taoist magicians were sought to provide charms against rain, drought, famine and devils; they also acted as mediums. Unlike the Taoist monks who lived in communities, practising asceticism and meditation, they lived as laymen among the members of their families and were married. Some of the leading magicians were summoned to the imperial court during the T'ang and Sung dynasties to provide help against floods, comets and droughts, receiving generous recognition for their services.

In the north, the Perfecting the True (Chuan-chen) sect was one of the leading groups. It was founded by Ch'iu Ch'ang-ch'un who in 1280 CE was invited by the emperor to live with eight disciples in the Temple of the White Cloud near Peking. This temple later became the centre of their activities. Their teaching sought to promote harmony with nature through tranquillity of mind, simplicity of life and asceticism. The members of the sect were hard workers who produced their own food and sought to be independent of outside help. They were all Taoist priests living in monasteries, followed a vegetarian diet and were celibate. They fasted on certain occasions, abstained from alcohol and tended to combine Confucian and Buddhist with Taoist practices.

There were many other sects; some, such as the Pervading Unity Tao (*I-kuan Tao*) and the

Society of the *Tao* and *Tê* (*Tao-tê she*), were secret. In general, unlike Buddhist priests, Taoist priests are not celibate and do not shave their heads but bind their hair in a knot. Sometimes, it was customary for a Taoist to leave his home to serve in a temple and then return to take up his normal life. Taoist priests may be seen alongside Buddhist ones in homes, particularly in connection with funerals. Some Taoist mediums are sought to assist in the rituals of *feng-shui* (wind and water) based on *yin-yang* dualism. These rituals are used to select graves and the sites of houses and mines.

TAOISM AND CHINA

Taoism in its older, cruder and more superstitious forms will no doubt die out under communism. The last head of the Cheng-i sect, the sixty-third Taoist 'pope' or Celestial Master, left the mainland of China in 1949 and became a refugee with some of his followers in Formosa. The traffic in charms and magic, including exorcism, and 'masses' for the dead, will diminish under the influence of the new training in China, but the influence of Taoism will still be found in many facets of Chinese life.

Taoism served as a bridge to link the outer search for immortality and the emphasis on moral living and 'acts of virtue'. Maspero claimed that while 'Confucianism tended to treat man as no more than a cog in the social machine, it was Taoism that brought a 'new attitude' to China in Han times, namely to practise virtue and avoid sin, to confess and repent of one's faults, to do good works, to nourish the famished and to clothe the naked, to care for the sick, to distribute one's fortune to the poor, and finally to do good in secret – without acclaim'.

As a peculiarly Chinese religion, Taoism expresses the Chinese veneration for nature in all its beauty and the desire for harmony both within man and in his relationships with others on a cosmic scale. Co-operation, toleration and schemes for social well-being were traits that were extolled, while in art Taoism inspired great painters and poets by its imaginative and aesthetic appeal. The struggle for purification and the meditative channels of its quietism were often of a high moral standard and called forth the best in the Chinese character.

It has to be recognized, however, that Taoism has also suffered much persecution, particularly on account of its secret societies, and its leaders have been imprisoned under the present regime. However, there has come a new recognition which enabled the China Taoist Association to be officially founded in Peking on 12 April 1957 when a conference was held, attended by Taoist priests and nuns from all over the country.

A Taoist priest at the Thousand Hills Park, Anshan, North Eastern China. Most of the temples of popular Chinese religion are administered by Taoist priests. They perform a vast array of rituals including exorcism, healing and blessing.

SHINTO

HISTORICAL OUTLINE

Shinto is usually regarded as a religion indigenous to Japan, which helps to distinguish it in particular from the forms of Buddhism practised there. For more than a thousand years Buddhism was the predominant religious influence in the lives of the Japanese people, and it was only in the seventeenth century CE that Shinto re-established itself as the national faith.

There are no reliable historical records before the fourth century CE, but it seems most likely that during the latter part of the first millennium BCE several large clans or tribal groups invaded Japan and, after a long period of fierce and almost continual fighting, drove the aboriginal Ainu people into the most inhospitable regions, themselves settling in three main areas. These were to the south-west on the island of Kyushu; at Izumo on the west side of the main island; and at Yamato situated at the northern end of the inland sea. The invading groups came from the mainland of north-eastern Asia, and from the south-east, bordering on the Pacific Ocean, bringing with them their religious beliefs and practices.

The settlers developed a rich store of legends and myths which became an integral part of their religion. Only gradually were the numerous clans and tribal groups, through warfare and intermarriage, brought under a central control with a supreme ruler to form the Japanese nation. Although tradition claims that Jimmu Tenno, a direct descendant of the sun-goddess Amaterasu, set up his throne as first Emperor of Japan in 660 BCE, it is highly probable that it was not until about the first century CE that the Yamato tribe gained an ascendancy and their overlord was recognized as emperor.

Belief

At the time of the initial invasion of the islands, the invaders' beliefs and worship centred on the powers of nature, for which an elaborate ritual had already developed that was presided over by a shamanistic type of priesthood. The priests were experts in divination by which they ascertained the will of the gods and spirits. There was an almost universal dread of pollution, and a corresponding necessity for ritual purification. This dread was particularly evident when a death occurred: the deceased was buried immediately, and after a period of mourning the whole family cleansed themselves by bathing in water. The home was often abandoned, and a new structure erected. In the case of a chieftain, as with the emperor of later times, this involved the abandonment of the old capital and its entire removal to another place. Their religion also involved an almost fanatical loyalty to the clan chiefs, whose wisdom and martial prowess evidenced their divine status.

By the fourth century CE, the Shinto religion was well established. The belief was inculcated that the islands of Japan were a special creation of the gods, from whom the Emperor and the people were all descended. Hence the name 'Shinto', derived from the Chinese characters *shen dao*, meaning 'the way of the gods'. The Japanese equivalent is *michi-no-kami*, in which the word *kami* is untranslatable: its root meaning is 'above', 'superior', and it refers to everything that is strange, mysterious, incomprehensible, fearful, powerful and worshipful. Consequently, the *kami* were gods, supernatural powers, forces of nature, even exceptionally great, wise and powerful humans. Traditionally in the Shinto pantheon there are some 800 myriads of *kami* – and about 200 are worshipped in Shinto temples and shrines.

THE THREE MAIN TYPES OF SHINTO

Shinto has thus been in existence from the beginning of Japanese history and may be roughly classified into State Shinto (*Kokka Shinto*), Sect Shinto (*Kyoha Shinto*), and Folk Shinto (*Minzoku Shinto*). All three types were

interrelated. It was, however, State Shinto which from the fourth to the twentieth centuries provided, in the person of a divine emperor, a unifying centre for the religious and cultural life of the Japanese nation.

By the fourth and fifth centuries CE, the cultural life of the Japanese had so richly developed that the state religion, although doctrinally weak, had become closely bound up with national traditions and social and political institutions. It possessed its own distinctive type of temple, four orders of priests, and highly developed ceremonial and ritualistic observances. There was a firm belief in the mysterious influence and power of the *kami*, who were dependable and trustworthy. The aim of religion was to co-operate with the *kami*, to live one's life in subservience to their will, to seek their approval and gain their protection. The *kami* had to be invoked, and this involved a trained priesthood. Communication with the *kami* demanded purity of mind without which the blessing invoked would be denied. The Japanese nation was the creation of the *kami*, and human beings were their offspring. Consequently, all humankind is sacred and possessed of a dignity and rights that must be respected. The object of purification, so prominently featured in Shinto rites, is to remove those impurities which stain

an individual's nature in daily contact with the world and with other people. Each person is part of a continuous stream of life which flows on through ancestors and posterity. The individual can make a contribution by living a life of truthfulness and sincerity, one which is in obedience to those superior powers by which all life is governed.

By 1945 there were 218 national and 110,000 local Shinto shrines. But State Shinto was of course based on the total identity of religion and State – and after the Second World War it was abolished.

Sect Shinto became effective only during the nineteenth century, mostly through the charismatic activity of outstanding personalities. For a while these movements were disapproved by the State, and suffered persecution, but they gradually gained official recognition. During the Meiji period (from 1868 onwards) thirteen major sects were approved, were organized into flourishing religious communities, and were systematized, claiming millions of adherents. A representative few of these sects are discussed on pages 292 and 293.

Folk Shinto, which includes simple religious practices performed daily before a domestic shrine, has no normal organizational structure. It is centred on the veneration of gods and spirits

A Shinto house shrine where offerings of food and drink are ritually made at the start of each day. There is no organized structure: Shinto has always seemed indifferent to any systematic order of beliefs. Yet it provides the individual with a vivid, if nebulous, poetic sense of the mystery of life and the universe. This is expressed in the ancient poem: 'Unknown to me who resideth here, tears flow from a sense of unworthiness and gratitude'.

Amaterasu is the supreme goddess, the sun-goddess, who is worshipped in the Imperial Temple of Isé.

which are deemed to be efficacious in promoting harmony and prosperity. In this largely rural and agricultural society, many rites and ceremonies were observed to foster the help and assistance of those *kami* which were responsible for providing good harvests and protection from malevolent forces in nature.

WRITINGS

Early Shinto literature

The strong appeal of Shinto to the imagination and religious faith of the Japanese people is in large measure due to their legends, traditions and myths. Their creation myths and aetiological myths were passed down from generation to generation by oral tradition and were finally written down in two major works: the Kojiki or 'Records of Ancient Events', and the Nihongi or 'Chronicles of Japan', chronicles from earliest times to 697 CE. The Kojiki was compiled by imperial order and completed in 712 CE. The Nihongi, in thirty extant books, was published in 720 and is attributed to Shotoku Daishi; almost all of it is written in Chinese. At that period Chinese was the language of polite society and Chinese culture was influential.

These works were followed by the compilation of the Kogoshui by Hirohari in 807, which is one of the chief literary sources for ancient Shinto mythology. The Engishiki or 'Chronicles of Engi' (because they originated in the Engi period, 901–22) was first published in 927. It is the source of information for Shinto rituals, giving minutely detailed descriptions of Shinto ceremonies. It also includes twenty-seven ritualistic prayers or *norito* to be intoned by priests in solemn services at the shrines.

The creation myths

The importance of these myths to Shinto and to the Japanese people lies in the fact that they explain how the Japanese islands were a special creation of the gods out of primaeval chaos. They are concerned only with Japan and its people (as though the rest of the world were of no conseqence), and they reflect an attitude to nature that is basically animistic.

Out of primeval slime the god Izanagi, 'the male who invites', and Izanami, 'the female who invites', created the islands of Japan and, by their union, a host of other deities. (These two probably represent the Sky Father and Earth Mother so prominent in the myths of other religions.) The last offspring of Izanami was the god called Kagu-Tsuchi, the fiery-heat god, by whose birth his mother was fatally burned and forced to descend into the underworld, the dark land of Yomi. In his grief and loss, Izanagi decided to follow her and bring her back to the upper world, but already decomposition had made her unsightly and she begged him not to look upon her. Nevertheless he did, and in her fury she had him chased out of Yomi and ordered his destruction. He escaped his pursuers by a stratagem: as he came up into the light he sealed off the underworld with a huge rock. Izanagi, now covered with pollution, went down to the ocean to bathe. By his washing the filth from his left eye, the greatest of all the deities, the sun-goddess Amaterasu, was produced. From the washing of his right eye came the moon-god Tsuki-yomi. And from the washing of his nostrils came the storm-god Susu-no-wo.

Much later, Amaterasu looked down from her high abode on the terrible disorder in the Japanese islands ruled over by the storm-god's son. She ordered her grandson Ni-ni-gi to descend and rule on her behalf. From him was descended the first divine-human Emperor Jimmu Tenno who, having unified under his rule the province of Yamato in the central island, gradually brought under his control the whole of Japan. According to Japanese mythology, the Emperor could thus trace his descent from the supreme goddess Amaterasu.

WORSHIP

Shinto is an inherently polytheistic religion. There are gods of thunder, lightning and rain, gods of vegetation and fertility, gods of food, healing and purification, gods of hearth and home. Various attempts have been made to rationalize the colourful myths which have captured the imagination and stirred the religious fervour of the people.

Apart from the elaborate state ceremonies and the religious festivals, the worship consists of simple acts performed by the individual at the shrine or by family groups in the home. Each village has its shrine or temple. Each home has its *kami-dana*, a simple shrine usually in the form of a temple, where offerings are presented daily by the head of the family. Such offerings consist of rice, salt and water, and on special days fruit, *saki* and other foods. The ceremony, attended by all members of the household, is simple, reverent and brief.

In great contrast to domestic Shinto was the highly organized and elaborate State Shinto, which from the first was nationally and politically orientated. At the end of the Second World War State Shinto as such was abolished, however, and only domestic and Sect Shinto were supposed to remain.

The temples and shrines of State Shinto were called *jinja*, meaning literally 'god houses'. Shinto temples are built of unpainted wood to ancient traditional design. They are usually rebuilt every few years, like the great imperial temple at Ise. There is a sacred enclosure, generally rectangular in shape. This is pierced on one side by a central opening at which stands the world-famous gateway or *torii*, from which a shaded path leads to the outer shrine or *haiden*. Here the worshipper – after a ritual washing and cleansing of the mouth, with frequent bowing, at a purification place – claps his hands, rings a bell, kneels reverently, makes his offering, and after a time of prayer quietly retires.

Beyond the *haiden*, and often connected to it by a short passage, lies the *hondon*, the most sacred part of the temple which contains the chief treasure of the shrine, the *shintai* or 'god body'. Although it is usually an object of little intrinsic value – a mirror, a sword, maybe just a pebble – it represents the invisible spiritual presence of the god. At the imperial temple at Ise the *shintai* is a mirror representing the sun-goddess Amaterasu. Only priests are allowed to enter the sacred *hondon*.

The *torii* or *tori-wi*, which have always been a distinguishing feature of Shinto temples, in their simplest form consist of two vertical posts supporting two horizontal ones; symbolically they represent bird-perches. According to Shinto mythology, it was the singing of birds which helped to invoke the return of the sun-goddess when, in her anger at the disorder in the world, she had withdrawn into a deep cavern and thus deprived the world of heat and light. The disorder had been caused by her brother, the storm-god. Originally made of unpainted wood, many of the *torii* in modern Japan are constructed of cement or bronze, and painted black and red. Each main Shinto temple generally

There are many types of shrine, from the Grand Shrine at Isé which has fourteen subsidiary shrines surrounding it, to primitive road-side shrines. Prayers are said at an outer shrine and simple offerings of food, money or even paper are made. The sacred part of the temple contains the shintai, or god body, where the god resides. However a shrine may be dedicated to a mountain or surrounding forest, when a special sanctuary would not be appropriate.

possesses three: the first being the gateway into the sacred enclosure, and the others spaced on the pathway that leads to the *haiden*.

Connected with Shinto worship is the *gohei* (a word of Chinese origin of which the Japanese equivalent is *mitegara*). It is at one and the same time both a symbolic offering, representing clothing offered to the god, and an indication of the presence of the *kami* within the shrine. It consists of an upright wand from which strips of paper hang down on either side, and it stands upon the altar in the temple. Today's worshippers often make offerings of money for which they receive pieces of the *gohei* from the temple to place on the *kami-dana* in the home. They believe that this ensures divine protection and good fortune. One means of purification is to shake the *gohei* over a person.

Down through the centuries, one of the most popular of Shinto gods has been Hachiman, the god of war who is also a protector of human life, a guardian deity and the patron of sailors and shipping. The origin of his worship is unknown; he is not mentioned at all in the Kojiki or the Nihongi. His first shrine was built at Usa, and his cult came into prominence after 720 CE. Almost half the state temples came to be dedicated to him.

Popular, too, among the peasantry in a predominantly agricultural community has been Inari, the god of rice, fertility and food. His shrines are usually painted black, and the pillars and horizontal beams bright red. The fox is regarded as his messenger, and many statues of foxes are accordingly associated with the shrines.

The Shinto priesthood

In ancient times the priesthood consisted of four orders, most priests were married and their office was hereditary. In the state rituals each order had a distinct part to play. Wearing their official priestly garments only when celebrating at the temples and at great religious ceremonies, they were: the Imbe or 'abstainers'; the Nakatomi or 'ritualists'; the Urabe or 'diviners'; and the Sarume or 'musicians'. The Nakatomi formed a hereditary corporation belonging to the imperial clan. They were the experts in ritual, had overall charge of the ceremonies, and read the *norito* or ritual prayers.

The State Shinto rituals

Most solemn and important of the State Shinto rituals was the *Oho-ruhe*, the 'great food offering' which was performed at the accession of a Mikado to the throne. Also twice yearly at the capital was the *Oho-narabi* or 'great purification ritual', when the Mikado proclaimed absolution from sins and impurities. Usually the ritual followed a pattern in which seven major acts were performed with great solemnity and dignity: purification; a request for the *kami* to attend; the presentation of symbolic offerings; the chanting of *norito*; divination to ascertain the will of the *kami*; the withdrawal of the offerings and the request for the *kami* to withdraw; and a sacred communal feast.

THE INFLUENCE AND DECLINE OF BUDDHISM

It was inevitable, when Buddhism became acceptable to the Japanese people and spread rapidly among all sections of the population from the Mikado downwards, becoming a dominant religious influence from the eighth century, that serious attempts should be made to bring about a fusion of the two religions. This was effected mainly by the priests of the Shingon Buddhist sect, the founding of which is attributed to Kobo Daishi (774–855). He taught the principles which led to the formation in the twelfth century of what is called Ryobu Shinto. Highly influenced by Buddhism, in the thirteenth century, due to certain developments it became the dominant form of Shinto. Joint Shinto and Buddhist sanctuaries were served by an amalgamated priesthood, and Buddhist rites were observed in Shinto shrines. The ethical content and spiritual outlook of Shinto were deepened.

But this accommodation was not to last. During the period of the Tokugawa Shogunate (1603–1867) Ryobu Shinto came under fierce attack, and practically disappeared as a system of doctrine and ceremony. Although the Mikado was titular head of the country, and regarded as divine because of his descent from the great goddess Amaterasu, from the twelfth century onwards political power was held by the military rulers (*shoguns*), and from the seventeenth century until the Meiji restoration in 1868 the *de facto* rulers of Japan were of the Tokugawa family. Influenced in particular by the works of three great contemporary scholars, they not only restored Shinto as the national religion of Japan, but proclaimed and emphasized the superiority of the native Japanese religion and also the people of Japan over all other religions and people in the world. And so, right up until the end of the Second World War, State Shinto was vigorously controlled by the government, in effect sometimes acting as the agent of government. It inculcated a system of national ethics, a programme of nationalistic rites and a cult of loyalty to the nation and its rulers, together with the spirit of *bushido*.

SECT SHINTO

In spite of official disapproval and even persecution, a large number of Shinto sects arose and flourished during the nineteenth century as religious ideas, stemming mainly from Buddhism and Christianity, filtered down to affect the lives of the common people. In general, the government found it politic to tolerate these sects, thirteen of which came to be officially recognized, as long as they conformed to the accepted code of beliefs and conduct. They were placed, together with Buddhism and Christianity, under the control of the Board of Education. A brief account of three of these important sects provides a fair indication of their main interests and appeal. They arose generally as a result of the visions, teachings and healing powers of charismatic leaders, saintly men and women of simple piety, often of humble origin.

Kurozumi-Kyo

This sect is named after its founder Kurozumi (1780–1850). In his day he was recognized as a saintly man who inspired others by his simplicity, devotion, moral strength and strict piety; he was known also for his impartial benevolence. Believing that a divine power from Amaterasu had taken possession of him, he taught that Amaterasu is the source of all life and the sustainer of the universe. There is an essential divinity in all life, and one must renounce self and seek for the control of the divine spirit over mind and body. He preached the blessings of cheerfulness, health and gratitude. It was believed that he performed many miracles of healing. In 1876 Kurozumi-Kyo was organized as an independent sect. Its devotional activities include early rising, sun-bathing and deep-breathing exercises, together with simple exercises to promote physical well-being.

Konko-Kyo

The founder of this sect, Kawale-Bunjiro (1814–83), received his teaching by revelation after suffering calamity, sickness and near-death. He was led to believe in One True God, and repudiated all forms of superstition. Thus this sect is farthest removed from traditional beliefs, popular magic and official rituals, and seems to have been influenced by Christianity. An illiterate farmer, Bunjiro lived a frugal life in communion with God and in the service of his fellow men. Two years after his death his teachings were gathered together in 182 precepts which came to be regarded by his followers as sacred scripture. Among his teachings were the beliefs that communion with God should be regarded as spontaneous and natural, and that formal rituals, and reliance on magic, charms and divination are unnecessary.

Tenri-kyo

Tenri-kyo – Heavenly Reason – became the most widespread and enduring of all the modern Shinto sects founded in the nineteenth century. It owes its origin and development to two remarkable women, and within ten years of its founding it had claimed 5 million adherents and 10,000 places of worship staffed by some 60,000 men and women. It remains strongly missionary, engaged in educational and social work.

A peasant woman named Kino (1756–1826) came to believe that she was called to transmit God's final message of salvation for all humankind. She attracted a considerable following which withstood harassment and persecution. After her death her followers organized themselves as monks, nuns and tertiaries. But the actual founding of Tenri-kyo is ascribed to another woman, Miki (1798–1887), who was brought up as a Buddhist of the Jodo sect. In 1838 she had a trance experience which revolutionized her life: she believed herself to be possessed by the spirit of the Lord of Heaven who commanded her to dedicate everything she possessed to the cause of suffering humanity. Mocked, persecuted and imprisoned, her ardent

faith and her powers of healing drew a large following. Her teachings stress the importance of mental and spiritual healing, for the soul of every individual is part of the omnipresent spirit of God. It is each member of the human race that creates his good or evil fate.

SHINTO AND THE MODERN WORLD

As a result of Japan's defeat in the Second World War State Shinto was disestablished, together with government support of shrines. The state rites performed by the emperor on behalf of all his people were henceforth to be private rites for the imperial family – this was written into the Constitution in 1947. The traumatic experiences of the war years led also to a proliferation of new sects, many of them again drawing heavily on Buddhist and Christian ideas, and some incorporating elements of scientific materialism. Nevertheless, an association of Shinto shrines was formed in 1946, to which at present about 80,000 shrines belong; about 1000 shrines remain independent. The number of believers in Shinto is thought to be about 60 million. Tenri-kyo in particular still maintains its appeal and strong missionary fervour.

Leading Shintoists are convinced that the way forward is not by syncretism but by mutual recognition and co-operation between world faiths as a path to harmonious relationships and the furtherance of world peace.

From earliest times there has always been an element of superstition in Shinto, though one sect in particular, the Konko-Kyo, has taught that magic and charms are unnecessary. Here paper fortunes are tied to a tree branch at a shrine. These are 'bad' fortunes which it is hoped will divert the bad luck from the person who has purchased them.

NEW RELIGIOUS MOVEMENTS

IN MODERN WESTERN SOCIETY

HISTORY AND DISTRIBUTION

The term 'new religious movement' is used to refer to a multitude of diverse groups that have appeared in the West since the Second World War. The term itself is a controversial one, for it can be argued with reason that several of the movements are not new, and several are not religious. Other labels that are sometimes applied include 'alternative movements', 'deviant religions' and, most commonly and most pejoratively, 'cults'.

Coming as they do from a wide range of traditions that they interpret and/or elaborate in a great variety of ways, it is impossible to generalize about the beliefs and practices of the new religions. Indeed, the only generalization that can safely be made about the movements is that any generalization about them is almost certain to be false.

Their diversity makes it difficult to describe the movements generically, but an initial distinction can be made between those that are derived from (and in some cases deviate from) the Christian tradition and those that come primarily from an eastern tradition. Amongst the former, one finds the Church of Armageddon (often referred to as the Love Israel Family), the Children of God (later called the Family of Love), the People's Temple, the Way International and, despite its Korean origins, the Unification Church; the latter group includes the Ananda Marga, the Brahma Kumaris, the Divine Light Mission, the Healthy, Happy, Holy Organization, the International Society for Krishna Consciousness (ISKCON), Rajneeshism and Sri Chinmoy from India, and the Soka Gakkai (Nichiren Shoshu), Rissō Kōsei Kai and various Zen Buddhist groups from Japan.

Movements that are sometimes referred to as para-religions, or collectively as the human potential movement, include Arica, EST (Erhard Seminars Training), Exegesis, Synanon, the Science of Creative Intelligence (Transcendental Meditation) and Silva Mind Control. Such groups typically have a closer connection with a particular technique (yoga, meditation, psychoanalysis, encounter group therapy etc) than with a dogmatic theological tradition. Another group of movements (such as the Arcane School, Eckankar and the Emin) falls within an esoteric tradition; and a further group encompasses various forms of satanism, paganism, occultism and witchcraft. It should be stressed however that many of the movements cannot be placed easily in any of these categories, that several can be placed in two or more categories and that some have altered quite markedly over a period of time (one example being the metamorphosis of Dianetics into the Church of Scientology).

Many of the movements were founded in the 1950s or earlier, but it was with the hippy counter-culture at the end of the 1960s that the movements (particularly those in California) began to attract widespread attention. Throughout the 1970s, their numbers increased until now there are estimated to be anything from a few hundreds to tens of thousands of such movements, much depending on how widely the term 'new religion' is defined. It is clear that in terms of membership the numbers have never been very high. Once again, however, definitions are important: 'members' may be fully committed, dedicating their whole lives to their movement (rather like monks or nuns); alternatively, they may be converted to a particular set of beliefs and attend services, but live and work 'outside' (like a member of a more conventional congregation); yet others may be little more than 'clients' who, having attended a course to 'gain enlightenment' or to learn a particular technique, have subsequently had little or no contact with the movement. The number of less committed ('Associate', 'Home Church' or 'congregational') members may reach some tens of thousands in a score or so of the more popular religious movements, and several hundreds of thousands of 'clients' may have had contact with the more popular human potential groups, but scarcely any of the new religions have succeeded in securing the long-term commitment of more than a few hundred full-time followers – many will have attracted only a few dozen. Prominent movements such as ISKCON and the Unification Church have never had as many as 10,000 full-time members in the West at any one time, although, when, one takes into account the high turnover rates which typify such movements, it is possible that 50,000 or so may have been members of each of them for a short period.

Some of the movements are so small that they will have only one address, others will have a few centres spread around a particular country, yet others will set up bases throughout the world in as many countries as they can. Most of the well known movements have had centres (some with no more than a couple of members) in the majority of states in Canada and the USA, in Australia and New Zealand and most of the countries of Western Europe.

California has been a particularly fruitful home for the movements. Some were actually founded there, others migrated from other parts of North America or from the East and, having collected the Californian imprint, spread throughout the rest of the continent and across the Atlantic. It would, however, be wrong to think of Europe merely as a host; it has also produced several indigenous movements.

LEADERS OF THE MOVEMENTS

Most of the movements have a leader who claims the authority of special revelations about, or insights into, or understanding of God (or gods), Holy Scripture, the nature of humanity, society, and the universe. Followers may see their leader in a variety of ways: Meher Baba, Bhagwan Rajneesh, Maharaj Ji (Divine Light Mission) and Haile Selasse (Rastafarianism) have all been honoured as gods; but he (or, occasionally, she) may be accepted as the Messiah (Sun Myung Moon of the Unification Church), as a religious philosopher (L. Ron Hubbard, founder of the Church of Scientology), as a miracle worker (Sai Baba), as a guru (His Divine Grace A. C. Bhaktivedanta Swami Prabhupada of ISKCON), as a Spiritual Master, a Teacher, an Enlightened One, an inspired father-figure – or as any combination of these roles. Most (though by no means all) of the leaders have managed to amass considerable personal wealth as the result of the fees charged for courses or through the fund-raising activities of their followers. One can pay several thousands of pounds for some of the courses on offer at the Church of Scientology's Manor at East Grinstead. Similarly high fees

were paid at the Rajneeshee ranch, Rajneeshpuram, in Oregon, and the Bhagwan's well-publicized fleet of over ninety Rolls Royces was one manifestation of the material advantages that can accrue to such charismatic leaders.

RITUAL

Some of the movements indulge in elaborate rituals, some have scarcely any. Chanting is an important feature for several of the movements, especially those from the East; the mantra chanted hundreds of times each day by members of ISKCON 'Hare Krishna, Hare Krishna, Krishna Krishna, Hare Hare, Hare Rama, Hare Rama, Rama Rama, Hare Hare' is thought to invoke

Six thousand couples, members of the Unification Church, married by their spiritual father Reverend Moon in the Olympic Stadium at Seoul, South Korea in 1982. In some new movements celibacy is practised and at the other extreme the Children of God at one time encouraged female members to employ sexual intercourse as a means of gaining new recruits.

Many of the new religious movements encourage meditation. A personal inner peace or an awareness of the cosmos are sought and some groups may use hallucinogenic drugs or ritual practices in order to heighten their perception. Fasting, quiet concentration or frantic shouting can all be part of a meditational experience. Here members of ISKCON are playing music which may accompany chanting of their mantra: 'Hare Krishna, Hare Krishna, Krishna Krishna, Hare Hare, Hare Rama, Hare Rama, Rama Rama, Hare Hare'.

Lord Krishna in person as well as in the consciousness of the devotee. That chanted by members of the Soka Gakkai (*Nam Myoho Renge Kyo*) not only encompasses the truths of the universe but also, it is believed, brings happiness, health and good fortune to the chanter. Meditation practices range from the stillness and quiet concentration practiced by Transcendental Meditators and the Brahma Kumaris to the frantic shouting and jumping engaged in by the Rajneeshees in the course of their dynamic or *kundalini* meditations.

A few of the movements use hallucinogenic drugs in ritual practices or in order to heighten their perception of either this world or the Beyond; others will indulge in fasting for the purposes of purification or as an exercise in self-denial. ISKCON is just one of the movements which expects its members to be vegetarians; it also demands that the devotees should not take drugs or alcohol, and that they should lead celibate lives except for the procreation of children within marriage. At the opposite extreme, female members of the Children of God are exhorted to become 'flirty fishers' or 'hookers for Jesus' by employing sexual intercourse as a method of gaining funds or new recruits. Baghwan Rajneesh has encouraged his followers to realize themselves through sexual abandonment; more recently, however the spread of sexually transmitted diseases amongst his followers and, in particular, the fear of AIDS has resulted in a more cautious and fastidiously hygienic approach to this particular form of self- and group-expression.

THE MOVEMENTS AND SOCIETY

The attitudes that the movements have towards the wider society again cover a wide spectrum. Some of the movements (such as the Divine Light Mission) are unlikely to espouse any particular political stance; others (such as the Children of God) have taken a revolutionary socialist position; yet others (such as the Unification Church) are fervently anti-communist. The Soka Gakkai is closely associated with Japan's third largest political party.

Wallis (1984) has drawn a distinction between three types of orientation towards the world: he calls movements that are fairly content with (or indifferent to) the existing social order 'world-accommodating' movements. In such movements as Neo-Pentecostalism, the Charismatic Renewal movement, Subud and the Aetherius Society, 'religion is not construed as a primarily social matter; rather it provides solace or stimulation to personal, interior life'. Into Wallis's second category, 'world-affirming' new religions, fall the members of the human potential movement whose beliefs are essentially individualistic: 'the source of suffering, of disability, of unhappiness, lies within oneself rather than in the social structure.' These movements claim that they can help the individual to cope with the world as they find it. The third type, the 'world-rejecting' new religion (ISKCON, the Children of God, the People's Temple and the Unification Church) is, Wallis suggests, much

THE LIFE CYCLE

Life cycle rites form an important part of religious practice, marking out significant stages in life and providing the means for formally incorporating people into religious communities and traditions. Birth is often marked by special ceremonies, such as baptism in Christianity and circumcision in Judaism. Attaining adulthood may be marked by religious rites, such as the giving of the sacred thread in Hinduism, Bar Mitzvah in Judaism, and, for some Christians, the act of confirmation. Marriage is regarded as an essentially religious rite, or even as a sacrament, in some religions (Hinduism, Christianity) but not in others (Buddhism). Great importance is attached to

This sixteenth-century mural in the Bellieu Church at Samakov, Bulgaria, provides a traditional picture of the baptism of Jesus by John in the river Jordan. John's baptism was a sign of repentance; Christian baptism was to take on a wider significance.

death in all religions. In secularized societies the apparent paradox often develops of people who seem to have rejected the practice of a religion still participating in some of its rites. In areas such as Hindu India or the Islamic world, however, social and religious practices are more closely related and are difficult to distinguish from one another.

LEFT An important life cycle rite in Judaism is the Bar Mitzvah ceremony, in which a boy at about the age of thirteen is received fully into the Jewish religious community. Here a Bar Mitzvah boy prays at the Western Wall in Jerusalem. Over his shoulders is the tallith, a fringed garment worn as a scarf or prayer shawl during the synagogue service; it has embroidered corners, from each of which is suspended a tzitzith, a cord of eight threads with five knots. On his head and his arm are tefillin, or phylacteries, small boxes containing a scriptural text.

RIGHT A group of Roman Catholic girls at their first communion in Paris. In the Catholic Church children have usually been confirmed between the ages of six and eight. In Protestant Churches confirmation or reception into full membership has normally been much later, on the assumption that this is a step for adults to take. In recent years, however, there has been much discussion within and between Churches about the respective roles of baptism and confirmation, and most church leaders and theologians would now agree that baptism (whether as an infant or an adult) is the one act of entry into church membership.

LEFT In this ceremony a boy is being initiated into the Parsi faith in Bombay. The Parsis are followers of Zoroaster whose ancestors fled from Iran to settle in the Gujarat and Bombay areas of India. The initiation ceremony, or naojit, takes place, as do all Parsi rituals, in the presence of the sacred fire. After saying a prayer and confessing his faith, the boy is clothed with the sudre, a thin white cotton garment worn next to the skin. Then he is invested with the kusti, a lambswool cord worn around the waist. The naojit is normally performed in the home when the child is between the ages of eight and thirteen. After the ceremony the initiate is considered to be morally responsible for his or her actions.

ABOVE *A member of an African Independent Church is baptized in the sea at Durban, South Africa. The ceremony of Christian baptism symbolizes the washing away of sin and also the idea of 'dying' to a worldly life and 'rising again' to a life lived 'in Christ' (Romans 6). It is also the act by which people are incorporated into the Church. So to the notion of baptism as a token of repentance there have been added ideas of baptismal regeneration and of a rite of entry into the Christian life and the Church. Many new Christian Churches and movements teach the necessity of adult baptism, and do not accept the more traditional practice of infant baptism. In some cases this gives rise to the practice of re-baptizing those baptized as infants, to the dismay of more traditional Churches.*

RIGHT *Initiation takes many forms. Sometimes it is the initiation of a person into a religious group; sometimes the initiation into a priesthood, monastic community or some other permanent leadership role. This picture of the initiation of a young man in a novice monk* (bhikkhu) *ceremony in Rangoon illustrates the second kind of initiation, in which a Buddhist lay person becomes a* bhikkhu. *In Burma and Thailand it is common for a man to become a monk for a limited period, so that the initiation ceremony may not be as final as it looks. In becoming a bhikkhu a Buddhist turns away from preoccupation with the world. This is symbolized by the taking of a bhikkhu's yellow or orange robe in place of ordinary clothes, and by keeping the head shaved as a demonstration of a lack of concern with worldly adornment.*

LEFT This Pakistani Muslim wedding illustrates a mixing of cultures. On the one hand is the Muslim tradition, with the marriage itself based upon the teaching of the Qur'an and the law of Shari'ah. On the other hand are customs which derive from the wider culture of the Indian sub-continent, illustrated here by the garland. The groom wears a mask and crown of flowers which will be removed when the bride is led to meet him. The bridegroom waits with the imam who will conduct the ceremony.

BELOW A Shinto wedding in Japan. Japanese weddings are often the result of arrangements between families, although Christian influence in Japan has increased the incidence of 'love' marriages – that is, marriages arranged directly between bride and groom, usually with parental approval. A Shinto wedding may be performed for non-adherents, including Buddhists. It will be held on an auspicious day, and the priest's role is especially one of purification in a ceremony designed to lead the couple safely through a period of transition.

LEFT Weddings in the USA may take place in a wide variety of settings, in church, at home, or elsewhere. The 'Chapel of Happiness' appears to be an accommodation of religious ideals with the fashions of secular American society geared to life, liberty, and the pursuit of happiness. The tension between religious and secular views of marriage is apparent in much of Western society, where the religious ideal is of a lifelong commitment to one marriage partner and the secular reality includes a high rate of divorce.

LEFT A Hindu wedding in south India. Most marriages in India are still arranged, and as much a matter of concern to the families as to the couple. Dowries are usually given by the bride's family to the bridegroom, in spite of government efforts to discourage the system. Marriage within caste groups remains normal practice, and is one way in which caste is maintained. The marriage ceremony is long and elaborate, with the Brahman priest chanting verses from the Vedas, and the couple processing around the sacred fire. Marriage is the time of greatest ritual purity for a Hindu.

BELOW A Sikh wedding has some features in common with a Hindu wedding, but there are also significant differences. Sikhs have shared the Indian practice of arranged marriages, and the notion that a marriage is at least as much a matter of family, as of individual, concern. Caste is not of religious significance in Sikhism, but marriages do often reflect caste traditions. The ceremomy is simpler, and normally takes place in the gurdwara. Gifts in the form of money are given by those present. Note that in both Hindu and Sikh weddings the bride wears red; white is the colour of mourning.

*The life cycle includes death as well as birth, initiation and
marriage. This unusual scene is of the bodies of Capuchin
monks at Palermo, Italy. The Capuchins are a strict
offshoot of the Franciscan Order, and follow a Rule
established in 1529. They were a powerful force during the
Counter-Reformation. Although cremation is now often
practised by Christians, Roman Catholics tend to prefer
burial; and some burial customs strongly reflect a belief in
the reconstitution of the body in a physical resurrection.*

more recognizably religious than the world-affirming type. It 'expects that the millennium will shortly commence or that the movement will sweep the world, and, when all have become members or when they are in a majority . . . a new world-order will begin, a simpler, more loving, more humane and more spiritual order in which the old evils and mistakes will be eradicated, and utopia will have begun'.

It has often been suggested that those who join new religions are drawn from the disadvantaged classes of society. This may have had some truth in it so far as earlier waves of new religions were concerned, but it would be difficult to describe the membership of the contemporary movements as either socially or materially oppressed. Although the Rastafarian movement is almost entirely composed of working-class blacks, and those who died with Jim Jones in Guyana were predominantly poor blacks, it is, generally speaking, the well-educated and well-to-do middle classes that provide the main source of recruitment for the new religions. Those who become fully committed members have tended to be young adults between the ages of eighteen and twenty-six; those in their thirties and forties are more likely to fall into one of the less demanding categories of membership.

Numerous theories, both complementary and contradictory, have been proffered to explain the rise of the new religions. Some theories might explain the rise of certain types of new religions, but not the emergence of others. It is, for example, difficult to accept that an explanation for the attraction of an authoritarian movement such as ISKCON, which advocates a hard-working, ascetic life devoted to God, would be appropriate to understand the attraction of an antinomian movement such as Rajneeshism, in which members are taught that the only truth is what one feels is the truth, and that the only person whom one ought to consider is oneself.

Some explanations focus on the individual membership, suggesting that it consists of people who, being rather weak, pathetic characters, are particularly susceptible to the hard sell of the movements, or who have some special needs or are seeking a particular set of answers. The more extreme of such explanations tend to 'medicalize' any kind of conversion to an unorthodox faith – or, in some cases, even a conversion to an orthodox religion. Needless to say, the reasons given by the members themselves are more likely to consist of a confession to a religious experience or understanding, or the sudden realization that they were faced with an inescapable truth.

Another set of explanations turns primarily to the social context within which the movements have emerged. Some, for example, point to the

effects of an increasingly industrialized, urbanized, technocratic and secular society in which religious questions and observances are pushed into a small corner of everyday life, in which the materialistic rat-race excludes spiritual values, in which the sense of community is lost and each individual is an alienated or anomic cog in a vast bureaucratic machine, in which rationality, calculability, relativism, impersonality and uncertainty reign supreme. In such a society, these theories argue, the new religions offer the attractions of caring communities in which loving relationships, religious understandings and spiritual values can develop within a context of certain, and usually simple, truths.

Throughout history new religions have been regarded with the utmost suspicion. The present wave offers no exception. Some of the movements are singled out for particular attention: the Unification Church, Scientology, ISKCON, the Children of God and the Rajneeshees are among those most frequently attacked by the media. But all the movements tend to be seen as tarred by the same brush, the sins (real and imagined) of one being visited on all the 'cults'. Common accusations include brainwashing, the use of deception, the breaking up of families, political intrigue, tax-evasion, drug-trafficking, violation of immigration laws, bizarre sexual practices and the exploitation of their membership by power-hungry leaders who live in the lap of luxury as a consequence of the vast wealth they have accumulated.

During the early 1970s, parents and other 'concerned persons' began forming a number of groups that are sometimes referred to generically as the 'anti-cult movement'. These groups disseminated literature warning readers about the dangers of the cults, supplied the media with 'atrocity stories' and engaged in political lob-

This young Rastafarian wears dreadlocks, the long hair that has become the outward sign of his religion. First known in Jamaica before World War II the movement has grown into an expression of many black people's search for identity. It is essentially a movement of peace and withdrawal from the commercial values of the world, of 'Babylon'. This retreat is signified in a desire to remove to the land of Jah, to Ethiopia whose Emperor Haile Selassie (pictured here) is believed to be the Living God. The title of his followers is derived from the Emperor's given name Ras Tafari.

The bodies of some members of the People's Temple at their jungle settlement in Jonestown, Guyana, South America, over nine hundred of whom committed mass suicide, or were murdered, in 1978 on the orders of their leader the Revd Jim Jones.

bying with aims such as the introduction of legislation that would allow members of 'destructive cults' to be placed under 'conservatorship orders'. There also grew up a small group of professional 'deprogrammers' who, for a price sometimes as high as thirty thousand dollars, will forcibly (and illegally) kidnap adult offspring away from movements of which their parents disapprove and keep them under lock and key until they (the deprogrammers) are satisfied that the 'patient' has returned to 'normal functioning'. Sometimes the 'deprogrammee' will renounce his or her faith within a couple of days and express gratitude for having been 'rescued'. Despite claims to the contrary, however, such deprogramming practices, apart from being illegal, are often (perhaps usually) ineffective, and can lead to increased antagonism between the parents and the son or daughter who returns to the movement.

When, in 1978, over 900 members of the People's Temple committed suicide or were murdered on the orders of their leader, the Reverend Jim Jones, there was a marked increase in the attention paid to anti-cult warnings of the danger of the cults. Several reports have been presented to government bodies, including the European Parliament, urging that the activities of the movements should be curtailed but, partly because of technical problems of drafting and partly because of the fears that have been voiced concerning the infringement of religious freedom, very little legislation has actually been

enacted with respect to the new religions *per se*. Furthermore, empirical studies that have been carried out on the movements and their membership suggest that many of the accusations do not stand up to close inspection, are grossly exaggerated, or could be applied equally well to more traditional religions. The fact remains, nonetheless, that small, inward-looking sects whose members believe that they have discovered the One Truth, frequently indulge in what seems to be fanatical behaviour, and this can, under certain circumstances, appear to pose a not inconsiderable threat to conventional society.

As time passes, however, the sectarian tendencies of such movements tend to undergo significant changes. The membership ages and the idealism of youth is frequently replaced by the pragmatism of a middle-age which has responsibilities for a future generation. Moreover, those born into a religion are rarely as committed to a socially deviant set of beliefs or way of life as are those who have themselves converted to the religion. Already it is possible to detect changes in the new religions. Some would seem to be fading away, losing more members than they can replace; others have become more accepting of and acceptable to the wider society. It is possible that those movements which survive until the end of the century will seem neither more nor less exotic or threatening than the Salvation Army, the Seventh-day Adventists or the Church of Latter Day Saints appear today.

NEW RELIGIOUS MOVEMENTS

AMONG PRIMAL PEOPLES

HISTORICAL OUTLINE AND PRESENT-DAY DISTRIBUTION

The expansion of the European peoples into other parts of the world, which began almost 500 years ago, has produced a series of new religious movements among primal or tribal peoples which, on the whole, are neither widely known nor appreciated.

These movements have taken many forms and a variety of names has been used to try to classify them: prophet, messianic, millennial and cargo cults; nativistic, acculturation and revitalization movements; and, most often in Africa, Independent Churches. Recently the term PRINERMS (Primal New Religious Movements) has been coined to cover the whole field. Such movements are worldwide, numerically significant, and expanding. It is estimated that in Africa alone there are around 10,000 distinct movements with perhaps as many as 20 million adherents in total.

In spite of their huge diversity, these movements have many things in common – principally the way in which they originated. They have arisen specifically from the interaction of a powerful, universal religion (usually Christianity) with a local, primal or tribal religion. In some cases, such interaction produces neither outright acceptance nor rejection of the incoming religion, but the emergence of a new synthesistic movement containing elements of both the old and the new.

The earliest recorded of these movements began in Guatemala in 1530, soon after the arrival of the Spanish; today, new movements are springing up, it sometimes seems, almost every day.

BELIEFS

Such is the variety of these movements that it is impossible to reduce their beliefs to anything approaching a single system. Their significant characteristic is the synthesis of the old and the new, but the proportion in which these are present varies greatly. This variety has led to a number of attempts to draw up a typology of such movements. One recent and widely accepted typology is that of Harold W. Turner, who attempts to place new religious movements among primal peoples on a spectrum, with the old primal religions at one end, and the new universal religion at the other. Within this spectrum Turner distinguishes four main types:

THE VARIOUS INTERACTIONS BETWEEN CHRISTIANITY AND THE TRIBAL RELIGIONS

ACCORDING TO THE TYPOLOGY OF HAROLD W TURNER

LOCAL RELIGION (PRIMAL OR TRIBAL)	NEO-PRIMAL MOVEMENTS ← INTENTION	SYNTHESIST MOVEMENTS ← → INTENTION	HEBRAIST MOVEMENTS → INTENTION	INDEPENDENT CHURCHES → INTENTION	INCOMING UNIVERSAL RELIGION (USUALLY WESTERN CHRISTIANITY)

Fasting, dancing and drug-taking may all play a part in the religious lives of primal societies. In many cases these lead to experiences of ecstatic possession as here at a service of the Brotherhood of the Cross and Star at Mill Hill, London.

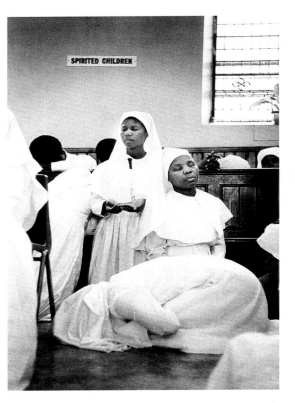

1 *Neo-primal* movements, concerned principally to remodel or revitalize traditional religion

2 *Synthesist* movements, seeking to create a new religious synthesis by drawing on both the old and the new traditions

3 *Hebraist* movements, heavily influenced by the Bible, particularly the Old Testament, but often giving a very limited place to Jesus Christ in their theology, and seeing themselves as the 'new people of God'

4 *Independent Churches*, substantially accepting the traditional teaching of Christianity and giving a central place to the Bible, Jesus Christ and the Holy Spirit, but attempting to interpret these teachings in a way which would be more relevant and meaningful to indigenous converts. Often such groups are led by highly charismatic figures who may be seen by their followers as prophets or even new Messiahs.

Briefly, one or two examples of general groups and particular movements fitting each of Turner's strata might be cited.

Neo-primal Many of the cargo cults of Melanesia could well feature in this category, as could many Native American movements, such as the Ghost Dance.

Synthesist Movements in this category can most readily be seen in Central and South America and the Caribbean where there is often a complex mixture of traditional beliefs, Western Christianity and African religion. Vodou

(voodoo) in Haiti is perhaps the best known example of this type. In North America, the Native American Church (sometimes known as the Peyote cult) could also be included.

Hebraist The Rastafarians of Jamaica might well fall into this category with their emphasis on Jah, and their belief in themselves as the true Israelites. However, there are less well known movements of this type, such as the Israelites of the New Universal Covenant in Peru, who celebrate the Passover, offer blood sacrifices and believe that the New Jerusalem will be in Peru.

Independent Churches In this group could be included many of the African Independent Churches, such as the Kimbanguist Church in Zaire, the Harrist Church in the Ivory Coast, and the Zion Christian Church in South Africa. But similar movements exist also in other parts of the world, such as the Christian Fellowship Church in the Solomon Islands.

ORGANIZATION

In size, such movements can vary from one worshipping group of a few individuals to large denominations with hundreds of thousands of members. The largest such movement is probably the Kimbanguist Church (l'Eglise de Jésus-Christ sur la Terre par le Prophète Simon Kimbangu), to which as many as 3,500,000 people may be affiliated in Zaire alone.

Again, while most PRINERMS remain essentially local, some have become international movements. The Church of the Lord (Aladura) operates not only in Nigeria, where it was founded in 1930, but in several other West African countries as well as in Britain, where it has been carried by Nigerian immigrants; the Iglesia ni Cristo from the Philippines claims members in more than twenty countries worldwide as well as in at least twenty states of the USA. Using Turner's spectrum it is possible to argue that the further removed a movement is from the primal, indigenous end and the nearer it approaches the new, incursive end of the spectrum, the more likely it is to spread beyond the immediate area in which it started.

Ecclesiastically, many new movements are centred upon a powerful, charismatic prophet-founder. Often such leaders feel the call to begin their movements as the result of a serious illness followed by a trance or vision; some even claim to have visited heaven and to have received a special commission from God. Such a pattern endows the leader with very great authority within the movement, which often thereafter adopts authoritarian and hierarchical patterns of leadership, commonly involving impressive titles and elaborate ecclesiastical vestments. These should not be seen primarily as imitations of western church patterns, but rather as attempts to express seriously and formally the claims which the movement is making for itself.

One further interesting organizational point is the number of women and young men who occupy positions of leadership in many PRINERMS. This can often be contrasted with the lack of such groups in leadership positions in many 'mainline' Churches.

WORSHIP

Several common features stand out from the otherwise amazing diversity of forms of worship in new religious movements. These include vitality, movement and colour; a frequent emphasis on the Spirit, and on healing; the use of indigenous music; and the mixing of traditional and Christian imagery and symbolism.

Traditional elements

Almost by definition most PRINERMS include some traditional elements, both in worship and belief. Sometimes, as in the neo-primal movements, the traditional element is uppermost, but it is often distinctly present in Independent Churches as well. The amaNazaretha – a Zulu independent Church founded by Isaiah Shembe in 1911 – has its own holy city and holy mountain (Ekuphakameni and Nhlangakazi) and its own special Zulu festivals; held in January and July. Its hymnology, although basically Christian, is also distinctly Zulu, containing many of the traditional Zulu names of God. Such traditional elements can be seen in many PRINERMS, especially in their hymns and prayers.

Liturgical practice

This varies greatly according to the self-understanding of the movement in relation to Christianity. For those who see themselves as Christians, the basic form of worship usually bears some resemblance to Western Christian worship, including hymns, prayers, a sermon, and quite often the sacraments of baptism and the eucharist. Frequently, baptism is by total immersion and is seen as the central sacrament; sometimes the eucharist is relegated to a comparatively minor role, or even omitted entirely. Occasionally, new sacraments may even be introduced. Elaborate vestments are a part of the ritual of many (although by no means all) Independent Churches, generally embroidered with symbolic patterns of which the cross, the circle, and the Star of David are the most common. Uniforms are quite often worn by the

whole congregation, not merely by the prophet-priest. In movements with a greater traditional element, such as Vodou in Haiti, many other symbols are used, a number of which have magical undertones. Fasting and dancing also play an important part in many PRINERMS.

Worship and drugs

In some movements drugs are used as an integral part of worship. This is not generally the rule, but where it is their use tends to be of central, and even sacramental, significance. In the Native American Church, the peyote cactus (which contains the drug mescaline) is chewed sacramentally during worship to produce a series of trance-like visions. Among Rastafarians the smoking of marijuana ('the holy herb' as they call it) is an integral part of religious ritual. To a lesser extent, the inhaling of the smoke from fires of *impepho* flowers is an important part of the New Year festival of the amaNazaretha.

Healing

In various forms, healing plays a central part in the worship of PRINERMS. Some may be regarded primarily as witch-finding movements, whose main purpose is to locate and remove disruptive social and magical forces within the community. The Mwana Lesa (Son of God) movement in Zambia in the 1920s, led by Tomo Nyirenda, was one such. More normally, healing is seen as an integral part of the salvific power claimed by the movement itself. It is sometimes carried out through prayer and the laying-on of hands during worship; often it involves ceremonies such as dancing, exorcism, and even animal sacrifices. There is generally a strong belief in the communal aspects of sickness and health in many new religious movements, although in practice healing is more ordinarily carried out on behalf of individuals.

A meeting of the Apostolic church in South Africa. Traditional African beliefs, particularly in the power of witchcraft, and in mediums, continue alongside participation in the rituals of the western church. Independent churches of this type are led by highly charismatic figures who may be seen by their followers as prophets or even new Messiahs while still giving central place to the bible, Jesus Christ and the Holy Spirit.

309

LEFT   Sympathetic magic is frequently used in rituals for healing, as here in Gran Canaria. A replica of the affected part of the body may be left at a shrine, or placed there as a thank offering after healing has taken place.

RIGHT   A black revivalist gathering in America. Being 'born again' or saved from sin; speaking in tongues, that is in unknown languages while in a state of inspiration; and trance-like states are all features of Christian-related sects, particularly among people of African descent.

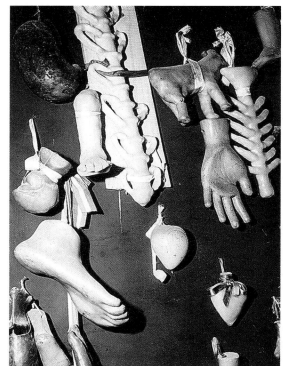

BUILDINGS

The place of buildings in the worship of new religious movements varies considerably. Some have no buildings at all, many others make use of only the simplest mud or wood structures. Often, the site of the place is more important than the buildings – for example, where a movement has its own holy mountain as in the Zulu independent Church of the amaNazaretha. Yet there are many forms of PRINERMS in which buildings do have a special significance. The cargo huts of the Melanesian cargo cults represent a focal point for the coming of the millennium, and sacred tepees form a central part of several Native American movements. Other movements vie with the formal world Churches in the elaborateness and size of their buildings. Many of the chapels of the Iglesia ni Cristo in the Philippines are air-conditioned with plush upholstered seats. The Kimbanguist Church in Zaire has recently erected a cathedral capable of containing 5,000 congregants.

RELATIONS WITH GOVERNMENTS

Many new religious movements among primal peoples first grew up during the colonial period and, indeed, several writers (notably Vittorio Lanternari) would attempt to explain the whole phenomenon as a reaction against colonialism or some related oppression. In any case, PRINERMS in their various manifestations were often regarded by colonial authorities with a high degree of suspicion occasionally bordering on paranoia. This was especially so with regard to movements with a high millenarian content, where the predicted 'end of the age' could be equated with the overthrow of an oppressive colonial government and the setting up of a new age of peace, prosperity and plenty. Such movements were particularly harshly treated and their leaders were generally imprisoned or deported. Elliot Kamwana Chirwa in Malawi and Simon Kimbangu in Zaire are two such examples; the general suspicion with which the cargo cults in Melanesia were regarded is another.

In the immediate post-colonial period, many of the new governments looked back on such movements as examples of proto-nationalism, seeing their leaders – Simon Kimbangu in Zaire, for example, and John Chilembwe in Malawi – as early nationalist heroes.

Today, those movements that are not actively anti-establishment tend to fight shy of direct involvement in politics. One notable exception has been the Iglesia ni Cristo in the Philippines, which for decades gave staunch electoral support to the Marcos regime. Generally speaking, however, such movements tend still to be misunderstood and even persecuted by governments in many parts of the world, despite the fact that many devote their energies to such apolitical activities as mental and physical healing.

WORLD AFFILIATIONS

At first sight, such movements as have been described above might appear to have little interest in, or need for, world affiliations. They are disparate, often highly individualistic, and with teachings specifically matched to the needs of the society amongst which they first arose.

Nevertheless, in the last twenty years, significant groups of these movements have begun both to seek for and to obtain wider ecclesiastical and geographical recognition. Primarily this tendency has occurred at the 'Independent Church' end of Turner's spectrum, among those movements which would regard themselves as Christians. It began first at national level, with the attempt by various independent Churches to gain admittance to local Christian Councils; such attempts were not always successful, but have gradually made progress over the last twenty years. Parallel to this development have been various attempts to create local councils of independent Churches; these have met with varying degrees of success.

At the international level, three developments should be noted. First there is the admittance to the World Council of Churches of a few of the larger African independent Churches. (The first to be so admitted was the Kimbanguist Church in 1969.) Secondly, there was the election of the primate of the Church of the Lord, Aladura, the Revd E. O. A. Adejobi, to a seat on the central committee of the WCC (in 1983). Thirdly, there was the formation in Cairo in 1978 of the Organization of African Independent Churches (now based in Nairobi).

Finally, the increasing cultural fluidity of the modern world and the considerable geographic immigration of primal peoples into Europe and North America since the end of the Second World War have carried several of these new religious movements into different parts of the world. Filipino new religious movements are now active throughout the USA; Rastafarians are to be found in the USA, the UK, South Africa, Zimbabwe and New Zealand; and many African independent Churches have branches in the major UK cities.

The only truly unique feature which gave rise to such movements – the dynamic interaction of primal and universal religious culture – is thus being continued, this time in the rich northern hemisphere, and may well have far-reaching implications and consequences for the development of religion there.

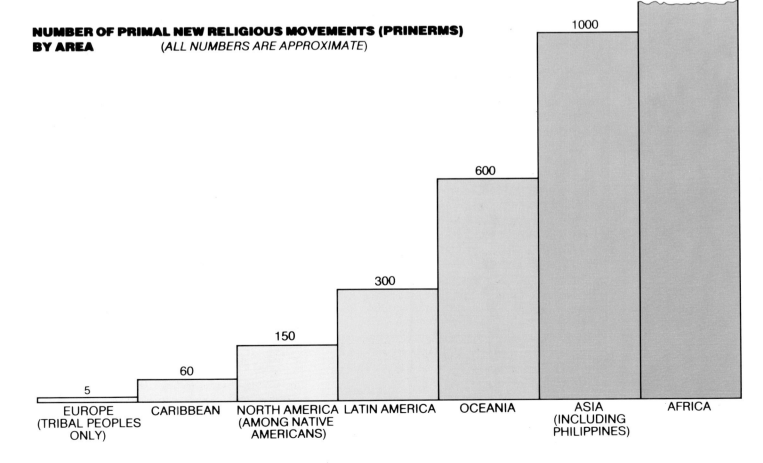

NUMBER OF PRIMAL NEW RELIGIOUS MOVEMENTS (PRINERMS) BY AREA *(ALL NUMBERS ARE APPROXIMATE)*

10,000

1000

600

300

150

60

5

EUROPE (TRIBAL PEOPLES ONLY) · CARIBBEAN · NORTH AMERICA (AMONG NATIVE AMERICANS) · LATIN AMERICA · OCEANIA · ASIA (INCLUDING PHILIPPINES) · AFRICA

CONCLUSION

RELIGION IN THE MODERN WORLD

In the preceding pages the great religious traditions have been dealt with separately, in their particular social and historical contexts. In this final section it will be appropriate to note how religions have become better known to each other in the modern world, how barriers between them have begun to break down, and how increasingly, as a result of closer contact, ideas are being shared. Greater contact between believers in different religious traditions has sometimes led to conflict; but it has also encouraged a convergence of religious thinking which is one feature of religion in the modern world.

THE MEETING OF EAST AND WEST

An appropriate starting point for the examination of this process is nineteenth-century India, where the British Raj was strengthening its political and economic control of the sub-continent, and where as a result two sets of influences were meeting and beginning to act upon each other. The influences can be variously described. They were on the one hand western and on the other hand eastern. They were on the one hand strongly influenced by the scientific and rational ways of thinking which have been an increasingly important part of what is conveyed by the word 'modern', and they were on the other hand still deeply imbued with traditional ways of thinking about the world and human destiny. They were on the one hand nominally Christian, and on the other hand mostly Hindu with a substantial Muslim minority. They were on the one hand capitalist and imperialist in their political and economic outlook and practice, and on the other hand almost feudal in relationships between peasants and landlords and in the exercise of social obligations. The meeting of these two different forces was to produce both baffled incomprehension and a stimulating conflict of ideas, beliefs, and social practices. And on both sides the meeting

was to lead to considerable changes, the final results of which have yet to be seen. The Indian experience provides an example, within a reasonably contained area, of the meeting of cultures and religions that was to be a marked feature of the nineteenth and twentieth centuries.

The Indian intellectual response to British influence was seen first among a small but influential group of Bengalis, who were affected by the modernizing influences of western thought and education, by criticisms of Hindu beliefs and practices which were offered by westerners in general and Christian missionaries in particular, and by the work of the Orientalists (most of them western) who went against the paternalistic western trend by commending Hindu scriptures and philosophy to the West.

At the beginning of the nineteenth century Hindu society was waiting to emerge from a long period of Muslim political dominance in India. There had been periods during the 800-year Muslim ascendancy when Hindus had been severely disadvantaged, especially in the leading urban centres. Hinduism had continued to flourish, especially in the villages where most of India's people are to be found, but the long Muslim hegemony in the sub-continent partly explains the low state of Hindu intellectual life during the late eighteenth and early nineteenth centuries, just when the force of western influence was beginning to be felt most strongly. The common European perception of India as a land permeated by superstition was fed by some of the features of village Hinduism as well as by western (and sometimes also Indian) ignorance of the great philosophical and intellectual traditions which lay behind common practice.

The early Bengali reformers (see Hinduism, pp. 186 to 207) responded to western criticism of Hinduism first by attempting to refine their faith by ridding it of what they believed to be superstitious and corrupt social practices. Ram Mohan Roy, the founder of the Brahmo Samaj, campaigned for reform of the marriage laws and attempted to present a rational and socially aware form of Hinduism not dissimilar to the

CONNECTIONS BETWEEN RELIGIONS

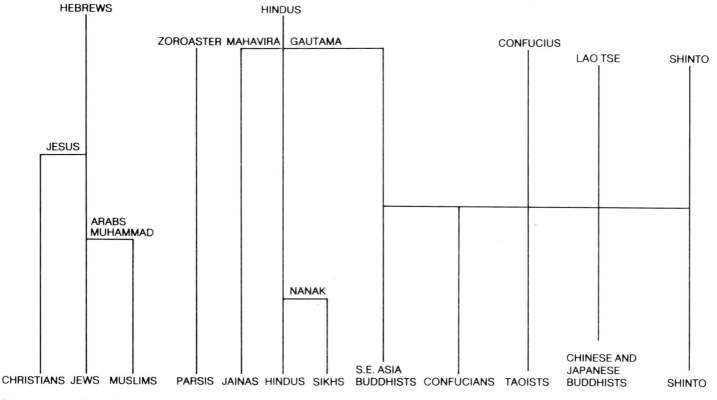

Unitarianism by which he was influenced. He showed great interest in other religions, and had considerable knowledge of Islam and Christianity. Part of his response to Christian influences was the writing of a book, *The Precepts of Jesus: the Guide to Peace and Happiness* which emphasized the ethical teaching of Jesus and seemed to Ram Mohan Roy to outline the area which Christianity and Hinduism could best share with each other. His gesture towards inter-religious co-operation, however, was met by vigorous criticism from Baptist missionaries in Bengal who objected to the presentation of Christianity as a religion of moral striving and humanistic values. For them, what was central to Christian faith – a belief in an objective atonement, appropriated by grace and faith – had been missed entirely from Roy's book. The difficulty of inter-religious dialogue became immediately and acutely apparent.

Ram Mohan Roy, stung by criticism of what he had conceived as an act of friendship towards Christian faith, began to move to a more robust defence of Hinduism. His immediate successor as leader of the Brahmo Samaj was a more traditional Hindu, but Keshab Chandra Sen, who became leader of a branch of the Samaj in 1865, tried quite deliberately to combine elements of Hinduism, Christianity and Islam. He founded 'The Church of the New Dispensation' which he optimistically regarded as the vehicle of a new religion which could bring together the

essential insights of all the world's faiths. The hope was short-lived, and was perhaps an early example of the difficulties of finding a common denominator among the immense variety of the world's religious traditions.

The early Brahmo Samaj reformers had reacted defensively to Christian faith and western influence. From around 1870, for a variety of reasons, the picture began to change, and a number of movements and individuals began to be more openly critical of Christianity and more assertive in their presentation of Hinduism as the equal of Christianity or even its superior.

The reassertion of Hindu teaching was given some stimulus by the beginnings of the Theosophical movement. In its origins a rather curious search by westerners for the powers believed to reside in certain eastern mystics, Theosophy developed into an eclectic movement which stressed the practical value of Hindu and Buddhist teaching about spiritual experience, and was a vehicle for the expression of western admiration for Indian religions. Recruits to the Theosophical Society in India included the Fabian and social reformer Annie Besant, who was critical of Christianity, supportive of Hindu culture, and both active and successful in Indian nationalist politics. Although Annie Besant was outstanding, there were many mature and educated people, Indian as well as western, who were attracted by Theosophy, and not least by its tolerant approach to all faiths.

Annie Besant (1847–1933) was converted to theosophy in 1889 on reading The Secret Doctrine *by Madame Blavatsky. In 1893 she travelled to India and through the Theosophical Society, of which she was a prominent member, helped to awaken an interest in Eastern religions in the West. She adopted Hinduism as her own basic religion.*

European interest in Indian religions developed during the nineteenth century and was by no means confined to such movements as Theosophy. Early European visitors to India were not always indifferent to Hinduism. The seventeenth-century Jesuit Roberto de Nobili, translator of Catholic writings into Tamil and the first European to learn Sanskrit, was a notable example of a missionary who took much trouble to understand and respond to the religious and cultural context in which he presented his message. The first English Protestant missionary to India, William Carey, also laboured to understand Indian languages and culture, and in time became the first professor of Bengali at the College of Fort William, an institution which for some years provided an education in Indian languages, culture and history for recruits to the East India Company's service. The College of Fort William was an important expression of the influence of the 'Orientalists' in British India: that is, those Britishers who themselves sought as complete an understanding as possible of Indian traditions and promulgated knowledge of Indian languages and writings among their fellow-countrymen. Some of these men were government servants and professional teachers; others were missionaries who, in seeking to communicate a Christian message that could be understood in Indian cultural contexts and in Indian languages, developed a profound knowledge of Indian traditions. Almost unconsciously such men became agents of inter-religious contact, some of them no doubt doing more to acquaint Europeans with Indian religious ideas than to propagate Christian notions among Hindus and Muslims.

When, in 1967, a Tamil nationalist government came to power in south India it decided to erect a number of statues of heroes of Tamil culture along the Marina in Madras. Eleven statues grace that long esplanade today, and curiously three of them are not of native-born Tamilians but of Christian missionaries – Dr G. U. Pope and Bishop Caldwell, both English Protestants, and Father Beschi, an Italian Jesuit. All three made major contributions to the development of Tamil language and literature by their translations and by the production of grammars and lexicons. Such work contributed much to inter-religious understanding, even if that were not its original intention. Their work in India was complemented by that of western-based scholars. The first translation into English of the *Bhagavad Gita*, now widely known in the West, was produced by Charles Wilkins in 1785. In the nineteenth century Max Müller made a great contribution to western knowledge of eastern classics with his important series 'The Sacred Books of the East', the first volume of which was published in 1879. Educated people in the West gradually came to have less and less excuse for thinking of Hinduism and Buddhism as simply 'heathen superstition'.

The progress towards sympathetic study of Indian culture by members of the British Raj received a set-back, however, when in 1835 the government decided to replace Persian, the language of government since Mughal times, with English, and to make English the medium of instruction in higher education in India. While this resolved a long debate between Orientalists and Anglicizers, in the longer term it not only encouraged a modernizing and westernizing of Indian education but also discouraged serious study of Indian traditions and perhaps even contributed to the growing racialist attitudes among the British in India during the second half of the nineteenth century. Nevertheless, European interest in the intellectual and practical traditions of Indian religions had been awakened which, despite the insularity of many Britains in India, continued to feed inter-religious and inter-cultural contact.

There was considerable response in India to western interest, and this encouraged among Hindus a growth of confidence, especially in their own traditions. The early phase of the nineteenth-century renaissance of Hinduism had been a matter largely of western-educated Hindus responding to one kind of inter-cultural contact. The later phase, from about 1870, was chiefly a matter of Hindus re-asserting the intrinsic values of their own traditions, and this led eventually to some Hindus proclaiming their faith in the West – and so to another kind of inter-religious contact.

The year that saw the foundation of the Theosophical Society in New York – 1875 – also witnessed the formation of the Arya Samaj in Bombay. The main purpose of the Arya Samaj was to recall Hindus to a purified version of their own faith and to resist the conversion of Hindus to Christianity and Islam. The Arya Samaj has been particularly influential in north-west India where it is still a potent force. But in its early years it was one among a number of expressions of a tendency for Hindus to be more openly critical of other religious traditions and to be more assertive in their presentation of Hinduism as equal, or even superior, to Christianity.

The Theosophical Society expressed a western admiration for things Indian, and the Arya Samaj a determination to resist foreign encroachments into Hindu territory. Another movement which had its beginnings in much the same period not only encouraged the reformulation and re-assertion of Hindu values but also became a Hindu missionary movement to the West. This was the Ramakrishna Mission, which sprang from the life and teaching of a simple Hindu temple priest and mystic, Sri Ramakrishna. Born Gadadhar Chatterji of a simple village family in Bengal, Ramakrishna became a temple priest at Dakshineswar near Calcutta. He had a number of intense spiritual experiences which drew people to his temple to listen to his teaching. Ramakrishna combined fervent devotional religion with a theoretical acceptance of the philosophy of *advaita vedanta*. He stressed the need for personal spiritual experience as the touchstone of true religion, and on the basis of his own spiritual experiences he declared that 'all religions are one'.

At his death in 1886 the leadership of the group that had gathered around Ramakrishna devolved upon Narendra Nath, later to be known as Swami Vivekananda. Vivekananda had had a western education, graduating from the Scottish Church College in Calcutta, and as a student he had attended meetings of the Brahmo Samaj. Attracted to Ramakrishna, he was advised to immerse himself in *advaita vedanta*, which he came to regard as the supreme expression of religion. He also drew from Ramakrishna a sense of the importance of spiritual experience and encouragement to explore further the claim that 'all religions are one'. In 1897 Vivekananda was instrumental in founding the Ramakrishna Mission, which became a most effective agent of social work and religious teaching in India and which also established centres in Europe and the USA for the propagation of Hindu teaching. Swami Vivekananda first visited the West as a delegate to the World Parliament of Religions held at Chicago in 1893, and there he combined a very effective presentation of Hinduism with a criticism of aspects of Christian missionary activity. In the West he claimed that Hinduism (as expressed particularly in *advaita vedanta*) was scientific, being based upon personal experiment and experience, and this he contrasted with religions of revelation which he suggested depended upon the blind acceptance of dogma. He emphasized the doctrinal tolerance of Hinduism, with its acceptance of many paths to the goal of liberation (although on closer examination his teaching suggests that *advaita* is superior to other paths), and contrasted this with the alleged intolerance of Christianity. In India his propagation of Hinduism abroad and his criticism of Christianity brought a delighted response from people who were beginning to emerge from a long period of cultural domination and who were searching for a cultural nationalism to complement political nationalism. Vivekananda encouraged people to think of themselves as the inheritors of a religion and culture which was in many respects superior to Christianity and to a western mode of life dominated, as he claimed, by materialism. His stirring call to his compatriots, 'Up India, and conquer the world with your spirituality', evoked an echo which sounded loudly in the nationalist movement. Abroad, Vivekananda's message, propounded after his early death in 1902 by the Ramakrishna Mission, attracted some notable western converts. It continued the process of inter-religious and inter-cultural contact which was to become a significant part of twentieth-century religious history.

Popularly, little had changed either in East or West. Village Hinduism continued its age-old traditions little affected by western influence or by Bengali intellectuals. Most European and American Christians continued to hold a triumphalist view of Christian mission little touched by the insights of Pope and Caldwell or the translations of Max Müller. But the seeds of change had been sown. By the end of the nineteenth century contact between the major religious traditions was greater than ever before, and knowledge of other people's religions was beginning to be a possibility for more than a rare handful of travellers. In the West, the scholarly study of religion developed in the twentieth century with the slow growth of 'Study of Religions' or 'History of Religions' as subjects offered by universities alongside the more traditional theology. Gradually people began to have the opportunity for serious study of religions other than Christianity and today, after a period of decline in formal adherence to Christian Churches, there are many Europeans and North Americans who know more about other world religions than they do about the Christian religion.

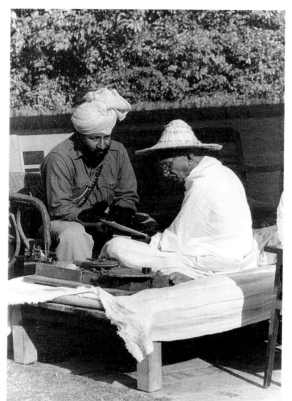

In India, the process of response and reaction to western influences can be traced through the twentieth century. Educated entirely in the West, Sri Aurobindo returned in 1893 to an India he could barely remember and, after a period as a political activist in Bengal, turned to a personal exploration of Hinduism as writer, mystic and guru. His writings include a fascinating integration of Indian and western ideas in his 'integral yoga', and his ideas have been put into practice in the Aurobindo Ashram and in the new town of Auroville at Pondicherry.

In most people's estimation the greatest Hindu of the twentieth century was Mahatma Gandhi, who is an interesting example of eclectic tendencies. In his formative years Gandhi was influenced not only by the Vaishnavism and Jainism of his native Gujarat but also by such Westerners as Tolstoy, Ruskin and Thoreau. He incorporated all these influences into his religious and political life, producing a model of neo-Hinduism in which religious tolerance was commended and conversion criticized but which retained high-caste values in, for example, an emphasis upon vegetarianism, celibacy and non-violence. Gandhi's borrowing from non-Hindu sources has been repaid many times over by people around the world who have received religious and moral inspiration and political guidance from the example of Gandhi's life.

In the twentieth century a number of Westerners have been attracted by the teaching of eastern religions and by the emphasis upon renunciation and personal spiritual experience, seeing in these values an antidote to the technology-dominated consumer society of the West (now increasingly found and zealously sought in the East as well, of course). A notable example of this tendency is Bede Griffiths, whose book *The Marriage of East and West* suggested that India could help the West recover the gentle, tolerant and female side of its corporate life which he believes has been overlaid with aggressive, assertive and masculine qualities. Yet the East continues to be influenced by the West, not least in an experience of political, social and economic development in which traditional cyclical views of history are being gradually superseded by linear views of progress.

THE ECUMENICAL MOVEMENT

For Christians, the nineteenth century had been the great century of mission. Missionary activity from Europe had accompanied or quickly followed voyages of discovery and trade from the sixteenth century onwards. The Society of Jesus, founded by Ignatius Loyola in 1534 and approved by Pope Paul III in 1540, provided the Roman Catholic Church with a body of dedicated men who were willing to go anywhere to proclaim the Catholic faith, and the Jesuits produced such able and imaginative sixteenth- and seventeenth-century missionaries as Matteo Ricci and Roberto de Nobili. But the nineteenth century saw a sudden and dramatic increase in missionary activity from Europe and North America. Many Protestant missionary societies were founded in the last decade of the eighteenth century: that of the English Baptists in 1792; the London Missionary Society (largely Congregational) in 1795; the Church Missionary Society (of the Church of England) in 1799. The Wesleyan Methodist Missionary Society was formed in 1813, although British Methodists date the inception of their overseas missionary activity from the visit of Thomas Coke to Antigua in 1786.

Following the establishment of Spanish and Portuguese overseas empires the Roman Catholic Church had expanded to take a dominant role in the religious life of central and southern America from the sixteenth century onwards. In the nineteenth century it was largely from the English-speaking world that missions spread across the globe, and only towards the end of that century was it accurate to speak of Christianity as a world-wide faith. For European and

North American Protestants the nineteenth century was a period of great confidence, fed not only by the religious certainty of the evangelicals but also by the success of western technology and the political and economic expansion which accompanied the burgeoning industrial revolution. Success in other areas encouraged the expectation of success in missionary enterprise. And even the ideas of evolution which were to become so dominant in the last quarter of the nineteenth century, and which appeared to threaten much current Christian thinking, supported the assumption that the progress of the Church, like the progress of everything emanating from the West, was certain and inevitable. This confidence was rewarded by a degree of success. By the end of the century the Church was planted in most countries of the world. But the expectation that Christianity would displace the other great world religions was not fulfilled, and that fact was to be significant in later Christian reassessments of 'mission'.

If the nineteenth century was the great century of mission, the most distinctive feature of twentieth-century church history has been ecumenism. The Ecumenical Movement (from the Greek word *oikumene*, or world-wide) was concerned to bring the many branches of the Church together in closer co-operation and, some hoped, in the unity of one Church.

The two themes of mission and unity were brought together at a conference held in Edinburgh in 1910. The Edinburgh gathering was called the World Missionary Conference, and its stated intention was to consider missionary problems in relation to 'the non-Christian world'. Among the declarations of the Conference was the aim 'to win the world for Christ in this generation', a sentiment which reflected the confidence and optimism of nineteenth-century Christianity and the expectation that Christianity would supplant other religions if only it were to be presented clearly and comprehensively in all the countries of the world. But it is a reflection of changing patterns both in Christianity and in the world's religious history that the lasting significance of the Edinburgh Conference did not have to do with missionary expansion but with the beginnings of the ecumenical movement. The Christian Churches did continue to expand both numerically and geographically as the twentieth century progressed, more than compensating for decline in Europe by growth in Africa and Asia. But the nineteenth-century optimism of European and American Churches which assumed that their faith would be accepted by the majority of the world's inhabitants was seen increasingly to be an ideal unlikely to be fulfilled, and the evangelical motive came to be overlaid more and more by a

desire to unite the Churches. Part of the argument for Church unity was that the division of the Church into many different bodies was an obstacle to effective evangelism in many areas where Christianity was a newcomer. But the medium was to become the message. As the twentieth century progressed ecumenism became an end in itself for many Christian leaders, and increasingly a preoccupation of Church assemblies. The Edinburgh Conference marked the end of the nineteenth century approach and the beginning of a different and major concern of twentieth-century Christianity.

A continuation committee was formed to carry forward some of the ideas that had been suggested at he Edinburgh Conference, among the most important of which was the hope of forming an International Missionary Committee as an agent of co-operation between different Churches and missionary societies. It was work towards this end that proved to be the most significant outcome of the Conference, encouraging the development of an impressive series of inter-church bodies, leading to the formation of the World Council of Churches.

The International Missionary Council owed its formation to a meeting held in Geneva in 1920 as a direct result of the Edinburgh Conference, and was formally constituted in October 1921. It brought together leaders of mostly western missionary societies to try to plan their work together, to co-operate where possible, and to avoid unnecessary duplication of effort. Concern about international co-operation after the First World War, a concern which led to the formation of the League of Nations, also encouraged Church leaders to think more seriously about co-operation between Christian Churches around the world. In January 1919 the Holy Synod of the Church of Constantinople (of the Eastern Orthodox Church), inspired by the

The Sixth Assembly of the World Council of Churches, Vancouver, Canada. Revd Elizabeth Lidell with the Archbishop of Canterbury, the Most Revd Robert Runcie and Revd Caroline Patriasina-Torch during the celebration of the Lima Liturgy.

THE WORLD COUNCIL OF CHURCHES

EDINBURGH, 1910

CONTINUATION COMMITTEE

INTERNATIONAL MISSIONARY COMMITTEE 1921

LIFE AND WORK 1925

FAITH AND ORDER 1927

WORLD COUNCIL OF CHURCHES 1948

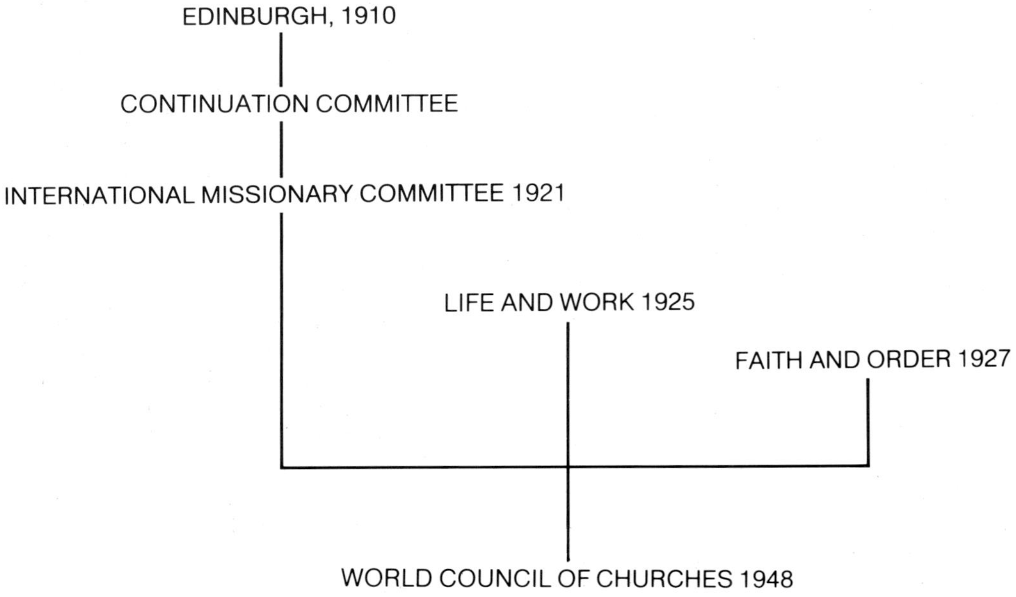

plans to form the League of Nations, decided to invite other Churches 'to consider seriously the matter of union of the different Christian Churches' and suggested the ultimate aim of 'the union of all Churches in Christian love'.

Initiatives in forming ecumenical bodies in this period came mostly from western, and especially European, Protestants however. Independently of the Constantinople suggestion but also inspired by secular progress towards international co-operation, the American J. H. Oldham, who had been secretary of the Edinburgh Conference, suggested the formation of a 'League of Churches'. Although that proposal was not immediately taken up, it formed part of the background to growing desires for interchurch co-operation which led to the formation of the Conference on Life and Work which first met at Stockholm in 1925 under the leadership of Archbishop Söderblom. 'Life and Work' was concerned with the relationship of Christianity to politics, society and economics. It established its own small secretariat for continuing work between conferences, and was one of the movements which eventually led to the formation of the World Council of Churches.

Similarly, a conference on Faith and Order (that is, matters to do with Christian doctrine and ecclesiology), held at Lausanne in 1927, developed into another agency of co-operation and provided another essential element for the work of the future World Council. The three bodies – the International Missionary Council, Life and Work, and Faith and Order – helped to establish both the need for and the initial pattern of the World Council of Churches, the formation of which, agreed before the outbreak of the

Second World War, was delayed by the war until 1948.

The period between 1920 and 1950 saw progress towards the establishment of ecumenical bodies (national councils of Churches as well as the World Council) which were not themselves Churches but which were formed from the official representatives of Churches and which attempted to speak and act on behalf of an increasingly wide range of member Churches. But the same period also witnessed much enthusiasm for a different and perhaps even more significant ecumenism, that is the formation of actual united Churches. The most notable example of this was the formation of the Church of South India in September 1947 from Anglican, Church of Scotland, Congregational, Methodist and Presbyterian Churches in south India together with the Basel Mission, the first union of Anglican and non-episcopal Protestant Churches. Followed in 1970 by the formation of the Church of North India (which also included Baptist Churches), these Indian Churches remain rare examples of this kind of union, although at least thirty united Churches have been formed on a more limited basis.

Among Roman Catholics the movement towards ecumenism was slower to gain impetus, but moved with impressive speed once the appropriate signals were given. The Second Vatican Council, which met between 1962 and 1965, issued an important decree on ecumenism and was responsible for creating a new climate of co-operation and friendliness between Roman Catholics and other Christians. Pope John XXIII had signalled his intention by inviting Orthodox and Protestant observers to be present at the

Council, and he established a Secretariat for Promoting Christian Unity. The Decree on Ecumenism asserted that 'Promoting the restoration of unity among all Christians is one of the chief concerns of the Second Sacred Ecumenical Synod of the Vatican', and the seriousness of that concern was shown by the way in which the Decree proceeded to speak of non-Catholic Christians no longer as apostates but as 'our separated brethren' whose Churches and Communities 'have by no means been deprived of significance and importance in the mystery of salvation'. Thus at least a conditional validity was accorded by Catholics to other Christian Churches. Much progress has been made since Vatican II in co-operation, theological discussion and consideration of ecumenical progress between Catholics and other Christians, one example of which is the work of the Anglican-Roman Catholic International Commission.

The Second Vatican Council was concerned not only with Christian ecumenism but also with a wider ecumenism. The Council issued a Declaration on the Relationship of the Church to Non-Christian Religions, and in May 1964 set up a secretariat for the development of relations with non-Christian religions. A particular concern of the Declaration was the relationship between Christianity and Judaism. Many, both among Christians and Jews, were disappointed that there was no expression of regret or penitence from the Council for anti-Jewish teaching and practices which are a sad part of the history of European Christianity. But there was some satisfaction with the Declaration's rather grudging statement that 'what happened in His [Christ's] passion cannot be blamed upon all the Jews then living, without distinction, nor upon the Jews of today'. On other religions more generally, the Council declared that 'the Catholic Church rejects nothing which is true and holy in these religions. She looks with sincere respect upon those ways of conduct and of life, those rules and teachings which, though differing in many particulars from what she holds and sets forth, nevertheless often reflect a ray of that Truth which enlightens all men'.

The two statements on ecumenism and on 'other religions' were of considerable significance and might be seen as being closely related to each other. In acknowledging the validity of other Christian bodies the Catholic Church was setting aside the tradition which had taught that 'there is no salvation outside the [Catholic] Church', and once that had been done it was a relatively small step further to recognize truth in non-Christian religions. Christian ecumenism and a wider ecumenism between Christianity and other religions may be seen as both part of one process.

Among the mainstream Christian Churches, then, ecumenism has been a major concern in the twentieth century. Probably most Christians, and certainly those involved in and enthusiastic for the ecumenical movement, see ecumenism as a rediscovery of an essential Christian truth. It reflects the belief that the Church is essentially one, and that the local Church should be all the Christian people of a particular place gathered together for worship and service. From this belief it follows that institutionalized divisions between Churches are a scandal and a denial of the Christian proclamation. Others – and there are critics of the ecumenical movement within and outside the Churches – have seen the desire for unity as an attempt on the part of Churches to huddle together for shelter from the chill winds of secularization now blowing in the West. This, however, may fail to take due account of the fact that the major successes of the movement have occurred so far in parts of the world other than those which have been most affected by secularization.

There is little doubt, however, that ecumenism is running out of steam in the final decades of this century. Anglicanism, in spite of its self-image as a *via-media*, has proved to be a major obstacle to reunion among Protestants. Anglicans now seem to look with increasing hope at the possibility of closer relations with Roman Catholics, although clearly formidable obstacles remain in the way of reunion between the two Churches.

Symbol of the Ecumenical Movement, the cross and the ship. The upright of the cross is at the same time the mast of the ship and the arms form a horizon. The forms surrounding the cross represent the sails and hull of the ship. The sail stands for the active present, the circumference for the world. The strongly-marked rudder is fixed in the centre of the cross. The rudder shows movement and direction towards the new. While this breaks the traditional symmetry it provides the impulse for the movement from the centre of the cross towards the circumference.

A WIDER ECUMENISM

Christian ecumenism has been only one part of a wider ecumenism that has been a notable feature of religion in the twentieth century. And since ecumenical means 'world-wide', it is appropriate to consider relations among religions as an important, indeed the most important, expression of ecumenism in the twentieth century.

Two religions with a long history of contact and conflict are Christianity and Judaism. Sadly, much of the suffering of Jewish people in the Dispersion took place under Christian rulers and among Christian people, and reflected not only hostility to the stranger based upon political and economic factors but also what James Parkes described as 'sustained theological denigration' of Jewish traditions. The Second World War and the appalling events of the Holocaust, in which six million Jews died under Nazi persecution, led some scholars to look afresh at elements in Christian teaching which may have encouraged hostility to Jewish people. This in turn led to institutional responses. Brief mention has

In 1986 a Roman Catholic Pope officially visited a Jewish synagogue. Pope John Paul II condemned persecution and anti-semitism 'at any time and by anyone' during his visit to Rome's central synagogue. Here he embraces Rabbi Elio Toaff.

been made already of the statement of the Second Vatican Council relating to Jewish people and Jewish faith. Protestant Churches, through the World Council of Churches, have made bolder declarations on this issue in a number of statements and publications from the time of the formation of the Council in 1948 onwards. The first Assembly of the World Council called upon all Churches represented there to denounce anti-semitism as irreconcilable with the practice of the Christian faith and a sin against God and man. The appeal was repeated at the Third Assembly in Delhi in 1961. In 1965 the World Council established a sub-department (the Consultation on the Church and the Jewish People) with special responsibility for encouraging dialogue between Christians and Jews. In Britain the Council of Christians and Jews, representative as its name suggests of both communities, accepts a special responsibility to encourage greater understanding, on both sides, between adherents of the two faiths.

Judaism and Christianity have lived for centuries in close proximity to one another. The same was true for centuries of Hinduism and Buddhism, and later of Islam and Hinduism in India, and of Taoism, Confucianism and Mahayana Buddhism in China. In most of these cases contact led at times to conflict, but also to some kinds of convergence: for example, Buddhism developed out of, or in reaction against, Hinduism, but also influenced important developments in Hindu philosophy; Islam and Hinduism often had an uneasy relationship in India, and yet the contact between members of the two communities greatly encouraged the development of certain kinds of Sufism. But it is also the case that for long periods of history major systems have been geographically separated from other great religious traditions and so

have not had to consider with any great urgency the question of how one faith relates to others. Such was the case of Christianity between the eighth and fifteenth centuries, when the 'Christendom' of Europe was largely sealed off from the larger world by the Mediterranean barrier of Islam. Such barriers have gradually been broken down, and in the twentieth century especially closer contact between adherents of different religions has led to growing knowledge and deeper understanding of other people's religious traditions. One example of this process already mentioned was the Hindu reaction to Christian mission in India exemplified in the Ramakrishna Mission. That, as we have seen, led to the establishment of centres in Europe and America where forms of Hinduism were taught and practised; and these were the forerunners of many other groups of Hindu origin (the Hare Krishna movement, for example) which have established themselves successfully in the West and gained western converts.

In the nineteenth century Christian missions often followed the routes of European traders, explorers and conquerors to Africa and Asia, and so were part of a limited movement of population from one part of the world to another. In the twentieth century movements of population have again led to a breaking down of geographical barriers between religions. There are now some seven million Muslims in western Europe, and probably more than a million Muslims in Britain. They include some western converts, but for the most part are the result of population movements from the Middle East, Pakistan and India. However, there has been much Islamic missionary activity in modern times, and this has resulted in significant numbers of conversions to Islam in Africa and in Europe. Sikhs have been notable in modern times for their willingness to migrate from the Punjab, settling in East Africa, many parts of South-East Asia, and New Zealand, Canada and Britain. Their movement has not only been followed by the establishment of Sikh gurdwaras but also in some cases by the establishment of Sikh Missionary Societies to commend the Sikh faith to non-Sikhs. Hindus have moved in considerable numbers, first to parts of South-East Asia and eastern and southern Africa, and in more recent times to Europe. There has also been a growing interest in Buddhism in the West, although that has been more a consequence of the movement of ideas than of the migration of people.

With the end of the colonial period, and the increasing freedom from foreign domination of Buddhist countries, Buddhism began to rediscover its own missionary intentions. A World Fellowship of Buddhists was founded in 1950, and delegates from 129 countries gathered at its

promote mutual understanding through such means as lectures, dialogue and inter-faith services. Sometimes mutual understanding is pursued through occasional gatherings of members and representatives of different faiths, such as the meeting between Christians, Hindus, Buddhists and Muslims at Ajaltoun in the Lebanon in 1970.

Christian response to greater knowledge of religions and increasing contact between adherents of different religions has been notable in two ways. There has been an official ecclesiastical response, as in the declaration of the Second Vatican Council. The success of the Ajaltoun Conference was one of the factors which inspired the World Council of Churches to establish its own 'Sub-unit on Dialogue with People of Living Faiths and Ideologies', and that Sub-unit has produced much valuable material on inter-faith matters and facilitated many useful meetings between representatives of different faiths. In 1978 the British Council of Churches established a Committee for Relations with People of Other Faiths, and that has helped to stimulate discussion of inter-faith matters and to keep before the British Churches the complex questions which arise when religions meet.

The second level of Christian response has been in theological discussion about the nature of Christian claims in relation to other religions. Some, such as Kraemer and Barth, have emphasized the view that the Christian Gospel contains the unique revelation of God to man, and that the teaching of other religions may not only have nothing to offer to those who live by the Gospel, but that such teaching might be positively harmful. Others (such as J. N. Farquhar) have thought of the relationship between Christianity and other religions in much the same way as Christians traditionally have thought of the relationship between Christianity and early Judaism – that is, that Christianity fulfils what has gone before. And at the opposite extreme from Barth and Kraemer, John Hick has propounded a view of Christianity in relation to other religions which appears to suggest that all religions may be regarded as equally, although differently, expressions of devotion and commitment to one God.

There are attitudes in other religions which seem in some respects to be similar to these varied Christian views. The consequences for dialogue of the Islamic claim for the finality of the revelation given through Muhammad and contained in the Qur'an may not appear to be very different from the implications of the views of Kraemer and Barth. And at the other extreme, the position of John Hick may appear to be a Christian version of the attitude to other religions of neo-Hinduism.

The Most Revd Desmond Tutu, Archbishop of Capetown, in 1986 appointed the first black archbishop of the Church of the Province of Southern Africa, and a fierce campaigner against apartheid.

first meeting in Kandy, Sri Lanka. Among the aims of the Fellowship was 'to strive to make known the sublime doctrine of the Buddha, so that its benign spirit of service and sacrifice may pervade the entire world'. A Lanka Dhamma Dhatta Society was founded in the same year with the specific intention of spreading the message of Buddhism in Germany. The idea that a country ravaged by war was in special need of the message of Buddhism no doubt reflected the conviction that Buddhism is particularly a religion of peace, and that there is an urgent need for Buddhist teaching with its emphasis upon the restraint of selfishness and desire, to be shared with the western world. In Burma, a Buddha Sasana Council was established in 1950 to encourage the spread of Buddhism at home and to send missions to other countries; and the Government of Thailand established a Religious Department which has sent Buddhist missionaries to Malaysia, Singapore, India, and Britain.

All this activity has encouraged the wider dissemination of religious ideas, and a breaking down of barriers which for long periods had effectively isolated some religions from contact with others. There have been deliberate attempts to bring together leaders of religious movements and thought. Sometimes this is achieved through organizations such as the World Congress of Faiths, which was founded in 1936 by Sir Francis Younghusband 'to instil a spirit of fellowship among mankind through religion'. Represented in Britain, France, Germany, Belgium, the Netherlands and India, the Congress strives to

Given the nature of religions, with their capacity for varieties of interpretation and expression, it is not surprising that there is no consistent view. But clearly there is now a much greater possibility of openness, and a greater willingness among religious believers to listen seriously to the claims of religions other than their own. This new kind of ecumenism is itself open to different interpretations. It may be seen as the result of the discovery of essential religious truths which override differences and which therefore tend to lead to the conclusion that religions are all essentially about the same kind of thing. Or it may be regarded as another example of that cultural and conceptual relativism which has been a feature of much twentieth-century thought. Whichever view is taken, it remains the case that religions are increasingly able to learn from one another, to be aware of other religious viewpoints, and to be less ready to dismiss what is found in other traditions.

Dialogue between adherents of different religions (and dialogue by its nature has to be between people rather than between 'religions') also enhances our understanding of the fact that religions are not necessarily homogeneous systems. There are great varieties of interpretation and expression within, as well as between, the major religious traditions. A recognition of the pluralism of religious belief and practice in most parts of the world encourages the perceptive observer to note that all religious traditions are themselves in some sense pluralistic.

RELIGION AND THE SECULAR WORLD

In the modern world religions have not only been in contact with one another; they have also faced an even more challenging encounter with secular thought. In the West much that is found in the philosophical traditions since the eighteenth century has been antithetical to religion and this has helped to formulate the secular cast of thought which has come to be commonly accepted, even by religious believers. Allied to this, the development and dissemination of scientific thought (including the popularization of Darwin's theory of evolution) further discouraged ideas of divine intervention. This combination of philosophical and scientific influence buttressed the increasingly secular, materialistic thought which grew in the West with the development of modern technology and which now pervades much of the world.

Yet religion does not inevitably disappear beneath the waves of secularism. In Russia and eastern Europe, where religious belief and practice has been subjected to sustained criticism from official sources, including educational authorities, it has proved to be surprisingly durable, and it may appear that some forms of religion actually become more vigorous in the face of opposition.

In the countries of western Europe, secular influences have had rather different effects on the Churches in different countries, but common to most of them (Ireland and Poland stand out as exceptions) is a trend of declining membership in the mainstream Churches. In recent years, however, there have been signs of growth in extreme evangelical Christian groups, such as Pentecostals, those related to the charismatic movement, and independent house Churches. All these share an emphasis upon personal spiritual experience and vigorous and exuberant worship – the Christian equivalent of Indian *bhakti*, perhaps – and clearly this is an attraction to many who find less satisfaction in more traditional forms of worship. An emphasis on experience and spirituality also appears to be part of the attraction of eastern religions in the West, whether Sufi Islam, Hare Krishna, or Buddhist meditation.

Some similar trends can be seen in the United States, although there secular influences appear to have had less adverse effects on religious institutions, and religious allegiance is more common than in much of western Europe. Churches and religious groups clearly play an important, although unofficial, role in national life. This role has sometimes taken the form of radical political protest made in the name of Christian conviction, as in much of the civil rights movement in the nineteen-sixties. But the American scene is also marked by the alliance of firm and often fundamentalist religious beliefs, joined with strongly nationalistic and right-wing political allegiance.

In the modern Islamic world religion appears to have gained, rather than lost, strength. There has been a resurgence of Islam to match the new economic power and political confidence of many Islamic countries. This has been a very positive influence in modern Islam, although no doubt public attention has focused largely upon the alliance of fanatical forms of Islam with political causes. In cases in which Muslims have migrated to non-Muslim areas, Islamic teaching and religious practice appear to have been important in providing identity and security. What will happen in the Islamic world when more critical modes of thought are applied to the Qur'an and the Shari'ah it is too soon to say; neither can we know to what extent the descendants of migrants will change or adapt by living in secular societies. For the moment, Islam is buoyant, full of life and confidence.

Hinduism and Buddhism show many signs of being able to adapt to changing situations. Buddhism appears to have particular attractions for secularized Westerners, perhaps partly because the essential teaching, of Theravada Buddhism especially, does not appear to demand belief in the supernatural, and also because of the apparent attraction of the emphasis of Zen upon an enlightenment obtained within the ordinary life of the world. But Buddhism has suffered considerable retrenchment in its traditional locations, and has been much weakened by political change and social upheaval in China, Tibet, Vietnam, Laos and Cambodia.

Many observers of early nineteenth-century India believed that Hinduism would disappear beneath the onslaught of western thought and Christian missionary activity, but in many ways Hindu religious traditions have appeared stronger in the twentieth century than they did in the nineteenth. A problem Hinduism has to contend with in India, however, is its connection with the caste system. Most converts from Hinduism to other faiths have been low-caste people among whom there is much dissatisfaction with high-caste Hinduism. Hinduism has not yet found a way of extending its tolerant attitudes towards religious belief to influence its rigid and often oppressive practice with regard to caste.

Historically, religions have demonstrated great capacity to change and adapt, and there is no reason to believe that they will not continue to do so. The great questions to which religion has sought to provide answers (or to which religion has seen itself as the vehicle of revealed answers) have not been answered satisfactorily elsewhere. The ability of science to give people greater control over their environment and to regulate life in hitherto unimagined ways is of profound significance. But the fundamental questions to which religions have always addressed themselves remain: questions about the meaning of time and death; about the possibility of an experience which has the power to connect the individual with a supernatural being or a super-mundane reality; about values which are absolute because they relate to absolute being or to transcendental realities.

In suggesting answers, religions may change and adapt, borrow from and share with one another, and seek common ground from which to address common questions. It is most unlikely that they will simply go away. As vehicles of experience and understanding, religions remain.

Dr Martin Luther King Jr leads a civil rights march in America in 1965. During this time he and many other black Christian ministers were instrumental in bringing about a change in the US government's civil rights policy though he himself did not live to see this come about. He was assassinated in Memphis, Tennessee in 1968.

FURTHER READING

INTRODUCTION: THE NATURE OF RELIGION

Brandon, S. G. F., *Man and His Destiny in the Great Religions*, Manchester (UK) 1962
Cerny, J., *Ancient Egyptian Religion*, London rpntd 1957
Eliade, M., *A History of Religious Ideas*, Vol 1, London 1979
Honko, L., (ed.), *Science and Religion: Studies in Methodology*, The Hague 1984
King, U., 'Historical and Phenomenological Approaches to the Study of Religion: Some major developments and issues under debate since 1950' in F. Whaling (ed.), *Contemporary Approaches to the Study of Religions*, Vol. 1, 'The Humanities', The Hague 1984
Lessa, W. A. and Vogt, E. Z., *Reader in Comparative Religion*, 3rd edn, New York 1972
Noss, J. B., *Man's Religions*, London 1974
Otto, R., *The Idea of the Holy*, Oxford (UK) 1923, London 1959
Ringgren and Ström, *Religions of Mankind Yesterday and Today*, London 1967
Sharpe, E. J., *Understanding Religion*, London 1983
Smart, N., *The Religious Experience of Mankind*, New York 1969, London 1971

JUDAISM

Abrahams, I., Bevan, E. R. and Singer, C., (eds), *The Legacy of Israel*, Oxford (UK) 1927
Buber, M., *Tales of the Hasidim*, New York, 1947
Bulka, R. P., (ed.), *Dimensions of Orthodox Judaism*, New York 1983
Danby, H. (trnsl.), *The Mishnah*, London 1933
Eban, A., *My People The Story of the Jews*, London 1969
Epstein, I., *Judaism*, London 1950
Epstein, I. (ed.), *The Talmud*, (35 vols), trnsl. London 1952
Friedlander, M., *The Jewish Religion*, London 1953
Guttmann, J., *Philosophies of Judaism*, trnsl. D. W. Silverman, Philadelphia 1964
Hertz, J. H., *Authorized Daily Prayer Book with Commentary*, London 1957
The Book of Jewish Thoughts, London 1917
Husik, I., *A History of Medieval Jewish Philosophy*, New York 1958
Jacobs, L., *A Jewish Theology*, London 1973
Principles of the Jewish Faith, London 1964
Joseph, M., *Judaism as Creed and Life*, London 1958
Levy, I., *The Synagogue: Its History and Functions*, London 1964
Maimonides, M., *Guide of the Perplexed*, trnsl. S. Pines, Chicago 1963
Mendes Flohr, P. R. and Reinharz, J., *The Jews in the Modern World*, Oxford 1980
Montefiore, C. G. and Loewe, H., *A Rabbinic Anthology*, London 1938
Raphael, C., *A Feast of History*, London 1972
Roth, C., *The Jewish Contribution to Civilization*, London 1956
A Short History of the Jewish People, London 1957
Roth, L., *Judaism, A Portrait*, London 1960
Scholem, G. G., *Major Trends in Jewish Mysticism*, London 1955
Wouk, H., *This is My God*, London 1973

ZOROASTRIANISM

Boyce, M., *A Persian Stronghold of Zoroastrianism*, Oxford (UK) 1977
Textual Sources for the Study of Zoroastrianism, Manchester (UK) 1984
Zoroastrians, Their Religious Beliefs and Practices, London 1979

Dhalla, M. N., *Zoroastrian Theology*, New York 1914
History of Zoroastrianism, New York 1938
Duchesne-Guillemin, J., *The Hymns of Zarathushtra*, 'Wisdom of the East' series, London 1952
The Western Response to Zoroaster, Oxford (UK) 1958
Hinnells, J. R., *Zoroastrianism and the Parsis*, London 1981
Insler, S., *The Gathas of Zarathushtra*, Leiden 1975
Jackson, A. V. W., *Persia Past and Present* (ch. 23–24), New York 1910
Zoroaster, The Prophet of Ancient Iran, New York, rpntd 1965
Jaeger, W., *Aristotle, Fundamentals of the History of his Development* (2nd edn), Oxford (UK) 1948
Karaka, D. F., *History of the Parsis* (2 vols), London 1884
Modi, J. J., *The Religious Ceremonies and Customs of the Parsis* (2nd edn), Bombay, rpntd 1979
Moulton, J. H., *The Treasure of the Magi, A Study of Modern Zoroastrianism*, Oxford (UK), rpntd 1971
Nanavutty, P., *The Parsis* (2nd edn), New Delhi 1980
Pangborn, C. R., *Zoroastrianism, A Beleagured Faith*, New Delhi 1982
Pavry, J. C., *The Zoroastrian Doctrine of a Future Life From Death to the Individual Judgement*, New York, rpntd 1975
West, M. L., *Early Greek Philosophy and the Orient*, Oxford (UK) 1971
Zaehner, R. C., *The Teachings of the Magi*, London, rpntd 1975

CHRISTIANITY

CHRISTIANITY TO THE ELEVENTH CENTURY

Altaner, B., *Patrology*, London 1960
Barraclough, G., *The Medieval Papacy*, London 1968
Chadwick, H., *The Early Church*, London 1968
Conzelmann, H., *History of Primitive Christianity*, London 1963
Deansley, M., *The Medieval Church* (9th edn), London 1963
Every, G., *The Byzantine Patriarchate (451–1204)*, London 1962
Frend, W. H. C., *The Rise of Christianity*, London 1984
Grant, R. M., *A Short History of the Interpretation of the Bible*, London 1965
Jedin, H., and Dolan, J., *History of the Church*, Vols 1–3, London 1980ff
Kelly, J. N. D., *Early Christian Doctrines*, 5th edn, London 1977
Knowles, D., *Christian Monasticism*, London 1969
Latourette, K., *A History of the Expansion of Christianity*, Vols 1–2, London 1938ff
Maxwell, W. D., *An Outline of Christian Worship, its Development and Forms*, London 1936
McEvedy, C., *The Penguin Atlas of Medieval History*, London 1961
van der Meer, F., and Mohrmann, C., *Atlas of the Early Christian World*, London 1958
Meyendorff, J., *Byzantine Theology*, New York 1974
Richardson, C. C., *The Church through the Centuries*, London 1938
Runciman, S., *The Eastern Schism*, Oxford (UK) 1955
Walker, W., *A History of the Christian Church*, Edinburgh and London, rev. edn 1958
Wand, J. W. C., *A History of the Early Church to AD 500*, London 1975

THE CHURCH OF THE EAST
The Eastern Orthodox Churches
Ware, T., *The Orthodox Church*, Harmondsworth 1963

The Independent Churches of Eastern Christianity
Atiya, A. S., *A History of Eastern Christianity*, New York 1968
Attwater, D., *The Christian Churches of the East* (2 vols), New York, rev. 1948–61

Butler, K. J., *Ancient Coptic Churches of the East* (2 vols), Oxford (UK) 1884
Day, P. D., *Eastern Christian Liturgies*, Shannon 1972
Hardy, E. R., *Christian Egypt*, New York 1952
Ormanian, M., *The Church of Armenia*, London, rev. 1955
Trimingham, J. S., *The Christian Church and Missions in Ethiopia*, London 1950

THE ROMAN CATHOLIC CHURCH

The Code of Canon Law in English Translation, London 1983
Dulles, Avery, *Models of the Church*, Dublin 1976
Guzie, Tad, *The Book of Sacramental Basics*, Ramsey (NJ) 1981
Holmes, J. Derek and Bickers, Bernard W., *A Short History of the Catholic Church*, Tunbridge Wells 1983
McCabe, Herbert, *The Teaching of the Catholic Church*, London 1985
Strange, Roderick, *The Catholic Faith*, Oxford 1986
Walsh, Michael, *An Illustrated History of the Popes*, London 1980

THE REFORMATION

Atkinson, J., *The Great Light*, London 1968
Martin Luther and the Birth of Protestantism, London 1966
Bainton, R. H., *Here I Stand*, London 1955
The Reformation of the 16th Century, London 1956
Chadwick, O., *The Reformation*, London 1964
Cross, Claire, *Church and People 1450–1660. The Triumph of the Laity in the English Church*, London 1976
Dickens, A. G., *The Counter Reformation*, Thames and Hudson 1968
Reformation and Society in 16th Century Europe, London 1967
Elton, G. R., *Reform and Reformation, England 1509–1558*, London 1977
Grimm, H., *The Reformation Era 1500–1650*, New York 1973
Hamilton, K. G., *History of the Moravian Church*, Bethlehem 1967
Hillebrand, J., *The Protestant Reformation*, London 1968
Kidd, B. J., *Documents Illustrative of the Reformation*, Oxford (UK) 1967
Rearden, B., *Religious Thought in the Reformation*, London 1981
Roper, Hugh Trevor, *Religion, the Reformation and Social Change*, London 1967
Rops, H. Daniel, *The Catholic Reformation*, London and New York 1962
Rupp, G., *Patterns of Reformation*, London 1969
Rupp, G., and Drewery, B., *Martin Luther*, London 1970
Schnattschneider, A. W., *Through Five Hundred Years*, Bethlehem 1956
Shawe, H., *Spirit of the Moravian Church*, London 1977
Southern, R. W., *Western Society and the Church in the Middle Ages*, London 1970
Williams, G. H., *The Radical Reformation*, London 1962
Scarisbrick, J. J., *The Reformation and the English People*, Oxford (UK), 1984

The Lutheran Churches
Arnold, D. W. H. and Fry, C. G., *The Way, the Truth, and the Life: An Introduction to Lutheran Christianity*, Grand Rapids 1982
Bergendoff, C., *The Church of the Lutheran Reformation: A Historical Survey of Lutheranism*, St Louis 1967
Bodensiek, J. H. (ed.), *The Encyclopedia of the Lutheran Church* (3 vols), Minneapolis 1965
The Book of Concord: A Handbook of the Evangelical Lutheran Church, Philadelphia 1959
Drummond, A. L., *German Protestantism Since Luther*, London 1951
Elert, W., *The Structure of Lutheranism*, St Louis 1962
Lutheran Directory: Part 1, *Lutheran Churches of the World*; Part 2, *The Lutheran World Federation*, Minneapolis 1964
Murray, R., *A Brief History of the Church of Sweden*, Stockholm 1969

Nelson, E. C. (ed), *The Lutherans in North America*, Philadelphia 1975
Pelikan, J., *From Luther to Kierkegaard*, New York 1950
Reformation of Church and Dogma, London 1983
Reed, L. D., *The Lutheran Liturgy*, Philadelphia 1947
Schlink, E., *The Theology of the Lutheran Confessions*, Philadelphia 1961
Schmid, H., *The Doctrinal Theology of the Evangelical Lutheran Church*, Minneapolis 1961
Vajta, V., *Luther on Worship*, Philadelphia 1958
Wentz, A. R., *A Basic History of Lutheranism in America* rev. edn, Philadelphia 1964

The Calvinist Churches

Henderson, G. D., *Presbyterianism*, Aberdeen 1954
Hunter, A. Mitchell, *The Teaching of Calvin*, London 1950
Maxwell, W. D., *An Outline of Christian Worship*, London 1936
McNeill, J. T., *The History and Character of Calvinism*, London 1954
Parker, T. H. L., *John Calvin: A Biography*, London 1975, Philadelphia 1976
Wendel, F., *Calvin*, London 1950

The Church of England and the Anglican Communion

Bromiley, G. W., *Archbishop and Martyr*, London 1956
The Church of England Year Book (annually)
Dickens, A. G., *The English Reformation*, London 1964
Henson, H. H., *The Church of England*, Cambridge (UK) 1939
Herklots, G. G., *Frontiers of the Church: The Making of the Anglican Communion*, London 1961
Iremonger, F. A., *Life of William Temple*, London 1948
Lloyd, R., *The Church of England 1900–1965*, London 1966
McAdoo, H. R., *The Spirit of Anglicanism. A Survey of Anglican Theological Method in the Seventeenth Century*, London 1965
Moorman, J. R. H., *A History of the Church in England*, London 1953, 1967
Neil, S., *Anglicanism*, London 1965

OTHER PROTESTANT CHURCHES AND CHRISTIAN-RELATED MOVEMENTS

Bacchiocchi, Samuele, *From Sabbath to Sunday: A Historical Investigation into the Rise of Sunday Observance in Early Christianity*, Rome 1977
Barker, Eileen, *The Making of a Moonie: Brainwashing or Choice*, Oxford (UK) 1984
Moonies in Action, Oxford (UK) (in preparation)
Ball, Bryan W., *Origin and History of Seventh-day Adventist Belief*, Cambridge (UK) 1981
Beasley, N., *The Cross and the Crown, The History of Christian Science*, Boston 1952, London 1953
Bloch-Hoell, N., *The Pentecostal Movement*, Oslo and London 1964
Bolam, C. G., Goring, J., Short, H. L., and Thomas, R., *The English Presbyterians from Elizabethan Puritanism to Modern Unitarianism*, London 1968
The Book of Mormon: Another Testament of Jesus Christ, Salt Lake City, rev. 1982
Braden, C. S., *Christian Science Today*, Dallas 1958, London 1959
Bromley, David and Shupe, Anson, *'Moonies' in America*, Beverley Hills 1979
Burleigh, J. H. S., *A Church History of Scotland*, London 1960
Cheyne, A. C., *The Transforming of the Kirk: Victorian Scotland's Religious Revolution*, Edinburgh 1983
Coad, F. R., *A History of the Brethren Movement*, Exeter (UK) 1976
Collier, Richard, *The General Next to God*, London 1965
Cousins, P., *The Brethren*, Exeter (UK) 1982
Coutts, Frederick, *No Discharge in This War*, London 1981
Curnock, N. (ed.), *The Journal of John Wesley* (8 vols), London 1938
Davies, R. E., *Methodism*, Harmondsworth 1963
Davies, R. E., George, A. R., and Rupp, G., *A History of the Methodist Church in Great Britain* Vol. 3, London 1983
Davies, R. E. and Rupp, G. (eds), *A History of the Methodist Church in Great Britain*, vol. 2 1978
Doctrine and Covenants of the Church of Jesus Christ of Latter-day Saints, Salt Lake City, rev. 1982
Fairbank, Jenty, *Booth's Boots*, London 1983
Forrester, D. and Murray, D. (eds), *Studies in the History of Worship in Scotland*, Edinburgh 1983
Gow, H., *The Unitarians*, London 1928
Hollenweger, W. J., *The Pentecostals*, Minneapolis and London 1972
Hinckley, Gordon B., *Truth Restored*, Salt Lake City 1979
History of the Salvation Army, The (6 vols), London 1947–78
Howick, E. K., *History of the Church* Vols I–VII, Salt Lake City 1970

Jones, C. E., *A Guide to the Study of the Pentecostal Movement*, Metuchen, (NJ) 1983
Kenworthy, Leonard S., *Quakerism: A study guide on the Religious Society of Friends*, Dublin (US)
Kew, Clifford, *Closer Communion*, London 1980
The Salvation Army, London 1977
Lofland, John, *Doomsday Cult*, Irvington (US), 2nd edn 1977
McLachlan, H. J., *Socinianism in 17th-Century England*, Oxford (UK) 1951
Moon, Sun Myung, *Divine Principle*, Washington DC 1973
Nicholl, J. T., *Pentecostalism*, New York 1966
Payne, E. A., *The Baptist Union. A Short History*, London 1958
The Fellowship of Believers, London 1952
Punshon, John, *Portrait in Grey: A short history of the Quakers*, London 1984
Slack, Kenneth, *The United Reformed Church*, London 1978
Spalding, Arthur, *Origin and History of Seventh-day Adventists*, Washington DC 1961
Sugden, E. H. (ed.), *The Standard Sermons of John Wesley* (2 vols), London 1956
Telford, J. (ed.), *The Letters of John Wesley* (8 vols), London 1931
Tolbert, R. G., *A History of the Baptists*, Philadelphia 1950
White, B. R., *History of the English Baptists*, London 1983
Wilbur, E. M., *A History of Unitarianism* (2 vols), Cambridge (US) 1946 and 1952
Wright, C., 'The Liberal Christians', *Essays on American Unitarian History*, Boston (US), 1970

ISLAM

Anderson, J. N. D., *Islamic Law in the Modern World*, London 1959
Andrae. Tor, *Mohammed, the Man and his Faith*, London 1936
Arberry, A. J., *Sufism*, London 1950
Brockelmann, Carl, *History of the Islamic Peoples*, London 1949
Coulson, N. J., *A History of Islamic Law*, Edinburgh 1964
Cragg, Kenneth, *Counsels in Contemporary Islam*, Edinburgh 1965
Fakhry, Majid, *A History of Islamic Philosophy*, London 1970
Gätje, Helmut, *The Qur'an and its Exegesis*, trnsl. Alford T. Welch, London 1971
Gibb, H. A. R., *Islam* (first pub. as *Mohammedanism*), London 1949
Holt, Lambton and Lewis (eds), *Cambridge History of Islam* (2 vols), Cambridge (UK) 1970
Ibn Ishaq, *The Life of Muhammad*, trnsl. A. Guillaum, London 1955
Jafri, S. Husain M., *Origins and Early Development of Shi'a Islam*, London 1979
Lings, Martin, *Muhammad*, London 1983
What is Sufism?, London 1975
McCarthy, Richard J. trnsl. *Freedom and Fulfillment*, Boston 1980
Morgan, Kenneth (ed.), *Islam – the Straight Path: Islam interpreted by Muslims*, New York 1958
Padwick, Constance, *Muslim Devotions*, London 1961
Qur'an, translations into English:
Arberry, A. J., *The Koran Interpreted*, London 1955
Dawood, N. J., *The Koran*, Harmondsworth 1956
Pickthall, Marmaduke, *The Meaning of the Glorious Koran*, London 1930
Schacht, Joseph, *An Introduction to Islamic Law*, Oxford (UK) 1964
Schimmel, Annemarie, *Mystical Dimensions of Islam*, Chapel Hill 1975
Smith, Wilfred Cantwell, Islam in Modern History, Princeton 1957
Shorter Encyclopaedia of Islam, Leiden 1953
Tabataba'i, 'Allamah, *Shi'ite Islam*, trnsl. S. H. Nasr, London 1975
Trimingham, J. S., *The Sufi Orders in Islam*, Oxford (UK) 1971
Watt, W. Montgomery, *Bell's Introduction to the Qur'an*, Edinburgh 1970
Islamic Philosophy and Theology (2nd edn.), Edinburgh 1985
Muhammad, Prophet and Statesman, London 1961
Wensinck, A. J., *The Muslim Creed*, Cambridge (UK) 1932

BABISM AND THE BAHA'I FAITH

Browne, E. G. (ed. and trans.), *The Taríkh-i-Jadíd or New History of Mírza 'Alí Muhammad the Báb*, by Mirza Huseyn of Hamadan, Cambridge (UK) 1893
Ferraby, John, *All Things Made New: A Comprehensive Outline of the Baha'i Faith* (rev. edn), London 1975
Nabíl, Muhammad Zarandi, *The Dawnbreakers: Nabíl's Narrative of the Early Days of the Bahá'í Revelation*, trnsl. and ed. by Shoghi Effendi. Wilmete 1932
Nicolas, A. L. M., *Séyyèd Ali Mohammed dit le Bâb*, Paris 1905
Smith, Peter, *The Babi and Baha'i Religions: From Messaianic Shi'ism to a World Religion*, Cambridge (UK) (in preparation)

HINDUISM

Babb, L. A., *The Divine Hierarchy*, New York 1975
Bharati, A., *The Tantric Tradition*, London 1975
Basham, A. L., *The Wonder That Was India*, London 1971
Basham, A. L., entry 'Hinduism, History of', in *Encyclopedia Britannica*, Macropaedia Vol. 8 (pp. 908–20), Chicago 1975
Brockington, J. L., *The Sacred Thread: Hinduism in its Continuity and Diversity*, Edinburgh 1981
Danielou, A., *Hindu Polytheism*, New York 1964
De Bary, W. T. (ed.), *Sources of Indian Tradition*, New York 1958
Eck, D. L., *Benares City of Light*, London 1983
Lannoy, R., *The Speaking Tree: A Study of Indian Culture and Society*, London 1971
Lewis, O., *Village Life in Northern India*, New York 1965
Michell, G., *The Hindu Temple: An Introduction to its Meaning and Form*, London 1977
O'Flaherty, W. D., *Asceticism and Eroticism in the Mythology of Siva*, New York 1973
Hindu Myths: A Sourcebook, Harmondsworth 1975
Parrinder, G., *The Indestructible Soul: The Nature of Man and Life after Death in Indian Thought*, London 1973
Pocock, D. F., *Mind, Body and Wealth. A Study of Belief and Practice in an Indian Village*, Oxford (UK) 1973
Radhakrishnan, S., *The Principal Upanishads*, London 1968
Smart, N., *Doctrine and Argument in Indian Philosophy*, London 1964
Walker, B., *Hindu World: An Encyclopaedic Survey of Hinduism* (2 vols.), London 1968
Williams, R. B., *A New Face of Hinduism: The Swaminarayan Religion*, Cambridge (UK) 1984
Zeahner, R. C., *Hinduism*, London 1962

JAINISM

Hay, S., 'Jain influences on Gandhi's early thought', in Ray, S. (ed.), *Gandhi, India and the World*, Philadelphia 1970 (pp. 29–38)
Jacobi, H., *Jaina Sutras* (2 vols), rpntd. New York 1968
Jain, J. P., *Religion and Culture of the Jains*, New Delhi 1975
Jaini, P. S., *The Jaina Path of Purification*, Berkeley 1979
Nevaskar, B., *Capitalism without Capitalists: The Jains of India and the Quakers of the West*, Westport 1971
Sangave, V. A., *Jaina Community: A Social Survey*, Bombay 1959
Schubring, W., *The Doctrines of the Jainas*, Delhi 1962
Shah, U. P., 'Jainism', in *Encyclopaedia Britannica*, Macropaedia Vol. 10, Chicago, 1975 (pp. 8–14)
Stevenson, M. A., *The Heart of Jainism*, rpntd. New Delhi 1970
Zimmer, H., 'Jainism', in *Philosophies of India* Part III, New York 1951 (pp. 181–279)

BUDDHISM

THE BUDDHA

Carruthers, M. B., *The Buddha*, Oxford 1983
Ling, T., *The Buddha*, Harmondsworth (UK) 1976
Rahula, W., *What the Buddha Taught*, London 1967
Saddhatissa, H., *The Buddha's Way*, London 1971

THERAVADA BUDDHISM

Aronson, H. B., *Love and Sympathy in Theravada Buddhism*, Delhi 1980
Carter, J. R., *Dhamma: Western Academic and Sinhalese Buddhist Interpretations*, Tokyo 1978
Collins, S., *Selfless Persons. Imagery and Thought in Theravada Buddhism*, Cambridge 1982
Conze, E., *A Short History of Buddhism*, London 1980
Jones, John Garrett, *Tales and Teachings of the Buddha*, London 1979
Masson, J., *The Noble Path of Buddhism*, Milton Keynes (UK) 1977
Robinson, R., *The Buddhist Religion*, California 1970
Saddhatissa, H., *Buddhist Ethics*, London 1970
Smith, B. L., *The Two Wheels of Dhamma*, Chambersburg (USA) 1972
Spiro, M., *Buddhism and Society*, London 1971
Tambiah, S. J., *World Conqueror and World Renouncer*, Cambridge 1976

MAHAYANA BUDDHISM

Blofeld, *The Way of Power*, London 1970
Chang, C. C., *A Treasury of Mahayana Sutras*, Pennsylvania 1983
The Hundred Thousands Songs of Milarepa (2 vols), Berkeley and London 1977
Ch'en, K., *Buddhism in China*, Princeton 1964

Collins, S., *Selfless Persons*, Cambridge (UK) 1982
Conze, E., *Buddhist Texts*, Oxford 1954
   Buddhist Thought in India, London 1962
Dasgupta, S. B., *An Introduction to Tantric Buddhism*, Berkeley and London 1974
Evans-Wentz, W. Y., *The Tibetan Book of the Dead*, Oxford (UK) 1969
Fung Yu-Lan, *A History of Chinese Philosophy* (2 vols), Princeton 1952
Govinda, Lama Anagarika, *Foundations of Tibetan Mysticism*, London 1969
Jones, J. Garrett, *Tales and Teachings of the Buddha*, London 1979
Snellgrove, D., *The Hevajra Tantra* (2 vols.), Oxford (UK) 1959
Suzuki, D. T., *Outlines of Mahayana Buddhism*, New York 1963
Trungpa, C., *Cutting Through Spiritual Materialism*, Colorado 1973
Trungpa, C. and Fremantle, F., *The Tibetan Book of the Dead*, Colorado and London 1975
Tucci, G., *The Religions of Tibet*, London 1980
Warder, A. K., *Indian Buddhism*, Delhi 1970

SIKHISM

Cole, W. O., *Sikhism and its Indian Context*, London 1984
Cole, W. O. and Sambhi, P. S., *The Sikhs: Their Religious Beliefs and Practices* (2nd edn.), London 1986
Harbans Singh, *The Heritage of the Sikhs*, Manchar 1985
Khushwant Sing, *A History of the Sikhs* (2 vols), Bombay 1977
McLeod, W. H., *Evolution of the Sikh Community*, Oxford 1976

CONFUCIANISM

Chang, C., *The Development of Neo-Confucian Thought*, New York 1977
Ching, J., *Confucianism and Christianity*, Tokyo and New York 1977
Creel, H. G., *Confucius: The Man and the Myth*, New York 1949
Dawson, R., *Confucius*, Oxford 1981
Hughes, E. R., *Chinese Philosophy in Classical Times*, London 1942
Levenson, J. R., *Confucianism and Its Modern Fate* (3 vols), Berkeley 1964
Shryock, J. K., *The Origin and Development of the State Cult of Confucianism*, New York, rpntd. 1966
Smith, D. H., *Chinese Religions*, London 1968
Smith, D. H., *Confucius*, London 1973
Waley, A., *The Analects of Confucius*, London 1938
Yang, C. K., *Religion in Chinese Society*, Berkeley 1961

TAOISM

Bonsall, B. S., *Confucianism and Taoism*, London 1934
Dore, H., *Researches into Chinese Superstitions*, trnsl. D. J. Finn, Vols I–X 1914–33
Fung Yu-lan, *A History of Chinese Philosophy* (2 vols), trnsl. D. Bodde, Princeton 1953
Giles, L., *Taoist Teachings*, London 1912
Graham, A. C., *The Book of Lieh-tzu*, London 1960
de Groot, J. J. M., *The Religious Systems of China*, Vols I–VI, Leyden 1892–1910
Maspero, H., *Le Taoïsme*, Vol II, Paris 1950
Needham, J., *Science and Civilization in China*, Vol II, Cambridge 1956
Waley, Arthur, *The Way and its Power*, London 1937
Welch, H., *Taoism, The Parting of the Way*, Boston 1966
Wing-tsit Chan, *Religious Trends in Modern China*, New York 1953
   The Way of Lao-tzu, New York 1963

SHINTO

Anesaki, M., *History of Japanese Religion*, London, rpntd. 1955
Aston, W. G., *Shinto: The Way of the Gods*, London 1905
Aston, W. G. trans., *Nihongi* (2 vols), London, rpntd. 1956
Hammer, R., *Japan's Religious Ferment*, London 1962
Herbert, J., *Shinto*, London 1967
Holtom, D. C., *The National Faith of Japan*, London, rpntd. 1965
Philippi, D. L. trns., *Kojiki*, London 1968

NEW RELIGIOUS MOVEMENTS IN MODERN WESTERN SOCIETY

Barker, Eileen, *Armageddon and Aquarius: New Religions in Contemporary Christendom*, Manchester (UK) (in preparation)
Barker, Eileen (ed.), *New Religious Movements: A Perspective for Understanding Society*, New York and Toronto 1982
   Of Gods and Men: New Religious Movements in the West, Macon (GA) 1984
Beckford, James A., *Cult Controversies: The Societal Response to New Religious Movements*, London and New York 1985
Bromley, David G. and Shupe, Anson D., *Strange Gods: The Great American Cult Scare*, Boston 1981
Glock, Charles Y. and Bellah, Robert N. (eds), *The New Religious Consciousness*, Berkeley, Los Angeles and London 1976
Robbins, Thomas and Anthony, Dick, *In Gods We Trust: New Patterns Of Religious Pluralism in America*, New Brunswick 1981
Shupe, Anson D., *Six Perspectives on New Religions: A Case Study Approach*, New York and Toronto 1980
Wallis, Roy, *The Elementary Forms of the New Religious Life*, London, Boston and Melbourne 1984
Wilson, Bryan R. (ed.), *The Social Impact of New Religious Movements*, Barrytown (NY) 1981

NEW RELIGIOUS MOVEMENTS AMONG PRIMAL PEOPLES

Barret, David B., *Schism and Renewal in Africa*, London 1968
Burridge, K., *New Heaven, New Earth*, Oxford (UK) 1969
Lanternari, Vittorio, *The Religions of the Oppressed*, London 1963
Morrish, Ivor, *Obeah, Christ and Rastaman*, Cambridge (UK) 1982
Sundkler, Bengt, *Bantu Prophets in South Africa*, London 1961
   Zulu Zion, London 1976
Turner, Harold W., *Religious Innovation in Africa*, Boston (USA) 1979
Wilson, Bryan R., *Magic and the Millennium*, London 1973

CONCLUSION: RELIGION IN THE MODERN WORLD

Abbot, W. M., *The Documents of Vatican II*, London 1967
Bapat, P. V., *2500 Years of Buddhism*, Delhi 1959
Edwardes, M., *In the Blowing Out of a Flame*, London 1976
Farquhar, J. N., *Modern Religious Movements in India*, London 1976
Hick, J. and Hebblethwaite, B. (eds), *Christianity and Other Religions*, London 1980
Kinnamon, M. and Best, T. F., *Called to be One in Christ: United Churches and the Ecumenical Movement*, Geneva 1985
Kopf, D., *The Brahmo Samaj and the Shaping of the Modern Indian Mind*, Princeton 1979
   British Orientalism and the Bengal Renaissance, California 1969
Neil, S., *A History of Christian Missions*, Harmondsworth 1977
de Silva, L., 'Buddhist–Christian Dialogue' in H. Jai Singh (ed.), *Inter-Religious Dialogue*, Bangalore 1967
Tinker, H., *The Banyan Tree; Overseas Emigrants from India, Pakistan and Bangladesh*, Oxford (UK) 1977
Visser't Hooft, W. A., *The Genesis and Formation of the World Council of Churches*, Geneva 1982
Voll, J. O., *Islam: Continuity and Change in the Modern World*, London 1982

GLOSSARY

Words requiring explanation or definition are listed in the glossary in alphabetical order. The chapter, or chapters, in which the word is primarily located are indicated by the following letters:

N	The nature of religion	Ba	Babism and the Baha'i Faith	Con	Confucianism
J	Judaism	H	Hinduism	T	Taoism
Z	Zoroastrianism	Jn	Jainism	Sh	Shinto
C	Christianity	B	Buddhism	NRM	New religious movements
I	Islam	S	Sikhism	MW	Religion in the modern world

Abbasid (I)	Muslim dynasty from 750–1258 CE (from 763 centred in Baghdad).
Abd-al-Muttalib (I)	grandfather of Muhammad.
'Abdul-Baha (Ba)	'Servant of Baha'. Title of Abbas Effendi (1844–1921), successor to Baha'u'llah as leader of the Baha'is.
abhuta-parikalpita (B)	the imagining of what does not exist.
Abidhamma (B)	'supplement to the Dhamma': the third of the three baskets of the Tipitaka.
Abraham (J)	the earliest patriarch.
Abu-Bakr (I)	successor to Muhammad as leader of the Islamic community and first caliph, 634–644 CE.
Abu-Lahab (I)	an uncle of Muhammad.
Abu-Talib (I)	an uncle of Muhammad.
achintya (B)	'unthinkable' or 'inconceivable': term used in Mahayana to describe the paradox between 'there is nothing to be done' and 'anything can be done'.
Adi Granth (S)	original name of the *Guru Granth Sahib* before it was assigned Guru status; it was compiled mainly by Guru Arjan and Guru Gobind Singh.
Advaita (H)	'non-dualism': doctrine of the fundamental identity of *Brahman* and *Atman*. Advaita Vedanta is one of the main schools of Indian philosophy.
advaya (B)	non-duality.
Aggadah (J)	non-legal aspect of Judaism.
ahimsa (Jn, B, H)	non-violence, non-injury to any living being: a central precept of Jainism; also found in Buddhism and Hinduism.
ahl-adh-dhimmi(s) (I)	protected minorities in areas of Muslim rule.
ahl-al-kitab (I)	'People of the Book': Muslims, but also Jews, Christians, and on occasion others who have their own scriptures.
Ahura Mazda (Z)	Avestan name used by Zarathushtra for God, Creator through his Holy Spirit of all that is good; in Middle Persian contracted to Ohrmazd (variants: Hormazd, Hormuzd).
Ainu (Sh)	aboriginal people of the Japanese islands, apparently of Caucasoid stock and appearance; a very few remain.

ajiva (Jn)	'non-living', lifeless: one of two Jaina categories describing creation – the other is *jiva*, 'living'.
Aladura (NRM)	'The Church of the Lord': an independent African church, founded in Nigeria in 1930. Now a member of the World Council of Churches.
al-Ash'ari (I)	founder of Sunnite theological school.
al-Farabi (I)	10th-century Muslim philosopher.
al-Ghazali (I)	leading Islamic philosopher who abandoned academic life to become a Sufi.
al-Hallaj (I)	a 10th-century Sufi of extreme views.
al-Hasan (I)	one of two sons of 'Ali, regarded by Shi'ites as a rightful successor to 'Ali as caliph.
al-Hasan al-Askari (I)	eleventh imam in Shi'ah Islam. d.874 CE,
al-Husayn (I)	son of 'Ali, and held by Shi'ites to be his rightful successor as caliph. Martyred 680 CE.
al-Tabari (I)	10th-century Muslim historian who wrote a major commentary on the Qur'an.
alaya-vijnana (B)	the storehouse of the Buddha consciousness.
Allah (I)	Arabic word for 'God'.
'Ali (I)	'Ali ibn-Abi-Talib. A cousin and son-in-law of Muhammad, 'Ali was caliph from 656 to 661 CE.
Amaterasu (Sh)	the sun-goddess, greatest of all Shinto divinities.
Amesha Spenta (Z)	'Holy Immortal': a beneficent divinity emanated by Ahura Mazda from an aspect of his own Being. The six Amesha Spentas form with him the divine Heptad.
Amitabha (B)	the Buddha who creates and sustains the pure land.
amrit (S)	'nectar': mixture of sugar and water used ritually in the Khalsa initiation ceremony.
ananda (H)	'bliss': term used for *Brahman*.
anatta (B)	the 'no self' doctrine of Buddhism, which maintains that there is no permanent or enduring reality that can be identified as the self.
anekantavada (Jn)	philosophy of the 'indefiniteness of being', seeing reality as subject to change through production, continuation and destruction.
Angra Mainyu (Z)	'Evil (or Hostile) Spirit': an uncreated Being, source of all evil, to combat whom this world has been created. In Middle Persian his name is contracted to Ahriman.
anicca (B)	impermanence, the characteristic of constant change and modification.
animism (N)	the theory that all objects, animate or inaminate, are inhabited by spirits; first enunciated by Sir Edward Tyler.
aparigraha (Jn)	non-owning, renunciation of possessions or of attachment to worldly goods.
apollinarianism (C)	the belief that the man Jesus had a completely divine and not a human spirit.
apostle (C)	one personally 'sent out' (Greek *apo-stellein*) as a witness to Jesus Christ, particularly one of the twelve (including Paul but not Judas) commissioned by Jesus to go out as missionaries to the world.
Apostles' Creed (C)	a statement of Christian faith dating from the late fourth century. The name reflects the belief that the creed expresses the faith of the Apostles.
apostolic succession (C)	unbroken line of ordination by the laying-on of hands believed to stretch back to one or more of the original apostles.
Aranyakas (H)	'forest treatises': philosophical texts following the Vedas and *Brahmanas*, culminating in the dialogues of the Upanishads.
Ardhamagadhi (Jn)	old language of Magadha, also called Jaina Prakrit.
Arianism (C)	philosophy of Arius (256–336) concerning the nature of Christ, that Jesus was of the highest order of being yet not the same as God.
Ark (J)	in synagogue, the holy container of the Torah scrolls.
Arminianism (C)	liberalist reaction to the original Calvinist doctrine of predestination, to the effect that by the actions of this life any individual is able to earn – or to lose – the chance of eternal salvation.

artha (H)	'wealth' or material gain, the second of the four Hindu aims in life.
arti (H)	ceremony of burning lights with which each act of worship (*puja*) is concluded.
Arya Samaj (MW, H)	a Hindu organization founded (in 1875) to recall Hindus to a purified form of their own faith, and to resist conversions to Christianity and Islam.
Aryans (H)	Indo-European invaders of India during the middle of the second millennium BCE who eventually merged with the non-Aryan population.
ash-Shafi'i (I)	Islamic jurist.
asha (Z)	in ancient Iranian tradition the principle of natural order, justice and truth.
Asha Vahishta (Z)	'Best Asha': the Amesha Spenta who represents this principle and who guards fire as his responsibility among the seven creations.
Ashkenazim (J)	Jewish community, originally of northern Europe, with characteristic interpretation of Jewish law.
ashramas (H)	the four stages in life for the twice-born upper castes; student, householder, forest-dweller and renunciate (*sannyasin*).
astika (H)	'orthodox': term applied to the six orthodox schools of Hindu philosophy; 'unorthodox' is *nastika*.
Atash Bahram (Z)	'Victorious Fire': a temple fire of the highest grade.
Atisha (B)	founder of Kadam pa school of Tibetan Buddhism.
atman (H)	'Universal Self', fundamentally identical with *Brahman*, the all-pervading soul of the universe.
Augsburg Confession (C)	statement of belief produced by Protestant leaders at the Diet of Augsburg (1530). Prepared by Martin Luther's friend Philip Melanchthon in a spirit of some conciliation, it was rejected by the Roman Catholic Church.
Augustine (C)	St Augustine of Hippo, 354–430: Bishop of Hippo Regius in north Africa, and major Christian theologian.
Aurobindo (MW–H)	Sri Aurobindo (1872–1950). Major Indian mystic and writer, and founder of the Aurobindo Ashram at Pondicherry.
autocephalous (C)	Greek word designating the system by which each Church (especially among the Eastern Orthodox) has a degree of independence and its own head (kephala).
avatar (H)	Avatara: descent or incarnation of a god, particularly Vishnu who is said to have ten *avatars*.
Avesta (Z)	the collected sacred texts of Zoroastrianism.
Avestan (Z)	otherwise unrecorded Eastern Iranian language in which the Avesta is composed.
avidya (H)	'ignorance': spiritual blindness about the fundamental human condition which is being one with *Brahman*.
ayatullah (I)	'Sign of God'. An honorific title of some senior mujtahid, or Muslim authorities, in Iran.
Bab (Ba)	the traditional intermediary between the Shi'i Hidden Imam and his followers.
Baha'u'llah (Ba)	'Glory' or 'Splendour' of God. A title given to Mirza Husaya 'Ali Nuri, founder of the Baha'i Faith.
bani (S)	'word', used to mean the complete expression (generally of God).
baptism (C)	one of the original seven sacraments of the old catholic Church still retained in most denominations; ritual ablution symbolizing the washing away of sin. Some denominations regard it as an initiation into the Church for infants, later to be confirmed in adulthood on a voluntary basis (then called confirmation); others believe only in adult ('believer's') baptism. Practices range from a token pouring of a cupful of water across the forehead to total immersion.
Bar Mitzvah (J)	a boy's initiation into Jewish adulthood.
bardo thodol (B)	the Tibetan 'Book of the Dead'.
Basil (St) (C)	one of the main proponents at the Council of Nicaea and a great organizer of monastic orders. He lived from about 330 to about 379.
basilica (C)	'palace': a great cathedral.
Bayan (Ba)	book written by the Bab (Sayid 'Ali Muhammad Shirazi), and containing doctrine of Babism.

Bhagavad Gita (H)	'Song of the Lord': famous Sanskrit poem, part of the epic *Mahabharata*. One of the best-known Hindu scriptures.
bhagvan (H)	term used for God.
Bhagwan Shree Rajneesh (H–NRM)	meditation centres based on the teachings of the modern Indian guru Bhagwan Shree Rajneesh; found widely in the West since the 1970s.
bhajan (H)	devotional song, accompanied by musical instruments.
bhakti (H)	worship or devotion; *bhakti yoga* is the path to liberation (*moksha*) by way of devotion to a personal god.
bhavana (B)	meditation, as on the wholesome deeds of Buddhism.
bhikkhu (B)	a Buddhist who enters the community of the Sangha, either temporarily or permanently, in order to live a celibate life devoted to exploring and practising the principles of Buddhism.
bhikkhuni (B)	female bhikkhu.
bhut (H)	a ghost. Belief in ghosts of, for example, those who died an unnatural death, is common in village Hinduism.
bija (B)	seed: in Vajrayana the mantra is the seed from which an inner light develops.
bodhi (B)	enlightenment.
bodhichitta (B)	the thought, or mind, of enlightenment.
Bodhidharma (B)	according to tradition, an Indian who first took Ch'an (Zen) Buddhism to China.
Bodhisattva (B)	'enlightenment being': one who wishes to attain enlightenment.
bodhisattva-charya (B)	the course of the Buddha: the six (or 10) perfections involved in being a Buddha.
Book of the Dead (N)	Egyptian text concerned with funerary ritual, written during the New Kingdom (*c*1600–1090 BCE).
Boxer Rebellion (T)	named from a secret society, whose followers were prominent in a nationalist revolt against foreign influences (1896–1900).
brahmachari (H)	celibate student: one who has taken a vow of celibacy; the first stage in life (*ashrama*).
Brahman 1. (H)	the Ultimate Reality, Universal Essence or Absolute of Hindu religion and philosophy; *nirguna brahman* (without strands or *gunas*) is *Brahman* without qualities or attributes; *saguna brahman* (with strands or *gunas*) is *Brahman* with qualities, which is important for a theistic understanding of the Absolute.
Brahman 2. (H)	highest Hindu caste grouping; traditionally priests or teachers, but also found in other occupations. Sometimes spelled 'Brahmin'.
Brahmanas (H)	series of ritual texts following the Vedas and explaining the significance of sacrifice.
Brahmanism (H)	also called Vedism; refers to the sacrificial religion of the Vedic period which was followed by early Hinduism.
Brahmo Samaj (MW–H)	Reformist Hindu society founded in 1828.
buddha darshana (B)	the sight of the Buddha; a visionary encounter with the Buddha.
budda-shabda (B)	the Buddha's voice, as heard in visionary experiences.
buddhata (B)	Buddhahood, or Buddha-nature.
bushido (Sh)	code of moral principles formulated by the *samurai*, warrior class of feudal Japan, combining militarism with frugality, honesty and charity.
Carey (MW)	William Carey, first English Protestant missionary to India in 1793.
caste (H)	term referring to the hereditary social system of India (cf. *varna* and *jati*): division of society into groups to which socio-religious values are ascribed.
catholic (C)	'universal' or 'general'. A title particularly applied to the western Church before the Reformation and commonly used of the Roman Catholic Church since then, although many Christian Churches regard themselves as 'catholic' in the sense of maintaining the universal faith of Christianity.
catholicos (C)	the equivalent of Patriarch in some Eastern and North American Churches.

Chalcedon (C)	town on the shore opposite Constantinople (Istanbul), site of the Fourth Christian Council in 451, and now called Kadikoy.
Ch'an (B)	school of Chinese Buddhism, known as Zen in Japan and more widely in other parts of the world. From ch'an-na, a Chinese reflection of the Sanskrit dhyana (meditation).
ch'I (T)	air, breath, inner essence and vital energy.
Ching T'u (B)	'Pure Land': a school of Chinese Buddhism.
Chinvat Bridge (Z)	bridge to be crossed by each soul after individual judgement, leading to heaven above or hell below.
chitta (B)	mind.
ch'ou Dynasty (T)	*c*1100–722 BCE.
Christ (C)	the term Christos means 'anointed' and was taken in translation as 'Christ' in reference to Jesus by the Christians.
Christology (C)	theories about the nature of the person of Christ, especially in his relationship to God the Father.
cit (H)	'consciousness': term applied to *Brahman*.
Coffin Texts (N)	texts of Egyptian religion, written during the Middle Kingdom (*c*2160–1788 BCE).
Communion (C)	*see* Eucharist.
confession (C)	also called 'penance'. One of the seven sacraments of the old catholic Church; the practice of recounting sins aloud, privately before a priest, and thereafter receiving absolution together with some form of actual penance. Also used for a statement of doctrine by many Protestant denominations.
confirmation (C)	one of the seven sacraments of the old catholic Church retained by a number of present-day denominations: the laying-on of hands on a candidate's head by a bishop, in confirmation that the candidate is voluntarily and acceptably thenceforward a member of the Church.
Counter-Reformation (C)	the reaction by the Roman Catholic Church in the face of the Protestant Reformation, itself a reformation of its own practices and a pruning of traditions.
creed (C)	a dogmatic statement detailing the exact tenets of religion. The creeds most commonly accepted by Christian denominations are the Apostles' Creed and the Nicene Creed; some denominations, however, see no point in any.
daeva (Z)	an old Indo-Iranian term for 'god' used by Zarathushtra for a group of amoral divinities whom he saw as agents of Angra Mainyu; in Middle Persian *dev*, meaning simply 'demon'.
dana (B)	'giving', as a Buddhist virtue.
Dancing Sorcerer (N)	figure in a painting in the Trois Frères caves in France, to which early religious significance is attached.
Dao (Con)	*see* Tao.
darshana (H)	manifestation or vision. Describes an audience with a saintly or otherwise important person, but refers particularly to the six 'viewpoints' of the different Hindu schools of philosophy.
Dhamma (B)	the teaching of the Buddha; Buddhist doctrine. Also the Pali form of dharma (Sanskrit).
dharma (B, H)	in Buddhism, dharma means whatever can be held before the mind, any object of awareness. In Hinduism, term describing both the absolute moral order and the right action of individuals in accordance with law and duty.
Dharma Shastras (H)	law books defining the rules of conduct; part of the sacred literature of the *Smriti* – best known are the *Laws of Manu*.
Dharmakara (B)	a monk who takes a vow to become a Buddha.
dhikr (I)	literally 'remembrance', especially of the name of God, and the practice in Sufism of reciting the name of God as a form of worship.
Diaspora (J)	the dispersion; the scattered nature of worldwide Jewry.
Digambara (Jn)	'sky-robed', i.e. naked; major Jaina sect in which nudity for monks was originally compulsory.

Divali or Dipavali (H)	'Feast of Lamps', widely celebrated all over India; according to one calendar, end of the Hindu old year and beginning of the new.
Donation of Constantine (C)	a document (probably fabricated) from the eighth or ninth centuries which sought to strengthen the power of the Church and especially of the Pope.
dukkha (B)	unsatisfactoriness; the suffering which arises from a desire for permanence in a world which is impermanent.
Durga Puja (H)	festival in honour of the goddess Durga, celebrated in autumn especially by Bengalis.
Dvaita (H)	dualism, the opposite of *advaita*. A school of philosophy founded by Madhva (13th century CE).
dvija (H)	'twice-born'; refers to the three upper *varna* groups.
ecumenical (oecumenical) (C, MW)	literally 'worldwide' or universal. The word is used to refer to major councils of the Christian Church, and in modern times to the movement for the reunion of churches.
Engishiki (Sh)	'Chronicles of Engi': liturgical Shinto texts also including 27 *norito*, published in 927 CE.
Episcopalianism (C)	term that outside the United Kingdom generally has the meaning equivalent to the Anglican Communion, but that literally connotes only a hierarchy of bishops or overseers.
Epistles (C)	the letters to Christians found in the New Testament. Those by Paul are addressed to specific Churches with specific instructions and encouragement. Some of the others are 'general epistles' meant to inspire any Church in which they are read aloud.
Eucharist (C)	literally 'thanks': the service of Communion, and especially within it the actual consumption of the Body and Blood of Christ, represented by (or, according to some denominations, co-existent as) bread and wine. Communion, partaken in this way, is one of the seven sacraments of the old catholic Church, and is retained by almost all denominations in one form or another; to some it is simply 'the sacrament'.
evangelist (C)	bringer of the 'good news', the gospel.
Farid (S)	Muslim Persian poet (*c*1150–*c*1230), mystical describer of Sufi religious experience.
Fatimid (I)	Islamic dynasty, founded in Tunisia and centred on Cairo.
Filioque clause (C)	the words 'and the Son' as added after 'who proceeds from the Father' in the Nicene Creed, accepted from very early times only by the Western Churches.
Fire Sermon (B)	sermon preached by the Buddha to a gathering of fire-worshipping ascetics.
Five Vows (Jn)	not to do violence; not to lie; not to steal; not to have sexual intercourse; and not to own possessions.
Folk Shinto (Sh)	the Shinto religion as practised domestically in individuals' homes before the *kami-dana*, in the hope particularly of harmony and prosperity.
Frasho-kereti (Z)	'making wonderful': the restoration of the world to its original state of perfect goodness after the final defeat of evil at the Last Day.
Ganapati Puja (H)	most important festival in Maharashtra, held in honour of the god Ganesha.
Gatha (Z)	'song', 'psalm': one of 17 short poetic works composed by Zarathushtra and preserved by inclusion in the *yasna*.
Gautama (B)	personal name of the Buddha. His family name was Siddharta.
gayatri mantra (H)	most sacred verse of the *Rig Veda*, also called the 'Mother of the Vedas'; it is addressed to the sun god and repeated several times daily by Brahmans.
Geluk pa (B)	school of Tibetan Buddhism which eventually became the dominant power in the land under the Dalai Lama.
Gentile (J)	used by Jews as a generic term for all non-Jews.
ghayba (I)	'seclusion'. The state of the twelfth imam (who is still to come) in Shi'ah Islam.
Gnosticism (C)	elitist concept of some early Christians who desired an esoteric religion for initiates involving secret mysteries.
gohei (Sh)	wand from which paper strips hang, symbolizing clothing offered to a god and protection to the offerer.

gopi (H)	wife or daughter of a cowherd, thus 'cowgirl' or 'milkmaid'; refers especially to the *gopis* of Vrindaban who played with Krishna.
gospel (C)	English translation of Greek original meaning 'good news' in reference to the message announced by Jesus of Nazareth.
grama devata (H)	'village godling'; minor village divinities.
granthi (S)	one who organizes and conducts services in a gurdwara.
Great Vows (Jn)	*see* Five Vows.
Gujarat (Z)	a state in north-west India.
gunas (H)	'strands': qualities or subtle elements which permeate primal matter. There are three gunas: goodness or brightness (*sattva*); passion or energy (*rajas*); and darkness or dullness (*tamas*).
gur- (S)	of a guru, of God.
gurdwara (S)	Sikh place of worship, administered by a committee.
guru (H)	teacher, spiritual guide.
Guru (S)	one of ten messengers or spokesmen of God's word.
Hadith (I)	Sometimes translated 'tradition'. Hadith is a collection of the sayings and acts of Muhammad used in interpretation of Islamic law.
haiden (Sh)	outer shrine at a temple.
hajj (I)	pilgrimage to Mecca. One of the five pillars of Islam.
Halakhah (J)	legal aspect of Judaism.
Hanbalites (I)	an Islamic legal rite, named after Ahmad ibn-Hanbal.
Harafites (I)	an Islamic legal rite which made much use of rational methods, and which became the official rite of the Ottoman empire.
Hare Krishna Movement (H–NRM)	also known as the International Society for Krishna Consciousness (ISKCON), a modern religious movement based on ecstatic devotion to Krishna; widely found in the West.
Hashim (I)	the Arabian clan to which Muhammad belonged.
Heptad (Z)	Ahura Mazda, his Holy Spirit and the six Amesha Spentas.
Hevajra Tantra (B)	a text of Vajrayana Buddhism.
Hijra (I)	migration of Muhammad and his followers from Mecca to Medina in 622 CE.
Hinayana (B)	'the lesser vehicle': a name given to the orthodox schools of early Buddhism by the Mahayanists.
Hishishiyyun (I)	'Hashish-men': Isma'ilites of Syria who gave their name to political assassination.
Holi (H)	colourful spring festival primarily celebrated in northern India.
Holy Communion (C)	the Eucharistic service, the Lord's Supper, the Mass; also within it the actual consumption of the Body and Blood of Christ, represented by (or, according to some denominations, co-existent as) bread and wine.
hondon (Sh)	most holy part of a temple, containing the *shintai*.
Hsien (T)	an immortal, sometimes used of a 'saint'.
hsing (B)	true nature.
Hua Yen (B)	school of Chinese Mahayana.
Hui-neng (B)	the sixth patriarch of Ch'an Buddhism.
Ibn Sina (Avicenna) (I)	11th-century Muslim philosopher and authority on medicine.
Ibn-Rush (Averroes) (I)	Muslim philosopher.
icon (C)	image or representation intended to recall to the believer aspects of devotion or of the life of Christ, his mother or the saints.

Iconoclastic Controversy (C)	seventh-century controversy over the use of icons in churches.
Iglesia ni Cristo (NRM)	an independent church founded in the Philippines, but now with a worldwide membership.
ijma (I)	consensus, either of the people as a whole or of jurists: a principle used in application of Islamic law.
ijtihad (I)	literally 'expanding effort'. A term used to describe the exercise of independent judgement by an Islamic jurist.
imam (I)	the leader of a congregation of Muslims. For Shi'ite Muslims there is a succession of Imams who are regarded as having special authority.
Imamites (I)	the most important surviving branch of Shi'ism.
Indra (Z)	ancient Iranian war-god, regarded in Zoroastrianism as a *daeva*.
Ioadites (I)	settled community which adopted a form of moderate Kharijism; now found in Oman and Algeria.
irja (I)	doctrine of 'postponement', probably in reference to the postponement of a decision as to whether a grave sinner was a believer or an unbeliever.
Ishwara (H)	'Lord': a term used for God.
Isis (N)	wife of Osiris.
ISKCON	*see* Hare Krishna Movement.
islam (I)	'surrender' or 'submission', in the sense of submission to Allah. Islam is also the term used for the faith of a Muslim.
Isma'ilite (I)	branch of Shi'ism in which Isma'il is regarded as the seventh Imam.
Isnad (I)	a chain of authorities used to confirm the status of a Hadith.
Israel (J)	original name of the patriarch Jacob, then applied to Hebrews.
istadevata (H)	family god, or one's own personally chosen deity.
istihsan (I)	'finding good': a method used in Islamic jurisprudence.
istislah (I)	a method similar to *istihsan* in Islamic jurisprudence, but which avoids the use of strict analogy.
Ithn'ashariyya (I)	'Twelvers': a branch of Shi'ism also known as Imamites, which held that there was a series of divinely supported Imams, each designating their successor.
jajmani system (H)	system of mutual rights and obligations; an intrinsic aspect of the working of the caste system at the village level.
Janamashtami (H)	fetival celebrating Krishna's birth.
Jataka (B)	the Jataka commentary is part of the fifth nikaya (or collection) of the Sutta Pitaka. It purports to tell stories of the past lives of the Buddha.
jati (H, Jn)	lineage or birth: the usual term for 'caste', of which the real division is not into four groups (cf. *varna*) but into many thousands, many of them regional. Although caste is essentially an aspect of Hindu social organization, its influence is widespread in Indian society generally.
Jats (S)	in north-western India, land-owners who believed in militaristic democracy.
Jehangir (S)	Mughal Emperor (1569–1627), successor to Akbar.
Jesus prayer (C)	invocation of the name of Jesus in a prayer which runs: 'Lord Jesus Christ, Son of God, have mercy on me, a sinner'.
Jimmu Tenno (Sh)	legendary first Emperor of 'all' Japan, by tradition responsible for unifying the country in 660 BCE.
jina (Jn)	'conqueror (of self)': one who has attained salvation (*moksha*) through spiritual liberation.
jiva (Jn)	'living': one of two Jaina categories describing creation. The other is *ajiva*, 'non-living'.
jnana (H)	knowledge or wisdom: *jnana yoga* is one of the three paths to liberation (*moksha*) based on meditation and renunciation.
John the Baptist (C)	Jewish preacher who offered baptism 'in repentance of sins' and declared himself to be the forerunner of the Messiah, the Christ.

ju-lai tsang (B)	'Buddha womb': the one absolute reality, according to the T'en T'ai school.
Ka'ba (I)	cube-shaped building within the great mosque at Mecca. The Ka'ba provides a physical focus for pilgrimage to Mecca and for Muslim prayer.
Kabir (S)	popular mystic poet (c1398–1518) who urged the equality of humankind.
kafir (I)	'unbeliever' (Arabic).
Kagyu pa (B)	school of Tibetan Buddhism.
Kalpa Sutra (Jn)	canonical text of the fourth century CE recounting the lives of the *Tirthankaras*.
kama (H)	love or desire: third of the four Hindu aims in life.
kami (Sh)	the gods and their powers – the mysterious, superior, controlling nature, occasionally seen as aspects of individual humans.
kami-dana (Sh)	the domestic shrine in an individual's home, before which offerings are presented daily by the head of the family.
karma (H, Jn, S)	action and the fruit of one's actions: the law of moral causation by which one's present life is strongly affected by one's deeds in previous lives. *Karma yoga*, the way of works, is one of the three paths to liberation (*moksha*) in Hinduism. In Jainism, subtle matter that adheres to and tarnishes the soul, which thus acquires first a spiritual then a physical body, so establishing the cycle of births and deaths.
karuna (B)	compassion: the desire to relieve suffering in others.
Keshab Chandra Sen (MW-H)	Hindu reformer and leader of the Brahmo Samaj who, in 1879, founded 'The Church of the New Dispensation' as an attempt to bring together the teaching of various religions.
Khadija (I)	wife of Muhammad.
khalifa (caliph) (I)	'successor' to Muhammad as leader of the Islamic community.
Khalistan (S)	Sikh national state, sought as political ambition by some Sikhs of particularly political aspiration.
Khalsa (S)	'pure': the community of initiated Sikhs, who at the age of puberty take the 'five Ks' as their uniform; male initiates take the name Singh, female initiates take the name Kaur.
khandha (B)	the aggregate of five constantly changing factors which make up the self: they are *rupa* (form); *vedana* (sensation); *sanna* (perceptions); *sankhara* (mental formations or volitional activities); and *vinnana* (consciousness).
Kharijites (I)	Muslim sects which advocated the exclusion of sinners from the community.
Kimbanguist (NRM)	'l'Église de Jésus-Christ sur la Terre par le Prophète Simon Kimbangu': an African independent church founded by Simon Kimbangu, with probably 3½ million adherents in Zaïre. Admitted to membership of the World Council of Churches in 1969.
koan (B)	Japanese form of the Chinese 'kung-an'. Literally, 'a magistrates table', or place where cases are tested in court. A koan is a question that cannot be answered by rational means.
Kojiki (Sh)	'Records of Ancient Events': ancient texts recounting creation and aetiological myths, completed in 712 CE but a compilation of much older oral traditions.
Kumbha Mela (H)	important festival held every 12 years, during which millions of Hindus bathe in the sacred river Ganges.
kusala kama (B)	wholesome deeds.
Lama (B)	head of Tibetan monastery.
Lankha Dhamma Dhatta Society (MW–B)	founded in 1950 in Sri Lanka, originally to spread the teaching of Buddhism in Germany.
Lao-Tzu (T)	lit. 'Old Master': an early philosopher, with a traditional birth-date (604 BCE). Reputed author of *Tao-tê Ching*.
Last Supper (C)	the meal detailed in the gospels just before Jesus's arraignment, and commemorated in the Eucharistic service, which is therefore also often called the Lord's Supper.
Legalists (Con)	school of philosophers who believed law – and particularly their own drastic penal code – more important than the individual.

li (T)	'form', outward appearance; sometimes used for 'inner law' of any particular object, its intrinsic essence.
Li Po (T)	leading poet of T'ang dynasty, 701–762 CE.
lingam (H)	phallic symbol closely associated with the god Shiva.
logos (C)	'word'. A Greek philosophical concept applied in Christian usage to express the belief that Jesus Christ is the Word of God made flesh.
loka (B)	the world; or the reality that people create for themselves.
Lord's Supper (C)	*see* Last Supper.
Lotus Sutra (B)	one of the earliest and most influential works of the Mahayana canon.
Luke (St) (C)	evangelist, friend and companion of St Paul on some of his travels, Hellenic and highly educated writer and diarist, apparently also a physician; the most accomplished journalist of the Bible.
madhahib (I)	legal schools, or 'rites', in Islam.
Madhyamaka (B)	school of Mahayana Buddhism that taught a 'middle way'.
Magadha (Jn)	ancient homeland of the Jainas, kingdom corresponding to the Patna and Gaya regions of present-day Bihar.
maghazi (I)	'raiding expeditions' engaged in by Arabs at the time of the rise of Islam, and by Muhammad and his followers against the Meccans between 622 and 630 CE.
magus (pl. magi) (Z)	priest of the Medes and Persians; for the Greeks a general term for a Zoroastrian priest.
Mahabharata (H)	one of the two great epics of India, it tells the story of the great war between the Pandavas and the Kauravas, and also contains the *Bhagavad Gita*.
Mahakashyapa (B)	a disciple of the Buddha, regarded as the first Zen (Ch'an) master.
Mahasanghika (B)	sect of early Buddhism from which Mahayana developed.
Mahavira (Jn)	'Great hero': title given to Vardhamana.
Mahayana (B)	the 'great vehicle' or 'way': the form of Buddhism which spread to China, Japan and Tibet.
Mahdi (I)	'guided one': the twelfth Imam of Shi'ite Islam who will return to lead and establish the faithful.
Maimonides (J)	medieval Egyptian Jewish sage.
Malakites (I)	an Islamic legal rite, or school, following Malik ibn-Anas.
mana (N)	Melanesian word referring to a mysterious power (of exorcism, spiritual healing, or even leadership) possessed by some people.
Manchu Dynasty (T)	1644–1911 CE.
mandala (B, H)	'circle': a symbolic diagram bounded by a circle, and believed to be a centre of psychic energy.
manmukh (S)	'Individual-centred' or 'Mind-centred', i.e. reliant on one's own powers.
mantra (B, H)	sacred verse from scriptures or sound used in meditation. In Hinduism, often taken from the Vedas; one of the most famous is the *gayatri mantra* addressed to the sun god.
Mass (C)	term used for the Eucharistic service in some denominations (chiefly Catholic) derived from the words at the end of the service in Latin: *Ite missa est*, generally apprehended to mean 'Go, it is the dismissal'.
matins (C)	service of morning prayer; not a Eucharistic service but one of devotion and praise.
Matthew (St) (C)	evangelist, almost definitely of orthodox Jewish background concerned above all to relate the events of Jesus's life and death to ancient Jewish prophetic scriptures.
Maya (B)	Mother of the Buddha.
maya (H)	divine power, often identified with the transient physical world in contrast to the unchanging Brahman; the term can also mean 'illusion'.
Mecca (I)	a place in Saudi Arabia, birthplace of Muhammad and focal point of Islam.

Medina (I)	city to the north of Mecca to which Muhammad and his followers fled in 622 CE.
Mencius (Con)	latinized form of Meng-zi, 'Master Meng' whose cognomen was in fact K'o, noted for his elaboration of Confucian principles, especially the basic goodness of human nature.
Messiah (C, J)	Christians believe Jesus of Nazareth to have been the Messiah, and to have inaugurated a provisional kingdom of God. In Jewish belief the Messiah is the anointed one, who will come to usher in a new age under the sovereignty of God.
mezuzah (J)	scriptural texts affixed to doorposts.
Midrash (J)	commentary on biblical text.
Milarepa (B)	teacher of Tibetan Buddhism, and founder of the Kagyu pa school.
Mimamsa (H)	'Enquiry': one of the six orthodox Hindu schools of philosophy, concerned mainly with the exegesis of Vedic texts.
Mishnah (J)	early compilation of Jewish law.
Mohists (Con)	closely-knit, disciplined and influential group, active 403–221 BCE, who practised self-denial and were anti-ritualistic. Their founder, Mo-zi, was famous for his doctrine of universal love – criticized by Confucians and Taoists alike.
moksha (H, Jn)	liberation from the cycle of rebirths (*samsara*), the ultimate aim of Hindu religion and philosophy. It can be reached by three different ways: knowledge (*jnana*), works (*karma*) or devotion (*bhakti*). In Jainism, salvation through liberation, as opposed to the perfect knowledge of *nirvana*.
monarchical episcopacy (C)	the belief that there is a transmission of true Christian faith through bishops, who are the successors to the Apostles and guardians of true Christian faith and practice.
monism (H, Z)	belief in a single primal being or force.
monophysite (C)	having only one nature: thus of Christ denying him either his humanity or his divinity (especially the former).
Monothelitism (C)	a seventh-century Christian heresy claiming only one will in Christ.
Moonies	*see* Unification Church.
Moses (J)	early leader of the Israelites.
mu'adhdhin (I)	*see* muezzin.
Mu'awiya (I)	the first Ummayad caliph (d.680 CE).
Mu'tazilites (I)	Muslim sect dating from the eighth century. They introduced concepts from Greek philosophy into their theology.
mudra (H)	gesture; widely used in Indian dance and sculpture.
muezzin (mu'adhdhin) (I)	person who calls the faithful to prayer from the minaret of a mosque.
Mughal Empire (S)	Indian empire established in 1526 under Babu. Mughal government, architecture and culture have left a lasting impression on India. Mughal power declined as European influence increased in India, but the last Mughal emperor was finally deposed only in 1858.
muhajirin (I)	emigrants from Mecca to Medina.
Muhammad (I)	prophet and founder of Islam, 570–632 CE.
mujtahid (I)	senior Iranian jurist.
Mula-Madhyamaka-Karika (B)	stanzas concerned with fundamental teaching of Madhyamaka.
Murji'ite (I)	Muslims who held to the doctrine of irja, or 'postponement'.
murti (H)	term referring to anthropomorphic statues and images of deities in Hindu worship.
Nagarjuna (B)	the leading exponent of Madhyamaka, born *c*150 CE.
Navaratri (H)	festival of nine nights devoted to the Mother Goddess: greatest festival of the Gujaratis, but widely celebrated throughout India. Also known as Durga Puja (especially in Bengal), and Ayudha Paja.

nayaka (B)	senior *bhikkhu* in Theravada Buddhist monastic community.
Nestorius (C)	bishop of Constantinople in the early fifth century whose view was that Jesus was essentially two 'persons', God and human, as separate entities; this persuasion was condemned at the Council of Ephesus (431) although that ruling has never been accepted by some churches.
New Testament (C)	the record of the revelation of Jesus Christ and its proclamation by the apostles. The 'Old Testament' in the Christian Bible is substantially the Hebrew Bible.
nibbana (B)	'blowing out': the state of enlightenment or liberation in which desires are extinguished. Nibbana is the Pali and 'nirvana' the Sanskrit form of the word.
Nicaea (C)	city in Turkey (now Iznik) from which the Nicene Creed took its name. Major Christian councils were held there in 325 and 787.
Nicene Creed (C)	fourth-century formulation of Christian belief, and a major statement of Christian orthodoxy.
Nihongi (Sh)	'Chronicles of Japan': ancient texts recounting legends and history from early times, published in 720 CE, but a compilation of much older oral traditions.
Ninety-Five Theses (C)	ninety-five points of argument compiled by Martin Luther suggesting that various practices of the catholic Church were non-scriptural, especially the sale of indulgences. He nailed his theses to the door of All Saints' Church at Wittenberg on the eve of an exhibition there of 'relics', thus beginning the process later to be seen as the Reformation.
Ninety-nine beautiful names	names of Allah used in Muslim devotion.
nirvana (B, Jn)	'blowing out': the state of enlightenment or liberation in which desires are extinguished. Nirvana is the Sanskrit and 'nibbana' the Pali form of the word. Also used in Jainism for the attainment of perfect knowledge and enlightenment.
Nobili (MW)	Roberto de Nobili (1577–1656). A Jesuit missionary who attempted to accommodate Christian teaching to a Hindu cultural setting in south India.
non-conformity (C)	general term for the resolution of Protestants in Britain during the 17th to 19th centuries not to belong to the Church of England.
norito (Sh)	ritual prayers.
Nyaya (H)	school of logic, one of the six orthodox systems of Hindu philosophy.
Nyingma pa (B)	school of Tibetan Buddhism.
Om (H)	most sacred word of the Hindus, symbolizing the Absolute. Composed of the sounds A, U, M, and a humming nasalization, it is said to represent the three oldest Vedas and also the three gods Brahma, Vishnu and Shiva.
Onam (H)	harvest festival celebrated in Kerala.
original sin (C)	Christian doctrine which maintains that sin, as the assertion of self over against the will of God, is inherently part of the human condition, vitiating any attempt on man's part to help himself spiritually. A consequence of the doctrine is that only God's grace can effect salvation.
Orthodox Judaism (J)	Judaism that accepts the doctrines and practices of ancient times.
Osiris (N)	legendary king of Egypt who, according to the Pyramid texts, was raised to life after a violent death to become god of the dead.
Padmasambhava (B)	Indian teacher invited to introduce Buddhism into Tibet.
Pahlavi (Z)	Iranian term for Middle Persian, the language in which most of the secondary Zoroastrian literature is preserved.
Pali (B)	the religious language of Theravada Buddhism, based on a vernacular of north India at or shortly after the life of the Buddha.
Paradise (Z)	word derived from Avestan *pairidaeza* (Old Persian *paridaisa*): a walled enclosure, park or garden.
Parameshvara (H)	'the highest Lord': a word used for God.
Paravritti (B)	transformation. A term used to describe the experience of 'seeing reality' in the Yogacharin school of Mahayana Buddhism.

Parshvanatha (Jn)	last-but-one patriarch of the Jainas, upon whose teachings Vardhamana based his own.
Parsis (Z)	'Persians': the name given in Gujarat to the Zoroastrian settlers from Iran; also spelled 'Parsees'.
Passion (C)	the suffering of Christ immediately before his death, particularly after being nailed to the cross.
Passover (J)	festival celebrating the Exodus from Egypt.
paticcasamappada (B)	theory of dependent origination or 'conditioned co-arising' in Theravada Buddhism.
Patristics (C)	the study of the 'Church Fathers': the early theological authorities and writers of the Christian Church in the period up to the seventh century.
Paul (St) (C)	Jewish Pharisee who became a Christian and (probably) martyr. He pioneered the Christian mission to non-Jews. His letters, contained in the New Testament, provide an important source of Christian theology.
Pelagianism (C)	the view expounded by the British theologian Pelagius (late fourth to early fifth century) that man can take fundamental steps towards his own salvation, without the prior action of divine grace. In this he opposed Augustine's doctrine of original sin.
Pentecost (J)	festival celebrating the receipt of the Ten Commandments which falls 50 days after Passover.
Peter (St) (C)	early leader of the Christian apostles and of the Jerusalem Church. It is widely held that Peter was martyred in Rome. Roman Catholics regard Peter as having been given a special authority reflected in the role of the Pope, the bishop of Rome.
Photian Schism (C)	ninth-century controversy in the Eastern Church occasioned by the appointment of Photius as Patriarch of Constantinople.
Pongal (H)	southern Indian harvest festival, celebrated in January.
pontiff (C)	the Pope; an alternative term derived from the Pope's title *pontifex*, 'bridge-builder'.
Pope, the (C)	from the latin 'Papa', 'father'. The title was once used generally of bishops in the Western Church, but it is now restricted to the bishop of Rome as the head of the Roman Catholic Church.
prabhasvara (B)	brightly shining, especially used in relation to the mind.
prajna (B)	wisdom.
Prakrit (Jn)	evolved form of Sanskrit in which Jaina, Buddhist and some Hindu scriptures were written.
prakriti (H)	matter or nature: one of the basic categories of Sankhya philosophy, the other being *purusha*, spirit.
pranidhana (B)	'fixation': the theory in Mahayana Buddhism that what the mind fixes upon becomes real.
prasada (H)	'grace': food offering made to a god, shared out among the devotees as a blessing.
predestination (C)	the doctrine held in various forms, particularly by Calvinists, that God has chosen his Elect from the beginning.
priesthood of all believers (C)	the idea that the priesthood is not restricted to those specifically ordained to be ministers, but that the laity may fulfil such functions if called upon to do so.
PRINEMS (NRM)	'Primal new religious movements': a term used to cover a wide range of new religious movements among primal peoples.
prophets (J)	series of religiously-inspired seers, some of whom foretold a Messiah.
Pseudo-Isidorian Decretals (C)	a collection of documents originally (and wrongly) attributed to St Isidore of Seville, but probably compiled in the ninth century. They were used to support claims for Papal authority.
puja (H)	'worship' at home or in the temple, to any deity. The term may refer to offerings of flowers, water and incense to images or a symbol of the god. As an act of ceremonial worship it consists of carefully graded actions, concluding with *arti*, a ceremony of lights.
pujari (H)	temple attendant or priest.
Puranas (H)	'Ancient': early medieval texts which contain important mythological material and belong to the *Smriti*. One of the best known is the *Bhagavata Purana*.
purification (Sh)	the means of freeing oneself from impurities, from the pollution of everyday life; an important aspect in Shinto.

purusha (H)	spirit: one of the basic categories of Sankhya philosophy, the other being *prakriti*.
Purushottama (H)	'Highest Spirit': a term used for God.
Pyramid Texts (N)	important texts of Egyptian religion, written *c*2400–2300 BCE.
Qadarites (I)	opponents of Umayyads, who asserted the doctrine of human free will.
qi'ra'at (I)	sets of readings from the Qur'an, and the order in which they are believed to have been revealed.
qi'yas (I)	analogy, a method used in Islamic legal discussions.
qibla (I)	niche in the wall of a mosque indicating the direction (of Mecca) to be faced in prayer.
Qur'an (Koran) (I, S)	the scripture of Islam, believed to be the revelation given to Muhammad by Allah.
Quraysh (I)	prominent tribe of Mecca at the time of Muhammad.
rabbi (J)	a teacher of the Torah.
Rajagaha (B)	town in north-west India where the first Buddhist Council met.
Ram Mohan Roy (MW–H)	a Bengali reformer of Hinduism and founder of the Brahmo Samaj (1772–1833).
Ramadan (I)	month during which Muslim fast is observed. The fast of Ramadan is one of the five pillars of Islam.
Ramakrishna (MW)	Sri Ramakrishna (1836–1886). Hindu mystic and an important figure in the 'Hindu renaissance'.
Ramakrishna Mission (H, MW)	reform movement and order of Indian ascetics founded by Vivekananda, inspired by the teaching of Ramakrishna, in 1897.
Ramayana (H)	one of the two great Indian epics. Its central characters are Rama and his wife Sita. The story is very popular, and a great dissemination of Hindu ideas and values among ordinary people.
Ramlila (H)	annual dramatic performance of the Ramayana story.
rasul Allah (I)	'the messenger of God': a title of Muhammad.
Reform Judaism (J)	Judaism that has adapted the doctrines and practices of ancient times for the modern age.
Reformation (C)	the 16th-century revolution within the Western catholic Church that resulted in the upsurge of Protestantism and the breaking away of a number of denominations then to fragment even further.
ren (Con)	the sum of all human virtues, variously translated as 'goodness', 'humanity', 'benevolence', etc.
Ridvan (Ba)	Baha'i festival marking the anniversary of Baha'u'llah's first declaration of his mission in 1863.
Rig Veda (Z)	oldest collection of Indian sacred texts.
Rishabhanatha (Jn)	the first Jaina *Tirthankara* (patriarch).
rita (H)	cosmic and moral order: Vedic term later replaced by *dharma*.
rupa (B)	form.
saccidananda (H)	term denoting Brahman, made up of *sat* (being), *cit* (consciousness) and *ananda* (bliss).
sacrament (C)	commonly defined as 'an outward and visible sign of an inward and spiritual grace': a ritual or ceremony that expresses visibly the conferring by the community of a spiritual benefit. In the old catholic Church there were seven: baptism, confirmation, holy orders, the Eucharistic service (Communion, Mass, the Lord's Supper, etc.) confession (penance), matrimony and unction (anointing, termed 'extreme unction' when administered to the dying. All have been retained by some denominations, notably the Roman Catholic and Orthodox Churches and the Anglican Communion. Others have reduced that figure, for example to three (the Lutheran Churches), or to two (the Calvinistic Churches and many others), or to none at all.
sadhu (H)	Hindu ascetic.
saki (Sh)	strong drink made from fermented rice.
Sakya pa (B)	school of Tibetan Buddhism.
Sakyamuni (B)	'The sage of the Sakyas': a nickname for the Buddha.
salat (I)	worship or prayer. One of the five pillars of Islam.

samadhi (B, H)	concentration. The final stage of Yoga in Hindu teaching. In Mahayana Buddhism, flexibility of the mind; fashioning the mind so that it may receive the attributes of the Buddha.
samsara (H)	transmigration: the continuous round of rebirths; also the constant change of the world.
samskaras (H)	Hindu life-cycle rites, sometimes called 'sacraments'.
sanatana dharma (H)	'eternal order': term used for Hinduism.
Sangha (Samgha) (B)	the community of bhikkhus (monks) in Buddhism.
Sanhedrin (J)	supreme court of Jewish law in Second Temple period.
Sankhya (H)	one of the six orthodox schools of Hindu philosophy, based on the dualism of matter (*prakriti*) and spirit (*purusha*).
Sannyasin (H)	renunciate or ascetic; traditionally the fourth stage in life.
Sanskrit (H, Jn)	early language of the Indo-Aryan subfamily in which many Hindu scriptures were written. Its earliest known form is called Vedic Sanskrit.
Sant (S)	holy person, person of obviously godly character and devotion (not necessarily of any specific religion).
Saoshyant (Z)	'He who will bring benefit': a term used especially of the future World Saviour, to be born of a virgin mother.
sat (H)	being, truth: a term used for *Brahman*.
sati (H, S)	former Hindu practice by which a widow went to her death, willingly or unwillingly, on the funeral pyre of her husband.
sawn (saum) (I)	fast, as in the fast of Ramadan.
Sayid 'Ali Muhammad Shirazi (Ba)	founder of Babism who claimed to be the Bab and was executed in Iran in 1850.
Second Coming (C)	the return of Jesus Christ in glory on the Last Day, in judgement over all humankind, sometimes called the Second Advent.
Sect Shinto (Sh)	the Shinto religion as it was divided into a number of sects, many of which incorporated ideas from elsewhere, especially Buddhism and Christianity.
See (C)	the area of jurisdiction of a bishop or archbishop.
sephardim (J)	community, originally of Spain, with characteristic interpretation of Jewish law.
Septuagint (C)	Greek translation of the Hebrew Bible.
Set (N)	brother and murderer of Osiris.
seven creations (Z)	in the ancient Iranian cosmogony the seven divisions of the physical world, created in the order: the sky, water, earth, plants, animals, humankind and fire. In Zoroastrianism each creation is assigned to the special guardianship of one of the Heptad.
shafi'ites (I)	an Islamic legal rite, or school, following 'ash-Shafi'i.
Shah Isma'il (I)	founder of Safavid dynasty, who made Imamism the official religion of his domains (Iran, or Persia) in 1301 CE.
shahada (I)	confession of faith, or witness. The first of the five pillars of Islam.
Shaivite (H)	worshipper of the god Shiva.
Shakta (H)	worshipper of the goddess or of *shakti*.
Shakti (H)	divine power or energy, deified as a goddess.
shaman (N, T)	sacred person who is believed to derive special power from direct contact with the supernatural.
Shandong (Con)	Chinese province between the Gulf of Chihli and the Yellow Sea, also spelled Shantung.
Shari'a (I)	the revealed law of Islam, which developed from the Qur'an, the Sunnah, and (in some traditions) ijma.
shastras (B)	'teaching': the textbooks of schools of Mahayana Buddhism.

Shaykhi (Ba)	sect of Iranian Shi'ite Islam, from which many early members of the Babi movement came.
Shembe, Isaiah (NRM)	founder of the Nazarite Church of the Shembe, an African independent church of the Zulu people.
Shi'ism (I)	party within Islam which developed from the experience of 'Ali and his followers.
Shi'ite (I)	a follower of the Islamic party of Shi'ism.
shih (B)	concrete particularity.
shila (B)	ethical conduct. In Mahayana, open-heartedness, or a willingness to receive.
shintai (Sh)	object that represents the invisible spiritual presence of a god within the *hondon* of a temple.
shirk (I)	ascribing partners to God; associating any person or thing with Allah. Shirk is a major sin in Islam.
Shogi Effendi Rabbani (Ba)	'Guardian of the cause of God'. Eldest grandson and successor to 'Abdul-Baha as leader of the Baha'is (d. 1957).
shraddha (B)	faith.
shraddha ceremony (H)	memorial service performed by Hindu males for their dead ancestors.
Shri Sathya Sai Baba (H)	modern Indian guru with a large following among Hindus in India and overseas.
Shruti (H)	'that which is heard': the sacred scriptures of Hinduism, especially the Vedas and Upanishads.
Shu-ching (T)	lit. 'Classic (*Ching*) of History', covering the period from 2300 to 600 BCE. One of the Five Classics.
shunyata (B)	the doctrine of emptiness in Mahayana Buddhism.
Shvetambara (Jn)	'white-robed': major sect in which the owning of a single white garment was held not to violate the principle of *aparigraha*.
siddha (Jn)	a free soul detached from the cycle of reincarnation and omniscient after enlightenment.
Siddharta (B)	the family name of the Buddha.
smriti (H)	'that which is remembered': writings of the Hindu religious tradition less sacred than the *Shruti*.
speaking in tongues (C)	ecstatic utterance in a trance-like state of emotional devotion to God. It is usually meaningless to listeners, consisting of an intoned jumble of syllables. In recent times found increasingly in Christian churches. Similar phenomena are found in many religions.
Sri Sarada Devi Math (H)	female branch of the Ramakrishna Mission, inspired by Ramakrishna's wife, founded in 1954.
State Shinto (Sh)	the Shinto religion as controlled by the government of Japan, headed both temporally and spiritually by the Emperor.
Stephen (St) (C)	early Christian martyr.
Sthanakavasis (Jn)	Jaina sect developed from the *Shvetambaras*, rejecting images and temple services.
Sthavira (B)	a sect of early Buddhism from which Theravada developed.
stupa (B)	a shrine or mound associated with sacred places or relics of the Buddha.
Subhi-i Azal (Ba)	'Morn of eternity': the appointed successor to the Bab, and half-brother to Baha'u'llah. Azal remained leader of the 'Azalis in Iran after a break with the Baha'is.
Sufism (I)	Islamic mystical movement.
Sukhavati-vyuha Sutra (B)	an early Mahayana writing.
sunna (I)	the example of Muhammad.
Sunnis (I)	the majority party within Islam.
sura (I)	a chapter of the Qur'an.
Sutra (Sutta) (B)	Buddhist scripture or text: theoretically, the words of the Buddha.
Sutra (H)	'thread': aphorism or short verse summarizing basic teaching.
Sutta Pitaka (B)	a collection of discourses which forms the second 'basket' of the Tipitaka.
Swaminarayan Sect (H)	sect founded in the early 19th century in Gujarat, now with a wide following among Gujaratis in India and overseas.

Tabernacles (J)	festival commemorating 40 years' wandering in the wilderness.
taboo (N)	Polynesian word for people or objects thought to be too dangerous to be associated with.
tafsir (I)	the interpretation or exegesis of the Qur'an.
Tallit (J)	prayer-shawl.
Talmud (J)	literary collection of ancient Jewish laws and practices.
Tanakh (J)	the Hebrew Bible.
T'ang Dynasty (T)	618–906 CE.
Tantra (H)	'loom': term that refers to a group of medieval Hindu scriptures and to rites (found also in Buddhism) concerned with the divine creative energy (*shakti*), partly yogic and orgiastic in character.
Tao (Dao) (Con, T)	'Road', 'Way', and thus by extension, 'method', 'principle'; hence not only the Way of the ancient sages but – as in Taoism – the unknowable Principle above and within all that exists. In Taoism applied mainly in philosophy and religion to schools of particular teachings, mainly of 'quietist' leanings.
Tao-tê Ching (T)	leading classical work of Taoism.
taqlid (I)	the following of precedents, and a principle in Islamic legal discussion.
tariqa (I)	a Sufi order.
Tathagata (B)	'the truly-arrived': a term used of the Buddha.
tathagata-garbha (B)	the embryonic Buddhu, or the Buddha-womb.
tathata (B)	reality, or 'suchness'.
tattva-darshana (B)	the seeing of reality.
te (T)	'virtue'. Sometimes translated as 'Power': active expression of moral endeavour.
Tefillin (J)	phylacteries containing sacred texts.
Ten Commandments (J)	laws believed to have been given by God personally to Moses.
Theopompos of Chios (Z)	Greek historian and orator, b.376 BCE.
Theosophical Society (MW–H)	founded in New York in 1875, but important in India as promoter of Indian (and largely Hindu) cultural and religious values.
Theravada (B)	'the way of the elders': the only extant form of Hinayana Buddhism.
Thirty-Nine Articles (C)	the articles accepted in 1571 as setting out the doctrine of the Church of England and included in the Book of Common Prayer. Based on an older compilation of 42 articles, their redefinition was supervised by Archbishop Matthew Parker under Queen Elizabeth I.
Three Jewels (Jn)	the triad of right faith, right knowledge and right conduct.
Tian (Con)	supreme deity presiding over the cosmos, other gods and spirits: Heaven.
t'ien T'ai (B)	school of Chinese Mahayana.
Tipitaka (B)	Buddhist scriptures.
Tirthankaras (Jn)	the 24 patriarchs of the Jainas (one a woman). The first was Rishabhanatha, the last Vardhamana Mahavira.
Torah (J)	originally the Pentateuch, the five books of Moses; then the body of Jewish teaching.
Transcendental Meditation (TM) (H)	contemplative method devised by the modern Indian guru Maharishi Mahesh Yogi and since the 1960s widely practised in the West.
transubstantiation (C)	concept held by some Catholic Christians that the 'substance' of the bread and wine used at the Eucharistic service becomes the 'substance' of the Body and Blood of Christ, although the 'accidents' of their outward forms remain the same. The alternative concept that the 'substance' of the bread and wine remains and, in addition, takes on the 'subtance' of the Body and Blood, is called consubstantiation.

Trent, Council of (C)	council of the Roman Catholic Church convened to debate the growing tide of Protestantism in the middle of the 16th century and held at Trento in northern Italy.
trikaya (B)	the three bodies of the Buddha in Mahayana doctrine: the conjured-up body (nirmana kaya); the body of blissful encounter (sambhoga kaya); the body of truth or reality (dharma kaya).
trimurti (H)	'one God in three forms': a triad of the gods Brahma, Vishnu and Shiva.
Trinity (C)	doctrine that there is one God, but that in the divine substance there are three co-equal and co-eternal Persons: the Father, the Son, and the Holy Spirit.
tulku (B)	a reincarnated person who maintains the constant presence in the world of an aspect of the Buddha. Since the sixteenth century, the Dalai Lama.
Twelve Tribes (J)	tribes of Israelites in the Promised Land, named after the sons of Jacob-Israel.
Tzitzit (J)	fringes on garments.
'Umar (ibn al-Khattab) (I)	caliph from 634 to 644 CE.
Ummayad (I)	Muslim dynasty which ruled from Damascus from 661 to 750 CE.
Unification Church (NRM)	'The Moonies': founded by Sun Myung Moon in Korea in 1954 but now with a worldwide membership.
Universal House of Justice (Ba)	from 1963 the supreme ruling body of the Baha'i Faith.
upanayana (H)	one of the important life-cycle rites (samskaras) for the boys of the three upper varna groups who are given the sacred thread.
Upanishads (H)	final section of the Vedas or 'Vedanta' containing some of the earliest philosophical thought of India, especially about Brahman and Atman, on which all later philosophical speculations are founded.
upashraya (Jn)	a (permanent) monastic building, monastery hall.
upaya (B)	device, method, or means.
upaya-kaushalya (B)	skill-in-means.
uposatha (B)	the Buddhist holy day, observed on the first, eighth, 15th and 23rd days of the lunar month.
usul al-fiqh (I)	Islamic jurisprudence.
'Uthman (I)	caliph 644–656 CE.
Vaisheshika (H)	also called 'Atomism': one of the six orthodox schools of Hindu philosophy, analysing elements into atoms and believing in a plurality of souls in the universe.
Vaishnavite (H)	devotee of Vishnu or of one of his avatars.
Vajrayana (B)	the Diamond Vehicle: a form of Buddhism based upon Tantric texts.
Vardhamana (Jn)	Prince and last Tirthankara of the Jainas, c540–468 BCE.
varna (H)	'colour': ancient term used for the theoretical rather than real division into classes or castes. The fourfold varna order goes back to Vedic times and comprises Brahmans (priests), Kshatriyas (warriors), Vaishyas (traders) and Shudras (serfs).
varnashramadharma (H)	important concept defining a person's duty (dharma) according to his or her class (varna) and stage in life (ashrama).
Vasubandhu (B)	one of the two founders of the Yogacharin school of Mahayana Buddhism.
Vedanta (H)	most significant of the six orthodox schools of Hindu philosophy, divided into several branches.
Vedas (H)	sacred scriptures (Shruti) of Hinduism brought to India by the invading Aryans. The corpus of Vedic literature (often simply called 'the Vedas') contains the four Vedas, Brahmanas, Aranyakas and Upanishads.
Vedic (H, Jn)	term descriptive of the civilization brought to India by the Indo-Aryan invaders during the second millennium BCE.
vespers (C)	service of evening prayer (also called evensong); not a Eucharistic service but one of devotion and praise.

Vinaya (B)	first of the 'three baskets' of the Tipitaka, concerned chiefly with monastic rules for *bhikkhus*.
Vishisht Advaita (H)	'qualified non-dualism': the system of Vedanta taught by Ramanuja (11th century CE).
vishuddha (B)	pure, especially in relation to the mind.
Visuddhi-magga (B)	a classical compendium of Theravada teaching compiled by Buddhaghosa in the fifth century CE.
Vivekananda (MW–H)	Swami Vivekananda (1863–1902). Founder of the Ramakrishna Mission, and initiator of the first Hindu 'mission' to the West.
Waldensians (C)	very early forerunners of the movement of the Reformation, flourishing mainly in the 13th century; ascetics, they repudiated many contemporary catholic practices later condemned by Protestants.
Warring States (T)	period known by these terms: 481–221 BCE.
Westminster Confession (C)	doctrinal statement of Presbyterianism, produced by the Westminster Assembly of Puritan clergymen convened by the Long Parliament, 1643–1649, and emphasizing the doctrine of predestination as expounded by John Calvin. It was adopted by the Church of Scotland in 1647.
World Congress of Faiths (MW)	founded in 1936 'to instil a spirit of fellowship among mankind through religion'.
World Council of Churches (MW)	formed in 1948 as an agency for co-operation among Christian denominations.
World Fellowship of Buddhists (MW)	founded in 1950 in Sri Lanka to promote Buddhist teaching throughout the world.
wu shing (T)	the five elements which form the universe, namely: water, fire, wood, metal and earth.
wu-wei (B, T)	lit. 'without action'. Used in Chinese Buddhism for 'nirvana'. In Taoism denoting a positive philosophy of non-assertion.
Yasna (Z)	'act of worship', the daily Zoroastrian religious service.
Yeshivah (J)	college for study of Torah.
yin-yang (Con, T)	opposing yet complementary forces of alternating growth and decay, light and dark, male and female, in nature; two principles of an early dualistic philosophy.
Yoga (H)	either one of the six orthodox schools of Hindu philosophy, based on Patanjali's *Yoga Sutra*, or more generally, the different methods of self-control and spiritual disciplines in Hinduism, such as *jnana yoga* or *bhakti yoga*.
Yogacharin (B)	a school of Mahayana Buddhism.
Yom Kippur (J)	festival and solemn fast ten days after Jewish New Year.
Yomi (Sh)	the underworld, domain of darkness and corruption.
yoni (H)	'female sexual organ': the base from which the phallic symbol of the *lingam* rises.
yuga (H)	cosmic age. There are four yugas in each cycle of the universe, ranging from the golden to the dark age (*Kali yuga*), the latter being the present age according to Hindu belief.
yung (B)	function.
Zaddik (J)	Hasidic saint and leader.
zakat (I)	Almsgiving; one of the five pillars of Islam.
Zand (Z)	'interpretation': the traditional exegesis of the Avesta by glosses, commentaries and translation.
Zarathushtra (Z)	priest, prophet and founder of the faith, known to the Greeks as Zoroaster. His name was popularized in German by Nietzsche in the form Zarathustra. His life-dates are uncertain, but most scholars agree on a date around or before 1000 BCE.
Zaydites (I)	a branch of Shi'ism which accepts as imam any member of the Prophet's family who by military force asserts his right to rule.
Zen (B)	Japanese form of Ch'an: a school of Mahayana Buddhism.
Zhou Dynasty (Con)	series of emperors, c1122–256 BCE that followed the Song Dynasty; sometimes spelled Chou.
zi (tsu) (Con)	master.

INDEX

ACKNOWLEDGEMENTS

The publishers would like to thank the following for providing the photographs listed on the pages below:

Biblioteca Ambrosiana, Milan 41; Bibliothèque Publique et Universitaire, Geneva 117; Bodleian Library, Oxford 80 right; British Library, London 72, 106, 218; Church of Jesus Christ of the Latter Day Saints 151; Edinburgh University Library 156; Werner Forman Archive 9, 104, 249; Giraudon 285; Sally and Richard Greenhill 45, 84, 148, 277, 280, 287, 296, 302 below left, 308 right; Sonia Halliday Photographs 22, 24, 59, 62 right, 73, 98, 100–1, 103 above, 105, 180, 220, 258 below right, 297, 298; Sonia Halliday Photographs/Laura Lushington 64; Robert Harding 19 below, 23, 60–1, 63, 101, 143 below left, 177, 181 above, 223 below, 299 above; Michael Holford 15, 137, 138 above, 139, 140, 141 below, 221, 222, 259, 260; Geoff Howard 20 above, 78, 94 left, 99 below, 124, 143 above left, 184, 258 above right, 264, 302, 311; Hutchison Picture Library 100 above, 102, 142, 143 above right, 206, 263 above right, 301, 303 below; Hutchison Picture Library/Sarah Errington 258 above left; Hutchison Picture Library/Patricio Goycolea 179 right; Hutchison Picture Library/Michael Macintyre 18, 263 above left; Andrzej Jarosewicz/David Williamson 62 left, 258 centre left; Dee Kongelige Bibliotek, Copenhagen 37; Library Committee of the Religious Society of Friends 135; The Macquitty International Photographic Collection 14, 39, 80 left, 83, 94 right, 162, 170, 189, 195, 201, 203 below, 216, 231, 247, 251, 252, 253, 255, 265, 267, 289, 291, 293, 304, 308 left; The Macquitty International Photographic Collection/British Museum, London 166; The Mansell Collection 123, 155; The Moravian Church 112; Musei Vaticani, Rome 70; National Gallery, London 57; National Spiritual Assembly of the Bahá'ís of the United Kingdom 174, 176; Network/Mike Abrahams 29, 33, 43, 44, 48, 50, 52, 204, 310; Network/Katalin Arkell 11; Network/Steve Benbow 305; Network/Barry Lewis 183 above; Novosti Press Agency 91; Oriental Museum, Durham 241; Bury Peerless 17, 19 above, 60 right, 61 below, 66, 138 below, 141 above, 144, 178, 197 left, 182 above, 187, 199, 203 above, 209, 213, 214, 217, 223 above, 224 below, 263, 299 below, 303 above; Figure 7:2 from *A Handbook of Living Religions* edited by John R. Hinnells (Viking Books, London 1984), copyright © John R. Hinnells and Penguin Books Ltd, 1984, illustrations by Raymond Turvey, p. 269. Reproduced by permission of Penguin Books Ltd 211; Caroline Penn 21 below, 77, 89; Pieterse Davison International Ltd. 58; Popperfoto 90, 314, 316, 323; Reflex Pictures/Carlos Guarita 321; Reflex Pictures/Denis Doran 20 below, 125, 129, 191, 268, 272; Rijksmuseum, Amsterdam 25; Salvation Army Archives and Information Services 145, 146; Schwizes Institut für Kunstwissenschaft, Zurich 113; Ronald Sheridan's Photo Library 8, 86, 107, 115, 219 below; Frank Spooner Pictures 88, 95, 159, 167, 172, 295, 306, 320; Dr. Jack Thompson 182 below; Times Newspapers Ltd./John Grimwade 161; Unterlinden Museum, Colmar/Bridgeman Art Library 68; Vautier-Decool 181 below; Vautier de Nanxe 21 above, 60 below, 97, 103 below, 219 above, 257, 302 below right; Victoria and Albert Museum, London 234, 239; Roger-Viollet 109 below; Jane Williams 109 above, 110; World Council of Churches 317.